KT-521-351

STREET ATLAS
Buckinghamshire

Contents

III Key to map symbols
IV-V Key to map pages
VI Administrative and post code boundaries
1 Street maps
214 Index of hospitals, railway stations, schools, shopping centres, street names and universities

PHILIP'S

First edition published 1993
Second edition published 1994
First colour edition published 1997
Reprinted 1998, 2000 by

George Philip Ltd, a division of
Octopus Publishing Group Ltd
2-4 Heron Quays
London E14 4JP

ISBN 0-540-07468-3 (pocket)

Printed and bound in Spain by Cayfosa

Digital Data

The exceptionally high-quality mapping
found in this book is available as
digital data in TIFF format, which is
easily convertible to other bit-mapped
(raster) image formats.

The index is also available in digital
form as a standard database table.
It contains all the details found in the
printed index together with the
National Grid reference for the map
square in which each entry is named
and feature codes for places of
interest in eight categories such as
education and health.

For further information and to discuss
your requirements, please contact
Philip's on 020 7531 8440 or
george.philip@philips-maps.co.uk

(22a)	**Motorway** (with junction number)
	Primary route (dual carriageway and single)
	A road (dual carriageway and single)
	B road (dual carriageway and single)
	Minor road (dual carriageway and single)
	Other minor road
	Road under construction
	Pedestrianised area
	Railway
	Tramway, miniature railway
	Rural track, private road or narrow road in urban area
	Gate or obstruction to traffic (restrictions may not apply at all times or to all vehicles)
	Path, bridleway, byway open to all traffic, road used as a public path
	The representation in this atlas of a road, track or path is no evidence of the existence of a right of way
102 **174**	**Adjoining page indicators**

	British Rail station
	Underground station
	Private railway station
	Bus, coach station
	Ambulance station
	Coastguard station
	Fire station
	Police station
+	**Accident and Emergency entrance to hospital**
H	**Hospital**
+	**Church, place of worship**
i	**Information centre**
P	**Parking**
PO	**Post Office**
Amersham & Wycombe Coll	**Important buildings, schools, colleges, universities and hospitals**
	County boundaries
Grand Union Canal	**Water name**
	Stream
	River or canal (minor and major)
	Water
	Tidal water
	Woods
	Houses
Berkhamsted Castle	**Non-Roman antiquity**
ROMAN VILLA	**Roman antiquity**

Abbr	Full	Abbr	Full
Acad	**Academy**	Mon	**Monument**
Cemy	**Cemetery**	Mus	**Museum**
C Ctr	**Civic Centre**	Obsy	**Observatory**
CH	**Club House**	Pal	**Royal Palace**
Coll	**College**	PH	**Public House**
Ent	**Enterprise**	Recn Gd	**Recreation Ground**
Ex H	**Exhibition Hall**	Resr	**Reservoir**
Ind Est	**Industrial Estate**	Ret Pk	**Retail Park**
Inst	**Institute**	Sch	**School**
Ct	**Law Court**	Sh Ctr	**Shopping Centre**
L Ctr	**Leisure Centre**	Sta	**Station**
LC	**Level Crossing**	TH	**Town Hall/House**
Liby	**Library**	Trad Est	**Trading Estate**
Mkt	**Market**	Univ	**University**
Meml	**Memorial**	YH	**Youth Hostel**

■ The small numbers around the edges of the maps identify the 1 kilometre National Grid lines

■ The dark grey border on the inside edge of some pages indicates that the mapping does not continue onto the adjacent page

The scale of the maps is 3.92 cm to 1 km (2½ inches to 1 mile)

0	¼	½	¾	1 mile
0	250m 500m	750m 1 kilometre		

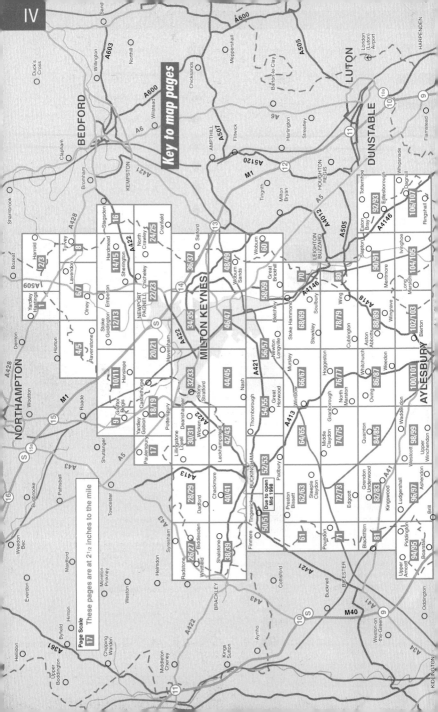

IV

Key to map pages

Page Scale
17 These pages are at 2½ inches to the mile

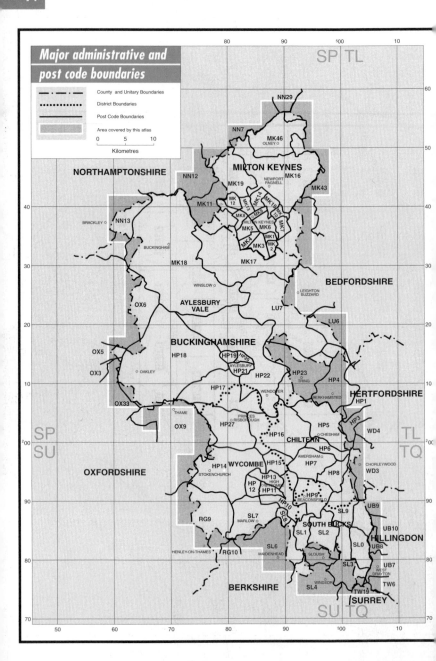

Major administrative and post code boundaries

— · — · — County and Unitary Boundaries

· · · · · · · · District Boundaries

Post Code Boundaries

Area covered by this atlas

0   5   10

Kilometres

NORTHAMPTONSHIRE

NN29

NN7

MK46
OLNEY ○

MILTON KEYNES

NN12

MK19

NEWPORT
PAGNELL ○

MK16

MK43

MK11

MK
12

MK8

MK
13

MK9

MK15

MK14

MK10

MILTON KEYNES

MK7

MK5

MK6

MK1

MK4

MK
2

MK3

BRACKLEY ○

NN13

BUCKINGHAM ○

MK18

MK17

BEDFORDSHIRE

WINSLOW ○

LEIGHTON
BUZZARD ○

OX6

AYLESBURY
VALE

LU7

LU6

BUCKINGHAMSHIRE

OX5

HP18

HP19

HP20

OX3

AYLESBURY

HP21

OAKLEY ○

HP22

HP23

TRING ○

HP4

HP17

WENDOVER ○

BERKHAMSTED ○

HERTFORDSHIRE

HP1

OX33

THAME ○

PRINCES
RISBOROUGH ○

HP5

CHESHAM ○

HP3

WD4

OX9

HP27

HP16

CHILTERN

HP6

WD3

OXFORDSHIRE

HP14
STOKENCHURCH ○

WYCOMBE

HP15

AMERSHAM ○

HP7

HP8

CHORLEYWOOD ○

HP
12

HP13

HIGH
WYCOMBE

HP11

HP9
BEACONSFIELD ○

UB9

HP10

SL9

UB10

RG9

SL7
MARLOW ○

SL8

SOUTH BUCKS

SL1

SL2

SL0

HILLINGDON

UB8

HENLEY-ON-THAMES ○

RG10

SL6
MAIDENHEAD ○

SLOUGH ○

SL3

UB7
WEST
DRAYTON

TW6

BERKSHIRE

SL4

WINDSOR ○

TW19

SURREY

SP TL

SP TL
SU TQ

SU TQ

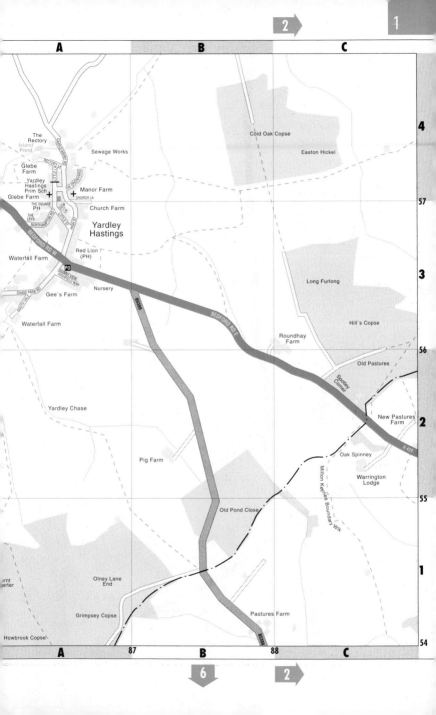

A B C

Bozeat

4

Horn Wood

Stocking Hollow

The Belts

57

The Lodge

Wold Barn

Santon

The Slipe

3

Bozeat Grange

Bozeat Wood

Nutwood Barn

The Oaks Wood

56

Northey Farm

Milton Keynes Boundary Wlk

Nun Wood

Three Shires Way

Threeshire Wood

2

New Pastures Farm

Lavendon Lodge Farm

Barslay Spinney

Warrington House

Broadlane Spinney

55

Nuniron Spinney

Nursery Nunirons

Park Far

1

The Nest Farm

Lower Farm

Castle Fa

Brickfield Plantation

Warrington House Farm

Warrington

54

D   **E**   **F**

Park
Wood

Austin's
Spinney

Allot
Gdns

4

Templegrove
Spinney

New
Buildings

Allot
Gdns

Manor
Farm

The Mansion

DICKENS CL 1
BRAMLEY CT 2

57

Harrold

PH
Sch

NEW RD

MOWHILLS

Coldharbour
Hill

Priory
Farm

3

Cracknell Hill
House

Cracknell
Hill

Middle
Farm

56

River Great Ouse

Carlton

Millholme
Island

Marsh
Farm

2

Harrold Lodge
Farm

Lavendon
Wood

Milton Keynes Boundary Wlk

55

Spring Close
Farm

Church
Farm

Southfields Farm
Cottage

Valley View
Farm

Tollgate
House

Snelson
Wood

Carlton Hall
Farm

Snelson
Cottages

Carltonhall
Wood

HARROLD RD

Snelson

Snelson
Cobs

CARLTON

1

54

D   **93**   **E**   **94**   **F**

D
E
F

The Paddock

Manor Farm

The Wold

Hay Copse

Yardley Chase

Church Slade

4

Biggin Lodge

Ravenstone Road Copse

Barnstaple Wood

Milton Keynes Boundary Wlk

53

Great Wood

Dinglederry

Ash Beds

Roadley's Brake

3

Hanger Spinney

Woodlands

52

Cheyney Farm

2

Parkfield Farm

Northend Farm

Milton Keynes Boundary Wlk

Cemy

51

Parkfield Spinney

Abbey Farm

Horseshoe Farm

THE CLOSE

PH

BAY LA.

Home Farm

THE CLOSE

WESTON RD

Spring Barn

Ravenstone

1

PO

Yew Tree Farm

COMMON ST

Sheep Dip

Mannings Farm

Lower Farm House

50

B526

D
84
E
85
F

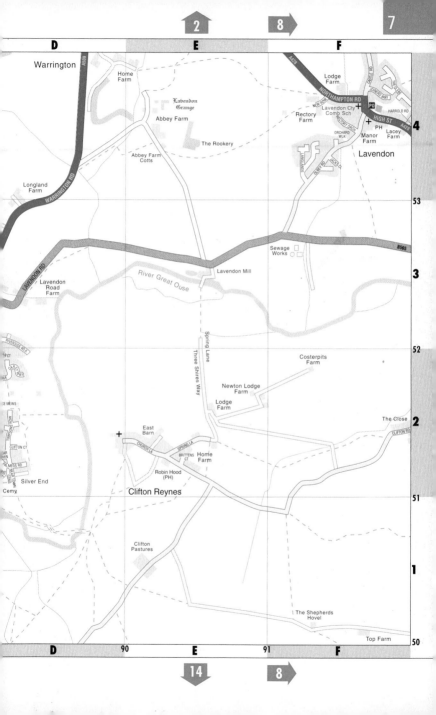

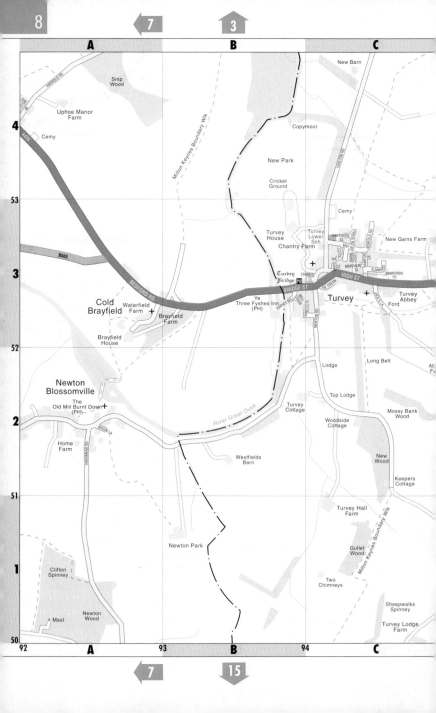

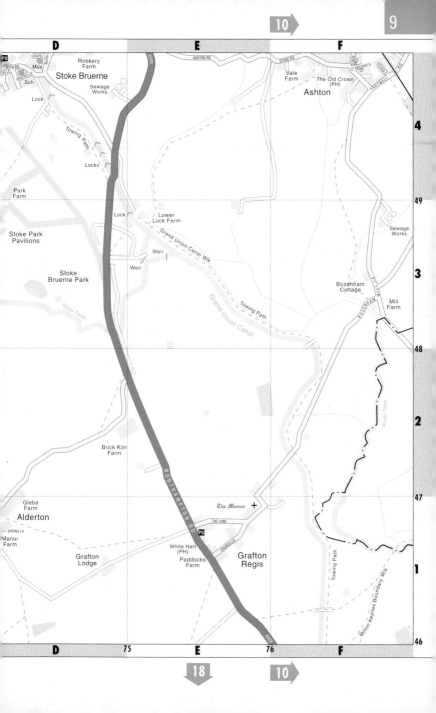

9

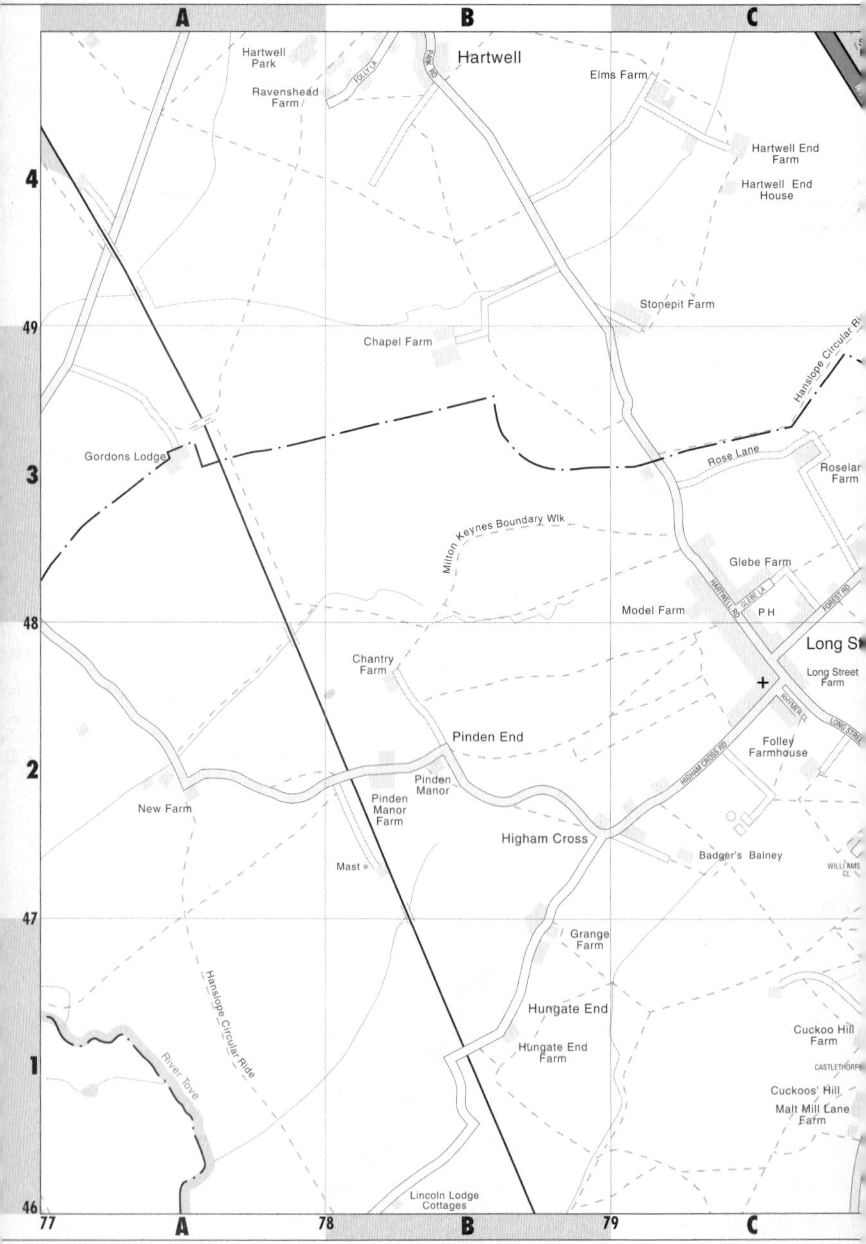

A
B
C
Hartwell Park
Ravenshead Farm
FOLLY LA
PARK RD
Hartwell
Elms Farm
Hartwell End Farm
Hartwell End House
4
Stonepit Farm
49
Chapel Farm
Hanslope Circular Ride
Gordons Lodge
3
Rose Lane
Roselar Farm
Milton Keynes Boundary Wlk
Glebe Farm
HARTWELL RD
GLEBE LA
FOREST RD
48
Model Farm
P H
Long St
Chantry Farm
Long Street Farm
RHYMER CL
LONG STREET
Pinden End
Folley Farmhouse
2
HIGHAM CROSS RD
Pinden Manor
New Farm
Pinden Manor Farm
Higham Cross
Badger's Balney
Mast
WILLIAMS CL
47
Grange Farm
Hanslope Circular Ride
Hungate End
Cuckoo Hill Farm
1
River Tove
Hungate End Farm
CASTLETHORPE
Cuckoos' Hill
Malt Mill Lane Farm
Lincoln Lodge Cottages
46
77
A
78
B
79
C

9

19

D   E   F

Jarvis's Wood

Salcey Green Farm

Forest Farm

Lodge Farm

Pinkard's Farm

Milton Keynes Boundary Wlk

4

Salcey Green

Stokepark Wood

Mast

49

3

Spinney Lodge

Littlewood Farm

48

Midshires Way

Hanslope Circular Ride

Yew Tree Farm

2

Stocking Green Farm

Hanslope

Woad Farm

Tathallend Farm

PH

Tathall End

Allot Gdns

47

MARKET SQ

PO

Maltings Farm House

Church End

Manor Farm

1

The Grove

Three Shires Way

Ivy Farm

Park Farm

46

D   81   E   82   F

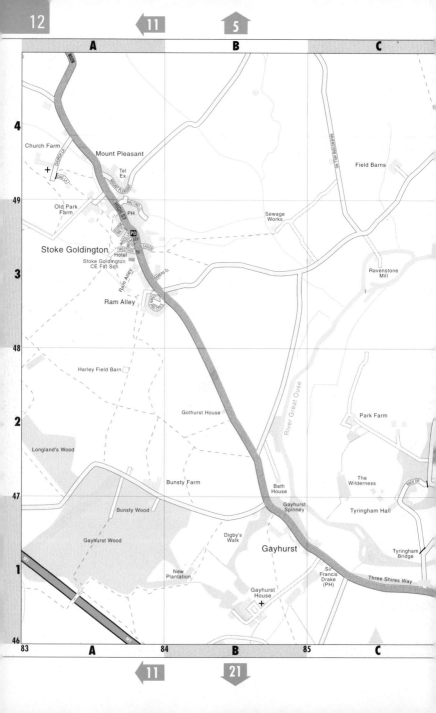

A B C

4

Church Farm

Mount Pleasant

Field Barns

Tel Ex

49

Old Park Farm

PH

Sewage Works

Stoke Goldington

Ravenstone Mill

Stoke Goldington CE Fst Sch

3

Ram Alley

48

Harley Field Barn

2

Gothurst House

Park Farm

Longland's Wood

River Great Ouse

The Wilderness

Bunsty Farm

47

Bunsty Wood

Bath House

Tyringham Hall

Gayhurst Spinney

Tyringham Bridge

Gayhurst Wood

Digby's Walk

Gayhurst

1

New Plantation

Sir Francis Drake (PH)

Three Shires Way

Gayhurst House

46

83

A

84

B

85

C

D
E
F

Caravan Park

Emberton
Emberton Cty Fst Sch

Manor Farm

HULTON DR
BATTLE CL

WEST FARM RD
THE CL
THE CLOSE
WEST PL
WEST LA
MAIN FARM CT.
HIGH ST
THE LODGE
PH

CHURCH LA

4

Woolwich Barn

Blackwell Spinney

49

Sowel Spinney

NEWPORT RD

Buryorchard Spinney

3

Filgrave

Rectory Farm

Manor Farm

TOWER CL

Lodge Spinney

A509

Ash Spinney

Filgrave Farm

48

oadmore Covert

Three Shires Way

Baker's Spinney

Fifty Acre Spinney

roadmore House

2

Blackthorn Covert

DUN LA

Ash Spinney

Hill Plantation

Reservoirs

47

FENCES LA

Fences Farm

Baker's Farm

VILLAGE CL

MARYOT CL

HIGH ST

FINCH RD

River Great Ouse

End Farm

WATER LA

THE BACK YD

LEYS CL

CARTERS CL

PO

1

Gallards Farm

Manor House

CREFTS END

MANOR CTYD

SHERINGTON RD

B526

46

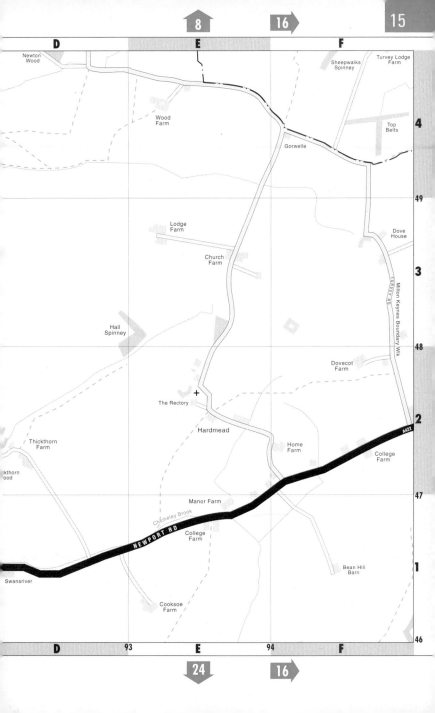

D
E
F

Newton
Wood

Sheepwalks
Spinney

Turvey Lodge
Farm

Wood
Farm

Top
Belts

4

Gorwelle

49

Lodge
Farm

Dove
House

Church
Farm

3

TURVEY RD

Milton Keynes Boundary Wlk

Hall
Spinney

48

Dovecot
Farm

The Rectory

+

2

A422

Hardmead

Thickthorn
Farm

Home
Farm

College
Farm

ckthorn
ood

47

Manor Farm

Chicheley Brook

NEWPORT RD

College
Farm

Bean Hill
Barn

1

Swansriver

Cooksoe
Farm

46

D
93
E
94
F

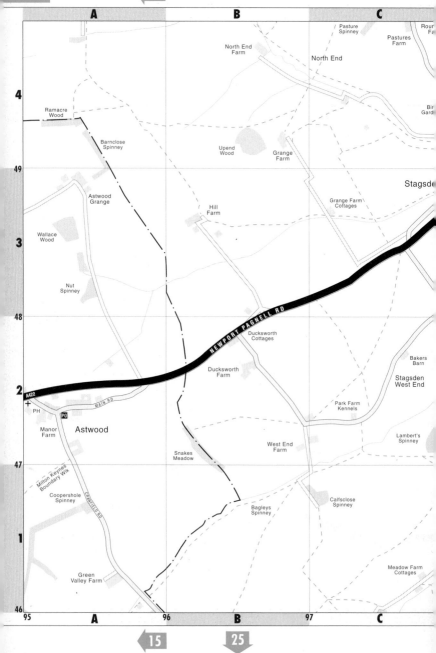

A

B

C

Pasture
Spinney

Rour
Fa

North End
Farm

Pastures
Farm

North End

4

Ramacre
Wood

Bir
Gard

Barnclose
Spinney

49

Upend
Wood

Grange
Farm

Stagsde

Astwood
Grange

Hill
Farm

Grange Farm
Cottages

3

Wallace
Wood

Nut
Spinney

48

NEWPORT PAGNELL RD

Ducksworth
Cottages

Bakers
Barn

Ducksworth
Farm

Stagsden
West End

2

A422

+

PH

MAIN RD

PO

Park Farm
Kennels

Manor
Farm

Astwood

Lambert's
Spinney

West End
Farm

47

Milton Keynes
Boundary Wlk

Snakes
Meadow

Coopershole
Spinney

CRANFIELD RD

Calfsclose
Spinney

Bagleys
Spinney

1

Green
Valley Farm

Meadow Farm
Cottages

46

95

A

96

B

97

C

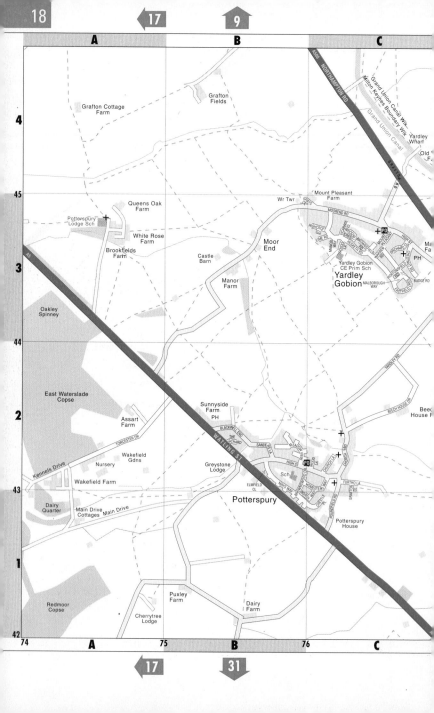

A
B
C

4

Grafton Cottage Farm

Grafton Fields

NORTHAMPTON RD

A508

Grand Union Canal Wlk
Milton Keynes Boundary Wlk
Grand Union Canal

Yardley Wharf

Old Fa

45

Queens Oak Farm

Wr Twr

Mount Pleasant Farm

MOOREND RD

PO

Potterspury Lodge Sch

White Rose Farm

Moor End

HIGHCROFT

Ma Fa

LIME RD

MANOR
HIGH ST

PH

Brookfields Farm

Castle Barn

Yardley Gobion
CE Prim Sch

3

A5

Manor Farm

Yardley
Gobion

MALBOROUGH WAY

BUDGE RD

FIELDS

Oakley Spinney

44

YARDLEY RD

East Waterslade Copse

Sunnyside Farm
PH

BEECH HOUSE RD

Beec House F

2

Assart Farm

TOWCESTER DR

BLACKWELL END

THE ORCHARD

WATLING ST

SANDE

MEADOW

HIGH ST

Nursery

Wakefield Gdns

Greystone Lodge

PO

CHURCHILL

FURTHO LA

Kennels Drive

Wakefield Farm

Sch

ELMFIELD CL

GRAFTON

43

Dairy Quarter

Main Drive Cottages
Main Drive

MACS WAY

DEAN LE

Potterspury

Potterspury House

1

Redmoor Copse

Puxley Farm

Dairy Farm

Cherrytree Lodge

42

74

A

75

B

76

C

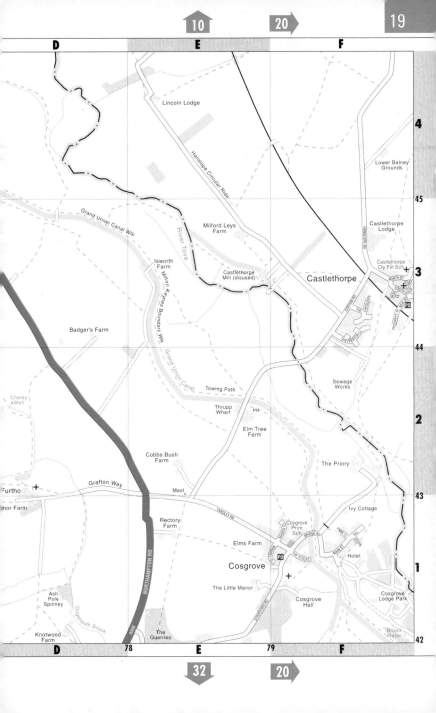

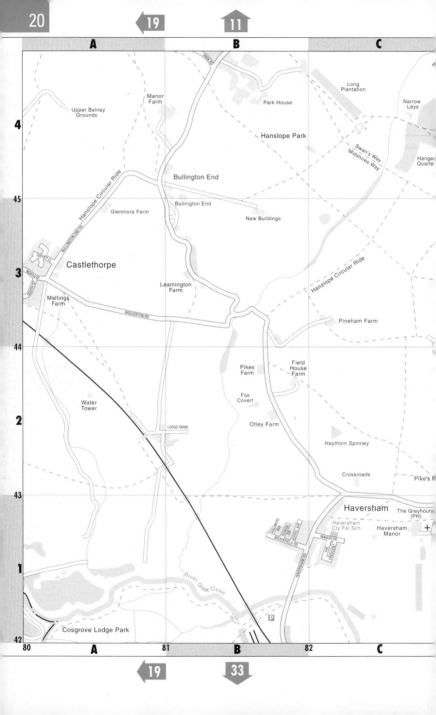

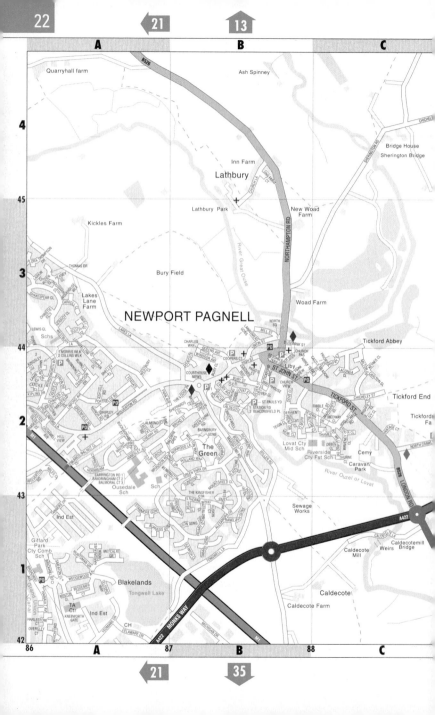

D
E
F

Up
End

The
Copse

A422

HALL LA
+ Chicheley
Hall

Little
End

Chicheley

CHICHELEY HILL

A509

BEDFORD RD

A422

4

Longclose
Spinney

CHICHELEY RD

Newfield
Spinney

Newfield
Farm

Sewage
Works

45

Far Farm

Mouthslade
Spinney

Chicheley Brook

3

Brookend
Farm

Hill Farm

Brook End

BROOK RD

44

Rectory
Farm

NORTH CRAWLEY RD

d Fields
arm

2

Tickford Lodge
Farm

43

Tickford Park
Farm

1

Tickford
Park

WOOD END LA

42

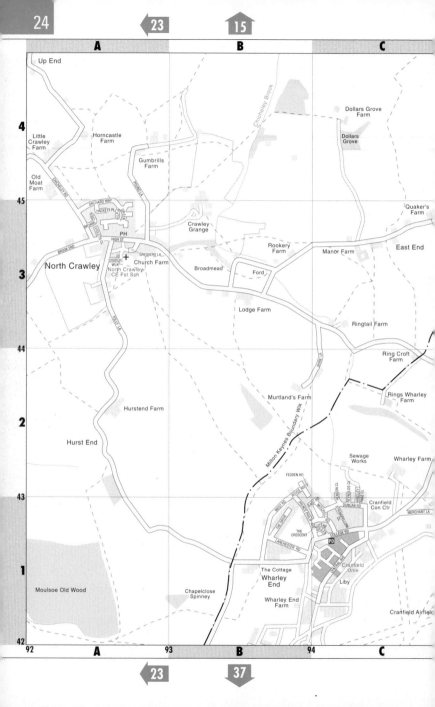

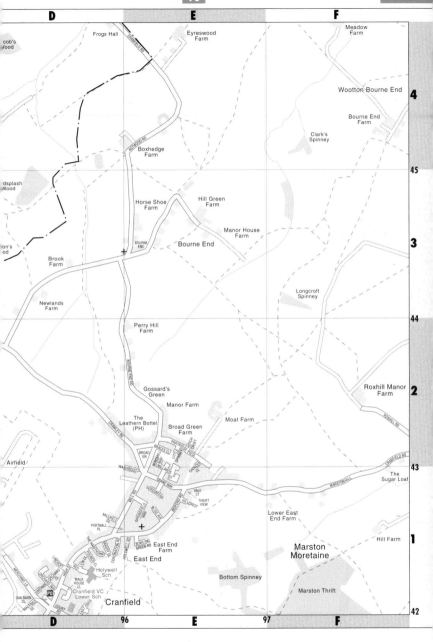

D   **E**   **F**

cob's
Wood

Frogs Hall

Eyreswood
Farm

Meadow
Farm

Wootton Bourne End

4

Bourne End
Farm

Clark's
Spinney

ASTWOOD RD

Boxhedge
Farm

dsplash
Wood

45

Hill Green
Farm

Horse Shoe
Farm

Manor House
Farm

on's
od

BOURNE
END

Bourne End

3

Brook
Farm

Longcroft
Spinney

Newlands
Farm

44

Perry Hill
Farm

BOURNE RD

Gossard's
Green

Roxhill Manor
Farm

2

Manor Farm

ROXHILL RD

The
Leathern Bottel
(PH)

Broad Green
Farm

Moat Farm

CRANLEY RD

CRANFIELD RD

HARTRIDGE
PIECE

PITCH
CROFT

PARTRIDGE
DRIFT

Airfield

BROAD
GN

MALLARD CL

CAMBRIDGE
CL

MARSTON HILL

The
Sugar Loaf

43

WASHINGLEYS

CRANE WAY

VALE
CT

LORDS MEAD

BEDFORD RD

BELCREST

THRIFT
VIEW

Lower East
End Farm

Hill Farm

MILLFIELD CL

PORTNALL
PL

BICKLING
GREEN RD

East End
Farm

1

THE MEADWAYS

East End

Marston
Moretaine

Holywell
Sch

OAK BARN
CL

MALTINGS
CL

WALK
HOUSE
CL

PO

Cranfield VC
Lower Sch

Bottom Spinney

Marston Thrift

Cranfield

42

D   96   **E**   97   **F**

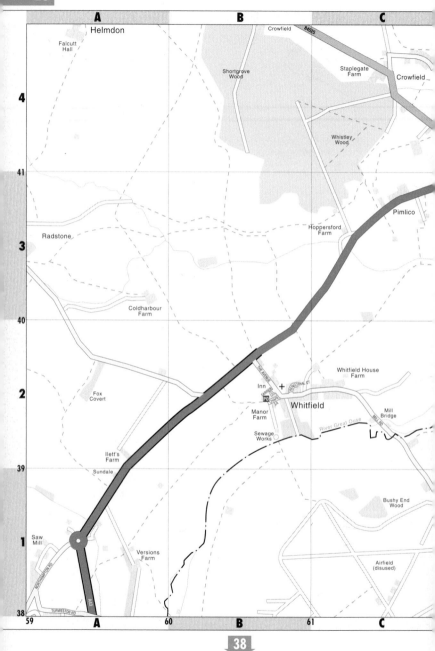

Helmdon
Falcutt Hall
Crowfield
B4525
Staplegate Farm
Crowfield
4
Shortgrove Wood
Whistley Wood
41
Pimlico
Radstone
Hoppersford Farm
3
Coldharbour Farm
40
Whitfield House Farm
THE AVENUE
2
Inn
MEMORIAL ST
Fox Covert
Whitfield
Manor Farm
Mill Bridge
River Great Ouse
MILL RD
Sewage Works
Ilett's Farm
39
Sundale
Bushy End Wood
Saw Mill
1
Versions Farm
Airfield (disused)
NORTHAMPTON RD
A43
38
TURWESTON RD
59   A   60   B   61   C

D

E

F

The Green Man Farm

The Green Man Inn

Needles Hall Farm

Brackley Heath

Manor Farm

Sewage Works

Kingshill Farm

Syresham

The King's Head (PH)

Syresham CE Prim Sch

PO

King's Hill Bridge

King's Hill

MAIN RD

4

Earl's Wood

Abbey Way House

Santhill Plantation

Wood Ground Plantation

41

gh Cross

Langley Farm

River Great Ouse

Syresham Fields Farm

Magdelen Spring Spinney

Home Wood

3

Briary Wood

French's Barn

Biddlesden Bridge

Castle Farm

Friday's Spinney

Biddlesden

40

Longmoor Spinney

Biddlesden House

Baker's Bridge

Westbury Circular Ride

Abbey House

2

Dropshort Farm

Biddlesden Park

Whitfield Wood

39

Wood Green

1

Airfield (disused)

Evershaw Farm

Den Farm

Woodgreen Farm

Westbury Circular Ride

Evershaw Copse

Ten Lands Copse

38

D

63

E

64

F

A

Works
Henwood Farm

Silverstone
Motor Racing
Circuit

Mary
Wood

Pentimore Wood

Airstrip

Farthing
Wood

4

Buttockspire Wood

Wetleys Wood

Golf Course

41

Swallowtail Wood   Old Red
Ditch

Red Ditches
Farm

CH

3

Hollyhill Wood

Point
Copse   Sawpit Wood

Thatcham Ponds
Farm

Blackpit
Farm

40

Westbury Circular Ride

Stowe Woods

Parkfields

Woodlands Farm

2

Three Parks Wood

39

Wolfe's
Obelisk

1

North Hill

Gorrell Farm

Dadford

Vancouver
Lodge

Grecian
Valley

38

65   **A**   66   **B**   67   **C**

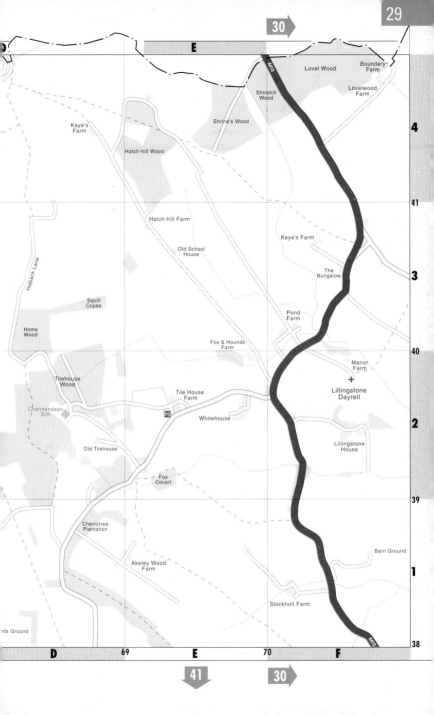

E

Boundary
Farm

Lovel Wood

Lovelwood
Farm

Shirehill
Wood

4

Kaye's
Farm

Shrine's Wood

Hatch-hill Wood

41

Hatch-hill Farm

Keye's Farm

Old School
House

3

The
Bungalow

Holback Lane

Squill
Copse

Pond
Farm

Home
Wood

Fox & Hounds
Farm

40

Manor
Farm

Tilehouse
Wood

Tile House
Farm

Lillingstone
Dayrell

Charmandean
Sch

PO

Whitehouse

2

Old Tilehouse

Lillingstone
House

Fox
Covert

39

Cherrytree
Plantation

Barn Ground

Akeley Wood
Farm

1

Stockholt Farm

...rts Ground

A
B
C

4

Manor
Cotts

Manor
House

The
Spinney

Manor
Lodge

Briary Wood
Farm

Briary
Lodge

West Ashalls
Copse

East Ashalls
Copse

Deanshanger Drive

Long
Copse

41

Valley
Farm

Bradley Fields
Farm

PO

Church Farm

Wicken Wood

3

Lillingstone
Lovell

Notamore
Copse

Glebe
Farm

Leckhampstead
Wood

Lilby
Wood

40

Hall Farm

Hill
Farm

2

39

1

Brook House
(Ruin)

Lodge
Farm

Wicken Road
Farm

The Shaw

Par
Cops

WICKEN RD

Pottery
Farm

Leckhampstead
House

Limes
End

LONG ROW

38

71
A
72
B
73
C

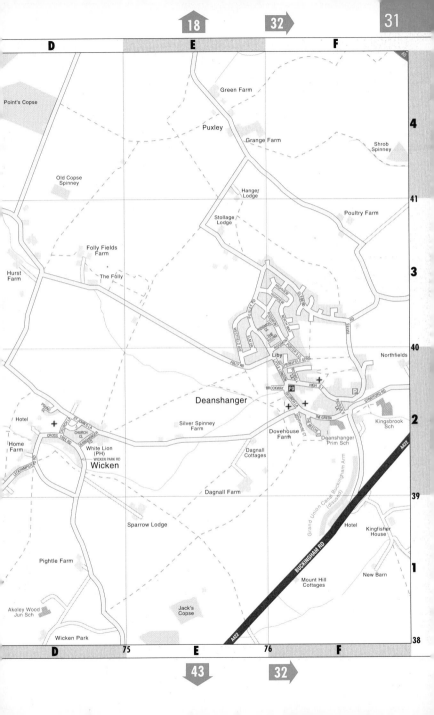

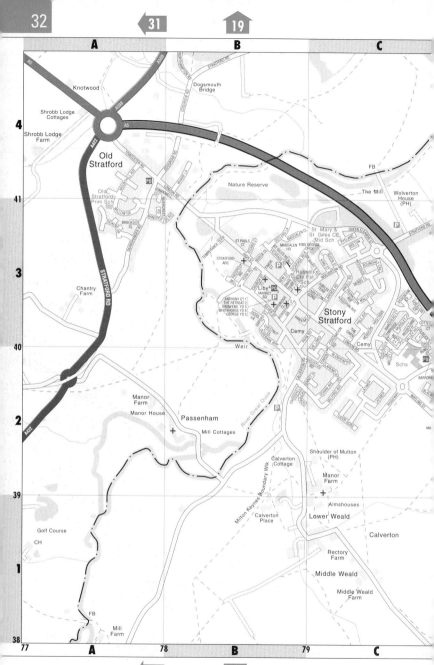

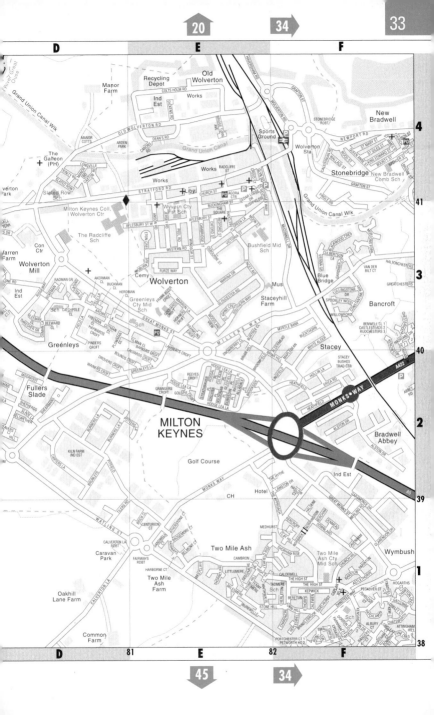

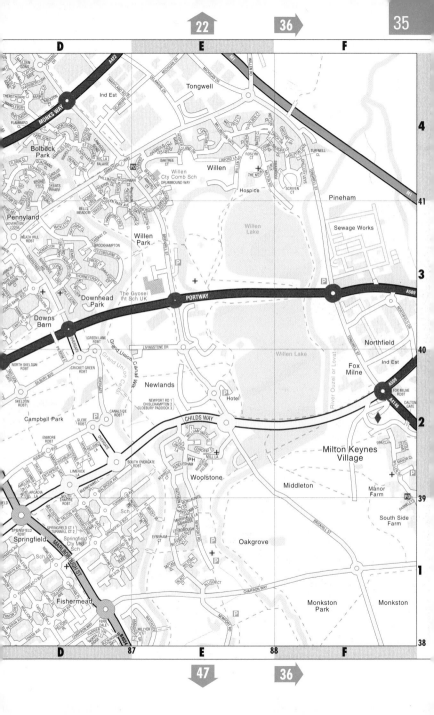

A
B
C

4

Hotel

COMPTON
CT   Moulsoe

Glebe
Farm

Church
Farm

NEWPORT RD

41

Hermitage
Farm

14

P

3

PORTWAY

A5130

Broughton
Barn

Old Covert

NORTHFIELD
RDBT

The Manor
House

Broughton Barns
Cotts

The
Old Rectory

Roundhill
Spinney

CHILDS RD

A509

CHICHELEY RD

40

Brooklands
Farm

New
Covert

Atterbury

Hotel

Broughton
Manor
Bsns Pk

Ravenstone
House

BROUGHTON RD

2

A4146

Broughton

Kingston
Bridge

MEADOW
LA

TONGWELL ST

39

GRIFFITH
GATE
RDBT

COLDWELL ST

Kingston
Bridge

Fen Farm

MONKSTON
RDBT

CHAFFRON WAY

MAIDSTONE RD

Kingston
Industrial
Estate

MANDEVILLE DR

NEWPORT RD

A5130

1

CHAFFRON WAY

NEWMARKET CT

CHIPPENHAM DR

WHITEHALL AVE

BALMERINO CL

ULVERSCROFT

LANERCOST
CRES

MARLBOROUGH ST

ST
BOTOLPHS

LAUNDE

CHETWODE AVE

HEYMONDHAM

A4146

WINCHESTER CIRC

BRINKLOW
RDBT

BRANSWORTH AVE

KINGSTON
RDBT

KINGSTON
RDBT

38

A421

STANDING WAY

ETHERIDGE AVE

89

A

90

B

91

C

D	E	F

Wood End Farm

Cranfield Airfield

Lower Wood

Cranfield Tech Pk

Stilliters Farm

Mast

Villa Pk **4**

Leys Farm

Conn's Farm

41

Broughton Grounds

Salford Wood

Holcotmoors Farm **3**

Holcotmoors Lodge

CRANFIELD RD

Whitsundoles Farm

Milton Keynes Boundary Wlk

40

College Farm

Rectory Farm

Mill Farm

2

Rooktree Farm

Salford

BROUGHTON RD

MILL LA

HONS LA

COURT

MANOR RD

Salfordford Bridge

Manor House

Inn

Waterhall

The Islands

Church Farm

39

Fox Covert

Water Hall Farm

Hulcot Manor

Hulcoté

1

Eagle Farm

Aspley Hall

CRANFIELD RD

Wavendon Lodge

LOWER END RD

Golf Course

A421

M1

38

D	93	E	94	F

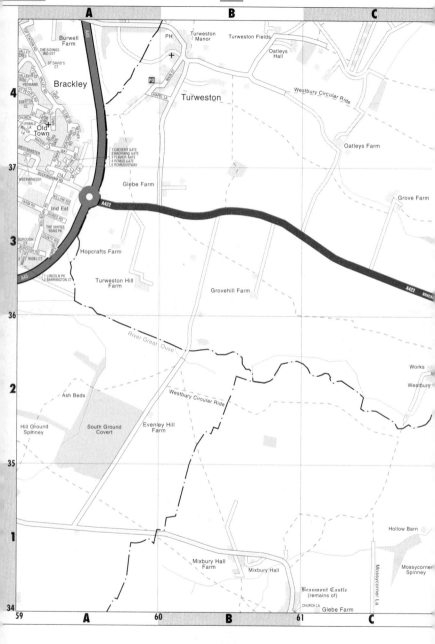

Brackley

Burwell
Farm

THE SIDINGS
IND EST

ST DAVID'S
CT

PH

Turweston
Manor

Turweston Fields

Oatleys
Hall

Westbury Circular Ride

PO

Turweston

Old
Town

1 CAESERS GATE
2 HADRIANS GATE
3 FLAVIUS GATE
4 REMUS GATE
5 ROMULUS WAY

Oatleys Farm

Grove
Farm

Glebe Farm

A422

Ind Est

A422

A422 BRACK

THE SHIRES
BSMS PK

Hopcrafts Farm

1 LINCOLN PK
2 BARRINGTON CT

Turweston Hill
Farm

Grovehill Farm

River Great Ouse

Works

Westbury

Ash Beds

Westbury Circular Ride

Hill Ground
Spinney

South Ground
Covert

Evenley Hill
Farm

Hollow Barn

Mixbury Hall
Farm

Mixbury Hall

Beaumont Castle
(remains of)

CHURCH LA

Glebe Farm

Mossycorner La

Mossycorner
Spinney

59   60   61

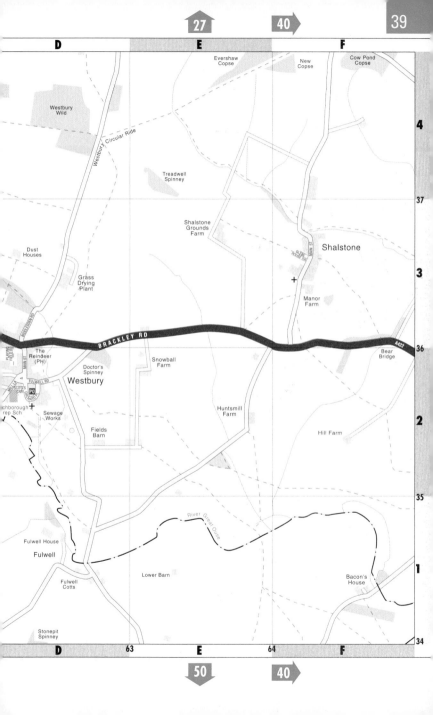

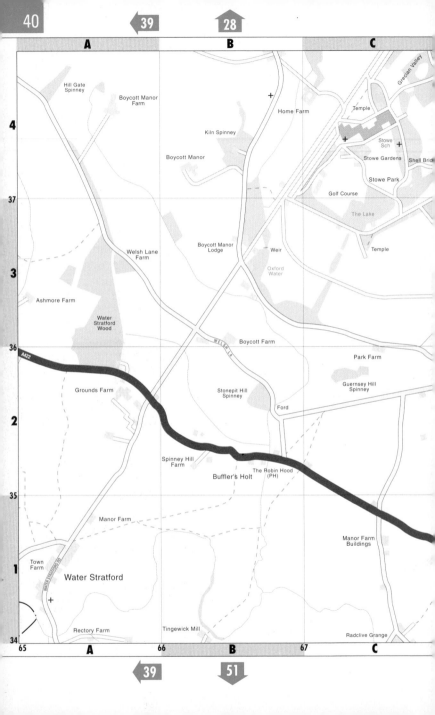

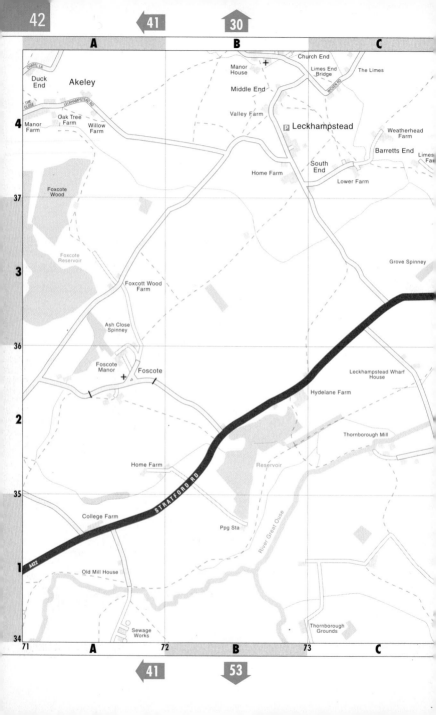

D
E
F

Little Oaken Copse

Rabbit Wood

Mount Mill Farm

Great Oaken Copse

4

Little Hill Farm

A422

37

River Great Ouse

Thornton Quabs

3

ord e

Weir

+

Thornton Coll (RC Convent Sch)

Thornton

Blackfields Farm

Thornton Park Farm

36

Home Farm

New Plantation

2

Village Farm Barn

Great Wood

Thornton Hall

35

Cowpen Wood

Tyrellcote Farm

Elder Spinney

THORNTON RD

1

Rogers Spinney

Langbridge Farm

34

D
75
E
76
F

A B C

4

Beachampton
Hall

Blacon
Spinney

Upper
Weald

Milton Keynes Boundary Wlk

Manor
Farm

Hill Farm

37

Beachampton

The Bell
(PH)

Home Farm

WATER LA

Red
House
Farm

Grange
Farm

Beachampton
Grove

Grove Farm

3

36

School
Furze

The Oaks

Potash
Farm

2

Furzenfield
Farm

35

Elm
Farm

Yew Tree
Farm

Basshill
Farm

WHADDON RD

1

THORNTON RD

Holywell
Cottages

Town's End

North Buckinghamshire Way

Holywell Farm

The
Hill

Nash

THORNBOROUGH RD

THORNBOROUGH RD

PH

HIGH ST

WINSLOW RD

Barnhi
Farm

34

77

A

78

B

79

C

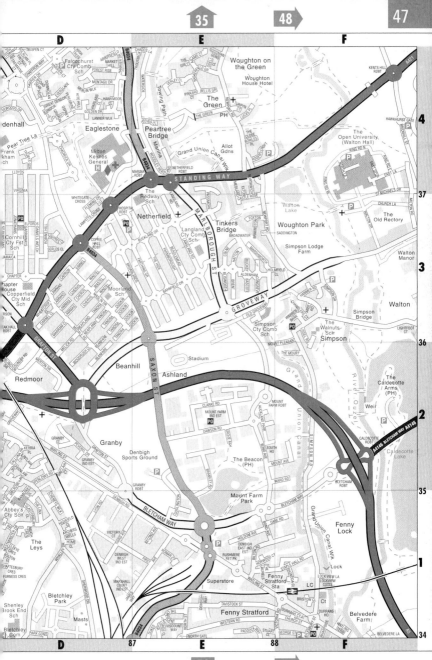

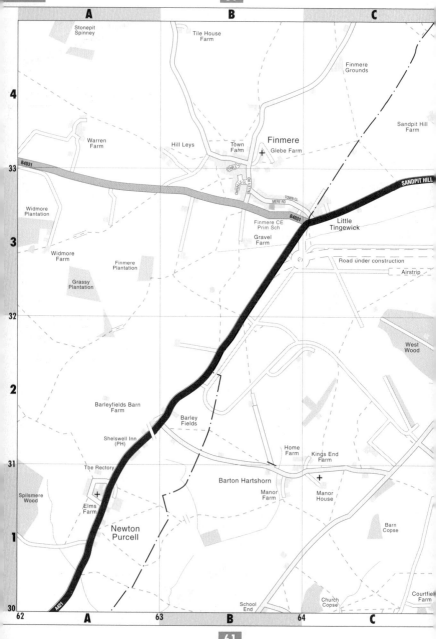

Stonepit
Spinney

Tile House
Farm

Finmere
Grounds

Sandpit Hill
Farm

4

Warren
Farm

Hill Leys

Town
Farm

Finmere

Glebe Farm

B4031

33

Widmore
Plantation

STABLE LA

CHURCH LA

MILL LA

TOWN CL

MERE RD

Finmere CE
Prim Sch

B4031

SANDPIT HILL

**Little
Tingewick**

3

Widmore
Farm

Finmere
Plantation

Gravel
Farm

Road under construction

Airstrip

Grassy
Plantation

32

West
Wood

2

Barleyfields Barn
Farm

Barley
Fields

Shelswell Inn
(PH)

Home
Farm

Kings End
Farm

31

The Rectory

Barton Hartshorn

Spilsmere
Wood

Elms
Farm

Manor
Farm

Manor
House

Barn
Copse

1

**Newton
Purcell**

School
End

Church
Copse

Courtfie
Farm

A421

30

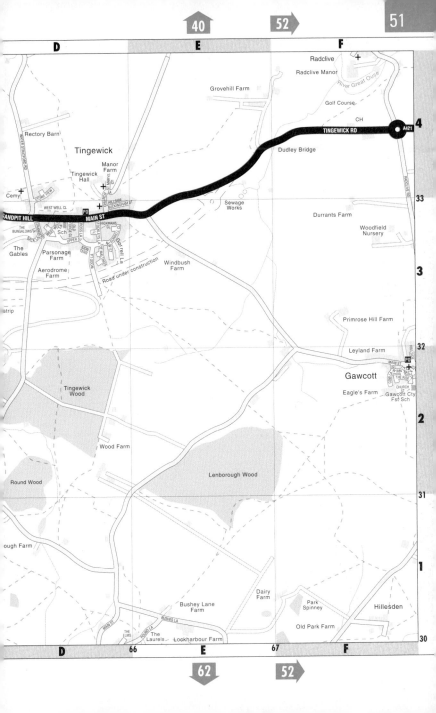

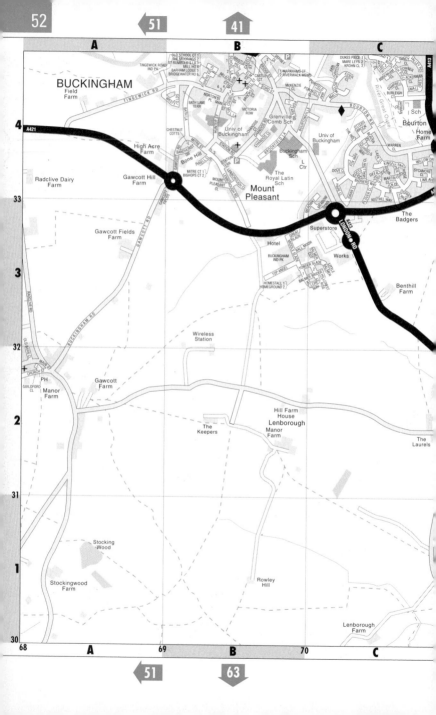

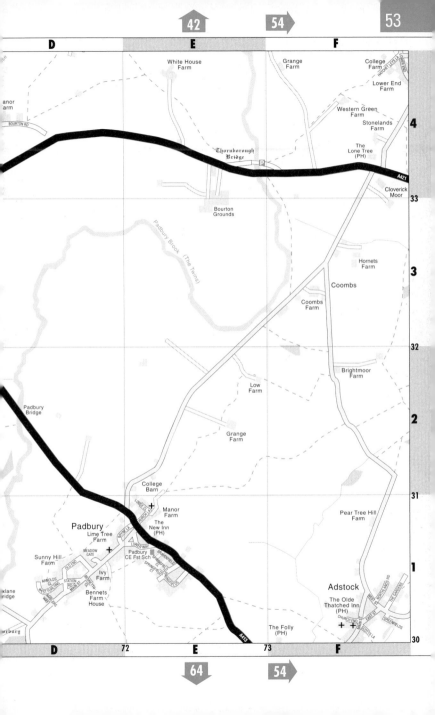

D   E   F

White House
Farm

Grange
Farm

College
Farm

LOWER END

HARDWICK RD

Lower End
Farm

BOURTON RD

anor
arm

Western Green
Farm

Stonelands
Farm

4

The
Lone Tree
(PH)

Thornborough
Bridge

P

A421

Cloverick
Moor

33

Bourton
Grounds

Padbury Brook (The Twins)

Hornets
Farm

3

Coombs

Coombs
Farm

32

Brightmoor
Farm

Low
Farm

Padbury
Bridge

2

Grange
Farm

College
Barn

31

LONG CL LA

NORTH END LA

Manor
Farm

Pear Tree Hill
Farm

Padbury

The
New Inn
(PH)

VICTOR LA

Lime Tree
Farm

MEADOW GATE

LOWER WAY

Padbury
CE Fst Sch

SPRINGFIELD
GARDENFIELD

Sunny Hill
Farm

OLD END

ARNOLDS

STATION RD

WEST FURLONG

MAIN ST

Ivy
Farm

WHITE DRIVE

Bennets
Farm
House

1

Adstock

xlane
ridge

The Olde
Thatched Inn
(PH)

CHURCH END

BRICK

FREE ST

NORTHLANDS RD

THE CHASERS

GREENFIELDS

PIGGOTTS LA

orbury

A413

The Folly
(PH)

30

D   72   E   73   F

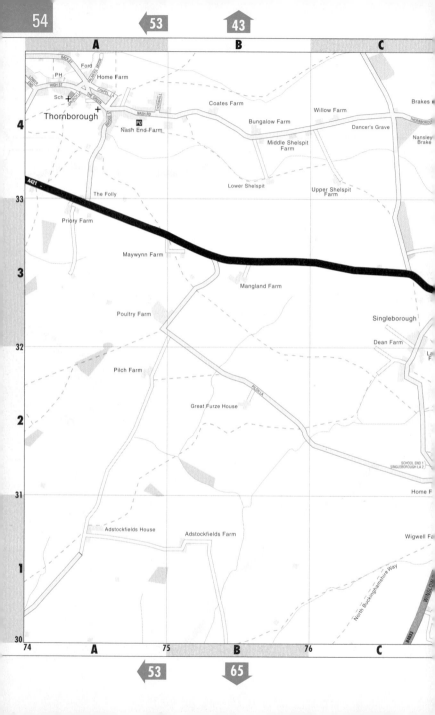

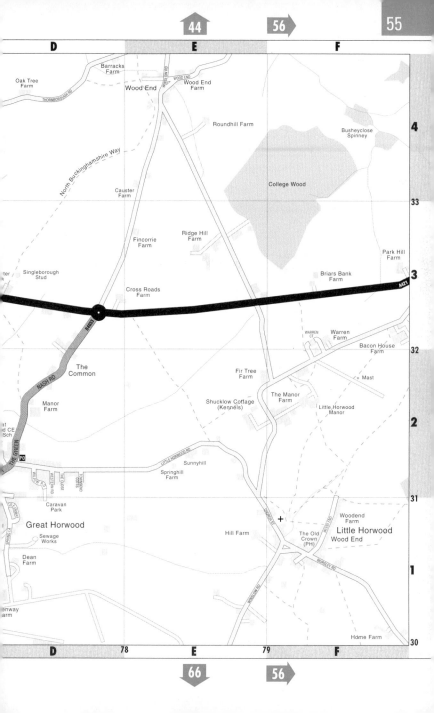

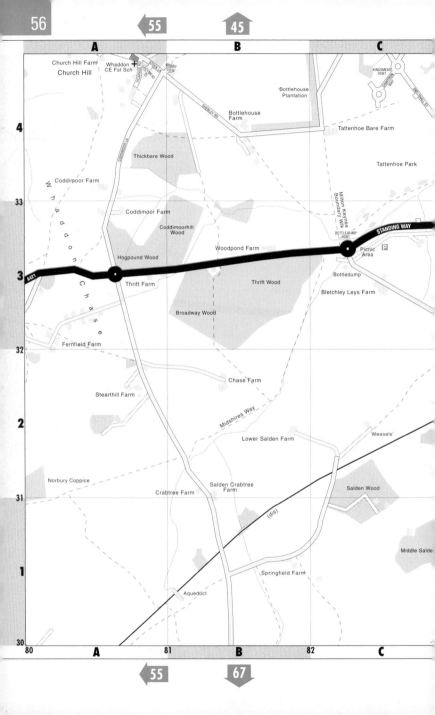

A **B** **C**

4

Church Hill Farm
Church Hill
Whaddon
CE Fst Sch

STOCK LA
CODIMOOR LA
BRIARY VIEW

SHENLEY RD

Bottlehouse
Plantation

Bottlehouse
Farm

KINGSMEAD
RDBT

CHARTHILL WAY

BRICKHILL ST

Tattenhoe Bare Farm

Thickbare Wood

Tattenhoe Park

W h a d d o n

Coddimoor Farm

33

Coddimoor Farm

Milton Keynes
Boundary Wlk

Coddimoorhill
Wood

STANDING WAY

BOTTLE DUMP
RDBT

Woodpond Farm

Hogpound Wood

Picnic
Area

P

C h a s e

3 A421

Thrift Farm

Bottledump

Thrift Wood

Bletchley Leys Farm

Broadway Wood

32

Fernfield Farm

Chase Farm

Stearthill Farm

Midshires Way

2

Lower Salden Farm

Weasels'

Norbury Coppice

Salden Crabtree
Farm

Salden Wood

31

Crabtree Farm

(dis)

Middle Salde

1

Springfield Farm

Aqueduct

30

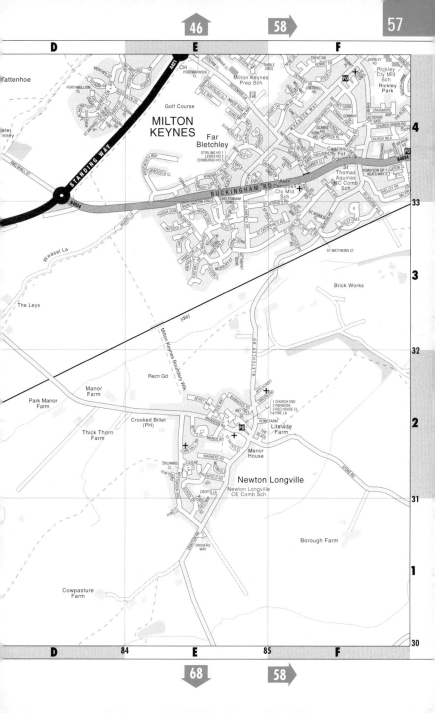

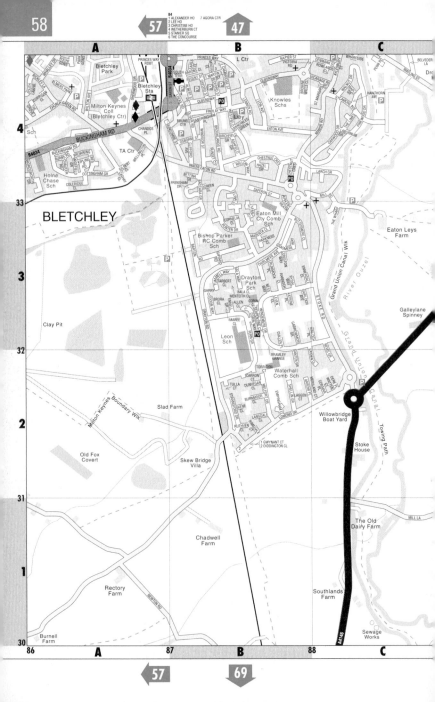

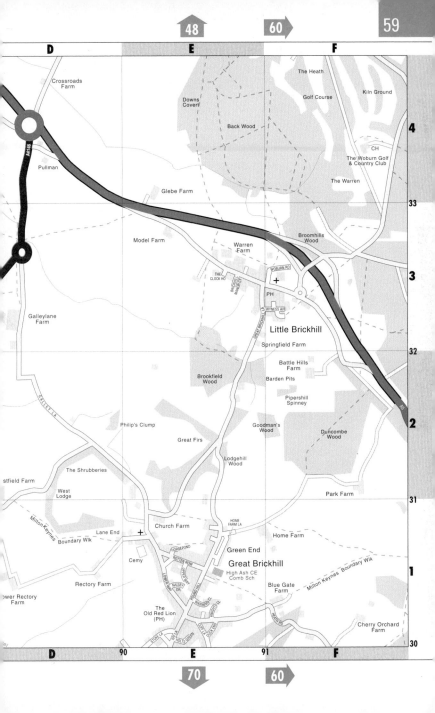

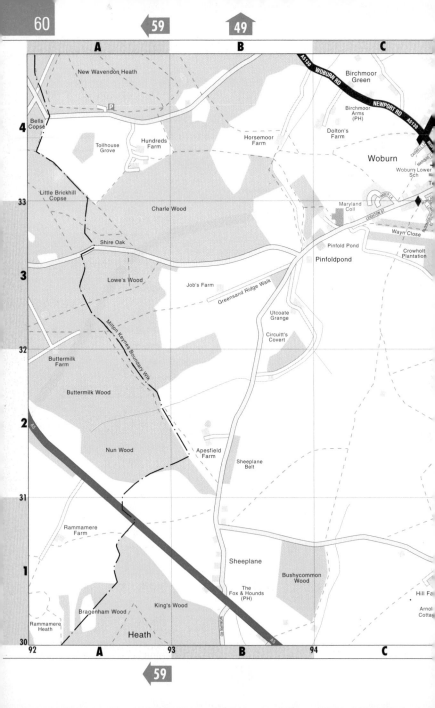

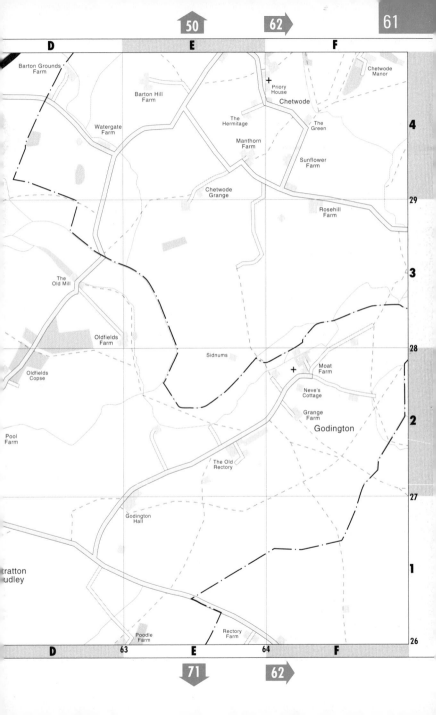

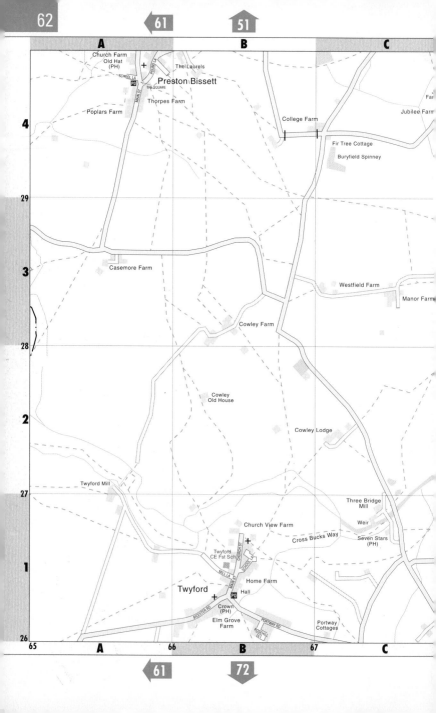

A   **B**   **C**

Church Farm
Old Hat
(PH)
The Laurels
SCHOOL LA
PO
Preston Bissett
THE SQUARE

Thorpes Farm

College Farm

Poplars Farm

Fir Tree Cottage

Buryfield Spinney

Jubilee Farm
Far

4

29

Casemore Farm

Westfield Farm

Manor Farm

3

Cowley Farm

28

Cowley
Old House

Cowley Lodge

2

Twyford Mill

Three Bridge
Mill

27

Weir

Church View Farm

Cross Bucks Way

Seven Stars
(PH)

Twyford
CE Fst Sch

1

Home Farm

Twyford

Hall

PO

Crown
(PH)

Portway Cottages

Elm Grove
Farm

PORTWAY RD

RIDGEHILL CL

BICESTER RD

MILL LA

MAIN ST

26

D   **E**   **F**

The Barracks

Brasses Spinney

Padbury Mill

West Hill Farm **4**

Lower Farm

Claydon Brook

PO

Orchard View

The Orchard

29

Home Farm

King's Bridge

Lower Kingsbridge Farm

Cross Bucks Way

Hillesden

Kingsbridge Cottage

Kingsbridge Farm **3**

Church-hill Farm

Sewage Works

28

Padbury Brook

Claydon Plank (FB)

Northend Farm

2

North End

Steeple Claydon

Allan Shaw Cty Comb Sch

SPORTSMAN CL

OLD SCHOOL YD

PH

Elm Tree Farm

27

West End

Liby

arhill

Hog Bridge

PO

Manor Farm

Willowvale Farm

Church End

QUEEN CATHERINE RD

Camp Close

1

Redland Bridge

Pear Tree House

(dis)

26

D   69   **E**   70   **F**

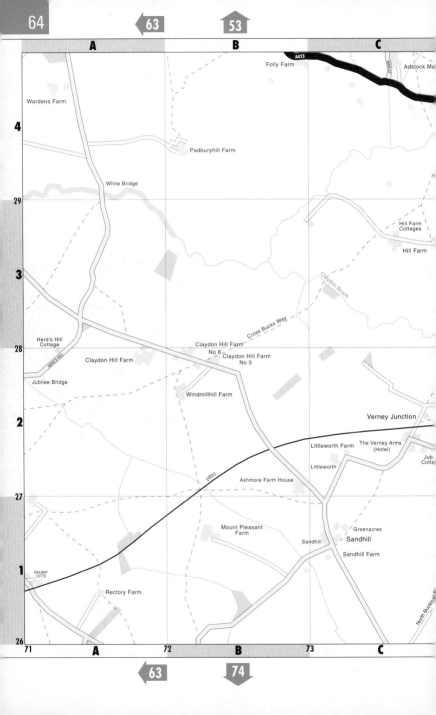

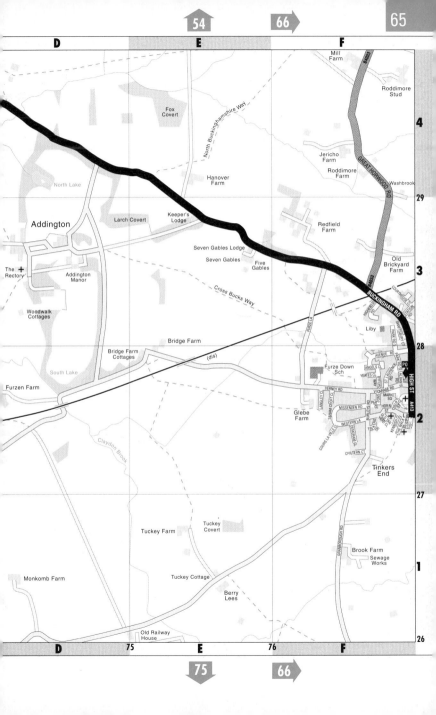

D   E   F

Mill Farm

Roddimore Stud

4

Fox Covert

North Buckinghamshire Way

Jericho Farm

Roddimore Farm

GREAT HORWOOD RD

B4033

Washbrook

North Lake

Hanover Farm

29

Addington

Larch Covert

Keeper's Lodge

Redfield Farm

The Rectory

Addington Manor

Seven Gables Lodge

Seven Gables

Five Gables

Old Brickyard Farm

BUCKINGHAM RD

B4033

3

Woodwalk Cottages

Cross Bucks Way

Bridge Farm

Liby

Bridge Farm Cottages

(dis)

Furze Down Sch

AVENUE RD

ANGELS CL

28

Furzen Farm

South Lake

YEATES CL

VERNEY RD

MARKET SQ

V.VICARAGE RD

PO

Glebe Farm

MISSENDEN RD

WESTERN LA

BUCKINGHAM RD

LANGLEY CL

SAHAM RD

PURLETS RD

HORN ST

HIGH ST

A413

BELL

2

CHILTERN CT

Tinkers End

27

Claydon Brook

Tuckey Covert

Tuckey Farm

GRANBOROUGH RD

Brook Farm

Sewage Works

1

Monkomb Farm

Tuckey Cottage

Berry Lees

26

Old Railway House

D   75   E   76   F

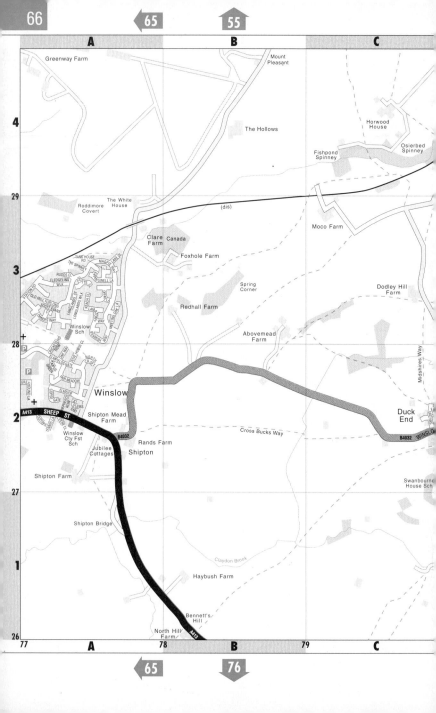

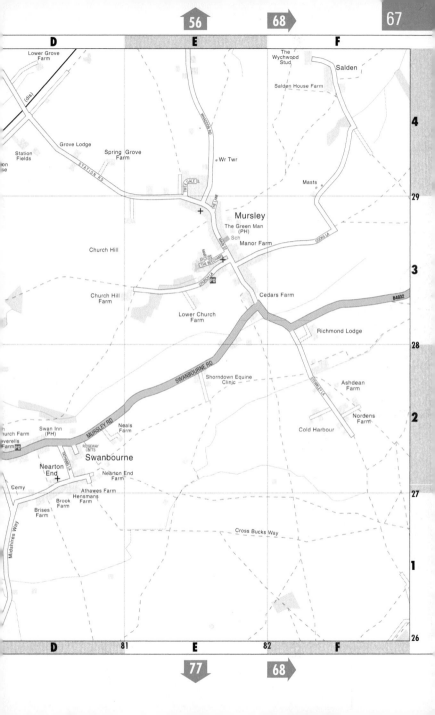

Lower Grove
Farm

(dis)

Station
Fields

Grove Lodge

STATION RD

Spring Grove
Farm

Church Hill

The
Wychwood
Stud

Salden

Salden House Farm

BRIGGOR RD

Wr Twr

TWITE DALE CL

THE LANE

Masts

Mursley

The Green Man
(PH)

Sch

Manor Farm

MAIN ST

THE BEECHAMS

CHURCH RD

PO

COOPS LA

Church Hill
Farm

Lower Church
Farm

Cedars Farm

B4032

Richmond Lodge

28

SWANBOURNE RD

Shorndown Equine
Clinic

STEWKLEY LA

Ashdean
Farm

MURSLEY RD

Swan Inn
(PH)

urch Farm

averells
Farm PO

Neals
Farm

RIDGEWAY
COTTS

Swanbourne

Nearton
End

PEOVERS LA

Nearton End
Farm

Cold Harbour

Nordens
Farm

Cemy

Brises
Farm

Brook
Farm

Athawes Farm
Hensmans
Farm

Midshires Way

Cross Bucks Way

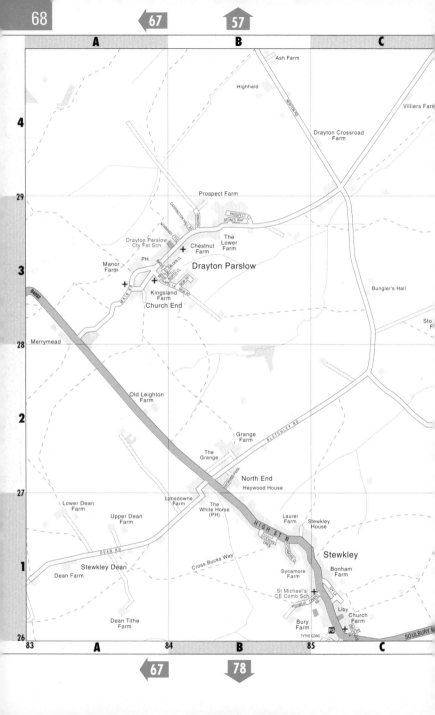

A   **B**   **C**

Ash Farm

Highfield

Villiers Farm

Drayton Crossroad Farm

4

29

Prospect Farm

PROSPECT CL

STONES WAY

CARRINGTON HILL RD

NEWMANS CL

HIGHFIELD

Drayton Parslow Cty Fst Sch

Chestnut Farm

The Lower Farm

The Lower Farm

Drayton Parslow

Manor Farm

PH

BATE'S CL

LOWNDES CL

GLEBE CL

NORTH RD

STAIRS LA

NEW RD

Bungler's Hall

3

B4032

Kingsland Farm

Church End

Sto P

28

Merrymead

Old Leighton Farm

2

BLETCHLEY RD

Grange Farm

The Grange

BEECHWOOD PARK

North End

Heywood House

Lower Dean Farm

27

Lansdowne Farm

The White Horse (PH)

Laurel Farm

Stewkley House

Upper Dean Farm

HIGH ST N

STOCKHALL CRES

SOULBURY RD

Stewkley

DEAN RD

Cross Bucks Way

1

Sycamore Farm

Bonham Farm

Stewkley Dean

Dean Farm

St Michael's CE Comb Sch

FISHWEIR CLOSE SO

Liby

Church Farm

MURSLEY RD

Dean Tithe Farm

Bury Farm

TYTHE GDNS

PO

SOULBURY

26

83   **A**   **84**   **B**   **85**   **C**

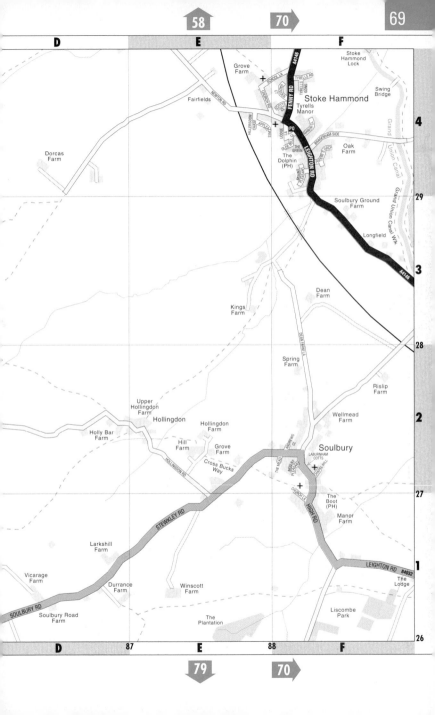

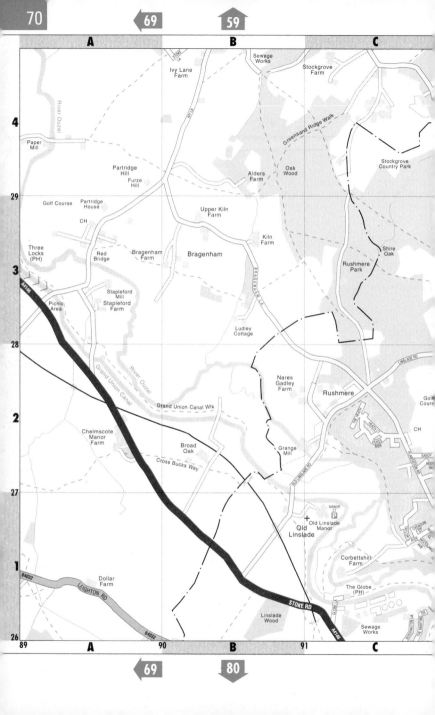

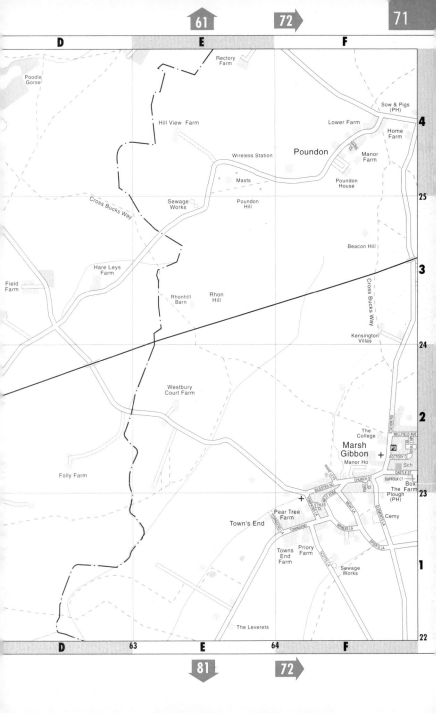

D
E
F

Poodle Gorse

Rectory Farm

Sow & Pigs (PH)

Hill View Farm

Lower Farm

Home Farm

4

Wireless Station

Poundon

Manor Farm

Masts

Poundon House

25

Cross Bucks Way

Sewage Works

Poundon Hill

Beacon Hill

3

Hare Leys Farm

Field Farm

Rhonhill Barn

Rhon Hill

Cross Bucks Way

Kensington Villas

24

Westbury Court Farm

2

The College

Marsh Gibbon

MILLFIELD AVE

PO

RECTORY CL.

Manor Ho

Sch

CASTLE ST

SUFFOLK CT.

Box Farm

The Plough (PH)

23

Folly Farm

BICESTER RD.

CHURCH ST

STYLES

Cemy

Pear Tree Farm

Town's End

TOWNSEND

WALES LA.

Towns End Farm

Priory Farm

Sewage Works

1

The Leverets

22

D
63
E
64
F

A **B** **C**

Cross Bucks Way
Red Furlong Farm

Rosehill Farm

Portway Rd
Portway Farm

Twyford Lodge

4

Grebe Lake

25

Lawn Farm

Hampden Hill
Charndon

Windmill Hill

Wootton Gn

Station House

3

Charndon Grounds

Main St

Middle Farm

Valley Farm

Hill Farm

24

2

Little Marsh Rd
Potts Cl
Swan Lane
Swan Farm
Little Marsh

Gubbinshole Ditch

Castle St

23

Castle St
Leopold Farm

Summerstown

Rectory Farm

Edgcott

1

New Swan Farm

Gubbin's Hole

Leyburne Cl
Rochester Rd

PO

Gubbins Hole Farm

Lower Farm
Grendon Rd

22

73
64

A
B
C
4
25
3
24
2
23
1
22
71
A
72
B
73
C
Home Farm
Cemy
PO
Middle Claydon
Weir
The Old Brick Yard (disused)
Claydon Park
Claydon House
Catherine Farm
South Lodge
Phoenix Fruit Farm
THREE POINTS LA
Home Wood
Muxwell Farm
Romer Wood
Balmore Wood
Greatsea Wood
Runt's Wood
Three Points La
Finemerehill House
Kitehill Farm
New Farm
SANDHILL RD
Verney Farm
VERNEY FARM CL
EMERALD CL
CHURC
ST MARYS CL
CHESTNUT VIEW
East Claydon
ST MARYS RD
Ivy Nook
East Claydon Cty Fst Sch
Botolph Farm
BOTYL RD
PO
Botolph Farm
Botolph Claydon
ORCHARD WAY
WEIR LA
Bernwood Farm
Claydon Lawn
Hogshaw Farm
Coppice Lowhill Farm
Hogshaw Farm

73
84

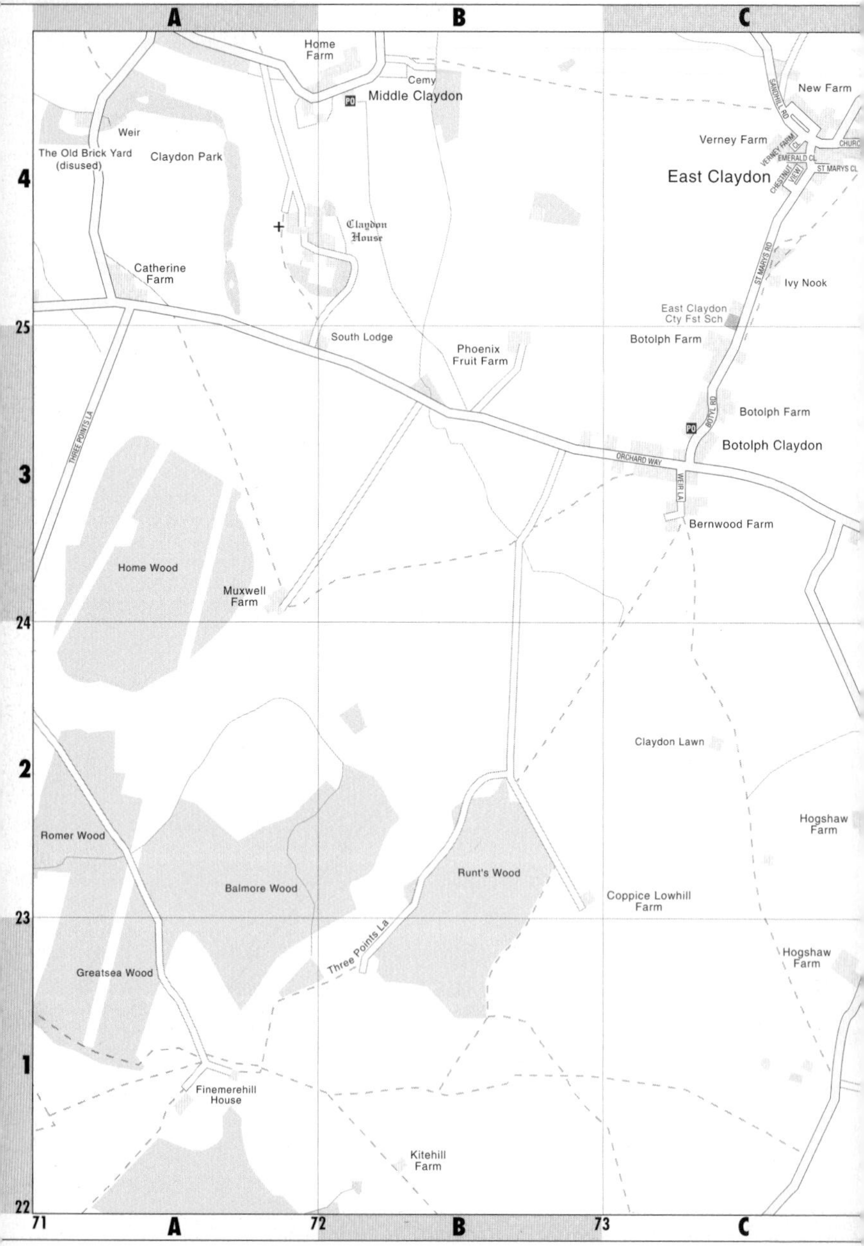

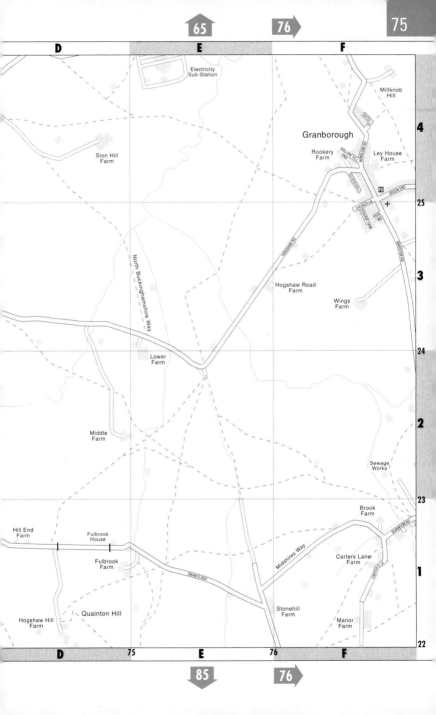

Electricity
Sub-Station

Millknob
Hill

4

Granborough

Sion Hill
Farm

Rookery
Farm

Ley House
Farm

HOLLOW HILL END

WINSLOW RD

GREEN END

PO

25

CHURCH LA

CHAPEL LA

PARK RD

MANSFIELD RD

North Buckinghamshire Way

Hogshaw Road
Farm

HOGSHAW RD

3

Wings
Farm

24

Lower
Farm

2

Middle
Farm

Sewage
Works

23

Hill End
Farm

Fulbrook
House

Brook
Farm

QUAINTON RD

Midshires Way

Carters Lane
Farm

Fulbrook
Farm

SWAN'S WAY

CARTERS LA

1

Stonehill
Farm

Manor
Farm

Hogshaw Hill
Farm

Quainton Hill

22

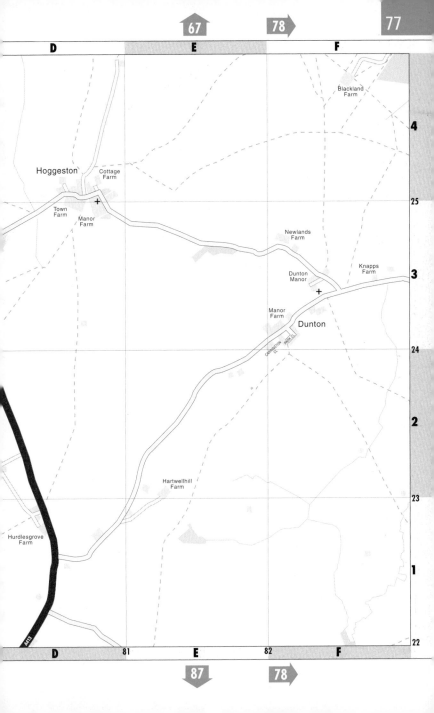

D
E
F

4

Blackland
Farm

25

Hoggeston
Cottage
Farm

Town
Farm
Manor
Farm

Newlands
Farm

Knapps
Farm

3

Dunton
Manor

Manor
Farm

Dunton

24

CARRINGTON CL.
PRIOR CL.

2

Hartwellhill
Farm

23

Hurdlesgrove
Farm

1

A413

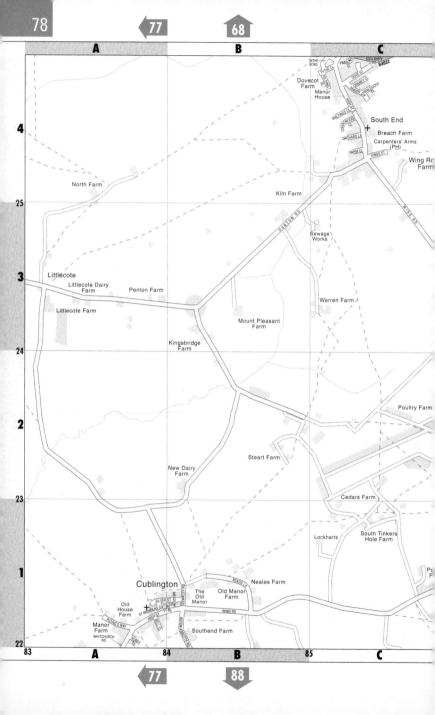

A   **B**   **C**

TYTHE GDNS

THE CL

DUKE ST

PARSONS

SOULBURY RD

B4032

BRACDE CL

SWALLOWS

PENNEL CL

Dovecot Farm

Manor House

MALTINGS CL

DOVEBRIDGE CL

South End

ORCHARD LA

Breach Farm

Carpenters' Arms (PH)

FARM CL

KINGS ST

Wing Rd Farm

4

North Farm

25

Kiln Farm

SUTTON RD

WING RD

Sewage Works

3

Littlecote

Littlecote Dairy Farm

Penton Farm

Warren Farm

Littlecote Farm

Mount Pleasant Farm

24

Kingsbridge Farm

2

Poultry Farm

Steart Farm

New Dairy Farm

23

Cedars Farm

Lockharts

South Tinkers Hole Farm

1

Neales Farm

READS LA

Cublington

SILVER ST

The Old Manor

Old Manor Farm

Old House Farm

ST NICHOLAS CL

HIGH ST

ASTON ABBOTTS RD

WING RD

BETTLE

Manor Farm

RUDDS & WAY

WHITCHURCH RD

HIGH ST

Southend Farm

22

83   **A**   **84**   **B**   **85**   **C**

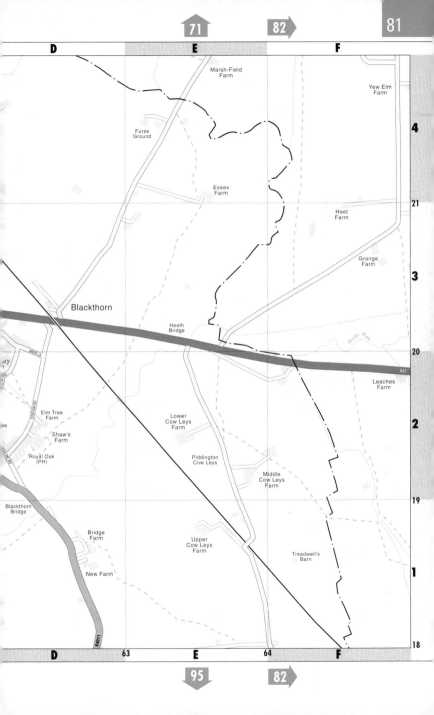

4

21

3

20

2

19

1

Marsh-Field
Farm

Yew Elm
Farm

Furze
Ground

Essex
Farm

Heet
Farm

Grange
Farm

Blackthorn

Heath
Bridge

River Ray

A41

Leaches
Farm

Elm Tree
Farm

Lower
Cow Leys
Farm

Shaw's
Farm

Piddington
Cow Leys

Middle
Cow Leys
Farm

Royal Oak
(PH)

Blackthorn
Bridge

Bridge
Farm

Upper
Cow Leys
Farm

Treadwell's
Barn

New Farm

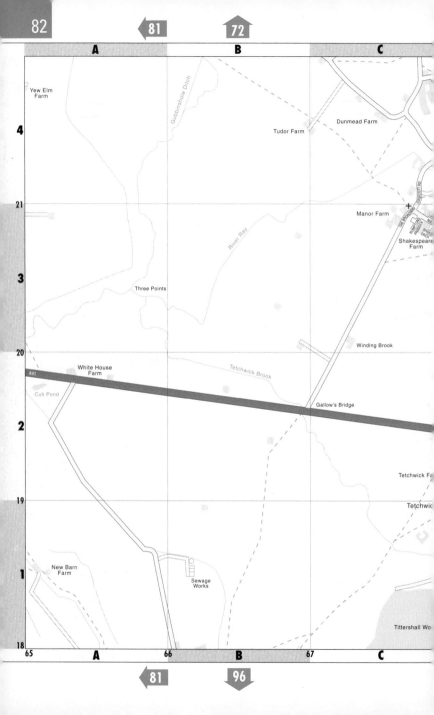

A
B
C

Yew Elm
Farm

Gubbinshole Ditch

Dunmead Farm

Tudor Farm

4

21

Manor Farm

River Ray

Shakespeare
Farm

3

Three Points

20

Winding Brook

White House
Farm

A41

Tetchwick Brook

Cub Pond

Gallow's Bridge

2

Tetchwick Fa

19

Tetchwi

New Barn
Farm

1

Sewage
Works

18

Tittershall Wo

D
E
F

4

Springhill
(H M Prison)

Spring Hill

Mill Hill

Hewin's
Wood

Lee Wood

Grendon Wood

River Ray

Grendon
Underwood

21

dle
m

The Swan
(PH)

MAIN ST

BAKER'S CT

OWNER'S CL

Grange
Farm

Bailey's
Farm

Butler's
Farm

Grove Farm

Oak Tree
Cottages

Doddershall Wood

Woodside Farm

3

Knapps Hook
Farm

Lawn
Farm

20

Pear Tree
Farm

Sharp's Hill

Sharpshill
Farm

Brick Kiln
Farm

Kingswood

GRENDON RD

Oving Hill Farm

2

Ham Home
Wood

Hamgreen
Wood

The Plough
and Anchor
(PH)

+

19

Rookery Farm

The
Crooked Billet
(PH)

Ham
Green

Kingswoodlane
Farm

Mercer's
Farm

Mercer's
Wood

KINGSWOOD LA

Glear
Farm

Collett Farm

1

Woodlands
Farm

Ham Farm

LC

PORTSMOUTH RD

Woodham

Little Yeat
Farm

A41

18

D
E
F

A
B
C

4

Finemere Wood

Dry Leys
Farm

River Ray

Shipton Lee

Woodlands
Farm

Middle Farm

Hill Farm

Lee House

21

Woodlands
Cottages

Lee Bridge Cottage

Grange

North
Farm

Grange
Farm

3

LEE RD

Railway
Cottage

Dodershall
House

20

Fieldside
Farm

Knapps Hook
Wood

2

Lower South
Farm

Upper South
Farm

Factory

Binwell
Farm

19

Quain
Railway C

Mast

1

Upper Barn
Farm

Lower
Farm

18

71
A
72
B
73
C

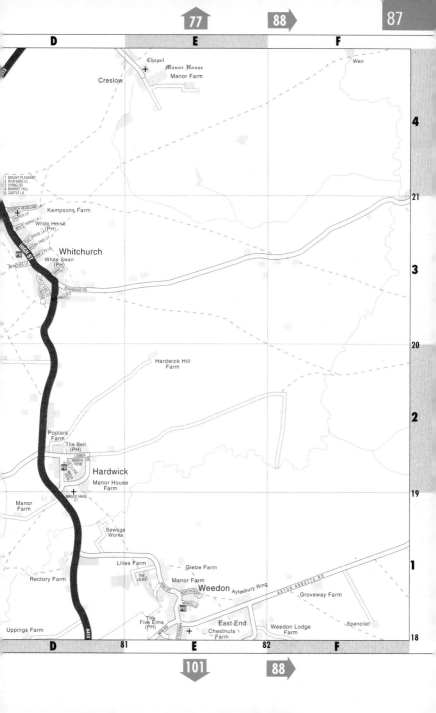

Creslow

Chapel

Manor House
Manor Farm

Weir

4

1 MOUNT PLEASANT
2 RICKYARD CL
3 OVING RD
4 MARKET HILL
5 CASTLE LA

Kempsons Farm

21

CHURCH HEADLAND LA
CHURCH LA
WHITE HORSE LA
POST OFFICE LA
BEECH TREE CT
HAWKEYS LA

White Horse
(PH)

HIGH ST

Whitchurch

PO

White Swan
(PH)

BLANCHES LA
BELL WALK

3

BUSHMEAD RD

SHMEAD

20

Hardwick Hill
Farm

2

Poplars
Farm

The Bell
(PH)

LOWER
NORTH
VIEW

BELL CL
WEST ST

Hardwick

PO

Manor House
Farm

19

Manor
Farm

MANOR FARM
CT

Sewage
Works

Lilies Farm

Glebe Farm

1

Manor Farm

THE
LAURELS

HIGH ST

Weedon

Aylesbury Ring

ASTON ABBOTTS RD

Groveway Farm

Rectory Farm

NORTHCROFT

NEWVILLE

PO

The
Five Elms
(PH)

STOCKAWAY

NEW RD

East End

Chestnuts
Farm

Weedon Lodge
Farm

Spencilet

Uppings Farm

18

A413

A **B** **C**

4

21

3

Sewage
Works

Red Barn

Red Barn
Farm

Vicarage
Farm

Longmoor
Farm

Works

Freemasons
Wood

Aston Abbotts +

Church
Farm

Home
Farm

The
Abbey

Bull & Butcher
(PH)

Norduck
Farm

20

Nashs
Farm

New
Zealand

Windmill Hill
Farm

WINGRAVE
CROSSROADS

2

Windmill
Hill

Fox
Covert

Barns
Farm

19

Lower Burston
Farm

Burston Hill
Farm

1

Burston Hill

Manor
Farm

Hale Farm

Aylesbury Ring

18

83 **A** 84 **B** 85 **C**

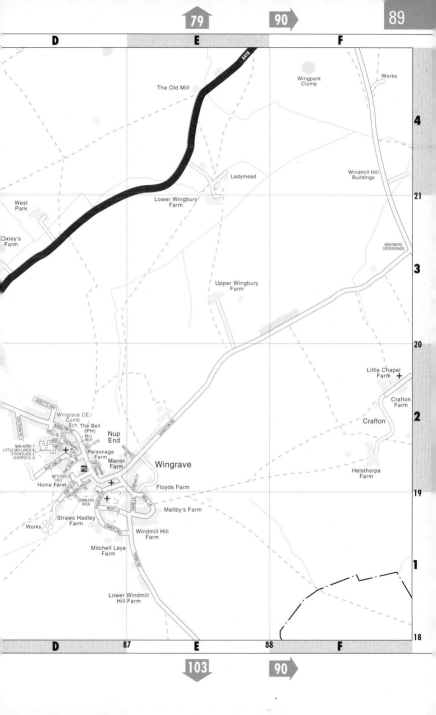

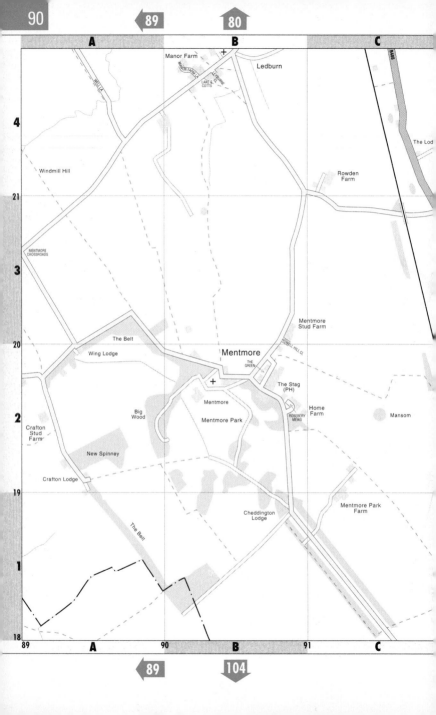

A   B   C

Manor Farm

Ledburn

WELL LA

MANOR FARM LA

LEYBURNE CL

LAKE & COTTS

The Lod

4

Windmill Hill

Rowden Farm

B488

21

MENTMORE CROSSROADS

3

Mentmore Stud Farm

The Belt

20

Wing Lodge

Mentmore

HORWELL HILL CL

THE GREEN

The Stag (PH)

Big Wood

Mentmore

Mentmore Park

Home Farm

Mansom

2

Crafton Stud Farm

New Spinney

ROSEBERY MEWS

Crafton Lodge

19

Cheddington Lodge

Mentmore Park Farm

The Belt

1

18

89   A   90   B   91   C

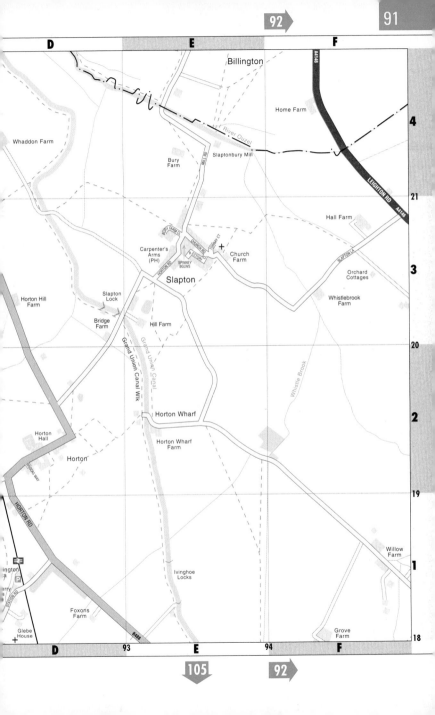

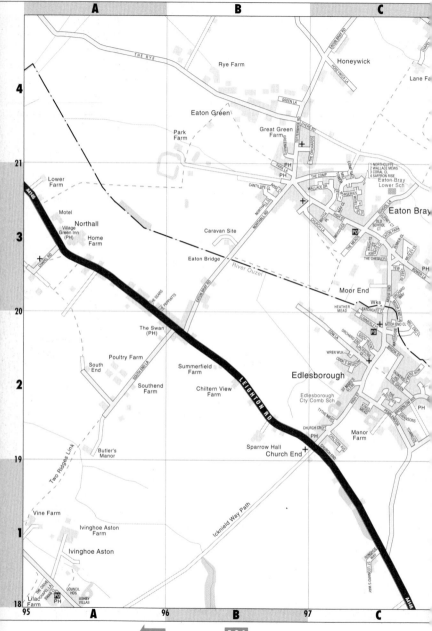

THE RYE

Rye Farm

Honeywick

Lane Fa

4

Eaton Green

Park
Farm

GREEN LA

Great Green
Farm

PH

PH

1 NORTHOLME
2 WALLACE MEWS
3 CORAL CL
4 SAFFRON RISE

Eaton Bray
Lower Sch

21

Lower
Farm

CANTILUPE CL

WALLACE DR

THE COMP

NORTHALL RD

Motel

Northall

Village
Green Inn
(PH)

Home
Farm

Caravan Site

Eaton Bray

OLD
SCHOOL
CT

PO

THE MEAD

THE CHEQUERS

3

Eaton Bridge

River Ouzel

EATON BRAY RD

YEW

Moor End

Wks

Moor End

HEATHER
MEAD

EATONGATE CT

PO

20

THE SLADE

THE SWAN
(PH)

ORCHARD END

CONE LA

GOOD INTENT

WREN WLK

COOK'S MEADOW

South
End

Poultry Farm

SOUTH MEAD

Edlesborough

2

Summerfield
Farm

Southend
Farm

Chiltern View
Farm

LEIGHTON RD

Edlesborough
Cty Comb Sch

ST MARGARETS

TYTHE MEAD

Butler's
Manor

Two Ridges Link

CHURCH CROFT

PH

Manor
Farm

19

Sparrow Hall

Church End

CHILTERN RISE

CHURCH END

Vine Farm

Icknield Way Path

1

Ivinghoe Aston
Farm

Ivinghoe Aston

ST EDMUND'S WAY

A4146

Lilac
Farm

THE GREEN

COUNCIL
HOS

ASHBY
VILLAS

PO

PH

18

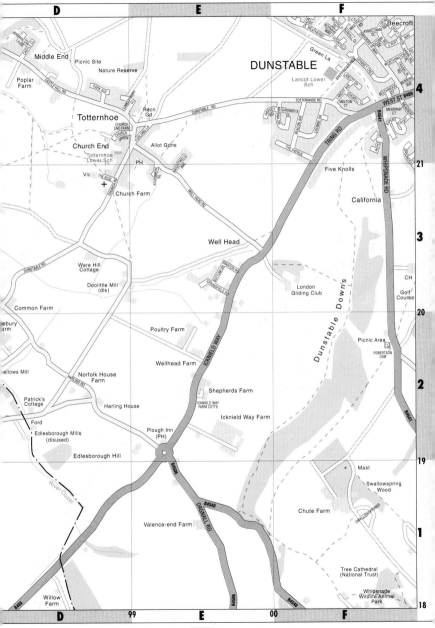

Beecroft

Middle End   Picnic Site

Nature Reserve

DUNSTABLE

Green La

Poplar Farm

Lancot Lower Sch

4

WEST ST B489

Totternhoe

Recn Gd

DUNSTABLE RD

TOTTERNHOE RD

B4541

WHIPSNADE RD

Church End   Allot Gdns

CHURCH END FARM

CHURCH GREEN

Totternhoe Lower Sch

PH

Vic

TRING RD

Five Knolls

21

California

Church Farm

WELL HEAD RD

3

Well Head

Ware Hill Cottage

MANTON RD

London Gliding Club

Dunstable Downs

CH

Doolittle Mill (dis)

DOOLITTLE LN

Golf Course

Common Farm

20

ebury arm

Poultry Farm

ICKNIELD WAY

Picnic Area

ROBERTSON CNR

ellows Mill

HARLING RD

Wellhead Farm

Norfolk House Farm

Shepherds Farm

2

B4541

Patrick's Cottage

Harling House

ICKNIELD WAY FARM COTTS

Icknield Way Farm

Ford

Plough Inn (PH)

Edlesborough Mills (disused)

19

Edlesborough Hill

B4506

Mast

River Ouzel

Swallowspring Wood

DAGNALL RD

Chute Farm

SWALLOWSPRINGS

B4540

1

Valence-end Farm

B489

Tree Cathedral (National Trust)

Whipsnade Wildlife Animal Park

Willow Farm

B4506

B4540

18

Astley Bridge Farm

River Ray

Murcott

Marlake House

Latchmeads

Whitecross Green

Manor Farm

Panshill Farms

Whitecross Green Wood

Nature Reserve

Upper Wood

Oriel Wood

Boarstall Lane

New Park Farm

Four Winds Farm

Upper Panshill Farm

The Plough (PH)

Offices

PALMER AVE

PATRICK HAUGH RD

Upper Arncott

Depot

CH

Arncott Hill

Arncott Wood

Arncott Hill Farm

Depot

ARNCOTT WOOD RD

Red House Farm

Oldhouse Spinney

Pans Hill

LC
LCs
LC

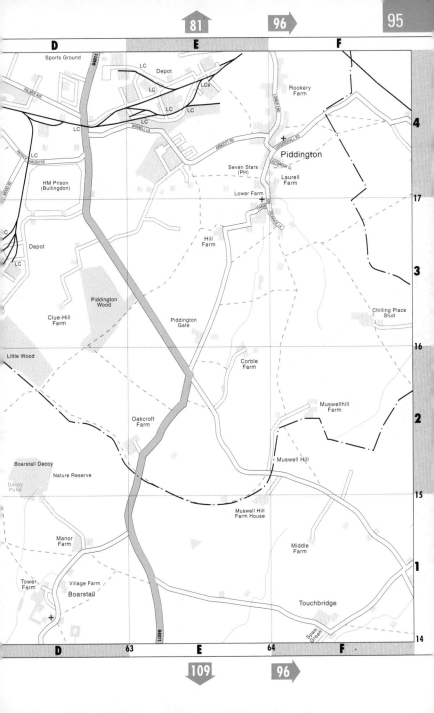

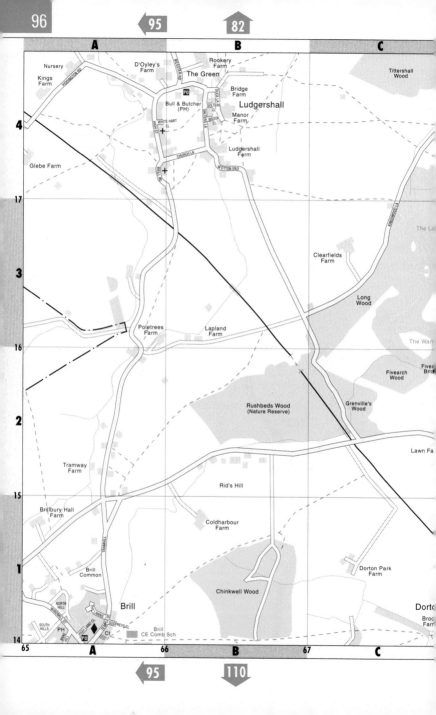

D
E
F

A41

4

17

3

16

2

15

1

14

KINGSWOOD LE

Yeat Farm

Moat Farm

Middle Farm

Wotton Brook

Hill Furlong Wood

Wotton House

Lodge Farm

Manor Farm

Grove Wood

Church Farm

Wotton Underwood

Sewage Works

The Row

Tramroad Ditch

Navigation Spinney

The Old Station

Thame Lodge

Cartersmead Spinney

Wotton Station House

Howe Wood

Berryfield Spinney

Hill Farm

East Farm

PO

The Red Lion (PH)

HILL COTTS

Ashendon

BRICK HILL

WOTTON RD

GREEN END

THE SQUARE

MAIN ST

FORGE CL

SPRING MDW

Sewage Works

Hill Farm

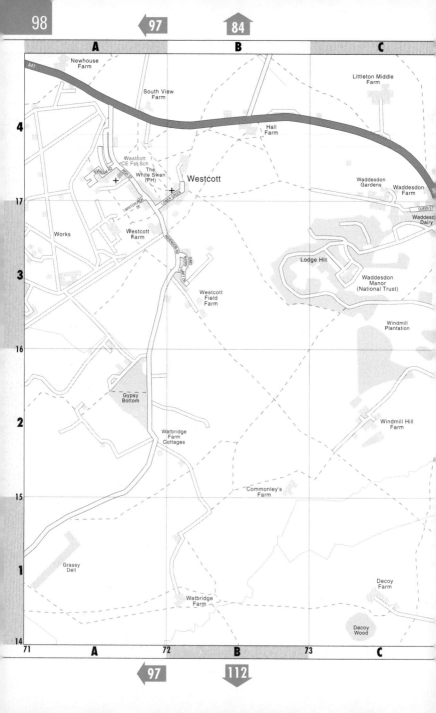

A41

Newhouse
Farm

South View
Farm

Littleton Middle
Farm

Hall
Farm

4

Westcott
CE Fst Sch

The
White Swan
(PH)

Westcott

Waddesdon
Gardens

Waddesdon
Farm

17

QUEEN ST

Waddesdon
Dairy

WHITCHURCH RD

LOWER GREEN

Works

Westcott
Farm

BOURNE RD

Lodge Hill

Waddesdon
Manor
(National Trust)

3

Westcott
Field Farm

Windmill
Plantation

16

Gypsy
Bottom

Windmill Hill
Farm

2

Watbridge
Farm
Cottages

Commonley's
Farm

15

1

Grassy
Dell

Decoy
Farm

Watbridge
Farm

Decoy
Wood

14

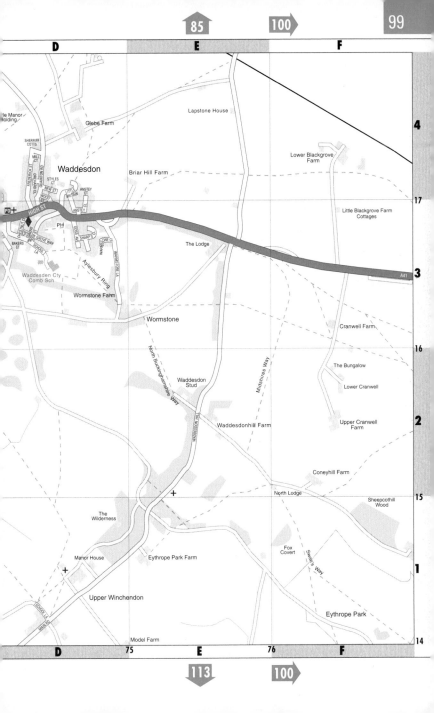

4

Lapstone House

Glebe Farm

Lower Blackgrove
Farm

SHERRIFF
COTTS
MILL
CT

Waddesdon

STYLES
CT
NEW ST
LITTLE
BRITAIN
ANSTEY
CT

Briar Hill Farm

17

PO

HIGH ST

ANSTEY
CT

Little Blackgrove Farm
Cottages

PH

GRS RD
SHARP'S

GROVE WAY

SCHOOL LA

WARMSTONE LA

CONE CL

The Lodge

A41

3

BAKERS
CT

Waddesdon Cty
Comb Sch

Aylesbury Ring

Cranwell Farm

Wormstone Farm

Wormstone

16

North Buckinghamshire Way

The Bungalow

Midshires Way

Waddesdon
Stud

Lower Cranwell

WADDESDON HILL

Waddesdonhill Farm

Upper Cranwell
Farm

2

Coneyhill Farm

15

North Lodge

Sheepcothill
Wood

The
Wilderness

Fox
Covert

Swan's Way

Manor House

Eythrope Park Farm

1

Upper Winchendon

Eythrope Park

SCHOOL LA

MAIN RD

Model Farm

14

D E F

4

17

3

16

2

15

1

14

Uppings Farm

Weedon Lodge Farm

Fields Farm

Evelyn's Patch

Grendon Hill Farm

River Thame

Weedon Hill

Weedon Hill Farm

St Peter's Church
(remains of)

Ski & Water Sports Ctr

AYLESBURY

Hotel

Holman's Bridge

Quarrendon

1 ANGUS RD
2 GUERNSEY CL
3 KERRY CL
4 HEREFORD WAY
5 DEVON RD
6 SUSSEX CL

BUCKINGHAM RD

Elmhurst

Dunsham La

3 BERKELEY RISE
4 HANOVER CL
5 BROMPTON CL

Sch

Sch

BICESTER RD

1 ALDERSON CL
2 WILLOW CT

Superstore Trad Est

Broadfields

Superstore

Griffin Ind Mall

HAYDON RD

Alfred Rose Park

RAINBOROUGH GDNS

Manor Park

St Andrews Way

The Courtyard

(Printers End)

Merlin Ctr

BIERTON RD

HM Young Offender Inst

Manor House

Park Sch

PARK ST

Pembroke Rd

NEW ST

D E F
81 82

Aylesbury Ring

Home
Farm

Rowsham

Hale Farm

Ridgeway

MANOR RD

A418

BENNETTS LA

Baileys
Farm

Seabrook
Farm

Rowsham
Bridge

4

17

Crane End
Farm

Aylesbury

Ring

Manor Farm

Church
Farm

Hulcott

3

Grove
Farm

New
Covert

16

CH

Golf
Course

GROVE LA

GUB LA

2

Badricks
Farm

Burcott

Bierton

PH

AYLESBURY RD

MARSHALLS LEA

Church Farm

St JAMES WAY

Bierton
CE Comb
Sch

15

1 OLDHAMS MEADOW
2 HONDUR CL
3 BIERTON RD

BROUGHTON
CROSSING

PH

POPLAR
CL

A418

1

MEADOW WAY

AYLESBURY

STOCKLAKE

DOUGLAS RD

STOCKLAKE

Grand Union Canal　Aylesbury Arm

Grand Union Canal Wlk

Towing Path

PARK STREET
IND EST

Bear Brook

Brook Farm

14

83　　　　　A　　　　　84　　　　　B　　　　　85　　　　　C

D
E
F

4

Thistlebrook
Farm

Boarscroft
Farm

ALNWICK RD

Whitewell Farm

17

Thistle Brook

Marstongate
Station

3

Aylesbury Ring

Folly
Farm

POTASH LA

16

Red House
Farm

Fox
Covert

2

15

Manor
Farm

Potash
Farm

Grange Farm

Rectory
Farm

Puttenham

Draytonmead
Farm

1

Works

COLLEGE RD

Merrymead Farm

Grand Union Canal
Aylesbury Arm

d Union Canal Wlk

Monks Court

14

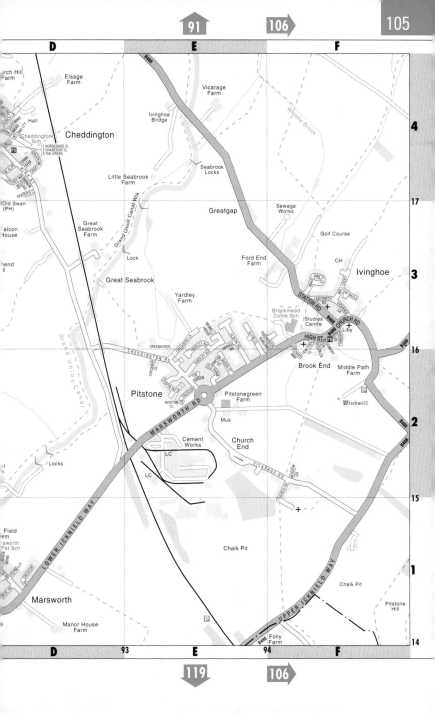

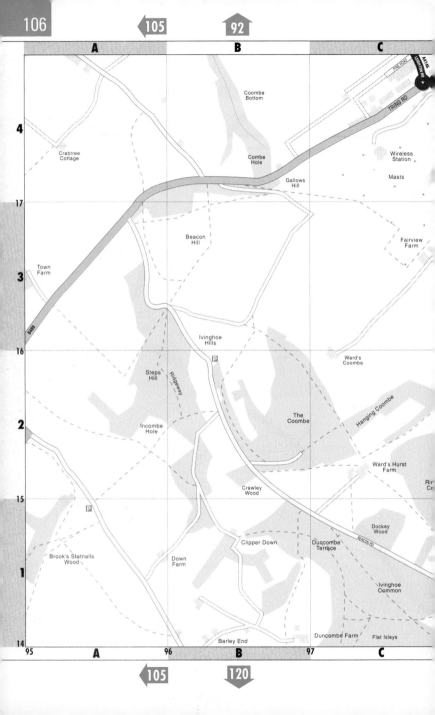

A

B

C

Coombe
Bottom

4

Crabtree
Cottage

Combe
Hole

Gallows
Hill

Wireless
Station

Masts

17

Beacon
Hill

Fairview
Farm

Town
Farm

3

B488

Ivinghoe
Hills

Ward's
Coombe

16

Steps
Hill

Ridgeway

The
Coombe

Hanging Coombe

2

Incombe
Hole

Ward's Hurst
Farm

Rir
Co

Crawley
Wood

15

Dockey
Wood

Clipper Down

Duncombe
Terrace

BEACON RD

Brook's Statnalls
Wood

Down
Farm

Ivinghoe
Common

1

Duncombe Farm

Flat Isleys

14

Barley End

D
E
F

Willow Farm

Dell Farm

Dukes Ave

Wood Lawn

The Green

Escarpment Ave

White Lion

Spicers Field

Central Paddock

Central Ave

Whipsnade Wildlife Animal Park

4

Miss Joans Ride

Round Close

Chiltern Farm

MAIN RD N

Lay Meadow

Hallcraft

Cut Throat Ave

Woodfield Paddock

Humphrey Talbot Ave

17

Collyers

Holly Frindle Paddock

Dagnall Paddock

Valley Cl

Bethshan Farm

Dagnall

DUNSTABLE RD

Lower Farm

Whipsnade Park Golf Course

3

HAMILTON CL

NELSON RD

Red Lion (PH)

PO

Highbury Farm

CH

Dagnall Farm

BLACK MEAD

HORSEMANS

Dagnall Cty Fst Sch

Cross Keys Farm

DagnallHall Farm

16

Hall

Cha Reetaa

RINGSHALL RD

MAIN RD S

STUDHAM LA

Sewage Works

2

Man's Grove

COMMON RD

Oakley Wood

gshall ppice

Well Farm

15

Meadow Farm

Levi Spring

HEMEL HEMPSTEAD RD

Ashridge Farm

Hall Farm

Lamsey Farm

Milebarn Farm

1

Ringshall

Hoo Wood

BEACON RD

A4146

Gade Plas

14

D
99
E
00
F

94

A B C

Old Arngrove

New Arngrove
Farm

Warren
Farm

Gardner's
Barn

Tippens
Copse

13

Nursery

Sermin's
Copse

Pasture
Farm

Studley
Farm

Danes Brook

Horton-cum-Studley

3

CHURCH LA

VENTFIELD
CL

MILL LA

PO

THE GREEN

FORGE CL

Manor
Far

New
Farm

Studley
Priory

PRIORY
CL

Moors
Farm

Hotel

Sewage
Works

12

Studley
Wood

P

Oakley
Wood

2

Corner
Farm

Nature Trail

Stanton
Little Wood

The
Moat

Nature Reserve

11

Bernwood Forest
(Nature Reserve)

Danesbrook
Farm

York's
Wood

1

Moorbirge Brook

Danes Brook

Oxfordshire Way

Beckley

Menmarsh
Guide Post

Hell
Coppice

Moorbirge
Bridge

10

59 A 60 B 61 C

122

B4011

Span Green

Danes Brook

4

Boarstall Wood
Cottage

Honeyburge

Nashway
Farm

Willow Close
Farm

13

FORESTERS

Fennemore
Farm

Boarstall Wood

Hillside
Farm

Slatters
Farm

Nap
Farm

3

Poplar
Farm

Denfield Farm

BICESTER RD

FELL VIEW

LITTLE LONDON GREEN

Little London
Farm

Little
London

BRILL RD

ARNCROLT CLOSE

BROADSIDE

THE TURNPIKE

Oakley
Common

Oakley

SUN CRES

MANOR RD

akley
Wood

OX.F ORD RD

P.O

Manor
Farm

B4011

12

ELMWOOD
CL

Royal Oak
(PH)

BRADLEY
CL

Oakley
Parochial
Comb Sch

Jericho
Farm

WORMINGHALL RD

MILL RD

ORCHARD
CL

FORGE CL

Smithy

MEADOW CL

Hedges
Farm

COLLEGE CRES

Sewage Works
(disused)

2

Moorley's
Farm

Shabbington Wood

Woodground
Farm

11

Waterslade
Farm

1

Airfield
(disused)

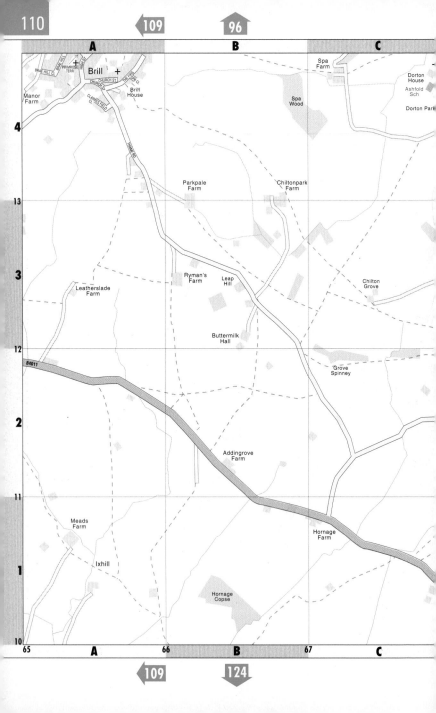

109
96

A   **B**   **C**

Manor
Farm

BRAE HILL CL
PRIMROSE
TERR
Brill
CHURCH ST
Brill
House
UPPER CL
HIGH ST
CLARKES FIELD
CL

Spa
Farm

Dorton
House

Ashfold
Sch

Dorton Park

Spa
Wood

4

THAME RD

Parkpale
Farm

Chiltonpark
Farm

13

3

Leatherslade
Farm

Ryman's
Farm

Leap
Hill

Chilton
Grove

Buttermilk
Hall

12

B4011

Grove
Spinney

2

Addingrove
Farm

11

Meads
Farm

Hornage
Farm

1

Ixhill

Hornage
Copse

10

65   **A**   66   **B**   67   **C**

D
E
F

Upper
Pollicott

Valley Farm

Upper
Pollicott
Farm

4

Arrow
Cotts

Lower Pollicott

13

Manor
Farm

Dorton Hill

3

Camp Farm

12

Gregorys
Farm

Townhill
Farm

Chilton
House

Chilton

Wurtemburg
Farm

Chilton
Grounds

2

BRILL RD

COLES
HILL

C.HAPEL LA

Sewage
Works

Canoncourt
Farm

THAME RD

PRINCES RD

Crawley
Farm

Wombwell's
Farm

11

Ashtree Tree
Cotts

Easington

EASINGTON LA

Lower
Farm

The Mole &
Chicken (PH)

Mount
Pleasant

1

10

D
69
E
70
F

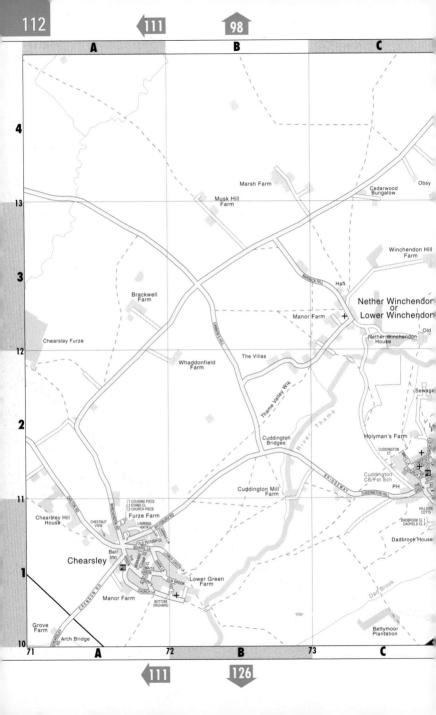

A B C

4

13 Marsh Farm
Musk Hill
Farm
Cedarwood
Bungalow
Obsy

Winchendon Hill
Farm

3 Brackwell
Farm
BADDICK HILL
Hall
Nether Winchendon
or
Lower Winchendon
Manor Farm
Chearsley Furze
Nether Winchendon
House
Old

12 CARTER'S LA
Whaddonfield
Farm
The Villas

Thame Valley Wlk
Sewage

River Thame

2 Holyman's Farm
CUDDINGTON
CT
Cuddington
Bridges
Cuddington
CE Fst Sch
PH
THE
PO
Cuddington Mill
Farm
BRIDGEWAY
CUDDINGTON HILL
GREEN

11 Cheasley Hill
House
1 COUSINS PIECE
2 EVANS CL
3 CHURCH PIECE
Furze Farm
CHESTNUT
VIEW
LAMMAS
PATH
AYLESBURY RD
HILLSIDE
COTTS
DADBROOK CL 1
DADFIELD CL 2
Dadbrook House

SCHOOL LA
OLD PLOUGH CL
Bell
Inn
Chearsley
PO
LOWER GREEN
LONG
GREEN
Lower Green
Farm
Dad Brook

1 Manor Farm
ELM BROOK CL
CHURCH LA
BOTTOM
ORCHARD

Grove
Farm
CHEARSLEY RD
Arch Bridge
Bettymoor
Plantation

10 71 72 73
A B C

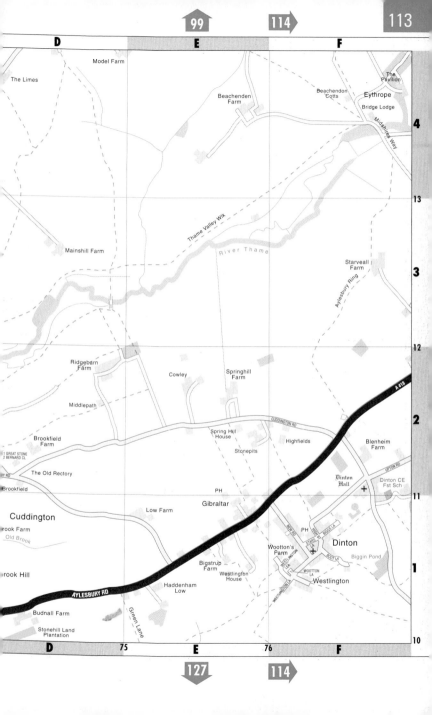

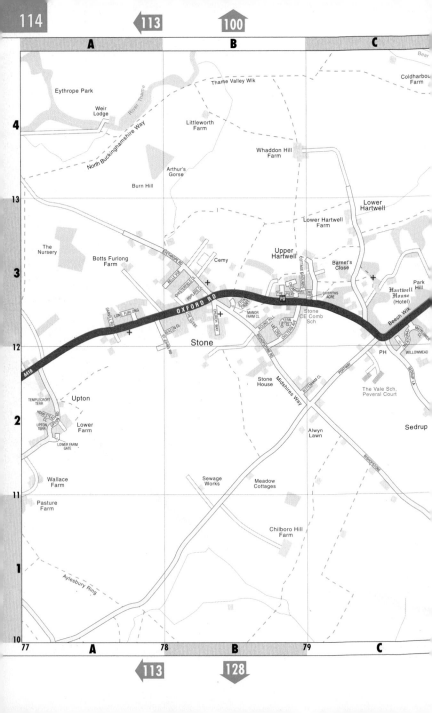

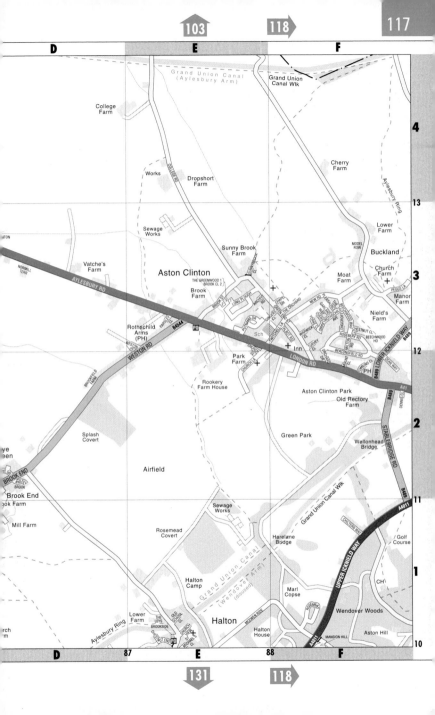

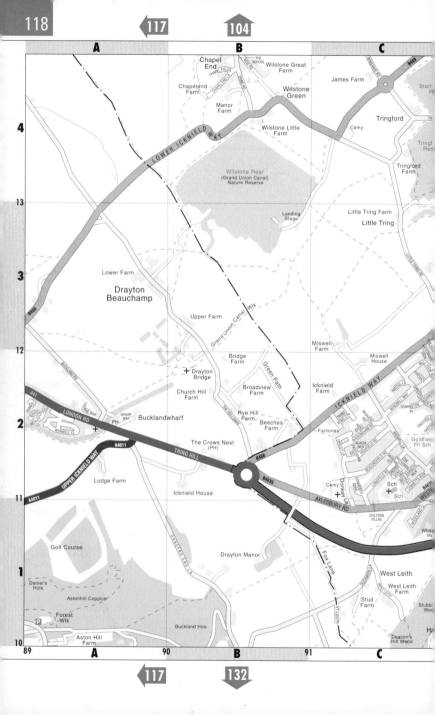

A
B
C

Golding's
Spring

Hanging
Isley

4
Aldbury
Nowers

Howlett's
Wood

Walk Wood

Moneybury Hill

Sallow Copse

Stocks
House

CH

Trin's Spring

Stock's Farm

Pitstone Common

Little
Stocks

Bridgewater
Monument

Golf Course

Picnic
Area

Visitors
Ctr

13

P

Ridgeway

Aldbury Common

Westland Farm

Aldbury
Sch

Town Farm

Thunderdell
Cottages

3
Church Farm

Inn

PO

Old Copse

STATION RD

Aldbury

Tring Sta

Hotel

MALTING LA

Brightwood

12

Rail Copse

NEWGROUND RD

The
Hangings

Tom's Hill

Tom's Hill House

2

The
Scrubs

Bottom
Spring

Broom
Spr

High Spring

11

Grand Union Canal Wlk

A4251

New
Ground
Farm

Norcott Hill

Northchurch Common

New
Ground

Grand Union Canal

Norcott Hall
Farm

Cow Roast
Lock

Norcott Court Farm

1
A1

Cow Roast

Norcott
Court

Hill Farm

The
Cow Roast
(Inn)

A4251

WHARF LA

B4506

10
95
A
96
B
97
C

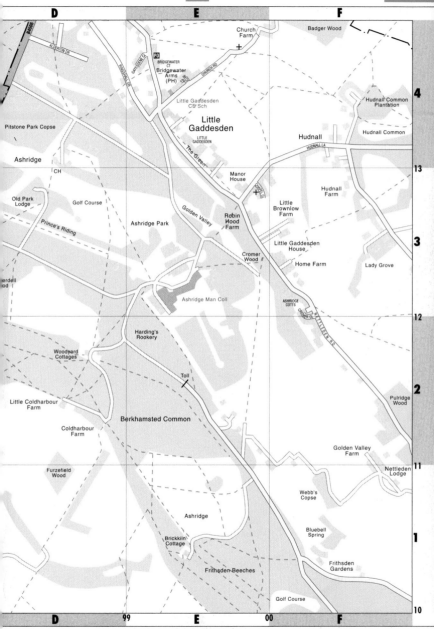

Badger Wood

Church Farm

B3506

ALDBURY DR

GADDESDEN LA

PO

BRIDGEWATER CL

Bridgewater Arms (PH)

CHURCH RD

Little Gaddesden CE Sch

4

Hudnall Common Plantation

Pitstone Park Copse

Little Gaddesden

LITTLE GADDESDEN

Hudnall

Hudnall Common

Ashridge

CH

The Green

13

Manor House

HUDNALL LA

Old Park Lodge

Golf Course

Golden Valley

Little Brownlow Farm

Hudnall Farm

Prince's Riding

Ashridge Park

Robin Hood Farm

Little Gaddesden House

3

erdell od

Cromer Wood

Home Farm

Lady Grove

Ashridge Man Coll

ASHRIDGE COTTS

12

Harding's Rookery

Woodyard Cottages

Toll

2

Little Coldharbour Farm

Pulridge Wood

Coldharbour Farm

Berkhamsted Common

Golden Valley Farm

Furzefield Wood

11

Nettleden Lodge

Webb's Copse

Ashridge

Bluebell Spring

1

Brickkiln Cottage

Frithsden Beeches

Frithsden Gardens

Golf Course

10

Moorbidge Brook

Clearsale   Hursthill

Wood Farm

Waterperry Common

4

Bernwood Forest

Commonleys Farm

Waterperry Wood

09

Polecat End

Park Farm

Park Farm House

Drunkard's Corner

3

Parson's Farm

Polecat End Hollows   Marsh Copse

Oxfordshire Way

Ledall Cottage

08

Holton Wood

Buryhook Barn

2

Holton Brook

Keeper's Cottage   Warren Farm

Pond Farm

Warren Wood

Old Park Farm

07

Lyehill Quarries (disused)

BURYHOOK CNR

Cottage Copse

Warwick Close Farm

Recn Gd

Wheatley Park Sch

Liby

Holton

The Rectory

Holton Place

1

John Watson Sch

Church Farm

Wheatley Campus (Brookes Univ)

Garden Copse

LONDON RD

COLLEGE CL

06

| 59 | A | 60 | B | 61 | C |

A B C

Woodway Farm

4

Westfield Farm

Lower
Peppershill
Farm

09

Peppershill

Crendon
House

Peppershill Farm

3

08

Peacehaven Farm

Marsh
Farm

Upper
Farm

2

Ickford

THE BURNHAMS

LOWER
FARM
CL

LONG CRENDON RD

Thame Valley Wlk

GOLDER'S CL
SCHOOL FIELD CL
BURNELL'S
SHELDON RD

MARSH RD

MORTON KING
CL

Sewage
Works

Shabbington

BULL CL

Ickford
Cty Comb
Sch

Little
Ickford

Rookery
Farm

THE VINE

JAMES WAY

Village
Farm

07

SCHOOL LA

ICKFORD RD

PO

River Thame

DUKES CL

CRABTREE CL

Franklins
Farm

1

Old
Fisherman
(PH)

River Thame

River Thame

Manor Farm

N
We

06

65 A 66 B 67 C

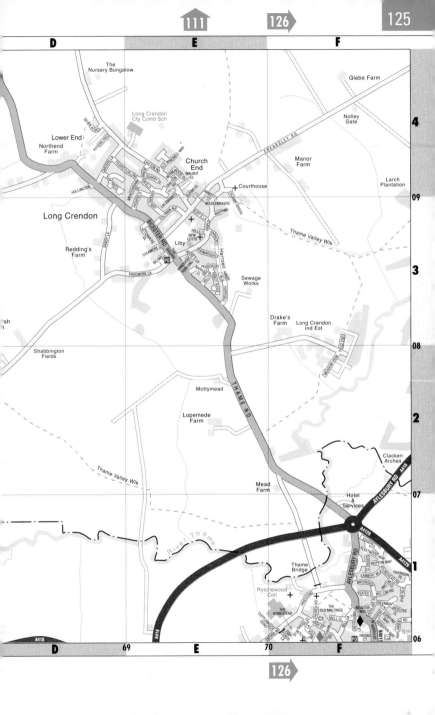

125

112

A　　　　　B　　　　　C

A418

Roundhill
Farm

Dad Brook

Long Mead
Copse

Yolsum
Plantation

4

Notley
Farm

Home
Copse

Notley
Abbey
(remains of)

Aylesbury & Thame
Airport

HADDENHAM AER
IND ES

Thame Valley Walk

09

Crosse's
Covert

WATERSIDE
YOLSUM
ASKETT CL
DOVECOTE
CL
DOVECOTE

SHERLEY
MARRIOTTS
MARRIOTTS CL
MARRIOTTS WAY
WYKEHAM WAY

P

Haddenham
& Thame
Parkway Sta

WYKEHAM GATE

GREENWAY
CLERKENWELL
COTTS

SOUTH END

Allot
Gdns

3

AYLESBURY RD

Fowlers Field

CROFT CLYD

THAME RD

SLADE HILL

STATION RD

SLADE HILL

08

Diggs

Scotsgrove
Cotts

Grove End
Farm

2

Scotsgrove
House

MILL LA

Dogkennel
Covert

A418

Scotsgrove
Mill

Tythrop Park
Farm

Decoy
Pond

Long
Covert

Ty
H

07

Sewage
Works

MOORE END LA

Tyt
Lo

1

A4129

1 RUSHALL RD
2 RUPERT WAY
3 SEDGEMOOR DR
4 DUNBAR DR
5 CHARLES DR

6 STUART WAY
7 CAVENDISH WLK
8 PENNINGTON PL
9 PELHAM RD
10 GLENHAM RD

Thame

Pilmoor
Arch

CLARENDON
DR

HAMILTON

GREVILLE WAY

A4129

Whites
Farm

Sch

OVERTON DR

KINGSEY RD

A4129

WINDMILL RD

06

71　　　　　A　　　72　　　　　B　　　73　　　　　C

125

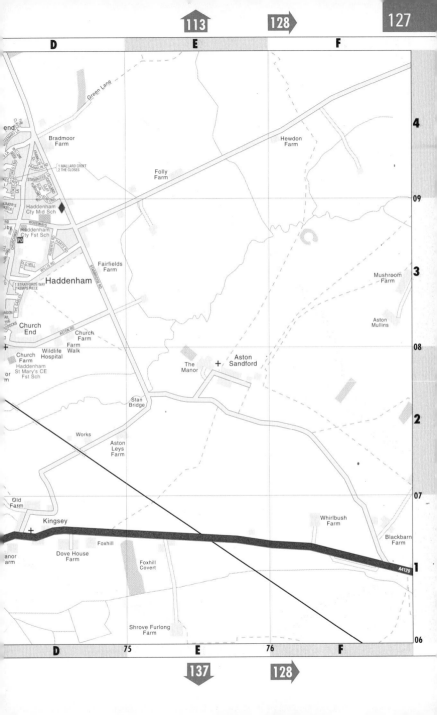

D E F

4

09

3

08

2

07

1

06

D 75 E 76 F

Green Lane

Bradmoor Farm

Hewdon Farm

1 MALLARD CROFT
2 THE CLOSES

Folly Farm

Haddenham Cty Mid Sch

Haddenham Cty Fst Sch

PO

OLD MILL

Fairfields Farm

1 STRATFORDS WAY
2 KEMPS PIECE

Haddenham

Mushroom Farm

Aston Mullins

Church End

Church Farm Walk

Church Farm

Wildlife Hospital

Haddenham St Mary's CE Fst Sch

The Manor

Aston Sandford

Stan Bridge

Works

Aston Leys Farm

Old Farm

Kingsey

Whirlbush Farm

Blackbarn Farm

Foxhill

Dove House Farm

Foxhill Covert

A4129

Shrove Furlong Farm

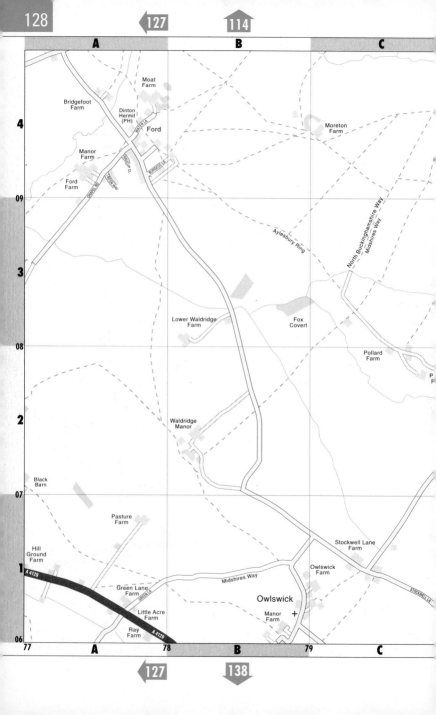

A   B   C

4

Bridgefoot
Farm

Moat
Farm

Dinton
Hermit
(PH)

Ford

WATER LA.

Moreton
Farm

Manor
Farm

PRIORS PL.

BURGESS LA.

09

Ford
Farm

CHAPEL RD.

LUCAS LE WAY

Aylesbury Ring

North Buckinghamshire Way

Midshires Way

3

Lower Waldridge
Farm

Fox
Covert

08

Pollard
Farm

P
F

2

Waldridge
Manor

Black
Barn

07

Pasture
Farm

Stockwell Lane
Farm

Hill
Ground
Farm

1

A 4129

Midshires Way

Owlswick
Farm

STOCKABELLA LA.

Green Lane
Farm

GREEN LA.

Owlswick

Little Acre
Farm

A 4129

Manor
Farm

Ray
Farm

06

77   A   78   B   79   C

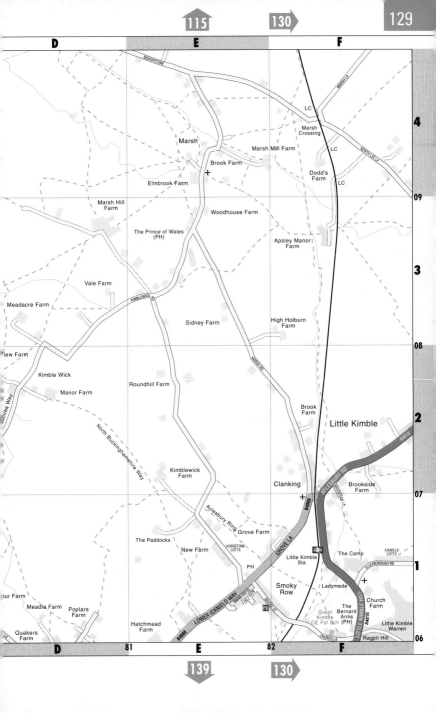

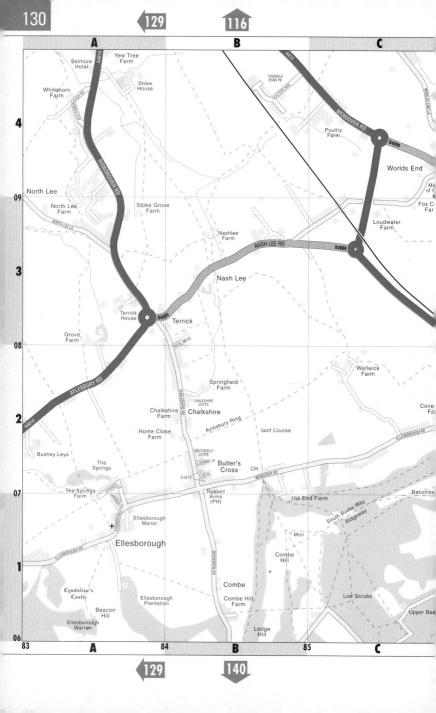

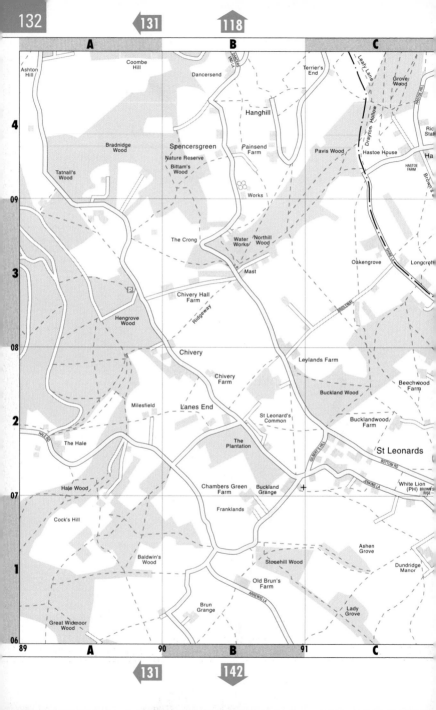

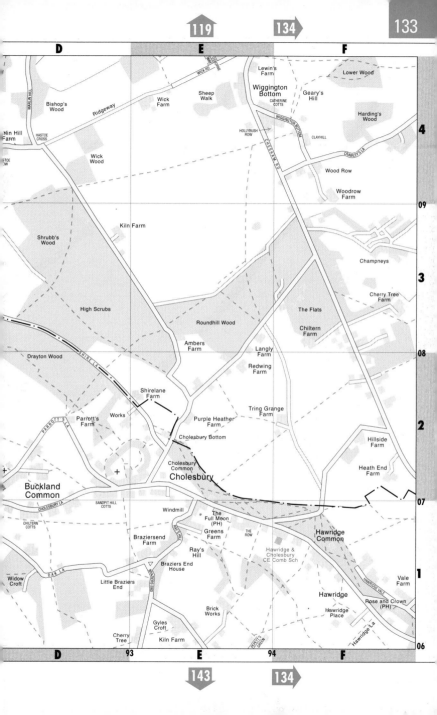

A B C

4

A41
M25?
ROUGH LA
Tinkers
Lodge
Northchu
Commo
Gorseside
Crawley's Lane
Farm
Hamberlins
Farm
Dudswell
Grand Union Canal
Grand Union Canal Wlk
River Bulbourne
HOME
FARM RD
White Farm
TRING RD
Hamberlins
House
OLD OAK
GDNS
NEW RD
HIGH ST
St Mary's
Sch

09

Hamberlins
Wood
COMPASS POINT 1
TUDOR ORCH 2
APPLECROFT 3
SEYMOUR CT 4

3

Newsetts Wood
Pea Lane
THE BENTONS 5
STONEY CL 6
CHILTERNS 7
THOMAS CT 8
Westfield
Fst Sch
Northchurch
BELL LA
Shootersway
Farmhouse
THE LARCHES
Woodcock
Hill
DURRANTS LA
The
Shrubbery
The
Lodge
Egerton-Rothesay
Mid & Upper Sch

08

Lodge
Farm
Oak Corner
COCK GR
Shootersway
Tring Lodge
Windbush
Gree
Fst
THE HEMMINGS
THE SPINNEY

2

Cock Grove
Rossway Home
Farm
Rossway
OAK WOOD
Marlin Chapel
Farm

07

HOG LA
Heath End
Glebe Farm
NORTHCHURCH LA
Pancake Wood
JOHNS LA

1

Hill Farm
The
Old Farm
Woodfield Spring
Farm
Hog Lane Farm
Johns Lane
Farm
Hockeridge Wood
Hockeridge Bottom
A41

Hadden's
Plantation

06

95 A 96 B 97 C

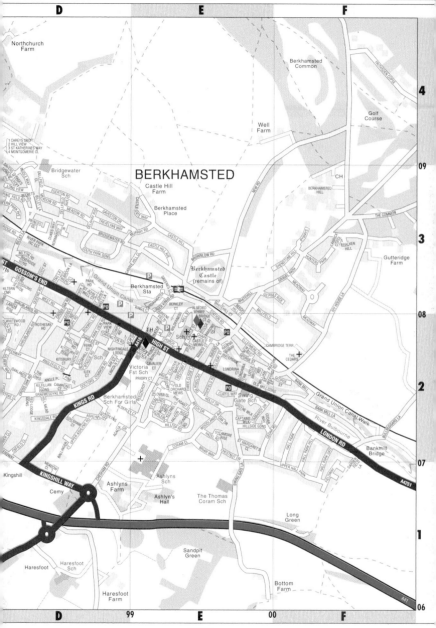

BERKHAMSTED

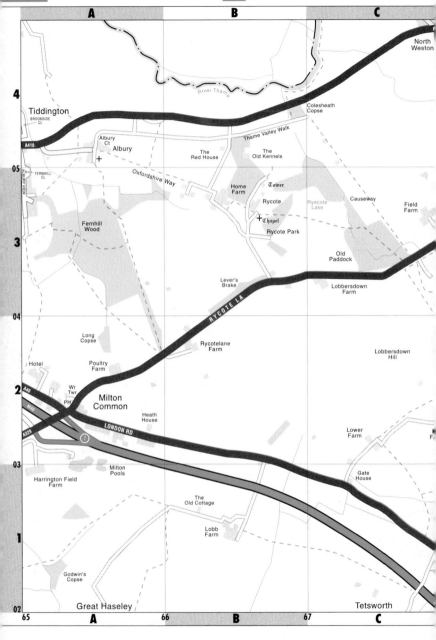

North Weston

4

Tiddington
BROOKSIDE CL

Colesheath Copse

Thame Valley Walk

A418

Albury Ct

Albury

The Red House

The Old Kennels

05

FERNHILL CL

ALBURY VIEW

Oxfordshire Way

Home Farm

Tower

Rycote

Ryecote Lake

Causeway

Field Farm

Fernhill Wood

Chapel

Rycote Park

Old Paddock

3

Lever's Brake

Lobbersdown Farm

04

RYCOTE LA

Long Copse

Rycotelane Farm

Lobbersdown Hill

Hotel

Poultry Farm

A40

Wr Twr

PH

Milton Common

Heath House

London Rd

A329

7

Lower Farm

F

03

Milton Pools

Harrington Field Farm

Gate House

The Old Cottage

1

Lobb Farm

Godwin's Copse

02

Great Haseley

Tetsworth

65   A   66   B   67   C

D **E** **F**

Bumpers

Grange Farm

Parkhill
Covert

Ilmer

Manor Farm

Upper
Farm

4

05

MANOR RD

North Mill
Farm

NORTH MILL RD

Penn Farm

3

Grovehill Farm

Hinton Crossing
Cottage

Grovehill
Covert

New Close Farm

04

Down
Covert

Whites Close

Cuttle Brook

New Close Farm Road

Forty Green

2

Fortygreen
Farm

Great
Covert

Sewage Works

FORTY GREEN

The Peacock
(PH)

Home Farm

03

Henton

Village Farm

College Farm

OLD ORCHARD

Emmington

Manor Farm

Rectory

Allnut's Farm

1

Church Covert

Westbrook
Farm

Upper Farm

LOWER ICKNIELD WAY

B 4009

B 4009

02

D **75** **E** **76** **F**

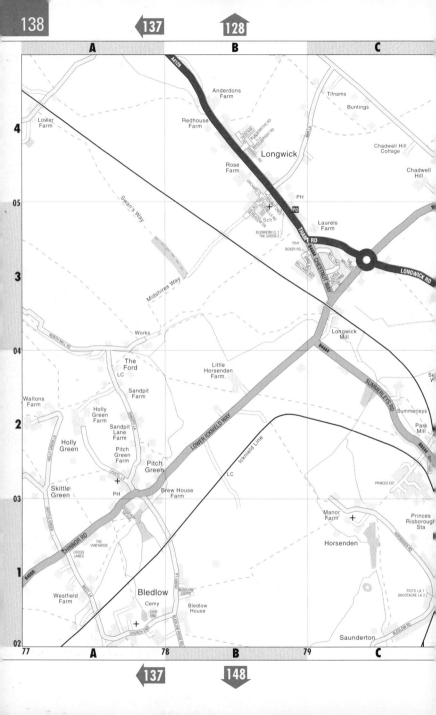

4

Lower
Farm

Anderdons
Farm

Tifnams

Buntings

Redhouse
Farm

Longwick

Chadwell Hill
Cottage

Chadwell
Hill

Rose
Farm

Swan's Way

05

PH

PO

Laurels
Farm

Sch

BLENHEIM CL 1
THE GREEN 2

Inn

BOXER RD

THAME RD

B4444 CHESTNUT WAY

LONGWICK RD

3

Midshires Way

Longwick
Mill

04

NORTH MILL RD

Works

B4444

The
Ford

LC

Little
Horsenden
Farm.

SUMMERLEYS RD

Summerleys

Waltons
Farm

Sandpit
Farm

Park
Mill

LOWER ICKNIELD WAY

B4444

2

Holly
Green
Farm

Sandpit
Lane
Farm

Icknield Line

HOLLY GREEN LA

Holly
Green

Pitch
Green
Farm

Pitch
Green

LC

PRINCES EST

03

CHAPEL LA

PH

Skittle
Green

Brew House
Farm

Manor
Farm

Princes
Risborough
Sta

Horsenden

CHINNOR RD

SKITTLE GREEN

CROSS
LANES

THE
VINEYARDS

HORSENDEN RD

B4009

1

Westfield
Farm

Bledlow

Cemy

BLEDLOW COPPS

PICTS LA 1
SHOOTACRE LA 2

Lyde
Enc

Bledlow
House

BLEDLOW RIDGE RD

BLEDLOW RD

02

Saunderton

77   **A**   78   **B**   79   **C**

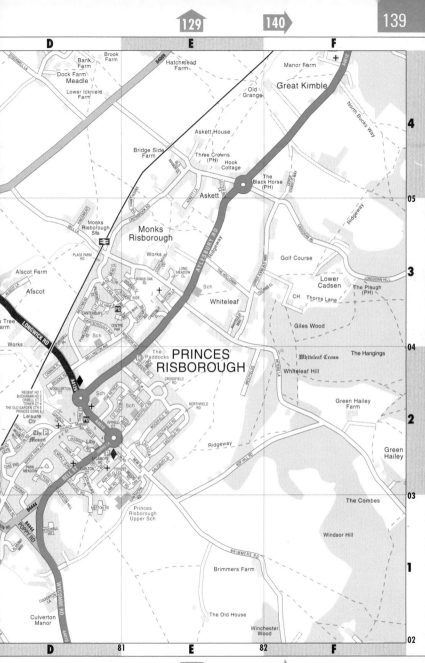

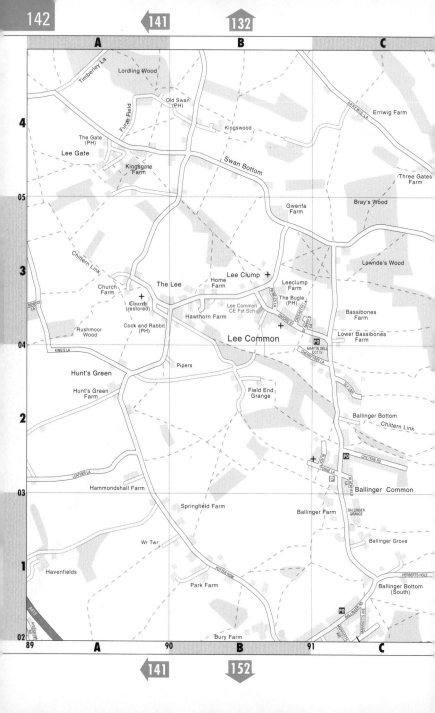

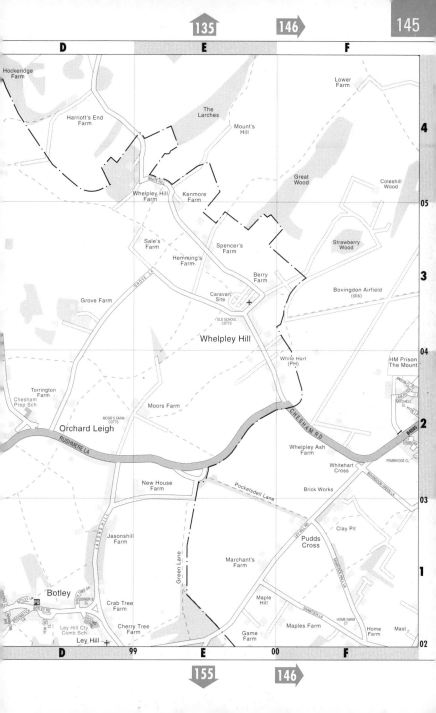

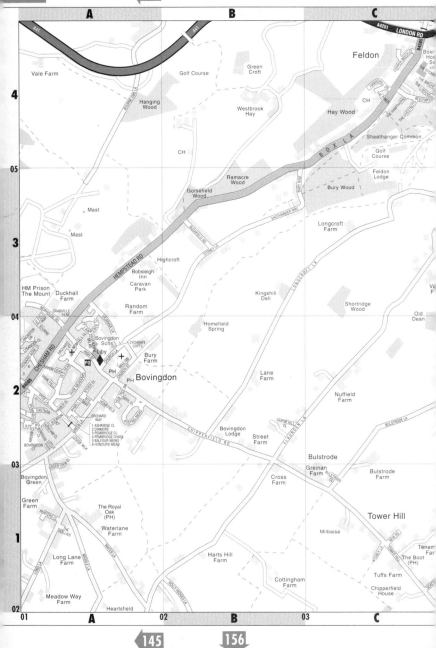

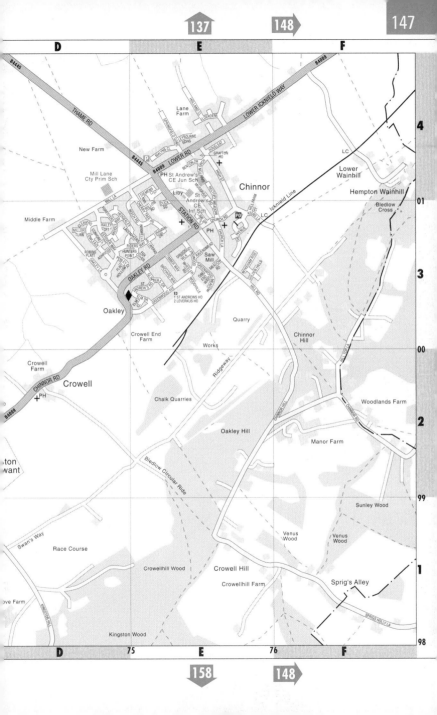

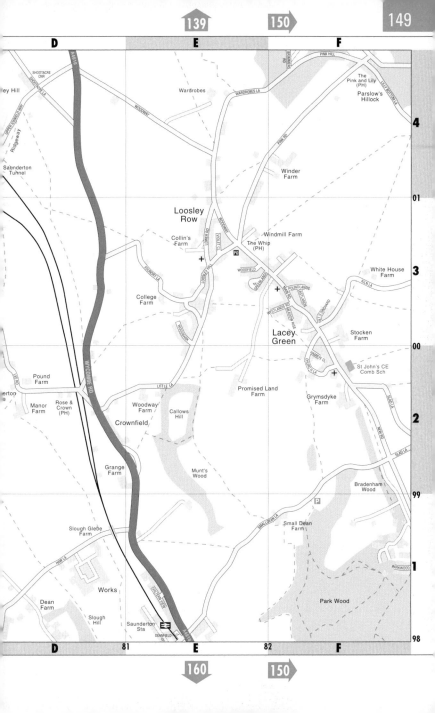

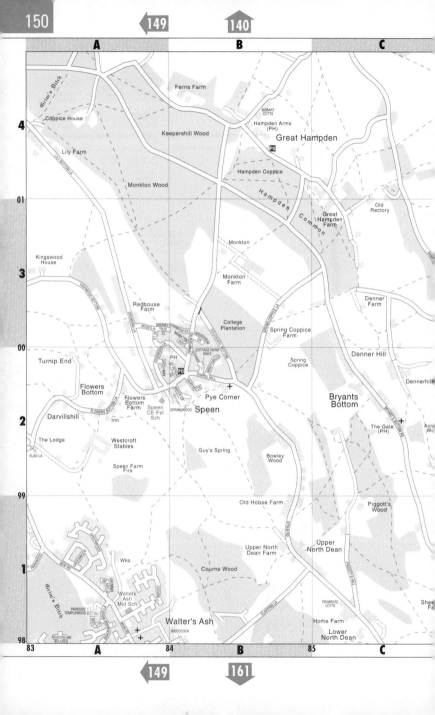

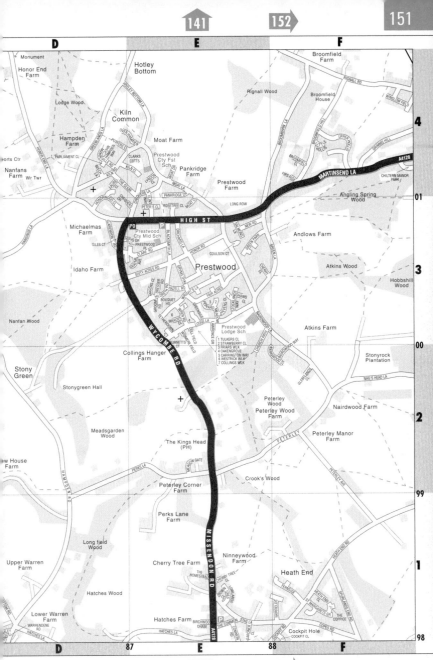

A   **B**   **C**

Mobwell
1 HEADLAND FIELD
2 WINSLOW FIELD
3 MOBWELL TERR
4 ROBSON CT

The Gateway Sch

POTTER ROW

Black Horse
(PH)

WATLINGTON
ELMHURST

Hill House

Sibley's
Coppice

South
Heath

FRITH HILL

Frith-hill

Middlegrove
Farm

Great
Missenden
CE Comb
Sch

Cudsden's
Farm

CHESHAM RD   Hyde End

OLD TOWN
FARM

Giby
THE
HERMITAGE
WHEELERS
YD

STATION APP
LINK RD

The Barley Mow
(PH)

The Hyde

CHILTERN MANOR
PARK

Great
Missenden
Sta

Chapel Farm

Rowen
Farm

TWITCHELL RD
COLVILLE
CT

Hyde
Farm

WHITEFIELD LA

Great
Missenden

Warren
Water

Rook Wood

Hedgemoor

The Misbourne
Sch

Mast

Wendover Woods
Pike Hill

The
Castle

Abbey
Park

GREEN LA

River Misbourne

ROD WOOD WAY

Sedges Farm

MISBOURNE AV
MAGPIE HEAD LA

H
The
Chiltern

Deep Mill
Farm

Francis
Plantation

John's
Plantation

NAG'S HEAD LA
PINES
WYCHWOOD
DENE RD
NEW RD
LARCHMOOR
SHEFFIELD

Little
Kingshill

HARE LANE END
HARE LA

Grange
Farm

Royal Oak
(PH)

DEEP MILL LA

Suffolk
Bridge

Full Moon
(PH)

GRANGE
COTTS
THE LINCOLNS

St
CHRISTOPHER'S
RD

STORR LA

MEADOW COTTS

WINDSOR LA

South Bucks Way

Little Boys Heath

HIGHMORE COTTS

SHEPHERDS LA
HEATHLAND RD

Ashwell
Farm

Orchard
Farm

Little Kingshill
Cty Comb
Sch

Boot
Farm

Kingshill
Farm

Affricks
Farm

Haleacre Wood

King Street Lane

Grubbins
Plantation

WHICHELL LA

Featherbed Lane

Copes
Farm

Keepers
Cottage

Coleman's Wood

Bear
Wo

Long Wood

FEATHERBED LA

BEAMOND E
LA

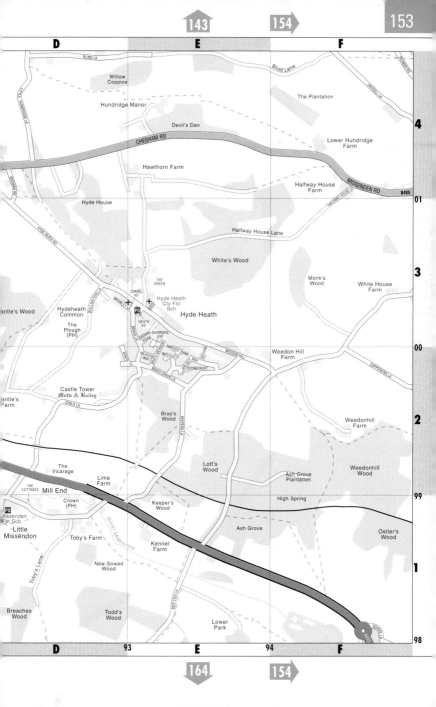

D   E   F

BLIND LA

Blind Lane

Willow
Coppice

The Plantation

Hundridge Manor

MITCHELL LA

FERNEY RD

Devil's Den

4

Lower Hundridge
Farm

CHESHAM RD

MISSENDEN RD

Hawthorn Farm

B485

Halfway House
Farm

HYDE HEATH RD

Hyde House

01

HALFWAY HOUSE LA

Halfway House Lane

BOTTOM RD

White's Wood

3

THE
GREEN

Monk's
Wood

White House
Farm

antle's Wood

CHAPEL
HO

BROW LA

Hydeheath
Common

Hyde Heath
Cty Fst
Sch

Hyde Heath

BULL BAITERS LA

The
Plough
(PH)

HEATH
RD

SAUNDERS
END

CEDARS
EDGE

Weedon Hill
Farm

00

BRAYS LA

HARVEST BANK

WEEDON HILL

COPPERKINS LA

MEADOWS
WAY

WE'ST LA

BRAYS
CL

STONECROFT

BRAYS GREEN LA

antle's
arm

Castle Tower
Motte & Bailey

CHALK LA

Bray's
Wood

KEEPERS LA

Weedonhill
Farm

2

The
Vicarage

Lott's
Wood

Weedonhill
Wood

Lime
Farm

Ash Grove
Plantation

THE
COTTAGES

Mill End

99

Crown
(PH)

Keeper's
Wood

High Spring

PO

Missendon
Fst Sch

Little
Missendon

Toby's Farm

Ash Grove

Ostler's
Wood

TOBY'S LANE

Kennel
Farm

RIVER MISBOURNE

1

New Sowed
Wood

MOP END LA

Breaches
Wood

Todd's
Wood

Lower
Park

98

D   93   E   94   F

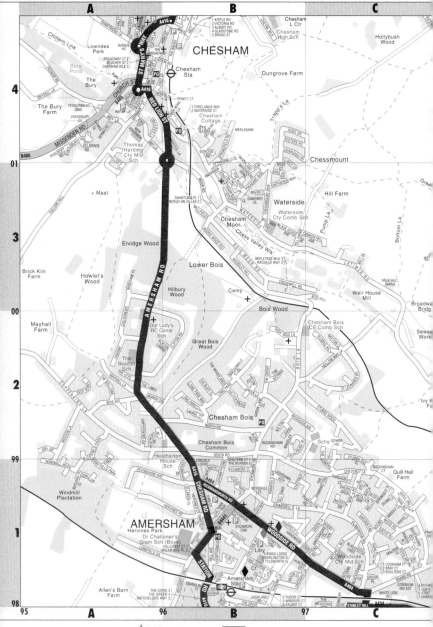

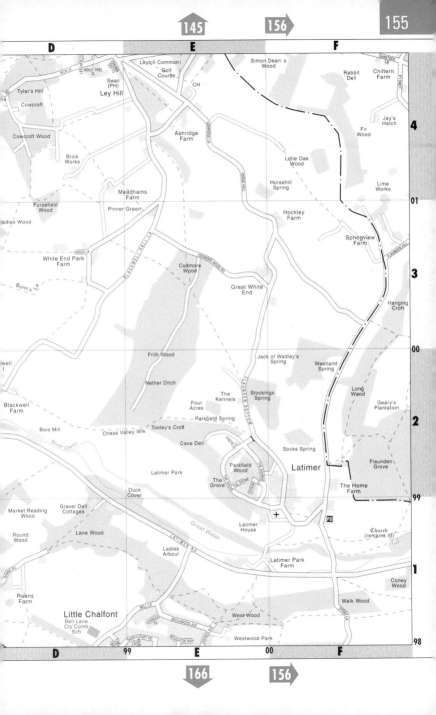

Oxgate
Farm

Venus Hill

Venus Hill
Farm

VENUS HILL LA

BRASIER LA

HOLLY HEDGES LA

Hollow
Hedge

Woodman's
Wood

Brazier
Farm

Chippe

New Maulden
Farm

Caravan
Site

Hogpits
Bottom

FLAUNDEN LA

LONG LA

BRICK LA

Bricklayers
Arms
(PH)

Lower Plantation

Cherry Trees
Farm

GILTSBERRY LA

Woodman's
Farm

WINDMILL HILL
HILL

LITTLE WINDMILL
HILL

DUNNY LA

4

Sharlow's
Farm

Green
Dragon
(PH)

FLAUNDEN HILL

Flaunden

Dale Farm

Holly Hedges

Whitedell
Farm

Newhouse
Farm

Bragman's
Farm

Rose Hall
Farm

Rosehall
Wood

BELSIZE
COTTS

Plough
(PH)

PICKET LA

PLOUGH LA

Belsize
Cotts

Pe
G

Belsize

01

3

Hollin's
Hall

Moonshine
Farm

Great Sarratt
Hall

00

Wireless
Station

Mast   Mast

Hanginglane
Wood

Oldcroft
Wood

Sarratt

2

Martin Top
Farm

Oldfield
Spring

Bramble
Croft

MODEL LA

DAWES LA

Dawes
Common

Baldwin's
Wood

Wallace's
Wood

Limeshill
Wood

Valley
Farm

Old Rectory

99

Mill
Farm

Chenies
Bottom

River Chess

HOLLOWAY LA

Chess Valley Wlk

Ford

Mount
Wood

Sarratt
Bottom

Chenies
Place

Mountwood
Farm

Nicholas
Spring

Church End

Goldingtons

CHUR
EN
COT

1

Greathouse
Farm

Chenies
Cty Comb Sch

Inn

Wyburn
Wood

Turveylane
Wood

98

Chenies

Resolution is perhaps not an organisation that many of us have heard of, but it is in fact the UK's largest organisation of family lawyers with approximately 6,000 members. It believes that family law disputes should be dealt with in a constructive way, designed to preserve people's dignity and to encourage agreements.

Resolution is the recognised voice of family law and has been influential in impacting many Government policies. All members must abide by its Code of Practice and to be accepted must demonstrate, by answering a series of questions their commitment to the Code.

It is of course still possible for your legal advisor to act in a firm fashion whilst abiding by the Code and at the end of the day all family lawyers will work to same set of rules when it comes to working out a division of finances, contact arrangements for any children or setting up a Pre-Nuptial Agreement.

Miss Hazel Page is a Solicitor and a Member of Resolution. For any enquiries please contact us on Hazel.page@ommlaw.law.co.uk or telephone 01525 378177.

resolution
first for family law
30 years

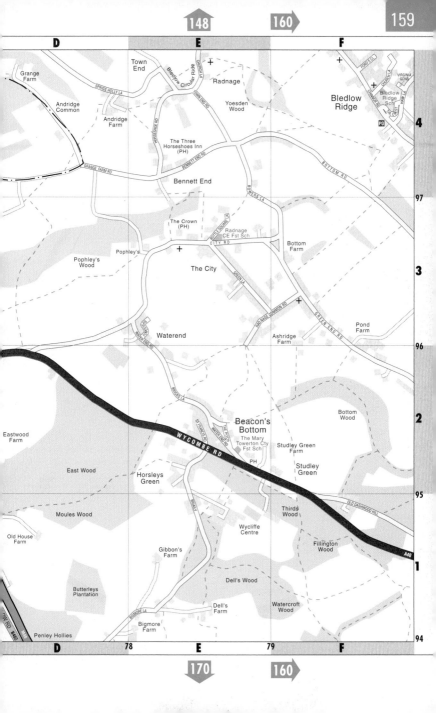

D · E · F

4

Little Stocking Wood

Timber Research & Development Ctr

The Coppice

Mast

The Black Lion (PH)

Great Moseley Farm

Naphill

Orchard Farm

Sch

Naphill Common

Little Moseley Farm

Chalkpit Wood

Coombe's Orchard

97

The Wheel (PH)

PO

Works

HYCHENDEN CL

Coombe Farm

COOMBE LA

Bradenham Hill Farm

PROSPECT COTTS

CHERRYCROFT DRI

VINCENTS WAY

Pimlock's Wood

Hogtrough Farm

Naphill Farm

3

Great Cookshall Wood

Cookshall Farm

Hunt's Hill

Kit's Wood

Oaks Wood

Woodcock Wood

Flagmore Wood

96

Le de Spencers Arms (PH)

Common Wood

Hanging Wood

Lee's Wood

Works

Downley Common

2

Downley Farm

Downley

KILN POND LA 1

TAYLORS TURN 2

Tilbury Wood

Wycombe West Sch & Collegiate Ctr

Manor Farm

PO

COMMON SIDE

Downley Cty Mid Sch

95

lint Hall Farm

Branch Wood

The Heights Sch

WOODCOTE GREEN

BURROWS WAY

SELWOOD WAY

MANOR VIEW HO

Little Tinker's Wood

WOODCOTE DN

WOODCOTE VIEW

SOUTH VIEW

HIGH WYCOMBE

Monument

CURLEW CL

PARTRIDGE WAY

KESTREL CL

TALBOT RD

WESTOVER CT

COLUMS

LYDEHURST CL

MOLE RUN

Great Tinker's Wood

FALCON RISE

West Wycombe Park

Sawmill House

WHITE CL DOWN

THE ACRES

MIDDLETON WAY

MERRY DOWN

Tinkers Wood Cty Comb Sch

Mast

1 ANTHONY CL
2 BRINDLEY AVE
3 STEPHENSON CL

1

River Wye

WEST WYCOMBE RD

A40

SOUTHFIELD RD

CHEVIOT

COTSWOLD WAY

BRECON CL

WYE

CHAPEL LA

MILL END RD

94

D · 84 · E · 85 · F

161
151

Great
Kingshill

Longrove
Plantations

PIPERS LA

Springfields

Lodge

Hughenden
Valley

Gomms
Wood

White Lion
(PH)

Sladmore
Farm

Hoppers
Farm

Hawbushes
Farm

Boss Lane
Farm

Great Kingshill CE
Combined Sch

PO

CRYERS HILL RD

Cryers
Hill

Widmer
End

Provost
Wood

Cemy

CRYERS HILL LA

Widmer End
Farm

Widmer End
Cty Comb Sch

Widmer
Farm

VALLEY RD

FOUR ASHES RD

Town
Wood

NORTH RD

Royal Standard
(PH)

Rec
Gd

The Park Cty
Mid Sch

The Cedar
Cty Fst Sch

Uplands

Church
Farm

Four
Ashes

Grange
Farm

Recreation
Ground

Millfield
Wood

Brands
House

Cockshoot
Wood

Hughenden
Manor

Masts

Hazlemere
CE Comb
Sch

Hughenden
Park
Sports
Ground

CHURCH LA

KINGSHILL RD

Terriers
Farm

Terriers

AMERSHAM RD

PO

Middle
Lodge

WHITE HILL

Green
Wood

Green
Hill

**HIGH
WYCOMBE**

GREEN HILL GATE 1
DUNWOOD RISE 2
DURLEY HOLLOW 3
THE RISINGS 4

THE
GREENACRES Royal
Gram Sch

BRUNSWICK CL

1 GERALDS CT
2 CHURCH CT

Terriers Cty
Mid Sch

HUGHENDEN RD

Wks

MELROSE
CT

MANOR
COURT YD

MAITLAND

Kingswood View

161
173

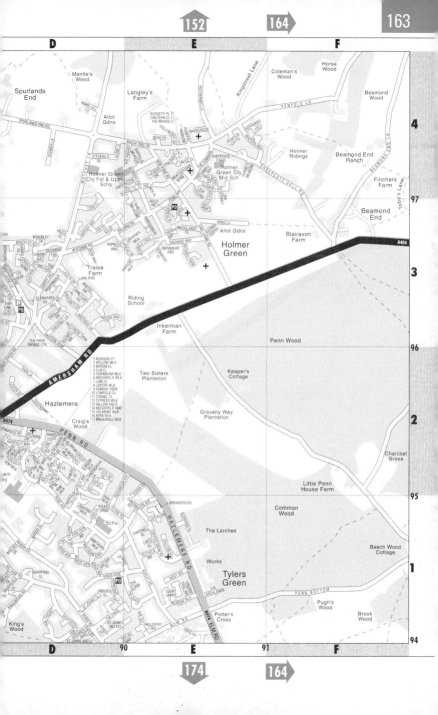

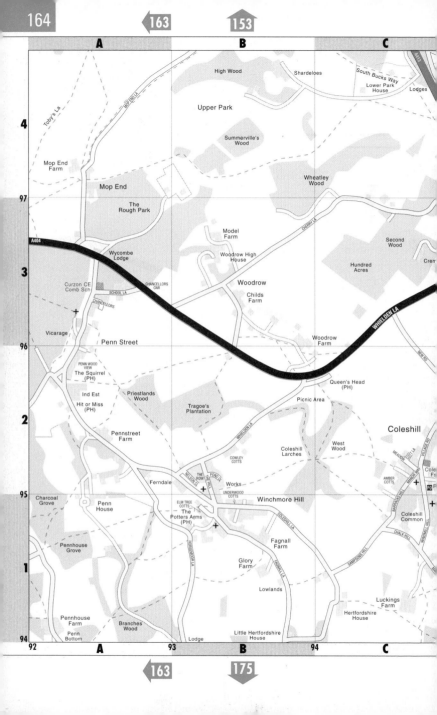

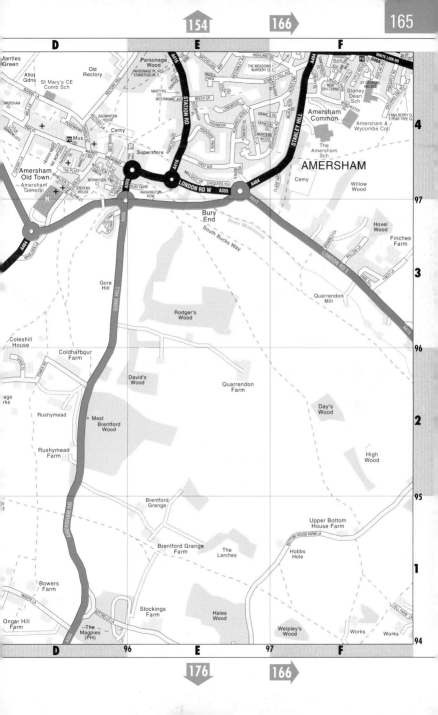

D

Mantles Green

Old Rectory

St Mary's CE Comb Sch

Allot Gdns

SCHOOL LA

Parsonage Wood

STATION RD

PARSONAGE PL
STANSTEAD PL 2

MARTYRS CT
WESTMOUNT AVE

BEECH GR

HIGHMOOR

HIGHVIEW PARK

HIGHLAND RD

THE MEADOWS 1
NURSERY CL 2

HAZELL PARK

Sch

F

WHITE LION RD

A404

PO

STANLEY HILL AVE

NEW CHILTERNS

Stoney Dean Sch

ST GEORGES IND EST

1 MULBERRY CL
2 PEAR TREE CL

4

Amersham Common

Amersham & Wycombe Coll

Mus

PO

Cemy

Superstore

A416

Amersham Old Town

Amersham General

H

Stevens House

NORWOODS

A355

Bury Farm

WASHINGTON ROW

LONDON RD W

A355

FIRST AVE

CHEQUERS HILL

WEST ACRES

A404

The Amersham

AMERSHAM

Cemy

STANLEY HILL

Willow Wood

97

A404

Bury End

River Misbourne

South Bucks Way

LONDON RD E

Hovel Wood

Finches Farm

WILLOW LA

FINCH LA

DANE CL

A413

Gore Hill

Quarrendon Mill

3

Coleshill House

GORE HILL

Coldharbour Farm

TOWER RD

Rodger's Wood

96

David's Wood

Quarrendon Farm

Day's Wood

age rks

Rushymead

Mast
Brentford Wood

2

Rushymead Farm

High Wood

AMERSHAM RD

95

Brentford Grange

Upper Bottom House Farm

BOTTOM HOUSE FARM LA

Brentford Grange Farm

The Larches

Hobbs Hole

1

Bowers Farm

MAGPIE LA

Ongar Hill Farm

A355

SCHOOL LA

The Magpies (PH)

Stockings Farm

Hales Wood

Welpley's Wood

Works

HILL FARM LA

Works

94

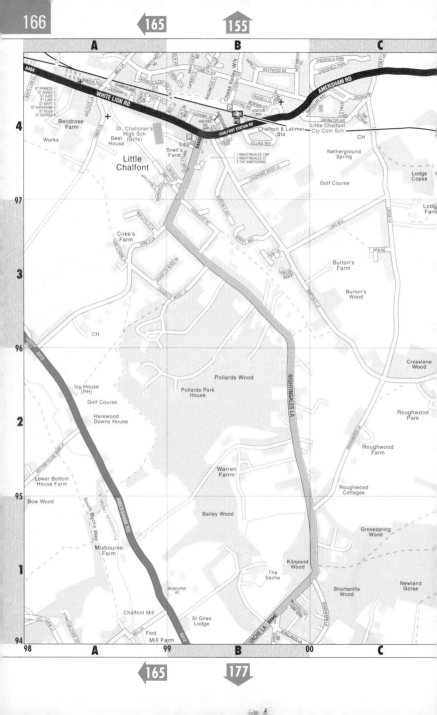

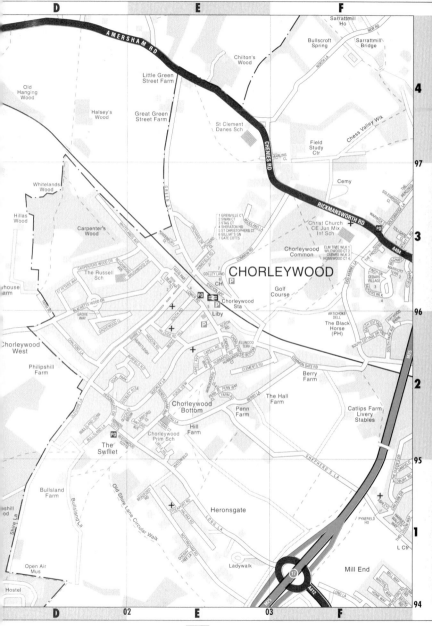

CHORLEYWOOD

D E F

4

97

3

96

2

95

1

94

AMERSHAM RD

Sarrattmill Ho

Bullscroft Spring

Sarrattmill Bridge

NEW RD

NORTH LA

Chilton's Wood

Little Green Street Farm

Old Hanging Wood

Halsey's Wood

Great Green Street Farm

St Clement Danes Sch

Chess Valley Wlk

Field Study Ctr

THE HEMMINGS

SOLESBRIDGE LA

CHENIES RD

MARLINS CL

RICKMANSWORTH RD

Cemy

Whitelands Wood

Hillas Wood

GREEN ST

Carpenter's Wood

1 GRENVILLE CT
2 SWAN CT
3 STAG CT
4 SHERATON HO
5 ST CHRISTOPHERS CT
6 GILLIAT'S GN
7 GATE COTTS

WOODLAND LA

ORCHARD DR

Christ Church CE Jun Mix Inf Sch

WARNICK CL

A404

PO

TOLLGATE

house Farm

The Russell Sch

CARPENTERS WOOD DR

ST PETERS RW

WHITELANDS RD

BLACKETTS WOOD DR

GROVE WAY

Chorleywood West

COLLEY LAND

SHIRE LA

BRUSHWOOD DR

STATION APP

CHORLEYWOOD

Chorleywood Common

ELM TREE WLK 1
WILDWOOD CT 2
CEDARS WLK 3
HOMEWOOD CT 4

THE PARADE

FINCH CT

CEDARS VILLAGE

JACOBS WLK

MARRIOTT TERR

HASELMERE PARK

PO

LONG RD

CH

P

Chorleywood Sta

Liby

Golf Course

DOG KENNEL LA

ARTICHOKE DELL

The Black Horse (PH)

SOUTH COTTAGE DR

SOUTH PARK AV

SOUTH RD

M25

Philipshill Farm

CHALFONT LA

SOUTH DOWNS

GROVEWOOD CL

SHIRE LA

COMMON RD

SOUTH RD

ELLWOOD TERR

HUBBARDS RD

CAPELL RD

GREEN ST

CLEMENTS RD

COMMON GATE RD

Berry Farm

Chorleywood Bottom

DUCHESS

BISSELL RD

BURTONS RISE

RIDGE LA

SWILLET RD

SHEPHERDS LA

CAPELL RD

PENN WAY

Penn Farm

The Hall Farm

Catlips Farm Livery Stables

Hill Farm

Chorleywood Prim Sch

PO

The Swillet

Bullsland Farm

BULLSLAND LA

Shire La

SHIRE LA

Old Shire Lane Circular Walk

BRINDLES RD

ROTHERFIELD RD

COBBS RD

CRESTA MW

Heronsgate

CHASE LA

SHEPHERDS LA

Ladywalk

Bullsland Farm

Open Air Mus

Hostel

PYNEFIELD HO

ASKEYS

L Ctr

MILL TOLLHSE

LONG LA

Mill End

A412

02 03

D E F

Portways

Oxfordshire Way

Shotridge Wood

Buckingham Bottom

Hungryhill Wood

Barnfield Hanging Wood

Mast

P

4

Christmas Common

Copper's Wood

Blackmoor Wood

Fox & Hounds (PH)

Mast

93

Prior's Grove

PH

Launder's Farm

Northend

Northend Farm

Queen Wood

The White Hart (PH)

HOLLOMBI LA

3

Fire Wood

92

Swain Wood

Greenfield

HOLLANDRIDGE LA

College Wood

Hollandridge Farm

Longhill Hanging Wood

Blundell

2

Turville Park Farm

Turville Park

91

Greenfield Wood

Roll's Shaw

Shambridge Wood

1

Pishill Bottom

Whitehill Shaw

B480

Whitelands House

Oxfordshire Way

Primrose Cottage

Pishill Bank

PH

B480

90

71

A

72

B

73

C

D **E** **F**

The Fox
(PH)

Cholsey
Farm

Ibstone
Common

4

Twigside
Bottom

GLEBE
COTTS

Great Wood

CHILTERN
COTTS

Ibstone

Hale Wood

Hellcorner
Farm

93

r Northend
Farm

Parsonage
Wood

Twigside
Farm

Harecramp
Cottages

Ibstone
CE Fst
Sch

Lower
Barn

3

Ibstone House

Grays Lane

Park
Wood

+

92

Manor Farm

Gilham
Copse

spinney
Farm

Turville
Wood

HOLLOWAY LA

Ashfield
Barn

2

Idlecombe
Farm

Idlecombe
Wood

Windmill
(dis)

Turville Valley
Farm

**Turville
Heath**

Turville
Grange

Turville +

SCHOOL LA

PH

SQUARE CLOSE
COTTS

91

Churchfield Wood

Summer
Heath

Tel
Ex

Rose Farm

Turville Court

DROVERS LA

Home Wood

1

Summerheath
Wood

Dolesden

DOLESDEN LA

Poynatts Wood

90

D 75 **E** 76 **F**

A

B

C

4

93

3

92

2

91

1

90

Barn Wood

Leygrove's Wood

Chequers Manor Farm

Blue Flag (PH)

MARLOW RD

Pound Wood

Watercroft Farm

Huckende Farm

Pound Farm

Cadmore End CE Comb Sch

Cadmore End

Old Ship (PH)

Kensham Farm

Cadmore End Common

CREDITOR LA

Hill Farm

Rackley's Farm

Bolter End

The Peacock (PH)

NEW RD

BOLTER END LA

Hanger Wood

Priestley's Farm

FININGS RD

Gravesend

Manor Farm

Mill Hanging Wood

Hanger Farm

FINGEST LA

Hanover Hill

Long Copse

Turville Hill

Fingest

The Chequers Inn (PH)

Fingest Wood

Mouseils Wood

Dovers Farm

Murrage Farm

WATERY LA

Maiden Farm

Spurgrove

SPURGROVE LA

The Prince Albert (PH)

Goddard's Wood

Adam's Wood

Little Frieth

PERRIN SPRINGS LA

Frieth

Poynatts Farm

Bottom Wood

Colliers Farm

FININGS GATE

HALLEY FIELD LA

PO

The Frog (PH)

Stud Farm

Lower Goddards Farm

SHOGMOOR LA

Upper Goddards

Maiden Farm

SHOGMOOR LA

Frieth CE Comb Sch

Skirmett

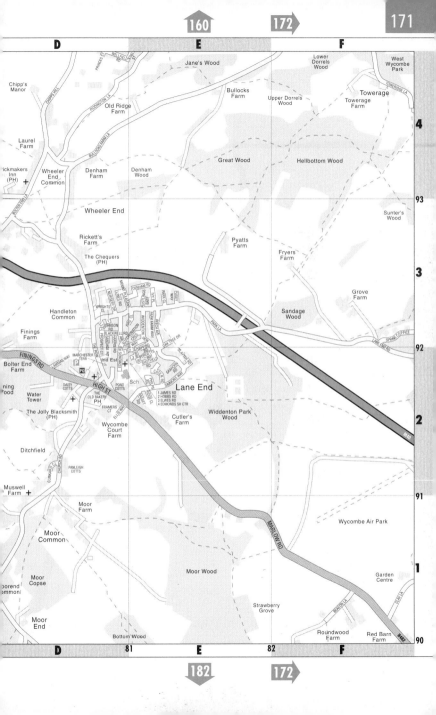

D E F

Chipp's Manor

Jane's Wood

Lower Dorrels Wood

West Wycombe Park

rickmakers Inn (PH)

Laurel Farm

Chipps Hill

PRINGE ST

WELLHILL LA

PRIORSITON LA

Old Ridge Farm

Bullocks Farm

Upper Dorrels Wood

Towerage

Towerage Farm

TOWERIDGE LA

4

BULLOCKS FARM LA

Wheeler End Common

Denham Farm

Denham Wood

Great Wood

Hellbottom Wood

Sunter's Wood

93

BOLTER END LA

Wheeler End

Rickett's Farm

The Chequers (PH)

Pyatts Farm

Fryers Farm

Grove Farm

3

DENHAM RD

Handleton Common

Finings Farm

PUSEY WAY

PARK LA

Sandage Wood

SPRING COPPICE

LANE END RD

92

FININGS RD

Bolter End Farm

ning ood

Water Tower

The Jolly Blacksmith (PH)

Wycombe Court Farm

TADDEAN WAY

HIGH ST

Daisy Cotts

Manchester Terr

rind Est

Sch

THE OLD BAKERY PH

FRAMERS CT

POND COTTS

ELLES WAY

Lane End

1 JAMES RD
2 HOBBS RD
3 ELWES RD
4 EDMONDS SH CTR

Widdenton Park Wood

M40

2

Ditchfield

Cutler's Farm

Muswell Farm

CHURCH RD

CHINNOR RD

PANLEIGH COTTS

Moor Farm

91

Moor Common

Wycombe Air Park

Moor Copse

MARLOW RD

1

Garden Centre

orend mmon

Moor End

Moor Wood

Strawberry Grove

BEACON LA

CAA LA

B482

Bottom Wood

Roundwood Farm

Red Barn Farm

90

D 81 E 82 F

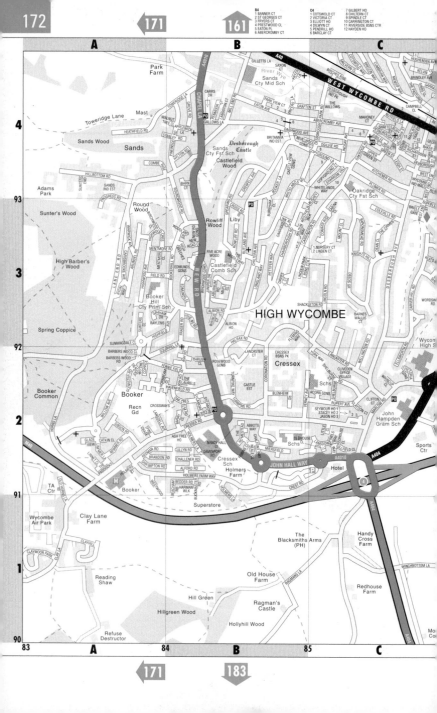

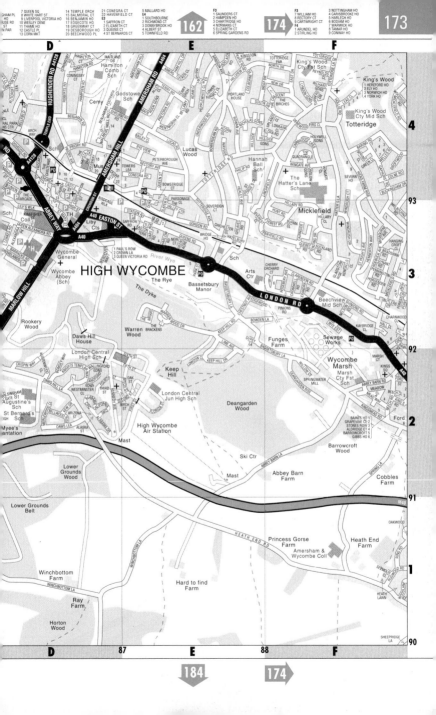

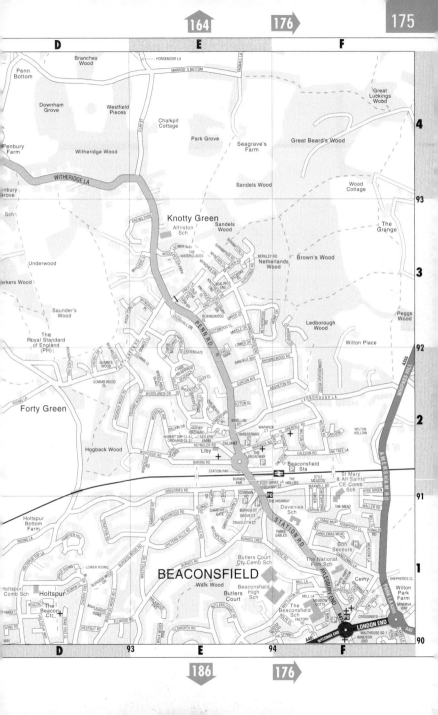

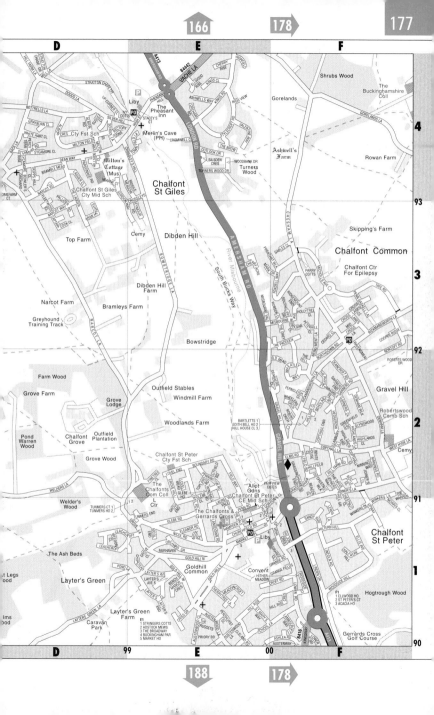

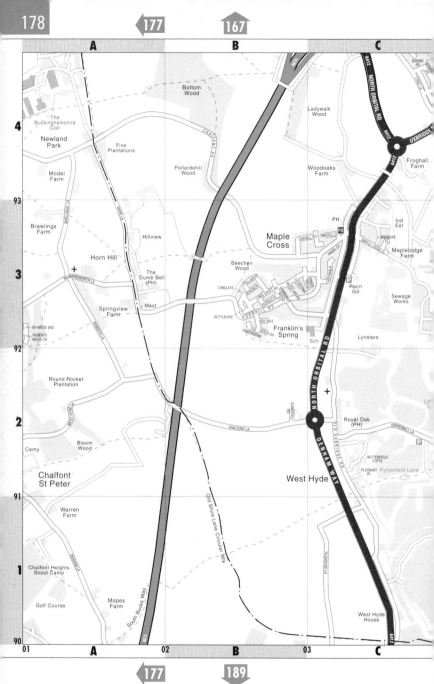

A B C

4

The Buckinghamshire Coll

Newland Park

Five Plantations

Bottom Wood

Ladywalk Wood

NORTH ORBITAL RD

A412

UXBRIDGE

A412

Froghall Farm

Model Farm

93

Pollardshill Wood

Woodoaks Farm

PH

Ind Est

Brawlings Farm

Hillview

PO

Longmore Cl

Oakhill Rd Oakhill Cl

Mapledge Farm

Horn Hill

Maple Cross

MAPLE LODGE CL

Sewage Works

3

The Dumb Bell (PH)

Beechen Wood

Recn Gd

LONGLEES

Franklin's Spring

Springview Farm

Mast

BUTTLEHIDE

ASH VALE

Sch

Lynsters

92

HAWTHORNS

BIRCH DW

Round Rocket Plantation

NORTH ORBITAL RD

2

CHALFONT LA

Royal Oak (PH)

COPPERMILL LA

Cemy

Bloom Wood

Old Shire Lane Circular Wlk

DENHAM WAY

OLD UXBRIDGE RD

BUTTERFIELD COTTS

Chalfont St Peter

PLEASANT PL

PYNESFIELD LAKE

West Hyde

91

Warren Farm

1

Chalfont Heights Scout Camp

South Bucks Way

TILEHOUSE LA

Golf Course

Mopes Farm

West Hyde House

A412

90

01 A 02 B 03 C

4

89

3

88

2

87

1

86

Balhams's Wood

Stonor House

Kildridge Wood

Stonor Park
(Deer Park)

Coxlease
Farm

Bosmore
Farm

Hanging
Wood

Jubilee
Plantation

Jackson's Farm

Fawley Bottom

Fawley Bottom
Farm House

Kitchener's
Firs

Eversdown

Drovers

Southend

Southend
Farm

Binfield Bottom

Great Wood

Kimble Farm

Gussetts
Wood

Upper Woodend
Farm

Lower Woodend
Farm

Roundhouse
Farm

The Walnut Tree
(PH)

Sunnyclose

Fawley Green
Farm

Fawley

Benhams

Brackenhill
Stud Farm

Vineyar
& Brewe

Luxters
Farm

Jubilee Plantat

Henleyhill Woo

Woodcocks
Bill

Highfield
Plantation

Great Wo

Red Hill

Pallbach Hill

A 74 75 **B** 76 **C**

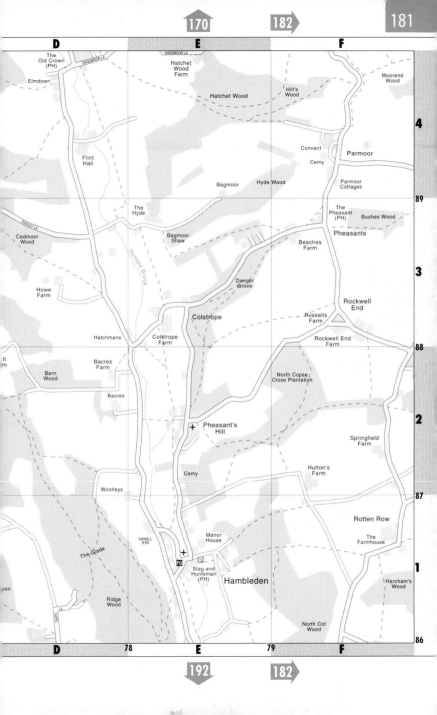

SHOGMOOR LA

The Old Crown (PH)

Elmdown

Hatchet Wood Farm

Hatchet Wood

Hill's Wood

Moorend Wood

4

Flint Hall

Convent

Parmoor

Cemy

Bagmoor

Hyde Wood

Parmoor Cottages

89

DUDLEY LA

The Hyde

The Pheasant (PH)

Bushes Wood

Cadmoor Wood

Bagmoor Shaw

Beeches Farm

Pheasants

3

Hamble Brook

Danger Grove

Howe Farm

Colstrope

Rockwell End

Russells Farm

Hatchmans

Colstrope Farm

Rockwell End Farm

88

Bacres Farm

Barn Wood

North Copse Close Plantation

Bacres

2

Pheasant's Hill

Springfield Farm

Cemy

Hutton's Farm

Woolleys

87

Rotten Row

The Farmhouse

VARNELL TERR

Manor House

PO

P

The Glade

Stag and Huntsman (PH)

Hambleden

1

DAIRY LA

Ridge Wood

Harcham's Wood

oir

North Cot Wood

86

A B C

Moorend Wood

Bottom Wood

Beacon Farm

Finnamore La

Beacon La

4

HM
Young Offender Inst
(Finnamore Wood Camp)

Finnamore Wood

Bluey's Farm

The Roost

89

Chisbridge Cross

Chisbridge

Shillingridge Wood

Copy

Holme Wood Cottage

Holme Wood

3

SHILLINGRIDGE PK

Woodlands

Denelands Farm

Holme Wood

Oaklands Farm

Kent's Wood

FRIETH RD

Hawkins Farm

Mundaydean Bottom

Bottom House

88

Woodend House

Fountain's

Woodend Farm

MARLOW COMM

Holywick

Arbon

Lower Woodend

2

Walnut Tree Farm

Heath Wood

Lord's Wood

Marlow Common

87

Homefield Wood

MARLOW COMM

Rogues Plantation

1

Davenport Wood

Bockmer End Farm

Pullingshill Wood

Bockmer End

BOCKMER LA

Bockmer House

Woodland Plain

Hook's Farm

Widefield

80 A 81 B 82 C

D E F

4

89

3

88

2

87

1

86

High Heavens Wood

Nuttings Wood

Linzees Firs

Widmere Farm

Juniper

Coldharbour

Highruse Wood

End Farm

High Rews Farm

Little Manor

Hatches Wood

Munces Wood

Marlow Bottom

Mast

Burford Cty Comb Sch

Seymour Court

Stowe

The Old Workhouse

Wymers Wood

Burroughs Grove Hill

Three Horseshoes (PH)

Juniper Hill

Bencombe Farm

Burroughs Grove

Wood Barn Farm

Kiln House

Capel Cillia

Great Marlow Stapleton Sch

Gypsy Lane

MARLOW ROAD

SEYMOUR COURT RD

MARLOW BOTTOM

SEYMOUR PLAIN

A404

A4155

Blount's Wood

Bovingdon Green

Blount's Farm

Woodside Farm

The Royal Oak (PH)

Marefield

Forty Green

Little House Farm

Spinfield

MARLOW

Spinfield Cty Comb Sch

St Peter's RC Comb Sch

Sir William Borlase's Gram Sch

Marlow CE Fst Sch

Holy Trinity CE Mid Sch

Fox Piece Cty Fst Sch

Fox Piece Cty Mid Sch

Marlow Com

Marlow Sta

Liby

Brewery

Court Garden L Complex

Marlow Weir

The Thames Path River Thames

HENLEY RD

WEST ST

SPITTAL ST

CHAPEL ST

LITTLE MARLOW RD

A4155

MUNDAYDEAN LA

D 84 E 85 F 86

E1
1 BRAEMAR CT
2 CHISWICK LODGE
3 LISTON CT
4 LIME BARN
E1
1 BEECH CT
2 VICTORIA CT
3 GLADE HO
4 ST JAMES CTYD

5 LEIGHTON HO
6 MONKSWOOD CT
7 LITTLE BOLTONS
8 PENN CT
9 TEMPLARS PL
10 TIERNEY CT
11 DUNSTABLE HO
F2
1 EASTWOOD CT
2 WILTSHIRE RD

3 MILE ELM
4 BEECHINGSTOKE
5 BUTLER CT
6 BYRON CT
7 MEAD CL
8 WILLOWMEAD RD
9 WILLOWMEAD SQ
10 WILLOWMEAD CL
11 ROMNEY CT
12 SHELLEY RD

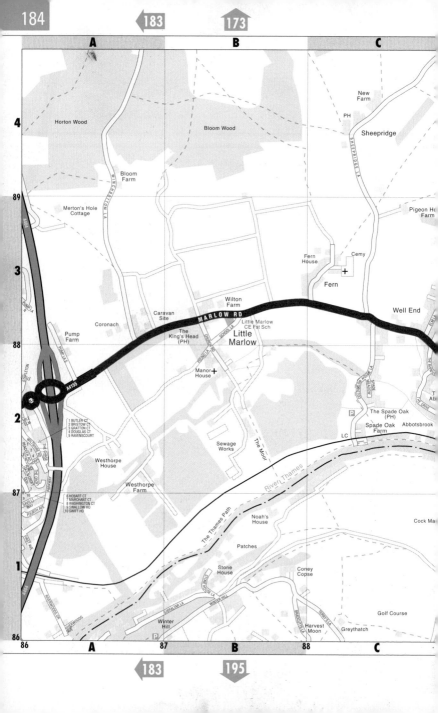

WHITE HILL

Golf Course

BOUNDARY RD

Glory Hill
Farm

Wooburn
Green

ckwell
Heath

Juniper Hill
Cty Comb
Sch

Juniper
Farm

Works

The Meadows
Cty Comb
Sch

WYCOMBE LA

Parklands

Clayfield
House

Old Meadows

HOLTSPUR LA

Westwinds

Ronald
Wood

River Wye

der
dge

THE COACH
HO
TUDOR
MILL

THE
HAWTHORNS

Unity
House

Claytons
Cty Comb
Sch
Resr

WOOBURN
MEWS

GREEN B4440

WOOBURN
MANOR PARK

BROAD
LA

Wooburn

1 UFTON COURT YD
2 UFTON CT

Wooburn
Park

Berghers
Hill

MARLOW RD

The Wye Valley
Sch

Farm
Wood

Liby

TOWN LA

Cores
End

Cemy

Wash Hill
Wood

Mast

THE PARADE

CORES END RD A4094

BROOKBANK

The
Swilley

STATION RD A4155

FURLONG

Works

Widmoor

Hedsor

Hawk's
Hill

The Chequers
(PH)

Hedsor
Farmhouse

Bourne
End

CAMDEN RD

Hollands
Farm

HAYWARD

1 COSTERS COTTS
2 BEACONSFIELD COTTS

White
Hill

Church Rd

Beeches Way

Woodman's Wood

HEDSOR RD

Mill
House

The Thames Path

River Thames

Merlins
Mead

FERRY LA A4094

Hedsor
Priory

Park Top

Hedsor
Court

4

89

3

88

2

87

1

86

ROWAN HO
OKERS CT
RUSSELL HO
RAY HO
GRANT HO
RCHARD HO
AILEY HO
BOURNE END BSNS CTR
GHAMS CT

10 HYLAND HO
11 FARRIER CT
12 MOUNT PLEASANT COTTS
13 SYCAMORE CL
14 THE WILLOWS
15 THE MAPLES
16 MEADOW BANK
17 THE COURTYARD

D **E** **F**

LONDON RD
A40

Stampwell Farm

Birchland Wood

Lower Pyebushes

FOXHILL LA

Pyebushes

PYEBUSH LA

Birch Wood

OXFORD RD

Hyde Farm

4

Hotel

Wapsey's Wood

Sand Pit

89

Green Broom

Further Warren Wood

Burtley Wood

Bower Wood Cotts

Cave Wood

Works

HEDGERLEY LA

3

Birchen Spring Coppice

Hillmotts Farm

Moat Farm

Slade Farm

Slade Wood

BLACKMOOR COMMON LA

WAPSEYS LA

88
M40

Bower Wood

Hillmotts Furze

Manor Farm

Hedgerley Green

Mount Pleasant Farm

Sutton's Wood

VILLAGE LA

Nature Reserve

Leith Grove

2

DORNEY HILL S

Pennlands Wood

MARSH LA

Hedgerley

White Horse (PH)

THE CHURCH HOLT
+

Pennlands Farm

Church Wood

HAREMEAD LA

Court Farm

KILN LA

Brick Mould (PH)

87

Kiln Wood

STEVENSON RD

Hanging Wood

Summerlins Wood

The Yew Tree (PH)

NURSERY CT

GREGORY RD

WILKINS RD

Hedgerley Park

COLINSWOOD RD

Hedgerley Hill

1

Egypt ods

Heathfield Wood

HOLLYBUSH CNR

PARISH LA

One Pin Farm

LONGFIELD

PO

EGYPT WOOD COTTS

EGYPT LA

CHRISTMAS LA

Colinswood

The One Pin (PH)

School Wood

WOOD END CL

COLLUM GREEN RD

Hedgerley Park Farm

WOODLAND SLADE

PUMSEY DR

A355

OTLEY HILL

86

D 96 **E** 97 **F**

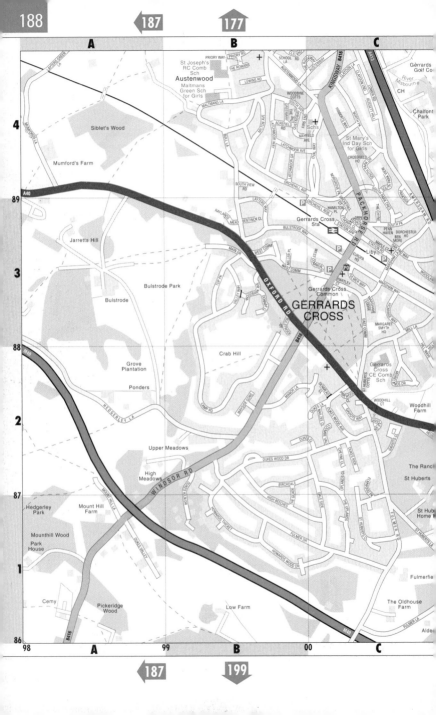

189

South Harefield

Langley Farm
Bourne Farm
Highbor
Breakspear Path
BREAKSPEAR RD N
Breakspear House
Nature Reserve

ST MARY'S RD
ST ANNE'S RD
CARDINAL RD
Broadwater Farm
BROADWATER LA
BEDLEY GRN
BALLE GRN
Broad Water

Park Lodge Farm Ctr

Bayhurst Wood (Countryside Park)

89

Battlesford Wood

Widewater Lock
WIDEWATER RSNS CTR

Lower Lodge

The Horse & Barge (PH)

Harefield Moor

Newyears Green
NEWYEARS GREEN LA

3

BROADWATER PARK
1 GREEN TILES LA
2 SHEEPCOTE GDNS
3 DENHAM GREEN LA
M12
Green Bridge

Grand Union Canal
Towing Path

Highway Farm

Braemar Farm

Savay Farm

88

DENHAM GLOUCESTER
Denham Sta

Dews Farm

Newyears Green Covert

2

Pyghtle Footpath

River Colne

Grand Union Canal Wlk

HARVIL RD

Research Farm

Camping Site

87

Copthall Covert

Golf Course

The White House
Denham

SOUTH BUCKS WAY

Court Farm

Denham Court
CH

Golf Course
CH

Harvil Farm

Copthall Farm

River Misbourne

Denham Country Park

THE DRIVE

1

Priory Covert

Colne Valley Park Visitor Ctr

CAMPION CL

Ickenham

ST GEORGE'S DR

SHOREDICHE CL 1
CAMPDEN RD 2

OXFORD RD

PRIORY

Fray's River

The Lea

Denham Lock

SWAKELEYS RD
THREE OA

86

189 201

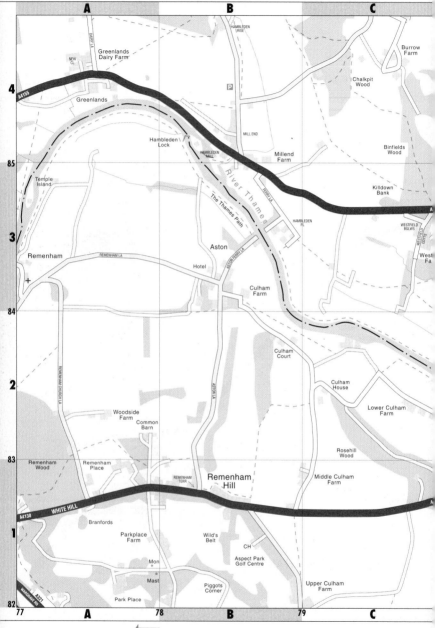

A B C

4

Greenlands
Dairy Farm
NEW
CL
DAIRY LA

A4155

Greenlands

HAMBLEDEN
RISE

P

BURROW
Farm

CHALKPIT
WOOD

Hambleden
Lock

MILL END

Millend
Farm

Binfields
Wood

85

River Thames

HAMBLEDEN
MILL

Temple
Island

The Thames Path

FERRY LA

Killdown
Bank

WESTFIELD
BGLWS

BETTS

West
Fa

3

Remenham

REMENHAM LA

Aston

HAMBLEDEN
PL

ASTON FERRY LA

Hotel

Culham
Farm

84

Culham
Court

2

REMENHAM CHURCH LA

Woodside
Farm

Common
Barn

ASTON LA

Culham
House

Lower Culham
Farm

83

Remenham
Wood

Remenham
Place

REMENHAM
TERR

Remenham
Hill

Rosehill
Wood

Middle Culham
Farm

A4130 WHITE HILL

Branfords

1

Parkplace
Farm

Wild's
Belt

CH

Aspect Park
Golf Centre

Upper Culham
Farm

Mon

Mast

Piggots
Corner

WARGRAVE RD

A321

Park Place

82

77 A 78 B 79 C

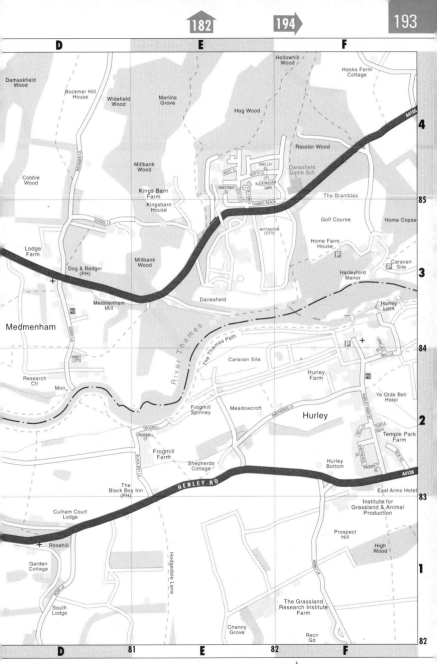

A · B · C

HIGHFIELD PARK

THE RUSHES

BEECHWOOD DR

A4155

Hooks Corner

A4155

THE HEIGHTS

Sentry Hill

4

Golf Course

Harleyford Lane

East Lodge

85

Low Grounds Farm

The Garden Cottage

Marina

Temple Lock

3

Weir

TEMPLE MILL ISLAND

TEMPLE LA

TEMPLE MILL COTTS

STABLE COTTS

Temple

Temple Park

The Thames Path

River Thames

TEMPLE LA

Caravan Site

84

Temple Farm

Sewage Works

2

HURLEY LA

Golf Course

A4130

83

Black Horse Lodge

HENLEY RD

CH

Speen Hill

1

Applehouse Hill Red Lion (PH)

Applehouse Farm

Hall Place (Berkshire Coll of Ag)

82

BURCHETT'S GREEN RD

A4155

PERCH CL

Lower Lodge

Pens Place

Stoney Ware

Bisham CE Cont Prim Sch

Bisham Abbey National Sports Ctr

Bisham Abbey

RIVERMEAD

MARSH MILL LA

QUARRY WOOD RD

Lock Island

Longridge Scout Bc Activity

Town Farm

VANSITTART RD

Bisham

Bisham GN

P

A308

Princess Elizabeth's Well

Fultness Wood

EAST PADDOCK

Inkydown Wood

Park Farm

Park Wood

The Lodge

MARLOW RD

Goulding's Wood

Hyde Farm

DUNGROVEHILL LA

Dungrovehill Wood

Lee Farm

Carpenter's Wood

Pinkneys Court

St Timothe

LEE LA

83 · A · 84 · B · 85 · C

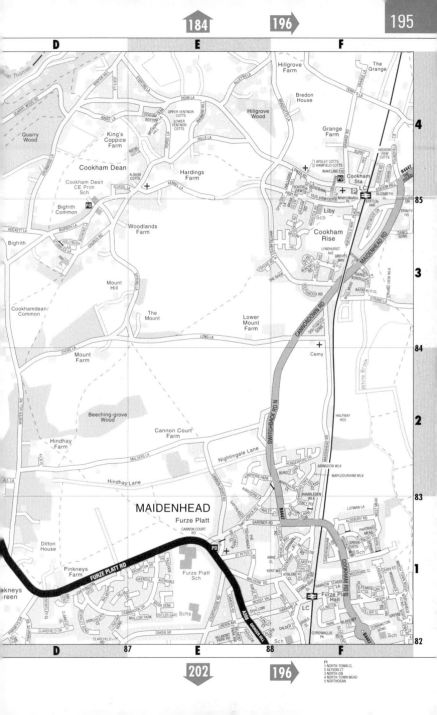

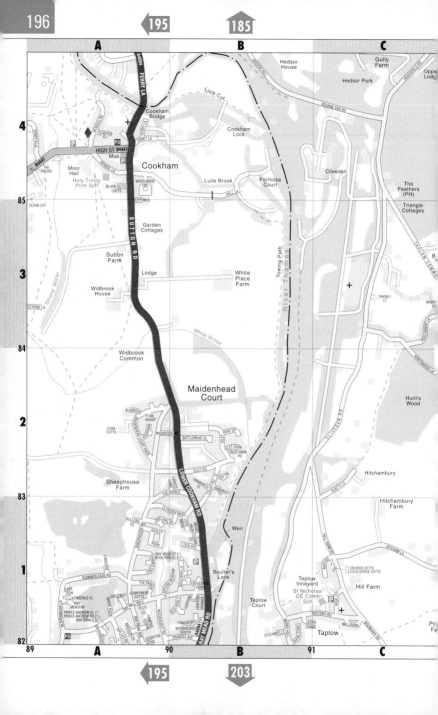

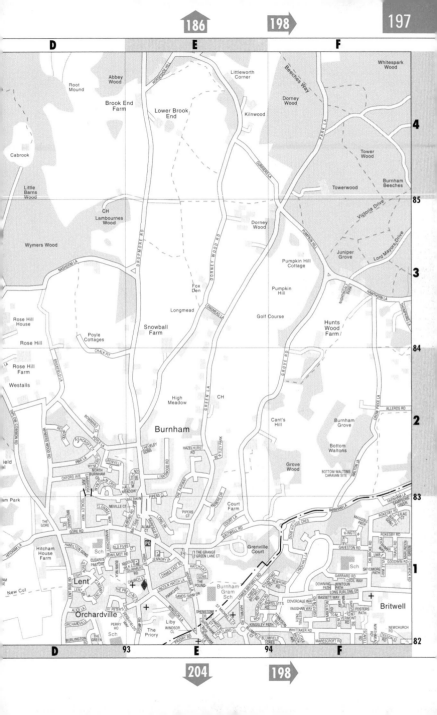

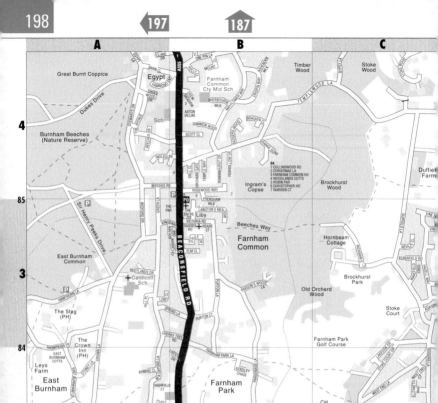

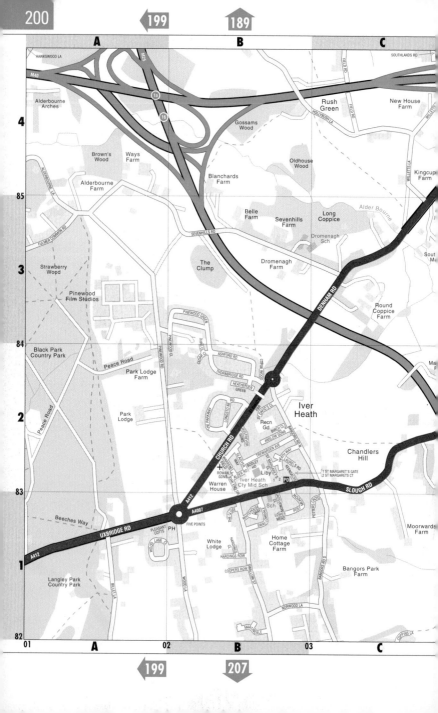

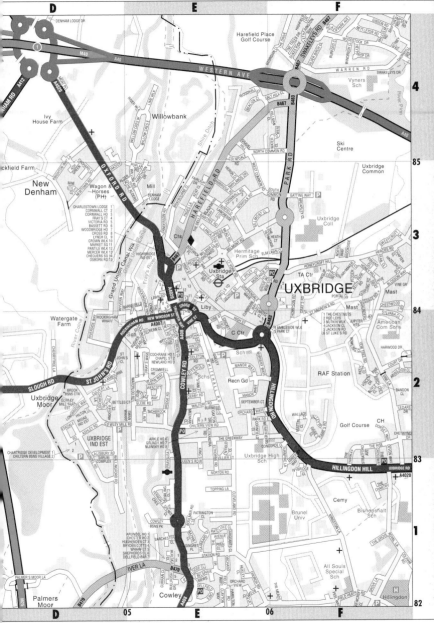

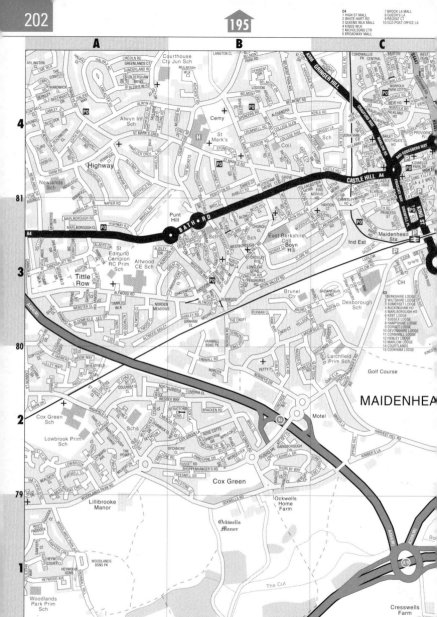

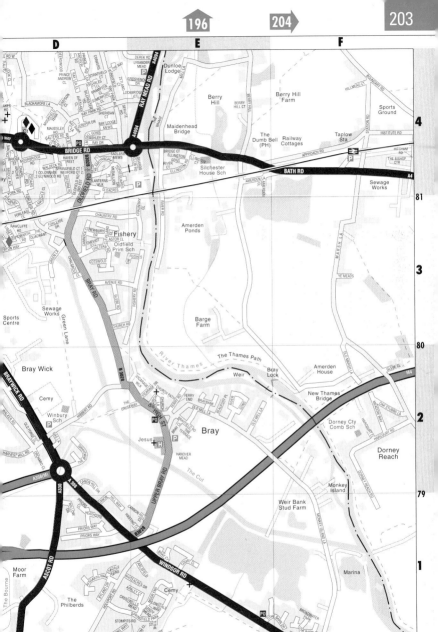

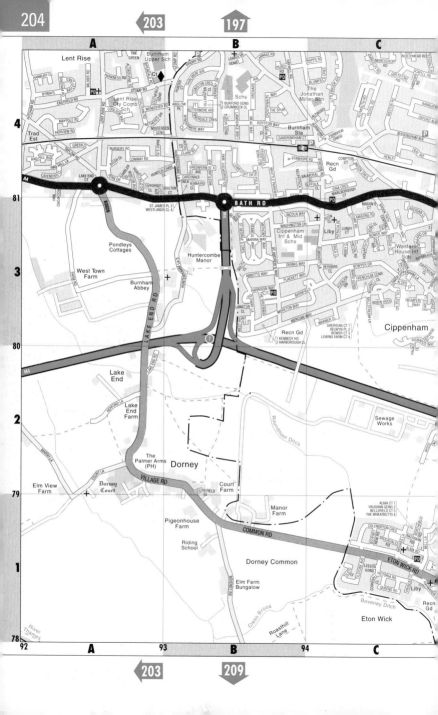

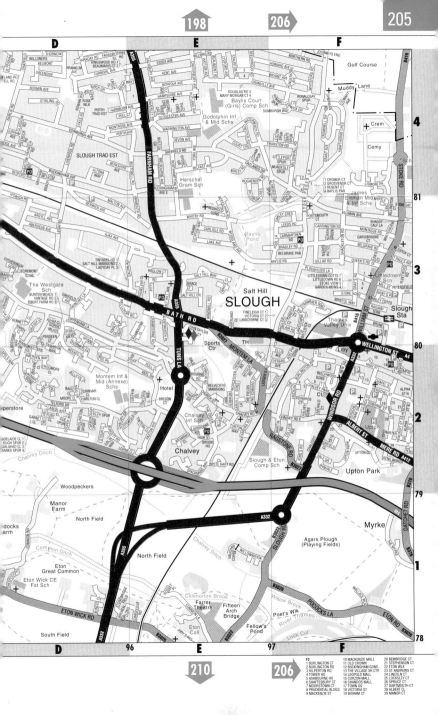

SLOUGH

Salt Hill

Chalvey

Upton Park

Woodpeckers

Manor Farm

North Field

North Field

Myrke

Agars Plough
(Playing Fields)

Eton Great Common

Eton Wick CE Fst Sch

South Field

Colenorton Brook

Farrer Theatre

Fifteen Arch Bridge

Fellow's Pond

Eton Coll

Poet's Wlk

River Thames

Lock Cut

F2
1 BURLINGTON CT
2 BURLINGTON RD
3 HILPERTON RD
4 TOWER HO
5 ASHBOURNE HO
6 SHAFTESBURY CT
7 MOORSTOWN CT
8 PRUDENTIAL BLDGS
9 MACKENZIE ST
10 MACKENZIE MALL
11 OLD CROWN
12 BUCKINGHAM GDNS
13 THE VILLAGE SH CTR
14 LEOPOLD MALL
15 CURZON MALL
16 CHANDOS MALL
17 TOWN SQ
18 VICTORIA CT
19 BISHAM CT
20 BEMBRIDGE CT
21 STEPHENSON CT
22 ETON WLK
23 ST ANDREWS CT
24 LINCOLN CT
25 LOCKSLEY CT
26 SPRUCE CT
27 DARTMOUTH CT
28 ALBERT CL
29 MANOR CT

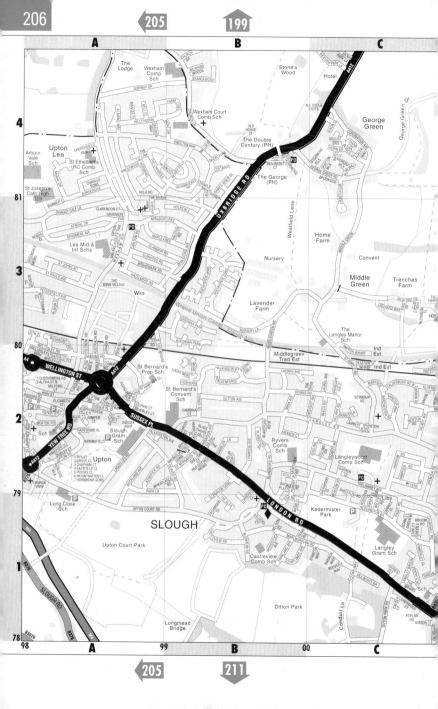

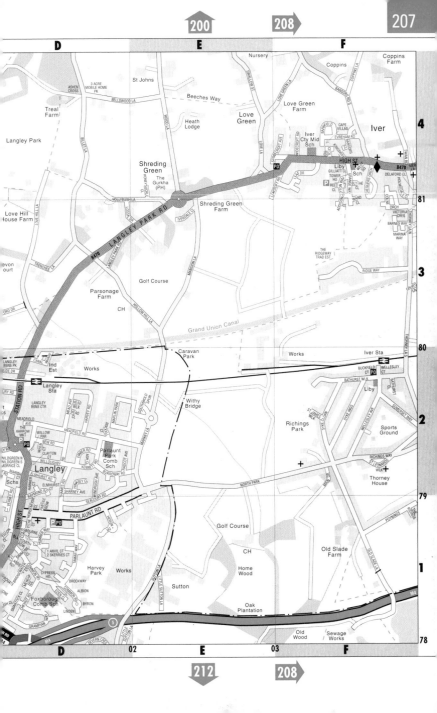

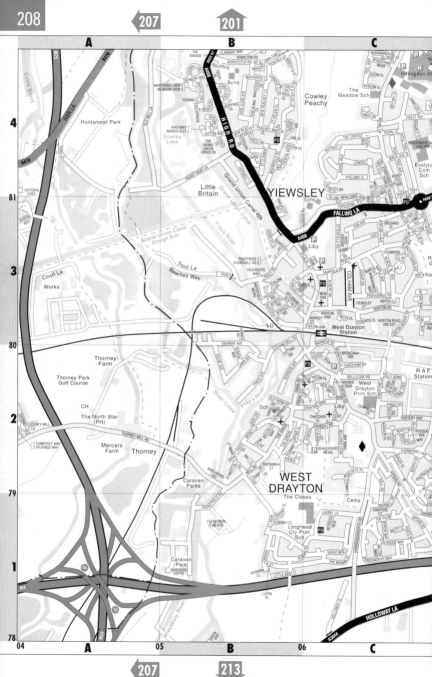

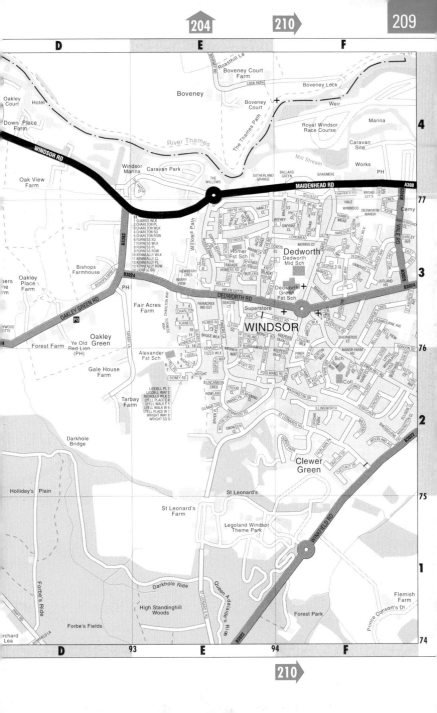

Roasthill La
Boveney Court Farm
LOCK PATH
Boveney Lock
Boveney
Boveney Court
Weir
Oakley Court
Hotel
Down Place Farm
Marina
Royal Windsor Race Course
Caravan Site
Works
PH
WINDSOR RD
River Thames
The Thames Path
MAIDENHEAD RD A308
Windsor Marina
Caravan Park
THE WILLOWS
SUTHERLAND GRANGE
BALLARD GREEN
GRASMERE
Mill Stream
Oak View Farm
Cemy

4

77

1 GUARDS WLK
2 CHARLTON PL
3 CHARLTON WLK
4 CHARLTON SQ
5 CHARLTON ROW
6 FURNESS SQ
7 FURNESS WLK
8 FURNESS ROW
9 FURNESS PL
10 KENNEALLY WLK
11 KENNEALLY CL
12 KENNEALLY PL
13 KENNEALLY ROW
14 LIDDELL SQ

Bishops Farmhouse

Oakley Place Farm

Dedworth
Dedworth Mid Sch

Homer Fst Sch

Dedworth Green Fst Sch

Forest Farm

Oakley Green
Ye Old Red Lion (PH)

PH

OAKLEY GREEN RD

PO

DEDWORTH RD

Superstore

WINDSOR

3

76

Fair Acres Farm

Alexander Fst Sch

CHARLTON
FAIRACRES IND EST
FURNESS

Coll

Gale House Farm

Tarbay Farm

LIDDELL PL 1
NICHOLLS WLK 3
LYELL PLACE 4
LYELL WALK E 5
LYELL WALK W 6
LYELL PLACE W 7
WRIGHT WAY 8
WRIGHT SQ 9

DUNCANNON CRES
STROUD
ROWLAND CL
FENNING
GILMAN CRES
PINER
POOLMANS RD
WASHINGTON DR
ILLINGWORTH

2

75

Darkhole Bridge

Holliday's Plain

St Leonard's

St Leonard's Farm

Legoland Windsor Theme Park

Clewer Green

WINKFIELD RD

Forest Park

Flemish Farm

Prince Consort's Dr

1

Darkhole Ride

Queen Adelaide's Ride

High Standinghill Woods

Forbe's Ride

Forbe's Fields

Orchard Lea

74

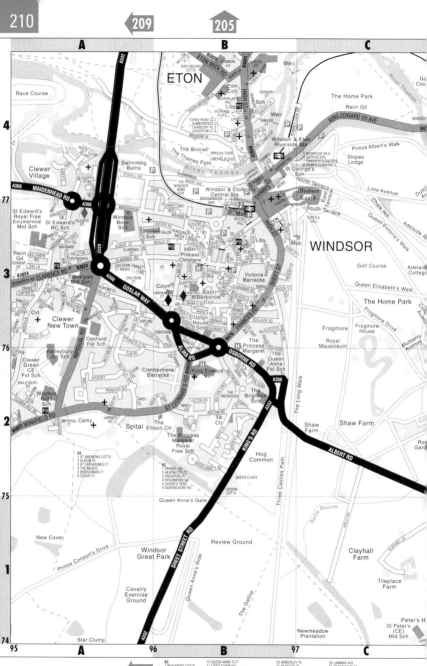

ETON

WINDSOR

Race Course

Clewer Village

Clewer New Town

Clewer Green

Windsor Great Park

Cavalry Exercise Ground

Star Clump

The Home Park

Prince Albert's Walk

Slopes Lodge

Lime Avenue

Windsor Castle

Golf Course

The Home Park

Frogmore

Royal Mausoleum

Shaw Farm

Clayhall Farm

Tileplace Farm

New Cover

Review Ground

Newmeadow Plantation

St Peter's (CE) Mid Sch

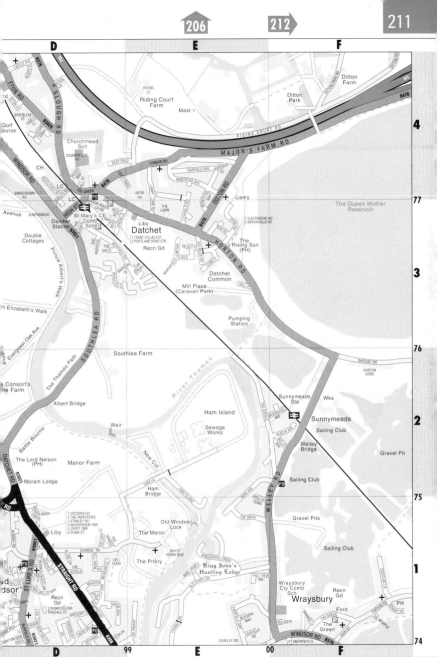

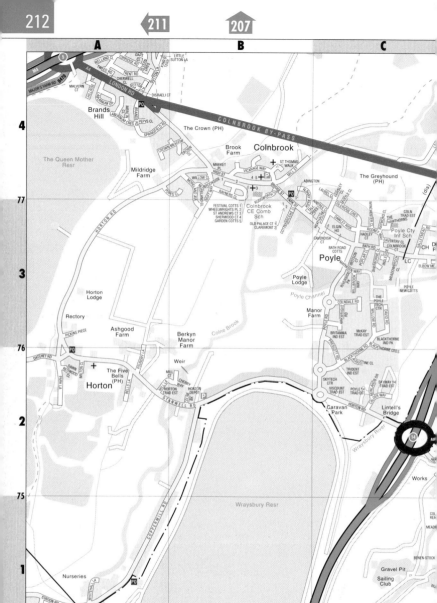

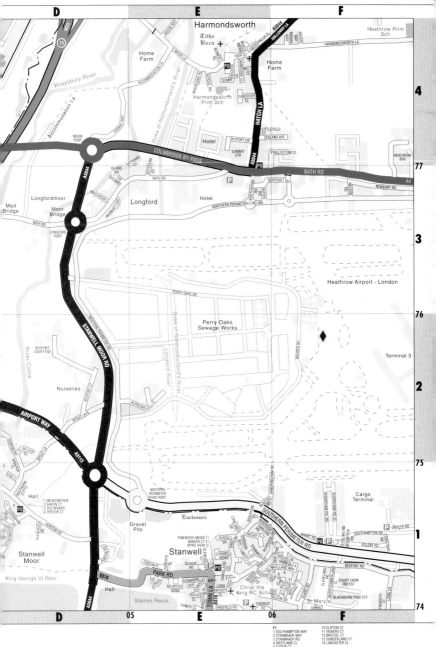

Harmondsworth

Tithe Barn

Home Farm

Wraysbury River

Home Farm

Heathrow Prim Sch

HARMONDSWORTH LA

Harmondsworth Prim Sch

Accommodation La

MOOR RDBT

COLNBROOK BY-PASS

Mad Bridge

Longfordmoor

Moor Bridge

LONGFORD RDBT

Longford

BATH RD

Hotel

Northern Perimeter O Rd (W)

NEWBURY RD

A4

Heathrow Airport - London

PERRY OAKS DR

Perry Oaks Sewage Works

Duke of Northumberland's River

Longford River

Terminal 3

River Colne

BEDFONT COURT EST

Nurseries

AIRPORT WAY

A3113

King George VI Resr

WESTERN PERIMETER BROAD RDBT

Enclosure

Cargo Terminal

SOUTHERN PERIMETER RD

Gravel Pits

Stanwell Moor

B378

PARK RD

Stanwell

Christ the King RC Sch

St Mary's Sch

Court Farm Ind Est

Blackburn Trad Est

Hall

Staines Resrs

Hall

1 MEADOWVIEW
2 SAXON CT
3 THE BRIARS
4 TREVOR CT

PINEWOOD MEWS 1
BAKERS CT 2
SPIRE VIEW 3

F1
1 SOUTHAMPTON WAY
2 STRANRAER WAY
3 STRANRAER RD
4 WESTLAND CL
5 TUDOR CT
6 WESSEX CT
7 SHACKLETON CT
8 VANGUARD HO
9 FLEETWOOD CT

10 CLIFTON CT
11 VICKERS CT
12 BRISTOL CT
13 SUNDERLAND CT
14 LANCASTER CL

Index

Street names are listed alphabetically and show the locality, the Postcode District, the page number and a reference to the square in which the name falls on the map page

Shaftesbury Ct **6** Slough SL1 .... 205 F2

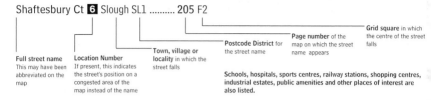

Grid square in which the centre of the street falls

Page number of the map on which the street name appears

Postcode District for the street name

Town, village or locality in which the street falls

Location Number
If present, this indicates the street's position on a congested area of the map instead of the name

Full street name
This may have been abbreviated on the map

Schools, hospitals, sports centres, railway stations, shopping centres, industrial estates, public amenities and other places of interest are also listed.

Abbreviations used in the index

App	Approach	Cl	Close	Ent	Enterprise	La	Lane	Rdbt	Roundabout
Arc	Arcade	Comm	Common	Espl	Esplanade	N	North	S	South
Ave	Avenue	Cnr	Corner	Est	Estate	Orch	Orchard	Sq	Square
Bvd	Boulevard	Cotts	Cottages	Gdns	Gardens	Par	Parade	Strs	Stairs
Bldgs	Buildings	Ct	Court	Gn	Green	Pk	Park	Stps	Steps
Bsns Pk	Business Park	Ctyd	Courtyard	Gr	Grove	Pas	Passage	St	Street, Saint
Bsns Ctr	Business Centre	Cres	Crescent	Hts	Heights	Pl	Place	Terr	Terrace
Bglws	Bungalows	Cswy	Causeway	Ho	House	Prec	Precinct	Trad Est	Trading Estate
Ctr	Centre	Dr	Drive	Ind Est	Industrial Estate	Prom	Promenade	Wlk	Walk
Cir	Circus	Dro	Drove	Intc	Interchange	Ret Pk	Retail Park	W	West
		E	East	Junc	Junction	Rd	Road	Yd	Yard
		Emb	Embankment						

Town and village index

Adstock	53 F1	Coleshill	164 C2	Haversham	20 C1	Moulsoe	36 B4	Stoke Mandeville	116 A1
Akeley	42 A4	Colnbrook	212 B4	Hedgerley	187 F2	Murcott	94 A2	Stoke Poges	198 C2
Aldbury	120 B3	Cookham	196 A4	Henley-on-Thames	191 E1	Mursley	67 E3	Stokenchurch	158 C3
Amersham	154 B1	Cookham Dean	195 D4	Henton	137 F1	Naphill	161 E4	Stone	114 B3
Ashendon	97 F1	Cosgrove	19 E1	High Wycombe	173 B3	Nash	44 B1	Stonor	179 F3
Ashley Green	144 C4	Cranfield	25 D1	Hoggeston	77 D4	New Denham	201 D3	Stony Stratford	32 C3
Ashton	9 F4	Cublington	78 A1	Holmer Green	163 E3	Newport Pagnell	22 B3	Swanbourne	67 D2
Aspley Guise	49 F2	Cuddington	113 D1	Holton	122 B1	Newton Blossomville	8 A2	Syresham	27 D4
Aspley Heath	49 D1	Dadford	28 B1	Horton	212 A2	Newton Longville	57 E2	Taplow	196 C1
Aston Abbots	88 B3	Dagnall	107 E3	Horton-cum-Studley	108 A3	Newton Purcell	50 A1	Thame	126 A1
Aston Clinton	117 E3	Datchet	211 E3	Hughenden Valley	162 A4	North Crawley	24 A3	Thornborough	54 A4
Astwood	16 A2	Deanshanger	31 E2	Hurley	193 F2	North Marston	76 A1	Thornton	43 E3
Aylesbury	115 E4	Denham	190 A1	Hyde Heath	153 E3	Northchurch	134 C3	Tiddington	136 A4
Ballinger Common	142 C2	Denham Green	189 F3	Ibstone	169 E4	Oakley	109 E3	Tingewick	51 D4
Beachampton	44 A3	Dinton	113 F1	Ickenham	190 C1	Oakley Green	209 D3	Totternhoe	93 D4
Beacon's Bottom	159 E2	Dorney	204 B2	Ickford	124 A2	Old Stratford	32 A4	Tring	119 D2
Beaconsfield	175 E1	Dorton	96 C1	Iver	207 F4	Old Windsor	211 D1	Turvey	8 C3
Beckley	108 A1	Drayton Beauchamp	118 A3	Iver Heath	200 B2	Olney	6 C2	Turweston	38 B4
Bellingdon	143 F4	Drayton Parslow	68 B3	Ivinghoe	105 F3	Oving	86 B4	Twyford	62 B1
Berkhamsted	135 E3	Dunstable	93 F4	Kingswood	83 D2	Padbury	53 D1	Tylers Green	163 E1
Biddlesden	27 E3	East Claydon	74 C4	Lacey Green	149 F3	Paulerspury	17 D4	Upper Arncott	94 C4
Bierton	102 A2	Eaton Bray	92 C3	Lane End	171 E2	Piddington (Bucks)	95 F4	Upper Winchendon	99 D1
Bisham	194 C4	Edgcott	72 C1	Lathbury	22 B4	Piddington (Northants)	4 A4	Uxbridge	201 F3
Blackthorn	81 D3	Edlesborough	92 C2	Latimer	155 F2	Pitstone	105 E2	Waddesdon	99 D4
Bledlow	138 A1	Ellesborough	130 A1	Lavendon	7 A4	Pottersspury	18 B1	Walter's Ash	150 B4
Bledlow Ridge	159 F4	Emberton	13 F4	Leckhampstead	42 C4	Poundon	71 F4	Walton	48 A3
Bletchley	58 A3	Eton	210 B4	Lee Common	142 B3	Poyle	212 C3	Warrington	7 D4
Boarstall	95 D1	Farnham Common	198 B3	Leighton Buzzard	80 C3	Preston Bissett	62 A4	Water Stratford	40 A1
Botley	145 D1	Farnham Royal	198 B2	Lewknor	157 D4	Prestwood	151 E3	Waterperry	123 D1
Bourne End	185 D1	Fawley	180 B1	Lillingstone Lovell	30 A3	Princes Risborough	139 E2	Wavendon	48 C4
Bovingdon	146 A2	Feldon	146 C4	Little Brickhill	59 F3	Puttenham	103 F1	Weedon	87 E1
Bow Brickhill	48 B1	Finmere	50 B4	Little Chalfont	166 A4	Quainton	85 D3	Wendover	131 E2
Brackley	38 A4	Flackwell Heath	185 D4	Little Chalfont	155 D1	Ravenstone	5 F3	West Drayton	208 B2
Brill	96 A1	Flaunden	156 A3	Little Gaddesden	121 E4	Remenham Hill	192 B1	Westbury	39 D2
Buckingham	52 A4	Ford	128 A4	Little Hampden	140 C2	Ringshall	107 D1	Westcott	98 B4
Buckland Common	133 D2	Frieth	170 C1	Little Horwood	55 F1	Rout's Green	148 C1	Weston Turville	116 C2
Burnham	197 E2	Fulmer	199 E4	Little Kimble	129 F2	Salford	37 E2	Weston Underwood	6 A1
Butler's Cross	130 B2	Gawcott	51 F2	Little Kingshill	152 A2	Sarratt	156 C2	Whaddon	45 D1
Castlethorpe	19 F3	Gerrards Cross	188 C3	Little Marlow	184 B3	Seer Green	176 B2	Whitchurch	87 D3
Chackmore	41 D2	Godington	61 F2	Long Crendon	125 D3	Shabbington	124 B2	Whitfield	26 B2
Chalfont St Giles	177 E4	Grafton Regis	9 F1	Long Marston	104 A2	Shalstone	39 F3	Wicken	31 D2
Chalfont St Peter	177 F1	Granborough	75 F4	Longwick	138 B4	Shenley Brook End	46 A1	Wigginton	119 E1
Chardon	72 C3	Great Brickhill	59 E1	Loosley Row	149 E3	Shenley Church End	45 F3	Wilstone	104 B1
Chartridge	143 E2	Great Horwood	55 D1	Loudwater	174 B1	Sherington	14 A1	Winchmore Hill	164 B2
Chearsley	112 A1	Great Kimble	129 F4	Ludgershall	96 B4	Slapton	91 E3	Windsor	210 C3
Cheddington	105 D4	Great Kingshill	162 C4	Maidenhead	202 C2	Slough	205 E3	Wing	79 F1
Chenies	156 B1	Great Missenden	152 A3	Maidenhead Court	196 B2	Soulbury	69 F2	Wingrave	89 E2
Chesham	144 B2	Grendon Underwood	83 D4	Maids Moreton	41 F2	South Harefield	190 B3	Winslow	66 A2
Chesham	154 B4	Haddenham	127 D3	Maple Cross	178 B3	South Heath	152 C4	Woburn	60 C4
Chicheley	23 E4	Halton	117 E1	Marlow	183 D1	Speen	150 B2	Woburn Sands	49 D3
Chilton	111 D2	Hambleden	181 E1	Marlow Bottom	183 E3	St Leonards	132 C2	Wooburn Green	185 F4
Chinnor	147 E4	Hanslope	11 D2	Marsh Gibbon	71 F2	Stagsden	16 C3	Worminghall	123 F3
Chipperfield	158 B3	Hardmead	15 E2	Marsworth	105 D1	Stanwell	213 A1	Wotton Underwood	97 E2
Cholesbury	133 E2	Hardwick	87 D2	Medmenham	193 D3	Steeple Claydon	63 E2	Wraysbury	211 F1
Chorleywood	167 B3	Harmondsworth	213 E4	Mentmore	90 B2	Stewkley	68 C1	Yardley Gobion	18 C3
Christmas Common	168 A4	Harrold	3 F3	Middle Claydon	74 B4	Stoke Bruerne	9 D4	Yardley Hastings	1 A3
Clifton Reynes	7 E2	Hartwell	10 B4	Milton Keynes	34 B3	Stoke Goldington	12 A3	Yiewsley	208 B4
Cold Brayfield	8 A3	Hastoe	132 C4	Milton Keynes Village	35 F2	Stoke Hammond	69 F4		

B Acre Mobile Home Pk
SL0 .... 207 D4
Abbey Barn La
High Wycombe HP11 ..... 173 F2
Little Marlow HP10 ..... 173 F2
Abbey Barn Rd HP11 ..... 173 F2
Abbey CI SL1 ..... 204 C3
Abbey Cotts SL7 ..... 193 D2
Abbey Rd La SL1 ..... 186 C1
Abbey Rd Aylesbury HP19 . 101 D1
Bourne End SL8 ..... 184 C3
Milton Keynes, Bradwell
MK13, MK6 ..... 34 A2
Milton Keynes, Simpson
MK6 ..... 47 F3
Syresham NN13 ..... 27 E4
Abbey Terr MK16 ..... 22 B2
Abbey Way Bisham SL7 ..... 194 B3
High Wycombe HP11 ..... 173 D3
Milton Keynes MK13 ..... 34 A3
Ravenstone MK46 ..... 5 F1
Abbey Wlk HP16 ..... 152 A4
Abbey's Cty Comb Sch
MK3 ..... 47 D1
Abbot Ridge HP18 ..... 125 E3
Abbot Wlk HP18 ..... 125 E3
Abbot's Wlk SL4 ..... 209 F3
Abbots CI MK13 ..... 34 A3
Abbots Way
Little Marlow HP12 ..... 172 B2
Princes Risborough HP27 . 139 E3
Abbotsfield MK6 ..... 47 D4
Abbotswood HP27 ..... 150 B2
Abbotts CI UB8 ..... 208 B4
Abbotts Rd HP20 ..... 101 F1
Abbotts Rd HP20 ..... 101 F1
Abbotts Vale HP5 ..... 144 B2
Abbotts Way Burnham SL1 . 204 B3
Wingrave HP22 ..... 89 D2
Abell Gdns SL6 ..... 195 D1
Abercromby Rd La SL2 ..... 172 C4
Abercromby Ct 6 HP12 .. 172 B4
Aberdeen Ave SL1 ..... 205 D3
Aberdeen CI MK3 ..... 46 C1
Abingdon CI UB10 ..... 201 F2
Abingdon Ox OX9 ..... 125 F1
Abingdon Wlk SL6 ..... 195 F2
Abington SL3 ..... 212 B4
Abney Court Dr SL8 ..... 185 D1
Abraham CI MK15 ..... 35 E3
Abrahams Rd RG9 ..... 191 E2
Abstacle Hill HP23 ..... 118 C2
Acacia RG9 ..... 191 E1
Acacia Ave
West Drayton UB7 ..... 208 C3
Wraysbury TW19 ..... 211 F2
Acacia Gr HP4 ..... 135 D2
Acacia CI 3 SL9 ..... 177 F1
Acacia Mews MK2 ..... 213 E4
Acacia Wlk HP23 ..... 118 C2
Accommodation La UB7 ..... 213 E4
Ackerman CI MK18 ..... 52 C4
Acorn CI HP13 ..... 173 E4
Acorn Gdns HP12 ..... 172 C2
Acorn Wlk MK9 ..... 34 C1
Acre Pas SL4 ..... 210 B3
Acre The SL7 ..... 183 F1
Acrefield Rd SL9 ..... 188 B4
Acres End HP7 ..... 165 F4
Acres The HP13 ..... 161 F1
Adam CI Aylesbury HP21 ... 116 A2
High Wycombe HP13 ..... 173 E4
Slough SL1 ..... 205 D3
Adams CI MK18 ..... 41 E1
Adams Ct MK6 ..... 47 E4
Adams Park HP12 ..... 172 A4
Adams Way HP23 ..... 119 D3
Addington CI SL4 ..... 210 A2
Addington Cotts HP22 ..... 131 D3
Addington Rd MK18 ..... 41 E1
Addison CI SL6 ..... 207 F3
Addison Ct SL6 ..... 196 A1
Addison Rd Chesham HP5 . 144 B1
Steeple Claydon MK18 ..... 63 E1
Adelaide CI SL1 ..... 205 D2
Adelaide Rd HP13 ..... 162 B1
Adelaide Sq SL4 ..... 210 B3
Adelphi Gdns SL6 ..... 205 F2
Adelphi St MK9 ..... 34 C2
Adkins CI HP19 ..... 100 C2
Admiral Way HP4 ..... 134 C3
Adstock Mews 2 SL9 ..... 177 E1
Adwell Sq RG9 ..... 191 E1
Adwycks CI MK5 ..... 45 F3
Agora Ctr
7 Milton Keynes, Bletchley
MK2 ..... 58 B4
Milton Keynes, Wolverton
MK12 ..... 33 E4
Ailward Rd HP19 ..... 101 D1
Ainsdale CI MK3 ..... 46 B1

Aintree CI
Milton Keynes MK3 ..... 57 E3
Stanwell SL3 ..... 212 C3
Airport Way TW19 ..... 213 D2
Aiston PI HP20 ..... 101 F1
Ajax Ave SL1 ..... 205 D3
Akeley CE Fst Sch MK18 .. 41 E4
Akeley Wood Jun Sch
MK18 ..... 31 D1
Akeley Wood Sch MK18 ... 41 E4
Akerman CI MK12 ..... 33 D3
Akister CI MK18 ..... 52 C4
Alabama Circ HP11 ..... 173 D2
Alabama Dr HP11 ..... 173 D2
Alan Wlk SL3 ..... 206 C4
Alaska St HP11 ..... 173 D2
Albany CI MK14 ..... 34 B4
Albany Gate HP5 ..... 144 A1
Albany Park SL3 ..... 212 B4
Albany PI HP19 ..... 101 D1
Albany Rd Old Windsor SL4 211 D1
Windsor SL4 ..... 210 B3
Albany Terr HP23 ..... 119 D3
Albert CI 28 SL4 ..... 210 B3
Albert PI SL4 ..... 205 D1
Albert Rd Chesham HP5 ... 154 B4
Henley-on-T RG9 ..... 191 F1
Old Windsor SL4 ..... 211 D1
West Drayton UB7 ..... 208 C3
Windsor SL4 ..... 210 C2
Albert St Aylesbury HP20 .. 116 A4
4 High Wycombe HP13 . 173 E4
Maidenhead SL6 ..... 202 C4
Milton Keynes MK2 ..... 58 B4
Slough SL1 ..... 205 F2
Tring HP23 ..... 119 D2
Windsor SL4 ..... 210 A3
Albion SL3 ..... 207 D1
Albion CI SL2 ..... 206 A3
Albion Cotts SL6 ..... 195 E4
Albion Cres HP8 ..... 177 D4
Albion PI
2 Milton Keynes MK9 ..... 35 D2
2 Windsor SL4 ..... 210 C2
Albion Rd
Chalfont St Giles HP8 ..... 177 D4
High Wycombe HP12 ..... 172 B3
Pitstone LU7 ..... 105 E3
Albright Dr MK20 ..... 115 F4
Albury CI MK48 ..... 33 F1
Albury View OX9 ..... 136 A3
Aldborough Spur SL1 ..... 205 F4
Aldbourne Rd SL1 ..... 204 A4
Aldbury Gdns HP23 ..... 119 D3
Aldbury Rd WD3 ..... 167 F1
Aldbury Sch HP23 ..... 120 B3
Aldebury Rd SL6 ..... 195 F1
Alden View SL4 ..... 209 E3
Aldene CI MK19 ..... 11 D2
Alder CI SL4 ..... 204 C3
Alder CI SL1 ..... 205 D3
Alder Rd Iver Heath SL0 .... 200 B2
New Denham UB9 ..... 201 E3
Alderbourne La Fulmer SL3 199 F4
Iver Heath SL0 ..... 200 A4
Alderbury Rd SL3 ..... 206 C2
Alderbury Rd W SL3 ..... 206 C2
Aldergill MK13 ..... 34 B3
Alderley CI MK4 ..... 135 C2
Aldermead MK12 ..... 33 F3
Alders The UB9 ..... 201 E3
Alderson CI HP19 ..... 101 D1
Aldin Ave N SL1 ..... 206 A2
Aldin Ave S SL1 ..... 206 A2
Aldrich Dr MK15 ..... 35 F4
Aldridge CI HP11 ..... 173 F2
Aldridge Rd SL2 ..... 198 A1
Aldridge St SL6 ..... 202 B3
Aldwycks CI MK5 ..... 45 F3
Alex Campbell Cty Mid Sch
MK3 ..... 57 F4
Alexander Ct SL4 ..... 209 E2
Alexander Ho 1 MK2 ..... 58 B4
Alexander Rd HP20 ..... 101 E1
Alexander St HP5 ..... 144 B1
Alexandra Ct LU7 ..... 80 C4
Alexandra Dr MK16 ..... 22 B1
Alexandra Park HP11 ..... 173 D3
Alexandra Rd
High Wycombe HP13 ..... 173 F3
Maidenhead SL6 ..... 202 B4
Slough SL1 ..... 205 E2
Uxbridge UB8 ..... 201 E2
Windsor SL4 ..... 210 B3
Alfloral Rd HP17 ..... 172 B2
Alfriston Sch HP9 ..... 175 E3
Alham Rd HP11 ..... 115 D3
Alice CI HP15 ..... 163 E4

Alice La SL1 ..... 197 D1
All Saints' Ave SL6 ..... 202 B4
All Saints CE Jun Sch SL6 202 B4
All Saints View MK5 ..... 46 A4
All Souls Cotts SL1 ..... 206 C4
All Souls Special Sch UB8 . 201 F1
Alladale PI MK12 ..... 33 E3
Anchor La 1 HP20 ..... 115 F4
Allanson Rd SL7 ..... 183 F2
Allen Ct MK2 ..... 58 B3
Allen Dr HP14 ..... 161 E4
Allenby Rd SL6 ..... 202 A4
Allerds Rd SL2 ..... 198 A2
Alleyns La SL6 ..... 195 E4
Allhusen Gdns SL3 ..... 199 F4
Allington Ct SL2 ..... 205 F3
Allison Ct MK15 ..... 35 E3
Allkins CI SL4 ..... 210 B3
Allonby Way HP21 ..... 116 A4
Allyn CI HP13 ..... 173 E4
Alma Ct Burnham SL1 ..... 197 E1
Eton SL4 ..... 204 C1
Alma Rd
Berkhamsted HP4 ..... 134 C3
Chesham HP5 ..... 144 B1
Eton SL4 ..... 204 C1
Windsor SL4 ..... 210 B3
Windsor SL4 ..... 210 B3
Almond CI
Newport Pagnell MK16 ..... 22 C4
Almond Rd SL1 ..... 197 E1
Almond Way HP27 ..... 139 E3
Almond Wlk HP15 ..... 163 D2
Almonds Gr SL2 ..... 206 A4
Almshouses SL4 ..... 210 B4
Almshouses The MK46 ..... 5 F1
Alnwick Rd HP13 ..... 103 F4
Alpha Ct MK1 ..... 47 E1
Alpha St N SL1 ..... 205 F2
Alpha St S SL1 ..... 206 A2
Alscot La HP27 ..... 139 D3
Alsford Wharf HP4 ..... 135 E3
Alston Dr MK13 ..... 33 F2
Alston Gdns SL6 ..... 202 C4
Althorpe Cres MK13 ..... 34 A3
Alton Bsns Pk HP19 ..... 101 D1
Alton Gate MK5 ..... 45 F2
Altona Rd HP10 ..... 174 B1
Altona Way SL1 ..... 205 D4
Atwood CI SL6 ..... 202 A3
Atwood Dr SL6 ..... 202 A3
Alwin CI HP21 ..... 115 E2
Alwins Field LU7 ..... 80 B4
Alwyn Inf Sch SL6 ..... 202 A4
Alwyn Rd SL6 ..... 202 A4
Alyngton MK4 ..... 53 D1
Alyson Ct 2 SL6 ..... 195 F1
Amanda Ct SL3 ..... 206 B2
Amber Cotts HP7 ..... 164 C2
Amberley CI SL6 ..... 196 B2
Amberley PI 20 SL4 ..... 210 B3
Amberley Rd SL2 ..... 205 D4
Amberley Way UB10 ..... 201 F1
Ambers Way MK18 ..... 53 D1
Ambleside HP21 ..... 116 A3
Ambleside Wlk UB8 ..... 201 E1
Ambridge Gr MK6 ..... 35 E1
Ambrose Ct MK15 ..... 35 D4
Amelias La MK9 ..... 35 D2
Amerden CI SL6 ..... 203 E4
Amerden La SL6 ..... 203 E4
Amerden Way SL1 ..... 205 D4
American Com Schs UB10 201 F2

Amersham & Wycombe Coll
Amersham HP7 ..... 165 F4
Flackwell Heath HP10 ..... 173 F1
Amersham & Wycombe Coll
Chesham Campus HP5 ..... 144 B2
Amherst Ct MK15 ..... 35 E4
Amy La HP5 ..... 154 A4
Ancastle Gr RG9 ..... 191 E1
Andermans SL4 ..... 209 E3
Anderson CI HP14 ..... 158 C2
Anding Way MK46 ..... 6 C2
Andover CI UB8 ..... 201 D2
Andrew Hill La SL2 ..... 187 E2
Andrews Ct LU7 ..... 80 C4
Andrews Croft MK14 ..... 34 C4
Andrews Way SL7 ..... 183 E4
Anershall HP22 ..... 89 D2
Angel CI MK15 ..... 35 E3
Angelica CI MK7 ..... 208 C4
Angelica CI MK7 ..... 48 A3
Angell Rd MK11 ..... 32 C3
Angels CI MK18 ..... 65 F2
Angle PI HP4 ..... 135 D2
Anglefield Rd HP4 ..... 135 D2
Anglesey Ct
Milton Keynes MK8 ..... 46 A4
Stokenchurch HP14 ..... 158 C3
Angood CI HP27 ..... 139 D2
Angstrom CI MK5 ..... 46 A3
Angus Dr MK3 ..... 46 C1
Angus Rd HP19 ..... 101 D2
Annan CI SL1 ..... 195 F1
Annes Gr MK14 ..... 21 E1
Annesley Rd MK16 ..... 22 C2
Anns CI Aylesbury HP21 ... 116 A2
Annslow Gdns SL0 ..... 200 B2
Anslow Pl SL1 ..... 204 B4
Anson CI Aylesbury HP21 .. 115 F2
Bovingdon HP1 ..... 145 F2
Anson Rd MK13 ..... 33 E3
Anstey Brook HP22 ..... 117 D2
Anstey CI HP18 ..... 99 D4
Anstey Ct HP18 ..... 99 D4
Anthony CI MK11 ..... 32 B3
Anthony CI MK11 ..... 32 B3
Antony Way SL1 ..... 204 B3
Anvil CI HP3 ..... 146 A2
Anvil CI SL3 ..... 207 D1
Anxey CI HP17 ..... 116 B3
Aplin Rd HP21 ..... 116 B3
Apple Tree Ave
Uxbridge UB8 ..... 208 C4
West Drayton UB8 ..... 208 C4
Apple Tree CI LU7 ..... 80 B4
Appleacres MK17 ..... 69 E4
Appleby Heath MK2 ..... 58 B3
Applecroft
Berkhamsted HP4 ..... 134 C3
Maidenhead SL6 ..... 202 B2
Newton Longville MK17 .... 57 F2
Applefield HP6 ..... 166 B4
Appleton CI HP7 ..... 166 B3
Appletree La SL3 ..... 206 B2
Appletree Wlk HP5 ..... 154 B3
Applewick La HP12 ..... 172 B4
Appleyard PI MK6 ..... 34 C1
Approach Rd SL6 ..... 203 F4
Approach The MK8 ..... 33 F1
Apsley Cotts SL4 ..... 195 F4
Apsley Ho SL1 ..... 206 A3
Aran Heights HP8 ..... 177 D3
Arborfield CI SL1 ..... 205 F2
Arbour Vale Sch SL2 ..... 205 F4
Arbour View HP7 ..... 166 A4
Arbroath CI MK3 ..... 46 C2
Arbrook Ave MK13 ..... 34 B2
Arcade The HP11 ..... 173 E4
Arcadia La MK9 ..... 35 D2
Arch Way
High Wycombe HP13 ..... 173 D4
Lacey Green HP27 ..... 150 A3
Archdale HP11 ..... 173 D2
Archer CI SL6 ..... 202 B4
Archer Terr UB7 ..... 208 C3
Archers Way HP14 ..... 171 D3
Archers Wells MK3 ..... 57 E3
Archive Rd HP22 ..... 117 E3
Arden CI HP23 ..... 146 A2
Arden Park MK12 ..... 33 D4
Ardenham La HP19 ..... 101 E1
Ardenham St HP19 ..... 101 E1
Ardrossan CI SL2 ..... 198 B1
Ardwell La MK12 ..... 33 D4
Argyle Ave HP19 ..... 101 D2
Argyll Ave SL1 ..... 205 D3
Aries Ho HP10 ..... 185 D4
Arizona St HP11 ..... 173 D2

Arkle Ho UB8 ..... 201 E2
Arkley Ct SL6 ..... 203 E1
Arkwright Rd SL3 ..... 212 C3
Arlington CI SL6 ..... 202 A4
Arlington Ct MK4 ..... 46 C2
Arlott Cres MK4 ..... 46 C4
Armourer Dr MK14 ..... 34 C3
Armstrong CI MK8 ..... 45 F3
Arncliffe Dr MK13 ..... 34 A3
Arncott Ho OX6 ..... 95 E4
Arncott Wood Rd OX6 ..... 94 C3
Arne La MK7 ..... 48 B3
Arnison Ave HP13 ..... 162 B1
Arnold CI HP21 ..... 116 B1
Arnold Ct HP21 ..... 115 F3
Arnold's Cotts HP16 ..... 143 D2
Arnolds CI MK18 ..... 53 D1
Arnott's Yd HP18 ..... 125 E3
Arrewig La
Drayton-Beauchamp HP23 132 B1
St Leonard HP5 ..... 142 C4
Arronmore Ho 12 HP10 ..... 174 A2
Arrow PI MK2 ..... 58 B2
Arthur Rd Slough SL1 ..... 205 E2
Windsor SL4 ..... 210 B3
Artichoke Dell WD3 ..... 167 F2
Arts Education Sch HP23 .. 119 D2
Arundel CI SL6 ..... 202 A4
Arundel CI MK3 ..... 206 B1
Arundel Gn HP20 .....* 101 F1
Arundel Gr MK3 ..... 57 F4
Arundel Ho
1 High Wycombe HP13 .. 173 F4
Uxbridge UB8 ..... 201 E1
Arundel Rd
High Wycombe HP12 ..... 172 A3
Uxbridge UB8 ..... 201 E1
Ascot Dr LU7 ..... 80 B3
Ascot Mews LU7 ..... 80 B3
Ascot Rd SL6 ..... 203 D1
Ascott CI HP20 ..... 101 F1
Ascott House (NT) 1 LU7 .. 80 A1
Ascott Rd HP20 ..... 101 F1
Ash CI Aylesbury HP20 ..... 102 A1
Slough SL3 ..... 207 D2
Walter's Ash HP14 ..... 161 A4
Ash Gr Amersham HP6 ..... 154 A2
Aylesbury HP21 ..... 116 A4
Stoke Poges SL2 ..... 198 C3
West Drayton UB8 ..... 208 C3
Ash Green SL0 ..... 201 D3
Ash Hill Rd MK6 ..... 22 A2
Ash La SL4 ..... 209 E3
Ash Mead Dr UB9 ..... 190 A4
Ash Rd
High Wycombe HP12 ..... 172 B2
Princes Risborough HP27 . 139 D2
Tring HP23 ..... 118 C2
Ash Tree Ho HP12 ..... 172 B2
Ash Vale WD3 ..... 178 B3
Ashbourne End HP21 ..... 115 E2
Ashbourne Gr SL6 ..... 202 B2
Ashbourne Ho 5 SL1 ..... 205 F2
Ashbrook Cty Fst Sch MK8 . 33 F1
Ashburnham CI MK3 ..... 46 B1
Ashburnham Cres LU7 ..... 80 C3
Ashby MK6 ..... 47 D4
Ashby Rd HP4 ..... 134 B4
Ashby Villas LU6 ..... 92 A1
Ashcroft Ct SL1 ..... 197 D2
Ashcroft Dr UB9 ..... 189 F2
Ashcroft Rd SL6 ..... 202 B4
Ashcroft Terr HP23 ..... 119 D3
Ashdown SL6 ..... 196 A2
Ashdown CI MK14 ..... 35 D4
Ashdown CI HP13 ..... 174 A4
Ashdown Rd UB10 ..... 201 F1
Ashdown Way HP6 ..... 154 B3
Ashen Cross SL3 ..... 207 D4
Ashenden Wlk SL2 ..... 198 B4
Ashendon Rd HP18 ..... 98 B3
Asheridge Rd HP5 ..... 144 A3
Ashfield MK14 ..... 34 B4
Ashfield CI HP5 ..... 163 D1
Ashfield Gr SL6 ..... 195 F1
Ashfield Rd HP5 ..... 144 B1
Ashfield Sch HP13 ..... 163 D2
Ashfold Sch HP18 ..... 110 C4
Ashford CI HP21 ..... 116 A3
Ashford La SL4 ..... 204 A2
Ashford Rise HP18 ..... 109 E3
Ashgrove MK18 ..... 63 E1
Ashgrove Gdns HP22 ..... 86 C4
Ashgrove Rd HP23 ..... 118 C2
Ashleigh CI HP7 ..... 165 F4
Ashley Ho HP10 ..... 185 F4

Ashley Cl LU7 .... 105 D4
Ashley Ct
  Maidenhead SL6 .... 203 D4
  Tylers Green HP10 .... 163 D1
  West Drayton UB7 .... 208 C3
Ashley Dr HP10 .... 163 E1
Ashley Green Rd HP5 .... 144 C3
Ashley Park SL6 .... 196 A1
Ashley Rd SL8 .... 201 D2
Ashley Row HP20 .... 102 A1
Ashleys WD3 .... 167 F1
Ashlyns Ct HP4 .... 135 D2
Ashlyns Rd HP4 .... 135 D2
Ashlyns Sch HP4 .... 135 E1
Ashmead Cty Comb Sch
  HP21 .... 115 E3
Ashmead La UB9 .... 190 A1
Ashotts La HP5 .... 143 D3
Ashpole Furlong MK5 .... 46 A4
Ashridge Cl 147 D3
Ashridge Cl
  Bovingdon HP3 .... 146 A2
  Milton Keynes MK3 .... 57 E4
Ashridge Cotts HP4 .... 121 F3
Ashridge La HP5 .... 155 E4
Ashridge Man Coll HP4 .... 121 E3
Ashridge Rise HP4 .... 134 C3
Ashton Pl SL6 .... 202 A3
Ashton Rd NN12 .... 9 A3
Ashtree Wlk HP15 .... 163 E1
Ashwell St **1** LU7 .... 80 C4
Ashwells HP10 .... 174 A4
Ashwells Manor Dr HP10 . 174 B4
Ashwells Way HP8 .... 177 E4
Ashwood MK 34 A4
Askett La HP27 .... 139 E4
Aspect Park Golf Ctr RG9 . 192 B1
Aspen Cl Aylesbury HP20 . 102 A1
  Slough SL2 .... 205 D4
  West Drayton UB7 .... 208 C3
Asplands Cl MK17 .... 49 D2
Aspley Ct MK17 .... 49 E2
Aspley Guise Lower Sch
  MK17 .... 49 F2
Aspley Guise Sta MK17 ..... 49 E3
Aspley Hill MK17 .... 49 E2
Aspley La MK17 .... 49 E1
Aspreys MK46 .... 6 C2
Assheton Rd HP9 .... 175 F2
Astlethorpe MK8 .... 33 E1
Astley Rd OX9 .... 126 A1
Aston Abbotts Rd
  Cublington LU7 .... 78 B1
  Weedon HP22 .... 87 F1
Aston Cl HP19 .... 101 D2
Aston Clinton Cty Comb Sch
  HP22 .... 117 E3
Aston Clinton Rd HP22 .... 116 C3
Aston Ferry La RG9 .... 192 B3
Aston Hill OX9 .... 157 F4
Aston La RG9 .... 192 B2
Aston Rd HP17 .... 127 D3
Aston Villas SL2 .... 198 B4
Astor Cl SL6 .... 203 D3
Astrope La HP23 .... 104 A2
Astwood Rd MK43 .... 25 E4
Atherstone Ct MK8 .... 33 E1
Atherton Cl TW19 .... 213 E1
Atherton Ct SL4 .... 210 B4
Athlone Cl SL6 .... 195 F1
Atkins Cl MK13 .... 34 A2
Atlas Ho HP5 .... 144 A1
Atterbrook MK13 .... 34 A2
Attingham Hill MK8 .... 34 A1
Attwells Yd UB8 .... 201 E3
Atwell Cl MK4 .... 45 F4
Auckland Cl SL6 .... 203 D4
Auckland Pk MK1 .... 47 E2
Auckland Rd HP13 .... 173 F3
Auden Cl MK16 .... 22 A3
Audley Dr SL6 .... 202 A3
Audley Mead MK13 .... 34 A2
August End SL3 .... 206 C4
Augustine Ct SL2 .... 212 C2
Augustus Rd MK11 .... 32 B2
Austen Ave MK46 .... 7 D2
Austen Pl HP19 .... 100 C1
Austenway SL9 .... 188 C4
Austenwood Cl
  Gerrards Cross SL9 .... 177 E1
  High Wycombe HP11 .... 173 D2
Austenwood La SL9 .... 188 B4
Austin Wray UB8 .... 201 E2
Austins Mead HP3 .... 146 A2
Australia Ave SL6 .... 202 C4
Australia Rd SL1 .... 206 A2
Austwick La MK4 .... 46 A1

Autumn Cl
  Aylesbury HP19 .... 101 D2
  Slough SL1 .... 204 C3
Autumn Wlk SL6 .... 202 A3
Auxiliaries Way UB9 .... 189 F3
Avalon Rd SL8 .... 185 D3
Avebury SL1 .... 205 D3
Avebury Bvd MK9 .... 34 C1
Aveling Rd HP13 .... 173 E3
Avenue Cl UB7 .... 208 B2
Avenue Ho HP5 .... 154 A4
Avenue Rd
  Buckingham MK18 .... 41 F2
  Maidenhead SL6 .... 203 D3
  Winslow MK18 .... 65 F2
Avenue The
  Amersham HP7 .... 154 B1
  Bourne End SL8 .... 185 D2
  Chinnor OX9 .... 147 E3
  Datchet SL3 .... 211 D3
  Dunstable LU6 .... 93 F4
  Farnham Common SL2 ..... 198 A4
  Maidenhead SL6 .... 196 B2
  Old Windsor SL4 .... 211 D1
  Princes Risborough HP27 . 139 E2
  Uxbridge UB8 .... 201 E1
  Whitfield NN13 .... 26 B2
  Worminghall HP18 .... 123 F3
  Wraysbury TW19 .... 211 E2
Averil Ct SL6 .... 204 B4
Avery Ave HP13 .... 161 E1
Avington MK8 .... 33 E1
Avocet Way HP20 .... 101 F2
Avon Cl
  Newport Pagnell MK16 .... 22 B2
  Slough SL1 .... 204 C3
Avon Gr MK3 .... 57 F4
Avon Pl HP21 .... 115 E2
Avonbury Ct NN13 .... 38 A3
Avondale SL6 .... 195 E1
Aylesbury Bsns Ctr HP19 . 101 D1
Aylesbury Coll HP21 .... 115 E4
Aylesbury Cres SL1 .... 205 E4
Aylesbury End HP9 .... 175 F1
Aylesbury Gram Sch (Boys)
  HP21 .... 115 F4
Aylesbury High Sch (Girls)
  HP21 .... 115 F4
Aylesbury Rd
  Aston Clinton HP22 .... 117 D3
  Bierton HP22 .... 102 A2
  Chearsley HP18 .... 112 A1
  Cuddington HP18 .... 113 D2
  Drayton Beauchamp HP23 118 C1
  Ellesborough HP17 .... 129 F2
  Great Kimble HP17 .... 129 F2
  Great Missenden HP16 .... 141 F1
  Haddenham HP17,HP18 ... 126 B3
  Princes Risborough HP27 . 139 E2
  Thame OX9 .... 126 B3
  Tring HP23 .... 118 C1
  Wendover HP22 .... 131 D3
  Wing LU7 .... 79 F1
Aylesbury St
  Milton Keynes, Bletchley
    MK2 .... 58 C4
  Milton Keynes, Wolverton
    MK12, MK2 .... 33 E3
Aylesbury St W MK12 ...... 33 E3
Aylesbury Sta HP21 .... 115 E4
Aylesweter HP20 .... 101 F2
Aylesworth Ave SL2 .... 198 A1
Aylward Gdns HP5 .... 144 A1
Aynho Ct MK8 .... 45 F4
Aynscombe Cl LU6 .... 93 F4
Ayr Way MK3 .... 46 C1
Ayres Cl HP21 .... 115 D3
Ayrshire Cl HP19 .... 101 D2
Aysgarth Park SL6 .... 203 D1
Azalea Cl HP15 .... 163 D2
Azalea Way SL3 .... 206 C4

Babington Rd HP22 .... 131 E3
Baccara Gr MK2 .... 58 B4
Bachelors Acre SL4 .... 210 B3
Back Dr MK16 .... 12 C2
Back La
  Chalfont St Giles HP8 ...... 177 D4
  Tingrick MK18 .... 51 D3
Back St Gawcott MK18 ..... 51 F2
  Stokenchurch HP14 .... 158 B3
  Thornborough MK18 .... 54 A4
  Wendover HP22 .... 131 D2
Backleys MK7 .... 48 A1
Backs The HP5 .... 154 B4
Bacombe La HP22 .... 131 A2
Bacon Hill MK46 .... 6 C2
Baconsmead UB9 .... 190 A1
Bad Godesberg Way SL6 . 202 C4
Bader Gdns SL1 .... 205 D2
Badgebury Rise SL7 .... 183 E4

Badgemoor La RG9 .... 191 E2
Badgemore Ct MK8 .... 33 E1
Badgemore Cty Prim Sch
  RG9 .... 191 E2
Badger Cl SL6 .... 202 B2
Badger Way HP15 .... 163 D3
Badgers Meadow HP22 ... 131 E3
Badgers Oak MK7 .... 48 A4
Badgers Way
  Buckingham MK18 .... 52 C4
  Marlow Bottom SL7 .... 183 E4
Badgers Wlk WD3 .... 167 F3
Badgers Wood SL2 .... 198 B4
Badminton Ho HP7 .... 165 D4
Badminton Rd SL6 .... 202 A3
Badminton View MK8 .... 34 A1
Badrick Rd HP19 .... 100 C1
Bagley Cl UB7 .... 208 C2
Bailey Cl
  High Wycombe HP13 .... 173 E4
  Maidenhead SL6 .... 202 C4
  Windsor SL4 .... 210 A3
Bailey Ho **7** SL8 .... 185 D2
Bailey's Ct **12** HP20 ..... 115 E4
Baily Ct MK5 .... 46 A3
Baines Ho HP11 .... 173 F2
Baird Cl SL1 .... 205 D2
Baker St
  High Wycombe HP11 .... 172 C4
  Waddesdon HP18 .... 99 D3
Baker's Orch HP10 .... 185 F3
Baker's Rd UB8 .... 201 E3
Bakers Cl MK16 .... 12 A3
Bakers Ct HP18 .... 99 D3
Bakers Walk HP22 .... 116 C1
Bakers Wood UB9 .... 189 D2
Bakery Cl Cranfield MK43 . 25 D1
  Grendon Underwood HP18 . 83 D3
Bala Cl MK2 .... 58 B3
Bala Way MK2 .... 58 B3
Balcary Gdns HP4 .... 134 C2
Baldways Cl HP22 .... 89 E2
Baldwin Cres MK16 .... 22 A2
Baldwin Rd
  Beaconsfield HP9 .... 176 A1
  Burnham SL1 .... 197 E1
Baldwin's Shore SL4 .... 210 B4
Balfe Mews MK7 .... 48 B2
Balfour Mews HP21 .... 146 A2
Balfour Pl SL7 .... 183 F2
Balham's La Ibstone RG9 . 179 F4
  Stoner RG9 .... 179 F4
Ball Moor MK18 .... 52 B3
Ballard Ct HP21 .... 116 A3
Ballard Green SL4 .... 209 F4
Ballinger Ct HP4 .... 135 D2
Ballinger Grange HP16 .... 142 C1
Ballinger Rd HP16 .... 142 C1
Balmer Bridge MK18 .... 52 C3
Balmer Cut MK18 .... 52 C3
Balmerino Cl MK10 .... 36 A1
Balmoral SL6 .... 195 D1
Balmoral Cl SL4 .... 204 C1
Balmoral Ct
  15 High Wycombe HP13 . 173 D4
  Newport Pagnell MK16 .... 22 A2
Balmoral Gdns SL4 .... 210 B2
Balsam Cl MK7 .... 48 A3
Bamford La MK43 .... 8 C3
Bamfords Yd MK43 .... 8 C3
Bampton Cl MK4 .... 46 C1
Banburies Cl MK3 .... 47 D1
Banbury Ave SL1 .... 204 C4
Bancroft Rdbt MK13 .... 34 A4
Bandon Cl UB10 .... 201 F2
Bangors Cl SL0 .... 207 F4
Bangors Rd N SL0 .... 200 B2
Bangors Rd S Iver SL0 ..... 207 F4
  Uxbridge SL0 .... 200 C1
Bank Green HP5 .... 143 E4
Bank Mill HP4 .... 135 F2
Bank Mill La HP4 .... 135 F2
Bank Rd HP10 .... 174 B4
Bank St HP10 .... 174 A2
Bankfield Rdbt MK9 .... 35 D2
Banks Rd HP17 .... 127 D3
Banks Spur SL1 .... 205 D2
Bankside HP22 .... 131 D3
Bankton Pl MK4 .... 46 B2
Bannard Rd SL6 .... 202 A3
Banner Ct **1** HP12 .... 172 B4
Bannister Cl SL3 .... 206 C2
Bantock Cl MK7 .... 48 A4
Bar La HP27 .... 138 C4
Barbers Mews MK14 .... 34 C3
Barbers Wlk HP23 .... 118 C2
Barbers Wood Cl HP12 ... 172 A2
Barbers Wood Rd HP12 ... 172 A2
Barbury Ct MK14 .... 35 D4
Barchester Cl UB8 .... 201 E1

Barchester Rd SL3 .... 206 C2
Barclay Ct **6** HP12 .... 172 C4
Bardney Cl SL6 .... 202 B2
Bardon Gn HP20 .... 101 F1
Barford MK11 .... 32 C2
Bargeman Rd SL6 .... 202 C3
Barham Lodge MK18 .... 52 B4
Baring Cres HP9 .... 175 E2
Baring Rd Beaconsfield HP9 175 E2
  High Wycombe HP13 .... 173 F4
Barkers Croft MK12 .... 33 E2
Barkestone Cl MK4 .... 46 B1
Barkham Cl LU7 .... 104 C4
Barkus Way HP14 .... 158 C3
Barlee Cres UB8 .... 208 B4
Barley Cl Lewknor OX9 .... 157 D4
  Tylers Green HP15 .... 163 D2
  Weston Turville HP22 ...... 116 C1
Barley Cres HP21 .... 115 E2
Barley Fields HP10 .... 185 F4
Barley Hill Cty Prim Sch
  OX9 .... 126 A1
Barleycroft MK4 .... 46 C2
Barlow Rd HP22 .... 131 E3
Barn Cl
  Farnham Common SL2 .... 198 A4
  Maidenhead SL6 .... 195 F1
Barn Ct HP27 .... 172 B4
Barn Dr SL6 .... 202 A2
Barn La RG9 .... 191 E2
Barn Rd HP27 .... 138 C3
Barnabas Rd LU7 .... 80 B3
Barnacre Cl UB8 .... 208 B4
Barnard Cres HP21 .... 115 F3
Barnards Hill SL7 .... 183 E1
Barncroft MK43 .... 8 C3
Barncroft Rd HP4 .... 134 C2
Barnes Ave HP5 .... 144 B1
Barnes Pl MK6 .... 46 C4
Barnes Wallis Ct MK17 .... 172 C3
Barnes Way SL0 .... 207 F3
Barnett Way HP22 .... 102 A2
Barnfield Iver SL0 .... 207 F4
  Slough SL1 .... 204 B3
Barnfield Cl SL6 .... 195 F3
Barnfield Dr MK6 .... 47 E3
Barnhill Cl SL7 .... 183 E2
Barnhill Gdns SL7 .... 183 E2
Barnhill Rd SL7 .... 183 E2
Barnsbury Ave HP20 .... 116 A4
Barnsbury Gdns MK16 .... 22 B2
Barnsdale Dr
  Shenley Brook End MK5 ... 46 A1
  Shenley Church End MK4 . 45 F1
Barnsfield Pl UB8 .... 201 E3
Barnstable Ct MK4 .... 46 A4
Baroma Way RG9 .... 191 F1
Barons Cl MK2 .... 58 B4
Barons Mead RG9 .... 191 E1
Baronsmead Rd HP12 ..... 172 C3
Barr's Rd SL6 .... 204 A4
Barrack Hill HP18 .... 112 C3
Barrack La SL4 .... 210 B3
Barracks Hill HP7 .... 164 C1
Barracks Rd HP11 .... 173 D3
Barrards Way HP9 .... 176 B2
Barrie Cl HP19 .... 100 C1
Barrington Ct NN13 .... 38 A3
Barrington Mews MK6 ..... 34 C1
Barrington Park Gdns
  HP8 .... 166 B1
Barrowcroft HP11 .... 173 F2
Barry Ave Eton SL4 .... 210 B4
  Milton Keynes MK13 .... 34 B4
Barry Cl HP12 .... 172 B2
Barry View SL4 .... 209 E3
Bartelotts Rd SL2 .... 197 F1
Bartholomew Cl MK7 ...... 48 A3
Bartholomew Tipping Way
  HP14 .... 158 C3
Bartlett Pl MK18 .... 41 F1
Bartletts SL9 .... 177 F2
Barton Rd
  Milton Keynes MK2 .... 58 B3
  Slough SL3 .... 206 C2
Barton Way HP13 .... 162 C1
Bartons Rd HP10 .... 163 D1
Bascote MK6 .... 47 E3
Base Cl **9** HP20 .... 101 F1
Basford Way SL4 .... 209 E2
Basildon Ct
  8 Leighton Buzzard LU7 . 80 C4
  Milton Keynes MK8 .... 45 F4
Basing Rd WD3 .... 167 F1
Baskerfield Gr MK6 .... 47 F4
Bass Mead SL6 .... 195 F3
Basset Rd HP14 .... 171 E2
Bassetsbury La HP11 ...... 173 F2
Bassett Ct
  7 Leighton Buzzard LU7 . 80 C4
  Newport Pagnell MK16 .... 22 B2

Bassett Rd
  Leighton Buzzard LU7 ...... 80 C4
  Uxbridge UB8 .... 201 E1
Bassett Way SL2 .... 197 F1
Batchelor Cl HP20 .... 101 F1
Batchelors Way
  Amersham HP7 .... 165 E4
  Chesham HP5 .... 144 A1
Bateman Dr HP21 .... 115 F3
Bates Cl Aylesbury HP20 . 101 F1
  Grainborough MK18 .... 65 F4
  Milton Keynes MK15 .... 35 E4
  Slough SL3 .... 206 C4
Bates Gdns MK17 .... 68 A3
Bates La HP22 .... 116 C1
Bath Cl SL6 .... 202 B3
Bath La MK18 .... 52 B4
Bath Lane Terr MK18 ...... 52 B4
Bath Rd Burnham SL1,SL6 . 204 B3
  Harmondsworth TW6, UB7 . 213 E3
  Maidenhead SL6 .... 202 B3
  Stanwell SL3 .... 212 C3
Bath Road Cotts SL3 ...... 212 C3
Bathurst Cl SL0 .... 207 F2
Bathurst Wlk SL0 .... 207 F2
Batt Furlong HP21 .... 115 F2
Battersby Mews HP21 ..... 115 E4
Battings Wood Gdns
  HP14 .... 161 E4
Battle Cl MK46 .... 13 F4
Battlemead Cl SL6 .... 196 B2
Baulk The Cheddington LU7 104 C4
  Ivinghoe LU7 .... 105 E2
Bawtree Rd UB8 .... 201 E3
Baxter Cl MK8 .... 45 F4
Bay Cl HP4 .... 135 D2
Bay La MK46 .... 5 E1
Bay Tree Cl
  Loudwater HP10 .... 174 A3
  Newton Longville MK17 .... 57 E2
Bay Tree Ct SL1 .... 197 E1
Bayard Ave MK14 .... 34 C2
Bayley Cres SL1 .... 204 A4
Bayley Gdns HP14 .... 161 E3
Bayley Hatch HP16 .... 152 B4
Baylis Court (Girls)
  Comp Sch SL1 .... 205 E4
Baylis Par SL1 .... 205 F4
Baylis Rd SL1 .... 205 F3
Bayman Manor HP5 .... 144 C3
Bayne Hill HP9 .... 176 B2
Bayne Hill Cl HP9 .... 176 B2
Baynham Mead MK7 .... 48 A4
Baysfarm Ct TW6 .... 213 E3
Beacham Rd HP22 .... 172 B2
Beachborough Prep Sch
  NN13 .... 39 D2
Beacon Ave LU6 .... 93 F4
Beacon Cl
  Beaconsfield HP9 .... 175 D3
  Chalfont St Peter SL9 ...... 177 F2
  Stone HP17 .... 114 B3
  Uxbridge UB8 .... 201 E4
Beacon Ct MK4 .... 46 B1
Beacon Ctr The HP9 .... 175 D3
Beacon Hill HP10 .... 174 A4
Beacon La HP7 .... 171 F1
Beacon Rd Ivinghoe HP4 . 106 C1
  Ringshall HP4 .... 106 C1
Beacon Sch The HP6 ...... 154 A2
Beacon Way HP23 .... 119 E3
Beaconsfield Ave HP13 ... 162 A1
Beaconsfield Com La SL2 . 187 E3
Beaconsfield Cotts SL8 ... 185 D1
Beaconsfield High Sch
  HP9 .... 175 D1
Beaconsfield Mews HP9 .. 186 A4
Beaconsfield Pl MK16 ..... 22 B2
Beaconsfield Rd
  Aston Clinton HP22 .... 117 F2
  Aylesbury HP21 .... 115 F4
  Farnham Common SL2 .... 198 B3
  Tring HP23 .... 118 C1
Beaconsfield Sch The
  HP9 .... 175 F1
Beaconsfield Sta HP9 ..... 175 F2
Beadlemead MK6 .... 47 E3
Beales La MK7 .... 48 A3
Bealings End HP9 .... 175 E3
Beamish Way MK18 .... 66 A3
Beamond End La
  Holmer Green HP16 .... 163 F4
  Hyde Heath HP16 .... 163 F4
Beanfare MK6 .... 47 D2
Bearbrook Cty Comb Sch
  HP21 .... 115 E4
Beauchamp Cl MK14 ...... 34 C3
Beaudesert Mews UB7 ... 208 C2
Beaufort Cl
  Aylesbury HP21 .... 116 B4
  Marlow SL7 .... 183 F1

Beaufort Dr MK15 .... 35 E4
Beaufort Gdns SL7 .... 183 F1
Beaufort Pl SL6 .... 203 E2
Beaulieu Cl SL3 .... 211 D3
Beaumaris Cl SL1 .... 205 E4
Beaumaris Gr MK5 .... 46 A3
Beaumont Cl SL6 .... 202 A2
Beaumont Cotts ■ SL4 .... 210 B3
Beaumont Ct SL3 .... 206 B4
Beaumont Rd Slough SL2 .... 205 E4
  Windsor SL4 .... 210 B3
Beaumont Rise SL7 .... 183 F1
Beaumont Way HP15 .... 162 C2
Beaver Cl MK18 .... 52 C4
Beaverbrook Ct MK3 .... 46 C1
Beck La MK15 .... 35 D4
Beckets Sq HP4 .... 135 D3
Beckins Way HP10 .... 185 E4
Beckinsale Gr MK8 .... 45 F4
Bedder Rd HP12 .... 172 B2
Bede Ct HP4 .... 121 E4
Bedfont Court Est TW19 ... 213 D2
Bedfont Ct TW19 .... 213 D2
Bedfont Rd TW19 .... 213 F1
Bedford Ave
  Little Chalfont HP6 .... 166 B4
  Slough SL1 .... 205 D4
Bedford Cl Chenies WD3 ... 156 A1
  Maidenhead SL6 .... 202 A2
Bedford Ct HP6 .... 166 B4
Bedford Dr SL2 .... 198 A3
Bedford Rd
  Aspley Guise MK17 .... 49 F3
  Cold Brayfield MK46 ...... 8 A3
  Cranfield MK43 .... 25 E1
  Sherington MK16 .... 14 A1
Bedford Rd E NN7 .... 1 B3
Bedford Rd W NN7 .... 1 A3
Bedford St
  M Keynes, Bletchley MK2 ... 58 B4
  M Keynes, Wolverton MK12 33 E1
  Woburn MK17 .... 60 C4
Bedgebury Pl MK7 .... 48 A4
Bedgrove Inf Sch
  HP21 .... 116 B3
Bedgrove Cty Fst Sch
  HP21 .... 116 B3
Bedgrove Cty Mid Sch
  HP21 .... 116 B3
Bedlam La MK16 .... 14 B1
Bedwins La SL6 .... 195 D3
Bedwyn Wlk HP21 .... 115 E2
Beech RG9 .... 191 E1
Beech Ave Lane End HP14 .. 171 E3
  Olney MK46 .... 6 C2
Beech Cl C Bierton HP22 ... 102 A2
  Buckingham MK18 .... 41 E1
  Flackwell Heath HP10 ..... 174 A1
  High Wycombe HP11 .... 173 F2
  Stokenchurch HP14 ...... 158 C2
Beech Ct ■ SL7 .... 183 F1
Beech Dr HP4 .... 135 E2
Beech Fern MK7 .... 48 A3
Beech Gr Amersham HP7 ... 165 E4
  Leighton Buzzard LU7 ...... 80 C4
Beech Green HP21 .... 115 E3
Beech Hill Ct HP4 .... 135 E3
Beech House Dr NN12 ...... 18 C2
Beech La Prestwood HP16 151 D4
  Seer Green HP9 .... 176 C2
Beech Leys MK18 .... 63 F2
Beech Park HP14 .... 150 A1
Beech Pk HP6 .... 155 D1
Beech Rd Aylesbury HP21 .. 115 E3
  Chinnor OX9 .... 147 E3
  High Wycombe HP11 .... 173 F2
  Newport Pagnell MK16 .... 22 A2
  Princes Risborough HP27 . 139 E2
  Slough SL3 .... 206 C2
Beech St HP11 .... 173 E2
Beech Tree Ct HP22 .... 87 D3
Beech Tree Rd HP15 ...... 163 E4
Beech Waye SL9 .... 189 D2
Beech Wlk HP23 .... 119 E2
Beechams The MK17 ...... 67 E3
Beechcroft HP4 .... 135 E2
Beechcroft Rd
  Chesham HP5 .... 144 A1
  Milton Keynes MK3 ...... 57 F3
Beeches Dr SL2 .... 198 A4
Beeches Gr HP15 .... 163 D1
Beeches Park HP9 .... 175 E1
Beeches Rd SL2 .... 198 A4
Beeches The
  Deanshanger MK19 ...... 31 F2
  Tring HP23 .... 119 E2
  Wendover HP22 .... 131 E3
Beechfield Way HP15 ...... 163 D2
Beechfields Wlk HP15 ...... 163 D2
Beechingstoke ■ SL4 .. 183 F2
Beechtree Ave SL7 .... 183 E3
Beechview Mid Sch HP13 . 173 F3

Beechwood Ave
  Chorleywood WD3 ...... 167 D3
  Little Chalfont HP6 ...... 155 E1
  Uxbridge UB8 .... 208 C4
Beechwood Cl HP6 .... 166 B4
Beechwood Comp Sch
  SL2 .... 198 A1
Beechwood Cotts WD3 .... 167 D2
Beechwood Ct LU6 .... 93 F4
Beechwood Dr
  Aldbury HP23 .... 120 B3
  Maidenhead SL6 .... 202 A3
  Marlow SL7 .... 194 A4
Beechwood Gdns SL1 ...... 205 F2
Beechwood Ho HP22 ...... 117 F3
Beechwood La HP22 ...... 131 E3
Beechwood Park HP3 ...... 146 C4
Beechwood Pk WD3 ...... 167 F3
Beechwood Pl ■ HP13 .... 173 D4
Beechwood Rd
  Beaconsfield HP9 .... 175 E1
  High Wycombe HP14 ...... 161 D1
  Slough SL2 .... 205 E4
Beechwood Way HP22 ...... 117 F3
Beecroft Way LU6 .... 93 F4
Beehive Cl UB10 .... 201 F3
Beel Cl HP6 .... 166 B4
Beeward Cl MK12 .... 33 D3
Bekonscot Ct MK14 .... 21 F1
Belfast Ave SL1 .... 205 E4
Belgrave Mews UB8 ...... 201 E1
Belgrave Par SL1 .... 205 F3
Belgrave Rd
  Aylesbury HP19 .... 101 D2
  Slough SL1 .... 205 F3
Bell Alley MK18 .... 65 F2
Bell Ave UB7 .... 208 C2
Bell Bsns Ctr SL6 .... 202 C3
Bell Cl Beaconsfield HP9 .. 175 F1
  Cublington LU7 .... 78 A1
  Drayton Parslow MK17 .... 68 A3
  Princes Risborough HP27 139 D2
  Slough SL2 .... 206 A4
  Thame OX9 .... 125 F1
Bell Cres HP27 .... 138 C3
Bell Ct SL6 .... 193 F2
Bell Gn HP3 .... 146 A2
Bell La Berkhamsted HP4 .. 134 C3
  Eton SL4 .... 204 C1
  Henley-on-T RG9 .... 191 F2
  Little Chalfont HP6 ...... 155 E1
  Princes Risborough HP27 139 D2
  Syresham NN13 .... 27 D4
  Thame OX9 .... 125 F1
Bell Lane Cty Comb Sch
  HP6 .... 155 D1
Bell Leys HP22 .... 89 D2
Bell St Henley-on-T RG9 .. 191 F1
  Maidenhead SL6 .... 202 C3
  Princes Risborough HP27 139 D2
Bell View SL4 .... 209 F3
Bell View Cl SL4 .... 209 F3
Bell Wlk HP22 .... 89 D2
Bellamy Rd HP13 .... 173 E4
Belleau Rd UB7 .... 208 C2
Belle Vue HP18 .... 114 B3
Bellfield Cty Mid Sch
  HP13 .... 173 D4
Bellfield Fst Sch HP13 .... 172 C4
Bellfield Rd HP13 .... 173 D4
Bellfounder Ho MK13 .... 34 A2
Bellis Gr MK6 .... 47 E4
Bells Hill SL2 .... 199 D3
Bells Hill Gn SL2 .... 199 D3
Bells La SL3 .... 212 A2
Bells Meadow MK15 ...... 35 D4
Bellsfield Ct SL4 .... 204 C1
Bellswood La SL0 .... 207 D4
Bellway MK17 .... 49 D3
Bellwether MK11 .... 33 D2
Bellwood Rise HP11 ...... 173 D2
Belmers Rd HP23 .... 119 E1
Belmont SL2 .... 205 D4
Belmont Cl UB8 .... 201 E3
Belmont Cres SL6 .... 202 B4
Belmont Ct MK8 .... 33 E1
Belmont Dr SL6 .... 202 B4
Belmont Park Ave SL6 .... 202 B4
Belmont Park Rd SL6 .... 202 B4
Belmont Rd Chesham HP5 144 A2
  Maidenhead SL6 .... 202 B4
  Uxbridge UB8 .... 201 E3
Belmont Vale SL6 .... 202 B4
Belsize Ave MK4 .... 35 D1
Belsize Cotts WD4 ...... 156 C4
Belton Rd HP4 .... 135 D3
Belvedere La MK17 ...... 58 C4
Belvedere Mansions SL1 . 205 E2
Belvedere Rdbt MK9 ...... 34 C2
Belvoir Ave MK4 .... 46 B1

Bembridge Ct ■ SL1 ...... 205 F2
Ben More SL9 .... 188 C3
Benbow Ct MK5 .... 46 A4
Benbow Way UB8 .... 208 B4
Bench Manor Cres SL9 .... 177 E1
Bencombe Rd SL4 .... 183 F3
Benen-Stock Rd TW19 .... 213 D1
Benham Cl HP5 .... 144 A1
Benhams La RG9 .... 180 B1
Benjamin Ho ■ HP13 .... 173 D4
Benjamin Rd HP13 ...... 173 D4
Benjamins Footpath HP13 173 D4
Bennet Cl MK1 .... 32 B2
Bennett End Rd HP14 .... 159 E4
Bennett's Hill MK18 ...... 76 B4
Bennetts HP5 .... 144 B1
Bennetts Cl Padbury MK18 . 53 D1
  Slough SL1 .... 205 D3
Bennetts La HP22 .... 102 C4
Benning Ave LU6 .... 93 F4
Benning Cl SL4 .... 209 F2
Bens Cl MK19 .... 19 F3
Benson Cl Slough SL2 .... 206 A3
  Uxbridge UB8 .... 208 C4
Bentall Cl MK15 .... 35 E4
Bentinck Cl SL9 .... 188 B3
Bentinck Rd UB7 .... 208 B3
Bentley Park SL2 .... 197 E2
Bentley Rd SL1 .... 205 D3
Benton Dr OX9 .... 147 E4
Bentons The HP4 .... 134 C3
Benwell Cl MK13 .... 33 F3
Benwells OX9 .... 147 E3
Berberis Cl MK7 .... 48 A3
Berbers Wlk UB7 .... 208 C1
Bercham MK8 .... 33 F1
Beresford Ave
  Aylesbury HP21 .... 101 D2
  Slough SL2 .... 206 B3
Beresford Rd WD3 ...... 167 F1
Beretun MK8 .... 33 F1
Bergamot Gdns MK7 .... 48 A3
Berkeley Ave HP5 ...... 143 F1
Berkeley Cl Chesham HP5 . 144 A1
  Stoke Goldington MK16 .... 12 A3
Berkeley Mews SL7 ...... 183 F1
Berkeley Rd
  Loudwater HP10 .... 174 B1
  Thame OX9 .... 126 A1
Berkeley Rise HP19 ...... 101 D1
Berkhamsted Rd HP5 .... 144 B1
Berkhamsted Hill HP4 .... 135 F3
Berkhamsted Sch HP4 .... 135 E4
Berkhamsted Sch For Girls
  HP4 .... 135 D2
Berkhamsted Sports Ctr
  .... 135 D3
Berkhamsted Sta HP4 .... 135 E3
Berkley Cl SL2 .... 202 A4
Berkley Ct HP4 .... 134 C3
Berkley Rd HP9 .... 175 E3
Berks Hill WD3 .... 167 E2
Berkshire Ave SL1 ...... 205 D4
Berkshire Coll of Art &
  Design SL1 .... 205 E2
Berkshire Lodge ■ SL6 .. 202 C3
Berling Rd MK8 .... 33 F1
Bernard Cl HP18 .... 112 C1
Bernard's Cl HP18 ...... 112 A1
Bernards Cl HP16 ...... 152 A4
Bernards Way HP10 .... 174 A1
Bernay Gdns MK15 ...... 35 D4
Bernwood Cl HP18 ...... 125 E4
Bernstein Cl MK7 .... 48 B2
Bernwood Forest
  (Nature Reserve) HP18 . 108 C1
Berries Rd SL6 .... 196 A4
Berry Field Cl HP21 .... 116 A4
Berry Field Park HP6 .... 154 A1
Berry Hill Cl SL6 .... 203 E4
Berry Hill Ct SL6 .... 203 E4
Berry La Aspley Guise MK17 . 49 F3
  Chorleywood WD3 ...... 167 E2
Berry Way MK17 .... 57 E2
Berryfield LU7 .... 104 C4
Berryfield Cty Fst Sch
  HP27 .... 139 E2
Berryfield Rd
  Aylesbury HP21 .... 101 D2
  Princes Risborough HP27 139 E2
Berrystead MK7 .... 48 A2
Berwald Cl MK7 .... 48 B2
Berwick Ave SL1 .... 205 D3
Berwick Cl
  Beaconsfield HP9 ...... 176 A1
  Marlow SL7 .... 183 E2
Berwick Ct SL7 .... 183 E2
Berwick La SL7 .... 183 E2
Berwick Rd SL7 .... 183 E2
Bessemer Cres HP19 .... 100 C1
Bessemer Ct MK14 ...... 22 A1

Bestobell Rd SL1 .... 205 E4
Betjeman Ct UB7 .... 208 B3
Bettgames Dr MK4 ...... 58 B4
Bettles Cl UB8 .... 201 E2
Bettles Cl HP23 .... 119 D2
Betty's La HP23 .... 119 D2
Betty's Cl MK17 .... 57 E2
Bevan Hill HP5 .... 144 A1
Bevelwood Gdns HP12 ... 172 B4
Beverley Cl HP12 .... 183 D1
Beverley Cl SL1 .... 206 A2
Beverley Gdns SL6 ...... 195 D1
Bevill's Cl MK6 .... 35 D1
Bewdley Dr LU7 .... 80 B4
Bexley St SL4 .... 210 B3
Beyners Green HP16 .... 152 A2
Bicester Rd
  Aylesbury HP18, HP19 ... 101 D1
  Long Crendon HP18 ...... 125 E4
  Ludgershall HP18 ...... 96 B4
  Marsh Gibbon OX6 ...... 71 F2
  Oakley HP18 .... 109 E3
  Twyford MK18 .... 62 B1
Bickleigh Cres MK4 ...... 46 B2
Biddlesden Rd NN13 .... 39 D3
Bideford Cl LU7 .... 80 B4
Bideford Gn LU7 .... 80 B4
Bideford Spur SL2 ...... 198 A1
Bierton CE Comb Sch
  HP22 .... 102 A2
Bierton Rd HP20 .... 101 F1
Bigfrith La SL6 .... 195 D3
Biggs La HP17 .... 113 F1
Bigmore La HP14 .... 170 A4
Billet La Berkhamsted HP4 135 D3
  Iver SL0 .... 207 D4
Billings Cl HP14 .... 158 C3
Billingwell Pl MK6 ...... 35 D1
Billwell HP18 .... 125 E3
Bilton Rd MK1 .... 47 E1
Bingham Cl MK4 .... 46 B1
Bingham Rd SL1 .... 204 A4
Binghams The SL6 ...... 203 D2
Birch Ave UB8 .... 208 C4
Birch Cl Amersham HP6 .. 154 C1
  Iver Heath SL0 .... 200 B2
Birch Cres UB10 .... 201 F2
Birch Gr Slough SL2 .... 205 E4
  Windsor SL4 .... 209 E3
Birch La HP3 .... 156 A4
Birch Rd HP4 .... 134 B4
Birch St HP11 .... 173 D2
Birch Tree Gr HP5 ...... 145 D1
Birch Way Chesham HP5 .. 144 B1
  Tylers Green HP15 ...... 163 D1
Birchdale SL9 .... 188 B2
Birchen Lee MK4 ...... 46 B1
Birches Rise HP12 ...... 172 C4
Birches The Feldon HP3 .. 146 C4
  High Wycombe HP13 .... 173 F4
Birchfield Gr MK2 ...... 58 B4
Birchington Rd SL4 .... 210 A3
Birchwood Chase HP15 .. 151 E1
Birchwood Cl HP22 ...... 172 A3
Bird Mount Cotts SL4 .... 210 B4
Birdcage Wlk HP13 ...... 173 D4
Birdlip La
  Milton Keynes Village MK7 . 48 A4
  Walton MK7 .... 48 A4
Birds La MK16 .... 12 A3
Birdwood Rd SL6 .... 202 A4
Birfield Rd HP10 .... 174 B1
Birinus Ct HP12 .... 172 B3
Birkdale Cl MK3 .... 57 E4
Birkett Way HP8 .... 166 B3
Birley Rd SL1 .... 205 E4
Bisham Abbey
  National Sports Ctr SL7 194 B3
  Bisham CE Prim Sch SL6 . 194 B4
  Bisham Ct Bisham SL7 .... 194 B3
  ■ Slough SL1 .... 205 F2
Bishop Ct SL6 .... 194 C3
Bishop Ct SL6 .... 202 B3
Bishop Ctr The SL6 .... 193 F3
Bishop Parker RC Comb Sch
  MK2 .... 58 B3
Bishop Wood Jun Sch
  HP23 .... 119 D2
Bishops Cl MK18 ...... 52 B4
Bishops Farm Cl SL4 .... 209 D3
Bishops Field HP23 .... 118 A2
Bishops Meadow HP22 .. 102 A2
Bishops Orch SL2 ...... 198 A1
Bishops Wlk
  Aylesbury HP21 .... 115 F3
  Woburn Sands MK17 ...... 49 D2
  Wooburn Green HP10 .... 185 F3
Bishopshalt Sch UB8 .... 201 F1

Bishopstone
  Milton Keynes MK13 .... 34 A3
  Stone HP17 .... 115 D1
Bishopstone Rd HP17 .... 114 B3
Bissley Dr SL6 .... 202 A2
Bit The HP23 .... 119 E1
Bittenham Cl HP17 ...... 114 C2
Bitterne Way ■ HP20 .... 101 F2
Bix Hill HP17 .... 191 D3
Black Acre Cl HP7 ...... 165 F4
Black Boy La SL6 .... 196 A4
Black Butts Cotts SL6 .. 196 A4
Black Horse Ave HP5 .... 154 B3
Black Horse Cl SL4 ...... 209 D3
Black Park Ctry Pk SL0 .. 200 A2
Black Park Rd Fulmer SL3 . 199 F2
  Slough SL3 .... 199 F2
Blackberry Cl MK7 ...... 48 A3
Blackburn Trad Est TW19 . 213 F1
Blackdown MK11 ...... 32 C2
Blacketts Wood Dr WD3 . 167 D3
Blackham La HP16 ...... 142 C2
Blackham Ct MK6 ...... 46 C4
Blackheath Cres MK13 .. 34 B2
Blackhill Dr MK12 ...... 33 D3
Blackichen Cl HP6 ...... 154 C1
Blackichen Cres HP6 .... 154 C1
Blackmoor Gate MK4 .... 46 B1
Blackmore Way UB8 .... 201 E3
Blackpool La SL2 .... 198 A2
Blacksmith La HP16 .... 151 E3
Blacksmith Row SL3 .... 207 D1
Blacksmith's La UB9 .... 189 E1
Blacksmiths Rd HP27 .... 138 B4
Blackthorn Cl OX6 ...... 81 D2
Blackthorn Dell SL3 .... 206 B2
Blackthorn Gr MK17 .... 49 D2
Blackthorne Cres SL3 ... 212 C3
Blackthorne Ind Pk SL3 . 212 C3
Blackthorne La HP16 .... 142 C2
Blackthorne Rd SL3 .... 212 C3
Blackwell End NN12 .... 18 B2
Blackwell Hall La
  Botley HP5 .... 155 D3
  Latimer HP5 .... 155 D2
Blackwell Rd HP14 ...... 171 D3
Blackwood Cres MK13 .. 33 F3
Blair Rd SL1 .... 205 F3
Blairmont St MK9 ...... 34 C2
Blake Way OX9 .... 126 A1
Blakedown Rd LU7 ...... 80 B3
Blakeney Cl
  Maidenhead SL6 ...... 195 F1
  Milton Keynes MK4 ...... 57 D4
Blakes Ho HP10 .... 174 B1
Blandford Cl SL3 .... 206 B2
Blandford Rd N SL3 .... 206 B2
Blandford Rd S SL3 .... 206 B2
Blatherwick Cl MK5 .... 45 F4
Blaydon Cl MK3 .... 57 E3
Bleak Hall Rdbt MK6 .... 47 D3
Bleasdale MK13 .... 34 B3
Bledlow Cotts HP27 .... 138 B1
Bledlow Ridge Cty Comb Sch
  HP14 .... 159 F4
Bledlow Ridge Rd HP27 .. 148 B4
Blenheim Ave MK11 .... 32 C2
Blenheim Cl
  Longwick HP27 .... 138 D3
  Slough SL3 .... 206 C3
Blenheim Pl
  Aylesbury HP21 .... 115 F3
  Syresham NN13 .... 27 E4
Blenheim Rd
  High Wycombe HP12 .... 172 B2
  Maidenhead SL6 .... 202 A4
  Slough SL3 .... 206 B1
Blenheim Rdbt MK1 .... 47 F2
Bletcham Way
  Bow Brickhill MK7 ...... 48 A2
  Milton Keynes MK1, MK7 . 47 F1
  Walton MK7 .... 48 A2
Bletchley Com Hospl MK3 47 D1
Bletchley Rd
  Newton Longville MK17 .. 57 E2
  Shenley Brook End MK5 .. 46 A2
  Stewkley LU7 .... 68 B2
Bletchley Sta MK3 ...... 58 A4
Blinco La SL3 .... 206 C4
Blind La Bourne End SL8 . 185 D3
  Chartridge HP16 ...... 153 D4
  Flackwell Heath HP10 .... 185 D3
Blind Pond Ind Est MK17 .. 48 B1
Bliss Ave MK43 .... 25 E1
Bliss Ct MK7 .... 48 B2
Blisworth MK6 .... 47 E3

Blondell Cl UB7 .... 213 E4
Bloomfield Rd SL6 .... 202 A3
Bloomsbury Cl MK17 .... 60 C3
Blossom Way UB10 .... 201 F3
Blucher St HP5 .... 154 A4
Bluebell Ct MK7 .... 48 A3
Blumfield Cres SL1 .... 204 C4
Blumfield Ct SL1 .... 197 E1
Blundells Rd MK13 .... 34 B3
Blyth Cl HP21 .... 115 E3
Blythe Cl Iver SL0 .... 207 F4
  Newport Pagnell MK16 .. 22 B2
Blyton Cl HP9 .... 175 F2
Boarlands Cl SL1 .... 204 C3
Boathouse Reach RG9 ...... 191 F1
Bobmore La SL7 .... 183 F2
Bockmer La SL7 .... 193 D4
Boddington Rd HP22 .... 131 E2
Bodenham Cl MK18 .... 52 C4
Bodiam Cl Aylesbury HP21 . 116 A3
  Shenley Church End MK5 . 46 A3
Bodiam Ho **6** HP13 ..... 173 F4
Bodle Cl MK15 .... 35 D3
Bodley Ho SL0 .... 200 B2
Bodmin Ave SL2 .... 205 D4
Bois Ave HP6 .... 154 A2
Bois Hill HP5 .... 154 C3
Bois La HP6 .... 154 B2
Bois Moor Rd HP5 .... 154 B3
Bolan Cl MK8 .... 45 F3
Bold's Ct SL2 .... 199 D3
Bolter End La HP14 .... 171 D3
Bolton Ave SL4 .... 210 B2
Bolton Cl MK3 .... 47 D1
Bolton Cres SL4 .... 210 B2
Bolton Rd SL4 .... 210 B2
Bon Secours Hospl HP9 .... 175 F1
Bond Ave MK1 .... 47 E2
Bond Cl UB7 .... 208 C4
Bonham Carter Rd HP22 .... 131 F4
Bonham Cl HP21 .... 115 D3
Bonnards Rd MK17 .... 57 E2
Bonnersfield HP18 .... 125 E4
Booker Ave MK13 .... 34 B2
Booker Hill Cty Comb Sch
  HP12 .... 172 A3
Booker Hospl HP12 .... 172 A2
Booker La HP12 .... 172 B4
Bookerhill Rd HP12 .... 172 B3
Booth La HP17 .... 113 F1
Booth Pl UB6 .... 92 C3
Borderside SL2 .... 206 A4
Borough Ct MK13 .... 38 A3
Borough Rd NN13 .... 38 A3
Borough Wlk MK14 .... 34 C2
Bosanquet Cl UB8 .... 201 E1
Boss La
  Great Kingshill HP14 .. 162 A4
  Hughenden Valley HP15 . 162 A3
Bossiney Pl MK6 .... 34 C1
Bossington La LU7 .... 80 C4
Boston Dr SL8 .... 185 D2
Boston Gr SL1 .... 205 E4
Boswell Ct MK18 .... 41 F1
Boswell La MK19 .... 31 F2
Boswick La HP4 .... 134 B4
Bosworth Cl MK3 .... 46 C1
Botley La HP5 .... 145 D1
Botley Rd HP5 .... 144 C1
Bottesford Cl MK4 .... 46 B1
Bottle Dump Rdbt MK17 .... 56 C3
Bottle Square La HP14 .... 159 F3
Bottom Cl LU6 .... 93 E3
Bottom House Fm La HP8 ... 155 F1
Bottom House La HP23 ..... 120 A1
Bottom La HP9 .... 176 B3
Bottom Orchard HP17 ...... 112 A1
Bottom Rd
  Bledlow Ridge HP14 .... 160 A3
  Buckland Common HP23 .. 133 D2
  Drayton Beauchamp HP23 132 C2
Bottom Waltons Caravan Site
  SL2 .... 197 F2
Bottrells La
  Amersham HP8 .... 176 C4
  Chalfont St Giles HP8 . 176 C4
Botyl Rd MK18 .... 74 C3
Boughton Way HP6 .... 155 E1
Boulmer Rd UB8 .... 201 E1
Boulters Cl
  Maidenhead SL6 .... 196 B1
  Slough SL1 .... 205 D2
Boulters Ct Amersham HP6 . 154 C1
  Maidenhead SL6 .... 196 B1
Boulters Gdns SL6 .... 196 B1
Boulters La SL6 .... 196 B1
Boulters Lock MK14 .... 21 F1
Boundary Cres MK11 .... 32 C3

Boundary Pl HP10 .... 185 E4
Boundary Rd Brackley NN13 38 A3
  Gerrards Cross SL9 .... 177 E2
  Taplow SL6 .... 203 F4
  Wooburn Green HP10 .... 185 E4
Boundary The MK6 .... 46 C4
Bounds Croft MK12 .... 33 E2
Bounty St MK13 .... 33 F4
Bouquet Ho HP16 .... 151 E3
Bourbon St HP20 .... 115 E4
Bourne Ave SL4 .... 210 B2
Bourne Cl SL8 .... 185 D3
Bourne End MK43 .... 25 D3
Bourne End Bsns Ctr **8**
  SL8 .... 185 D2
Bourne End La HP1 .... 146 A4
Bourne End Rd
  Bourne End SL6 .... 196 C4
  Cranfield MK43 .... 25 E2
  Taplow SL6 .... 196 C4
Bourne Rd
  Berkhamsted HP4 .... 134 C3
  Slough SL1 .... 205 E2
Bourne The HP1 .... 146 A2
Bourton Low MK7 .... 48 A3
Bourton Meadow Comb Sch
  MK18 .... 52 C4
Bourton Rd MK18 .... 52 C4
Bourtonville MK18 .... 52 B4
Bouverie Way SL3 .... 206 C1
Boveney Cl SL1 .... 205 D2
Boveney New Rd SL4 .... 204 C1
Boveney Rd SL4 .... 204 C1
Boveney Wood La SL1 ...... 186 B1
Bovingdon Cl HP3 .... 146 A2
Bovingdon Green La HP3 ... 145 F2
Bovingdon Hts SL7 .... 183 D1
Bovingdon Inf Sch HP3 .... 146 A2
Bovingdon Jun Mix Sch
  HP3 .... 146 A2
Bow Brickhill Cty Fst Sch
  MK17 .... 48 B1
Bow Brickhill Rd MK17 .... 48 C2
Bow Brickhill Sta MK7 .... 48 A1
Bowden La HP11 .... 173 E3
Bowen Cl MK7 .... 48 B3
Bower Cl LU6 .... 92 C3
Bower Ct SL1 .... 204 C3
Bower La LU6 .... 92 C3
Bower Way SL1 .... 204 C3
Bowerbank Ct **18** HP20 . 101 F1
Bowerdean Rd HP13 .... 173 E4
Bowers La HP14 .... 159 E4
Bowes Cl MK16 .... 22 B2
Bowes-Lyon Cl **7** SL4 .. 210 B3
Bowl Rdbt The MK5 .... 46 B3
Bowland Dr MK4 .... 46 A1
Bowler Lea HP13 .... 161 E1
Bowler Rd HP21 .... 115 F2
Bowler's Orch HP14 .... 177 D4
Bowles Pl MK6 .... 47 E4
Bowling Alley HP22 .... 86 B4
Bowling Ct RG9 .... 191 E2
Bowling Gr HP14 .... 158 B3
Bowling Green Rd MK43 .... 25 E1
Bowmans Cl SL1 .... 197 D2
Bowmont Dr HP21 .... 115 E2
Bowood Ct MK8 .... 33 F1
Bowood La
  Lee Common HP16 .... 141 F3
  Wendover HP16 .... 141 F3
Bowry Dr TW19 .... 211 F1
Bowstridge Ct HP13 .... 173 E4
Bowstridge La HP8 .... 177 E3
Bowyer Cres UB9 .... 189 F3
Bowyer Dr SL1 .... 204 C3
Bowyers Mews MK14 .... 34 C3
Box La HP3 .... 146 C4
Box Tree Cl HP5 .... 154 B3
Boxberry Gdns MK7 .... 48 A3
Boxer Rd HP27 .... 138 C3
Boxmoor House Special Sch
  HP3 .... 146 C4
Boxwell Rd HP4 .... 135 D2
Boxwood Cl UB7 .... 208 C2
Boyce Cres MK7 .... 48 B3
Boycott Ave MK6 .... 34 C1
Boyle Cl UB10 .... 201 F2
Boyn Hill Ave SL6 .... 202 B3
Boyn Hill Cl SL6 .... 202 B3
Boyn Hill Rd SL6 .... 202 B3
Boyn Valley Rd SL6 .... 202 B3
Boyndon Rd SL6 .... 202 B4
Boyne Hill CE Inf Sch SL6 202 B3
Bozenham Mill La
  Ashton NN7 .... 9 F3
  Grafton Regis NN7 ..... 9 F3
Bracken Cl SL2 .... 198 B4
Bracken Hill HP4 .... 135 F3

Bracken Rd SL6 .... 202 B2
Bracken Way HP10 .... 185 D4
Brackenforde SL3 .... 206 B2
Brackens The HP11 .... 173 E3
Brackenwood HP14 .... 161 E4
Brackley Dr HP15 .... 163 D3
Brackley La MK18 .... 73 D3
Brackley Rd
  Buckingham MK18 .... 41 D1
  Chackmore MK18 .... 41 D1
  Holmer Green HP15 ..... 163 D3
  Westbury NN13 .... 39 D3
Bradbery WD3 .... 178 B3
Bradbourne Dr MK7 .... 48 A2
Bradbury Cl MK13 .... 34 A2
Bradbury Gdns SL2 .... 199 E4
Bradcutts La SL6 .... 195 F4
Braddenham Wlk HP21 ...... 116 B3
Braddons Furlong HP18 .... 125 E3
Braden Cl HP21 .... 116 A3
Bradenham Beeches HP14 ... 161 D4
Bradenham La SL7 .... 194 B3
Bradenham Rd HP14 .... 161 D2
Bradenham Wood La
  HP14 .... 161 D4
Bradfield Ave MK18 .... 41 E1
Bradford Gdns MK5 .... 46 A2
Bradford Rd Heron WD3 .... 167 E3
  Slough SL1 .... 205 D4
Bradley Cl HP18 .... 109 E3
Bradley Gr MK4 .... 46 A1
Bradley Rd SL1 .... 205 F3
Bradshaw Cl SL4 .... 209 F3
Bradshaw Rd HP13 .... 173 F3
Bradshaw Waye UB8 .... 208 C4
Bradwell Common Bvd
  MK13 .... 34 B2
Bradwell Rd
  Milton Keynes, Bradville
  MK13, MK5 .... 34 A3
  Milton Keynes, Loughton
  MK13, MK5 .... 46 A4
Bradwell Village Cty Mid Sch
  MK13 .... 34 A2
Brae Hill HP18 .... 110 A4
Brae Hill Cl HP18 .... 110 A4
Braemar Ct **1** SL7 ..... 183 E1
Braemar Gdns SL1 .... 205 D2
Bragenham La
  Leighton Buzzard MK17,LU7 70 B3
  Soulbury MK17,LU7 ..... 70 B3
Bragenham Side MK17 ...... 69 F4
Brahms Cl MK7 .... 48 B3
Braid The HP5 .... 144 C1
Brakynbery HP14 .... 134 C4
Bramber Cl MK3 .... 57 F4
Bramber Ct SL1 .... 204 C3
Bramble Ave MK14 .... 34 C2
Bramble Cl
  Chalfont St Peter SL9 . 177 E2
  Uxbridge UB8 .... 208 C4
Bramble Cres HP15 .... 163 E3
Bramble Dr SL6 .... 202 A2
Bramble La HP27 .... 165 F3
Bramble Mead HP8 .... 177 D4
Brambles The UB7 .... 208 C1
Brambleside HP10 .... 174 A2
Brambling HP20 .... 101 F2
Bramcote Cl HP13 .... 116 B4
Bramley Cl SL6 .... 202 B2
Bramley Ct MK43 .... 3 F3
Bramley End HP16 .... 151 D1
Bramley Grange MK2 .... 58 B2
Bramley Rd MK1 .... 47 E2
Brammas Cl SL1 .... 205 E2
Brampton Ct
  Maidenhead SL6 .... 203 D4
  Milton Keynes MK13 .... 34 A3
Branch Rd HP10 .... 174 A1
Brandon Rd HP12 .... 172 A2
Brands Hill Ave HP13 ..... 162 B1
Brands Rd SL3 .... 212 A4
Brandville Rd UB7 .... 208 C2
Bransgill Ct MK13 .... 34 A2
Bransworth Ave MK7 .... 48 B4
Braunston MK6 .... 47 E3
Bravenfield MK18 .... 53 E1
Bray Cl SL6 .... 203 E2
Bray Ct Amersham HP6 ..... 154 C1
  Maidenhead SL6 .... 203 E1
Bray Rd SL6 .... 203 D3
Braybank SL6 .... 203 E2
Braybrooke Dr MK4 .... 46 C2
Brayfield Rd SL6 .... 203 E2
Brays Cl HP6 .... 153 E2
Brays Green La HP6 .... 153 E2
Brays La HP6 .... 153 E3
Brays Meadow HP6 .... 153 E2

Brayton Ct MK5 .... 46 B3
Braywick Rd SL6 .... 203 D2
Braywood Cotts SL4 .... 209 D3
Braziers End HP5 .... 133 E1
Breachwell Pl LU7 .... 91 D1
Breakspear Rd N UB9 ...... 190 C4
Breakspear Rd S UB10 ..... 190 C1
Bream Cl SL7 .... 194 B4
Breamore Ct MK8 .... 45 F4
Brearley Ave MK6 .... 46 C4
Brearley Cl UB8 .... 201 F3
Brecon Cl SL1 .... 205 E2
Brecon Way HP13 .... 172 C4
Bredward Cl SL1 .... 197 D1
Brenchwood Cl HP13 .... 161 E1
Brendon Ct MK4 .... 46 B1
Brent MK6 .... 47 E3
Brent Rd SL8 .... 185 D2
Brentwood Way HP21 .... 116 A3
Breton MK11 .... 32 C3
Brewhouse La HP22 .... 88 C1
Briaily HP14 .... 159 E1
Briar Cl SL6 .... 204 A4
Briar Dene SL6 .... 195 E1
Briar Glen SL6 .... 195 F3
Briar Hill MK12 .... 33 F2
Briar Way
  Berkhamsted HP4 .... 135 E2
  Slough SL2 .... 205 D4
Briars The
  High Wycombe HP11 ..... 173 E3
  Holmer Green HP15 ..... 163 E4
  Slough SL3 .... 206 C1
Stanwell TW19 .... 213 D1
Briarswood HP15 .... 163 D2
Briarwood Ct HP14 .... 158 C3
Briary Vew MK17 .... 56 A4
Brices Meadow MK5 .... 46 A2
Brick Cl MK11 .... 33 E1
Brick Hill HP18 .... 97 F1
Brick Kiln La HP22 .... 102 A2
Brickfield La SL1 .... 197 D2
Brickfields Way UB7 ...... 208 C2
Brickhill Manor Ct MK17 .. 59 E3
Brickhill St
  Bow Brickhill MK7 ..... 48 A2
  Milton Keynes MK15 .... 35 E3
  Milton Keynes Village
  MK10, MK15 .... 35 F1
  Walton MK7 .... 48 A2
Bricks La HP14 .... 159 E2
Brickwell Wlk HP15 .... 163 D2
Bricstock HP22 .... 88 B2
Briden's Way HP17 .... 126 C3
Bridge Ave Cookham SL6 ... 195 F3
  Maidenhead SL6 .... 203 D4
Bridge Bank Cl HP11 ...... 174 A2
Bridge Cl SL1 .... 204 C3
Bridge Ct
  Berkhamsted HP4 .... 135 E2
  Maidenhead SL6 .... 203 E4
Bridge Ho HP13 .... 173 E3
Bridge Pl HP6 .... 154 C1
Bridge Rd Cosgrove MK19 .. 19 F1
  Ickford HP18 .... 123 F1
  Maidenhead SL6 .... 203 D4
  Uxbridge UB8 .... 201 E2
Bridge St
  Berkhamsted HP4 .... 135 E2
  Buckingham MK18 .... 52 B4
  Colnbrook SL3 .... 212 B4
  Great Kimble HP17 ..... 129 E1
  High Wycombe HP11 ..... 173 D4
  Leighton Buzzard LU7 .. 80 C4
  Maidenhead SL6 .... 203 D4
  Milton Keynes MK13 .... 33 F4
  Olney MK46 .... 6 C2
  Thornborough MK18 ..... 54 A4
  Turvey MK43 .... 8 B3
Bridge Turn Ave MK12 ..... 33 E4
Bridgeford Ct MK6 .... 46 C4
Bridgegate Bsns Pk HP19 .. 101 D1
Bridgeman Ct **5** SL4 ... 210 A3
Bridgeman Dr SL4 .... 210 A3
Bridgestone Dr SL8 .... 185 E2
Bridgewater Ct
  Little Gaddesden HP4 .. 121 E4
  Slough SL3 .... 207 D1
Bridgewater Hill HP4 ..... 134 C4
Bridgewater Ho MK18 ...... 52 B4
Bridgewater Rd HP4 .... 135 D3
Bridgewater Sch HP4 ...... 135 D3
Bridgewater Terr SL4 ..... 210 B3
Bridgewater Way SL4 ...... 210 B3
Bridgeway
  Cuddington HP18 .... 112 C2
  Milton Keynes MK13 .... 34 A4
Bridle Cl Maidenhead SL6 . 195 F1
  Milton Keynes MK13 .... 34 A3
Bridle Gate HP11 .... 172 C3
Bridle Manor HP22 .... 131 E4

Bridle Rd SL6 .... 195 F3
Bridle Way HP4 .... 135 D3
Bridleway
  Drayton Beauchamp HP23 132 C3
  Weston Turville HP22 .. 116 C1
Bridleways HP22 .... 131 D3
Bridlington Spur SL1 ..... 205 D2
Bridport Way SL2 .... 198 A3
Briery Way HP6 .... 154 C1
Brighton Spur SL2 .... 198 A1
Brightwell Ave LU6 .... 93 E4
Brigidine Sch The SL4 .... 210 B2
Brill CE Comb Sch HP18 ... 96 A3
Brill Cl Maidenhead SL6 .. 202 B2
  Marlow SL7 .... 183 E1
Brill Pl MK13 .... 34 B2
Brill Rd Chilton HP18 .... 111 D2
  Ludgershall HP18 ...... 96 A4
  Oakley HP18 .... 109 F3
Brimmers Hill HP15 .... 162 C3
Brimmers Rd HP27 .... 139 E1
Brimstone Wlk HP4 .... 134 C3
Brindlebrook MK8 .... 33 F1
Brindley Ave HP13 .... 161 F3
Brinklow Rdbt MK10 .... 36 A3
Bristle Hill MK18 .... 52 B4
Bristol Cl TW19 .... 213 F3
Bristol Way **2** TW19 ... 213 F1
Bristol Way SL1 .... 205 F3
Bristow Cl MK2 .... 47 F1
Bristow Ct SL7 .... 184 A2
Britannia Cl UB7 .... 208 B2
Britannia Ind Est
  High Wycombe HP12 ..... 172 B4
Stanwell SL3 .... 212 C3
Britannia Rd HP15 .... 144 B1
Britannia St HP20 .... 115 F4
Britnell Ct HP14 .... 158 C3
Britten Gr MK7 .... 48 B3
Brittens Cl MK43 .... 7 E2
Brittons La MK17 .... 37 E2
Britwell Rd SL1 .... 197 E1
Broad Arrow Cl MK14 ...... 34 C4
Broad Dean MK6 .... 47 D4
Broad Gn MK43 .... 25 E2
Broad La HP10 .... 186 A3
Broad Ley's SL4 .... 209 F4
Broad Leys HP27 .... 139 D2
Broad Oak SL2 .... 198 B1
Broad Oak Ct SL2 .... 198 B3
Broad Piece MK15 .... 35 D4
Broad Platts SL3 .... 206 B2
Broad Rush Gn LU7 .... 80 C4
Broad St Chesham HP5 ..... 144 B3
  Newport Pagnell MK16 .. 22 B2
  Syresham NN13 .... 27 D4
Broadfields HP19 .... 101 D1
Broadfields Ct HP19 ...... 101 D1
Broadlands MK6 .... 47 D3
Broadlands Ave HP5 .... 144 B3
Broadmark Rd SL2 .... 206 A3
Broadview Rd HP5 .... 144 A2
Broadwater
  Berkhamsted HP4 .... 135 E3
  Milton Keynes MK6 ..... 47 E3
Broadwater Gdns UB9 ...... 190 B4
Broadwater La UB9 .... 190 B4
Broadwater Park
  Denham Green UB9 ...... 190 A3
  Maidenhead SL6 .... 203 F1
Broadway Amersham HP7 .... 165 D4
  Maidenhead SL6 .... 202 C4
Broadway Ave MK14 .... 21 F1
Broadway Cl HP7 .... 165 D4
Broadway Ct HP5 .... 154 A4
Broadway Mall **6** SL6 .. 202 C4
Broadway Par UB7 .... 208 C2
Broadway The
  Beaconsfield HP9 ...... 175 E2
  Chesham HP5 .... 154 A4
  8 Gerrards Cross SL9 177 E1
  Grendon Underwood HP18 82 C3
Brocas St SL4 .... 210 B4
Brocas Terr SL4 .... 210 B4
Brocas Way SL1 .... 91 D2
Brock La SL6 .... 202 C4
Brock La Mall **7** SL6 .. 202 C4
Brockhampton MK15 .... 35 D3
Brockhurst Rd HP5 .... 144 B1
Brockway SL3 .... 207 D1
Brockwell MK16 .... 22 B2
Broddick Ho **10** HP10 .. 174 A2
Broken Furlong SL4 .... 205 D1
Broken Gate La UB9 .... 189 E2
Bromham Mill MK14 .... 21 F1
Bromley HP22 .... 104 A2
Bromley La HP16 .... 153 D3
Brompton Cl HP19 .... 101 D1
Brompton Cres HP19 .... 101 D1
Brompton Dr SL6 .... 195 E1
Bromycroft Rd SL2 .... 198 A1

ronsdon Way UB9 .... 189 F1
ronte CI HP19 .... 100 C1
room Bsns Ctr UB8 .... 201 D2
rook CI
 Aston Clinton HP22 .... 117 E3
 Ludgershall HP18 .... 96 B4
rook Cres SL1 .... 204 C4
rook End
 North Crawley MK16 .... 24 A3
 Weston Turville HP22 ...... 117 D2
rook Ho SL1 .... 205 E2
rook La
 Berkhamsted HP4 .... 135 D3
 Harrold MK43 .... 3 F4
 Newton Blossomville MK43 .. 8 A2
 Thame OX9 .... 125 F1
rook Path SL1 .... 204 C3
rook St
 Aston
 Edlesborough LU6 .... 92 C2
 High Wycombe HP11 ...... 173 D4
 Tring HP23 .... 119 D2
 Windsor SL4 .... 210 B3
rookbank HP10 .... 185 E2
rookdene CI SL6 .... 195 F1
rooke CI MK3 .... 57 F4
rooke Furmston PI SL7 .. 183 F2
rooke Rd HP27 .... 139 D2
rookfield CI HP23 .... 119 D2
rookfield Farm HP22 .... 111 E3
rookfield Ho SL3 .... 211 E3
rookfield La MK18 .... 52 B4
rookfield Rd
 Haversham MK19 .... 20 B1
 Newton Longville MK17 .... 57 E2
 Wooburn Green HP10 ...... 185 E2
rookhouse Dr HP10 .... 185 E2
rooklands Rd MK2 .... 58 B4
rooklyn Way SL2 .... 208 B2
rookmead Comb Sch
 LU7 .... 105 F3
rooks Ct MK18 .... 52 B4
rookside Colnbrook SL3 .. 212 B4
 Halton HP22 .... 117 E1
 Lillingstone Lovell MK18 .... 30 A3
 Loudwater HP10 .... 174 B1
 Milton Keynes MK12 .... 33 E2
 Oakley HP18 .... 109 E3
 Slough SL3 .... 206 C4
 Thame OX9 .... 125 F1
 Uxbridge UB10 .... 201 F3
 Weston Turville HP22 ...... 117 D1
rookside Ave TW19 .... 211 F2
rookside CI
 Old Stratford MK19 .... 32 A3
 Tiddington OX9 .... 136 A4
rookside La HP17 .... 127 F2
rookside Terr SL1 HP21 .. 115 F4
rookward Cty Mid Sch
 MK14 .... 34 C4
rookway MK19 .... 31 F2
room CI HP15 .... 163 D2
room Hill Cookham SL6 .. 195 F3
 Stoke Poges SL3 .... 199 D3
room Ho SL3 .... 206 C1
roombarn La HP16 .... 151 F4
roomfield MK12 .... 33 E2
roomfield CI HP16 .... 151 F4
roomfield Hill HP16 .... 151 F4
roomlee MK13 .... 34 A3
roomstick La HP5 .... 145 D1
rora CI MK4 .... 58 B3
rotheridge Ct HP21 ...... 115 D3
rough CI MK5 .... 46 A3
roughton Ave HP20 .... 116 A4
roughton CI HP22 .... 102 A2
roughton Crossing HP22 102 B1
roughton Cty Fst Sch
 HP20 .... 116 A4
roughton Cty Mid Sch
 HP20 .... 116 A4
roughton La
 Aylesbury HP20 .... 116 B4
 Bierton HP20 .... 116 B4
roughton Manor Bsns Pk
 MK10 .... 36 A2
roughton Rd
 Aylesbury HP20 .... 116 A4
 Milton Keynes Village MK10 36 A2
 Salford MK17 .... 37 E2
roughton The HP8 .... 177 E4
rown's Rise HP23 .... 132 C2
rownaker Ct MK14 .... 34 C3
rowne Wills MK2 .... 58 B4
rownfield Gdns SL6 ...... 202 C3
Browning CI MK10 .... 52 A2
Browning Cres MK3 .... 58 A4
Brownlow La LU6 .... 92 C2
Brownlow La LU7 .... 105 D4
Brownlow Rd HP4 .... 135 E3
Brownlow Rise LU6 .... 93 D4

Browns Rd
 Chartridge HP16 .... 153 D4
 Holmer Green HP15 .... 163 E3
Browns Way MK17 .... 49 F3
Browns Wood Rdbt MK7 .. 48 B3
Brownsfield Rd NN12 ...... 18 C3
Brownswood Dr NN12 ...... 18 B2
Brownswood Rd HP9 ...... 175 F2
Broxbourne CI MK14 ...... 21 F1
Bruce CI SL1 .... 205 D3
Bruce Wlk SL4 .... 209 D2
Brucewood Par SL7 .... 183 F3
Bruckner Gdns MK7 .... 48 B3
Brudenell SL4 .... 209 F2
Brudenell Dr
 Milton Keynes Village MK7 .. 48 B4
 Stoke Mandeville HP22 .... 116 A1
Brunel CI SL6 .... 202 C3
Brunel Ctr Maidenhead SL6 202 B3
 Milton Keynes MK2 .... 58 B3
Brunel Rd Aylesbury HP19 . 100 C1
 High Wycombe HP13 ...... 161 F1
 Maidenhead SL6 .... 202 B3
Brunel Univ UB8 .... 201 F1
Brunel Way SL1 .... 205 F3
Brunleys MK1 .... 58 A3
Brunswick CI HP19 .... 101 D2
Brunswick PI HP13 .... 162 B1
Brushford CI MK4 .... 46 B3
Brushwood Dr WD3 .... 167 F4
Brushwood Mid Sch HP5 144 C1
Brushwood Rd HP5 .... 144 B1
Bryans Cres MK16 .... 24 A3
Bryanston Ave HP20 ...... 101 F1
Bryant Ave SL2 .... 205 F3
Bryant's Bottom Rd HP16 150 C2
Bryant's Acre HP22 .... 131 D3
Bryden Cotts UB8 .... 201 E1
Bryer PI SL4 .... 209 E2
Bryne La MK18 .... 44 C3
Bryony CI UB8 .... 208 C4
Bryony PI MK14 .... 34 C3
Bryony PI MK14 .... 34 C3
Bryony PI MK14 .... 34 C3
Bsns Village The SL2 .... 206 A3
Buccleuch Rd SL3 .... 211 D4
Buchan Cl UB8 .... 201 F1
Buchanan Ho HP27 .... 139 D2
Buchanan Rd OX6 .... 94 C4
Buckby MK6 .... 47 E3
Buckfast Ave MK3 .... 47 D1
Buckfield Ct SL0 .... 207 F2
Buckingham Ave SL1 ...... 205 D4
Buckingham Ave E SL1 .. 205 E4
Buckingham CI HP13 .... 174 A4
Buckingham Ct
 Amersham HP6 .... 154 C1
 Newport Pagnell MK16 .... 22 A2
Buckingham Gate
 Medmenham SL7 .... 193 E4
 Milton Keynes MK6 .... 35 D1
Buckingham Gdns SL1 .. 205 F2
Buckingham Ho
 Amersham 154 B2
 Maidenhead SL6 .... 202 C3
Buckingham Ind Pk MK18 52 B3
Buckingham Mid Sch MK18 41 F1
Buckingham Pl SL9 ...... 177 E1
Buckingham Pl HP11 .... 173 D4
Buckingham Rd
 Brackley NN13 .... 38 A3
 Deanshanger MK19 .... 31 F1
 Edgcott HP18 .... 72 C1
 Gawcott MK18 .... 52 A3
 Milton Keynes
 MK17, MK19, MK3 .... 57 E4
 Steeple Claydon MK18 .... 63 F2
 Tring HP23 .... 118 C2
 Wicker MK19 .... 31 F1
 Winslow MK18 .... 65 F3
Buckingham Sch MK18 .. 52 B4
Buckingham St
 Aylesbury HP20 .... 101 D1
 Milton Keynes MK12 .... 33 E4
 Tingewick MK18 .... 51 D3
Buckinghamshire Coll of H Ed
 HP11 .... 173 D3
Buckinghamshire Coll The
 SL9 .... 178 A4
Buckland Ave SL6 .... 206 A2
Buckland Cres SL4 .... 209 F3
Buckland Dr MK6 .... 47 E3
Buckland Rd HP22 .... 118 A2
Bucklebury CI SL6 .... 203 E1
Buckley CI MK11 .... 32 C2
Buckman CI MK12 .... 33 D3
Buckmaster Rd HP18 .... 172 B2
Buckthorn MK12 .... 33 F3
Budge Rd NN12 .... 18 C3
Buffins SL6 .... 196 C1
Bulbourne CI HP4 .... 134 C3

Bulbourne CI HP23 ...... 119 D4
Bulbourne Rd HP23 ...... 119 E4
Bulkeley Ave SL4 .... 210 A2
Bull La Gerrards Cross SL9 188 B4
 High Wycombe HP11 .... 173 E4
Bulbaiters La HP6 .... 153 D3
Bullbeggars La HP4 ...... 135 F2
Bullfinch Gdns 13 HP20 .. 101 F2
Bullington End Rd MK19 .. 20 A3
Bullocks Farm La HP14 .. 171 D4
Bullrush Gr UB8 .... 201 E1
Bulls La HP18 .... 124 A2
Bullsland Gdns WD3 ...... 167 D2
Bullsland La WD3 .... 167 D2
Bulstrode CI W10 .... 146 C1
Bulstrode Ct SL9 .... 188 B3
Bulstrode La W04 .... 146 C2
Bulstrode Way SL9 .... 188 B3
Bunby Rd SL2 .... 198 C3
Bunces CI SL4 .... 205 D1
Bunces Ct HP20 .... 101 E1
Bungalows The MK18 .... 51 D3
Bunhill CI LU6 .... 93 F4
Bunkers La LU7 .... 80 B3
Bunstrux HP23 .... 119 D2
Bunsty Ct MK11 .... 32 C2
Bunten Meade SL1 .... 205 D3
Bunswick PI HP13 .... 162 B1
Bunyan CI HP23 .... 119 D3
Burano CI MK7 .... 48 B3
Burchard Cres MK5 .... 46 A3
Burchett's Green Rd SL6 . 194 B1
Burcot Gdns SL6 .... 195 F2
Burcott CI HP22 .... 102 B2
Burcott La HP22 .... 102 B2
Burdeleys La MK5 .... 46 A2
Burdett Ho HP11 .... 173 D4
Burdett 11 HP11 .... 161 D4
Burdock CI MK16 .... 21 F2
Burewelle MK8 .... 33 F1
Burfield Rd
 Chorleywood WD3 .... 167 E2
 Old Windsor SL4 .... 211 D1
Burford CI Ickenham UB10 .201 F4
 Marlow Bottom SL7 .... 183 E3
Burford Cty Comb Sch
 SL7 .... 183 E3
Burford Gdns SL1 .... 204 B4
Burgess Gdns MK16 ...... 22 A1
Burgess La HP17 .... 128 A4
Burgess Wood Gr HP9 .. 175 D1
Burgess Wood Rd S HP9 . 175 D1
Burgett Rd SL1 .... 205 D2
Burghley CI MK8 .... 45 F4
Burholme MK4 .... 46 A4
Burkes CI HP9 .... 186 A4
Burkes Cres HP9 .... 175 E1
Burkes Ct HP9 .... 175 E1
Burkes Par HP9 .... 175 E1
Burkes Rd HP9 .... 175 E1
Burleigh CI MK18 .... 52 C4
Burleigh Piece MK18 .... 52 C4
Burleys Rd MK18 .... 65 F2
Burlington Ave SL1 .... 205 F2
Burlington Ct 11 SL1 .... 205 F2
Burlington Rd
 Burnham SL1 .... 197 D1
 Slough SL1 .... 205 F2
Burma CI HP13 .... 173 F3
Burn Wlk SL1 .... 197 D1
Burners La MK11 .... 33 D2
Burners La S MK11 ...... 33 D2
Burnetts CI SL4 .... 209 F3
Burnetts Ct HP16 .... 151 E3
Burnetts Rd SL4 .... 209 F3
Burnham Ave HP9 .... 176 A1
Burnham Beeches
 (Nature Reserve) SL2 .. 198 A4
Burnham CI
 Bourne End SL8 .... 185 D2
 High Wycombe HP12 .... 172 A3
 Windsor SL4 .... 209 E3
Burnham Dr MK13 .... 34 B2
Burnham Field HP22 ...... 116 C4
Burnham Gram Sch SL1 .. 197 E2
Burnham La SL1 .... 204 B4
Burnham PI NN13 .... 27 D4
Burnham Rd
 Beaconsfield HP9 .... 186 C3
 Hughenden Valley HP14 . 162 A3
 Westcott HP18 .... 98 A4
Burnham Sta SL1 .... 204 B4
Burnham Upper Sch SL1 .. 204 A4
Burnham The HP18 ...... 124 B2
Burnmoor CI MK2 .... 58 B2
Burns CI
 Long Crendon HP18 .... 125 E4
 Newport Pagnell MK16 .... 22 A2
Burns CI HP21 .... 115 F3
Burns Rd MK3 .... 58 A4
Burnt Oak SL6 .... 195 F4
Burren The HP6 .... 154 B1

Burroughs Cres SL8 ...... 185 D2
Burroway Rd SL3 .... 207 D2
Burrows CI
 Tylers Green HP10 .... 163 E1
 Woburn Sands MK17 ...... 49 D3
Burrows Field CI TW6 .. 213 E2
Burrows Ho HP13 .... 161 F1
Burt's La HP18 .... 125 E3
Burton Rd HP22 .... 139 E3
Burton Way SL4 .... 209 F2
Burton's La HP8 .... 166 B3
Burton's Way HP8 .... 166 B2
Burtree CI MK12 .... 33 E2
Bury Ave MK16 .... 22 B2
Bury CI MK16 .... 22 B2
Bury Farm HP7 .... 165 E4
Bury Farm CI LU7 .... 115 F2
Bury La HP5 .... 154 A4
Bury Lawn Sch
 Ind Co Ed Day Sch MK13 . 34 B4
Bury Rise HP3 .... 146 B3
Bury St MK16 .... 22 B2
Buryhook Cnr OX33 ...... 122 B1
Busby CI MK8 .... 45 F4
Buscot PI MK8 .... 45 F4
Bush The HP17 .... 126 C3
Bushel Wharf HP23 ...... 119 D3
Bushes La MK18 .... 51 F1
Bushey Bartrams MK5 .. 46 A2
Bushey CI
 Buckingham MK18 .... 41 F1
 High Wycombe HP12 .... 172 C4
Bushfield Mid Sch MK12 . 33 E3
Bushfield Rd HP19 .... 146 B3
Bushfields MK12 .... 33 E4
Bushmead CI HP22 .... 86 B3
Bushmead Rd HP22 ...... 87 D2
Bushy CI MK3 .... 47 D2
Buslins La HP5 .... 144 A2
Butcher La MK5 .... 45 F2
Bute Brae MK3 .... 46 B2
Butler CI SL7 .... 184 A2
Butlers CI Amersham HP6 . 154 A1
 Windsor SL4 .... 209 E3
Butlers Court Cty Comb Sch
 HP9 .... 175 E1
Butlers Court Rd HP9 .... 175 E1
Butlers CI HP13 .... 173 F3
Butlers Gr MK14 .... 34 B4
Butterfield Rd HP10 ...... 185 E2
Butterfield CI MK15 ...... 35 E1
Butterfield Cotts WD3 .. 178 C2
Butterfly Rd HP14 .... 158 C2
Buttermere HP21 .... 116 A4
Buttermere Ave SL1 ...... 204 B4
Buttermere CI MK2 ...... 58 B3
Buttfurlong HP17 .... 127 D4
Buttlehide WD3 .... 178 B3
Buzzacott La MK4 .... 46 B3
By-Wood End SL9 .... 178 A3
Byebend CI SL2 .... 198 A2
Bycell Rd MK18 .... 41 E3
Bye Gn HP22 .... 117 D2
Byerly PI MK14 .... 34 C3
Byford Way MK18 .... 65 F2
Byland Dr SL6 .... 203 D1
Byrd Cres MK7 .... 48 B3
Byres The HP17 .... 126 C3
Byron CI MK3 .... 207 D1
Byron CI 6 Marlow SL7 .. 183 F2
 Milton Keynes MK3 .... 57 F4
Byron Dr MK16 .... 22 A2
Byron Rd HP21 .... 115 F3
Byron Way UB7 .... 208 C1
Byward CI MK14 .... 34 C4
Byways Berkhamsted HP4 . 135 F3
 Burnham SL1 .... 204 A4

Cadman Sq MK6 .... 46 B3
Cadmore End CE Comb Sch
 HP14 .... 170 B3
Cadsdean Rd HP27 .... 139 F3
Cadwell Dr SL6 .... 202 B2
Caernarvon Cres MK3 .... 57 F4
Caesars CI MK3 .... 57 F4
Caesars Gate NN13 .... 38 A3
Cages Wood Dr SL2 ...... 198 A4
Cairngorm Gate MK6 ...... 46 B3
Cairngorm PI SL2 .... 198 B1
Cairnside HP13 .... 173 F3
Caithness CI MK3 .... 46 C1
Calamus CI MK7 .... 48 A3
Calbroke Rd SL2 .... 197 F1
Caldecote La MK16 .... 22 C1
Caldecote St MK16 .... 22 B2
Caldecott CI MK17 .... 48 A2
Caldecotte Lake Dr MK7 .. 48 C2
Caldecotte Rdbt MK7 ...... 47 F2
Calder CI SL6 .... 195 F1
Calder Ct Maidenhead SL6 . 195 E1
 Slough SL3 .... 206 C1

Calder Gdns LU7 .... 80 A4
Calder Vale MK3 .... 46 C1
Calder Way SL3 .... 212 C2
Caldwell MK8 .... 33 E1
Caldicot CI MK4 .... 116 A3
Caldicott Sch SL2 .... 198 A3
Caledon CI HP9 .... 175 F2
Caledon Rd HP9 .... 175 F2
Caledonian Rd MK13 ...... 33 F4
Calewen MK8 .... 33 F1
California Circ HP13 ...... 173 D2
Callis Farm CI TW19 ...... 213 F1
Calluna Dr MK3 .... 47 D2
Calumet HP9 .... 175 E2
Calvards Croft MK12 ...... 33 E2
Calverleigh Cres MK4 .... 46 B2
Calverley Cres HP13 ...... 161 F1
Calverton La Rdbt MK11 . 33 E1
Calverton Rd MK13 .... 32 B2
Calves CI MK5 .... 46 A2
Cam Ct MK3 .... 57 F4
Cam Mead HP21 .... 116 A3
Camber CI MK3 .... 57 F4
Camberton Rd LU7 .... 80 C3
Camborne Ave HP21 .... 116 A3
Cambria CI SL3 .... 206 B2
Cambridge Ave
 Burnham SL1 .... 197 D2
 Slough SL1 .... 205 D4
Cambridge CI
 Aylesbury HP20 .... 101 F1
 Harmondsworth UB7 ...... 213 E4
Cambridge Close Trad Est
 HP20 .... 101 F1
Cambridge Cres HP13 .. 173 F4
Cambridge Ho 2 SL4 .... 210 B3
Cambridge 7 HP20 ...... 115 E4
Cambridge Rd
 Beaconsfield HP9 .... 175 E1
 Marlow SL7 .... 183 E1
 Uxbridge UB8 .... 201 E3
Cambridge St
 Aylesbury HP20 .... 101 F1
 M Keynes, Bletchley MK2 .. 58 B4
 M Keynes, Wolverton
 MK12 .... 33 E3
Cambridge Terr HP4 ...... 135 E4
Camden MK8 .... 33 E1
Camden Ct HP19 .... 101 E1
Camden PI SL8 .... 185 D2
Camden Rd SL6 .... 195 E1
Cameron Rd HP5 .... 144 B1
Camlet Gr MK14 .... 34 B4
Camley Gdns SL6 .... 202 A4
Camm Ave SL4 .... 209 F2
Camomile CI MK7 .... 48 B3
Camomile Way UB7 ...... 208 C3
Camp Rd SL9 .... 188 B2
Campbell CI
 Buckingham MK18 .... 52 C4
 High Wycombe HP13 .... 172 C4
Campbell Dr HP9 .... 175 E3
Campbells Ride HP15 .... 163 E4
Campden Rd UB10 .... 190 C1
Camperdown SL6 .... 196 A1
Camperdown Ho 30 SL4 . 210 B3
Campion MK14 .... 21 F1
Campion CI
 Aylesbury HP20 .... 116 B4
 Denham UB9 .... 190 A1
 Uxbridge UB8 .... 208 C4
Campion Rd HP15 .... 162 C3
Campions Ct HP4 .... 135 D3
Canada Rd SL1 .... 206 A2
Canal Wharf SL3 .... 207 D2
Canalside Rdbt MK9 ...... 35 D2
Candlemas La HP9 .... 175 F1
Candlemas Mead HP9 .. 175 F1
Candlewicks MK7 .... 48 A3
Candover CI UB7 .... 213 E4
Candytuft Green HP15 .. 162 C3
Cane End HP27 .... 139 D2
Canford Ct HP21 .... 115 F3
Cannock CI SL6 .... 203 D3
Cannock Rd HP20 .... 101 F2
Cannon Court Rd
 Cookham SL6 .... 195 F3
 Maidenhead SL6 .... 195 E2
Cannon La HP10 .... 203 E1
Cannon La SL6 .... 202 A3
Cannon Mill Ave HP5 .... 154 C3
Cannon's Hill HP18 ...... 112 D3
Cannon's Orch HP22 ...... 85 D2
Cannondown Rd SL6 ...... 195 F3
Canon Harnett Ct MK11 . 32 C3
Canon Hill Dr SL6 .... 203 D2

Canon Hill Way SL6 .... 203 D1
Canon's Cloisters SL4 .... 210 B4
Canons Rd MK12 .... 33 E4
Canterbury Ave SL2 .... 198 B1
Canterbury Cl
  Amersham HP7 .... 165 F4
  Princes Risborough HP27 139 D3
Cantilupe Cl LU6 .... 92 B3
Cantle Ave MK14 .... 35 D3
Cantley Cl HP20 .... 101 F1
Cape Villas SL0 .... 207 F4
Capel Cl MK18 .... 41 F4
Capel Dr MK14 .... 34 C4
Capell Ave WD3 .... 167 E2
Capell Rd WD3 .... 167 E2
Capell Way WD3 .... 167 E2
Capitol Dr MK14 .... 34 C3
Caplan Wlk MK8 .... 33 F1
Capps La HP16 .... 143 D3
Capricorn Ho HP10 .... 185 D4
Capron MK5 .... 47 D3
Captain Cook Cl HP8 .... 177 D3
Captain's Cl HP5 .... 144 A2
Captains Wlk HP4 .... 135 E2
Caraway Cl MK7 .... 48 A2
Cardigan Cl
  Milton Keynes MK3 .... 46 C1
  Slough SL1 .... 204 C2
Cardinals Wlk SL6 .... 204 B4
Cardwell Cl MK4 .... 46 B1
Carey Cl Aylesbury HP21 .... 115 E1
  Windsor SL4 .... 210 A2
Carey Way MK46 .... 7 D2
Careys Croft HP4 .... 135 D4
Carhampton Ct MK4 .... 46 B2
Carisbrooke Ave HP12 ..... 172 A3
Carisbrooke Cl SL6 .... 202 B3
Carisbrooke Ct
  Buckingham MK18 .... 41 F1
  Slough SL1 .... 205 F3
Carisbrooke Ho **4** HP13 .. 173 F4
Carleton Gate MK15 .... 35 F4
Carlina Pl MK14 .... 34 B2
Carlisle Rd SL1 .... 205 E3
Carlton Cl
  Aylesbury HP19 .... 101 D1
  Newport Pagnell MK16 ..... 22 C2
Carlton Ct HP27 .... 139 D2
Carlton Ho TW19 .... 213 E1
Carlton Rd Slough SL2 ..... 206 A3
  Turvey MK43 .... 8 C4
Carlyle Ave HP21 .... 115 F4
Carlyle Cl MK16 .... 22 A2
Carman Ct HP23 .... 118 C2
Carmarthen Rd SL1 .... 205 F3
Carnation Way HP21 .... 115 F3
Carne The MK11 .... 32 C3
Carnot Cl MK5 .... 46 A3
Carnoustie Cl MK3 .... 57 E4
Caroline Cl UB7 .... 208 B2
Caroline Cl SL7 .... 183 F2
Caroline Haslett
  Cty Comb Sch MK5 ...... 46 A3
Carolus Creek MK15 .... 35 D4
Carpenter Ct MK14 .... 11 D1
Carpenters Wood Dr
  WD3 .... 167 D3
Carpenters Yd HP23 .... 119 D2
Carr Cl HP19 .... 101 D1
Carrick Rd MK6 .... 11 D1
Carriers Cl MK19 .... 11 D1
Carrington Ave HP10 .... 185 D4
Carrington Cl MK18 .... 77 F3
Carrington Cres HP22 ...... 117 E3
Carrington Ct **16** HP12 .. 172 C4
Carrington Cty Fst Sch The
  HP10 .... 174 A1
Carrington Cty Mid Sch The
  HP10 .... 185 D4
Carrington Hall Rd MK17 ... 68 B3
Carrington Pl
  Holmer Green HP15 .... 163 E4
  Tring HP23 .... 119 D3
Carrington Rd
  Aylesbury HP21 .... 115 E3
  High Wycombe HP12 .... 172 B3
  Newport Pagnell MK16 ..... 22 A2
  Slough SL1 .... 205 D3
Carrington Way HP16 .... 151 E3
Carroll Cl MK16 .... 22 A3
Carron Cl LU7 .... 80 B4
Carron Ct MK42 .... 58 B2
Carrs Dr HP12 .... 172 B4
Carter Cl SL4 .... 210 A3
Carter Wlk HP10 .... 174 B4
Carter's La HP4 .... 75 F1
Carteret Cl MK15 .... 35 F4
Carters Cl MK16 .... 13 F1

Carters La
  Long Crendon HP18 .... 125 D4
  Milton Keynes MK11 ...... 32 B2
  Quainton HP22 .... 85 F3
Carters Meadow MK18 ...... 76 A1
Carters Ride HP22 .... 116 A1
Cartmel Cl MK3 .... 57 E3
Cartwright Ct **9** HP13 .... 173 F3
Cartwright Pl MK6 .... 46 C4
Cartwright Rd MK11 .... 172 C3
Carvers Mews MK14 .... 34 C3
Cascadia Cl HP11 .... 174 A1
Cashmere Cl MK5 .... 46 A2
Casterton Cl MK13 .... 34 B2
Castle Ashby Rd NN7 .... 1 A4
Castle Ave Datchet SL3 .... 211 D4
  West Drayton UB7 .... 208 C3
Castle Cl
  Marsh Gibbon OX6 .... 72 A2
  Totternhoe LU6 .... 93 D4
  Wing LU7 .... 79 F2
Castle Ct
  13 Aylesbury HP20 ...... 115 E4
  Buckingham MK18 .... 52 B4
  Maidenhead SL6 .... 202 B4
Castle Dr SL6 .... 202 B4
Castle Est HP12 .... 172 B2
Castle Gate Way HP4 .... 135 E3
Castle Hill
  Berkhamsted HP4 .... 135 E3
  High Wycombe HP13 ...... 173 D4
  Maidenhead SL6 .... 202 C4
  Windsor SL4 .... 210 B3
Castle Hill Ave HP4 .... 135 E3
Castle Hill Cl HP4 .... 135 E3
Castle Hill Rd LU6 .... 93 D4
Castle Hill Terr SL6 .... 202 C4
Castle La HP22 .... 86 C3
Castle Lodge SL6 .... 202 C4
Castle Meadow CI MK16 .... 22 C2
Castle Mews
  Berkhamsted HP4 .... 135 E2
  Maidenhead SL6 .... 202 C4
Castle Park Rd HP22 .... 131 D3
Castle Pl **12** HP13 .... 173 D4
Castle Rose MK6 .... 47 E3
Castle St Aylesbury HP20 .. 115 E4
  Berkhamsted HP4 .... 135 E2
  Buckingham MK18 .... 52 B4
  High Wycombe HP13 ...... 173 D4
  Marsh Gibbon OX6 .... 72 A2
  Slough SL1 .... 205 F2
  Wingrave HP22 .... 89 D2
Castle View Gdns HP21 .... 172 B4
Castlefield Comb Sch
  HP12 .... 172 B3
Castlefields HP22 .... 116 B2
Castles Cty Fst Sch MK3 ... 57 F4
Castlesteads MK13 .... 173 E4
Castlethorpe Cty Fst Sch
  MK19 .... 19 F3
Castlethorpe Rd MK19 .... 11 D1
Castleton Ct SL7 .... 183 F1
Castleview Comb Sch SL3 .. 206 B1
Castleview Ho **11** SL4 .... 210 B3
Castleview Rd SL3 .... 206 B1
Caswell La MK17 .... 60 C4
Catchpole Cl MK12 .... 33 D3
Cater Rd HP14 .... 171 E2
Cathay Cl MK3 .... 58 A4
Catherine Cotts HP23 ...... 133 E4
Catherine Ct MK18 .... 41 F1
Catherines Cl HP27 .... 208 B2
Catkin Cl HP12 .... 172 A2
Causeway The
  Maidenhead SL6 .... 203 E2
  Marlow SL7 .... 183 F1
Cautley Cl HP22 .... 85 D3
Cavalier Cl HP4 .... 135 E2
Cavalier Rd OX9 .... 126 A1
Cavalry Cres SL4 .... 210 B2
Cavendish Cl Burnham SL6 204 A4
  Little Chalfont HP6 .... 166 A4
  Wendover HP22 .... 131 D3
Cavendish Ct
  Milton Keynes MK5 ...... 46 A4
  Stanwell SL3 .... 212 C3
Cavendish Rd HP5 .... 154 B4
Cavendish Wlk OX9 .... 126 A1
Cavenham MK6 .... 34 B4
Cavenham Gn **1** HP20 .... 101 E1
Cawardon MK13 .... 34 B4
Cawcott Dr SL4 .... 209 F3
Caxton Ct RG9 .... 191 F1
Caxton Dr UB8 .... 201 E2
Caxton Rd MK12 .... 33 D4
Ceadar Rd HP4 .... 135 F2
Cecil Rd SL0 .... 207 F4
Cecil Way SL2 .... 197 F1
Cecily Ct MK5 .... 46 A3
Cedar RG9 .... 191 E1

Cedar Ave
  Holmer Green HP15 .... 163 D3
  West Drayton UB7 .... 208 C2
Cedar Chase SL6 .... 196 B1
Cedar Cl Aylesbury HP20 ... 102 A1
  Iver Heath SL0 .... 200 B2
Cedar Ct
  High Wycombe HP13 ...... 173 D4
  Maidenhead SL6 .... 202 B4
  Marlow SL7 .... 183 F1
  6 Windsor SL4 .... 210 A3
Cedar Dr Cookham SL6 ..... 195 F4
  Marlow Bottom SL7 .... 183 E4
Cedar Gr Amersham HP7 ... 165 E4
  Chartridge HP5 .... 143 E4
Cedar Lodge Dr MK12 ...... 33 E4
Cedar Terr HP11 .... 172 C4
Cedar Way
  Berkhamsted HP4 .... 135 E2
  Slough SL3 .... 206 C1
Cedars Cl Akeley MK18 ..... 41 F4
  Chalfont St Peter SL9 .... 177 F3
Cedars Cty Comb Sch
  MK16 .... 22 C2
Cedars Cty Fst Sch The
  HP15 .... 162 C3
Cedars Dr UB10 .... 201 F2
Cedars Rd SL6 .... 203 D4
Cedars Ridge HP16 .... 153 E3
Cedars The
  Berkhamsted HP4 .... 135 F2
  Wendover HP22 .... 131 D3
Cedars Upper Sch
  & Comm Coll The LU7 .... 80 C3
Cedars Village WD3 .... 167 F3
Cedars Way
  Leighton Buzzard LU7 ..... 80 C3
  Newport Pagnell MK16 .... 22 B2
Cedars Wlk WD3 .... 167 F3
Ceely Rd HP21 .... 115 E3
Celandine Ct MK7 .... 48 A3
Celina Cl MK2 .... 58 B4
Cell Farm SL4 .... 211 D1
Cell Farm Ave SL4 .... 211 D1
Centenary Bsns Pk RG9 ... 191 F1
Centenary Way HP6 .... 154 C1
Central Ave MK43 .... 24 C1
Central Dr SL1 .... 204 C3
Central Est SL6 .... 202 C4
Central Pk Bsns Ctr HP13 173 D4
Centre Par HP27 .... 139 D3
Centre The SL2 .... 198 B3
Centre Wlk HP15 .... 163 D2
Centurion Ct MK11 .... 33 E1
Century Ave MK6 .... 46 C4
Cestreham Cres HP5 .... 144 B1
Chackmore CE Fst Sch
  MK18 .... 41 D2
Chadbone Cl HP19 .... 115 E4
Chadds La MK6 .... 47 D4
Chadwell Path HP21 .... 116 B3
Chadwick Dr MK6 .... 47 D4
Chadwick St HP13 .... 162 B1
Chaffinch HP27 .... 101 F2
Chaffron Way
  Milton Keynes MK6 ...... 47 D4
  Milton Keynes Village
  MK6, MK10, MK15 .... 35 E1
  Shenley Brook End MK6 ... 46 B3
Chairborough Rd HP12 .... 172 B3
Chalcot Pl MK8 .... 45 F4
Chalcott SL1 .... 205 F2
Chalet Cl HP4 .... 134 C2
Chalfont Ave HP6 .... 166 B4
Chalfont Cl MK13 .... 34 A3
Chalfont La
  Chorleywood WD3 .... 167 D2
  Maple Cross SL9, WD3 ... 178 B2
Chalfont & Latimer Sta
  HP6 .... 166 B4
Chalfont Park Golf Club
  HP8, HP9 .... 176 C3
Chalfont Rd
  Maple Cross SL9, WD3 .... 178 B4
  Seer Green HP9 .... 176 B3
Chalfont St Giles
  Cty Jun Sch HP8 .... 177 D4
Chalfont St Giles
  Cty Prim Sch HP8 .... 177 D4
Chalfont St Peter
  CE Mid Sch SL9 .... 177 E1
Chalfont St Peter
  Cty Fst Sch SL9 .... 177 E2
Chalfont Station Rd HP6 .. 166 B4
Chalfont Way HP12 .... 172 B2
Chalfonts Com Coll The
  SL9 .... 177 E2
Chalfonts & Gerrards Cross
  Hospl The SL9 .... 177 E1
Chalford HP10 .... 185 F3
Chalgrove Cl HP18 .... 203 D3

Chalgrove End HP22 .... 116 A1
Chalgrove Rd OX9 .... 126 A1
Chalgrove Wlk HP21 .... 115 E3
Chalk Farm Rd HP14 .... 158 B3
Chalk Hill Chesham HP5 .... 144 A1
  Coleshill HP7 .... 164 C1
Chalk La HP6 .... 153 D2
Chalk Pit La SL1 .... 197 D2
Chalkdell Dr MK5 .... 45 F2
Chalklands SL8 .... 185 D2
Chalkshire Cl HP22 .... 131 D3
Chalkshire Cotts HP17 .... 130 B2
Chalkshire Rd HP17 .... 130 B2
Challacombe MK4 .... 46 B1
Challener Rd HP12 .... 172 B2
Challow Cl SL6 .... 195 E1
Chalmers Ave MK19 .... 20 B1
Chaloner Cl HP21 .... 115 E3
Chaloner Rd HP21 .... 115 E3
Chaloners Hill MK18 .... 63 E2
Chalvey Gdns SL1 .... 205 F2
Chalvey Gr SL1 .... 205 D2
Chalvey Inf Sch SL1 .... 205 E2
Chalvey Park SL1 .... 205 F2
Chalvey Rd E SL1 .... 205 F2
Chalvey Rd W SL1 .... 205 E2
Chalwell Ridge MK5 .... 46 A2
Chamberlain Rd HP19 .... 101 D1
Champflower MK4 .... 46 B2
Chancellors HP7 .... 164 A3
Chancellors Cnr HP7 .... 164 A3
Chancery Cl MK13 .... 34 A3
Chancery Pl SL4 .... 210 B4
Chandlers Ct MK6 .... 47 E3
Chandos Cl
  Buckingham MK18 .... 52 B4
  Little Chalfont HP6 .... 155 E1
Chandos Ct SL6 .... 52 B4
Chandos Ho **16** SL1 .... 205 F2
Chandos Pl
  Milton Keynes MK2 ...... 58 A4
  Wendover HP22 .... 131 D2
Chandos Rd MK18 .... 52 B4
Channer Dr
  Tylers Green HP10 .... 163 D1
  Tylers Green HP10 .... 174 A4
Chantry Cl
  West Drayton UB7 .... 208 B3
  Windsor SL4 .... 210 A3
  Woburn Sands MK17 ...... 49 D3
Chantry Rd HP19 .... 101 E2
Chantry Sch UB7 .... 208 C3
Chantry The
  11 Aylesbury HP20 ...... 115 E4
  Uxbridge UB8 .... 201 F1
Chapel Arches SL6 .... 203 D4
Chapel Cl HP4 .... 121 E3
Chapel Crofts HP4 .... 134 C3
Chapel Dr HP22 .... 117 F3
Chapel End La HP23 .... 118 B4
Chapel Fields HP23 .... 118 B4
Chapel Hill
  Lacey Green HP27 .... 150 B2
  Soulbury LU7 .... 69 F2
  Windsor SL4 .... 210 B3
Chapel Ho HP16 .... 153 E3
Chapel La Akeley MK18 ..... 41 F4
  High Wycombe HP12 ...... 172 B4
  Ivinghoe LU6 .... 92 A1
  Long Marston HP23 .... 104 A2
  Stoke Bruerne NN12 .... 9 D4
  Stoke Mandeville HP22 .... 116 A1
  Stoke Poges SL2 .... 199 D3
  Thornborough MK18 ...... 54 A4
  Totternhoe LU6 .... 92 C4
  Turweston NN13 .... 38 A4
  Walter's Ash HP14 .... 161 E4
  Wendover HP22 .... 131 D2
  Whitfield NN13 .... 26 B4
Chapel Rd Dinton HP17 .... 128 A4
  Edlesborough LU6 .... 92 B3
  Flackwell Heath HP10 .... 185 D4
Chapel Sq LU7 .... 68 C1
Chapel St
  Berkhamsted HP4 .... 135 E2
  High Wycombe HP13 ...... 161 E2
  Marlow SL7 .... 183 F1
  Slough SL1 .... 205 F2
  Tring HP23 .... 118 C2
  Uxbridge UB8 .... 201 E2
  Woburn Sands MK17 ...... 49 D2
Chaplin Gr MK8 .... 45 E4
Chapman Ave MK14 .... 35 D3
Chapman Cl UB7 .... 208 C2
Chapman La
  Bourne End SL8 .... 185 D3
  Flackwell Heath HP10 .... 185 D3

Chapmans Cres HP5 .... 144 A2
Chappel Meadow HP23 ... 119 D3
Chapter MK6 .... 47 D1
Chapter Cl UB10 .... 201 F3
Chapter Mews SL4 .... 210 B4
Charbray Cres MK5 .... 46 A3
Chardacre MK8 .... 33 F1
Charlbury Rd UB10 .... 190 C1
Charles Cl HP21 .... 116 A1
Charles Dr OX9 .... 126 A1
Charles Gdns SL2 .... 206 A4
Charles Ho **9** SL4 .... 210 B3
Charles St
  Berkhamsted HP4 .... 135 D2
  Tring HP23 .... 119 D2
  Windsor SL4 .... 210 B3
Charles Way MK16 .... 22 B2
Charlestown Lodge UB8 ... 201 E1
Charlock Ct MK14 .... 21 F4
Charlotte Cl LU7 .... 77 F4
Charlton SL4 .... 209 E1
Charlton Cl Slough SL1 ... 205 D2
  Swanbourne MK17 .... 66 C2
Charlton Pl **2** SL4 .... 209 E1
Charlton Row **5** SL4 ..... 209 E1
Charlton So **4** SL4 .... 209 E1
Charlton Way SL4 .... 209 E1
Charlton Wlk **3** SL4 ...... 209 E1
Charmandean Sch MK18 ... 29 D2
Charmfield Rd HP21 .... 116 A1
Charnwood Cl HP13 .... 173 F3
Charsley Cl HP6 .... 166 B4
Charter Cl SL1 .... 205 F2
Charter Dr HP6 .... 154 C1
Charter Rd SL1 .... 204 C3
Chartley Ct MK5 .... 46 A2
Chartridge Cty Comb Sch
  HP16 .... 143 E2
Chartridge Development
  UB8 .... 201 D2
Chartridge Grange Dr
  HP16 .... 143 E2
Chartridge Ho **3** HP13 .. 173 F4
Chartridge La
  Chartridge HP5,HP16 ..... 143 F3
  Chesham HP5,HP16 .... 143 F3
Chartwell Gate HP9 .... 175 E3
Chartwell Rd MK16 .... 22 C2
Chase Ave MK7 .... 48 A2
Chase Cl HP7 .... 165 D2
Chase Park Rd NN7 .... 1 A4
Chase The Chesham HP5 .. 144 A2
  Marlow SL7 .... 184 A2
  Tylers Green HP10 .... 163 E3
Chaseside Cl LU7 .... 105 D4
Chatfield SL2 .... 205 D4
Chatham Ct SL1 .... 206 A2
Chatsworth MK8 .... 33 F1
Chatsworth Cl SL6 .... 202 B3
Chaucer Cl
  Berkhamsted HP4 .... 134 C1
  Newport Pagnell MK16 .... 22 A2
Chaucer Dr HP21 .... 115 F3
Chaucer Rd MK3 .... 58 A4
Chauntry Rd SL6 .... 203 D3
Chawton Cres MK8 .... 33 F1
Cheapside La UB9 .... 189 F3
Chearsley Rd HP18 .... 113 E4
Cheddington Cty Comb Sch
  LU7 .... 105 D4
Cheddington La
  Long Marston HP23 .... 104 B3
  Marsworth HP23 .... 104 B3
Cheddington Rd LU7 .... 105 E2
Cheddington Sta LU7 ...... 91 D1
Chelmsford Ct **33** SL4 .... 210 B3
Chelsea Green LU7 .... 80 B3
Cheltenham Gdns MK3 .... 57 E3
Cheney Cl LU7 .... 78 A1
Cheney Way HP20 .... 101 F1
Cheney Wlk **3** HP20 ...... 101 F1
Cheneys Wlk MK3 .... 47 D1
Chenies Ave HP6 .... 166 B3
Chenies Cty Comb Sch
  WD3 .... 156 A3
Chenies Par HP6 .... 166 B4
Chenies Rd WD3 .... 167 E4
Chepping Cl HP10 .... 163 D3
Chepstow Dr MK3 .... 57 E3
Chequers Cl LU7 .... 105 E2
Chequers Dr HP16 .... 151 E3
Chequers La Ibstone HP14 170 A3
  Lane End HP14 .... 172 A3
  North Crawley MK16 ...... 24 A2
  Pitstone LU7 .... 105 E3
  Prestwood HP16 .... 151 E4
Chequers Orch SL0 .... 207 F4
Chequers Sq UB8 .... 201 E1
Chequers St HP21 .... 115 F2

hequers The
Castlethorpe MK19 ...... 19 F3
Eaton Bray LU6 ...... 92 C3
herington Gate SL6 ...... 195 D1
heriton MK4 ...... 46 C2
herleton MK8 ...... 33 F1
herries The SL2 ...... 206 A4
herry Acre SL9 ...... 177 E3
herry Ave SL3 ...... 206 B2
herry Cl
Flackwell Heath HP10 ...... 185 D4
Prestwood HP16 ...... 151 E3
herry Dr HP9 ...... 175 D2
herry Gdns HP23 ...... 118 C2
herry Gr HP15 ...... 163 E3
West Drayton UB7 ...... 208 C1
herry La Amersham HP7 . 164 B3
herry Lane Jun & Inf Sch
UB7 ...... 208 C1
herry Leys MK18 ...... 63 F2
herry Orch
Amersham HP6 ...... 154 C2
Olney MK46 ...... 6 C2
Stoke Poges SL2 ...... 199 E3
West Drayton UB7 ...... 208 C2
herry Orchard Ct HP13 ... 173 F3
herry Rd MK16 ...... 22 A2
herry Rise
Chalfont St Giles HP8 ... 177 E4
Flackwell Heath HP10 ... 185 D4
herry St HP10 ...... 174 A2
herry The HP13 ...... 161 F1
herry Tree Ave UB8 ...... 208 C4
herry Tree Cl
Great Kingshill HP15 ... 151 E1
Hughenden Valley HP14 . 162 A4
Lacey Green HP27 ...... 150 A3
herry Tree La
Buckland Common HP23 . 133 D2
Fulmer SL3 ...... 199 F3
Heron WD3 ...... 167 E1
Lee Common HP16 ...... 146 C2
herry Tree Rd
Chinnor OX9 ...... 147 E3
Farnham Common SL2 .... 198 B3
herry Tree Way HP10 ... 163 E1
herry Tree Wlk
Chesham HP5 ...... 144 B1
Leighton Buzzard LU7 ..... 80 C4
Wendover HP22 ...... 131 D3
herry Way
Holmer Green HP15 ...... 163 D3
Horton SL3 ...... 212 B2
herrycroft Dr HP14 ...... 161 E3
herrytree La
Gerrards Cross SL9 ...... 177 E1
Iver Heath SL0 ...... 201 D2
herrywood Cl HP9 ...... 176 B3
herrywood Gdns HP10 .. 185 D4
herwell Cl
Maidenhead SL6 ...... 203 D4
Slough SL3 ...... 212 A4
herwell Ho MK3 ...... 57 F4
herwell Rd
Aylesbury HP21 ...... 115 E3
Bourne End SL8 ...... 185 D2
hesham Ave MK13 ...... 34 B2
hesham Bois CE Comb Sch
HP6 ...... 154 C2
hesham Cottage Hospl
HP5 ...... 154 B4
hesham High Sch HP5 .. 144 B1
hesham L Ctr HP5 ...... 154 B4
hesham La
Chalfont St Peter SL9 ... 177 F3
Wendover HP22 ...... 131 D3
hesham Park Com Coll
HP5 ...... 144 A1
hesham Prep Sch HP5 .. 145 D2
hesham Rd
Amersham HP6 ...... 154 B4
Berkhamsted HP4 ...... 135 D1
Bovingdon HP3 ...... 145 F2
Chartridge HP5 ...... 143 F4
Hyde Heath HP16 ...... 153 E4
Wigginton HP23 ...... 133 E4
hesham Sta HP5 ...... 154 B4
heshire CI SL1 ...... 206 A2
heslyn Gdns MK14 ...... 35 D4
hesney Wold MK6 ...... 35 E1
hess CI Latimer HP5 ...... 155 E2
Stoke Mandeville HP21 ... 115 D2
hessbury CI HP5 ...... 154 A4
hessbury Rd HP5 ...... 154 A4
hessfield Park HP6 ...... 166 C4
hessmount Rise HP5 ...... 154 B4
hester CI MK3 ...... 57 E4
hester Ho UB8 ...... 201 E1
hesterfield CI SL5 ...... 205 E4
hesterfield CI HP18 ...... 114 B3
hesterfield Cres LU7 ...... 79 F2

Chesterfield Pl HP21 ...... 115 D4
Chesterholm MK13 ...... 33 F3
Chesterton Cl HP5 ...... 144 A1
Chesterton Green HP9 .... 175 F2
Chestnut Ave
Chesham HP5 ...... 144 B1
High Wycombe HP11 ...... 173 E3
Slough SL3 ...... 206 C2
West Drayton UB8 ...... 208 B2
Chestnut Cl
Amersham HP6 ...... 154 B1
Aston Clinton HP22 ...... 117 F3
Chalfont St Peter SL9 ... 177 F1
Dagnall HP4 ...... 107 E3
Maidenhead SL6 ...... 196 A1
Medmenham SL7 ...... 193 E4
Milton Keynes MK11 ...... 32 B3
Newton Longville MK17 ... 57 E1
Princes Risborough HP27 139 E3
Waddesdon HP18 ...... 99 D3
Chestnut Cotts MK18 ...... 52 B4
Chestnut Cres
Aylesbury HP21 ...... 115 D3
Milton Keynes MK2 ...... 58 B4
Chestnut Dr
Berkhamsted HP4 ...... 135 E2
Princes Risborough HP27 139 D2
Windsor SL4 ...... 209 F2
Chestnut End HP22 ...... 117 E1
Chestnut Hill LU7 ...... 80 B4
Chestnut La
Amersham HP6 ...... 154 C1
Holmer Green HP15 ...... 163 D3
Chestnut Lane Cty Fst Sch
HP6 ...... 154 C2
Chestnut Leys MK18 ...... 63 F2
Chestnut Rd
Beaconsfield HP9 ...... 175 D1
Princes Risborough HP27 139 D2
Yardley Gobion NN12 ... 18 C3
Chestnut Rise LU7 ...... 80 B4
Chestnut View
Chearsley HP18 ...... 112 A1
East Claydon MK18 ...... 74 C4
Chestnut Way
Halton HP22 ...... 131 E4
Longwick HP27 ...... 138 C3
Stoke Mandeville HP22 ... 116 A1
Chestnut Wlk SL9 ...... 177 F2
Chestnuts The Feldon HP3 146 C4
Uxbridge UB10 ...... 201 F3
Chestwood Gr UB10 ...... 201 F3
Chettle Pl NN12 ...... 18 C1
Chetwode Ave MK10 ...... 36 A1
Chetwode Cl MK18 ...... 41 F1
Chetwynd Dr UB10 ...... 201 F2
Chevalier Gr MK18 ...... 45 E4
Cheveley Gdns SL1 ...... 197 F2
Cheviot Cl
High Wycombe HP13 ...... 161 F1
Leighton Buzzard LU7 ..... 80 B4
Maidenhead SL6 ...... 203 D3
Cheviot Rd SL3 ...... 207 D1
Cheyne Cl Amersham HP6. 154 B2
Buckingham MK18 ...... 52 C3
Gerrards Cross SL9 ...... 188 C2
Pitstone LU7 ...... 105 C2
Cheyne Wlk HP5 ...... 154 B4
Chicheley Hall MK16 ...... 23 E4
Chicheley Hill MK16 ...... 23 E4
Chicheley Rd
Chicheley MK16 ...... 23 F4
North Crawley MK16 ...... 23 F4
Chicheley St MK16 ...... 22 C2
Chievely Ct MK4 ...... 46 B1
Chilcote La HP7 ...... 166 A4
Childs Way
Milton Keynes MK10, MK9 46 A2
Shenley Brook End MK5 ... 46 A2
Chillery Leys MK15 ...... 35 F4
Chiltern Ave
Amersham HP6 ...... 154 B1
Edlesborough LU6 ...... 92 C2
High Wycombe HP12 ...... 172 B3
Stone HP17 ...... 114 B4
Chiltern Cl
Holmer Green HP15 ...... 163 E4
Princes Risborough HP27 139 D2
Stone HP17 ...... 114 B3
Chiltern Cnr HP4 ...... 135 C2
Chiltern Commerce Ctr
HP5 ...... 144 A1
Chiltern Cotts
Buckland Common HP23 .. 133 D1
Ibstone HP14 ...... 169 E4
Chiltern Ct Amersham HP6. 154 B1
Chesham HP5 ...... 144 A1
8 High Wycombe HP12 ... 172 C4

Chiltern Ct
Wendover HP22 ...... 131 D3
Windsor SL4 ...... 210 A3
Winslow MK18 ...... 65 F2
Chiltern Ct Mews SL4 ..... 210 A3
Chiltern Dr WD3 ...... 167 F1
Chiltern Gate Sch HP12 .. 172 C2
Chiltern Gn HP10 ...... 185 D4
Chiltern Hill SL9 ...... 177 F2
Chiltern Hills Rd HP9 .... 175 E1
Chiltern Hospl The HP16 . 152 B2
Chiltern Manor Park HP16 152 A4
Chiltern Par HP6 ...... 154 B1
Chiltern Park Ave HP4 ... 135 D3
Chiltern Rd Amersham HP6 154 A2
Burnham SL1 ...... 204 A4
Maidenhead SL6 ...... 203 D3
Marlow SL7 ...... 183 E1
South Heath HP16 ...... 142 C2
Wendover HP22 ...... 131 D3
Wingrave HP22 ...... 89 D2
Chiltern Ridge HP14 ...... 158 B2
Chiltern St HP21 ...... 115 F3
Chiltern View HP14 ...... 149 E1
Chiltern View Rd UB8 .... 201 E2
Chiltern Villas HP23 ...... 118 C1
Chiltern Way
Aston Clinton HP22 ...... 117 E1
Tring HP23 ...... 119 E3
Chilterns HP4 ...... 134 C3
Chilterns CI HP10 ...... 185 D4
Chilterns Park SL8 ...... 185 D3
Chilterns The HP13 ...... 173 D4
Chilton Cl HP10 ...... 163 E1
Chilton Ct SL6 ...... 204 B4
Chilton Rd Chearsley HP18 112 A1
Chesham HP5 ...... 144 B1
Long Crendon HP18 ...... 125 E4
Chilwick Rd SL2 ...... 197 F3
Chiltern Rd SL7 ...... 172 C3
Chinalls Cl MK18 ...... 50 B3
Chingle Croft MK4 ...... 46 B1
Chinnor Hill OX9 ...... 147 F2
Chinnor Rd Bledlow HP27 . 138 A1
Bledlow Ridge HP14 ...... 148 B2
Chinnor OX9 ...... 147 D2
Chippendale Cl HP11 ...... 173 F2
Chippendale Waye UB8 ... 201 E3
Chippenham Dr MK10 ...... 36 B1
Chipperfield Cl SL3 ...... 34 A4
Chipperfield Rd HP3 ...... 146 B2
Chipping Vale MK4 ...... 46 B1
Chipps Hill HP14 ...... 171 D4
Chipstead SL9 ...... 177 E1
Chislehampton MK15 ...... 35 E2
Chiswick Cl MK5 ...... 45 F2
Chiswick Lodge 2 SL7 ... 183 E1
Choke La SL6 ...... 195 D2
Cholesbury La HP23 ...... 133 D1
Chorley Rd HP14 ...... 160 C2
Chorleywood Bottom WD3 167 E2
Chorleywood Prim Sch
WD3 ...... 167 E2
Chorleywood Sta WD3 .... 167 E3
Chrislaine CI TW19 ...... 213 E1
Christ Church CE
Jun Mix Inf Sch WD3 ... 167 F3
Christ the King RC Sch
TW19 ...... 213 F1
Christchurch Ho 18 HP21 ... 115 F3
Christchurch Rd HP23 .... 118 C2
Christian Ct MK15 ...... 35 E4
Christian Sq SL4 ...... 210 B3
Christie Cl MK16 ...... 22 A3
Christine Ho 3 MK2 ...... 58 B4
Christmas La SL2 ...... 187 E1
Christopher Cl HP14 ...... 161 E4
Christopher Ho 6 SL2 ... 198 B4
Church Ave RG9 ...... 191 F1
Church Cl
Aston Clinton HP22 ...... 117 E3
Cuddington HP18 ...... 112 C2
Eton SL4 ...... 210 B4
Maidenhead SL6 ...... 202 B3
Maids Moreton MK18 ...... 41 F2
Uxbridge UB8 ...... 201 D2
West Drayton UB7 ...... 208 C2
Wicker MK19 ...... 31 D2
Church Cotts SL6 ...... 196 C1
Church Croft LU6 ...... 92 C2
Church Ct HP13 ...... 162 B1
Church Dr SL6 ...... 203 E2
Church End Adstock MK18 ... 53 F1
Bledlow HP27 ...... 138 A1
Edlesborough LU6 ...... 92 C2
Newton Longville MK17 ... 57 E1
Pottersbury NN12 ...... 18 C2
Sherington MK16 ...... 14 A1
Steeple Claydon MK18 .... 63 E3
Syresham NN13 ...... 27 E4
Wavendon MK17 ...... 48 C4

Church End Cotts WD3 ... 156 C1
Church End Farm LU6 ..... 93 D4
Church End Rd MK5 ...... 46 A2
Church Farm Cl HP22 ..... 102 A2
Church Farm Cres MK14 ... 34 C4
Church Gr
Little Chalfont HP6 ...... 166 C4
Slough SL3 ...... 206 B4
Church Green
Long Crendon HP18 ...... 125 E4
Totternhoe LU6 ...... 93 D4
Church Green Rd MK3 ..... 58 A4
Church Headland La HP22 . 87 D3
Church Hill Akeley MK18 ... 29 E1
Aspley Guise MK17 ...... 49 F3
Cheddington LU7 ...... 105 D4
Ellesborough HP17 ...... 130 A1
Milton Keynes MK8 ...... 33 F1
South Harefield UB9 ...... 190 B4
Stoner RG9 ...... 179 E4
Whaddon MK17 ...... 45 D1
Church Holt The SL2 ...... 187 E2
Church La Alderton NN12 .... 9 D1
Aston Clinton HP22 ...... 117 E2
Berkhamsted HP4 ...... 135 E2
Bledlow Ridge HP14 ...... 159 F4
Bledlow Ridge HP14 ...... 159 F4
Bovingdon HP3 ...... 146 A2
Brackley NN13 ...... 38 B1
Chearsley HP18 ...... 112 A1
Cheddington LU7 ...... 105 D4
Chinnor OX9 ...... 147 D3
Clifton Reynes MK43 ...... 7 E2
Deanshanger MK19 ...... 31 F2
Eaton Bray LU6 ...... 92 C3
Edgcott HP18 ...... 72 C1
Emberton MK46 ...... 13 F4
Gerrards Cross SL9 ...... 177 E1
Grafton Regis NN12 ...... 9 E1
Granborough MK18 ...... 75 F3
Great Horwood MK17 ...... 55 D2
Great Kimble HP17 ...... 129 F1
High Wycombe HP14 ...... 161 D1
Holmer Green HP15 ...... 162 B2
Horton-cum-S OX33 ...... 108 A3
Lacey Green HP27 ...... 149 F2
Ludgershall HP18 ...... 96 B4
Maidenhead SL6 ...... 203 E2
Marsworth HP23 ...... 104 C1
Milton Keynes MK5 ...... 46 A4
Mursley MK17 ...... 67 E3
Newport Pagnell MK16 .... 22 B4
Oving HP22 ...... 86 B4
Padbury MK18 ...... 53 E1
Pottersbury NN12 ...... 18 C2
Princes Risborough HP27 139 D2
Slough SL2 ...... 206 B4
Soulbury LU7 ...... 69 E1
South Heath HP16 ...... 152 A4
Stoke Bruerne NN12 ...... 9 F4
Stoke Goldington MK16 ... 12 A4
Stoke Poges SL2 ...... 198 C1
Thornborough MK18 ...... 54 A4
Uxbridge UB8 ...... 201 D2
Walter's Ash HP14 ...... 161 F3
Walton MK7 ...... 47 F3
Wendover HP22 ...... 131 E2
Weston Turville HP22 ..... 116 C1
Whaddon MK17 ...... 45 D1
Whitchurch HP22 ...... 87 D3
Wicker MK19 ...... 31 D2
17 Windsor SL4 ...... 210 B3
Yardley Hastings NN7 ...... 1 A4
Church Lees MK14 ...... 21 E1
Church Pas MK16 ...... 22 B2
Church Path
Maidenhead SL6 ...... 203 E2
Prestwood HP16 ...... 151 E3
Stokenchurch HP14 ...... 158 B3
Church Piece HP18 ...... 112 A1

Church Rd
South Harefield UB9 ...... 190 B4
Stoke Hammond MK17 ... 69 E4
Stokenchurch HP14 ...... 158 B3
Thame OX9 ...... 125 F1
Totternhoe LU6 ...... 93 D3
Tylers Green HP10 ...... 174 C4
Uxbridge UB8 ...... 201 E1
West Drayton UB7 ...... 208 C2
Church Row SL2 ...... 199 E4
Church Sq
High Wycombe HP11 ...... 173 D4
Leighton Buzzard LU7 ..... 80 C3
Church St
Amersham HP7 ...... 165 D4
Aspley Guise MK17 ...... 49 F3
9 Aylesbury HP20 ...... 115 E4
Bovingdon HP3 ...... 146 A2
Brill HP18 ...... 110 A4
Buckingham MK18 ...... 52 B4
Burnham SL1 ...... 197 E1
Chesham HP5 ...... 154 A4
Gawcott MK18 ...... 52 A2
Henley-on-T RG9 ...... 191 E1
High Wycombe
HP11, HP14 ...... 173 D4
Little Horwood MK17 ..... 55 F1
Maids Moreton MK18 ...... 41 F2
Marsh Gibbon OX6 ...... 72 F2
Milton Keynes, Fenny Stratford
MK2 ...... 47 F1
Milton Keynes, New Bradwell
SL3 ...... 33 F4
Milton Keynes, Stony Stratford
MK11 ...... 32 B3
Milton Keynes, Wolverton
MK12 ...... 33 E4
North Marston MK18 ...... 76 A1
Olney MK46 ...... 7 D2
Princes Risborough HP27 139 D2
Quainton HP22 ...... 85 D3
Slough, Chalvey SL1 ...... 205 F2
Slough, Upton Park SL1 ... 205 F2
South Heath HP16 ...... 152 A4
Stokenchurch HP14 ...... 158 B3
Tingewick MK18 ...... 51 D3
Twyford MK18 ...... 62 B1
15 Windsor SL4 ...... 210 B3
Wing LU7 ...... 79 F1
Wingrave HP22 ...... 89 D1
Winslow MK18 ...... 65 F2
Church Terr SL4 ...... 209 F3
Church View
Brackley NN13 ...... 38 A4
Halton HP22 ...... 117 E1
Long Marston HP23 ...... 104 A2
Newport Pagnell MK16 .... 22 B2
Slough SL1 ...... 206 A2
Steeple Claydon MK18 .... 63 F1
Church View Ct LU7 ...... 80 C3
Church Views SL6 ...... 202 C4
Church Way
East Claydon MK18 ...... 74 C4
Stone HP17 ...... 114 B3
Church Wlk
Milton Keynes MK3 ...... 57 F4
North Crawley MK16 ...... 24 A3
Weston Turville HP22 ..... 116 C1
Church Yard HP23 ...... 119 D2
Churchfield Mews SL6 ..... 206 A4
Churchfield Rd SL9 ...... 177 E1
Churchill Ave HP21 ...... 115 E3
Churchill CI HP10 ...... 185 D4
Churchill Ct 7 HP21 ...... 115 F3
Churchill Dr
Beaconsfield HP9 ...... 175 E3
Marlow SL7 ...... 183 F2
Churchill Ho UB7 ...... 208 B3
Churchill Rd SL3 ...... 206 C1
Churchmead Sch SL3 ..... 211 D4
Churchmere Wlk HP11 .... 115 E3
Churchside HP15 ...... 163 E4
Churchway HP17 ...... 127 D4
Chyne The SL9 ...... 188 C3
Cinnamon Gr MK7 ...... 48 A3
Cippenham Inf Sch SL1 ... 204 B3
Cippenham La SL1 ...... 205 D3
Cippenham Mid Sch SL1 ... 204 B3
City Rd HP14 ...... 159 E3
Clailey Ct MK11 ...... 32 C3
Claires Court Sch SL6 ..... 196 A1
Clammas Way UB8 ...... 208 B4
Clapham Pl MK13 ...... 34 B1
Clappers Meadow SL6 .... 196 B1
Clappins La HP14 ...... 161 E4
Clapton App HP10 ...... 185 E4
Clare Dr SL2 ...... 198 A4
Clare Park HP7 ...... 165 F4

Clare Rd Maidenhead SL6 ... 202 B3
Prestwood HP16 ... 151 E3
Slough SL6 ... 204 B4
Stanwell TW19 ... 213 F1
Clarefield Cl SL6 ... 195 D1
Clarefield Dr SL6 ... 195 D1
Claremont SL3 ... 212 B3
Claremont Ave MK11 ... 32 C2
Claremont Ct HP21 ... 115 F3
Claremont Gdns SL7 ... 183 F1
Claremont Rd Marlow SL7 . 183 F1
Windsor SL4 ... 210 B3
Clarence Cres SL4 ... 210 B3
Clarence Ct
Maidenhead SL6 ... 202 C4
Windsor SL4 ... 210 A3
Clarence Rd
Berkhamsted HP4 ... 135 E2
Henley-on-T RG9 ... 191 E1
Milton Keynes MK11 ... 32 C3
Windsor SL4 ... 210 A3
Clarendon Ct SL2 ... 206 A3
Clarendon Dr
Milton Keynes MK8 ... 33 F1
Thame OX9 ... 126 A1
Clarendon Rd
High Wycombe HP13 ... 173 F3
Prestwood HP16 ... 151 D3
Claridge Dr MK10 ... 36 A4
Clarke Ct HP20 ... 101 F1
Clarke Dr HP13 ... 174 A3
Clarke Rd MK1 ... 47 E2
Clarke Wlk ☑ HP20 ... 101 F1
Clarke's Spring HP23 ... 119 F3
Clarkes Dr UB8 ... 208 C4
Clarkes Field Cl HP18 ... 110 A4
Clarks Cotts HP16 ... 151 E4
Classon Cl UB7 ... 208 C2
Clauds Cl HP15 ... 163 D3
Claverton Cl HP3 ... 146 A2
Clay Acre HP5 ... 144 B1
Clay Cl HP10 ... 185 D4
Clay Hill MK8 ... 33 F1
Clay La Marlow Bottom SL7 172 A1
Wendover HP22 ... 131 E3
Clay St HP9 ... 175 E4
Claycots Cty Fst & Mid Schs
SL2 ... 198 A1
Claycots Inf & Mid Sch
SL2 ... 198 A1
Claycutters MK18 ... 66 A2
Claydon Cl HP21 ... 115 E3
Claydon Ct HP12 ... 172 C2
Claydon End SL9 ... 188 C4
Claydon House MK18 ... 74 B4
Claydon La SL9 ... 188 C4
Claydon Path HP21 ... 115 F2
Clayfield Rd HP22 ... 131 E4
Clayfields HP10 ... 163 E1
Clayhall La SL4 ... 210 C1
Clayhill
Marlow Bottom SL7 ... 172 A1
Wigginton HP23 ... 119 E4
Claymoor Park SL7 ... 172 A1
Clays The HP17 ... 127 D4
Clayton Ct SL3 ... 207 D2
Clayton Gate MK14 ... 35 D4
Clayton Way UB8 ... 201 E1
Clayton Wlk HP6 ... 166 B4
Claytons Cty Comb Sch
SL8 ... 185 D3
Claytons Meadow SL8 ... 185 D2
Clearbrook Cl HP10 ... 174 A2
Cleanes Pasture SL1 ... 197 D1
Cleavers OX9 ... 147 D3
Cleavers Ave MK14 ... 34 C2
Cleeve Cres MK3 ... 47 D1
Clegg Sq MK5 ... 46 A3
Cleland Rd SL9 ... 177 E1
Clement Pl ☑ HP23 ... 119 D2
Clementi Ave HP15 ... 163 E4
Clements Cl SL1 ... 206 A2
Clements La OX6 ... 71 F1
Clements Rd
Chorleywood WD3 ... 167 E2
Henley-on-T RG9 ... 191 E2
Clerkenwell Cotts HP17 ... 126 C3
Clerkenwell Pl MK6 ... 35 D2
Cleve Ct SL4 ... 209 F2
Clevehurst Cl SL3 ... 199 D3
Cleveland MK4 ... 34 A3
Cleveland Cl
Maidenhead SL6 ... 203 D3
Wooburn Green HP10 ... 185 F4
Cleveland Dr LU7 ... 80 B4
Cleveland Pk
Aylesbury HP20 ... 101 F2
Stanwell TW19 ... 213 F1

Cleveland Pl ☑ HP20 ... 101 F2
Cleveland Rd
Aylesbury HP20 ... 101 F2
Uxbridge UB8 ... 201 E1
Clewer Ave SL4 ... 210 A3
Clewer Ct Rd SL4 ... 210 A4
Clewer Fields SL4 ... 210 B3
Clewer Green CE Fst Sch
SL4 ... 210 A2
Clewer Hill Rd SL4 ... 209 F2
Clewer New Town SL4 ... 210 A3
Clewer Park SL4 ... 210 A4
Clifden Rd HP18 ... 123 E3
Clifford Ave MK ... 58 B4
Clifford Rd HP27 ... 139 D2
Clifford Way SL8 ... 185 D3
Clifton Cl SL6 ... 203 D2
Clifton Ct
High Wycombe HP12 ... 172 C2
Olney MK46 ... 7 D2
☑ Stanwell TW19 ... 213 F1
Clifton Gn HP19 ... 101 D1
Clifton Lawns HP6 ... 154 B2
Clifton Lodge SL4 ... 205 D3
Clifton Rd Amersham HP6 ... 154 B2
Newton Blossomville MK43 ... 7 F2
Slough SL1 ... 206 A2
Clifton Rise SL4 ... 209 E3
Cline Ct MK8 ... 45 F3
Clinkard Cl HP14 ... 171 D2
Clinton Cres HP21 ... 116 A4
Clive Ct SL1 ... 205 E2
Cliveden SL6 ... 196 C4
Cliveden Mead SL6 ... 196 C4
Cliveden Office Village
HP12 ... 172 C2
Cliveden Rd SL6 ... 196 C2
Clivemont Rd SL6 ... 202 C4
Clock Ho The MK17 ... 59 E3
Cloebury Paddock MK15 ... 35 E2
Cloister Garth HP4 ... 135 E2
Cloisters The HP13 ... 162 B1
Clonmel Way SL1 ... 197 D1
Close The Akeley MK18 ... 42 A4
Ashendon HP18 ... 97 F1
Bierton HP22 ... 102 A2
Bourne End SL8 ... 185 D3
Burnham SL1 ... 204 B3
Great Horwood MK17 ... 55 D2
Iver Heath SL0 ... 200 B1
Milton Keynes, Bradwell
MK13, MK17, MK6 ... 34 A2
Milton Keynes, The Green
MK6 ... 47 E4
Olney MK46 ... 6 A1
Ravenstone MK46 ... 5 F1
Whitchurch HP22 ... 87 D2
Closes The HP17 ... 127 D4
Cloudberry MK7 ... 48 A3
Cloutsham Cl MK4 ... 46 B2
Clover Cl MK5 ... 46 A4
Clover La HP21 ... 115 F3
Club Cotts MK17 ... 49 D2
Clyde Pl MK3 ... 46 C1
Clydesdale Pl MK14 ... 34 C2
Coach Ho The
☑ High Wycombe HP10 . 174 A2
Wooburn Green HP10 ... 185 F3
Coach Ride SL7 ... 183 E2
Coachmaker Ct MK14 ... 34 C3
Coachman's Lodge ☑ SL4 210 B3
Coat Wicks HP9 ... 176 B2
Coates La HP13 ... 162 A1
Cobb Cl SL3 ... 211 E3
Cobb Hall Rd MK17 ... 57 E2
Cobb Rd HP4 ... 134 C3
Cobbetts Mount MK18 ... 63 E1
Cobbetts Ride HP23 ... 118 C2
Cobblers Cl SL2 ... 198 A2
Cobblers Wick HP22 ... 89 D2
Cobblershill La
Prestwood HP16 ... 141 D2
Wendover HP16 ... 141 D2
Cobbs Gdn MK46 ... 6 C2
Cobden Cl UB8 ... 201 E2
Coberley Cl MK15 ... 35 D3
Cochran Cl MK8 ... 45 F4
Cochrane Ho UB8 ... 201 E2
Cock Gr HP4 ... 134 B2
Cock La HP10, HP13 ... 174 A3
Cockerill Gr MK5 ... 46 B3
Cockett Rd SL3 ... 206 C2
Cockpit Cl HP15 ... 163 F3
Cockpit Rd HP14 ... 162 B4
Coddimoor La MK17 ... 56 B4
Codmore Cross HP5 ... 144 B3
Codmore Wood Rd HP5 ... 155 E3
Coe Spur SL1 ... 205 D2
Coffee Hall Rdbt MK6 ... 47 E3
Cofferidge Cl MK11 ... 32 B3
Coftards SL2 ... 206 B4

Cogan Ct MK8 ... 45 F4
Cogdells Cl HP16 ... 143 D2
Cogdells La HP16 ... 143 D2
Coggeshall Gr MK7 ... 48 B4
Coke's Farm La HP7 ... 166 A3
Coke's La Amersham HP7 . 166 A3
Little Chalfont HP7 ... 166 A3
Cokers Ct ☑ SL8 ... 185 D2
Colborne Rd HP13 ... 173 E4
Cold Grove Cotts SL6 ... 196 C1
Cold Harbour CE Comb Sch
MK3 ... 46 C2
Coldeaton La MK4 ... 46 B2
Coldharbour Way HP21 ... 115 D3
Coldmoorholme La SL8 ... 184 C2
Coldmoreham Yd HP7 ... 165 D4
Cole Rd HP21 ... 115 E3
Colehatch Bottom HP27 ... 150 B3
Colenorton Cres SL4 ... 204 C1
Coleridge Cl
Milton Keynes MK4 ... 58 A4
Newport Pagnell MK16 ... 21 F2
Coleridge Cres SL3 ... 212 C3
Coleridge Way UB7 ... 208 C1
Coles Hill HP18 ... 111 D2
Colesbourne Dr MK15 ... 35 D3
Coleshill CE Fst Sch HP7 .. 164 C2
Coleshill La HP7 ... 164 B1
Coleshill Pl MK13 ... 34 B2
Colet Rd HP22 ... 131 E3
Coleville Rd HP21 ... 172 C3
Colgrain St MK9 ... 35 D2
Colham Ave UB7 ... 208 C3
Colham Mill Rd UB7 ... 208 B3
Colham Rd UB8 ... 201 F1
Colin Way SL1 ... 205 D2
Colinswood SL2 ... 187 D1
Colinswood Rd
Beaconsfield SL2 ... 187 D1
Farnham Common SL2 . 187 D1
Hedgerley SL2 ... 187 D1
College Ave
Maidenhead SL6 ... 202 C4
Slough SL1 ... 205 F2
College Cl OX33 ... 122 B1
College Cres Oakley HP18 . 109 F2
Windsor SL4 ... 210 B3
College Glen SL6 ... 202 B4
College Lake Wildlife Ctr
HP23 ... 119 E4
College Rd
Aston Clinton HP22 ... 117 E4
Cranfield MK43 ... 24 C1
Maidenhead SL6 ... 202 C4
Slough SL1 ... 204 C3
College Rise SL6 ... 202 B4
Colley Hill MK13 ... 34 A2
Colley Hill UB8 ... 201 E2
Colley Land WD3 ... 167 E3
Collier Cl SL6 ... 195 F1
Collings Walk HP16 ... 151 E3
Collingwood Cl HP13 ... 174 A3
Collins Ho ☑ HP11 ... 173 D4
Collins Wlk MK16 ... 22 A2
Collinswood Rd ☑ SL2 ... 198 B4
Collum Green Rd
Farnham Common SL2 .... 187 E1
Stoke Poges SL2 ... 187 E1
Collyer Rd HP14 ... 158 C2
Coln Cl SL6 ... 202 C4
Coln Trad Est SL3 ... 212 C3
Colnbrook By-Pass
Colnbrook SL3, TW6 ... 212 B4
Slough SL3 ... 212 B4
Colnbrook CE Comb Sch
SL3 ... 212 C4
Colnbrook Ct SL3 ... 212 C3
Colndale Rd SL3 ... 212 C3
Colne Mk6 ... 47 E4
Colne Ave UB7 ... 208 B2
Colne Bank SL3 ... 212 B2
Colne Orch SL0 ... 207 F3
Colne Park Cvn Site UB7 .. 208 B1
Colne Reach TW19 ... 212 C1
Colne Valley Park Visitor Ctr
UB9 ... 190 A1
Colnedale Rd UB8 ... 201 E4
Colonial Rd SL1 ... 206 A2
Colonnade SL6 ... 203 D4
Colsons Way MK46 ... 6 C3
Colston Bassett MK4 ... 46 B1
Coltman Ave HP18 ... 125 E3
Colts Holm Rd MK12 ... 33 E4
Coltsfoot Dr UB8 ... 208 C4
Coltsfoot Pl HP27 ... 150 B3
Columbia Pl MK9 ... 35 D2
Columbine Rd HP15 ... 162 C3
Colville Ct HP16 ... 152 A4
Combe Martin MK4 ... 46 B2

Combe Rise HP12 ... 172 A4
Combermere Cl SL4 ... 210 A3
Comfrey Cl MK7 ... 48 A3
Comfrey The HP20 ... 101 F2
Common Field HP23 ... 119 E3
Common Gate Rd WD3 ... 167 F2
Common La Burnham SL1 186 B1
Eton SL4 ... 205 E1
Milton Keynes, Bradwell
MK13, MK5 ... 34 A2
Milton Keynes, Loughton
MK5 ... 46 B4
Common Rd
Chorleywood WD3 ... 167 E3
Dagnall HP4 ... 107 F2
Dorney SL4 ... 204 B1
Eton SL4 ... 205 D1
Flackwell Heath HP10 ... 185 D4
Great Kingshill HP15 ... 151 E1
Slough SL3 ... 207 D1
Common Side HP13 ... 161 F2
Common St MK46 ... 5 E1
Common The
Berkhamsted HP4 ... 135 F3
Chipperfield WD4 ... 156 C4
Flackwell Heath HP10 ... 185 D4
Great Kingshill HP15 ... 151 E1
Holmer Green HP15 ... 163 E3
Common Wood SL2 ... 198 B4
Como Rd HP20 ... 116 A4
Comp Gate LU6 ... 92 C3
Comp The LU6 ... 92 C3
Compass Point HP4 ... 134 C3
Compton Ct Moulsoe MK16 . 36 B4
Slough SL1 ... 204 C4
Compton Dr SL6 ... 202 A4
Compton Rd HP22 ... 131 E3
Concorde Cl UB10 ... 201 F2
Concorde Rd SL6 ... 202 B2
Concorde Way SL1 ... 205 E2
Concourse The ☑ MK2 ... 58 B4
Concra Pk MK7 ... 49 E2
Condor Cl MK6 ... 47 F4
Conegar Ct SL1 ... 205 F3
Conegra Ct ☑ HP13 ... 173 D4
Conegra Rd HP13 ... 173 E4
Coneyeere MK46 ... 7 D2
Congreve MK6 ... 47 E3
Conifer Rise HP12 ... 172 C3
Conifers The SL6 ... 202 A4
Conigre OX9 ... 147 D3
Coningsby Cl SL6 ... 202 B2
Coningsby Ct HP13 ... 173 D4
Coningsby Rd HP13 ... 162 A1
Coniston Cres SL1 ... 204 B4
Coniston Gn HP20 ... 101 E2
Coniston Rd LU7 ... 80 B4
Coniston Way MK2 ... 58 B3
Conkers SL6 ... 203 D4
Connaught Cl SL6 ... 195 F1
Connaught Gdns HP4 ... 134 C3
Connaught Rd
Aylesbury HP20 ... 116 B4
Slough SL1 ... 206 A2
Conniburrow Bvd MK14 ... 34 C2
Conniston Cl SL7 ... 183 D1
Consort Way UB9 ... 189 F3
Constable Cl MK14 ... 34 C4
Constable Pl HP19 ... 100 C1
Constable's Croft OX6 ... 94 C4
Constantine Way HP13 ... 173 F2
Convent Rd SL4 ... 210 A3
Conway Cl Aylesbury HP21 115 F4
Loudwater HP10 ... 174 B1
Milton Keynes MK5 ... 57 F4
Conway Cres MK3 ... 57 F4
Conway Cl SL9 ... 189 D2
Conway Ho ☑ HP13 ... 173 F4
Conway Rd SL4 ... 204 B1
Cook Cl MK7 ... 48 A2
Cook's Meadow LU6 ... 92 C2
Cookfield Cl LU6 ... 93 F4
Cookham Ct HP6 ... 154 C1
Cookham Dean Bottom La
SL6 ... 195 E4
Cookham Dean CE Prim Sch
SL6 ... 195 E4
Cookham Lodge ☑ SL6 ... 202 C3
Cookham Rd SL6 ... 195 F2
Cookham Rise Cty Prim Sch
SL6 ... 195 F3
Cookham Sta SL6 ... 195 F4
Cooks Cl NN7 ... 1 A4
Cooks La MK17 ... 67 F3
Cookshall La HP14 ... 161 D1
Coombe Ave HP22 ... 131 D2
Coombe Cl HP22 ... 116 B3
Coombe Dr LU6 ... 93 F4
Coombe Gdns
Berkhamsted HP4 ... 134 C3
Hughenden Valley HP14 .. 162 A3

Coombe La HP14 ... 161 F2
Coombe Vale SL9 ... 188 C2
Cooper Rd RG9 ... 191 E3
Cooper Ridge SL9 ... 177 F1
Cooper Way SL1 ... 205 D2
Cooper's Court Rd HP14 .. 158 B3
Cooper's Yd HP20 ... 101 E2
Coopers Ct MK16 ... 22 B2
Coopers Mews MK14 ... 34 C3
Coopers Row SL0 ... 200 B3
Coots Cl MK18 ... 52 C2
Copeland Cl MK7 ... 48 B3
Copes Haven MK5 ... 46 A3
Copes Rd HP15 ... 151 F2
Copes Shroves HP15 ... 162 C2
Copmans Wick WD3 ... 167 E3
Copners Dr HP15 ... 163 E1
Copners Way HP15 ... 163 D3
Copper Beech Cl
Feldon HP1 ... 146 C4
Windsor SL4 ... 209 E2
Copperfield Cty Mid Sch
MK6 ... 47 D3
Copperfields
Beaconsfield HP9 ... 175 F3
High Wycombe HP12 ... 161 D3
Copperkins Gr HP6 ... 154 A3
Copperkins La HP6 ... 154 A4
Coppermill La WD3 ... 178 C3
Coppermill Rd Horton SL3 212 A4
Wraysbury TW19 ... 212 A4
Coppice Cl HP20 ... 102 A4
Coppice Farm Rd HP10 ... 163 E3
Coppice The
Great Kingshill HP15 ... 151 F2
High Wycombe HP12 ... 172 A3
☑ Seer Green HP9 ... 176 B3
Walter's Ash HP14 ... 161 D4
West Drayton UB7 ... 208 C4
Wigginton HP23 ... 119 E4
Coppice Way
Aylesbury HP20 ... 102 A4
Hedgerley SL2 ... 187 E3
Coppidwell Dr HP21 ... 116 A4
Coppin La MK13 ... 34 A4
Coppinger Ct UB7 ... 208 C2
Coppins Cl HP4 ... 134 C2
Coppins La SL0 ... 207 F4
Copse Cl Marlow SL7 ... 183 E1
Slough SL1 ... 204 C1
West Drayton UB7 ... 208 B1
Copse Gate MK18 ... 66 A4
Copse Hill Cl HP3 ... 146 B3
Copse La HP9 ... 176 C3
Copse The Amersham HP7 154 B4
Beaconsfield HP9 ... 175 E3
Copse Way HP5 ... 144 A4
Copse Wood SL0 ... 200 B3
Copthall Cl SL9 ... 177 F1
Copthall Cnr SL9 ... 177 F1
Copthall Ho SL6 ... 203 D4
Copthall La SL9 ... 177 F1
Copthorn Cl SL6 ... 202 A4
Copyground Cl HP12 ... 172 C4
Copyground La HP12 ... 172 C4
Coral Cl LU6 ... 92 C3
Coram Cl HP4 ... 135 E2
Corbet Ride LU7 ... 80 B4
Corbet Sq LU7 ... 80 B4
Corbett Cl MK15 ... 35 E3
Cordain Ho HP9 ... 175 E3
Cordwainer Ct MK14 ... 34 C4
Cordwallis Est SL6 ... 202 C4
Cordwallis Pk SL6 ... 195 F1
Cordwallis Rd SL6 ... 202 C4
Cordwallis St SL6 ... 202 C4
Cores End Rd SL8 ... 185 D3
Corfe Cl HP21 ... 116 A4
Corfe Cres MK3 ... 57 F4
Corfe Gdns SL1 ... 205 D3
Corfe Pl SL6 ... 202 A3
Coriander Ct MK7 ... 48 A4
Corin Cl MK2 ... 58 B4
Corin Way MK2 ... 58 B4
Corinium Ind Est HP6 ... 154 C4
Corn Hill MK8 ... 33 F1
Corn Mkt ☑ HP11 ... 173 D4
Cornbrook Rd HP21 ... 115 E3
Cornbury Cres MK15 ... 35 D3
Corncrake ☑ HP20 ... 101 F2
Cornel Cl HP15 ... 163 D4
Cornel Ho ☑ SL4 ... 210 B3
Cornelia Cl MK2 ... 58 B3
Cornerways HP27 ... 150 B3
Cornfield Cl UB8 ... 201 E4
Cornfield Cres HP4 ... 134 B4
Cornhill Cty Fst Sch MK6 ... 47 D3
Cornwall Ave SL2 ... 198 B4
Cornwall Cl Eton SL4 ... 204 C2
Maidenhead SL6 ... 195 F1
Cornwall Ct UB8 ... 201 E4

Cornwall Gr MK3 .... 46 C1
Cornwall Ho UB8 .... 201 E3
Cornwall Lodge 11 SL6 .... 202 C3
Cornwall Rd SL1 .... 201 E3
Cornwall Rd SL4 .... 211 D1
Coronation Ave SL3 .... 206 C4
Coronation Cotts MK18 .... 41 F4
Coronation Cres HP14 ...... 171 E3
Coronation Pl MK18 .... 63 E1
Coronation Rd
  Cranfield MK43 .... 25 C1
  High Wycombe HP12 ...... 172 B2
  Milton Keynes MK1 .... 32 C3
Coronation Villas HP21 .... 115 F4
Corporation St SP13 .... 173 D4
Corrigan Cl MK3 .... 58 A4
Corsham Ct MK3 .... 33 F1
Cosgrove Prim Sch MK19 .. 19 F1
Cosgrove Rd MK19 .... 32 B4
Costers Cotts SL8 .... 185 D1
Cotes Way LU7 .... 79 F2
Cotman Cl MK12 .... 33 D3
Cotswold Cl
  Maidenhead SL6 .... 203 D3
  Slough SL1 .... 205 D2
  Uxbridge UB8 .... 201 E2
Cotswold Ct 11 HP12 ...... 172 C4
Cotswold Dr LU7 .... 80 B4
Cotswold Gn HP20 .... 101 F1
Cotswold Way HP13 .... 172 C4
Cottage Farm Waye HP27 .. 150 B2
Cottage Grounds HP18 .... 114 B3
Cottage Park Rd SL2 .... 187 E1
Cottages The HP16 .... 153 D1
Cottesbrooke Cl SL3 .... 212 B3
Cottesloe Cl LU7 .... 79 F2
Cottesloe Ct MK11 .... 32 C3
Cottesloe Rd HP21 .... 115 F3
Cottesloe Sch The LU7 .... 79 F1
Cottingham Sr MK43 .... 58 A4
Cottisford Cres MK14 ...... 21 F1
Cotland Clay HP17 .... 127 D4
Coulson Ct HP16 .... 151 E3
Coulson Way SL1 .... 204 A4
Council Hos LU6 .... 92 A1
Countisbury MK4 .... 46 B1
Country Life Ho SL3 .... 211 D4
County Rd NN13 .... 38 A3
Cours La Ville Cl MK18 .... 65 F2
Court Cl Aylesbury HP21 .. 115 F4
  High Wycombe HP13 ...... 161 E1
  Maidenhead SL6 .... 203 E1
  Princes Risborough HP27 139 D2
Court Cnr MK46 .... 6 C2
Court Cres SL1 .... 205 E4
Court Dr Maidenhead SL6 . 196 B2
  Uxbridge UB10 .... 201 F2
Court Farm La SL1 .... 205 D3
Court Farm Ind Est TW19 . 213 F1
Court Garden L Complex
  SL7 .... 183 E1
Court La Burnham SL1 .... 197 E1
  Dorney SL4 .... 204 A2
  Iver SL0 .... 207 F3
Court Lawns HP10 .... 163 E1
Court Rd Cranfield MK43 .. 25 D1
  Maidenhead SL6 .... 196 B2
Court The MK17 .... 37 E2
Courteneys Lodge MK4 .... 46 C2
Courtfield Dr SL6 .... 202 B3
Courtfield Gdns UB9 .... 190 A1
Courthouse Cl MK18 .... 125 E4
Courthouse Cl MK18 .... 65 F3
Courthouse Cty Jun Sch
  SL6 .... 202 A4
Courthouse Mews MK16 ... 22 B2
Courthouse Rd SL6 .... 202 B4
Courtlands
  Leighton Buzzard LU7 .... 80 C3
  Maidenhead SL6 .... 202 C3
Courtlands Ave SL3 .... 206 B3
Courtmoor Cl HP27 .... 139 D3
Courtneidge Cl LU7 .... 78 C4
Courtyard Cl HP6 .... 154 B1
Courtyard The
  Aylesbury HP19 .... 101 E1
17 Bourne End SL8 .... 185 D2
Cousins Cl UB7 .... 208 C3
Cousins Dr HP20 .... 101 F1
Cousins Piece HP18 .... 112 A1
Coventon Rd HP19 .... 101 E1
Coverack Pl MK4 .... 57 D4
Coverdale MK13 .... 34 B3
Coverdale Way SL2 .... 197 F1
Covert Cl HP4 .... 134 B3
Covert Rd HP4 .... 134 B3
Cow La Edlesborough LU6 . 92 C2
  Gawcott MK18 .... 51 F2
  Tring HP23 .... 119 E2
Cowdray Cl MK15 .... 35 E2
Cowleaze OX9 .... 147 D3

Cowley Bsns Pk UB8 ...... 201 E1
Cowley Ct HP22 .... 102 A2
Cowley Cotts HP7 .... 164 B2
Cowley Cres UB8 .... 208 B4
Cowley Int Sch UB8 .... 208 B4
Cowley Mill Rd UB8 .... 201 D2
Cowley Mill Trad Est UB8 201 D2
Cowley Rd UB8 .... 201 E2
Cowley Rd MK46 .... 22 A2
Cowper Rd
  Berkhamsted HP4 .... 135 D2
  Chesham HP5 .... 144 A1
  Olney MK46 .... 6 C3
  Slough SL2 .... 198 A1
Cowpers Ct SP MK46 ...... 7 D3
Cowper's House Mus MK46 6 C2
Cowpers Orch MK46 ...... 6 A1
Cowslip Cl UB10 .... 201 F3
Cowslip Rd HP15 .... 162 C3
Cox Green La SL6 .... 202 B2
Cox Green Rd SL6 .... 202 B2
Cox Green Sch SL6 ...... 202 C2
Coxborrow Cl SL6 .... 195 F4
Coxfield Cl HP14 .... 158 C3
Coxwell Cl MK18 .... 41 F1
CR Bates Ind Est HP14 .. 158 C3
Crab Tree Cl
  Beaconsfield HP9 .... 175 D1
  Olney MK46 .... 6 C3
Crabs Gr HP22 .... 86 C4
Crabtree Cotts HP27 ..... 139 D1
Crabtree La MK17 .... 49 E4
Crabtree Rd HP27 .... 127 D3
Craddocks Cl MK13 ...... 34 A2
Cradley Wlk HP20 .... 101 F2
Craigleith Ct HP9 .... 175 E1
Craigmore Ave MK3 ..... 57 F4
Craigwell Ave HP7 ...... 116 B4
Cranberry Cl MK7 .... 48 A3
Cranborne Ave MK4 ..... 45 F1
Cranbourne Ave SL4 ... 209 F3
Cranbourne Cl SL1 ...... 205 E3
Cranbourne Rd SL1 .... 205 E3
Cranbrook MK17 .... 37 E3
Cranbrook Dr SL6 ...... 195 E1
Crane Way MK43 .... 25 E1
Cranes Cl MK43 .... 8 C3
Cranesbill Pl MK14 ..... 34 C2
Cranfield Con Ctr MK43 24 C1
Cranfield Rd Astwood MK16 16 A1
  Moreton MK43 .... 25 F2
  Moulsoe MK16 .... 36 C4
  Salford MK17 .... 37 E3
  Wavendon MK17 .... 49 D4
Cranfield Tech Pk MK17 .. 37 E4
Cranfield Univ MK43 ..... 25 D1
Cranfield VC Lower Sch
  MK43 .... 25 C1
Craufurd Ct SL6 .... 202 C4
Craufurd Rise SL6 ...... 202 C4
Craven The MK13 .... 34 B2
Crawley Rd Cranfield MK43 25 F3
  Woburn MK17 .... 60 C4
Crayle La HP23 .... 133 F4
Crayle St SL2 .... 198 A1
Creed St MK12 .... 33 E4
Creighton Rd HP18 ..... 83 F1
Crendon Rd HP18 ...... 112 A1
Crendon St HP13 .... 173 D3
Crenwell Cl MK5 .... 46 A2
Crescent Dale SL6 ..... 202 C2
Crescent Dr SL6 .... 202 C4
Crescent The
  Cranfield MK43 .... 24 C1
  Haversham MK19 ...... 20 C1
  High Wycombe HP13 .... 173 F4
  Maidenhead SL6 .... 202 C4
  Marsworth HP23 .... 105 F2
  Milton Keynes, Fenny Stratford
    MK2 .... 47 E1
  Milton Keynes, Giffard Park
    MK14 .... 21 F1
  Pitstone LU7 .... 105 E2
  Princes Risborough HP27 139 E2
  Slough SL3 .... 205 F2
Crescent Villas 5 SL4 .. 210 B3
Creslow Cl MK1 .... 32 C3
Cress Rd SL1 .... 205 D2
Cressex Bsns Pk HP12 .. 172 B2
Cressex Cl HP12 .... 172 B2
Cressex Sch HP12 ..... 172 B2
Cressey Ave MK5 ...... 46 A1
Cressington Pl SL8 ... 185 D2
Cresswell Rd HP5 ..... 154 B3
Cresswell Row SL7 .... 183 E1
Cresswell Way HP15 .. 163 E4
Cresswells Mead HP10 203 E1
Crest Rd HP12 .... 172 B2
Crest The HP14 .... 159 F4
Creswick Meadow HP21 116 A3

Crew Curve HP4 .... 134 C4
Cricket Field Rd UB8 .. 201 E2
Cricket Green Rdbt MK9 35 D2
Cricket Ground HP14 .. 158 B3
Cricketers Row MK14 .. 66 A2
Cricketfield Rd UB7 .... 208 B1
Cricklebeck MK13 ...... 34 A3
Crimp Hill SL4 .... 211 D1
Crisp Rd RG9 .... 191 E2
Crispin Cl HP9 .... 175 E2
Crispin Field LU7 ..... 105 E2
Crispin Rd MK13 ...... 34 A4
Crispin Way
  Farnham Common SL2 . 198 B4
  High Wycombe HP11 .. 173 D2
Criss Gr SL9 .... 177 E1
Crocketts La HP16 .... 142 B3
Crocus Dr HP21 ...... 115 D3
Croft Cl SL4 .... 211 D1
Croft Ct 11 HP21 .... 115 F4
Croft Ctyd HP17 ..... 126 C3
Croft Green LU6 ..... 93 F4
Croft Meadows LU7 .. 105 D4
Croft Rd Aylesbury HP21 115 E4
  Gerrards Cross SL9 .. 177 F1
Croft The
  Maidenhead SL6 ..... 202 B3
  Marlow SL7 .... 184 A2
Crofters Cl SL4 ..... 211 D1
Crofthill Rd SL2 .... 198 A1
Crofton Ho HP11 .... 174 A2
Crofts End MK16 .... 14 A1
Crofts La MK17 ..... 57 E2
Croftwood HP13 .... 173 F4
Cromarty Ct MK3 .. 46 C2
Cromer Cl HP4 ..... 121 F2
Cromer Rd SL4 .... 205 F4
Cromhamstone HP18 114 B3
Cromwell Ave
  Aylesbury HP19 .... 101 E1
  Newport Pagnell MK16 22 A2
  Thame OX9 .... 126 A1
Cromwell Cl HP8 ... 177 E4
Cromwell Ct MK18 . 41 F1
Cromwell Dr SL1 ... 205 D3
Cromwell Gdns SL7 183 F1
Cromwell Ho
  Chesham HP5 ...... 144 B1
  Uxbridge UB8 ...... 201 E2
Cromwell Rd
  High Wycombe HP13 173 F3
  Maidenhead SL6 ... 202 B4
  Marlow SL7 .... 183 F1
Cropredy Ct MK18 .. 41 F1
Cropwell Bishop MK4 34 B3
Crosby Cl HP9 ..... 186 C4
Crosby Ct MK8 .... 45 F3
Crosland Rd HP21 . 116 A3
Cross Cl HP13 ..... 161 E1
Cross End MK17 ... 44 C4
Cross La Beaconsfield HP9 186 C4
  Tingewick MK18 ... 51 D3
  Weston Underwood MK46 6 A1
Cross Lanes
  Bledlow HP27 ...... 138 B4
  Chalfont St Peter SL9 177 F3
Cross Lanes Cl SL9 177 F3
Cross Meadow HP5 143 F1
Cross Oak La SL4 .. 210 A3
Cross Oak Rd HP4 . 135 D2
Cross Rd
  High Wycombe HP12 172 B3
  Uxbridge UB8 ...... 201 E1
Cross St
  Newport Pagnell MK16 22 B2
  Uxbridge UB8 ...... 201 E1
Cross Tree Rd MK19 31 D2
Crossfield Cl HP4 . 134 C2
Crossfield Ho SL9 . 188 C4
Crossfield Rd HP27 139 D2
Crosshills MK11 ... 32 B2
Crosslands MK14 . 34 C4
Crossley's Hill HP14 177 E4
Crossleys HP5 .... 144 C1
Crossway HP5 .... 144 C1
Crossway The UB10 201 F2
Crossways
  Beaconsfield HP9 . 175 F1
  Berkhamsted HP4 . 134 C2
  High Wycombe HP12 172 B3
Crossways St 51 SL4 210 B3
Crosthwaite Way SL1 204 B4
Crow La MK17 ..... 49 D4
Crow Piece La SL2 197 E2
Crowborough La MK7 48 A4
Crowbrook Rd HP27 139 E3
Crown Cl SL3 ..... 212 B4
Crown Cotts Botley HP5 155 D4
  Windsor SL4 ...... 210 B3
Crown Ct HP14 ... 161 D1

Crown La Burnham SL2 .. 198 A2
  High Wycombe HP11 .. 173 D3
  Maidenhead SL6 ...... 203 D4
  Marlow SL7 .... 183 E1
  Tylers Green HP10 ... 174 C4
Crown Leys HP20 ...... 101 F1
Crown Meadow SL3 ... 212 A4
Crown Rd SL7 .... 183 E1
Crown Rose Ct 5 HP23 . 119 D2
Crown Way SL1 ...... 208 C3
Crown Wlk
  Milton Keynes MK9 .. 34 C2
  Uxbridge UB8 .... 201 E3
Crownhill Rdbt MK8 .. 45 F4
Crowther Ct MK5 ... 46 A1
Croxley CI 4 LU7 ... 80 C4
Croxley Rise SL6 ... 202 B3
Croydon Ct MK4 ... 57 D4
Cruickshank Gr MK8 45 F4
Crummock Cl SL1 .. 204 B4
Crummock Pl MK2 . 58 B3
Crutches La HP9 .. 176 C2
Cryers Hill La HP15 162 B3
Cuba Cotts SL6 .... 196 A2
Cubb Field HP21 ... 115 D4
Cublington Rd HP22 88 B3
Cuddington CE Fst Sch
  HP18 .... 112 C2
Cuddington Ct HP18 . 112 C2
Cuddington Hill HP18 112 C2
Cuddington Rd HP18 . 113 F2
Cuff La MK17 ..... 59 E1
Culbertson La MK13 . 33 F3
Culham Dr SL6 ... 195 E3
Cullen Pl MK2 .... 58 B3
Cullen's Pass SL6 . 202 C3
Culley Way SL6 ... 202 A2
Cullyn Rd HP12 .. 172 B2
Culmstock Cl MK4 46 B1
Culrain Pl MK12 .. 33 E2
Culvers Croft HP9 . 175 E2
Culvert La UB8 .. 201 D2
Culverton Hill HP27 139 D3
Culverton La HP27 139 D1
Cumberland Ave SL2 198 B1
Cumberland Cl
  Aylesbury HP21 ... 116 A4
  Little Chalfont HP6 166 A4
Cumbria Cl
  Maidenhead SL6 .. 202 B2
  Milton Keynes MK3 . 46 C1
Cumbrian Way
  High Wycombe HP13 172 C4
  Uxbridge UB8 ..... 201 E3
Curlew HP20 ..... 101 F2
Curlew Cl
  Berkhamsted HP4 . 135 E2
  High Wycombe HP11 161 E1
Curls La SL6 ...... 202 C2
Curls Rd SL6 ..... 202 B2
Curran Cl UB8 ... 201 E1
Currier Dr MK14 . 34 C3
Curriers La SL1 .. 197 E4
Curtis Cotts HP5 . 144 C4
Curtis Croft MK5 . 46 A2
Curtis Way HP4 . 135 E3
Curzon Ave
  Beaconsfield HP9 . 175 E2
  Tylers Green HP15 163 E1
Curzon CE Comb Sch HP7 164 A3
Curzon Cl HP15 .. 163 E1
Curzon Gate Ct HP14 158 C3
Curzon La HP7 ... 164 A3
Curzon Mall 15 SL1 205 F2
Cutlers Mews MK14 . 34 C3
Cuttlebrook Gdns OX9 125 F1
Cyclamen Pl HP21 115 D3
Cypress Cl SL3 ... 207 D1
Cypress Wlk HP15 . 163 D2

Dacre Rd HP21 .... 131 F4
Dadbrook HP18 ... 112 C1
Dadbrook Cl HP18 . 112 C1
Dadfield Cl HP18 .. 112 C1
Dag La MK16 ..... 12 A4
Dagmar Rd SL4 ... 210 B3
Dagnall Cres SL8 . 185 D2
Dagnall Cty Fst Sch HP4 107 E3
Dagnall Rd Eaton Bray LU6 . 93 E1
  Olney MK46 ...... 6 C2
Dair House Sch SL2 198 B2
Dairy La RG9 ..... 192 A4
Dairymeade HP27 150 B2
Daisy Cotts HP14 . 171 D2
Dale Cl HP13 ..... 174 A4
Dale Cl SL1 ...... 205 E2
Dale Side SL9 .... 188 C1
Dalesford Rd HP21 116 A2
Dalgin Pl MK9 ... 35 D2
Dalston Cl HP20 . 101 F1
Dalton Gate MK10 35 F2

Dalvina Pl MK12 ... 33 E2
Daly Way HP20 ... 116 A4
Damson Gr SL1 ... 205 E2
Dancers End La HP23 118 B1
Dandridge Cl SL3 . 206 B3
Dandridge Dr SL8 . 185 E2
Dane Cl HP27 .... 165 F3
Dane Ct HP21 .... 115 E2
Dane Rd MK1 .... 47 F1
Danes Cl SL6 .... 202 B4
Danes Gdns SL6 . 195 F3
Danesfield Comb Sch SL7 193 F4
Daneswood HP14 . 49 D1
Daniels Welch MK6 47 D3
Danstead Way MK8 45 E4
Dansteed Way MK13, MK8 34 B2
Dansteed Way MK8 45 E4
Danvers End MK23 119 E3
Darby Lodge HP13 174 A4
Darin Cl MK8 .... 45 F1
Dark La Chearsley HP18 112 A1
  Oving HP22 ..... 86 B4
  Wingrave HP22 .. 89 E1
Darley Cl HP21 .. 116 A3
Darley Gate MK14 35 D3
Darley's Cl HP18 . 83 D3
Darling's La SL6 . 194 C1
Darlington Cl HP6 154 B1
Darnel Cl MK6 ... 47 D3
Darr's La HP4 ... 134 B3
Darrell Cl SL3 ... 206 C3
Darsham Wlk HP5 154 A4
Dart Cl Aylesbury HP21 115 E3
  Newport Pagnell MK16 22 B2
  Slough SL3 ..... 212 A4
Dartmouth Ct 27 SL1 205 F2
Dartmouth Rd MK4 46 C2
Darvell Dr HP5 .. 144 A1
Darvill Rd HP18 . 114 A3
Darvill's La SL1 . 205 E2
Darvills Meadow HP15 163 E4
Darwin Rd SL3 .. 206 C2
Dashfield Gr HP15 162 C3
Dashwood Ave HP12 172 B4
Dashwood Cl SL3 206 B1
Datchet Pl SL3 .. 211 D3
Datchet Rd Datchet SL3 205 F1
  Eton SL3 .... 205 F1
  Horton SL3 ..... 211 F2
  Old Windsor SL4 211 D2
  Windsor SL4 .... 210 C3
Datchet Sta SL3 . 211 D3
Daubeney Gate MK5 45 F3
Davenies Sch HP9 175 F1
Davenport Lea MK7 48 A3
Davenport Rd HP12 172 C3
Daventry Cl SL3 . 212 C3
David Cl HP21 ... 116 A2
David Rd SL3 ... 212 C3
Davies Cl HP20 . 115 E4
Davies Ct HP12 . 172 B3
Davies Way HP10 174 A4
Davis Cl SL7 .... 183 F1
Davy Ave MK5 .. 46 B3
Dawe's Cl UB10 . 201 F2
Dawe's Rd UB10 . 201 F2
Dawes Cl HP5 .. 154 A4
Dawes East Rd SL1 197 E1
Dawes La WD3 . 156 C2
Dawes Moor Cl SL2 206 B4
Dawley Ride SL3 212 C3
Dawn Redwood Cl SL3 212 A3
Daws Hill La HP11 173 D2
Daws Lea HP11 . 173 D2
Dawson Cl SL4 . 210 A3
Dawson Rd MK1 47 E2
Daylesford Ct MK15 35 D3
de Clare Ct MK18 41 F1
De Havilland Way TW19 213 F1
De Montfort Univ MK7 48 A4
Deacon Cl HP22 172 A2
Deacon Cl SL4 . 209 E3
Deacon St SL4 . 183 E1
Deadhearn La HP8 166 C1
Deal Ave SL1 .. 204 C4
Dean Cl Aylesbury HP21 116 A2
  High Wycombe HP12 172 C3
  Uxbridge UB10 . 201 F4
  Windsor SL4 .... 209 E2
Dean Farm La LU7 .. 69 F2
Dean Field HP21 146 A2
Dean La SL6 .... 195 E4
Dean Rd LU7 ... 68 A1
Dean St SL7 .... 183 E1
Dean The HP22 89 D2
Dean Way
  Aston Clinton HP22 117 F2
  Chalfont St Giles HP8 177 D4
  Holmer Green HP15 163 D3
Dean Wood Rd HP9 176 B1

Dean's Cloisters SL4 ...... 210 B4
Dean's Rd MK12 .... 33 E4
Deanacre Cl SL9 .... 177 F2
Deancroft Rd SL9 .... 177 F2
Deanfield HP14 .... 160 A4
Deanfield Ave RG9 .... 191 E1
Deanfield Cl
　Bledlow Ridge HP14 ...... 149 E1
　Marlow SL7 .... 183 E2
Deanfield Rd RG9 .... 191 E1
Deangarden Rise HP11 .... 173 F2
Deans Cl Amersham HP6 .. 154 C1
　Stoke Poges SL2 .... 199 D2
　Tring HP23 .... 119 D2
Deans Furlong HP23 .... 119 D2
Deans Meadow HP4 .... 107 E3
Deanshanger Prim Sch
MK19 .... 31 F2
Deanshanger Rd
　Old Stratford MK19 .... 32 A3
　Wicker MK19 .... 31 D2
Deansway HP5 .... 144 A1
Dearing Cl **12** HP20 ...... 101 F1
Deben Cl MK16 .... 22 C2
Decies Way SL2 .... 199 D2
Dedmere Cl SL7 .... 183 F1
Dedmere Rd SL7 .... 183 F1
Dedmere Rise SL7 .... 183 F1
Dedworth Dr SL4 .... 209 F3
Dedworth Green Fst Sch
SL4 .... 209 F3
Dedworth Manor SL4 ...... 209 F3
Dedworth Mid Sch SL4 .... 209 F3
Dedworth Rd SL4 .... 209 E3
Deeds Gr HP12 .... 172 C3
Deena Cl SL1 .... 204 C3
Deep Acres HP6 .... 154 A2
Deep Field SL3 .... 211 D4
Deep Mill La HP16 .... 152 B2
Deepdale MK13 .... 34 B3
Deer Park Wlk HP5 .... 144 C2
Deer Wlk MK9 .... 34 C2
Deerfern Cl MK14 .... 21 F1
Deerfield Cl MK18 .... 52 C4
Deermead HP16 .... 152 A2
Deerswood La SL6 .... 196 A1
Deethe Cl MK17 .... 49 D3
Delafield Cl HP14 .... 158 C2
Delaford Cl SL0 .... 207 F4
Delahay Rise HP4 .... 135 D3
Delamere Cl HP20 .... 101 F1
Delamere Gdns LU7 .... 80 B4
Delaware Dr MK15 .... 35 D4
Delius Cl MK7 .... 48 B2
Dell Cl SL2 .... 198 B4
Dell Field HP16 .... 151 E3
Dell Lees HP9 .... 176 B2
Dell Rd Berkhamsted HP4 . 134 B4
　West Drayton UB7 .... 208 C2
Dell The Aylesbury HP20 .. 102 A1
　Chalfont St Peter SL9 .... 177 F2
　Maidenhead SL6 .... 202 A1
　Tylers Green HP10 .... 163 E1
　Uxbridge UB8 .... 201 E3
Dellfield HP5 .... 144 A1
Dellfield Ave HP4 .... 135 D3
Dellfield Cl HP4 .... 135 D3
Dellfield Cres UB8 .... 201 E1
Dellfield Par UB8 .... 201 E1
Dells MK46 .... 6 C2
Dellside UB9 .... 190 B3
Delmeade Rd HP5 .... 154 A4
Deltic Ave MK13 .... 34 A1
Demoram Cl MK18 .... 65 F2
Denbigh East Ind Est MK1 .. 47 E1
Denbigh Hall MK1 .... 46 C2
Denbigh Hall Dr MK3 ...... 46 C2
Denbigh Rd
　Milton Keynes MK1 .... 47 D1
　Thame OX9 .... 126 A1
Denbigh Sch MK5 .... 46 A3
Denbigh Way MK2 .... 47 E1
Denbigh West Ind Est MK1 . 47 D1
Denborough Cres SL6 ..... 202 B3
Denby Walk HP20 .... 116 A4
Denchworth Ct MK4 .... 46 B1
Dene Cl Winslow MK18 .... 66 A2
　Woburn Sands MK17 ..... 49 E2
Dene The MK18 .... 63 E2
Denewood HP13 .... 173 F4
Denham Ave UB9 .... 189 F2
Denham Cl Denham UB9 .. 190 A1
　Maidenhead SL6 .... 202 B3
　Milton Keynes MK13 ..... 57 E4
Denham Ctry Pk UB9 ...... 190 A1
Denham Ctry Pk Vstr Ctr ∗ UB9 .. 189 F1
Denham Golf Club Sta
UB9 .... 189 E2

Denham Green Cl UB9 ..... 190 A2
Denham Green La UB9 .... 189 F3
Denham La SL9 .... 178 A1
Denham Lodge UB9 .... 201 E3
Denham Lodge Dr UB9 .... 190 A1
Denham Rd
　Iver Heath SL0 .... 200 C3
　Lane End HP14 .... 171 E3
Denham Sta UB9 .... 190 A2
Denham View MK18 .... 75 F3
Denham Way
　Denham SL1 .... 190 A1
　Maple Cross WD3 .... 178 C2
Denham Wlk SL9 .... 177 F2
Denison Ct MK7 .... 48 B3
Denmark St
　High Wycombe HP11 ..... 173 D4
　Maidenhead SL6 .... 202 C4
　Milton Keynes MK2 .... 58 C4
Denmead MK8 .... 33 F1
Denmead Cl SL3 .... 188 C2
Dennis Cl
　Aston Clinton HP22 ...... 117 F2
　Drayton Beauchamp HP23 118 A2
Dennis Way SL1 .... 204 B3
Denny Rd SL3 .... 206 C1
Denny's La HP4 .... 134 C1
Depot Rd SL6 .... 203 D3
Derby Rd UB8 .... 201 E2
Dere Pl MK2 .... 58 C2
Derehams Ave HP10 .... 174 B2
Derehams La HP10 .... 174 B2
Derek Rd SL6 .... 203 E4
Deri Dene Cl TW19 .... 211 E3
Derwent Cl
　Little Chalfont HP6 ...... 166 A4
　Newport Pagnell MK16 .. 22 B2
Derwent Dr Burnham SL1 . 204 B4
　Maidenhead SL6 .... 202 B4
　Milton Keynes MK3 ...... 57 F4
Derwent Rd LU7 .... 80 A4
Desborough Ave HP11 .... 172 C3
Desborough Gn HP20 ...... 101 E1
Desborough Ho **19** HP13 . 173 D4
Desborough Ind Pk HP12 . 172 C4
Desborough Park Rd HP12 172 C4
Desborough Rd HP11 ...... 172 C4
Desborough Sch SL6 ...... 202 C3
Desborough St HP11 ...... 172 C4
Deseronto Wharf (Ind Est)
SL3 .... 206 C2
Develin Cl MK14 .... 34 C4
Devereux Pl HP19 .... 101 D1
Devereux Rd SL4 .... 210 B3
Deverill Rd HP21 .... 115 E2
Devon Ave SL1 .... 205 E4
Devon Cl MK3 .... 46 C1
Devon Rd HP19 .... 101 D2
Devon Way UB10 .... 201 F2
Devonshire Ave HP6 ...... 154 A1
Devonshire Cl
　Amersham HP6 .... 154 B1
　Farnham Common SL2 .. 198 A2
Devonshire Gn SL2 .... 198 A2
Devonshire Lodge **10** SL6 . 202 C3
Dexter Ave MK6 .... 46 C4
Dexter Ho MK6 .... 46 C4
Dhoon Rise SL6 .... 202 C3
Diamond Rd SL1 .... 206 A2
Diana Cl SL3 .... 206 C4
Diane Cl HP21 .... 116 A2
Diane Wlk HP21 .... 116 A2
Dickens Cl MK43 .... 3 F3
Dickens Dr MK13 .... 32 A3
Dickens Rd MK12 .... 33 E4
Dickens Way HP19 .... 100 C1
Dicks Way HP19 .... 100 C2
Diddington Cl MK2 .... 58 B2
Dilwyn Ct **4** HP12 .... 172 C4
Dingle Dell LU7 .... 70 C1
Dinglederry MK46 .... 6 C2
Dinmore HP3 .... 145 F2
Dinton CE Fst Sch HP17 .. 113 F2
Disraeli Cres HP13 .... 161 F1
Disraeli Ct SL3 .... 212 A4
Disraeli Park HP9 .... 175 E2
Ditchingham Cl HP21 ..... 115 D4
Ditton Park Rd SL3 .... 211 F4
Ditton Rd Datchet SL3 .... 211 E3
　Slough SL3 .... 206 B1
Divine Mercy Coll RG9 ... 191 F3
Dixie Cl HP20 .... 102 B1
Dixie La MK7 .... 48 B3
Dobbins La HP22 .... 131 D3
Dobson's La RG9 .... 191 F4
Doctors' Common Rd
HP4 .... 135 D2
Dodds La HP8 .... 177 D4
Dodkin MK6 .... 47 D3
Dodman Gn MK4 .... 57 D4
Dodsfield Rd SL2 .... 198 A1

Dog Kennel La WD3 .... 167 F3
Doggett St LU7 .... 80 C4
Doggetts Farm Rd SL9 .... 188 A3
Doggetts Wood Cl HP8 ... 166 B3
Doggetts Wood La HP8 ... 166 B3
Dolben Cl MK15 .... 35 E4
Dolesden La RG9 .... 169 E1
Dollicot HP17 .... 126 C4
Dolphin Ct
　High Wycombe HP11 ..... 174 A2
　Slough SL1 .... 206 A2
Dolphin Pl HP21 .... 115 F3
Dolphin Rd SL1 .... 206 A2
Dolphin Sq **3** HP23 ...... 119 D2
Don The MK3 .... 46 B1
Donnay Cl SL9 .... 188 B3
Donnington MK13 .... 34 A3
Donnington Gdns SL6 ..... 195 F1
Donnybrook Ho **3** HP13 . 173 E4
Doon Way MK2 .... 58 B3
Dorchester Ave MK3 .... 47 D1
Dorchester Cl
　Maidenhead SL6 .... 195 D1
　Stoke Mandeville HP22 .. 116 A1
Dorchester Ho SL9 .... 188 C3
Doreen Cl MK2 .... 58 B4
Dorking Pl MK5 .... 46 A2
Dormans Cl MK10 .... 36 A1
Dormer Ave LU7 .... 79 F2
Dormer Cl HP21 .... 115 D3
Dormer Ct **4** HP20 .... 101 F1
Dormer La HP15 .... 163 D4
Dornels SL2 .... 206 B4
Dorney Cl SL4 .... 204 A2
Dorney Cty Comb Sch
SL4 .... 203 F2
Dorney End HP5 .... 144 A1
Dorney Hill S HP9 .... 187 D2
Dorney Pl MK13 .... 34 B2
Dorney Reach Rd SL4 ..... 203 F2
Dorney Wood Rd SL1 ..... 197 E3
Dorrells Rd HP27 .... 138 B3
Dorrien's Croft HP4 .... 134 C4
Dorset Cl
　Berkhamsted HP4 .... 134 C3
　Milton Keynes MK3 .... 46 C1
Dorset Lodge **9** SL6 ..... 202 C3
Dorset Pl HP21 .... 116 B3
Dorset Rd SL4 .... 210 B3
Dorset Way UB10 .... 201 F2
Dorton Cl MK8 .... 33 F1
Dorton Rd HP18 .... 111 D2
Douglas Ct SL7 .... 184 A2
Douglas Gdns HP4 .... 135 D3
Douglas La TW19 .... 211 F1
Douglas Pl MK6 .... 46 C4
Douglas Rd
　Aylesbury HP20 .... 102 A1
　Slough SL2 .... 205 E4
　Stanwell TW19 .... 213 E1
Doune Ho MK3 .... 46 C1
Dove Ave HP20 .... 101 F2
Dove Cl Aylesbury HP21 .. 115 E3
　Buckingham MK18 .... 52 C4
　Newport Pagnell MK16 .. 22 B2
Dove Ct HP9 .... 175 E2
Dove Ho HP20 .... 101 F2
Dove House Cl
　Edlesborough LU6 .... 92 C2
　Winslow MK18 .... 65 F2
Dove House Cres SL2 ..... 197 F1
Dove Pk WD3 .... 167 D2
Dove St LU7 .... 78 C4
Dovecot Rd HP13 .... 173 D4
Dovecote
　Haddenham HP17 .... 126 C3
　Newport Pagnell MK16 .. 22 B2
Dovecote Cl
　Haddenham HP17 .... 126 C3
　Princes Risborough HP27 139 E3
Dovehouse Cl MK19 .... 31 F2
Dovehouse Rd **3** HP13 .. 173 D4
Doveleat OX9 .... 147 E4
Dover Gate MK3 .... 57 F4
Dover Hedge HP21 .... 116 B4
Dover Rd SL1 .... 204 C4
Dowding Rd UB10 .... 201 F3
Dowler Ct HP9 .... 175 E3
Dower Park SL4 .... 209 F2
Down Pl SL4 .... 209 D4
Downdean MK6 .... 47 D4
Downer Cl MK18 .... 52 C4
Downham Rd MK17 .... 49 E2
Downing Path SL2 .... 197 F1
Downings Wood WD3 ..... 178 B3
Downland MK8 .... 33 F1
Downley Ave MK13 .... 34 B2
Downley Cl HP13 .... 161 E1
Downley Cty Mid Sch
HP13 .... 161 E2
Downley Rd HP14 .... 161 E3

Downs Barn Cty Fst Sch
MK14 .... 34 C3
Downs Park HP13 .... 161 F1
Downs Rd SL3 .... 206 B2
Downs View MK17 .... 48 B1
Dr Challoner's Gram
Sch (Boys) HP6 .... 154 B1
Dr Challoner's High
Sch (Girls) HP7 .... 166 A4
Dragon Tail HP17 .... 127 D3
Drake Ave SL3 .... 206 B1
Drake's Rd HP7 .... 165 F4
Drakeloe Cl MK17 .... 60 C4
Drakes Mews MK8 .... 45 F3
Drakewell Rd MK17 .... 48 B1
Drayton Cl UB7 .... 208 C1
Drayton Gdns UB7 .... 208 C2
Drayton Park Comb Sch
MK2 .... 58 B3
Drayton Parslow Cty Fst Sch
MK17 .... 68 B3
Drayton Rd
　Aylesbury HP20 .... 101 E1
　Milton Keynes MK2, MK3 .. 58 B3
　Newton Longville MK17 .. 57 E1
Dresser Rd HP16 .... 151 E3
Drew Meadow SL2 .... 198 B4
Drews Park HP9 .... 175 E3
Drey The SL9 .... 177 F3
Drift Rd SL4 .... 209 D1
Drift Way SL3 .... 212 B4
Drive The Amersham HP7 . 154 B1
　Bourne End SL8 .... 184 C2
　Chalfont St Peter SL9 ... 177 F2
　Cranfield MK43 .... 24 B1
Dromenagh Sch SL0 ...... 200 C3
Dropmore Cty Fst Sch
SL1 .... 186 B1
Dropmore Rd SL1 .... 197 E3
Drovers Croft MK12 ...... 33 D2
Drovers La RG9 .... 169 D1
Drovers Way Dunstable LU6 93 F4
　Newton Longville MK17 .. 57 E1
　Seer Green HP9 .... 176 B2
Druids Wlk OX9 .... 147 E3
Drummond Ho **4** SL4 ... 210 B2
Drummond Ride HP23 .... 119 D3
Drummond Way MK15 ... 35 E4
Drydell La HP5 .... 153 F4
Dryden Cl
　6 Aylesbury HP20 ..... 101 F1
　Newport Pagnell MK16 .. 22 B2
Du Pre Wlk HP10 .... 185 E2
Duchess Gr MK7 .... 48 B4
Duck End MK17 .... 59 E1
Duck La Ludgershall HP18 .. 96 B4
　Woburn MK17 .... 60 C4
Duckmore La HP23 .... 118 C1
Dudley Cl MK18 .... 76 A1
Dudley Ct SL1 .... 206 A2
Dudley Hill MK5 .... 46 A3
Dudley La RG9 .... 181 D3
Dudswell La HP4 .... 134 B4
Duffield La SL2 .... 198 C3
Duffield Park SL2 .... 199 D1
Duke St Aspley Guise MK17 .49 E2
　Eton SL4 .... 210 B4
　Henley-on-T RG9 .... 191 F1
　High Wycombe HP13 .... 173 E3
　Princes Risborough HP27 139 D2
Dukes Cl
　Gerrards Cross SL9 ...... 188 B2
　Shabbington HP18 .... 124 B3
Dukes Dr MK2 .... 47 E1
Dukes La SL9 .... 188 C2
Dukes Piece MK18 .... 52 C4
Dukes Pl SL7 .... 183 E1
Dukes Ride
　Gerrards Cross SL9 ...... 188 C2
　Ickenham UB10 .... 201 F4
　Leighton Buzzard LU7 .. 70 C2
Dukes Valley SL3 .... 188 A1
Dukes Way HP4 .... 135 D3
Dukes Wood Ave SL9 .... 188 C2
Dukes Wood Dr SL9 ...... 188 B2
Dulverton Ct LU7 .... 80 B4
Dulverton Dr MK4 .... 46 B2
Dulwich Cl MK16 .... 22 B1
Dumfries Cl MK3 .... 46 C2
Dunbar Cl
　Milton Keynes MK3 ...... 57 E4
　Slough SL2 .... 206 A3
Dunbar Dr OX9 .... 126 A1

Duncan Gr MK5 .... 45 F3
Duncan Rd MK43 .... 24 C1
Duncannon Cres SL4 ..... 209 E2
Dunchurch Dale MK7 ..... 48 A3
Duncombe Cl HP6 .... 154 C1
Duncombe Rd HP4 .... 134 C3
Duncombe St MK2 .... 58 B4
Duncroft SL4 .... 209 F2
Dundale Jun Mix Inf Sch
HP23 .... 119 D3
Dundale Rd HP23 .... 119 D2
Dundee Rd SL1 .... 205 D4
Dungrovehill La SL6 ...... 194 B2
Dunholme End SL6 .... 202 B2
Dunkeld Ho **11** HP10 ... 174 A2
Dunkery Beacon MK4 .... 46 B2
Dunny La WD4 .... 156 C4
Dunsby Rd MK6 .... 47 D2
Dunsham La HP20 .... 101 F1
Dunsley Pl HP23 .... 119 D2
Dunsmore Ave HP27 ...... 139 E3
Dunsmore Ride HP27 .... 139 E3
Dunstable Ho **11** SL7 ... 183 F1
Dunstable Rd Dagnall HP4 . 107 E4
　Eaton Bray LU6 .... 93 D3
　Totternhoe LU6 .... 93 E4
Dunster CH MK4 .... 46 C2
Dunster Gdns SL1 .... 205 D3
Dunston Hill HP23 .... 119 D2
Dunton Rd LU7 .... 78 B3
Dunvedin Pl MK12 .... 33 E2
Dunvegan Cl MK2 .... 58 B2
Dunwood Cl SL6 .... 202 B3
Dunwood Rise HP13 ..... 162 A1
Duparc Cl MK7 .... 48 B3
Dupre Cres HP9 .... 176 A1
Durgate MK7 .... 48 A4
Durham Ave SL1 .... 205 D4
Durley Hollow HP13 ...... 162 A1
Durrans Ct MK2 .... 47 F1
Durrans Ho MK2 .... 47 F1
Durrants La HP4 .... 134 C3
Durrants Path HP5 .... 144 A2
Durrants Rd HP4 .... 134 C3
Durrell Cl LU7 .... 80 C4
Dutch Barn Cl TW19 ..... 213 E1
Dutton Way SL0 .... 207 F4
Dyers Mews MK14 .... 34 C3
Dyers Rd LU6 .... 92 B4
Dyersdale MK13 .... 34 B3
Dyson Cl SL4 .... 210 A2

Eagle Wlk MK9 .... 34 C2
Eagles Rd HP20 .... 116 A4
Eames Cl HP20 .... 101 F2
Earl Cl HP13 .... 162 A1
Earl Howe Rd HP15 ...... 163 E3
Earls Cl MK2 .... 58 B4
Earls Ct SL1 .... 204 C1
Earls Willow MK13 .... 34 A4
Earlsfield SL3 .... 203 E1
Earlswood Ct HP21 .... 116 A3
Easington La HP18 .... 111 D3
East Berkshire Coll
　Maidenhead SL6 .... 202 B1
　Slough SL3 .... 207 D2
　Windsor SL4 .... 210 B1
　Windsor, Clewer Green
　SL4 .... 209 F2
East Burnham Cotts SL2 . 198 A1
East Burnham La SL2 .... 198 A1
East Chapel MK4 .... 57 D4
East Claydon Cty Fst Sch
MK18 .... 74 C1
East Common SL9 .... 188 C2
East Cres SL4 .... 209 F4
East Dales MK13 .... 34 B3
East Dr
　High Wycombe HP13 .... 173 F4
　Stoke Poges SL2 .... 198 C1
East Hills MK43 .... 25 D1
East La MK7 .... 47 F4
East Paddock SL6 .... 194 C2
East Rd Cranfield MK43 .. 24 B1
　Maidenhead SL6 .... 202 C2
　West Drayton UB7 .... 208 C2
East Ridge SL8 .... 185 D2
East Spur MK1 .... 47 F1
East St Adstock MK18 .... 53 F4
　Chesham HP5 .... 154 A4
　Olney MK46 .... 6 C1
East Way HP9 .... 175 D4
Eastbourne Rd SL1 .... 205 D3
Eastbridge SL2 .... 206 A1
Eastbrook Cl OX6 .... 95 F1
Eastbury Ct MK4 .... 46 B1
Eastcote Rd HP21 .... 116 A3
Eastcroft SL2 .... 198 A4
Eastergate HP9 .... 175 E3
Eastern Dene HP15 .... 163 D4
Eastern Dr SL8 .... 185 D3

astern St HP20 .... 101 F1
astfield CI SL1 .... 206 A2
astfield Cres NN12 .... 18 C3
astfield Dr MK19 .... 11 D2
astfield Rd
  Aylesbury HP20 .... 116 A4
  Burnham SL1 .... 204 A4
  Princes Risborough HP27 .... 139 E2
astlands HP27 .... 149 F3
astnor HP3 .... 146 A2
aston St HP11 .... 173 D3
aston Terr HP13 .... 173 E3
astwick Cres WD3 .... 178 C4
astwood CI ▪ SL7 .... 183 F2
astwood Rd HP14 .... 158 C2
aton Ave
  High Wycombe HP12 .... 172 B4
  Milton Keynes MK7 .... 58 B4
aton Bray Lower Sch LU6 . 92 C3
aton Bray Rd
  Edlesborough LU6 .... 92 B3
  Totternhoe LU6 .... 92 C4
aton Mill Cty Comb Sch
  MK2 .... 58 B4
aton Park LU6 .... 92 C3
aton Pl ▪ HP12 .... 172 B4
aton Rd HP21 .... 115 E4
atongate CI LU6 .... 92 C3
eble CI HP21 .... 115 E2
ebenezer Ho HP10 .... 174 B1
bsworth CI SL6 .... 196 B2
iddington Ct MK4 .... 46 B1
iddy St HP4 .... 135 D3
den CI Slough SL3 .... 207 D1
  Stoke Mandeville HP21 .... 115 E2
den Wlk MK3 .... 46 C1
dgar Rd UB7 .... 208 C3
dge Hill Ct MK18 .... 41 F1
dgecombe Rd HP21 .... 116 A3
dgecote MK8 .... 46 A4
dgecote Ho ▪ HP13 .... 173 E2
dgecott Rd HP18 .... 82 C4
dghill OX9 .... 125 F1
dgewood HP11 .... 173 E3
dinburgh Ave SL1 .... 205 D4
dinburgh Dr UB9 .... 189 F3
dinburgh Ho MK3 .... 57 E4
dinburgh Pl HP21 .... 115 E3
dinburgh Rd
  Maidenhead SL6 .... 195 F1
  Marlow SL7 .... 183 F2
dison Sq MK5 .... 46 B3
dith Bell Ho SL9 .... 177 F2
dith Rd SL6 .... 202 A4
dlesborough Cty Comb Sch
  LU6 .... 92 C2
dlyn CI HP4 .... 134 C3
dmonds CI MK18 .... 41 F1
dmonds Rd HP14 .... 171 D2
dmonds Sh Ctr HP14 .... 171 D2
dmund Ct MK5 .... 45 F4
dmunds CI HP12 .... 172 B3
dmunds Gdns HP21 .... 172 B3
dmunds Way SL2 .... 206 A4
drich Ave MK6 .... 46 C4
dward CI HP21 .... 116 A2
dward Wlk HP21 .... 116 A2
dwards CS SL1 .... 205 F2
dwin CI MK17 .... 48 B1
dy Ct MK5 .... 34 A1
elbrook Ave MK13 .... 34 B3
eles CI HP19 .... 100 C2
gerton CI NN13 .... 38 A4
gerton Gate MK5 .... 46 A4
gerton Rd
  Berkhamsted HP4 .... 135 D3
  Slough SL2 .... 197 F1
gerton-Rothesay Lower Sch
  HP4 .... 135 D2
gerton-Rothesay Mid &
  Upper Sch HP4 .... 134 C2
ghams CI HP9 .... 175 E2
ghams Ct ▪ SL8 .... 185 D2
ghams Wood Rd HP9 .... 175 E2
gmont Ave MK11 .... 32 C3
aremont Gdns SL1 .... 205 D3
ypt La SL2 .... 187 D1
yyp Wood Cotts SL2 ... 187 D1
der CI MK18 .... 52 C4
ght Acres Burnham SL1 . 197 D1
ring HP23 .... 119 D2
angeni Cty Mid Sch
  HP6 .... 154 C2
bow Meadow SL3 .... 212 C1
der CI Loudwater HP10 ... 174 A2
  West Drayton UB7 .... 208 C3
der Gate Milton Keynes,
  Rooksley MK9 .... 34 B1
  Milton Keynes, Winterhill
  MK9 .... 46 B4
der Way HP15 .... 163 D2

Elderdene OX9 .... 147 E4
Elderfield Rd SL2 .... 198 C3
Eldridge La HP17 .... 130 B2
Eleanor CI MK17 .... 60 C4
Eleanor Gdns HP21 .... 115 F3
Eleanor Rd SL9 .... 177 E1
Eleanor Wlk MK17 .... 60 C4
Elfords MK6 .... 47 D3
Elgar Gr MK7 .... 48 B2
Elgin Ho SL3 .... 212 C3
Elgiva La HP5 .... 154 A4
Elham Way HP21 .... 116 B2
Eliot CI Aylesbury HP19 ... 100 C1
  Newport Pagnell MK16 .... 21 F3
Elizabeth CI
  Aylesbury HP21 .... 116 A2
  Cookham SL6 .... 195 F4
Elizabeth Ct
  ▪ High Wycombe HP13 .. 173 E3
  ▪ Slough,
  Wycombe Marsh HP13 .. 173 F3
  Slough SL1 .... 206 A2
Elizabeth Dr HP23 .... 119 D3
Elizabeth Rd Marlow SL7 . 183 F2
  Stokenchurch HP14 .... 158 C2
Elizabeth Way SL2 .... 198 C2
Elkins Rd SL2 .... 187 F1
Ellen Pl HP21 .... 115 E3
Ellen Rd HP21 .... 115 E3
Ellen Wlk HP21 .... 115 D3
Ellenstow MK13 .... 34 A2
Ellerburn Pl MK4 .... 46 B1
Ellery Rise RG9 .... 170 C1
Ellesborough Rd
  Ellesborough HP17 .... 130 A1
  Great Kimble HP17 .... 129 F1
  Wendover HP22 .... 131 D2
Ellesmere CI LU6 .... 93 E3
Ellesmere Rd HP4 .... 135 E2
Elliman Ave SL2 .... 205 F3
Ellington Ct SL6 .... 203 E4
Ellington Gdns SL6 .... 203 E4
Ellington Park SL6 .... 195 F1
Ellington Prim Sch SL6 .. 195 F1
Ellington Rd SL6 .... 203 E4
Elliot Dr SL7 .... 183 F2
Elliots CI UB8 .... 208 B4
Elliott Ho ▪ HP11 .... 172 C4
Ellis Ave
  Chalfont St Peter SL9 .... 177 F1
  Slough SL1 .... 205 F2
Ellis Way HP14 .... 171 D2
Ellisgill Ct MK13 .... 34 A2
Ellison CI SL4 .... 209 F2
Ellison Ho ▪ SL4 .... 210 B3
Ellsworth Rd HP11 .... 172 C2
Ellwood Terr WD3 .... 167 E2
Ellwood Ho ▪ SL9 .... 177 F1
Ellwood Rd HP9 .... 175 D1
Ellwood Rise HP8 .... 177 E4
Elm Brook CI HP18 .... 112 B1
Elm CI Amersham HP6 ..... 154 B1
  Chinnor OX9 .... 147 E3
  Ellesborough HP17 .... 130 B2
  Farnham Common SL2 .. 198 B3
  Newton Longville MK17 ... 57 E1
  Tylers Green HP15 .... 163 D2
  Weston Turville HP22 .... 116 C1
Elm Croft SL3 .... 212 B2
Elm Ct HP17 .... 130 B2
Elm Dr Chinnor OX9 .... 147 E3
  Deanshanger MK19 .... 31 E3
Elm Farm Rd HP21 .... 116 A3
Elm Gn HP21 .... 115 E4
Elm Gr Berkhamsted HP4 .. 135 E2
  Maidenhead SL6 .... 202 C4
  West Drayton UB8 .... 208 C3
  Woburn Sands MK17 ..... 49 D2
Elm La SL8 .... 184 C3
Elm Lawn CI UB8 .... 201 F3
Elm Rd
  High Wycombe HP12 ..... 172 B2
  Princes Risborough HP27 . 139 D2
  Tylers Green HP10 .... 174 B4
  Windsor SL4 .... 210 A2
Elm St MK18 .... 52 B4
Elm Tree Cotts HP17 ..... 130 B2
Elm Tree Wlk
  Chorleywood WD3 .... 167 F3
  Tring HP23 .... 119 D3
Elm Trees HP18 .... 125 D4
Elmar Gn SL2 .... 198 A1
Elmdale Gdns HP27 .... 139 D2
Elmers CI MK19 .... 31 E4
Elmers Park MK3 .... 58 A4
Elmfield CI NN12 .... 18 B2
Elmfields Gate MK18 ..... 66 A2
Elmhurst HP16 .... 152 A4
Elmhurst CI
  High Wycombe HP13 .. 162 B1
  Milton Keynes MK4 ..... 46 C2

Elmhurst Ct SL3 .... 207 D2
Elmhurst Cty Fst Sch
  HP20 .... 101 F1
Elmhurst Cty Mid Sch
  HP20 .... 101 E1
Elmhurst Rd
  Aylesbury HP20 .... 101 F1
  Slough SL3 .... 207 D2
Elmore Dr MK16 .... 6 C2
Elmridge Ct MK4 .... 46 B1
Elms Dr SL8 .... 185 E2
Elms Rd SL9 .... 177 F2
Elms The
  ▪ Leighton Buzzard LU7 .. 80 C4
  Milton Keynes MK5 ..... 57 F4
  Preston Bissett MK18 .... 51 D1
Elmshott CI HP10 .... 163 D1
Elmshott La SL1 .... 204 C3
Elmside MK18 .... 66 A2
Elmslie CI SL6 .... 202 C4
Elmtree Ct HP16 .... 152 A4
Elmtree Cty Inf Sch HP5 . 144 A1
Elmtree Green HP16 ..... 152 A4
Elmtree Hill HP5 .... 144 A1
Elmwood Maidenhead SL6 . 196 A2
  Turvey MK43 .... 8 C3
Elmwood CI HP18 .... 109 E3
Elmwood Park SL9 .... 188 C2
Elmwood Rd SL2 .... 206 A3
Elora Rd HP13 .... 173 F4
Elruge CI UB7 .... 208 B2
Elsmore CI HP21 .... 116 A2
Elthorne Rd UB8 .... 201 E2
Elthorne Way MK16 .... 22 B1
Elton MK6 .... 47 E4
Elton Dr SL6 .... 202 B4
Elwes Rd HP14 .... 171 E2
Ely Ave SL1 .... 205 E4
Ely CI HP7 .... 165 F4
Ely Ho HP13 .... 173 F4
Ember Path HP21 .... 115 E2
Ember Rd SL3 .... 207 D2
Emberton Ctry Pk MK46 ... 6 C1
Emberton Cty Fst Sch
  MK46 .... 6 C1
Emberton Gdns MK11 ..... 32 C3
Emerald CI MK18 .... 74 C4
Emerald Ct SL1 .... 205 F2
Emerson Ct HP10 .... 185 F3
Emerson Valley Comb Sch
  MK4 .... 46 B1
Emerton Ct HP4 .... 134 C4
Emerton Garth HP4 ..... 134 C4
Emlyns Bldgs SL4 .... 210 B4
Emma Rothschild Ct HP23 119 D3
Emperor CI HP4 .... 135 D3
Empingham Ct MK2 ..... 58 B2
Enborne CI HP21 .... 115 E2
Enfield Chase MK13 ..... 34 B3
Enfield CI UB8 .... 201 E2
Engaine Dr MK5 .... 45 F4
English Gdns TW19 ..... 211 E1
Enmore Gate MK9 .... 35 D2
Enmore Rdbt MK9 .... 35 D2
Ennell Gr MK2 .... 58 B3
Ennerdale CI SL7 .... 184 B4
Ennerdale Cres SL1 ..... 204 B4
Ensbury Wlk HP20 .... 101 F1
Enstone Rd UB10 .... 190 C1
Enterprise La MK9 .... 35 D2
Epsom CI LU7 .... 80 B2
Epsom Gr MK3 .... 57 E3
Eriboll CI LU7 .... 80 A3
Erica CI SL1 .... 204 C3
Erica Rd MK12 .... 33 F2
Eridge Gn MK7 .... 48 A4
Errington Dr SL4 .... 210 A3
Esk Way MK3 .... 46 C1
Eskdale Ave HP5 .... 144 B1
Eskdale Gdns SL6 .... 203 D1
Eskdale Lodge HP6 ..... 154 B1
Eskdale Rd
  Stoke Mandeville HP22 .. 116 A1
  Uxbridge UB8 .... 201 D2
Essendon Ct MK11 .... 32 C3
Essex Ave SL2 .... 205 E4
Essex CI MK3 .... 46 C1
Essex Ho ▪ HP20 .... 101 E1
Essex Rd HP5 .... 144 B1
Estcourt Dr HP15 .... 162 C3
Eston Ct MK13 .... 34 A3
Estover Way OX9 .... 147 D3
Etheridge Ave MK7 ..... 48 A4
Ethorpe MK8 .... 33 F1
Ethorpe CI SL9 .... 188 C3
Ethorpe Cres SL9 .... 188 C3
Eton CI SL3 .... 211 D4
Eton Coll SL4 .... 210 B4
Eton Cres MK12 .... 33 E3
Eton Ct SL4 .... 210 B4

Eton End PNEU Sch SL3 ... 211 D4
Eton Pl SL7 .... 183 E1
Eton Porny CE Comb Sch
  SL4 .... 210 B4
Eton Rd SL3 .... 211 D4
Eton Sq SL4 .... 210 B4
Eton Wick CE Fst Sch SL4 205 D1
Eton Wick Rd SL4 .... 205 D1
Eton Wlk ▪ SL1 .... 205 F2
Eunice Gr HP5 .... 154 B4
Europa Ho Sl 188 C3
Evans CI Aylesbury HP21 .. 116 A2
  Chearsley HP18 .... 112 A1
Evans Gate MK6 .... 46 C4
Evelyn CI LU7 .... 79 F1
Evelyns CI UB8 .... 208 C4
Evelyns Com Sch UB8 .... 208 C4
Evenlode SL6 .... 202 C4
Evenlode CI HP21 .... 115 E3
Evenlode Rd SL8 .... 185 D2
Everard Ave SL1 .... 205 F2
Exmoor Gate MK4 .... 46 C1
Eyethrope Rd HP18 ..... 114 A3
Eynsford Terr UB7 .... 208 C4
Eynsham Ct MK15 .... 35 D1
Eyre Gn SL2 .... 198 A1

Factory Yd HP9 .... 175 F1
Fadmoor Pl MK4 .... 46 A2
Fagnall La HP7 .... 164 B1
Fair Acres HP16 .... 151 E3
Fair Leas HP5 .... 144 A1
Fair Meadow MK18 ..... 66 A2
Fair Mile Aylesbury HP21 .. 116 A4
  Henley-on-T RG9 .... 191 E2
Fair Ridge HP11 .... 172 C2
Fair View Cotts
  Chalfont St Peter SL9 .... 177 F2
  Cookham SL6 .... 195 F4
Fairacre SL6 .... 202 B3
Fairacres Ind Est SL4 ..... 209 F3
Fairacres SL2 .... 198 A1
Fairfax MK13 .... 34 B3
Fairfax Cres HP20 .... 101 F1
Fairfax Mews HP7 .... 165 D4
Fairfield App TW19 ..... 211 E1
Fairfield Ave Datchet SL3 .. 211 E4
  Farnham Common SL2 .. 198 B3
Fairfield CI Datchet SL3 ... 211 E4
  Olney MK46 .... 7 D2
Fairfield Rd Burnham SL1 . 197 E1
  Paulerspury NN12 .... 17 D4
  Uxbridge UB8 .... 201 E3
  West Drayton UB7 .... 208 C3
  Wraysbury TW19 .... 211 E1
Fairfields HP15 .... 151 F1
Fairford Cres MK15 .... 35 D3
Fairford Rd SL6 .... 202 C4
Fairhaven SL9 .... 177 E1
Fairlawn Pk SL4 .... 209 F2
Fairlea SL6 .... 202 B3
Fairlie Rd SL1 .... 205 D4
Fairlight Ave SL4 .... 210 B3
Fairlight Dr UB8 .... 201 E3
Fairmile Ct RG9 .... 191 E2
Fairthorn CI HP23 .... 118 C2
Fairview La HP10 .... 174 A1
Fairview Rd Burnham SL6 . 204 A4
  Slough SL2 .... 197 F1
Fairway HP27 .... 139 D2
Fairway Ave UB7 .... 208 B3
Fairway CI UB7 .... 208 B3
Fairway The Burnham SL1 . 197 E2
  Flackwell Heath HP10 .... 185 E4
  Maidenhead SL6 .... 202 A2
  Uxbridge UB10 .... 201 F2
Fairways MK8 .... 33 E1
Fairways Rdbt MK8 .... 33 E1
Falaise MK15 .... 35 D4
Falcon Ave MK6 .... 35 D1
Falcon Dr TW19 .... 213 F1
Falcon Ridge HP4 .... 135 E2
Falcon Rise HP13 .... 161 F2
Falcon The HP20 .... 101 F1
Falcons Croft HP10 ..... 185 F4
Falkland Ho SL6 .... 202 C4
Fall CI HP19 .... 101 E2
Falling La UB7 .... 208 C3
Fallow Field HP15 .... 163 D2
Falmouth Pl MK6 .... 34 C1
Falmouth Rd SL1 .... 205 D4
Fane Way SL6 .... 202 B3
Fantail La HP23 .... 118 C2

Far Furlong CI HP21 ..... 115 E2
Faraday CI SL2 .... 205 D4
Faraday Dr MK5 .... 46 B3
Faraday Rd
  Aylesbury HP19 .... 101 D1
  Slough SL2 .... 205 D4
Farinton MK8 .... 33 F1
Farm CI
  High Wycombe HP13 .... 174 A4
  Little Chalfont HP6 ..... 166 B4
  Maidenhead SL6 .... 203 E1
  Maidenhead, Highway SL6 202 A4
  Stewkley LU7 .... 78 C4
Farm Cres SL2 .... 206 B4
Farm Dr SL4 .... 211 D1
Farm Gr HP9 .... 175 E3
Farm La HP9 .... 176 B2
Farm Lea HP10 .... 185 F4
Farm Pl Berkhamsted HP4 . 134 C3
  Chinnor OX9 .... 137 F1
Farm Rd Bourne End SL8 .. 184 C2
  Brackley NN13 .... 38 A3
  Chorleywood WD3 .... 167 D3
  Maidenhead SL6 .... 202 A4
Farm Way TW19 .... 212 C1
Farm Yd SL4 .... 210 B4
Farmborough MK6 .... 47 E3
Farmborough CI HP20 .... 102 A1
Farmers CI SL6 .... 202 A2
Farmers Way
  Maidenhead SL6 .... 202 A2
  Seer Green HP9 .... 176 B2
Farnburn Ave SL1 .... 205 D4
Farndale Gdns HP15 ..... 163 D3
Farnham CI HP3 .... 146 A2
Farnham Common Cty
  Fst Sch SL2 .... 198 A4
Farnham Common Cty
  Mid Sch SL2 .... 198 B4
Farnham Common Ho ▪
  SL2 .... 198 B4
Farnham La SL2 .... 198 A2
Farnham Park La SL2 ..... 198 B2
Farnham Rd SL1, SL2 ..... 205 E4
Farnley Rd HP20 .... 101 F1
Farrer CI NN13 .... 26 B2
Farrer Theatre SL4 .... 205 E1
Farrier CI ▪ SL4 .... 185 D2
Farrier Pl MK14 .... 35 D3
Farthing Gr MK6 .... 47 E3
Farthing Green La SL2 ... 199 D2
Farthingales The SL6 ..... 203 D4
Fassets Rd HP11 .... 174 A1
Faulkner Way HP13 ..... 161 E2
Faulkner's Way LU7 ..... 80 C4
Favell Dr MK4 .... 46 C2
Faversham CI HP23 .... 119 D2
Fawcett Rd SL4 .... 210 A3
Fawley Bottom La RG9 ... 180 A1
Fawley CI SL6 .... 195 E1
Fawley Court RG9 .... 191 F3
Fawsley CI SL3 .... 212 C4
Featherbed La HP15 ..... 163 E4
Featherstone Rd MK12 ... 33 D3
Fedden Ho MK43 .... 24 B2
Fegans Ct MK11 .... 32 B3
Felbridge MK7 .... 48 B4
Felden La HP3 .... 146 C4
Fells CI HP18 .... 125 E3
Fences La MK16 .... 13 D1
Fennel Dr MK13 .... 34 C2
Fennels Farm Rd HP10 ... 174 A1
Fennels Rd HP11 .... 174 A1
Fennels Way HP10 ..... 174 A1
Fennimore CI HP18 ..... 109 E2
Fennings The HP6 .... 154 B2
Fenny Rd MK17 .... 69 F4
Fenny Stratford Sta MK1 ... 47 F1
Fennymere MK8 .... 33 E1
Fenton Ct MK8 .... 45 F4
Fern Ct MK4 .... 135 D2
Fern Dr SL6 .... 204 A4
Fern Gr MK2 .... 58 B3
Fern La HP17 .... 127 D3
Fern Wlk HP15 .... 163 D2
Fernborough Haven MK4 .. 46 B1
Ferndale MK6 .... 35 D1
Ferndale CI HP14 .... 158 C2
Ferndale Cres UB8 .... 201 E1
Ferne Furlong MK46 ..... 6 C3
Fernes CI UB8 .... 208 B4
Fernhill CI OX9 .... 136 A3
Fernhurst CI HP9 .... 175 F1
Fernie Fields HP12 ..... 172 B2
Fenlea CI HP10 .... 174 A1
Fernley Ct SL6 .... 195 E1
Ferns The HP9 .... 175 F1

Fernside
Great Kingshill HP15 .... 151 F1
Holmer Green HP15 .... 163 D3
Fernsleigh Cl SL9 .... 177 F2
Fernwood Sch MK17 .... 49 D1
Ferrers Ave UB7 .... 208 B2
Ferry End SL6 .... 203 E2
Ferry La Bourne End SL8 ...... 185 D1
Cookham SL6 .... 196 A4
Hambleden RG9 .... 192 B3
Mednemham SL7 .... 193 D3
Ferry Rd SL6 .... 203 E2
Festival Cotts SL3 .... 212 B4
Field Cl Aylesbury HP20 .... 102 A1
Chesham HP5 .... 144 C2
Ickford HP18 .... 124 A2
Sherington MK16 .... 14 A1
Field End HP18 .... 125 F3
Field End Cl HP23 .... 119 E1
Field Hurst SL3 .... 206 C1
Field La MK12 .... 33 D3
Field Rd Denham UB9 .... 189 F1
High Wycombe HP12 .... 172 A3
Murcott OX6 .... 94 A3
Field Way Aylesbury HP20 ... 102 A1
Bovingdon HP1 .... 146 A3
Gerrards Cross SL9 .... 177 F2
Uxbridge UB8 .... 201 E1
Field Wlk MK9 .... 34 C2
Fieldfare HP20 .... 101 F2
Fieldhead Gdns SL8 .... 185 D2
Fieldhouse Ind Est SL7 .... 183 F1
Fieldhouse La SL7 .... 183 F1
Fieldhouse Way SL7 .... 183 F1
Fielding Rd SL6 .... 202 A4
Fields End HP23 .... 119 D3
Fields The SL1 .... 205 E2
Fieldway Amersham HP7 ...... 165 D3
Berkhamsted HP4 .... 135 F1
Wigginton HP23 .... 119 E1
Fifth St HP11 .... 173 E2
Filey Spur SL1 .... 205 D2
Filmer Rd SL4 .... 209 E3
Finch Cl MK10 .... 35 F2
Finch Cres LU7 .... 80 C3
Finch Cl SL6 .... 202 B3
Finch End HP10 .... 174 B4
Finch Gn WD3 .... 167 F3
Finch La Amersham HP7 ...... 166 A4
Beaconsfield HP9 .... 175 E3
Little Chalfont HP7 .... 166 A4
Finch Rd HP4 .... 135 D2
Findlay Way MK2 .... 58 B4
Fineleigh Cl SL1 .... 205 F3
Fingest La Frieth HP14 .... 170 C2
Lane End HP14 .... 170 B2
Fingle Dr MK13 .... 33 F4
Finians Cl UB10 .... 201 F3
Finings Rd HP14 .... 171 D2
Finmere CE Prim Sch
MK18 .... 50 B3
Finmere Cres HP21 .... 116 B3
Fir Tree Ave SL2 .... 198 C1
Fir Tree Cotts HP14 .... 161 D4
Fircroft Cl SL2 .... 199 D3
Fire La MK17 .... 57 E2
Firs Ave SL4 .... 209 F2
Firs Cl High Wycombe HP13 173 F4
Iver Heath SL0 .... 200 B2
Lane End HP14 .... 171 E3
Tylers Green HP13 .... 163 D1
Whitchurch HP27 .... 87 D3
Firs Ct Amersham HP6 .... 154 B1
Bierton HP22 .... 102 B2
Firs Dr SL3 .... 206 C3
Firs End SL9 .... 188 B4
Firs Rise HP16 .... 151 F4
Firs The Bierton HP22 .... 102 B2
Brill HP18 .... 110 A4
Maidenhead SL6 .... 202 C4
Wigginton HP23 .... 119 E1
Firs View Rd HP15 .... 163 D1
Firs Wlk HP15 .... 163 D1
First Ave Amersham HP7 ...... 165 E4
Marlow SL7 .... 184 A1
Milton Keynes MK1 .... 47 E1
First Cres SL1 .... 205 E4
First St HP11 .... 173 E2
Firview Ct SL7 .... 183 F1
Fish Ponds La OX9 .... 125 F1
Fisherman's Way SL8 .... 185 D2
Fishermans Cl MK46 .... 6 C2
Fishermans Retreat SL7 ...... 183 F1
Fishermead Bvd MK6 .... 35 D1
Fishers Field MK18 .... 52 B4
Fishery Rd SL6 .... 203 D3
Fishguard Spur SL1 .... 206 A2
Fishweir LU7 .... 68 B1

Five Acre Wood HP12 .... 172 B3
Five Acres Chesham HP5 ..... 154 B3
Wooburn Green HP10 .... 185 F4
Five Points SL0 .... 200 B2
Flaggs Meadow MK46 .... 6 C2
Flambard Cl MK15 .... 35 D4
Flamborough Spur SL1 .... 205 D2
Flamingo Zoo Pk MK46 .... 6 A2
Flaunden Bottom HP5 .... 155 F2
Flaunden Hill HP3 .... 156 A3
Flaunden La HP3 .... 146 B2
Flavius Gate NN13 .... 38 A4
Flaxbourne Ct MK7 .... 48 B4
Flaxen Field HP22 .... 116 C1
Fledgeling Wlk MK18 .... 66 A3
Fleet Cl Buckingham MK18 .... 41 F1
Walter's Ash HP14 .... 161 F4
Fleet Rd HP20 .... 101 E1
Fleet St MK6 .... 35 D1
Fleetbrook Ho SL3 .... 211 E3
Fleetwood Cl HP8 .... 177 D3
Fleetwood Rd SL2 .... 205 F3
Fleetwood Way OX9 .... 125 F1
Fleming Dr MK6 .... 47 D3
Fleming Way HP12 .... 172 B3
Fletcher Cl HP19 .... 100 C2
Fletchers Mews MK14 .... 34 C3
Flint Hollow OX9 .... 147 D3
Flint St HP17 .... 127 D3
Flint Way HP16 .... 151 E4
Flintergill Ct MK13 .... 34 A2
Flintlock Cl TW19 .... 213 D2
Flitcroft Lea HP13 .... 173 D4
Flitton Ct MK11 .... 32 C3
Flora Thompson Dr MK16 ..... 21 F3
Florence Ave SL6 .... 203 D4
Florida St HP11 .... 173 E2
Florin Cl MK15 .... 35 D4
Flowers Bottom La HP27 . 150 A2
Folding Cl LU7 .... 78 C4
Foley Cl HP9 .... 176 C4
Foliejohn Way SL6 .... 202 A1
Folkestone Ct SL3 .... 207 D1
Follet Cl SL4 .... 211 D1
Folly La Hartwell NN7 .... 10 B4
North Crawley MK16 .... 24 A3
Folly Rd MK19 .... 31 E2
Fontwell Cl SL6 .... 202 A4
Fontwell Dr MK3 .... 57 E4
Forbes Cl MK4 .... 46 B1
Ford La SL0 .... 208 A4
Ford St Buckingham MK18 ..... 52 B4
High Wycombe HP11 .... 173 F2
Ford Way HP13 .... 161 F2
Ford's Cl HP14 .... 159 F4
Fordcombe Lea MK7 .... 48 A4
Fore End UB9 .... 189 F1
Forelands Way HP5 .... 154 B4
Forest Cl
Princes Risborough HP27 . 139 D2
Wendover HP22 .... 131 D2
Forest Point HP13 .... 173 F3
Forest Rd Hanslope MK19 .... 10 C3
Piddington (Northants) NN7 . 4 A4
Windsor SL4 .... 209 F3
Forest Rise MK6 .... 47 D4
Forest Way HP13 .... 174 A4
Foresters
Beacon's Bottom HP14 ...... 159 E3
Chinnor OX9 .... 147 D3
Forfar Dr MK3 .... 46 C1
Forge Cl Ashendon HP18 ...... 97 F1
Holmer Green HP15 .... 163 E3
Horton-cum-S OX33 .... 108 A3
Marsh Gibbon OX6 .... 71 F2
Oakley HP18 .... 109 E2
Steeple Claydon MK18 .... 63 F2
Forge Dr SL2 .... 198 B3
Forge End HP7 .... 165 D4
Forge Rd HP14 .... 161 E4
Forge The MK46 .... 13 F4
Forgetts Rd HP14 .... 171 E2
Forlease Cl SL6 .... 203 D3
Forlease Dr SL6 .... 203 D3
Forlease Rd SL6 .... 203 D3
Formby Cl MK3 .... 57 E4
Forrabury Ave MK13 .... 34 A2
Fort End HP17 .... 127 D3
Fortescue Dr MK5 .... 46 A3
Fortuna Ct MK7 .... 48 B3
Forty Green OX9 .... 137 F2
Forty Green Dr SL7 .... 183 D1
Forty Green Rd HP9 .... 175 E2
Foscote Rd MK18 .... 41 F2
Foscott Way MK18 .... 41 F1
Foster Ave SL4 .... 209 F2
Foster Cl HP20 .... 101 F2
Fosters La MK13 .... 34 A2
Fosters Path SL2 .... 197 F1

Fotherby Ct SL6 .... 203 D3
Fotheringay Gdns SL1 .... 205 D3
Fotherley Rd WD3 .... 178 C4
Founders Dr UB9 .... 189 F3
Foundes Meadow MK14 .... 34 C3
Foundry La Horton SL3 .... 212 A2
Lacey Green HP27 .... 149 E3
Fountain Gdns SL4 .... 210 B2
Fountain Ct MK14 .... 34 C4
Four Ashes Rd HP15 .... 162 B3
Fourth Ave SL7 .... 184 A1
Fourth St HP11 .... 173 D2
Fowler MK14 .... 34 C3
Fowler Rd HP21 .... 115 E4
Fowlers Farm Rd HP14 .... 158 C2
Fox Cl HP23 .... 119 E1
Fox Cover OX9 .... 147 E3
Fox Field HP15 .... 162 C3
Fox Hill Cl HP13 .... 162 A1
Fox La HP15 .... 163 D3
Fox Milne Rdbt MK10 .... 35 F3
Fox Piece Cty Fst Sch SL7 . 183 F2
Fox Piece Cty Mid Sch SL7 183 F2
Fox Rd Holmer Green HP15 163 D3
Slough SL3 .... 206 B1
Wigginton HP23 .... 119 E1
Fox Way MK18 .... 52 C4
Foxborough Cl SL3 .... 207 D1
Foxborough Comb Sch
SL3 .... 207 D1
Foxcovert Rd MK5 .... 45 F2
Foxdell Way SL9 .... 177 F3
Foxes Piece SL7 .... 183 F2
Foxgate MK16 .... 22 C2
Foxglove HP21 .... 115 D3
Foxherne SL3 .... 206 B2
Foxhill MK46 .... 6 C3
Foxhollow Dr SL2 .... 198 B4
Foxhunter Dr MK13 .... 34 C3
Foxleigh HP11 .... 173 D2
Foxton MK6 .... 47 E3
Framers Ct HP14 .... 159 E3
Framewood Manor SL2 .... 199 E3
Framewood Rd SL2, SL3 ..... 199 E3
Framlingham Ct MK5 .... 46 A3
Frampton Ct UB9 .... 189 F3
France Furlong MK14 .... 34 C3
Frances Ave SL6 .... 196 B1
Frances Rd SL4 .... 210 B3
Frances St HP5 .... 144 B1
Franchise St HP5 .... 144 B1
Francis Cl MK5 .... 46 A3
Francis Edmonds Cty
Comb Sch HP14 .... 171 D2
Francis Way SL1 .... 204 B3
Frank Atter Croft MK12 .... 33 E3
Frank Lunnon Cl SL8 .... 185 E2
Frank Sutton Way SL1 .... 205 E3
Franklin Ave SL2 .... 205 D4
Franklin Cl HP17 .... 127 D4
Franklin Ct HP17 .... 154 B1
Franklins Croft MK12 .... 33 E3
Franklyn Cres SL4 .... 209 E2
Frankston Ave MK11 .... 32 C3
Frankswode Ave UB7 .... 208 C4
Frascati Way SL6 .... 202 C4
Fraser Rd HP12 .... 172 B3
Fraucup Cl HP17 .... 128 A4
Fray's Ct UB8 .... 201 E3
Fray's Waye UB8 .... 201 E2
Frays Ave UB7 .... 208 B2
Frays Cl UB7 .... 208 B2
Fraylesa UB8 .... 201 E2
Frederick Pl HP11 .... 174 A2
Frederick St HP18 .... 99 D4
Fredericks Ct HP9 .... 186 A4
Freeman Cl MK12 .... 33 D3
Freeman Ct HP5 .... 144 B3
Freemans Cl SL2 .... 199 D3
Freemans Gdns MK46 .... 7 D2
Freemantle Rd HP21 .... 115 F3
Fremantle Rd HP13 .... 162 C1
Frenchum Gdns SL1 .... 204 C3
Frensham Dr MK2 .... 58 B4
Frensham Wlk SL2 .... 198 B3
Friarage Rd HP20 .... 116 C4
Friars Field HP4 .... 134 C4
Friars Furlong HP18 .... 125 D4
Friars Gdns HP14 .... 162 A4
Friars Sq HP20 .... 116 C4
Friars Walk HP16 .... 151 E3
Friars Wlk HP23 .... 119 D2
Friarscroft Way HP20 .... 115 E4
Friary Dr TW19 .... 211 E1
Friary Gdns MK16 .... 22 B1
Friary The SL4 .... 211 E1
Friday Cl OX9 .... 125 F1

Friday St Henley-on-T RG9 . 191 F1
Leighton Buzzard LU7 .... 80 C4
Frieth CE Comb Sch HP14 . 170 C2
Frieth Rd Marlow SL7 .... 182 C3
Marlow Bottom SL7 .... 182 C2
Frith Hill HP16 .... 152 A4
Frithe The SL2 .... 206 A4
Frithsden Copse HP4 .... 135 F4
Frithwood Cres MK7 .... 48 A4
Frog La HP18 .... 112 C2
Froggy La UB9 .... 189 E1
Frogmill SL6 .... 193 E2
Frogmill Ct SL6 .... 193 E2
Frogmoor HP13 .... 173 D4
Frogmore Cl
Hughenden Valley HP14 .... 162 A4
Slough SL1 .... 205 D2
Frogmore St HP23 .... 119 D2
Frome Cl HP21 .... 115 E3
Fromer Rd HP10 .... 185 E2
Froxfield Cl MK4 .... 46 B1
Fryday St MK6 .... 46 C1
Fryer Cl HP5 .... 154 B3
Fryers Cl HP12 .... 172 B4
Fryers La HP12 .... 172 B4
Frymley Hill SL4 .... 209 E3
Fulbrook Mid Sch MK17 .... 49 D3
Fullbrook Cl SL6 .... 203 D4
Fuller's Cl HP5 .... 154 A3
Fullers Hill Chartridge HP5 154 A3
Chesham HP5 .... 154 A3
Fullers Yd SL6 .... 196 A1
Fulmar Pl HP20 .... 101 F2
Fulmer Chase SL3 .... 199 E4
Fulmer Common Rd SL3 ..... 199 F3
Fulmer Cty Prim Sch SL3 ... 199 F4
Fulmer Dr SL9 .... 188 B1
Fulmer La SL9 .... 189 D1
Fulmer Rd SL3 .... 188 C1
Fulmer St
Milton Keynes MK4 .... 46 B2
Shenley Church End
MK8, MK5 .... 45 F2
Fulmer Way SL3 .... 188 C3
Fulwell Cl MK14 .... 34 C4
Fulwell Rd NN13 .... 39 D2
Fulwood Ct TW19 .... 213 F1
Fulwoods Dr MK6 .... 47 D4
Furlong Cl SL8 .... 185 D2
Furlong Cres HP17 .... 115 D1
Furlong La SL6 .... 93 E4
Furlong Rd SL6 .... 195 D2
Furlong The HP23 .... 119 D2
Furness SL4 .... 209 E3
Furness Pl SL4 .... 209 E3
Furness Row SL4 .... 209 E3
Furness Sq SL4 .... 209 E3
Furness Wlk SL4 .... 209 E3
Furnival Ave SL2 .... 205 E4
Furrow Cl HP21 .... 115 E2
Furrow Way SL6 .... 202 A2
Furrows The UB9 .... 190 B3
Furtho La NN12 .... 18 C2
Fury Ct MK8 .... 45 F2
Furze Down Sch MK18 .... 65 F2
Furze La MK18 .... 65 F2
Furze Platt Halt SL6 .... 195 F1
Furze Platt Inf Sch SL6 .... 195 F1
Furze Platt Jun Sch SL6 ..... 195 F1
Furze Platt Rd SL6 .... 195 F1
Furze Platt Sch SL6 .... 195 F1
Furze View WD3 .... 167 E2
Furzeham Rd MK4 .... 46 B2
Furzefield Rd HP9 .... 175 E3
Furzeham Rd UB7 .... 208 C2
Furzen Cl SL2 .... 198 A1
Fuzzen Rdbt MK4 .... 46 B2
Fuzzens Wlk SL4 .... 209 F3
Fyfield Barrow MK7 .... 48 A3
Fyne Dr LU7 .... 80 B4

Gable Thorne MK7 .... 48 B3
Gables Cl
Chalfont St Peter SL9 .... 177 F3
Datchet SL3 .... 211 D4
Maidenhead SL6 .... 203 D4
Gables Meadow HP15 .... 163 E3
Gables The
Haddenham HP17 .... 127 D3
Leighton Buzzard LU7 .... 80 C3
Gabriel Cl MK7 .... 48 B3
Gaddesden Cres MK7 .... 48 B3
Gadge Cl OX9 .... 125 F1
Gadsden Cl MK43 .... 25 E2
Gadsden Ct MK17 .... 69 F1
Gage Cl SL6 .... 202 C2
Gage St SL9 .... 177 F2
Gainsborough Cl MK8 .... 45 F1
Gainsborough Dr SL6 .... 202 B2

Gainsborough Hill RG9 .... 191 F1
Gainsborough Pl HP19 .... 100 C2
Gainsborough Rd
Aylesbury HP21 .... 115 F
Henley-on-T RG9 .... 191 E
Gairloch Ave MK2 .... 58 B
Galahad Cl SL1 .... 205 D
Gallagher Cl MK8 .... 45 F
Galley Hill MK11 .... 32 C
Galley La
Great Brickhill MK17 .... 59 D
Little Brickhill MK17 .... 59 D
Galleymead Rd SL3 .... 212 C
Galloway HP19 .... 101 D
Galloway Cl MK3 .... 46 C
Gallows La HP12 .... 172 B
Gallys Rd SL4 .... 209 E
Galsworthy Pl HP19 .... 100 C
Galvin Rd SL1 .... 205 E
Gamnel Terr HP23 .... 119 D
Gandon Vale HP13 .... 173 D
Ganton Cl MK3 .... 46 B
Garamonde Dr MK8 .... 33 F
Garbo Cl MK8 .... 45 E
Garden Cl Halton HP22 .... 131 E
Maidenhead SL6 .... 202 A
Garden Cotts SL3 .... 212 B
Garden Field La HP4 .... 135 F
Garden Ho HP10 .... 174 A
Garden Mews SL1 .... 205 F
Garden Reach HP8 .... 166 B
Gardener Wlk HP15 .... 163 E
Gardens Ct HP14 .... 158 C
Gardens The Adstock MK18 . 53 F
Ickenham UB10 .... 190 C
Gardiner Ct MK13 .... 33 F
Gardner Cl Aylesbury HP19 101 D
Great Kingshill HP15 .... 151 E
Gardner Rd SL6 .... 195 F
Gardner's Cl LU6 .... 93 F
Garfield Pl HP20 .... 210 E
Garland Way HP22 .... 117 F
Garners Cl SL9 .... 177 F
Garners End SL9 .... 177 F
Garners Rd SL9 .... 177 F
Garnet Cl SL1 .... 205 D
Garnet Ct SL7 .... 183 E
Garrard Rd SL2 .... 197 F
Garratts Way HP13 .... 173 D
Garraways MK6 .... 47 D
Garrett Cl HP5 .... 154 E
Garron Cl HP21 .... 115 E
Garrowmore Gr MK2 .... 58 E
Garry Cl MK2 .... 58 B
Garson Gr HP5 .... 144 A
Garston MK8 .... 33 F
Garth The HP16 .... 152 A
Garthwaite Cres
Shenley Brook End MK5 ...... 46 A
Shenley Church End MK5 .... 45 A
Garvin Ave HP9 .... 175 F
Gas La SL6 .... 203 D
Gascon's Gr SL2 .... 198 A
Gaskin Ct MK14 .... 35 D
Gatcombe MK8 .... 33 F
Gate Cotts WD3 .... 167 E
Gatehouse Cl HP19 .... 101 E
Gatehouse Rd HP19 .... 101 E
Gatehouse Sch (Boarding)
MK13 .... 34 A
Gatehouse Way HP19 .... 101 D
Gatesbury Pl HP27 .... 139 D
Gatesdene Cl HP4 .... 121 E
Gateway Sch The HP16 .... 152 A
Gatewick Cl SL1 .... 205 E
Gatewick La MK7 .... 48 A
Gatting Way UB8 .... 201 F
Gatward Ave SL6 .... 202 A
Gaveston Dr HP4 .... 135 D
Gaveston Rd SL2 .... 197 F
Gaviots Cl SL9 .... 188 E
Gaviots Green SL9 .... 188 E
Gaviots Way SL9 .... 188 E
Gawcott Cty Fst Sch MK18 . 51 F
Gawcott Fields MK18 .... 52 A
Gawcott Rd MK18 .... 52 A
Gawdrey Cl HP5 .... 154 E
Gayal Croft MK5 .... 46 A
Gayhurst Rd HP23 173
Gayton Cl HP6 .... 154 C
Gell Cl UB10 .... 190 C
George Cl SL7 .... 183 e
George Green Rd SL3 .... 206 E
George Inn Pl MK16 .... 12 A
George Lee HP14 .... 160 E
George Rd HP14 .... 158 C
George St
Aylesbury HP20 .... 115 F
Berkhamsted HP4 .... 135 D
Chesham HP5 .... 144 E
High Wycombe HP11 .... 172 A

George St
  Milton Keynes MK2 .... 47 F1
  Uxbridge UB8 .... 201 E3
Wing LU7 .... 79 F1
  Woburn MK17 .... 60 C4
George V Rd SL4 .... 210 B4
George's Yd MK11 .... 32 B3
George's Hill HP15 .... 162 C3
Georges Dr HP10 .... 185 E4
Georgian CI UB10 .... 201 F4
Geralds Ct HP13 .... 162 B1
Geralds Rd HP13 .... 162 B1
Gerard CI MK13 .... 34 A4
Gerards Cross Rd SL2 .... 199 D4
Germain St HP5 .... 154 A4
Germains CI HP5 .... 154 A4
Germander Park Cty Fst Sch
  MK13 .... 34 B2
Germander PI MK14 .... 34 B2
Gerrards Cross CE Comb Sch
  SL9 .... 188 C2
Gerrards Cross Golf Course
  Chalfont St Peter SL9 ..... 177 F1
Gerrards Cross Sta SL9 ... 188 C3
Gershwin Ct MK7 .... 48 B2
Gervaise CI SL1 .... 204 C3
Gib La HP22 .... 102 B2
Gibbings CI MK18 .... 76 A2
Gibbs CI HP13 .... 172 C4
Gibbs Ho HP11 .... 174 A2
Gibbwin MK14 .... 34 C4
Gibraltar La SL6 .... 184 B1
Gibson Ct SL3 .... 206 C1
Gibson La HP17 .... 127 D3
Gibson PI TW19 .... 213 E1
Gibson Rd
  High Wycombe HP12 ...... 172 A2
  Ickenham UB10 .... 201 F4
Gibsons Green MK13 ...... 34 B2
Giffard Park Cty Comb Sch
  MK14 .... 22 A1
Giffard Park Rdbt MK14 ... 21 F2
Giffard Rd MK2 .... 58 B3
Giffard Way HP18 .... 125 E4
Gifford Gate MK14 .... 34 C4
Gifford PI MK18 .... 41 F1
Gilbert CI MK3 .... 58 A4
Gilbert Ho HP11 .... 172 C4
Gilbert Scott Rd MK18 .... 41 E1
Gilbert Way HP4 .... 135 D2
Gilbert's Hill HP23 .... 132 C2
Gilbey Wlk HP10 .... 185 E2
Gilders Mews MK14 .... 34 C3
Giles Ct HP16 .... 151 D3
Gilletts La HP13 .... 161 E1
Gillfield CI HP12 .... 172 C2
Gilliat Rd SL1 .... 205 F3
Gilliat's Gn WD3 .... 167 E3
Gilliatt CI SL0 .... 207 F4
Gilman Cres SL4 .... 209 E2
Gilmore CI SL3 .... 206 B2
Gilmore Rd HP20 .... 101 F2
Gilpin Way MK46 .... 7 D2
Gilpin's Ride HP4 .... 135 F3
Gingers CI HP27 .... 137 E3
Gisburn Ct HP13 .... 34 A3
Glade Ho SL7 .... 183 F1
Glade Rd SL7 .... 183 F1
Glade The SL0 .... 188 B1
Glade View HP12 .... 172 A2
Gladstone CI MK16 .... 22 B2
Gladstone Ind Est SL6 .... 202 C4
Gladstone Rd HP5 .... 144 B1
Gladstone Rise HP13 ...... 173 F3
Gladstone Way SL1 .... 205 D3
Glaisyer Way SL0 .... 200 B2
Glamis Ho MK3 .... 57 F4
Glamorgan CI MK3 .... 46 C1
Glanmor Rd SL2 .... 206 A3
Glasgow Rd SL1 .... 205 D4
Glastonbury CI MK3 .... 47 D1
Glastonbury Thorn Cty
  Fst Sch MK5 .... 46 A3
Glazier Dr MK14 .... 115 E2
Glebe De Dorney SL6 ...... 203 F2
  Gerrards Cross SL9 .... 177 E2
  Holmer Green HP15 ...... 163 D4
  Maids Moreton MK18 ..... 41 F2
  Milton Keynes MK5 .... 46 A4
  Pitstone LU7 .... 105 E3
Glebe Cotts HP14 .... 169 E4
Glebe Dr Brackley NN13 ... 38 A4
  Old Windsor SL4 .... 211 D1
Glebe Ho SL9 .... 177 E2
Glebe House Dr MK18 ..... 39 F3
Glebe La MK19 .... 10 C3
Glebe Rd Deanshanger MK19 31 F3
  Gerrards Cross SL9 .... 177 E1
  Maidenhead SL6 .... 203 D3
  Uxbridge UB8 .... 201 E2

Glebe Rdbt MK9 .... 35 D2
Glebe The Lavendon MK46 .. 7 F4
  Lewknor OX9 .... 157 D4
  Prestwood HP16 .... 151 E4
  Walter's Ash HP14 .... 161 E3
  West Drayton UB7 .... 208 C1
  Weston Turville HP22 .... 116 C1
Glebe Way MK6 .... 154 B2
Glebelands CI HP10 .... 174 B4
Glebelands CI HP16 .... 151 F2
Gledfield PI MK12 .... 33 E2
Gleeman CI MK12 .... 33 D3
Glen The SL3 .... 206 B1
Glenavon Gdns SL3 .... 206 B2
Gleneagles CI
  Milton Keynes MK3 .... 57 E4
  Stanwell TW19 .... 213 E1
Glenfield CI HP21 .... 116 A3
Glenham Rd OX9 .... 126 A1
Glenhaven Dr TW19 .... 213 D1
Glenister Rd Chesham HP5 . 144 B2
  High Wycombe HP12 ..... 172 A2
Glenmore CI HP10 .... 174 A1
Glenmore Ho HP10 .... 174 A2
Glentworth PI SL1 .... 205 E3
Glenwater Ho HP15 ...... 163 D3
Glenwoods MK16 .... 22 B2
Glentham Gr OX9 .... 147 E3
Globe La LU7 .... 70 C1
Glory CI HP10 .... 185 F4
Glory Hill La HP9 .... 185 F4
Glory Mill La HP10 .... 185 F4
Gloucester Ave SL1 ...... 205 E4
Gloucester Ct UB9 .... 190 A2
Gloucester PI SL4 .... 210 B3
Gloucester Rd
  Maidenhead SL6 .... 195 F1
  Milton Keynes MK12 ..... 33 E3
Glovers Ct HP20 .... 101 F1
Glovers La MK13 .... 34 A2
Glyn Sq MK12 .... 33 E4
Glyn Sq MK12 .... 34 A4
Glynswood
  Chalfont St Peter SL9 ... 177 F2
  Chinnor OX9 .... 147 E3
  High Wycombe HP13 ..... 162 A1
Glynwood Ho SL6 .... 203 D4
Goathland Croft MK4 ..... 46 A1
Goddards Croft MK12 .... 33 E3
Godfreys CI Rd SL8 ...... 185 D3
Godolphin Inf Sch SL1 ... 205 E4
Godolphin Mid Sch SL1 .. 205 E4
Godolphin Rd
  Seer Green HP9 .... 176 B2
  Slough SL1 .... 205 E3
Godstowe Sch HP13 ..... 173 D4
Godwin CI MK7 .... 48 B4
Godwin Rd HP19 .... 100 C1
Gold Crest SL8 .... 185 D3
Gold Hill E SL9 .... 177 E1
Gold Hill N SL9 .... 177 E1
Gold Hill W SL9 .... 177 E1
Gold Ho HP15 .... 163 E3
Gold Oak Wlk MK9 ...... 34 C2
Gold St MK19 .... 11 D1
Golden Ball La SL6 ...... 195 D2
Golden Dr MK6 .... 47 D4
Golden Hills OX9 .... 147 E3
Golden Miller Ct LU7 .... 79 F1
Golden Oak SL2 .... 198 B3
Golden Riddy LU7 .... 80 C4
Golders CI HP18 .... 123 F2
Goldfield Inf Sch HP23 .. 118 C2
Goldfield Mid Sch SL1 ... 205 E4
Goldfield Rd HP23 ...... 118 C2
Goldilocks MK7 .... 48 A3
Goldlake Ct UB9 .... 189 F2
Goldmark CI MK7 .... 48 B3
Goldsmith Dr MK16 .... 21 F2
Goldsworthy Way SL1 .. 204 B4
Golspie Croft MK12 .... 33 E2
Gomm Rd HP10 .... 174 A2
Gomm's Wood HP9 .... 175 D2
Gomms Wood CI HP9 .. 175 D2
Good Intent LU6 .... 92 C2
Goodman Gdns MK6 ... 47 E4
Goodman Park SL2 .... 206 B3
Goodwick Gr MK4 ...... 57 D4
Goodwin Meadows HP10 .. 185 F3
Goodwin Rd
  Aylesbury HP19 .... 115 E4
  Slough SL1 .... 197 F1
Goodwins Mead LU7 ... 105 D4
Goodwood MK8 .... 45 F4
Goodwood Rise SL7 ... 183 E4
Goose Acre Botley HP5 .. 145 D1
  Cheddington LU7 .... 105 D4
Goose Gn SL2 .... 198 A2
Goosen Gn HP21 ...... 116 B3

Goran Ave MK11 .... 32 C2
Gordale MK13 .... 34 B3
Gordon Rd Chesham HP5 .. 154 B4
  High Wycombe HP13 .... 173 E3
  Maidenhead SL6 .... 202 B4
  West Drayton UB7 ...... 208 C3
  Windsor SL4 .... 209 F3
Gordon Way HP8 .... 177 D4
Gordon's CI SL9 .... 177 F1
Gore Hill HP7 .... 165 D3
Gore Rd SL1 .... 197 D1
Gore The SL1 .... 197 D1
Gorelands La SL9 ...... 177 F4
Gorell Rd HP9 .... 176 A1
Goring MK14 .... 34 B4
Gorman PI MK2 .... 58 C2
Gorrell CI MK18 .... 51 D3
Gorricks MK11 .... 32 B2
Gorse Meade SL1 ..... 205 D3
Gorse Rd SL6 .... 195 F3
Gorse Wlk
  Tylers Green HP15 ..... 163 D2
  West Drayton UB7 ..... 208 C4
Goslar Way SL4 .... 210 A3
Gosling Gn SL3 .... 206 C2
Gosling Gdns HP13 ... 161 E1
Gosling Rd SL3 .... 206 C2
Goslington MK1 .... 47 E1
Goss Ave HP18 .... 99 D3
Gossage Rd UB10 .... 201 F3
Gossmore CI SL7 ..... 183 F1
Gossmore La SL7 ..... 183 F1
Gossmore Wlk SL7 ... 183 F1
Gossom's End HP4 ... 135 D3
Gossoms Ryde HP4 .. 135 D3
Goswell Hill SL4 ...... 210 B3
Goswell Rd SL4 .... 210 B3
Governors Ave UB9 .. 189 F3
Governors Ct HP4 .... 154 C1
Gower Ho HP6 .... 154 C2
Gowers Field HP20 ... 101 E1
Gowers The HP6 ..... 154 C1
Goya PI MK19 .... 100 C1
Grace Ave MK6 .... 46 C4
Grace Ct SL1 .... 205 D3
Graces CI MK43 ...... 25 E2
Graces Maltings HP23 . 119 D2
Graeme Ave HP16 ... 151 E3
Graemesdyke Rd HP4 . 135 D2
Grafham CI MK14 .... 35 D4
Grafton CI
  Maidenhead SL6 .... 195 F1
  Pottersbury NN12 ..... 18 C2
  Slough SL3 .... 206 C4
Grafton Gate MK9 .... 34 B1
Grafton Orch OX9 .... 147 E4
Grafton Park MK9 .... 34 B1
Grafton Rd
  Aylesbury HP19 .... 101 D1
  Yardley Gobion NN12 . 18 C4
Grafton St
  Milton Keynes, Bradwell
    MK6 .... 34 A2
  Milton Keynes, Winterhill
    MK6 .... 46 C4
Graham CI SL6 .... 202 B3
Graham Dr HP12 .... 172 A3
Graham Rd SL6 ..... 195 F3
Grampian Gdns MK6 . 46 C4
Grampian Way SL3 .. 207 D1
Granary Mill MK5 ... 45 F4
Granborough Rd
  North Marston MK18 .. 76 A1
  Winslow MK18 .... 65 F1
Granby CI MK1 ...... 47 D2
Granby Ind Est MK1 . 47 D2
Granby Rdbt MK1 ... 47 D2
Grand Union Office Pk The
  UB8 .... 208 B4
Granes End MK14 .. 34 C4
Grange CI
  Gerrards Cross SL9 ... 177 F1
  Leighton Buzzard LU7 . 80 B3
  Maids Moreton MK18 . 41 F1
  Wraysbury TW19 ..... 211 F1
Grange Cotts HP16 . 152 A2
Grange Dr HP10 .... 185 E2
Grange Farm Rd HP14 . 159 D4
Grange Fields SL0 .. 177 F1
Grange Gdns
  Farnham Common SL2 . 198 B4
  Wendover HP22 ...... 131 D3
Grange La SL6 ..... 195 F4
Grange Rd Cookham SL6 . 195 F4
  Gerrards Cross SL9 ... 177 F1
  Henley-on-T RG9 ..... 191 F1
  Holmer Green HP15 .. 162 C3
  Milton Keynes MK3 .. 57 F4
  Pitstone LU7 .... 105 E3

Grange Rd
  Tring HP23 .... 119 E2
  Tylers Green HP15 .. 162 C2
  Wilstone HP23 ...... 104 B1
Grange Sch The HP21 . 115 F3
Grange The Burnham SL1 . 197 E1
  Old Windsor SL4 .... 211 D1
Grange Way SL0 .... 207 F4
Grangers Croft MK12 . 33 E2
Grant Ave SL1 ...... 205 F4
Grant Ho SL8 .... 185 D2
Grantham Ct MK5 .. 46 B3
Granville Ave SL2 .. 205 E4
Granville Dene HP1 . 146 A3
Granville PI HP20 .. 115 E4
Granville Rd HP4 ... 134 C3
Granville Sq MK15 . 35 E4
Granville St HP20 .. 115 E4
Grapevine CI HP11 . 173 F2
Grasmere Aylesbury HP21 116 A3
  Windsor SL4 .... 209 F4
Grasmere Ave SL2 . 206 A3
Grasmere Par SL2 . 206 A3
Grasmere Way
  Leighton Buzzard LU7 . 80 B4
  Milton Keynes MK2 .. 58 B3
Grass Hays HP21 .. 116 B4
Grasscroft MK4 .... 46 C2
Grassingham End SL9 . 177 F2
Grassingham Rd SL9 . 177 F2
Grassington MK13 . 34 A3
Grasslands HP20 .. 102 A1
Grassy La SL6 ..... 202 C4
Grattan Ct SL7 .... 184 A2
Gratton Dr SL4 .... 209 F2
Gravel Hill
  Chalfont St Peter SL9 . 177 F2
  Henley-on-T RG9 ... 191 E1
  Uxbridge UB8 .... 201 E4
Gravel Path HP4 ... 135 F3
Gravel Wlk MK46 .. 13 F4
Graveney PI MK6 .. 35 D1
Gray's La SL4 ..... 169 E4
Gray's PI SL2 ..... 205 F3
Gray's Rd Slough SL1 . 205 F3
  Uxbridge UB10 ..... 201 F3
Grayburn CI HP8 .. 177 D4
Grayling CI SL7 ... 194 B4
Grayling Ct SL7 ... 194 B4
Grayling Rd HP4 .. 134 C3
Grays CI NN12 .... 17 E4
Grays La
  High Wycombe HP13 . 161 E1
  Paulerspury NN12 .. 17 E4
  Yardley Gobion NN12 . 18 C3
Grays Park Rd SL2 . 199 D1
Grays Wlk HP5 .... 144 A1
Great Benty UB7 .. 208 C1
Great Brickhill La MK17 . 59 E3
Great Denson MK6 . 47 D4
Great Ground MK14 . 34 C4
Great Hill Cres SL6 . 202 B3
Great Hivings HP5 . 144 A2
Great Horwood CE Comb Sch
  MK17 .... 55 D2
Great Horwood Rd MK18 . 65 F4
Great Kimble CE Fst Sch
  HP17 .... 129 F1
Great Kingshill CE Comb Sch
  HP15 .... 162 B3
Great La HP22 .... 102 A2
Great Linford Cty Comb Sch
  MK14 .... 34 C4
Great Marlow Sch SL7 . 183 F2
Great Missenden CE Comb
  Sch HP16 .... 152 A4
Great Missenden Sta
  HP16 .... 152 A4
Great Monks St
  Milton Keynes, Wolverton
    MK12 .... 33 D4
  Milton Keynes, Wymbush
    MK8 .... 33 F1
Great Slade MK18 . 52 B3
Great Stone HP18 . 112 C2
Great Western St MK9 . 33 F3
Greatchesters MK13 . 33 F3
Greaves Rd HP13 .. 173 E3
Greble CI HP20 .... 101 F2
Grecian St HP20 .. 116 A4
Green Acre CI HP22 . 86 C4
Green Acres CI SL1 . 204 A4
Green CI Burnham SL1 . 204 A4
  High Wycombe HP13 . 161 E1
  Maidenhead SL6 ... 195 F1
Green Common La HP10 . 186 B2
Green Cres HP10 .. 185 E4
Green Dragon La HP10 . 185 D3
Green East Rd HP9 . 176 C2
Green End MK43 .. 76 A4

Green End Rd HP14 .... 159 F3
Green End St HP22 .... 117 F3
Green Farm Rd MK16 ..... 22 B2
Green Hill HP13 .... 162 A1
Green Hill CI HP13 .... 162 B1
Green Hill Gate HP13 ..... 162 A1
Green La Amersham HP6 .. 154 C1
  Aspley Guise MK17 ...... 49 F2
  Bledlow Ridge HP14 ..... 159 E3
  Bovingdon HP3 .... 146 A2
  Burnham SL1 .... 197 E2
  Datchet SL3 .... 211 D3
  Eaton Bray LU6 .... 92 B4
  Farnham Common SL2 .. 198 A3
  Ivinghoe LU7 .... 105 F3
  Latimer HP5 .... 155 D3
  Longwick HP27 .... 128 A1
  Maidenhead SL6 .... 203 D3
  Milton Keynes MK12 .... 33 E3
  Prestwood HP16 .... 151 F3
  Stokenchurch HP14 .... 158 B3
  Upper Arncott OX6 ..... 94 C4
  Windsor SL4 .... 210 A3
Green Lane Ct HP6 .... 154 B2
Green Lane Ct SL1 .... 197 E1
Green Lane Rdbt MK9 .... 35 D2
Green Leys
  High Wycombe HP13 .... 161 E1
  Maidenhead SL6 .... 195 F1
Green North Rd HP9 ..... 176 C2
Green Park HP16 .... 151 E3
Green Park Cty Comb Sch
  MK16 .... 23 A2
Green Park Dr MK16 ..... 22 B2
Green Rd HP13 .... 162 B1
Green St
  Chorleywood WD3 ...... 167 E3
  High Wycombe HP11 ... 172 C2
  Tylers Green HP15 ..... 162 C2
Green Street Cty Fst Sch
  HP11 .... 172 C4
Green The
  Amersham HP6, HP7 ... 154 B1
  Aston Abbots HP22 .... 88 B3
  Burnham SL1 .... 197 D1
  Chearsley HP18 .... 112 A1
  Cheddington LU7 ...... 105 D4
  Cosgrove MK19 .... 19 F1
  Cranfield MK43 .... 24 C1
  Cuddington HP18 ..... 112 C2
  Datchet SL3 .... 211 D4
  Deanshanger MK19 ... 31 F2
  Edlesborough LU6 .... 92 C2
  Great Horwood MK17 . 55 D2
  Hanslope MK19 .... 11 D1
  Horton-cum-S OX33 .. 108 A3
  Hyde Heath HP16 ..... 153 E3
  Longwick HP27 .... 138 B3
  Mentmore LU7 .... 90 B2
  Milton Keynes, Loughton
    MK5 .... 46 A4
  Milton Keynes, The Green
    MK6 .... 47 E4
  Newport Pagnell MK16 . 22 B2
  Paulerspury NN12 .... 17 D4
  Pitstone LU7 .... 105 E2
  Quainton HP22 ...... 85 D3
  Slough SL1, SL3 ..... 205 E2
  Stoke Hammond MK17 . 69 F4
  Thornborough MK18 . 54 A4
  Turvey MK43 .... 8 C3
  West Drayton UB7 ... 208 B2
  Wooburn Green HP10 . 185 F3
  Wraysbury TW19 .... 211 F1
Green Tiles UB9 .... 189 F2
Green Tiles La UB9 .... 189 F3
Green Verges SL7 .... 183 F2
Green View HP20 .... 102 A1
Green View CI HP3 ... 146 A1
Green Way MK17 .... 57 E2
Green West Rd HP9 . 176 C2
Greenacre SL4 ...... 209 F3
Greenacres Ave UB10 . 190 C1
Greenacres CI HP10 .. 163 D1
Greenacres The HP13 . 162 B1
Greenbury CI WD3 .. 167 E3
Greendale Mews SL2 . 206 A3
Greene Field Rd HP4 . 135 E2
Greene Wlk HP4 .... 135 E2
Greenes Ct HP4 .... 135 E3
Greenfern Ave SL1 . 204 B4
Greenfell End SL9 .. 177 F2
Greenfield Rd MK16 . 22 A2
Greenfields Adstock MK18 53 F1
  Maidenhead SL6 .... 203 D3
  Upper Arncott OX6 .. 94 C4
Greenhill CI MK5 ... 46 A4

Greenlands
Flackwell Heath HP10 ...... 185 D4
Lacey Green HP27 .... 149 E3
Greenlands Cl MK16 .... 22 C2
Greenlands Ct SL6 .... 202 A4
Greenlands La HP16 .... 151 D4
Greenlaw Pl MK3 .... 47 D2
Greenleaf Ct SL3 .... 211 D4
Greenleas Lower Sch LU7 ... 80 B4
Greenleys Cty Fst Sch
 MK12 .... 33 E3
Greenleys Cty Mid Sch
 MK12 .... 33 E2
Greenleys La MK12 .... 33 E2
Greenock Rd SL1 .... 205 D4
Greenridge HP10 .... 174 A4
Greens Keep HP17 .... 126 C3
Greenside Bourne End SL8 . 185 D3
 Prestwood HP16 .... 151 E3
 Slough SL2 .... 205 D4
Greenside Hill MK4 .... 46 A1
Greenway
 Berkhamsted HP4 .... 135 D2
 Chesham HP5 .... 144 A2
 Great Horwood MK17 .... 55 D1
 Haddenham HP17 .... 126 C3
Greenway Ct **18** HP13 .... 173 D4
Greenway Cty Fst Sch
 HP5 .... 144 A2
Greenway Cty Prim Sch
 HP4 .... 135 D2
Greenway Fst Sch HP4 ...... 134 C2
Greenway Par HP5 .... 144 A2
Greenway The
 Gerrards Cross SL9 .... 188 B4
 High Wycombe HP13 .... 173 D4
 Slough SL1 .... 204 B3
 Tring HP23 .... 118 C3
 Tylers Green HP10 .... 163 D1
 Uxbridge UB8 .... 201 E2
Greenway Wlk MK18 .... 41 F1
Greenways
 Bow Brickhill MK17 .... 48 B1
 Eaton Bray LU6 .... 92 B4
Greenways Dr SL6 .... 202 A4
Greenwich Gdns MK16 .... 22 B1
Greenwood HP14 .... 150 A1
Greenwood Ave OX9 .... 147 E3
Greenwood Cl
 Amersham HP6 .... 154 C1
 5 Seer Green HP9 .... 176 B2
Greenwood Meadow OX9 . 147 E3
Greenwood Pl MK18 .... 63 E2
Greenwood The HP22 .... 117 E3
Greenyard The NN7 .... 1 A4
Greetham Rd HP21 .... 116 B3
Gregories Dr MK7 .... 48 B3
Gregories Farm La HP9 ..... 175 E1
Gregories Rd HP9 .... 175 E2
Gregory Dr SL4 .... 211 D1
Gregory Rd SL2 .... 187 E1
Grenadine Way HP23 .... 119 D3
Grendon Rd Edgcott HP18 .. 72 C1
Grendon Underwood Cty
 Comb Sch HP18 .... 83 D3
Grendon Way HP22 .... 102 A2
Grenfell Ave
 High Wycombe HP12 .... 172 B4
 Maidenhead SL6 .... 202 C3
Grenfell Pl SL6 .... 202 C3
Grenfell Rd
 Beaconsfield HP9 .... 175 F2
 Maidenhead SL6 .... 202 C3
Grenville Ave HP22 .... 131 D4
Grenville Cl SL1 .... 197 D2
Grenville Comb Sch MK18 .. 52 B4
Grenville Ct WD3 .... 167 E2
Grenville Gn HP21 .... 115 E2
Grenville Rd
 Aylesbury HP21 .... 115 E3
 Buckingham MK18 .... 41 E1
Grenville Way OX9 .... 126 A1
Gresham Ct HP4 .... 135 D2
Gresham Rd SL1 .... 205 D4
Greyhound La Thame OX9 . 125 F1
 Winslow MK18 .... 66 A2
Greys Hill RG9 .... 191 E1
Greys Rd RG9 .... 191 E1
Greys The MK6 .... 47 E4
Greystoke Cl HP4 .... 135 D2
Greystoke Rd SL2 .... 204 C4
Griffetts Yd HP5 .... 144 A1
Griffin Cl Maidenhead SL6 . 202 C3
 Slough SL1 .... 205 D2
Griffin Ind Mall HP19 .... 101 D1
Griffin La HP19 .... 101 D1
Griffith Gate MK10 .... 36 A2

Griffith Gate Rdbt MK10 ..... 36 A2
Griffith Ho HP10 .... 174 B1
Griffiths Acre HP18 .... 114 C3
Griffon Cl MK6 .... 47 D4
Griggs Orch MK16 .... 14 A1
Grimbold Ct MK15 .... 35 E4
Grimmer Cl HP19 .... 100 C2
Grimms Hill HP16 .... 151 F4
Grimms Meadow HP14 ..... 150 A1
Grimsdell's La HP6 .... 154 B1
Grimsdyke Rd HP23 .... 119 E1
Gringer Hill SL6 .... 202 C4
Grizedale MK13 .... 34 A3
Groom Rd HP16 .... 151 E3
Groombridge MK7 .... 48 A4
Grooms Cotts HP5 .... 145 D1
Grooms Ct **3** HP10 .... 174 A2
Groomsby Dr LU7 .... 105 F3
Grosmont Cl MK4 .... 46 A1
Grosvenor Cl SL0 .... 200 B1
Grosvenor Ct SL1 .... 205 F4
Grosvenor Ct SL6 .... 203 E4
Groundsel Cl MK7 .... 48 A3
Grove Ash MK1 .... 47 E2
Grove Cl
 Gerrards Cross SL9 .... 177 E1
 Slough SL1 .... 206 A2
Grove Ct
 Beaconsfield HP9 .... 175 E1
 Bierton HP22 .... 102 B3
 Maidenhead SL6 .... 202 B4
Grove End SL9 .... 177 E1
Grove Gdns HP23 .... 119 D3
Grove Hill SL9 .... 177 E2
Grove Ind Sch The MK5 ...... 46 B4
Grove La
 Ashley Green HP5 .... 145 E3
 Gerrards Cross SL9 .... 177 E1
 Great Kimble HP17 .... 129 F1
 Uxbridge UB8 .... 201 F1
Grove Park HP23 .... 119 E3
Grove Rd Amersham HP6 .. 154 C1
 Beaconsfield HP9 .... 175 F1
 Burnham SL1 .... 197 F2
 Henley-on-T RG9 .... 191 F1
 High Wycombe HP12 .... 172 B4
 Maidenhead SL6 .... 202 C4
 Tring HP23 .... 119 E3
 Turvey MK43 .... 8 C3
 Tylers Green HP15 .... 162 C2
 Uxbridge UB8 .... 201 E3
 Windsor SL4 .... 210 B3
Grove Road Prim Sch
 HP23 .... 119 E3
Grove The Amersham HP6 154 B2
 Latimer HP5 .... 155 E2
 Milton Keynes, Bradwell
 MK13, MK17, MK3 .... 34 A2
Grove The
 Milton Keynes, Rickley Park
 MK3 .... 58 A4
 Newport Pagnell MK16 ...... 22 A2
 Slough SL1 .... 206 A2
 Tring HP23 .... 119 E3
 Uxbridge UB10 .... 201 F1
 Waddesdon HP18 .... 99 D3
Grove Way
 Chorleywood WD3 .... 167 D2
 Uxbridge UB8 .... 201 E3
 Waddesdon HP18 .... 99 D3
Grovelands HP11 .... 173 D3
Groves Cl SL8 .... 185 E2
Groves Rd HP22 .... 131 F4
Groves Way SL6 .... 195 F3
Grovesbrook MK17 .... 48 B1
Groveway
 Milton Keynes MK6 .... 47 E3
 Milton Keynes Village MK6 . 47 E3
 Walton MK6 .... 47 E3
Growewood Cl WD3 .... 167 D2
Grubbins La HP27 .... 150 A3
Grubwood La SL6 .... 195 D4
Grundy Ho UB8 .... 201 E2
Gryms Dyke HP16 .... 151 E3
Guards Club Rd SL6 .... 203 E4
Guards Rd SL4 .... 209 E3
Guards Wlk **1** SL4 .... 209 E3
Guernsey Cl HP19 .... 101 D2
Guest Gdns MK13 .... 34 A4
Guildford Cl MK18 .... 52 A2
Guillemot Way HP20 .... 101 F2
Guinea Orch MK46 .... 6 C2
Guinions Rd HP13 .... 173 F3
Guise Ct MK17 .... 49 F2
Gull Way **9** HP20 .... 101 F2
Gun La MK16 .... 14 A1
Gundale Ct MK4 .... 46 A1
Gunmaker Ct MK14 .... 34 B4
Gunthorpe Rd SL7 .... 184 A2
Gurnard Cl UB7 .... 208 B3
Gurnards Ave MK6 .... 35 D1

Gurnells Rd HP9 .... 176 B3
Gurney Cl
 11 Aylesbury HP20 .... 101 F1
 Beaconsfield HP9 .... 175 E1
 Milton Keynes MK5 .... 46 A4
Gurney Ct LU6 .... 92 C3
Gurneys Meadow HP15 .... 163 E4
Guttmann Rd HP21 .... 115 F3
Gwendale SL6 .... 195 E1
Gweneth Ct SL7 .... 183 E2
Gwent Cl SL6 .... 202 A2
Gwynant Ct MK2 .... 58 B2
Gwynne Cl Tring HP23 ..... 119 D3
 Windsor SL4 .... 209 F3
Gynant Rd HP13 .... 173 F3
Gyosei Int Sch UK The
 MK15 .... 35 E3
Gypsy La
 Aspley Guise MK17 .... 49 F2
 High Wycombe HP11 .... 173 E3
 Marlow SL7 .... 183 F2
 Stoke Poges SL2 .... 187 F1

Haberley Mead MK13 .... 34 A2
Hackett Pl MK16 .... 24 A3
Haddenham Aerodrome
 Ind Est HP17 .... 126 C4
Haddenham Cty Fst Sch
 HP17 .... 127 D3
Haddenham Cty Mid Sch
 HP17 .... 127 D3
Haddenham St Mary's
 CE Fst Sch HP17 .... 127 D2
Haddenham & Thame
 Parkway Sta HP17 .... 126 C3
Haddington Cl
 Milton Keynes MK3 .... 46 C1
 Wendover HP22 .... 131 E3
Haddington Way HP20 ...... 102 A1
Haddon MK8 .... 45 F4
Haddon Rd
 Chorleywood WD3 .... 167 E2
 Maidenhead SL6 .... 202 B3
Hadfield Rd TW19 .... 213 E1
Hadley Ct SL3 .... 212 C3
Hadley Pl MK13 .... 34 B2
Hadlow Ct SL1 .... 205 E3
Hadrians Dr MK3 .... 34 A3
Hadrians Gate NN13 .... 38 A4
Hag Hill La SL6 .... 204 A4
Hag Hill Rise SL6 .... 204 A4
Haglis Dr HP22 .... 131 D2
Haig Dr SL1 .... 205 D2
Hailey Cft OX9 .... 147 D3
Haileybury Ct SL4 .... 210 A2
Haileybury Jun Sch SL4 ... 210 A2
Hainault Ave MK14 .... 22 A1
Haines Cl HP19 .... 100 C1
Haines Rd HP15 .... 162 C3
Haithwaite MK8 .... 33 E1
Haldene MK8 .... 33 F1
Hale SL4 .... 209 F3
Hale Ave MK11 .... 32 C3
Hale La HP22 .... 131 F2
Hale Leys Ctr HP20 .... 115 E4
Hale Rd HP22 .... 131 E2
Hale St HP20 .... 115 F4
Hales Croft HP21 .... 116 A2
Halfacre Hill SL9 .... 177 F1
Halfway Hos SL6 .... 195 F2
Halfway House La HP5 ..... 153 F4
Halifax Cl SL8 .... 185 E2
Halifax Ho HP6 .... 166 B4
Halifax Rd Heron WD3 ..... 167 E1
 High Wycombe HP12 .... 172 B3
 Maidenhead SL6 .... 202 A4
Halifax Way SL6 .... 202 A4
Halings La UB9 .... 189 F4
Halkingcroft SL3 .... 206 B2
Hall Cl High Wycombe HP13 173 F3
 Maids Moreton MK18 .... 41 F2
Hall Ct SL3 .... 211 D4
Hall La MK16 .... 23 E4
Hall Meadow SL1 .... 197 D2
Hall Park HP4 .... 135 F2
Hall Park Gate HP4 .... 135 F2
Hall Park Hill HP4 .... 135 F2
Hall Place (Berkshire
 Coll of Ag) SL6 .... 194 A1
Halldore Hill SL6 .... 195 F4
Halls Cnr HP10 .... 174 A1
Halswell Pl MK10 .... 36 A1
Halton Cty Comb Sch
 HP22 .... 130 A2
Halton La Halton HP22 ..... 131 D4
 Wendover HP22 .... 131 D4
Halton Wood Rd HP22 ..... 131 E3
Haltonchesters MK13 .... 33 F3
Haly Cl MK13 .... 34 A2
Ham Island SL4 .... 211 E2
Ham La SL4 .... 211 E2

Hamberlins La HP4 .... 134 A4
Hamble Dr HP21 .... 115 E3
Hambleden Mill RG9 .... 192 B4
Hambleden Pl RG9 .... 192 B3
Hambleden Rise RG9 .... 192 B4
Hambleden Wlk HP21 ...... 115 E3
Hambledon Cl HP21 .... 116 A3
Hambleton Gr MK4 .... 46 A1
Hambling Pl LU6 .... 93 F4
Hamburg Croft MK5 .... 46 A2
Hambye Cl HP27 .... 149 F2
Hamer Cl HP3 .... 146 A2
Hamfield Cotts SL6 .... 195 F4
Hamilton Ave RG9 .... 191 F1
Hamilton Cl HP4 .... 107 E3
Hamilton Comb Sch HP13 173 D4
Hamilton Comb Sch
 (Annexe) HP13 .... 173 D4
Hamilton Ct
 Aylesbury HP19 .... 101 E1
 High Wycombe HP13 .... 173 D4
Hamilton Gdns SL1 .... 197 D1
Hamilton La MK3 .... 57 E3
Hamilton Mead HP21 .... 146 A2
Hamilton Pk SL6 .... 202 A3
Hamilton Rd
 Berkhamsted HP4 .... 135 D2
 High Wycombe HP13 .... 162 B1
 Slough SL1 .... 205 D4
 Thame OX9 .... 125 E4
 Uxbridge UB8 .... 201 E1
Hamlins MK6 .... 47 D3
Hammersley La HP10 .... 174 A3
Hammerwood Gate MK7 .... 48 A4
Hammond Cres MK15 .... 35 D3
Hammond End SL2 .... 198 A4
Hampden Ave HP5 .... 144 A1
Hampden Cl
 Aylesbury HP21 .... 115 E3
 Stoke Poges SL2 .... 199 D1
Hampden Gdns HP21 .... 115 E3
Hampden Hill
 Beaconsfield HP9 .... 175 D1
 Charndon OX6 .... 72 C1
Hampden Ho **2** HP21 ...... 173 F3
Hampden Rd
 Aylesbury HP21 .... 115 E3
 Gerrards Cross SL9 .... 177 E1
 High Wycombe HP13 .... 173 D4
 Hughenden Valley HP16 .. 151 D2
 Lacey Green HP27 .... 150 B3
 Maidenhead SL6 .... 202 A4
 Prestwood HP16 .... 151 D2
 Slough SL3 .... 206 C2
 Stoke Mandeville HP22 ... 116 A1
 Wendover HP22 .... 131 E3
Hampshire Ave SL1 .... 205 E4
Hampshire Ct MK3 .... 46 C1
Hampshire Lodge **8** SL6 . 202 C3
Hampson Cl MK13 .... 34 A3
Hampstead Gate MK13 ...... 34 B2
Hampton MK8 .... 46 A4
Hampton Cl HP21 .... 116 A1
Hanbury Cl SL1 .... 204 A4
Handel Mead MK7 .... 48 A4
Handley Page Cl MK43 ...... 24 C2
Handy Cross HP11 .... 172 C2
Hangar Rd UB9 .... 189 F4
Hanging Croft Cl HP13 ..... 173 F3
Hangings La HP16 .... 151 D3
Hanley Cl SL4 .... 209 E3
Hanmer Rd MK6 .... 47 F3
Hannah Ball Cty Fst Sch
 HP13 .... 173 F3
Hannon Rd HP21 .... 115 E3
Hanover Cl
 Aylesbury HP19 .... 101 D1
 Slough SL1 .... 206 A2
 Windsor SL4 .... 209 F3
Hanover Ct
 8 Aylesbury HP21 .... 115 E4
 Leighton Buzzard LU7 ...... 80 B4
 Milton Keynes MK14 .... 34 B4
 Tylers Green HP15 .... 163 D2
Hanover Mead SL6 .... 203 E2
Hanover Way SL4 .... 209 F3
Hanscomb Cl MK15 .... 35 E1
Hanslope Cty Comb Sch
 MK19 .... 11 D2
Hanslope Rd MK19 .... 19 F3
Hanson Cl UB7 .... 208 C2
Hanson Way HP21 .... 116 A2
Harborne Ct MK8 .... 33 E1
Harborough Cl SL3 .... 204 B3
Harbourne Cl HP21 .... 115 E2
Harby Cl MK4 .... 46 B1
Harcourt Cl Dorney SL4 ... 203 F2
 Henley-on-T RG9 .... 191 E1
Leighton Buzzard LU7 ..... 80 C4

Harcourt Gn HP19 .... 101 D1
Harcourt Rd Dorney SL4 ... 203 F2
 Stokenchurch HP14 .... 158 C2
 Tring HP23 .... 119 E2
 Windsor SL4 .... 209 F3
Hardenwaye HP13 .... 162 C1
Harding Rd Chesham HP5 . 144 B1
 Milton Keynes Village MK7 148 B1
Hardings Cl SL0 .... 200 B1
Hardings Row SL0 .... 200 B1
Hardmead Rd MK43 .... 8 A2
Hardwick Cl SL6 .... 202 A4
Hardwick Mews MK17 .... 49 D2
Hardwick Pl MK17 .... 49 D2
Hardwick Rd MK17 .... 49 D2
Hardwicke Gdns HP6 ...... 154 C1
Hardy Cl Aylesbury HP21 .. 115 F3
 Slough SL1 .... 205 D3
Hare Cl MK18 .... 52 C4
Hare La HP16 .... 152 A2
Hare Lane End HP16 .... 152 A2
Hare Shoots SL6 .... 202 C3
Harebell Cl MK7 .... 48 A3
Harebell Wlk HP15 .... 162 C3
Hareden Croft MK4 .... 46 A1
Harefield Place Golf Course
 UB10 .... 201 E4
Harefield Rd
 Maidenhead SL6 .... 202 A4
 Uxbridge UB8 .... 201 E3
Harehatch La SL2 .... 186 C2
Harescombe Cl HP9 .... 175 E2
Haresfoot Sch HP4 .... 135 D1
Harewood Pl SL1 .... 206 A2
Harewood Rd HP8 .... 166 B3
Hargrave Rd SL6 .... 202 B4
Hargreaves Nook MK14 .... 22 A1
Harkness Cl MK2 .... 58 B3
Harkness Rd SL1 .... 204 A4
Harlans Cl MK6 .... 47 D4
Harlech Ho **5** HP13 .... 173 F4
Harlech Pl MK3 .... 57 F4
Harlestone Ct MK14 .... 22 A1
Harling Rd LU6 .... 93 D2
Harlow Rd HP13 .... 173 E3
Harman Wlk HP12 .... 172 B2
Harmondsworth La UB7 ... 213 F4
Harmondsworth Prim Sch
 UB7 .... 213 E4
Harnett Dr MK11 .... 32 C3
Harper Cl OX6 .... 94 B4
Harpers La MK14 .... 34 C4
Harpsden Rd HP20 .... 101 F2
Harrier Cl HP20 .... 101 F2
Harrier Cl MK6 .... 47 D4
Harrier Dr MK6 .... 47 D4
Harries Cl HP5 .... 144 A1
Harries Way HP15 .... 163 D3
Harriet Walker Way WD3 .. 167 F1
Harrington Cl SL4 .... 209 F2
Harris Ct **8** HP20 .... 101 F1
Harris Rd HP14 .... 171 D3
Harrison Cl MK5 .... 46 B3
Harrison Pl OX9 .... 125 F1
Harrison Way SL1 .... 204 B3
Harroell HP18 .... 115 E4
Harrogate Ct SL3 .... 207 D1
Harrold Priory Mid Sch &
 Harrold Lower Sch MK43 ... 3 F3
Harrold Rd MK46 .... 8 A4
Harrow Cl
 Aylesbury HP21 .... 115 F2
 Maidenhead SL6 .... 195 F1
Harrow La SL6 .... 195 F1
Harrow Mkt The SL3 .... 207 D2
Harrow Rd SL3 .... 206 C2
Harrow Yard HP23 .... 119 D2
Harrow Yd **9** HP23 .... 119 D2
Harrowden MK13 .... 34 A4
Hart St RG9 .... 191 F1
Hartdames MK5 .... 46 A2
Hartfield Cl MK7 .... 48 A4
Harthmoor Cl HP14 .... 158 C2
Hartland Cl SL1 .... 205 E3
Hartley MK14 .... 34 C4
Hartley Cl SL3 .... 199 E2
Hartley Copse SL4 .... 211 D1
Hartley Ct SL9 .... 188 C3
Harts Rd HP17 .... 127 D3
Hartwell Cl HP10 .... 163 E1
Hartwell Dr HP9 .... 175 E2
Hartwell End HP21 .... 115 D4
Hartwell Rd Ashton NN7 .... 9 F4
 Hanslope MK19 .... 10 C3
Hartwort Cl MK7 .... 48 A3
Harvard Cl MK14 .... 21 F1
Harvest Bank HP6 .... 153 E2
Harvest Hill SL8 .... 185 E3
Harvest Hill Rd SL6 .... 202 C2
Harvester Cl MK12 .... 33 D3
Harvey Orch HP9 .... 175 E2

arvey Rd
Aylesbury HP21 .... 115 F3
Dunstable LU6 .... 93 E4
Slough SL3 .... 207 D2
arvil Rd Ickenham UB10 .... 190 C2
South Harefield UB9 .... 190 C2
arwich Rd SL2 .... 205 D4
arwood Dr UB10 .... 201 F2
arwood Rd SL7 .... 183 E1
arwood St MK13 .... 34 A4
asgill Ct MK13 .... 34 A2
aslemere Rd SL4 .... 210 A3
aslow Ct MK8 .... 33 F2
asting Cl SL6 .... 203 E1
astings MK11 .... 32 C3
astings Meadow SL2 .... 199 F2
astoe Cross HP23 .... 133 D4
astoe Farm HP23 .... 132 C4
astoe Hill
  Drayton Beauchamp HP23 132 C4
  Hastoe HP21 .... 119 D1
  Hastoe La HP21 .... 119 D1
  Hastoe Park HP20 .... 101 F1
  Hastoe Row HP23 .... 133 D4
atch La
  Bledlow Ridge HP14 .... 160 A2
  Harmondsworth UB7 ...... 213 E4
  Windsor SL4 .... 210 A3
atch The SL4 .... 209 E4
atches La HP15 .... 162 A4
atchet Leys La MK18 .... 53 F4
atchgate Gdns SL1 .... 197 E1
atchlands MK8 .... 33 F1
atfield Cl SL6 .... 202 B3
atfield Rd SL2 .... 206 A2
athaway Ct MK8 .... 45 F4
atter's La HP13 .... 173 F4
atter's Lane Sch The
  HP13 .... 173 F4
atton MK6 .... 47 E3
atton Ct SL2 .... 198 B1
atton Ct SL4 .... 210 B3
atton Gr UB7 .... 209 D2
auksbee Gdns MK5 .... 46 B3
avelock Cres SL6 .... 202 A4
avelock Gr LU7 .... 101 E1
avelock Rd SL6 .... 202 A4
avelock St HP20 .... 101 E1
aven Ct Rest SL6 .... 203 D4
aven Shaw Cl HP21 .... 116 A3
avenfield Ct ■ HP13 ...... 173 D4
avenfield Rd HP22 .... 172 B2
aversham Cty Fst Sch
  MK19 .... 20 C1
aversham Rd MK19 .... 20 B1
aw La HP14 .... 149 D1
awfinch ■ HP20 .... 101 F2
awker Cl SL3 .... 207 D2
awkhurst Gate MK7 .... 47 F4
awkins Cl MK11 .... 32 B3
awkmoor Cl MK6 .... 47 D4
awkmead Av MK6 .... 46 C2
awks Hill SL8 .... 185 E1
awkshill Dr HP1 .... 146 C4
awkshill Rd SL2 .... 198 A1
awkslade Furlong HP21 . 115 E2
awksmoor Cl HP13 .... 173 D4
awkswood MK4 .... 6 C3
awkswood La SL9 .... 199 F4
awkwell Dr HP23 .... 119 E2
awkwell Estate MK19 ..... 32 A4
awleys La HP22 .... 87 D1
awridge & Cholesbury
  CE Comb Sch HP5 .... 133 F1
awridge La
  Chartridge HP5 .... 143 F4
  Cholesbury HP5 .... 143 F4
awridge Vale HP5 .... 133 F1
awthorn Ave MK2 .... 58 C4
awthorn Cl
  Aylesbury HP20 .... 101 F1
  Marlow SL7 .... 183 F2
  Turvey MK43 .... 8 C3
awthorn Cres HP15 .... 163 D1
awthorn Dr UB9 .... 201 E3
awthorn La SL2 .... 198 A3
awthorn Pl HP10 .... 174 B4
awthorn Rd HP27 .... 139 E2
awthorn Way
  Chesham HP5 .... 144 B1
  Wing LU7 .... 79 F2
awthorn Wlk HP15 .... 163 D1
awthorne Cl LU7 .... 90 C4
awthorne Cres
  Slough SL1 .... 205 F4
  West Drayton UB7 .... 208 C2
awthorne Gdns HP10 .... 174 A1
awthorne Rd HP13 .... 174 A3
awthorns The
  Berkhamsted HP4 .... 135 D3
  Cranfield MK43 .... 25 D1

Hawthorns The
  Feldon HP3 .... 146 C4
  Little Chalfont HP6 .... 166 B4
  Maple Cross WD3 .... 178 B3
  Princes Risborough HP27 139 E3
  Stanwell SL3 .... 212 C3
  Wooburn Green HP10 .... 185 F3
Hawtrey Cl SL1 .... 206 A2
Hawtrey Rd SL4 .... 210 B3
Hay La SL3 .... 199 E4
Hayden Ho 12 HP11 .... 172 C4
Haydock Cl MK3 .... 57 E3
Haydon Abbey Cty Comb Sch
  HP19 .... 116 C4
Haydon Cl SL6 .... 202 C3
Haydon Rd HP19 .... 101 E1
Hayes Pl SL7 .... 183 E1
Hayes Rd MK19 .... 31 F3
Hayfield Dr HP15 .... 163 D1
Hayles Field RG9 .... 170 C1
Haymaker Cl UB10 .... 201 F3
Haymill Rd SL1, SL2 ...... 197 E1
Haynes Cl
  Bow Brickhill MK17 .... 48 B1
  Slough SL3 .... 206 C1
Haynes Mead HP4 .... 135 D3
Hayse Hill SL4 .... 209 E3
Haystacks The HP13 ..... 173 E4
Haythorp Cl MK15 .... 35 D3
Hayward Pl SL8 .... 185 E1
Haywards Cft RG9 .... 191 E1
Haywards Croft MK12 ... 33 D3
Haywards Mead SL4 ..... 204 C1
Haywood Park
  Chorleywood WD3 .... 167 F2
  Stewkley LU7 .... 68 B2
Haywood Way HP19 .... 100 C2
Hazel Ave HP21 .... 116 A4
Hazel Cl SL3 .... 183 E3
Hazel Ct WD3 .... 178 C3
Hazel Gr MK2 .... 58 B4
Hazel Rd HP4 .... 135 C2
Hazelbury Rd HP13 .... 173 E3
Hazelcroft Cl UB10 .... 201 F3
Hazeldene HP22 .... 131 E2
Hazelhurst Dr HP21 ...... 116 A3
Hazelhurst Rd SL1 .... 197 E2
Hazell Cl SL6 .... 203 D4
Hazell Park HP7 .... 165 E4
Hazell Rd HP16 .... 151 E3
Hazell Way SL2 .... 198 C3
Hazelmere Rd SL2 .... 206 A3
Hazelwood MK14 .... 34 C4
Hazelwood Cl HP5 .... 144 B1
Hazely HP23 .... 119 E2
Hazlemere CE Comb Sch
  HP15 .... 162 C2
Hazlemere Rd HP10 ...... 163 D3
Hazlemere View HP15 .. 163 D3
Hazlerig Cl HP21 .... 115 F3
Hazley Wlk MK18 .... 41 F1
Headington Cl SL6 .... 202 A4
Headington Rd SL6 .... 202 A4
Headland Cl HP16 .... 152 A4
Healey Ave HP13 .... 173 E4
Heaney Cl MK16 .... 22 A3
Hearn Cl HP15 .... 162 C1
Hearn's Meadow HP9 .... 176 B2
Hearne Ct HP8 .... 177 D4
Hearne Dr SL6 .... 203 D1
Hearne Pl MK4 .... 46 C4
Hearne's Cl HP9 .... 176 B3
Heath Cl Aylesbury HP21 116 A3
  Holmer Green HP15 ...... 163 D3
  Stanwell TW19 .... 212 C4
  Woburn Sands MK17 ..... 49 E2
Heath Ct
  Leighton Buzzard LU7 .... 70 C2
  Uxbridge UB8 .... 201 F3
Heath End Cl HP15 .... 151 F1
Heath End Rd
  Flackwell Heath HP10 ... 173 E1
  Great Kingshill
    HP15, HP16 .... 151 F1
  Little Kingshill HP16 ..... 151 F1
  Little Marlow HP10 .... 173 E1
Heath La MK17 .... 49 D1
Heath Lawn HP10 .... 173 F1
Heath Rd Beaconsfield HP9 185 F4
  Great Brickhill MK17 ..... 59 F1
  Hyde Heath HP6 .... 153 E3
Heath The LU7 .... 70 C2
Heath Way SL0 .... 200 B2
Heath Way SL3 .... 212 B2
Heathcote Cl SL6 .... 203 D1
Heathcote Ct 2 SL4 ...... 210 B2
Heathcote Way UB7 ...... 208 B3
Heathcroft MK14 .... 34 C4
Heather Cl UB8 .... 208 C4
Heather La UB7 .... 208 C4
Heather Mead LU6 .... 92 C3

Heather Wlk
  Aylesbury HP21 .... 115 D3
  Tylers Green HP15 .... 163 D2
Heatherden Green SL0 .. 200 B2
Heatherside Gdns SL2 .. 198 C3
Heatherton House Sch
  HP6 .... 154 B2
Heatherton Pk HP6 .... 154 A2
Heathfield MK12 .... 33 F2
Heathfield Rd
  High Wycombe HP12 .... 172 A4
  Taplow SL1 .... 186 A1
Heathlands Dr SL6 .... 202 A3
Heathrow Bvd UB7 .... 213 D3
Heathrow Cl TW6 .... 213 D3
Heathrow Prim Sch UB7 213 F4
Heavens Lea SL8 .... 185 E1
Hedge Lea HP10 .... 185 D4
Hedgerley Gn HP9 .... 187 E3
Hedgerley Hill SL2 .... 187 E1
Hedgerley La
  Beaconsfield HP9 .... 187 E3
  Gerrards Cross HP9 ...... 187 E3
Hedgerows The MK4 .... 46 C2
Hedges Cft MK5 .... 46 A3
Hedingham Ct MK5 .... 46 A3
Hedingham Mews SL6 ... 202 B4
Hedley Cl HP23 .... 118 A2
Hedley Rd HP10 .... 185 D4
Hedsor Hill SL8 .... 185 E1
Hedsor La Bourne End
  HP10 .... 185 F1
  Taplow SL1 .... 185 F1
Hedsor Rd SL8 .... 185 D1
Hedsor View Cotts SL6 . 195 F4
Heelands Cty Fst Sch MK13 34 A2
Heights Sch The HP13 ... 161 E1
Heights The SL7 .... 194 A4
Hele Ct MK7 .... 48 A2
Helen Cotts SL4 .... 209 E3
Helena Rd SL4 .... 210 B3
Helford Cl HP21 .... 115 E2
Helford Pl MK6 .... 35 D1
Hellyer Way SL8 .... 185 E2
Helston La SL4 .... 210 A3
Helston Pl MK6 .... 34 C1
Hemel Hempstead Rd HP4 107 F1
Hemingway Rd HP19 ..... 100 C1
Hemmings The HP4 .... 134 C2
Hemmingway Cl MK16 ... 21 F3
Hemp La HP23 .... 119 F1
Hempson Ave SL3 .... 206 B2
Hempstead Rd HP3 .... 146 A3
Hemwood Rd SL4 .... 209 E2
Hencroft St N SL1 .... 205 F2
Hencroft St S SL1 .... 205 F2
Henders MK11 .... 32 C3
Hendon Way TW19 .... 213 E1
Hendons Way SL6 .... 203 D1
Hendrix Dr MK8 .... 45 E4
Henley Coll The (Deanfield
  Bldgs) The RG9 .... 191 E1
Henley Coll The (Rotherham
  Bldgs) RG9 .... 191 E1
Henley Coll The (Southfield
  Bldgs) RG9 .... 191 E1
Henley Lodge 12 SL6 .... 202 C3
Henley Rd Bisham SL6 . 194 A1
  Hurley SL6 .... 193 E2
  Marlow SL7 .... 194 A4
  Slough SL1 .... 204 C4
Henley Trinity Prim Sch
  RG9 .... 191 E1
Hennerton Way HP13 .... 173 F3
Henrietta Rd SL9 .... 201 E1
Henry Rd Aylesbury HP20 116 A4
  Slough SL1 .... 205 E2
Henson Cl HP43 .... 24 C2
Hepleswell MK8 .... 33 F1
Hepplewhite Cl HP13 .... 173 E4
Herbert Rd HP13 .... 174 A4
Herberts Hole HP16 ...... 142 C1
Hercies Rd UB10 .... 201 F3
Herd's Hill MK18 .... 64 A2
Herdman Cl MK12 .... 33 D3
Hereford Ho HP13 .... 173 F4
Hereford Way HP19 .... 101 D2
Heritage Cl UB8 .... 201 E1
Heritage Gate HP10 ...... 174 C2
Heritage House Sch HP5 144 B1
Hermitage Cl SL3 .... 206 B2
Hermitage La SL4 .... 210 A2
Hermitage Prim Sch SL4 210 A2
Hermitage The
  Great Missenden HP16 . 152 A4
  Uxbridge UB8 .... 201 E1
Heron Cl Aylesbury HP20 116 B4
  Uxbridge UB8 .... 208 B3
Heron Dr SL3 .... 207 D1
Heron The HP20 .... 101 F2
Herons Elm HP4 .... 134 C4

Herons Pl SL7 .... 183 F2
Heronsgate Cty Comb Sch
  MK7 .... 48 A3
Heronsgate Dr WD3 ...... 167 D2
Herriot Cl MK16 .... 22 A3
Herschel Gram Sch SL1 205 E4
Herschel Park Dr SL1 .... 205 F2
Herschel St SL1 .... 205 F2
Herston Cl HP21 .... 116 A3
Hertford Pl MK3 .... 46 C1
Hervines Ct HP6 .... 154 B1
Hervines Rd HP6 .... 154 B1
Hesketh Rd NN12 .... 18 C3
Het's Orch HP27 .... 149 F3
Hetherington Cl SL2 ...... 197 F1
Hetherington Way UB10 . 201 F4
Hetton Cl MK13 .... 34 B2
Heusden Way SL9 .... 188 C2
Hever Cl SL6 .... 202 B3
Hewgate Ct RG9 .... 191 F1
Hexham Gdns MK18 .... 57 E3
Heybridge Cres MK7 .... 48 A2
Heynes Gn SL6 .... 202 A2
Heythrop Dr UB10 .... 201 F4
Heywood Ave SL6 .... 202 A1
Heywood Court Cl SL6 .. 202 A1
Heywood Gdns SL6 .... 202 A1
Hibbert Rd SL6 .... 202 B1
Hibbert's Alley 23 SL4 .. 210 B3
Hibberts Way SL9 .... 188 C3
Hickmans Cl MK18 .... 51 D3
Hickox Ct HP10 .... 185 F4
Hicks Farm Rise HP13 .. 173 F4
Hide The MK6 .... 47 E3
Higgs Ct MK5 .... 46 A4
High Ash CE Comb Sch
  MK17 .... 59 E1
High Beeches
  Gerrards Cross SL9 ...... 188 B1
  High Wycombe HP12 .... 172 B3
High Bois La HP6 .... 154 B2
High Coppice HP7 .... 165 E4
High Halden MK7 .... 48 A3
High Heavens Wood SL7 183 E1
High Land Cl HP18 .... 96 A1
High Moors HP22 .... 131 D4
High Rd Cookham SL6 ... 195 F3
  Soulbury LU7 .... 69 F1
  Uxbridge UB8 .... 208 B4
High St Amersham HP7 . 165 D4
  Aston Rowant OX9 .... 147 D2
  Aylesbury HP20 .... 115 F4
  Berkhamsted HP4 .... 135 C3
  Bovingdon HP3 .... 146 A2
  Brill HP18 .... 110 A4
  Buckingham MK18 .... 41 E1
  Burnham SL1 .... 197 E1
  Chalfont St Giles HP8 .. 177 E4
  Cheddington LU7 .... 105 D4
  Chesham HP5 .... 154 A4
  Chinnor OX9 .... 147 E4
  Colnbrook SL3 .... 212 B4
  Cookham SL6 .... 196 A4
  Cranfield MK43 .... 25 D1
  Cublington LU7 .... 78 A1
  Datchet SL3 .... 211 D3
  Deanshanger MK19 .... 31 F2
  Dinton HP17 .... 113 F1
  Eaton Bray LU6 .... 92 C3
  Edlesborough LU6 .... 92 C2
  Emberton MK46 .... 13 F4
  Eton SL4 .... 210 B4
  Gerrards Cross SL9 ...... 177 F1
  Great Horwood MK17 .... 55 D2
  Haddenham HP17 .... 126 C3
  Hanslope MK19 .... 11 D1
  Harmondsworth UB7 .... 213 E4
  Harrold MK43 .... 3 F3
  Haversham MK19 .... 21 D2
  High Wycombe HP11 .... 173 D3
  High Wycombe, Downley
    HP13 .... 161 E2
  Iver SL0 .... 207 F4
  Ivinghoe LU7 .... 105 F3
  Lane End HP14 .... 171 D2
  Lavendon MK46 .... 7 F4
  Leighton Buzzard LU7 ... 80 F2
  Lewknor OX9 .... 157 D4
  Long Crendon HP18 ..... 125 E3
  Ludgershall HP18 .... 96 A4
  Maidenhead SL6 .... 203 E2
  Marlow SL7 .... 183 F1
  Milton Keynes, Great Linford
    MK14 .... 21 F1
  Milton Keynes, New Bradwell
    MK13 .... 33 F4
  Nash MK17 .... 44 B1
  Newport Pagnell MK16 ... 22 B2
  North Crawley MK16 ...... 24 A3
  North Marston MK18 ...... 76 A1
  Olney MK46 .... 6 C2

Har – Hig **229**

High St
  Paulerspury NN12 .... 17 E4
  Pottersputy NN12 .... 18 B2
  Prestwood HP16 .... 151 E3
  Princes Risborough HP27 139 D2
  Sherington MK16 .... 13 F1
  Slough, Langley SL3 ..... 207 D1
  Slough, Upton SL1, SL3 205 F2
  South Heath HP16 .... 152 A4
  Stanwell TW19 .... 213 E1
  Stoke Goldington MK16 . 12 A3
  Syresham NN13 .... 27 D4
  Taplow SL6 .... 196 C1
  Thame OX9 .... 125 F1
  Thornborough MK18 ...... 54 A4
  Tring HP23 .... 119 D2
  Turvey MK43 .... 8 C3
  Uxbridge UB8 .... 201 E3
  Waddesdon HP18 .... 99 D3
  Weedon HP22 .... 87 E1
  Wendover HP22 .... 131 D2
  West Drayton UB7 .... 208 C3
  Westcott HP18 .... 98 A4
  Weston Underwood MK46 .. 6 A1
  Whaddon MK17 .... 45 D1
  Whitchurch HP22 .... 87 D3
  Windsor SL4 .... 210 B3
  Wing LU7 .... 79 F1
  Wing, Burcott LU7 .... 79 E2
  Winslow MK18 .... 65 F2
  Woburn MK17 .... 60 C4
  Woburn Sands MK17 ..... 49 D2
  Wraysbury TW19 .... 211 F1
  Yardley Gobion NN12 ... 18 C3
  Yardley Hastings NN7 ..... 1 A3
High St N ■ SL6 .... 202 C4
High St N SL7 .... 68 B1
High St S Olney MK46 ..... 6 C2
  Stewkley LU7 .... 78 C4
High St The MK8 .... 33 E1
High Town Rd SL6 .... 202 C4
High Trees MK6 .... 47 D4
High View HP8 .... 177 E4
High View Cl SL7 .... 183 E4
High Wycombe CE Comb Sch
  HP11 .... 173 D3
High Wycombe Sta HP13 173 D4
Higham Cross Rd MK19 .. 10 C2
Higham Mead HP5 .... 144 B1
Higham Rd HP5 .... 144 B1
Highbeeches Cl SL2 ...... 183 E4
Highbridge Ind Est UB8 . 201 E3
Highbridge Rd HP21 ...... 115 F4
Highbridge Wlk ■ HP21 . 115 F4
Highbury La MK19 .... 35 D2
Highcroft Cl NN12 .... 18 C3
Highfield
  Chalfont St Giles HP8 .. 177 E4
  Long Crendon HP18 ..... 125 E4
Highfield Ave HP12 .... 172 A3
Highfield Cl
  Amersham HP6 .... 154 B1
  Milton Keynes MK3 .... 47 D1
  Newport Pagnell MK16 ... 22 C2
Highfield Ct Burnham SL2 198 A2
  Tylers Green HP15 .... 163 D2
Highfield Dr UB10 .... 190 C1
Highfield La SL6 .... 202 A2
Highfield Park SL7 .... 194 A4
Highfield Pk SL7 .... 183 D1
Highfield Rd
  Berkhamsted HP4 .... 135 E2
  Bourne End SL8 .... 185 D2
  Chesham HP5 .... 144 A1
  Flackwell Heath HP10 ... 185 D4
  Maidenhead SL6 .... 202 A4
  Princes Risborough HP27 139 E2
  Tring HP23 .... 118 C2
  Wigginton HP23 .... 119 E1
  Windsor SL4 .... 209 F2
  Winslow MK18 .... 65 F3
Highfield Way
  Tylers Green HP15 .... 163 D2
  Yardley Hastings NN7 ..... 1 A3
Highgate Over MK7 .... 48 A3
Highgrove Hill MK8 .... 45 F4
Highgrove Park SL6 ...... 202 C4
Highland Cl MK3 .... 46 C2
Highland Rd HP7 .... 165 E4
Highlands
  Flackwell Heath HP10 .. 185 D4
  High Wycombe HP13 .... 174 A3
Highlands Cl SL9 .... 177 F2
Highlands End SL9 .... 177 F2
Highlands La SL9 .... 177 F2
Highlands Rd
  Buckingham MK18 .... 41 F1
  Seer Green HP9 .... 176 B3

Highlea Ave HP10 .... 185 D4
Highmoor HP7 .... 165 E4
Highmore Cotts HP16 ..... 152 C2
Highover Park HP7 .... 165 E4
Highview MK19 .... 31 F3
Highway Ave SL6 .... 202 A3
Highway Ct
  Beaconsfield HP9 .... 175 E2
  Chesham HP5 .... 144 B1
Highway Rd SL6 .... 202 A3
Highway The HP9 .... 175 E1
Highwood Ave HP12 ...... 172 A3
Highwood Bottom HP27 .. 150 A3
Highwood Cres HP12 ..... 172 A3
Highwoods Cl SL7 .... 183 E4
Highwoods Dr SL7 .... 183 E4
Highworth Cl HP13 .... 162 C1
Hilbury Cl HP6 .... 154 B2
Hilda Wharf HP20 .... 115 F4
Hildreth Rd HP16 .... 151 E3
Hiljon Cres SL9 .... 177 F1
Hill Ave Amersham HP6 .. 154 B1
  Holmer Green HP15 ...... 163 D3
Hill Cl HP10 .... 185 F4
Hill Cotts HP18 .... 97 F1
Hill Farm MK18 .... 76 A1
Hill Farm App HP10 .... 185 F4
Hill Farm Ct OX9 .... 147 E3
Hill Farm La HP8 .... 166 A1
Hill Farm Rd
  Chalfont St Peter SL9 ... 177 F2
  Chesham HP5 .... 154 B3
  Marlow Bottom SL7 .... 183 F3
  Taplow SL6 .... 196 C1
Hill Farm Way HP15 .... 163 D2
Hill Gr SL9 .... 177 F1
Hill House Cl SL9 .... 177 F1
Hill Mead HP4 .... 135 D2
Hill Meadow HP7 .... 164 C2
Hill Pl SL2 .... 198 A3
Hill Rd Chinnor OX9 ...... 147 E3
  Lewknor OX9 .... 157 D4
  Lewknor OX9 .... 157 E3
Hill Rise SL9 .... 177 E1
Hill Rise Cres SL9 .... 177 F1
Hill Side LU7 .... 104 C4
Hill St HP13 .... 174 A3
Hill The Coleshill HP7 .... 164 B2
  Syresham NN13 .... 27 D4
Hill Top Dr SL7 .... 183 D1
Hill Top La OX9 .... 147 F2
Hill View Berkhamsted HP4 135 D3
  Great Kimble HP17 .... 129 F1
  Newport Pagnell MK16 .... 22 A2
  Oakley HP18 .... 109 E3
Hill View Rd TW19 .... 211 E1
Hill Waye SL9 .... 188 C2
Hillary Cl Aylesbury HP21 .. 116 A3
  High Wycombe HP13 ...... 173 F3
Hillary Rd
  High Wycombe HP13 ...... 173 F3
  Slough SL3 .... 206 C2
Hillbottom Rd HP12 .... 172 A4
Hillcrest MK43 .... 25 E1
Hillcrest Ave SL6 .... 195 F3
Hillcrest Cl MK5 .... 46 A3
Hillcrest Ct HP6 .... 154 B1
Hillcrest Rise MK18 .... 52 C3
Hillcrest Way MK18 .... 52 C3
Hillcrest Waye SL9 .... 188 C3
Hillcroft Rd Chesham HP5 .. 144 B1
  Tylers Green HP10 .... 163 E1
Hillersdon SL2 .... 206 A4
Hillersdon Chase MK17 ... 69 E4
Hillesden Way MK18 .... 41 F1
Hillfield Cl HP13 .... 161 F1
Hillfield Rd SL9 .... 177 F2
Hillfield Sq SL9 .... 177 F2
Hilliard Dr MK13 .... 34 A2
Hilliards Rd UB8 .... 208 B4
Hillier Rd HP21 .... 115 E2
Hillingdon Hill UB10 ...... 201 F1
Hillingdon Hospl U88 .... 208 C4
Hillingdon Rd UB10 .... 201 F2
Hillington Cl HP21 .... 115 D4
Hillman Cl UB8 .... 201 F4
Hillmead Ct SL6 .... 203 F4
Hillrise SL3 .... 212 A4
Hills Cl MK14 .... 34 C4
Hills La SL6 .... 195 E4
Hillside Chesham HP5 ..... 144 A2
  Gawcott MK18 .... 51 F2
  High Wycombe HP13 ...... 173 E4
  Maidenhead SL6 .... 202 B3
  Slough SL1 .... 205 F2
  South Harefield UB9 ...... 190 B3
  Tingewick MK18 .... 51 D3

Hillside Cl
  Chalfont St Giles HP8 .... 177 D4
  Chalfont St Peter SL9 .... 177 F2
  Upper Arncott OX6 .... 94 C4
Hillside Cotts HP18 .... 112 C1
Hillside Gdns
  Berkhamsted HP4 .... 135 E2
  High Wycombe HP13 ...... 173 E4
Hillside Rd
  Chorleywood WD3 .... 167 E2
  Marlow SL7 .... 183 F2
  Tylers Green HP10 .... 163 D1
Hilltop HP18 .... 125 E3
Hilltop Ave MK18 .... 41 F1
Hilltop Fst Sch SL4 .... 209 F2
Hilltop Rd HP4 .... 135 E2
Hillview MK16 .... 14 A1
Hillview Rd HP13 .... 173 E4
Hillway Amersham HP7 ... 165 D3
  Woburn Sands MK17 .... 49 D3
Hillwerke SL9 .... 147 E3
Hillyer Ct MK6 .... 47 E1
Hilperton Rd 3 SL1 .... 205 F2
Hilton Ave HP20 .... 101 F1
Hilton Cl UB8 .... 201 D2
Himley Green LU7 .... 80 B3
Hindemith Gdns MK7 .... 48 B3
Hindhead Knoll MK7 .... 48 A3
Hinksey Cl UB9 .... 190 B4
Hinksey Cl SL3 .... 207 D2
Hinton Cl HP13 .... 162 A1
Hinton Rd Slough SL1 .... 204 C3
  Uxbridge UB8 .... 201 E2
Hipwell Ct MK46 .... 6 C2
Hitcham House SL1 .... 197 D1
Hitcham La Burnham SL1 .. 197 D1
  Taplow SL6 .... 196 C1
Hitcham Rd SL1 .... 204 A4
Hither Meadow SL9 .... 177 F1
Hithercroft Rd HP13 ...... 161 F1
Hithermoor Rd TW19 ..... 213 D1
Hiving's Hill HP5 .... 144 A1
Hivings Park HP5 .... 144 A2
HM Prison
  (Bullingdon) OX6 .... 95 D3
HM Prison (The Mount)
  HP1 .... 145 F2
HM Young Offender Inst
  (Grendon) HP18 .... 123 D1
HM Young Offender Inst
  (Winnamore Wood Camp)
  SL7 .... 182 B4
Hoathly Mews MK7 .... 48 A4
Hobart Cl HP13 .... 162 C1
Hobart Cotts HP16 .... 150 B4
Hobart Cres MK15 .... 35 D4
Hobart St SL7 .... 184 A2
Hobart Rd HP13 .... 162 B1
Hobarts Dr UB9 .... 189 F3
Hobbis Dr SL6 .... 202 A3
Hobbs Rd HP14 .... 171 E2
Hobsons Wlk HP23 .... 118 C3
Hockett La Bisham SL6 ... 195 D3
  Cookham SL6 .... 195 D3
Hockley La SL2 .... 199 D3
Hockliffe Brae MK7 .... 48 A3
Hodder La MK4 .... 46 A3
Hodds Wood Rd HP5 ..... 154 B3
Hodge Lea La MK12 .... 33 E2
Hodgemore Ct MK14 .... 21 F1
Hoe Meadow HP9 .... 175 E2
Hog Hall La HP4 .... 107 F2
Hog La Ashley Green HP5 .. 144 B4
  Berkhamsted HP5 .... 134 C1
Hogarth Cl SL1 .... 205 D2
Hogarths Ct MK8 .... 33 F1
Hogback Wood Rd HP9 .. 175 D2
Hogfair La SL1 .... 197 E1
Hogg La HP15 .... 163 E3
Hoggshill Rd HP16 .... 152 A3
Hogshaw Rd MK18 .... 75 F3
Hogtrough La HP22 .... 131 E1
Holdom Ave MK1 .... 47 E1
Holes La MK46 .... 6 C2
Holiday La MK19 .... 10 C2
Holland Cl Chinnor OX9 ... 147 E4
  Wendover HP22 .... 131 D2
Holland Rd
  Aylesbury HP19 .... 101 D1
  Marlow SL7 .... 183 F2
Holland Way MK16 .... 22 B2
Hollandridge La RG9 .... 168 B2
Holliday Cl MK8 .... 45 F4
Holliday St HP4 .... 135 E2
Hollies The
  Beaconsfield HP9 .... 175 F2
  Bovingdon HP3 .... 146 A1
  Tring HP23 .... 119 D2
  Wigginton HP23 .... 119 E1
Hollin La MK12 .... 33 F2
Hollingdon Rd LU7 .... 69 E2

Hollington HP18 .... 125 D4
Hollinwell Cl MK3 .... 46 B1
Hollis Rd HP13 .... 173 F4
Hollister Chase MK5 .... 46 A2
Hollow Hill End MK18 ..... 75 F4
Hollow Hill La SL0 .... 207 E3
Hollow Rise HP13 .... 162 A1
Hollow Way HP5 .... 143 F1
Hollow Way La
  Amersham HP6 .... 154 C2
  Chesham HP5 .... 154 C2
Hollow Wood MK46 .... 6 C2
Holloway Cl UB7 .... 208 C1
Holloway Dr MK18 .... 41 F1
Holloway La Chenies WD3 .. 156 B1
  Ibstone RG9 .... 169 E2
  West Drayton UB7 .... 208 C1
Holloway The
  Drayton Beauchamp HP22 118 B2
  Princes Risborough HP27 . 139 E3
Holly Cl
  Farnham Common SL2 ... 198 B4
  Shenley Church End MK8 ... 45 F3
Holly Cres SL4 .... 209 F2
Holly Dr Aylesbury HP21 .. 115 F3
  Berkhamsted HP4 .... 135 E2
  Maidenhead SL6 .... 202 C4
  Windsor SL4 .... 210 C1
Holly End HP14 .... 161 E4
Holly Gdns UB7 .... 208 C2
Holly Green La HP27 ...... 138 A2
Holly Hedges La HP3 ...... 156 B4
Holly Pl HP11 .... 174 A2
Holly Tree Cl HP5 .... 155 D4
Holly Tree La HP18 .... 112 C2
Holly Wlk MK17 .... 49 D1
Hollyberry Gr HP15 .... 163 E4
Hollybush Cnr SL2 .... 187 E1
Hollybush Hill SL2 .... 199 D3
Hollybush La
  Amersham HP6 .... 154 B2
  Cookham SL6 .... 195 D3
  Denham UB9 .... 200 C4
  Iver SL0 .... 207 D4
Hollybush Rd HP5 .... 144 A2
Hollybush Row HP23 ...... 133 E4
Hollyfield HP23 .... 119 E3
Hollyfield Cl HP23 .... 119 E3
Hollytree Cl SL9 .... 177 F1
Holm Gate MK5 .... 46 A3
Holman St HP19 .... 101 E1
Holmanleaze SL6 .... 203 D4
Holmdale SL2 .... 206 B3
Holmer Green Cty Fst Sch
  HP15 .... 163 D4
Holmer Green Cty Mid Sch
  HP15 .... 163 E4
Holmer Green Rd HP15 ... 163 D2
Holmer Green Upper Sch
  HP15 .... 163 E4
Holmer Pl HP15 .... 163 E4
Holmfield Ct HP21 .... 172 A2
Holmers Farm Way
  High Wycombe HP12 ...... 172 B2
  Little Marlow HP12 .... 172 B2
  Marlow Bottom HP12 ..... 172 B2
Holmers La
  High Wycombe HP12 ...... 172 B2
  High Wycombe HP12 ...... 172 B2
Holmewood MK4 .... 46 C2
Holmfield Cl MK6 .... 47 E3
Holmlea Rd SL3 .... 211 E3
Holmlea Wlk SL3 .... 211 E3
Holmoak Wlk HP15 .... 163 D2
Holmsdale Cl SL0 .... 207 F4
Holmwood Cl SL6 .... 202 A3
Holmwood Cty Fst Sch
  MK8 .... 33 F1
Holne Chase Cty Comb Sch
  MK3 .... 58 A4
Holt Cres MK7 .... 48 B2
Holt Gr MK5 .... 46 A2
Holt The MK18 .... 52 C4
Holton Hill MK4 .... 46 B1
Holton Rd MK8 .... 41 E1
Holts Green MK17 .... 59 E1
Holtspur Ave HP10 .... 185 F4
Holtspur Cl HP9 .... 186 A4
Holtspur Cty Comb Sch
  HP9 .... 175 D1
Holtspur La HP10 .... 185 F3
Holtspur Top La HP9 ...... 175 D1
Holtspur Way HP9 .... 175 D1
Holy Family RC Sch The
  SL3 .... 206 C1
Holy Thorn La MK5 .... 45 F3
Holy Thorne La MK5 .... 46 A3
Holy Trinity CE Mid Sch
  SL7 .... 183 E2
Holy Trinity Prim Sch SL6 .. 196 A4
Holyhead Cres MK4 .... 57 E4

Holyport Rd SL6 .... 203 D1
Holyrood MK8 .... 45 F4
Holywell Gdns HP13 ...... 173 F4
Holywell Pl MK6 .... 35 E1
Holywell Rd MK43 .... 25 E1
Holywell Sch MK43 .... 25 D1
Home Cl Milton Keynes MK3 47 D1
  Weston Turville HP22 ..... 116 C1
Home Farm MK17 .... 57 E2
Home Farm Cl
  Bovingdon HP3 .... 145 F1
  Emberton MK46 .... 13 F4
Home Farm La MK17 .... 59 E1
Home Farm Rd HP4 .... 134 B4
Home Farm Way SL3 ...... 199 E2
Home Field MK7 .... 48 A2
Home Meadow SL2 .... 198 B2
Home Meadow Dr HP10 .. 185 D4
Home Way WD3 .... 167 F1
Homefarm Ct HP8 .... 177 D4
Homefield P3 .... 146 A2
Homefield Ct LU4 .... 158 C2
Homefield Rd WD3 .... 167 E3
Homelands Gdns HP15 ... 162 B4
Homers Rd SL4 .... 209 E3
Homeridings Ho MK13 ..... 34 A2
Homers Rd SL4 .... 209 E3
Homestall MK6 .... 46 A4
Homestall Cl MK5 .... 46 A4
Homestead Cl HP17 .... 114 A2
Homestead Rd SL6 .... 202 B2
Homestead The
  Great Kingshill HP15 ..... 151 E1
  Little Marlow HP12 .... 172 B2
  Shenley Church End MK5 ... 46 A3
  Thame OX9 .... 125 F1
Homestead Way NN12 .... 18 C2
Homeward Ct MK5 .... 46 A4
Homewood SL3 .... 206 B4
Homewood Ct WD3 .... 167 F3
Hondur Cl HP20 .... 102 A1
Honey Banks HP22 .... 131 E2
Honey Hill UB10 .... 201 F3
Honey La SL6 .... 193 F1
Honey Way HP14 .... 161 D4
Honeycroft Hill UB10 ..... 201 F3
Honeypot Cl MK13 .... 34 A2
Honeysuckle Cl SL0 .... 207 E4
Honeysuckle Fld HP5 ..... 144 B1
Honeysuckle Rd HP15 .... 162 C4
Honeywick La LU6 .... 92 C4
Honiton Ct MK7 .... 48 B4
Honor End La HP16 .... 151 D4
Honor Rd HP16 .... 151 E3
Honorwood Cl HP16 ...... 151 D3
Honours Mead HP1 .... 146 A2
Hoods Farm Cl HP22 ..... 102 B2
Hooper Gate MK15 .... 35 D4
Hop Gdns RG9 .... 191 E1
Hopcraft Cl OX6 .... 94 C4
Hopkins Cl MK10 .... 36 A1
Hopkins Ct HP20 .... 101 F1
Hoppers Meadow MK5 ..... 46 A4
Hoppers Way HP15 .... 162 B4
Hopton Rd OX9 .... 126 A1
Horn La MK11 .... 32 B3
Horn St MK18 .... 65 F2
Hornbeam MK16 .... 22 A3
Hornbeam Cl HP12 .... 172 A2
Hornbeam Gdns SL1 ...... 206 A2
Hornbeam Wlk HP15 ...... 163 D2
Hornbill Cl UB7 .... 208 B4
Hornby Chase MK4 .... 46 C1
Horners Croft MK12 .... 33 E3
Hornhill Rd WD3 .... 178 B3
Horns La
  High Wycombe HP12 ...... 172 A2
  Princes Risborough HP27 139 D2
Horse Hill HP5 .... 155 E4
Horsefair Gn MK11 .... 32 B3
Horseguards Dr SL6 ...... 203 D4
Horsemoor Cl SL3 .... 207 D1
Horsemoor La HP7 .... 164 B1
Horsenden Rd
  Bledlow HP27 .... 138 C1
  High Wycombe HP13 ...... 173 F3
Horsepond MK7 .... 59 E1
Horseshoe Cl LU7 .... 105 D4
Horseshoe Cloisters 12
  SL4 .... 210 B3
Horseshoe Cres HP9 ..... 175 F1
Horseshoe Hill SL1 .... 197 E4
Horseshoe Rd HP14 ...... 159 E4
Horsetone Cotts HP17 ... 129 E1
Horsleys WD3 .... 178 B2
Horton Bridge Rd UB7 ... 208 C3
Horton Cl Maidenhead SL6 196 B1
  West Drayton UB7 .... 208 C3
Horton Depot SL3 .... 212 B2
Horton Gate MK14 .... 21 F1

Horton Gdns SL3 .... 211 F2
Horton Grange SL6 .... 196 B1
Horton Ind Pk UB7 .... 208 C3
Horton Par UB7 .... 208 C3
Horton Rd Datchet SL3 ... 211 E3
  Horton SL3 .... 212 A3
  Ivinghoe LU7 .... 91 E3
  Slapton LU7 .... 91 E3
  Stanwell TW19 .... 213 D2
  West Drayton UB7 .... 208 C3
Horton Road Ind Est UB7 . 208 C3
Horton Trad Est SL3 .... 212 B2
Hortonsfield Rd NN12 .... 18 C3
Horwood Ct MK1 .... 47 E1
Hospital Circular Rd HP22 131 E3
Hospital Hill HP5 .... 154 B4
Hospital Rdbt MK6 .... 47 D3
Hotch Croft MK43 .... 25 E2
Hotley Bottom La HP16 ... 151 E4
Houghton Ct MK8 .... 45 F4
Housman Cl MK16 .... 22 A3
Houston Ct 33 SL4 .... 210 B3
How's Cl UB8 .... 201 E2
How's Rd UB8 .... 201 E2
Howard Agne Cl HP1 ..... 146 A2
Howard Ave
  Aylesbury HP21 .... 116 A3
  Slough SL2 .... 205 F4
Howard Cres HP9 .... 176 B3
Howard Est The HP5 ...... 144 B3
Howard Rd Chesham HP5 . 144 A2
  Seer Green HP9 .... 176 B3
Howard Way MK16 .... 23 D2
Howards Thicket SL9 ...... 188 B3
Howards Wood Dr SL9 ... 188 B3
Howarth Rd SL6 .... 203 D3
Howe Dr HP9 .... 175 F2
Howe Hill La HP15 .... 163 D4
Howell Hill Cl LU7 .... 90 B3
Howland Pl MK17 .... 60 C4
Hoylake Cl MK3 .... 57 E4
HRH Princess Christians Hospl
  SL4 .... 210 B3
Hubbard Cl MK18 .... 41 F1
Hubbards Ct WD3 .... 167 E3
Hubbards Rd WD3 .... 167 E3
Huckleberry Cl HP7 .... 175 E2
Hubert Rd SL3 .... 206 B3
Huckleberry Cl MK7 .... 48 A4
Hudnall La HP4 .... 121 F1
Hudson La MK8 .... 45 E4
Hudsons Ave UB9 .... 189 F1
Hughenden Ave HP11 .... 173 D4
Hughenden Ct UB8 .... 201 E2
Hughenden Cty Fst Sch
  HP14 .... 162 A1
Hughenden Gn HP21 ..... 115 F3
Hughenden Rd
  High Wycombe HP13 ...... 162 A2
  Slough SL1 .... 205 E2
Hughendon Cl SL6 .... 202 B4
Hulbert End HP21 .... 116 B1
Hulcombe Wlk HP20 ...... 101 F1
Hull Cl Aylesbury HP21 ... 115 F3
  Slough SL1 .... 205 E2
Hulton Dr MK46 .... 13 F
Humber Dr HP21 .... 115 E
Humber Way
  Milton Keynes MK3 .... 46 C1
  Slough SL3 .... 207 D3
Hundred Acres La HP7 ... 165 E2
Hungerford Ave SL2 ...... 205 F
Hungerford Dr SL6 .... 195 F
Hungerford Ho MK4 .... 46 B
Hunsdon Cl MK14 .... 34 B
Hunstanton Way MK3 ...... 57 E
Hunt Rd HP13 .... 173 F
Hunt's La SL6 .... 196 C
Hunter Cl SL1 .... 204 B
Hunter Dr MK2 .... 58 B
Hunter St MK18 .... 52 B
Huntercombe Cl SL6 ...... 204 B
Huntercombe La N SL1 ... 204 B
Huntercombe La S SL6 ... 204 B
Hunters Cl Bovingdon HP3 146 A
  Chesham HP5 .... 144 A
  Tring HP23 .... 119 C
Hunters Hill HP13 .... 173 F
Hunters Mews SL4 .... 210 B
Hunters Park HP4 .... 135 F
Hunters Point OX9 .... 147 F
Hunters Reach MK13 .... 34 A
Huntingbrooke MK8 .... 45 F
Huntingdon Cres MK3 ...... 57 F
Huntley Cl HP13 .... 162 B
Hunts Hill La HP14 .... 161 F
Huntsman Gr MK14 .... 22 A
Huntsmans Cl HP4 .... 107 F
Huntswood La
  Burnham SL6 .... 196 C
  Taplow SL6 .... 196 C

Hurley High St SL6 .... 193 F2
Hurley La Bisham SL6 .... 194 A2
Hurley SL6 .... 194 A2
Hurlstone Gr MK4 .... 46 B2
Hurst Rd SL1 .... 204 B4
Hurstfield Dr SL6 .... 204 A4
Hurstleigh WD3 .... 167 E2
Hutchings CI MK5 .... 46 A4
Hutchings Rd HP9 .... 175 E3
Hutton Ave MK6 .... 34 C1
Hutton Way MK17 .... 49 D3
Huxley CI
  Newport Pagnell MK16 .... 21 F2
  Uxbridge UB8 .... 201 E1
Hyacinth Dr UB10 .... 201 F3
Hychenden CI HP14 .... 161 F3
Hyde CI MK16 .... 22 B1
Hyde Green
  Beaconsfield HP9 .... 175 F2
  Marlow SL7 .... 183 F1
Hyde Heath Cty Fst Sch
  HP16 .... 153 E3
Hyde Heath Rd HP16 .... 153 D3
Hyde La Bovingdon HP3 .... 146 A2
  South Heath HP16 .... 152 C3
Hyde Meadows HP3 .... 146 A2
Hyde The HP22 .... 116 C1
Hyland Ho [10] SL8 .... 185 D2
Hyllie CI SL4 .... 209 F3
Hylton Rd HP12 .... 172 B4
Hyrons CI HP6 .... 154 C1
Hyrons Ct HP6 .... 154 C1
Hyrons La HP6 .... 154 B1
Hythe The MK8 .... 33 F2

Ibotson Ct SL3 .... 212 C3
Ibstone Ave MK13 .... 34 B2
Ibstone CE Fst Sch HP14 ...... 169 E3
Ibstone Rd HP14 .... 158 B2
Ickfield Gn HP23 .... 119 D3
Ickford Cty Comb Sch
  HP18 .... 124 A2
Ickford Rd
  Shabbington HP18 .... 124 B1
  Worminghall HP18 .... 123 F3
Icknield CI
  Aston Rowant OX9 .... 147 D2
  Wendover HP22 .... 131 E3
Icknield Cotts HP17 .... 129 F1
Icknield Cty Mid Sch
  HP27 .... 139 D3
Icknield Gn HP23 .... 119 D3
Icknield Way
  Eaton Bray LU6 .... 93 E2
  Tring HP23 .... 118 C2
Icknield Way Farm Cotts
  LU6 .... 93 E2
Iffley CI UB8 .... 201 E3
Ilchester CI SL6 .... 202 B3
Ilex CI HP15 .... 163 D2
Ilex CI HP4 .... 135 D2
Illingworth SL4 .... 209 F2
Illingworth PI MK6 .... 46 C4
Imperial CI
  Henley-on-T RG9 .... 191 F1
  Windsor SL4 .... 210 A2
Imperial Rd SL4 .... 210 A3
In The Ray SL6 .... 203 D4
Independent Bsns Pk
  HP14 .... 158 B3
India Rd SL1 .... 206 A2
Ingleglen SL2 .... 198 A4
Ingleside SL3 .... 212 C3
Ingleton CI MK13 .... 34 B2
Ingram Ave HP21 .... 116 B3
Inholder Ct MK14 .... 34 C3
Inkerman Dr HP15 .... 163 D3
Inkerman Rd SL4 .... 204 C1
Inkerman Terr HP5 .... 154 B3
Inn Farm Ct MK16 .... 22 B4
Innings Gate RG9 .... 170 C1
Inniscrown Ho SL3 .... 211 D4
Institute Rd Burnham SL6 ..... 203 F4
  Marlow SL7 .... 183 F1
  Taplow SL6 .... 203 F4
Intalbury Ave HP19 .... 101 D1
Inverness CI MK3 .... 46 C1
Inwood CI SL6 .... 195 D3
Iona Cres SL1 .... 204 C4
Ipswich Rd SL1 .... 205 D4
Ireland CI MK7 .... 48 B2
Ireton Ct OX9 .... 125 F1
Iris CI HP21 .... 115 D3
Ironmonger Ct MK14 .... 34 C3
Irvine Dr HP22 .... 116 A1
Irving Cres LU7 .... 105 D4
Irving Dale MK7 .... 48 C3
Isaacson Dr MK7 .... 48 B3
Isambard CI UB8 .... 201 E1
Isis CI HP21 .... 115 E2
Isis Way SL8 .... 185 D2

Isis Wlk MK3 .... 46 C1
Island Ho TW6 .... 213 D3
Island The MK18 .... 63 E1
Islet Park Sch SL6 .... 196 B2
Islet Park Dr SL6 .... 196 B2
Islet Park Ho SL6 .... 196 B2
Islet Rd SL6 .... 196 B2
Islingbrook MK5 .... 46 A2
Ivanhoe CI UB8 .... 208 B4
Iver Cty Fst Sch SL0 .... 207 F4
Iver Cty Mid Sch SL0 .... 207 F4
Iver Heath Cty Fst Sch
  SL0 .... 200 B1
Iver Heath Cty Mid Sch
  SL0 .... 200 B2
Iver La Iver SL0 .... 208 A4
  Uxbridge SL0 .... 208 A4
Iver Sta SL0 .... 207 F2
Iverdale CI SL0 .... 207 E3
Ives Rd SL3 .... 207 D2
Ivester Ct LU7 .... 80 C3
Ivinghoe View HP20 .... 102 A1
Ivinghoe Way LU6 .... 92 C1
Ivins Rd HP9 .... 175 D1
Ivy CI MK16 .... 22 C2
Ivy Cotts HP8 .... 177 E2
Ivy Cres SL1 .... 204 C3
Ivy House La HP4 .... 135 F3
Ivy La Bierton HP22 .... 102 B1
  Great Brickhill MK17 .... 70 A4
  Newton Longville MK17 .... 57 E2
  Stewkley LU7 .... 68 C1
  Wing LU7 .... 79 E2
Ivy PI HP14 .... 171 E3
Ivybridge CI UB8 .... 201 F1
Ivyhill Ct HP27 .... 139 D2

Jack's La MK43 .... 8 C3
Jacks CI MK4 .... 7 F4
Jackson CI UB10 .... 201 F3
Jackson Ct HP15 .... 163 D2
Jackson Ind Est SL8 .... 185 D1
Jackson Rd
  Aylesbury HP19 .... 101 D2
  Uxbridge UB10 .... 201 F3
Jacksons CI LU6 .... 92 C2
Jacob CI SL4 .... 209 F3
Jacobs CI MK4 .... 34 B4
Jakes Ho SL6 .... 203 D4
Jamaica MK6 .... 47 D3
James CI
  Holmer Green HP15 .... 163 D3
  Marlow SL7 .... 183 F2
James Elliman Inf Sch
  SL2 .... 205 F4
James Elliman Mid Sch
  SL2 .... 205 F4
James Martin CI UB9 .... 190 A3
James Rd HP14 .... 171 D2
James St SL4 .... 210 B3
James Way MK1 .... 47 D1
Jane CI HP21 .... 116 A2
Jansel Sq HP21 .... 116 A3
Jardine Cotts SL2 .... 199 D4
Jarman CI MK18 .... 52 C4
Jarratt Ho SL4 .... 210 A2
Jarry CI SL7 .... 183 F2
Jarvis CI HP21 .... 116 A3
Jasmine CI HP21 .... 116 A2
Jasmine Cres HP27 .... 139 D2
Jason Ho HP12 .... 172 C2
Jasons Hill HP5 .... 145 D1
Jeeves CI MK6 .... 47 E4
Jefferson CI SL3 .... 207 D1
Jeffries CI SL8 .... 185 D1
Jellicoe CI SL1 .... 205 D2
Jenkins CI MK5 .... 45 F3
Jenkins Ct HP22 .... 89 E2
Jenkins La HP23 .... 132 C2
Jenna Way MK16 .... 23 D2
Jenner Rd HP21 .... 115 F3
Jennery La SL1 .... 197 E1
Jennings MK14 .... 34 B4
Jennings Field HP10 .... 185 E4
Jennings Wharf SL4 .... 210 B4
Jerome CI SL7 .... 183 F2
Jersey Rd MK12 .... 33 E3
Jesse's La HP18 .... 125 E3
Job's La SL6 .... 195 D4
John Colet Sch HP22 .... 131 E3
John Hall Way
  High Wycombe HP12 .... 172 B2
  Little Marlow HP12 .... 172 B2
John Hampden Cty Fst Sch
  HP22 .... 131 D3
John Hampden Gram Sch
  HP11 .... 172 C2
John Hampden Way
  HP16 .... 151 D4
John Hellins Prim Sch
  NN12 .... 18 B2

John Taylor Ct SL1 .... 205 E3
John Watson Sch OX33 .... 122 A1
Johns La HP5 .... 134 C1
Johnson Rd HP14 .... 171 D3
Johnsons Field MK46 .... 6 C2
Johnston PI MK6 .... 46 C4
Joiner's Ct Botley HP5 .... 145 D1
  Chalfont St Peter SL9 ...... 177 F2
Joiner's La SL9 .... 177 F2
Joiners Way
  Chalfont St Peter SL9 ...... 177 F2
  Lavendon MK46 .... 7 F4
Jonathan Ct SL6 .... 202 C4
Jonathan Miller Sch The
  SL1 .... 204 C4
Jonathans MK6 .... 47 D3
Jones Way SL2 .... 187 E1
Slough SL3 .... 207 D2
Jordans Cty Fst Sch HP9 ...... 176 C2
Jordans La HP9 .... 176 C2
Jordans Way HP9 .... 176 C2
Joules CI MK5 .... 46 B3
Jourdelay's Pas SL4 .... 210 B4
Journeys End SL2 .... 205 F4
Jubilee Rd
  High Wycombe HP11 .... 172 C4
  High Wycombe, Downley
  HP13 .... 161 F1
  Stokenchurch HP14 .... 158 C2
Jubilee Terr MK11 .... 32 C3
Judge's La LU7 .... 80 C3
Judy's Pas SL4 .... 205 E1
Juniper CI HP15 .... 163 D2
Juniper Ct SL1 .... 206 A2
Juniper Dr
  High Wycombe HP12 .... 172 B3
  Maidenhead SL6 .... 203 D4
Juniper Gdns MK7 .... 48 A4
Jupiter Hill Cty Comb Sch
  HP10 .... 185 D4
Juniper La HP10 .... 185 E4
Juniper Rd SL7 .... 183 E3
Jupiter Hts UB10 .... 201 F2
Juson's Glebe HP22 .... 131 E3
Jutland Ho SL4 .... 209 F3

Kalman Gdns MK7 .... 48 B3
Kaplan CI MK5 .... 46 A3
Katherine CI
  Tylers Green HP10 .... 174 B4
  Walton MK7 .... 48 A2
Katrina PI MK2 .... 58 B3
Kaybridge CI HP13 .... 173 F3
Kaywood CI SL3 .... 206 B2
Keach CI MK18 .... 66 A3
Keasden Ct MK4 .... 46 A1
Keaton Ct MK8 .... 45 E4
Keats CI
  High Wycombe HP11 .... 172 C3
  Newport Pagnell MK16 .... 22 A2
Keats La SL4 .... 210 B4
Keats Way
  Milton Keynes MK3 .... 57 F4
  West Drayton UB7 .... 208 C1
Keble CI HP21 .... 115 D4
Keble CI SL6 .... 202 C4
Keel Dr SL1 .... 205 E2
Keeler CI SL4 .... 209 F2
Keen's CI HP13 .... 162 C1
Keens La OX9 .... 147 E3
Keensacre SL0 .... 200 B2
Keep Hill Dr HP11 .... 173 E2
Keep Hill Rd HP11 .... 173 E3
Keeper's CI LU7 .... 105 D4
Keepers Farm CI SL4 .... 209 F3
Keepers La HP6 .... 153 E2
Keinches La HP22 .... 87 D3
Keith Park Rd UB10 .... 201 F3
Kelburn Ct MK4 .... 45 F3
Kellan Dr MK6 .... 35 D1
Kelpatrick Rd SL1 .... 204 B4
Kelsey CI SL6 .... 202 B2
Kelso CI MK3 .... 57 E3
Kelvin CI HP13 .... 172 C4
Kelvin Dr MK5 .... 46 B3
Kemble CI MK15 .... 35 D3
Kemps Piece HP7 .... 127 D3
Kempton Gdns MK3 .... 57 E3
Kempsey Chase SL2 .... 198 B2
Kenchester MK13 .... 33 F3
Kendal CI Aylesbury HP21 .... 116 A3
  Slough SL2 .... 206 A3
Kendal Dr SL2 .... 206 A3
Kendal Gdns LU7 .... 80 B4
Kendalls CI HP13 .... 173 F3
Kendrick Rd SL3 .... 206 A2
Kenilworth CI SL1 .... 205 F2
Kenilworth Dr
  Aylesbury HP19 .... 101 D1
  Milton Keynes MK3 .... 57 F4
Kenneally SL4 .... 209 E3
Kenneally CI [11] SL4 .... 209 E3
Kenneally PI [12] SL4 .... 209 E3

Kenneally Row [13] SL4 .... 209 E3
Kenneally Wlk [14] SL4 .... 209 E3
Kennedy Ave HP11 .... 173 D2
Kennedy CI
  Farnham Common SL2 .... 198 B3
  Maidenhead SL6 .... 202 B3
  Marlow SL7 .... 183 F2
Kennedy CI [5] LU7 .... 80 C4
Kennedy Ho SL1 .... 204 B3
Kennel La SL6 .... 195 E4
Kennet CI Aylesbury HP21 .... 115 E2
  High Wycombe HP13 .... 162 B1
Kennet Dr MK3 .... 57 F4
Kennet PI MK3 .... 57 F4
Kennet Rd SL6 .... 202 C4
Kennett Rd Bourne End
  SL8 .... 185 D2
  Slough SL3 .... 207 D2
Kennington CI MK16 .... 22 B2
Kennish CI MK18 .... 65 F2
Kensington Dr MK8 .... 33 F1
Kent Ave SL1 .... 205 E4
Kent CI UB8 .... 201 E3
Kent Lodge [6] SL6 .... 202 C3
Kent Way SL6 .... 195 F1
Kentmere Rd HP21 .... 116 A4
Kenton CI SL7 .... 182 A3
Kenton CI HP19 .... 101 E1
Kenton La SL4 .... 209 F3
Kents Hill Cty Fst Sch MK7 ... 48 A4
Kents Hill Rdbt MK7 .... 47 F4
Kents Rd MK14 .... 34 B4
Kenway Dr HP7 .... 166 A4
Kenwell Ct MK15 .... 35 E2
Kenwood Gate MK6 .... 35 D1
Kenwood CI SL6 .... 202 A4
Kenwood Dr WD3 .... 178 C4
Keppel Ave MK19 .... 20 B1
Keppel St SL4 .... 210 B3
Kepwick MK8 .... 33 F1
Kercroft MK8 .... 33 F1
Kernow Cres MK6 .... 35 D1
Kerria PI MK3 .... 47 D2
Kerry Ct HP19 .... 101 D2
Kersey MK14 .... 34 B4
Kesters Rd HP5 .... 154 B4
Kestrel CI
  Berkhamsted HP4 .... 135 E2
  High Wycombe HP13 .... 161 E1
Kestrel Dr HP15 .... 163 D3
Kestrel Path SL2 .... 197 F1
Kestrel Way
  Aylesbury HP20 .... 101 F2
  Buckingham MK18 .... 52 C4
Keswick Ct SL2 .... 205 F3
Keswick Rd SL2 .... 11 D1
Ketchmere CI HP18 .... 125 E3
Ketelbey Nook MK7 .... 48 C3
Ketton CI MK15 .... 35 E4
Kew CI MK8 .... 33 F1
Kew Gr HP11 .... 173 D2
Keyes Way MK18 .... 41 F1
Keynes CI MK16 .... 22 C2
Keys La SL6 .... 202 C3
Khasiaberry MK7 .... 48 A3
Kidd CI MK8 .... 45 F3
Kidderminster Rd SL2 .... 198 B1
Kidwells CI SL6 .... 202 C4
Kidwells Park Dr SL6 .... 202 C4
Kildonan PI MK12 .... 33 E2
Kilfillan Gdns HP4 .... 135 D2
Killarney Dr SL6 .... 202 C4
Kiln Ave HP6 .... 155 E1
Kiln CI HP6 .... 151 E4
Kiln Croft CI SL7 .... 184 A2
Kiln Ct HP9 .... 186 A4
Kiln Farm Ind Est MK11 .... 33 D2
Kiln Farm Rdbt MK11 .... 33 D2
Kiln La Botley HP5 .... 155 D4
  Bourne End SL8 .... 185 E2
  Hedgerley SL2 .... 187 E2
  Lacey Green HP27 .... 149 F3
Kiln PI SL6 .... 195 D2
Kiln Pond La HP13 .... 161 E2
Kiln Rd HP10 .... 161 D4
Kiln The HP5 .... 144 B1
Kilner Rd HP21 .... 116 A3
Kilnwood HP14 .... 150 A1
Kilpin Green MK16 .... 24 A3
Kimbells CI HP18 .... 124 B1
Kimber CI SL4 .... 210 A2
Kimber's La SL6 .... 202 C2
Kimberley CI SL3 .... 206 C1
Kimberley Dr SL6 .... 201 F1
Kimblewick Rd HP17 .... 129 E3
Kimbolton Ct MK14 .... 35 D4
Kincardine Dr MK6 .... 46 C2
Kindleton MK14 .... 34 C4
Kinellan CI HP9 .... 175 E2
King Charles CI MK18 .... 41 F1
King Edward Ave HP21 .... 116 A4

King Edward Ct [14] SL4 ...... 210 B3
King Edward St
  Milton Keynes MK13 .... 33 F4
  Slough SL1 .... 205 E2
King Edward VII Ave
  SL4, SL3 .... 210 C4
King Edward VII Hospl
  SL4 .... 210 B2
King George Cres MK11 .... 32 C3
King George V Rd HP6 .... 154 B1
King John's CI TW19 .... 211 E1
King St Chesham HP5 .... 154 A4
  High Wycombe HP14 .... 160 B1
  Maidenhead SL6 .... 202 C3
  Milton Keynes MK11 .... 32 C3
  Tring HP23 .... 119 D2
King Stable St SL4 .... 210 B4
King's Gr SL6 .... 202 C3
King's La
  Great Missenden HP16 .... 141 E1
  Lee Common HP16 .... 141 F4
  South Heath HP16 .... 152 C4
  Wendover HP16 .... 141 E1
King's Rd Aylesbury HP21 .... 116 B3
  Henley-on-T RG9 .... 191 E1
  High Wycombe HP11 .... 173 F2
  Slough SL1 .... 205 F2
  Uxbridge UB8 .... 201 E2
  Windsor SL4 .... 210 B2
  Windsor SL4 .... 210 B3
King's Road Ho [27] SL4 ...... 210 B3
King's Terr SL3 .... 212 A4
King's Wood Cty Fst Sch
  HP13 .... 173 F4
King's Wood Cty Mid Sch
  HP13 .... 173 F4
Kingfisher HP20 .... 101 F2
Kingfisher Ct
  High Wycombe HP11 .... 173 D3
  Slough SL2 .... 198 A1
Kingfisher Ctr The MK16 .... 22 B1
Kingfisher Ho [6] HP10 .... 174 A2
Kingfisher Rd MK18 .... 52 C4
Kinghorn La SL6 .... 195 E2
Kinghorn Park SL6 .... 195 E2
Kings CI Beaconsfield HP9 .... 186 A4
  Chalfont St Giles HP8 ...... 177 E4
  Henley-on-T RG9 .... 191 E1
  Worminghall HP18 .... 123 E3
Kings Ct HP4 .... 135 E3
Kings Farm Rd WD3 .... 167 E2
Kings Hall Par HP22 .... 131 D2
Kings La SL6 .... 195 D4
Kings Lodge HP6 .... 154 B1
Kings Mead LU6 .... 92 C2
Kings Meadow HP22 .... 102 B2
Kings Oak Ct HP27 .... 139 E3
Kings Rd
  Berkhamsted HP4 .... 135 D2
  Chalfont St Giles HP8 ...... 177 E4
  West Drayton UB7 .... 208 C2
Kings Ride HP10 .... 163 D1
Kings Sq HP11 .... 173 F2
Kings St LU7 .... 78 C4
Kings Wlk [4] SL6 .... 202 C4
Kings Wood SL7 .... 193 E4
Kingsbridge MK4 .... 46 B1
Kingsbrook Sch MK19 .... 31 F2
Kingsbury HP20 .... 115 E4
Kingsbury Ct [8] HP20 .... 115 E4
Kingsbury Ct SL4 .... 211 D1
Kingscale Rd HP4 .... 135 D2
Kingscote Sch SL9 .... 188 C4
Kingsdale Rd HP4 .... 135 D2
Kingsey Rd OX9 .... 126 B1
Kingsfield SL4 .... 209 E3
Kingsfold MK13 .... 34 A4
Kingshill Rd
  High Wycombe
  HP13, HP15 .... 162 B2
  Holmer Green HP13,HP15 .... 162 B2
Kingshill Way HP4 .... 135 D1
Kingsland Rd HP21 .... 116 A2
Kingsley CI MK16 .... 21 F2
Kingsley Cres HP11 .... 172 C3
Kingsley Dr SL7 .... 183 E3
Kingsley Path SL2 .... 197 F1
Kingsley Wlk HP23 .... 119 D2
Kingsmead HP27 .... 139 D3
Kingsmead Office Campus
  HP11 .... 174 A2
Kingsmead Rd
  High Wycombe HP11 .... 173 F2
  Loudwater HP10 .... 174 A2
Kingsmead Rdbt MK4 .... 56 C4
Kingston Ave
  Milton Keynes MK11 .... 32 C3
  West Drayton UB7 .... 208 C3
Kingston Hill OX9 .... 158 A4

Kingston La Uxbridge UB8 .... 201 F1
West Drayton UB7 .... 208 C2
Kingston Rd HP13 .... 162 B1
Kingston Rdbt MK19 .... 38 B1
Kingsway
Farnham Common SL2 ...... 198 B3
Gerrards Cross SL9 .... 188 C4
Iver SL0 .... 207 F4
Kingswood Ave HP19 .... 174 A4
Kingswood Creek TW19 .... 211 E1
Kingswood Ct SL6 .... 202 C3
Kingswood Ho SL1 .... 205 E4
Kingswood La HP18 .... 96 C3
Kingswood Par SL7 .... 183 E3
Kingswood Rd HP10 .... 163 D1
Kingswood View HP13 .... 162 C1
Kinloch HP12 .... 58 C3
Kinnaird CI SL1 .... 204 B4
Kinnear CI MK8 .... 45 F4
Kinross Dr MK3 .... 46 C1
Kinson Gn HP20 .... 101 F2
Kipling Ct SL4 .... 210 A3
Kipling Dr MK16 .... 21 F2
Kipling Rd MK3 .... 58 A4
Kippell Hill MK46 .... 6 C3
Kirke CI MK5 .... 46 A3
Kirkeby CI MK14 .... 34 B3
Kirkstall PI MK6 .... 46 B4
Kirkwall Spur SL1 .... 205 F4
Kirtle Rd HP5 .... 144 B1
Kirtlington MK15 .... 35 D3
Kitchener Rd HP11 .... 172 C4
Kite Field HP4 .... 134 C4
Kite Hill MK6 .... 47 D4
Kitsbury Ct HP4 .... 135 D2
Kitsbury Rd HP4 .... 135 D2
Kitsbury Terr HP4 .... 135 D2
Kittiwake HP20 .... 101 F2
Klondyke SL7 .... 183 E1
Knapp Gate MK5 .... 45 F4
Knaves Beech HP10 .... 174 B1
Knaves Beech Ind Est
HP10 .... 174 B1
Knaves Beech Way HP10 .... 174 B1
Knaves Hill LU7 .... 80 B4
Knaves Hollow HP10 .... 174 B1
Knebworth Gate MK14 .... 22 A1
Knighton Way La SL0 .... 201 D3
Knights CI Eaton Bray LU6 .. 92 C3
Great Brickhill MK17 .... 59 E1
Windsor SL4 .... 209 E3
Knights Ct LU6 .... 92 C3
Knights Hill HP17 .... 114 B3
Knights PI ⬛ SL4 .... 210 B3
Knights Templar Way
HP11 .... 173 D2
Knoll The MK17 .... 49 D1
Knolls CI HP22 .... 89 D2
Knolton Way SL2 .... 206 B4
Knottocks CI HP9 .... 175 E3
Knottocks Dr HP9 .... 175 E3
Knottocks End HP9 .... 175 E3
Knowl Gate MK5 .... 46 B4
Knowland Way UB9 .... 189 F3
Knowles CI UB7 .... 208 C3
Knowles Cty Fst Sch MK2 ... 58 B4
Knowles Cty Mid Sch MK2 .. 58 B4
Knowles Green MK2 .... 58 B4
Knowlhill Rdbt MK5 .... 46 B3
Knowsley CI SL6 .... 195 D1
Kola Ho SL2 .... 206 A3
Kop Hill Rd HP27 .... 139 E2
Krohn CI MK3 .... 52 C4
Krypton CI MK5 .... 46 B3
Kynaston Ave HP21 .... 115 F2
Kynaston Sch HP21 .... 115 F2

La Roche CI SL3 .... 206 B2
Laburnham Cotts LU7 .... 69 F2
Laburnham Rd SL6 .... 202 C3
Laburnum Ave UB7 .... 208 C3
Laburnum CI SL7 .... 183 F2
Laburnum Cres SL3 .... 212 A4
Laburnum Gr
Milton Keynes MK2 .... 58 C4
Slough SL3 .... 212 A4
Laburnum Rd HP12 .... 172 B3
Lace Mews MK46 .... 7 D2
Lacemakers Chinnor OX9 .... 147 E3
Long Crendon HP18 .... 125 E4
Lacey Dr HP14 .... 161 F4
Laceys Dr HP15 .... 163 D3
Lacy Dr MK15 .... 35 D4
Ladbroke CI HP20 .... 101 F1
Ladbrooke Rd SL1 .... 205 E2
Ladyday PI SL1 .... 205 E3
Ladymead CI MK17 .... 56 A4
Ladysmith Rd LU7 .... 105 F3

Ladywalk WD3 .... 178 C3
Laggan Rd SL6 .... 195 F1
Laggan Sq SL6 .... 195 F1
Laggen Ct MK4 .... 58 B2
Lagger CI HP8 .... 177 D4
Lagger The HP8 .... 177 D4
Lagonda CI MK16 .... 22 C2
Laiden CI MK2 .... 58 B2
Lake Ave SL1 .... 205 E3
Lake CI MK18 .... 66 A3
Lake End Ct SL6 .... 204 A4
Lake End Rd SL4,SL6 .... 204 A3
Lake View SL6 .... 196 A1
Lake's Cotts LU7 .... 90 B4
Laker CI MK6 .... 46 C4
Lakes La Beaconsfield HP9 .. 186 C4
Newport Pagnell MK16 ...... 22 A3
Lakeside Maidenhead SL6 ... 196 A1
Tring HP23 .... 119 D3
Lakeside Dr SL2 .... 198 C2
Lakeside Est SL3 .... 213 D4
Lakeside Rd SL3 .... 212 C4
Lamb CI MK16 .... 22 A2
Lamb La MK7 .... 48 B4
Lambe Rd HP22 .... 131 E3
Lamberhurst Gr MK7 .... 48 A4
Lambert Ave SL3 .... 206 C2
Lambert Wlk OX9 .... 125 F1
Lamberts Croft MK12 .... 33 E3
Lambourn Ct MK4 .... 46 B1
Lambourne Ave HP21 .... 115 E2
Lambourne Ct UB8 .... 201 D2
Lambourne Dr SL6 .... 202 B2
Lambridge La RG9 .... 191 E2
Lambridge Wood Rd
RG9 .... 191 D2
Lambscroft Way SL2 .... 177 F1
Lambtons Way MK18 .... 66 A3
Lamesley Ho SL6 .... 202 C3
Lammas MK6 .... 47 D3
Lammas Ave ⬛ SL4 .... 210 B3
Lammas Ct SL4 .... 210 B3
Lammas La HP18 .... 112 A1
Lammas Path HP18 .... 112 A1
Lammas Rd
Cheddington LU7 .... 105 D4
Slough SL1 .... 204 B4
Lammas Way
Lane End HP14 .... 171 D2
Loudwater HP10 .... 174 B1
Lampitts Cross MK6 .... 47 D3
Lamport Ct MK8 .... 46 A4
Lamva Ct MK11 .... 32 C3
Lancaster Ave SL2 .... 198 B1
Lancaster CI ⬛ TW19 .... 213 F1
Lancaster Ct HP12 .... 172 B2
Lancaster Dr HP11 .... 145 F2
Lancaster Gate MK3 .... 57 F4
Lancaster Rd
Aylesbury HP21 .... 116 A3
High Wycombe HP12 .... 172 C2
Maidenhead SL6 .... 202 A4
Uxbridge UB8 .... 201 E3
Lancaster Ride HP10 .... 174 A4
Lancastria Mews SL6 .... 202 B4
Lance Way HP13 .... 174 A3
Lancelot CI SL1 .... 205 D2
Lanchester Rd MK43 .... 24 B1
Lancot Ave LU6 .... 93 F4
Lancot Dr LU6 .... 93 F4
Lancot Lower Sch LU6 ...... 93 F4
Lancotbury CI LU6 .... 93 D4
Lancresse CI UB8 .... 201 E3
Lander Rd HP19 .... 100 C2
Landsborough Gate MK15 ... 35 E4
Lane End HP4 .... 134 C2
Lane End Rd HP12 .... 172 A3
Lane The
Grafton Regis NN12 .... 9 F3
Mursley MK17 .... 67 E3
Lane Wood CI HP7 .... 165 F4
Lanercost Cres MK10 .... 36 A1
Lanfranc Gdns MK15 .... 35 D4
Langcliffe Dr MK13 .... 34 B3
Langdale CI
Maidenhead SL6 .... 203 D3
Milton Keynes MK2 .... 58 B2
Langdale Ho HP11 .... 174 A2
Langdale Lodge HP10 .... 174 A2
Langdon Ave HP21 .... 116 A3
Langdon St HP23 .... 119 D2
Langland Cty Comb Sch
MK6 .... 47 E3
Langland Ho MK6 .... 47 E3
Langland Rd MK6 .... 47 E3
Langlands MK4 .... 7 F4
Langley Broom SL3 .... 206 C1
Langley Bsns Ctr SL3 .... 207 D2
Langley Bsns Pk SL3 .... 207 D2
Langley CI MK18 .... 65 F2
Langley Cnr SL3 .... 199 F3

Langley Gram Sch SL3 ...... 206 C1
Langley Manor Sch The
SL3 .... 206 C3
Langley Park Ctry Pk SL0 .. 200 A1
Langley Park Rd SL0 .... 207 E3
Langley Rd SL3 .... 206 C2
Langley St SL3 .... 207 D2
Langley Way SL7 .... 183 E1
Langleywood Cty Comb Sch
SL3 .... 206 C2
Langston Ct HP12 .... 172 B4
Langstone CI HP20 .... 101 F2
Langstone Ct ⬛ HP20 ...... 101 F2
Langton CI
Maidenhead SL6 .... 202 B4
Slough SL1 .... 204 B3
Langton Dr MK8 .... 33 F2
Langton's Meadow SL2 ..... 198 B3
Lanner Wlk MK6 .... 47 D4
Lanrick Copse HP4 .... 135 F3
Lansdell Ave HP12 .... 172 A2
Lansdown Rd SL9 .... 177 E1
Lansdowne Ave SL1 .... 205 F3
Lansdowne Ct SL1 .... 205 F3
Lansdowne Cty Mid Sch
HP12 .... 172 B2
Lansdowne Rd
Aylesbury HP20 .... 101 E1
Chesham HP5 .... 144 B1
Lansdowne Way HP21 .... 172 C2
Lanterns Wlk SL6 .... 203 D4
Lanthorn CI MK14 .... 34 C3
Lappetts La HP16 .... 152 C4
Larch CI Aylesbury HP20 .... 102 A1
Slough SL2 .... 205 D4
Tylers Green HP10 .... 163 E1
Larch Gr MK2 .... 58 C4
Larch Rise HP4 .... 135 D3
Larches The
Berkhamsted HP4 .... 134 B3
Holmer Green HP15 .... 163 E4
Larchfield Prim Sch SL6 .... 202 C2
Larchfield Rd SL6 .... 202 C3
Larchlands The HP10 .... 163 E1
Larchmoor Pk SL2 .... 199 D4
Larchwood HP16 .... 152 A2
Lark CI MK18 .... 52 C4
Lark Rise HP15 .... 163 D3
Lark Vale HP20 .... 101 F2
Larkfield CI HP13 .... 162 C1
Larkin CI MK16 .... 22 A3
Larkings La SL2 .... 199 E3
Larks Rise HP16 .... 154 B3
Larkspur Ave MK14 .... 34 C3
Larkspur Way HP15 .... 162 C3
Larvic Rd HP21 .... 115 E3
Larwood PI MK6 .... 34 C1
Lasborough Rd MK10 .... 36 B1
Lascelles CI MK15 .... 35 D4
Lascelles Rd SL3 .... 206 A2
Laser CI MK5 .... 46 B3
Lashlake Rd OX9 .... 125 F1
Lassell Gdns SL6 .... 203 D4
Lastingham Gr MK4 .... 46 A1
Latchmoor Ave SL9 .... 188 B4
Latchmoor Gr SL9 .... 188 B4
Latchmoor Way SL9 .... 188 B4
Latimer MK11 .... 32 C2
Latimer CI HP6 .... 166 B4
Latimer Ct HP20 .... 116 A4
Latimer Rd Chesham HP5 .. 155 E1
Latimer HP5 .... 155 E1
Latimer Way HP9 .... 175 E3
Laud's CI RG9 .... 191 E1
Launceston Ct MK5 .... 46 A3
Launde MK10 .... 36 A1
Laurel Ave SL3 .... 206 C2
Laurel CI Prestwood HP16 .. 151 D4
Shenley Church End MK8 ... 45 E4
Stanwell SL3 .... 212 C4
Laurel Ct HP6 .... 154 B2
Laurel Dr Loudwater HP10 .. 174 A2
Walter's Ash HP14 .... 161 E4
Laurel La UB7 .... 208 C1
Laurel Rd SL9 .... 177 E1
Laurel Way ⬛ HP21 .... 115 F4
Laurels Rd SL0 .... 200 B2
Laurels The
High Wycombe HP12 .... 172 B2
Milton Keynes MK1 .... 47 E1
Lautrec Way HP19 .... 100 C1
Lavender CI HP21 .... 115 D3
Lavender Gr MK7 .... 48 A3
Lavender Rd UB8 .... 208 C4
Lavender Way HP15 .... 162 C4
Lavender Wlk HP21 .... 115 D3
Lavendon Cty Comb Sch
MK46 .... 7 F4
Lavendon Rd MK46 .... 7 D3
Lawford Ave WD3 .... 167 E2
Lawford CI WD3 .... 167 E2

Lawkland SL2 .... 198 B1
Lawn Ave UB7 .... 208 B2
Lawn CI SL3 .... 211 E4
Lawn Hill HP18 .... 73 D1
Lawn Rd UB8 .... 201 E3
Lawn The SL3 .... 211 E3
Lawns The Brill HP18 .... 96 A1
Tylers Green HP10 .... 163 D1
Lawnsmead Gdns MK16 .... 22 B3
Lawrence Ct SL4 .... 210 B3
Lawrence Gr HP16 .... 151 E3
Lawrence Way SL1 .... 204 B4
Laws CI MK43 .... 8 C3
Lawsone Rise HP13 .... 162 A1
Laxton Gn SL6 .... 202 B2
Lay Rd HP19 .... 101 D1
Layter's Ave HP9 .... 177 E1
Layter's Ave S SL9 .... 177 E1
Layter's CI SL9 .... 177 E1
Layter's End SL9 .... 177 E1
Layters Green La SL9 ...... 177 D1
Layters Way SL9 .... 188 B3
Lea CI SL7 .... 183 E3
Lea Inf Sch SL2 .... 206 A3
Lea Mid Sch SL2 .... 206 A3
Leach Rd HP21 .... 115 E4
Leachcroft SL9 .... 177 D1
Leacroft CI UB7 .... 208 C3
Leacroft Rd SL0 .... 207 F4
Leadenhall Rdbt MK6 .... 46 C4
Leaders CI HP22 .... 89 D2
Leaf leaf Rise MK8 .... 33 E1
Leafy La HP23 .... 118 C1
Leaholme Gdns SL1 .... 204 B4
Leapingwell La MK18 .... 66 A3
Leas CI HP13 .... 173 F4
Leas Dr SL0 .... 207 F4
Leaside MK16 .... 12 A3
Leasowe PI MK13 .... 34 B2
Leather La HP16 .... 142 A2
Leaver Rd RG9 .... 191 E1
Leckhampstead Rd
Akeley MK18 .... 42 A4
Wicker MK19 .... 31 D2
Ledborough La HP9 .... 175 F2
Ledborough Wood HP9 ..... 175 F2
Ledburn Gr LU7 .... 80 C3
Ledbury MK14 .... 21 F1
Ledeview Ct ⬛ HP10 .... 174 A2
Ledger's Rd SL1 .... 205 E2
Lee Common CE Fst Sch
HP16 .... 142 B3
Lee Cres HP17 .... 114 B3
Lee Farm CI HP5 .... 145 D1
Lee Ho ⬛ MK2 .... 58 B4
Lee La Bisham SL6 .... 194 C1
Maidenhead SL6 .... 194 C1
Lee Rd Aylesbury HP21 .... 115 E3
Bledlow Ridge HP27 .... 148 C3
Quainton HP22 .... 85 D3
Leeches Way LU7 .... 105 D4
Leeds Rd SL1 .... 205 F3
Lees CI SL6 .... 202 A3
Lees Gdns SL6 .... 202 A3
Lees Wlk SL7 .... 183 E1
Leeson Gdns SL4 .... 204 C1
Legoland Windsor Theme
Park SL4 .... 209 E1
Leicester CI RG9 .... 191 E2
Leigh Hill MK4 .... 46 B1
Leigh Park SL3 .... 211 D4
Leigh Rd SL1 .... 205 D3
Leigh Sq SL4 .... 209 E3
Leigh St HP11 .... 172 C4
Leighton Buzzard Sta LU7 .. 80 C4
Leighton Gdns MK12 .... 196 A1
Leighton Ho ⬛ SL7 .... 183 F1
Leighton Rd SL2 .... 80 C3
Leighton Rd
Edlesborough LU6 .... 92 B2
Leighton Buzzard LU7 ...... 80 C4
Soulbury LU7 .... 70 A1
Stoke Hammond MK17 ..... 69 F4
Wing LU7 .... 80 A2
Wingrave HP22 .... 89 E2
Leighton St MK17 .... 60 C3
Leiston Spur SL1 .... 205 F4
Leisure Plaza MK9 .... 46 B4
Leith CI SL1 .... 206 A3
Lembrook Wlk HP21 .... 115 E3
Lenborough CI MK18 .... 52 B4
Lenborough La MK18 .... 51 E4
Lenborough Rd MK18 ...... 52 B4
Lennon CI MK8 .... 45 F4
Lennox Rd MK2 .... 58 B4
Lent Gn SL1 .... 197 D1
Lent Green La SL1 .... 197 D1
Lent Rise Cty Comb Sch
SL1 .... 204 A4
Lent Rise Rd SL1 .... 197 D1
Lenthall CI MK13 .... 34 A2

Leon Ave MK2 .... 58 B4
Leon Sch MK2 .... 58 B3
Leonards CI HP18 .... 72 C1
Leopard Dr MK15 .... 35 D4
Leopold Mall ⬛ SL1 .... 205 F2
Leopold Rd LU7 .... 80 B4
Lerwick Dr SL1 .... 205 F4
Lester CI MK7 .... 48 B4
Lester Gr HP15 .... 163 D2
Lesters Rd SL6 .... 195 E3
Letchfield HP5 .... 155 D4
Letter Box La HP27 .... 139 E4
Leven CI
Leighton Buzzard LU7 ...... 80 A4
Milton Keynes MK2 .... 58 B3
Leverkus Ho ⬛ OX9 .... 147 E3
Levings CI HP19 .... 101 D2
Lewes Ho MK3 .... 57 E4
Lewins Farm Ct SL1 .... 204 C3
Lewins Rd SL9 .... 188 B4
Lewins Way SL1 .... 204 C3
Lewis CI MK16 .... 21 F3
Lewis La SL9 .... 177 F1
Lewknor CI OX9 .... 157 D4
Lewknor Prim Sch OX9 ..... 157 D4
Lexham Gdns HP6 .... 154 B1
Lexington Ave SL6 .... 202 B3
Ley Hill Cty Comb Sch HP5 145 D1
Ley Hill Rd HP5,HP3 .... 145 F1
Leybourne Gdns OX9 .... 147 E4
Leyburne CI LU7 .... 90 B4
Leyfield Rd HP21 .... 115 F3
Leyland PI MK6 .... 47 D3
Leylands La SL3 .... 212 C2
Leys Ct MK5 .... 46 A4
Leys Rd MK5 .... 46 A4
Leys The Amersham HP6 ... 154 A2
Halton HP22 .... 117 E1
Tring HP23 .... 119 D2
Woburn Sands MK17 .... 49 D2
Leys View MK16 .... 13 F1
Leywood CI HP7 .... 165 F4
Libra Ho HP10 .... 185 D4
Lichfield Down MK7 .... 48 A3
Lichfield Ho HP21 .... 115 F3
Lichfield Rd SL3 .... 211 E3
Liddall Way UB7 .... 208 C3
Liddell SL4 .... 209 E3
Liddell PI SL4 .... 209 E2
Liddell Sq ⬛ SL4 .... 209 E3
Liddell Way SL4 .... 209 E2
Liffre Dr HP22 .... 131 D3
Lightfoot Ct MK7 .... 47 F3
Lightlands La SL6 .... 195 F3
Ligo Ave HP22 .... 116 B1
Lilac CI MK17 .... 57 E2
Lilac Ct SL2 .... 197 F1
Lilac PI UB7 .... 208 C3
Lilies The HP22 .... 87 E1
Lillibrooke Cres SL6 .... 202 A2
Lilly Bottom La HP27 .... 150 A4
Lillyfee Farm La HP10 ...... 186 A3
Lily's Wlk HP11 .... 173 D3
Limbaud CI MK7 .... 48 A3
Lime Ave
Buckingham MK18 .... 52 C4
High Wycombe HP11 .... 173 E3
West Drayton UB8 .... 208 C3
Lime Barn ⬛ SL7 .... 183 E1
Lime CI
Newport Pagnell MK16 .... 22 A2
Tylers Green HP15 .... 163 D2
Lime Gr Chinnor OX9 ...... 147 E3
Leighton Buzzard LU7 ..... 80 C4
Woburn Sands MK17 ...... 49 D2
Lime Rd
Princes Risborough HP27 .. 139 D2
Yardley Gobion NN12 ...... 18 C3
Lime St MK46 .... 6 C2
Lime Tree CI HP15 .... 162 B4
Lime Tree Wlk HP7 .... 165 F4
Lime Wlk Maidenhead SL6 .. 202 A4
New Denham UB9 .... 201 E4
Limerick La MK9 .... 35 D2
Limes Ave HP21 .... 116 A4
Limes The Amersham HP6 .. 154 A2
Milton Keynes, Fenny Stratford
MK2 .... 58 C3
Milton Keynes, Stony Stratford
MK11 .... 32 C3
Limes Way HP18 .... 124 B1
Limmer La HP12 .... 172 A4
Limmers La HP15 .... 162 B4
Lincesdale Gr MK5 .... 46 A4
Linchfield HP13 .... 173 F4
Lincoln MK14 .... 34 B4
Lincoln CI HP22 .... 116 A1
Lincoln Ct
Berkhamsted HP4 .... 135 D2
⬛ Slough SL1 .... 205 F1

Lincoln Hatch La SL1 .... 197 E1
Lincoln Park HP7 .... 165 F4
Lincoln Park Bsns Ctr
　HP12 .... 172 B3
Lincoln Pk NN15 .... 38 A3
Lincoln Rd
　Chalfont St Peter SL9 ...... 177 F1
　High Wycombe HP12 .... 172 C3
　Maidenhead SL6 .... 202 A4
Lincoln Way SL1 .... 204 B3
Lincolns The HP16 .... 152 A2
Lincombe Slade LU7 .... 80 C4
Lincroft MK43 .... 25 D1
Linden SL3 .... 207 D1
Linden Ave SL6 .... 195 E1
Linden Ct HP12 .... 172 B3
Linden Dr
　Chalfont St Peter SL9 ...... 177 F1
　Farnham Common SL2 ...... 198 B2
Linden End HP21 .... 115 F3
Linden Gr MK14 .... 34 C4
Linden Lea HP22 .... 131 D3
Linden Way HP17 .... 128 A4
Linden Wlk HP15 .... 163 D2
Lindens The HP3 .... 146 C4
Lindo Cl HP5 .... 144 A1
Lindsay Ave HP12 .... 172 C4
Lindsay Cl TW19 .... 213 E1
Lindsey Rd UB9 .... 190 A1
Lines Hill HP22 .... 88 A2
Lines Rd HP14 .... 171 D3
Lines The HP22 .... 88 B2
Linfields HP7 .... 166 B4
Linford Ave MK16 .... 22 A2
Linford La
　Milton Keynes, Willen
　MK15 .... 35 E4
　Milton Keynes, Woolstone
　MK15 .... 35 E2
Lingfield MK12 .... 33 F2
Lingfield Cl HP13 .... 174 A3
Lingholm Cl SL6 .... 202 B3
Link Rd Datchet SL3 .... 211 E3
　High Wycombe HP12 .... 172 B3
　South Heath HP16 .... 152 A4
Link The
　Holmer Green HP15 .... 163 D3
　Slough SL2 .... 206 A4
Link Way UB9 .... 190 A3
Links Rd HP10 .... 185 E4
Links Way HP10 .... 185 D4
Linkswood Rd SL4 .... 197 E2
Linnet Cl HP12 .... 172 A2
Linnet Dr HP18 .... 98 B3
Linnington Ave HP5 .... 145 D1
Linslade Lower Sch LU7 .... 80 B4
Linslade Mid Sch LU7 .... 80 C3
Linslade Rd LU7 .... 70 C2
Lintlaw Pl MK3 .... 47 D2
Linton Cl MK13 .... 34 B2
Lintott Ct TW13 .... 213 E1
Linx The MK3 .... 47 D1
Lionel Ave HP22 .... 131 D3
Lionel Cl HP22 .... 131 D3
Lipscomb La MK5 .... 46 A4
Lipscome Dr MK18 .... 41 F1
Lisburn Path [1] HP20 .... 101 F1
Lisle Rd HP13 .... 162 A1
Lisleys Field HP15 .... 162 B4
Lismore Pk SL2 .... 205 F4
Lissel Rd MK6 .... 47 F3
Lisset Rd SL6 .... 203 D3
Lister Gn HP21 .... 115 F3
Liston Ct [3] SL7 .... 183 E1
Liston Rd SL7 .... 183 E1
Litcham Spur SL1 .... 205 E4
Little Balmer MK18 .... 52 C3
Little Benty HP21 .... 208 B1
Little Boltons [7] SL7 .... 183 F1
Little Bridge Rd HP4 .... 135 E2
Little Britain HP18 .... 99 D4
Little Buntings SL4 .... 209 F2
Little Chalfont Cty Comb Sch
　HP6 .... 166 C4
Little Chapels Way SL1 .... 205 D2
Little Chartridge Ct HP5 .... 144 A1
Little Cl
　Flackwell Heath HP10 .... 185 D3
　High Wycombe HP12 .... 172 C2
Little Gaddesden HP4 .... 121 E4
Little Gaddesden CE Sch
　HP4 .... 121 E4
Little Greencroft HP5 .... 144 A2
Little Habton MK4 .... 46 A1
Little Ham La HP27 .... 139 D3
Little Hame MK10 .... 35 F2
Little Hampden Cl HP22 ...... 131 D2
Little Hill WD3 .... 167 E2
Little Hivings HP5 .... 144 A2
Little Hollis HP16 .... 151 F4
Little Hoo HP23 .... 118 C2

Little Horwood Rd
　Great Horwood MK17 .... 55 E2
　Little Horwood MK17 .... 55 F4
Little Hundridge La HP16 ... 153 D4
Little Kimble Hill HP17 .... 129 F1
Little Kimble Sta HP17 .... 129 F1
Little Kingshill Cty Comb Sch
　HP16 .... 152 A1
Little La
　Bledlow Ridge HP27 .... 149 E2
　Great Kimble HP27 .... 149 E2
　Yardley Hastings NN7 .... 1 A4
Little Linford La MK16,MK19 ... 21 F2
Little London
　Deanshanger MK19 .... 31 F2
　Whitchurch HP22 .... 87 D3
Little London Green HP18 109 F3
Little Marlow CE Fst Sch
　SL7 .... 184 B3
Little Marlow Rd SL7 .... 183 F2
Little Marsh Rd OX6 .... 72 A2
Little Meadow MK5 .... 46 B4
Little Missenden CE Fst Sch
　HP16 .... 153 D1
Little Mollards HP22 .... 89 D2
Little Orchard Cl HP27 .... 138 C3
Little Orchards HP20 .... 101 F2
Little Park Bovingdon HP3 . 146 A2
　Princes Risborough HP27 . 139 E2
Little Reeves Ave HP7 .... 165 F4
Little Shardeloes HP7 .... 165 D4
Little Spinney MK43 .... 25 E2
Little Spring HP5 .... 144 A2
Little St NN7 .... 1 A3
Little Stanton MK13 .... 34 B4
Little Stocking MK5 .... 46 A2
Little Sutton La
　Slough, Brands Hill SL3 ... 212 A4
　Slough, Sutton SL3 .... 207 E1
Little Tring Rd HP22 .... 118 C3
Little Twye Rd HP23 .... 132 C2
Little Windmill Hill WD4 ... 156 C4
Little Woodlands SL4 .... 209 F2
Littlebrook Ave SL2 .... 204 C4
Littlecote MK8 .... 34 A1
Littledown Cotts SL1 .... 205 F3
Littledown Rd SL1 .... 205 F3
Littledown Sch SL1 .... 205 F3
Littlefield Ct UB7 .... 213 E4
Littlemarsh MK7 .... 48 A3
Littlemere MK8 .... 33 E1
Littleport Spur SL1 .... 205 F4
Littlewood HP14 .... 158 C3
Littleworth LU7 .... 79 F2
Littleworth Rd
　Burnham SL1 .... 186 B1
　High Wycombe HP13 .... 161 F1
Litton Ct HP10 .... 174 B1
Liverpool Rd SL1 .... 205 D4
Liverpool Victoria Ho [9]
　HP13 .... 173 D4
Livesey Hill MK5 .... 46 A3
Livingstone Dr MK15 .... 35 E3
Lloyds MK6 .... 47 D4
Loakes Ho HP11 .... 173 D3
Loakes Rd HP11 .... 173 D3
Lochinvar Cl SL1 .... 205 D2
Lochnell Rd HP4 .... 134 C3
Lochy Dr LU7 .... 80 B4
Lock Ave SL6 .... 196 B1
Lock Bridge Rd SL8 .... 185 D2
Lock La SL6 .... 202 B2
Lock Mead SL6 .... 196 B1
Lock Path SL4 .... 209 E4
Lock Rd SL7 .... 183 F1
Lock View La MK1 .... 47 F1
Lockbridge Ct SL6 .... 203 E4
Locke Gdns SL3 .... 206 B2
Locke Rd MK2 .... 58 B4
Lockets Cl SL4 .... 209 E3
Locksley Ct [25] SL1 .... 205 F2
Lockton CM MK4 .... 46 A2
Lockview Cotts MK1 .... 47 F1
Lodden Cl HP21 .... 115 E2
Loddon Dr SL6 .... 202 B4
Loddon Rd SL8 .... 185 D2
Loddon Spur SL1 .... 205 F4
Lodge Cl Marlow SL7 .... 183 F1
　Padbury MK18 .... 53 E1
　Slough SL1 .... 205 E2
　Uxbridge UB8 .... 201 E1
Lodge Farm MK19 .... 20 B2
Lodge Gate MK14 .... 34 C4
Lodge La
　Little Chalfont HP8 .... 166 C3
　Prestwood HP16 .... 151 E3
　Stoke Hammond MK17 .... 69 F4
Lodge Park The MK16 .... 22 B2
Lodge Way SL4 .... 209 F2
Lodgings of the Military
　Knights [13] SL4 .... 210 B3

Lodore Green UB10 .... 190 C1
Lollards Cl HP6 .... 154 B1
Lombardy Dr HP4 .... 135 E2
Lomond Dr
　Leighton Buzzard LU7 .... 80 B4
　Milton Keynes MK2 .... 58 B2
London Central High Sch
　HP11 .... 173 D2
London Central Jun
　High Sch HP11 .... 173 E2
London Ct HP21 .... 115 F4
London End
　Beaconsfield HP9 .... 175 F1
　Newton Longville MK17 ..... 57 E2
　Woburn MK17 .... 60 C3
London End La MK17 .... 48 B1
London Rd
　Beaconsfield HP9 .... 187 D4
　Berkhamsted HP4 .... 135 F2
　Buckingham MK18 .... 52 C3
　Chalfont St Giles HP8 ...... 177 F4
　Datchet SL3 .... 211 E4
　Drayton Beauchamp HP22 118 A2
　Feldon HP1 .... 146 C4
　Great Haseley OX9 .... 136 A2
　Great Missenden HP16 ...... 152 A3
　High Wycombe HP11 .... 173 F3
　Holton OX33 .... 122 A1
　Little Kingshill HP16 .... 152 A3
　Milton Keynes MK5 .... 46 A4
　Milton Keynes Village MK10 36 A3
　Newport Pagnell MK16 ...... 22 C1
　Old Stratford MK19 .... 32 B4
　Slough SL3 .... 206 C1
　Tring HP23 .... 119 E2
　Wendover HP22 .... 141 E3
London Rd E HP7 .... 165 F3
London Rd W HP7 .... 165 E4
Londrina Cl HP4 .... 135 E2
Londrina Terr HP4 .... 135 E2
Long Ayers MK7 .... 48 A2
Long Cl SL2 .... 198 A3
Long Close Sch SL3 .... 206 A2
Long Crendon Cty Comb Sch
　HP18 .... 125 E4
Long Crendon Ind Est
　HP18 .... 125 F3
Long Crendon Rd HP18 ..... 124 B2
Long Croft Rd WD3 .... 178 B3
Long Dr SL1 .... 197 E1
Long Furlong
　Haddenham HP17 .... 126 C3
　Stone HP18 .... 114 A3
Long Furlong Dr SL2 .... 197 F1
Long Grove HP9 .... 176 B2
Long La Bovingdon HP3 ..... 155 F4
　Cookham SL6 .... 195 E3
　Flaunden HP3 .... 155 F4
　Heron WD3 .... 167 E1
　Olney MK46 .... 6 C2
Long Ley LU7 .... 105 D4
Long Marston Jun Mix
　Inf Sch HP23 .... 104 A2
Long Marston Rd HP23 ...... 104 C1
Long Massey MK46 .... 6 C3
Long Meadow
　Aylesbury HP21 .... 116 A3
　Chesham HP5 .... 144 B2
Long Meadow Cl HP27 .... 139 E3
Long Orchard Dr HP10 ...... 174 B4
Long Park HP6 .... 154 B2
Long Park Cl HP6 .... 154 B2
Long Park Way HP6 .... 154 B2
Long Plough HP22 .... 117 E3
Long Readings La SL2 .... 198 A1
Long Ride HP27 .... 139 E2
Long Row
　Leckhampstead MK18 .... 30 C1
　Prestwood HP16 .... 151 E3
Long Street Rd MK19 .... 11 D2
Long View HP4 .... 135 D3
Long Wall HP17 .... 126 C3
Long Wlk HP6 .... 166 C3
Long Wood Dr HP9 .... 176 C2
Longbottom La
　Beaconsfield HP9 .... 176 B2
　Seer Green HP9 .... 176 B2
Longbridge Cl HP23 .... 119 D3
Longbridge Way UB8 .... 201 D2
Longcroft HP22 .... 117 F3
Longcroft Ave HP21 .... 131 E3
Longcroft La HP3 .... 146 B3
Longcross MK15 .... 35 D3
Longdown Hill HP27 .... 139 F3
Longfellow Dr MK16 .... 22 A2
Longfield Hedgerley SL2 ... 187 E1
　Little Kingshill HP16 .... 152 A2
Longfield Dr HP6 .... 154 A1
Longfield Gdns HP23 .... 118 C2
Longfield Rd Chesham HP5 143 F1
　Tring HP23 .... 118 C2

Longfoot La NN12 .... 17 E4
Longford Rdbt TW6,UB7 .... 213 D3
Longhedge MK7 .... 48 A1
Longland Way HP12 .... 172 B3
Longlands CM MK18 .... 66 A3
Longlands Wlk MK18 .... 66 A3
Longleat Ct MK8 .... 33 F1
Longleat Gdns SL6 .... 202 B3
Longlees WD3 .... 178 B3
Longmead SL4 .... 209 F3
Longmead La SL1 .... 197 E3
Longmead Prim Sch LU7 ... 208 C1
Longmore Ct WD3 .... 178 C3
Longridge Scout Boating
　Activity Ctr SL6 .... 194 C4
Longstone Rd SL0 .... 200 B2
Longview HP9 .... 185 F4
Longville MK12 .... 33 D4
Longwick CE Comb Sch
　HP27 .... 138 B3
Longwick Rd
　Longwick HP27 .... 139 D3
　Princes Risborough HP27 139 D3
Longwood La HP7 .... 165 E4
Longworth Dr SL6 .... 196 B1
Lonsdale Cl SL6 .... 196 A1
Lonsdale Way SL6 .... 203 E1
Loosen Dr SL6 .... 202 A2
Loosley Hill HP27 .... 149 E3
Lord Grey Sch MK3 .... 46 C1
Lord Knyvett Cl TW19 .... 213 E1
Lords Cl MK2 .... 47 F1
Lordsmead MK43 .... 25 E1
Lorne Pl MK14 .... 35 D3
Loring Rd
　Berkhamsted HP4 .... 135 E2
　Dunstable LU6 .... 93 F4
　Windsor SL4 .... 209 F3
Lorne Cl SL1 .... 205 D2
Lorraine Cl HP13 .... 173 F4
Loseley Cl MK8 .... 33 F1
Losfield Rd SL4 .... 209 F3
Lothersdale MK13 .... 34 A3
Lothian Cl MK3 .... 46 C1
Lott Meadow HP21 .... 115 E2
Lott Wlk HP21 .... 115 E2
Louches La HP14 .... 161 E3
Loudhams Rd HP6 .... 166 B4
Loudhams Wood La HP6 .... 166 B4
Loudwater Comb Sch
　HP11 .... 174 A1
Loughton Cty Comb Sch
　MK5 .... 46 A4
Loughton Rd MK13 .... 34 A2
Loughton Rdbt MK8 .... 45 F4
Louisa Cotts [8] HP23 .... 119 D2
Louise Wlk HP3 .... 146 A2
Lovat City Mid Sch MK16 ..... 22 B2
Lovat St MK16 .... 22 B2
Lovatt Dr MK3 .... 57 F4
Love Green La SL0 .... 207 F4
Love Hill La SL3 .... 207 D3
Love La SL0 .... 207 E4
Lovejoy La SL4 .... 209 E3
Lovel End SL9 .... 177 E2
Lovel Mead SL9 .... 177 E2
Lovel Rd SL1 .... 177 E1
Lovelace Cl SL6 .... 193 F2
Lovett Gdns SL6 .... 196 B2
Lovett Rd SL9 .... 190 B4
Lovibonds Ave UB7 .... 208 C4
Lowbrook Cl HP21 .... 116 A2
Lowbrook Dr SL6 .... 202 A2
Lowbrook Prim Sch SL6 .... 202 A2
Lowdell Cl UB7 .... 208 C4
Lowdon Cl HP11 .... 173 E2
Lower Boynden Rd SL6 ..... 202 C3
Lower Britwell Rd SL2 .... 197 E1
Lower Church St
　Cuddington HP18 .... 112 C2
　Stokenchurch HP14 .... 158 C3
Lower Cippenham La
　SL1 .... 204 C3
Lower Cl HP21 .... 115 D4
Lower Cookham Rd SL6 ..... 196 B1
Lower Dr HP9 .... 175 E3
Lower Eighth St MK9 .... 34 C1
Lower End Ashendon HP18 .. 97 F1
　Piddington OX6 .... 95 F4
　Thornborough MK18 .... 53 F4
　Wingrave HP22 .... 89 D1
Lower End Rd MK17 .... 49 D4
Lower Farm Cl HP18 .... 124 B2
Lower Farm Gate HP17 ..... 114 A2
Lower Fourth St MK9 .... 34 B1
Lower Furney Cl HP13 .... 173 E4
Lower Gn HP18 .... 112 C2
Lower Green HP18 .... 98 B4
Lower Green La HP18 .... 112 B1
Lower Hammersley La
　HP10 .... 174 A2

Lower Icknield Way
　Aston Clinton HP22 .... 117 E2
　Chinnor OX9 .... 147 E4
　Drayton Beauchamp HP22 118 B4
　Great Kimble HP17 .... 129 E1
　Marsworth HP22,HP23 ...... 118 B4
　Princes Risborough HP27 138 B2
　Wilstone HP22,HP23 .... 118 B4
Lower King's Rd HP4 .... 135 E3
Lower Lees Rd SL2 .... 198 A1
Lower Lodge La HP15 .... 163 D3
Lower Mead SL0 .... 200 B1
Lower Ninth St MK9 .... 34 C1
Lower Pound La SL7 .... 183 E1
Lower Rd Blackthorn OX6 ... 81 D2
　Chinnor OX9 .... 147 E4
　Chorleywood WD3 .... 167 E3
　Cookham SL6 .... 195 F4
　Denham Green UB9 .... 189 E2
　Gerrards Cross SL9 .... 188 C4
　Lacey Green HP27 .... 149 E3
　Stoke Mandeville HP22 .... 115 F2
　Whitchurch HP22 .... 87 D2
Lower Ridge SL8 .... 185 D2
Lower Riding HP9 .... 175 D1
Lower Second St MK9 .... 34 B1
Lower St Paulersbury NN12 . 17 D4
　Quainton HP22 .... 85 D3
Lower Stonehayes MK14 ...... 34 C4
Lower Tenth St MK9 .... 34 C1
Lower Third St MK9 .... 34 B1
Lower Ventnor Cotts SL6 .. 195 E4
Lower Way
　Great Brickhill MK17 .... 59 E1
　Padbury MK18 .... 53 E1
Lowes Cl HP14 .... 158 B3
Lowestoft Dr SL1 .... 204 B4
Lowfield Cl HP15 .... 163 D2
Lowfield Way HP15 .... 163 D2
Lowland Rd MK4 .... 57 E4
Lowlands Cres HP15 .... 151 E1
Lowlands Dr TW19 .... 213 E1
Lowman Way HP21 .... 115 E2
Lowndes Ave HP5 .... 144 A1
Lowndes Way MK18 .... 66 A3
Lownes Gr MK5 .... 45 F4
Loxbeare Dr MK4 .... 46 B2
Loxboro Hill HP14 .... 160 B2
Loxley Rd HP14 .... 134 C3
Loxwood Cl HP3 .... 146 C4
Loyne Ct LU17 .... 80 B4
Lucas Pl MK6 .... 47 E4
Luccombe MK4 .... 46 B2
Lucky La or Cock La HP20 101 E1
Lucy La MK5 .... 46 A4
Ludgate Milton Keynes MK6 . 46 C4
　Tring HP23 .... 118 C2
Ludgershall Rd OX6 .... 95 F4
Ludlow Cl MK3 .... 57 F4
Ludlow Ho SL6 .... 202 C3
Ludlow Mews HP10 .... 174 A2
Ludlow Pl HP20 .... 116 A4
Ludlow Rd SL6 .... 202 C3
Luff Cl SL4 .... 209 F2
Lufford Park MK14 .... 34 C4
Luker Ave RG9 .... 191 E2
Lukes La HP23 .... 104 B2
Lukes Lea HP23 .... 105 D1
Lullingstone Dr MK12 .... 33 F3
Lumber La NN12 .... 17 D4
Lundholme MK13 .... 34 A3
Lundy Ct SL1 .... 204 C3
Lupin Cl UB7 .... 208 B1
Lupin Ct HP21 .... 115 D3
Lupin Wlk HP21 .... 115 D3
Lutman La SL6 .... 195 F1
Lutyens Gr MK7 .... 48 B3
Lychgate Cotts HP3 .... 146 A2
Lycrome La HP5 .... 144 B2
Lycrome Rd HP5 .... 144 C2
Lyde End HP27 .... 138 A1
Lydford Ave SL2 .... 205 E4
Lydiard MK8 .... 33 F1
Lydiard Cl HP21 .... 116 A2
Lydsey Cl SL2 .... 198 A1
Lye Green Rd HP5 .... 144 C1
Lyell Pl E SL4 .... 209 E2
Lyell Pl W SL4 .... 209 E2
Lyell Rd SL4 .... 209 E3
Lyell Walk E SL4 .... 209 E2
Lyell Walk W SL4 .... 209 E2
Lyme Ave HP4 .... 134 B4
Lynch Cl UB8 .... 201 E3
Lynch Hill La SL2 .... 197 F1
Lynch Hill Sch SL2 .... 197 F1
Lynch The UB8 .... 201 E3
Lyndhurst Ave SL6 .... 195 F3
Lyndhurst Cl HP13 .... 161 E1

Lyndhurst Rd HP5 .... 144 A1
Lyndon Cl HP16 .... 151 E4
Lyndon Gdns HP13 .... 173 F4
Lyndwood Dr SL4 .... 211 D1
Lyndwood Par SL4 .... 211 D1
Lyneham Gdns SL6 .... 195 D1
Lynher Cl HP21 .... 115 E2
Lynmouth Cres MK4 .... 46 B2
Lynott Cl MK8 .... 45 F3
Lynton Gn SL6 .... 202 C4
Lynton Rd HP5 .... 144 B2
Lynwood Ave SL3 .... 206 B2
Lynwood Rd HP21 .... 116 A3
Lyon Rd MK1 .... 47 D1
Lysander Cl HP1 .... 146 A2
Lysander Mead SL6 .... 203 E4

Mables The HP22 .... 131 E3
Macdonald Cl HP6 .... 154 B3
Mackenzie Mall **10** SL1 .. 205 F2
Mackenzie St **9** SL1 .... 205 F2
Maclaren Ct MK6 .... 46 C4
Madeira Wlk SL4 .... 210 B3
Madeley Cl HP6 .... 154 B2
Madeley Rd HP11 .... 115 F3
Magdalen Cl
  Milton Keynes MK11 .... 32 B3
  Syresham NN13 .... 27 E4
Magdalen Ho MK11 .... 32 B3
Magenta Cl MK2 .... 58 B3
Magnolia Dene HP15 .... 162 C1
Magnolia Gdns SL3 .... 206 B2
Magnolia St UB7 .... 208 B1
Magpie Cl HP10 .... 174 A1
Magpie La Coleshill HP7 .. 165 D1
  Flackwell Heath HP10 ..... 174 A1
  Loudwater HP10 .... 174 A2
Magpie Way Slough SL2 ... 197 F1
  Winslow MK18 .... 66 A3
Mahler Cl MK7 .... 48 B3
Mahoney Cl HP11 .... 172 C4
Maidenhead Ave MK13 .... 34 B2
Maidenhead Coll
  Claires Court Girls SL6 .... 202 C4
Maidenhead Court Park
  SL6 .... 196 A2
Maidenhead Rd
  Cookham SL6 .... 195 F3
  Oakley Green SL4 .... 209 F4
  Windsor SL4 .... 209 F4
Maidenhead Sta SL6 .... 202 C3
Maidstone Rd MK10 .... 36 B1
Main Dr
  Gerrards Cross SL9 .... 188 B3
  Iver SL0 .... 207 F2
Main Par WD3 .... 167 E3
Main Rd Astwood MK16 ...... 16 A2
  Drayton Parslow MK17 ...... 68 A3
  Grendon Underwood HP18 . 83 D3
  Lacey Green HP27 .... 149 F3
  Syresham NN13 .... 27 E4
  Waddesdon HP18 .... 99 D1
  Walter's Ash HP14 .... 161 E4
Main Rd N HP4 .... 107 D3
Main Rd S HP4 .... 107 E2
Main St Adstock MK18 .... 53 F1
  Ashendon HP18 .... 97 F1
  Beachampton MK19 .... 44 A3
  Chackmore MK18 .... 41 D2
  Charndon OX6 .... 72 C3
  Cosgrove MK19 .... 19 F1
  Gawcott MK18 .... 51 F2
  Mursley MK17 .... 67 E3
  Padbury MK18 .... 53 D1
  Preston Bissett MK18 .... 62 A4
  Shalstone MK18 .... 39 F3
  Tingewick MK18 .... 51 D3
  Turweston NN13 .... 38 B4
  Twyford MK18 .... 62 B1
  Westbury NN13 .... 39 D2
  Weston Turville HP22 ..... 116 C1
Maitland Dr HP13 .... 173 D4
Maitland Rd HP22 .... 131 E4
Major's Farm Rd SL3 .... 211 E4
Malbons Ct MK6 .... 46 C4
Malborough Way NN12 ...... 18 E2
Malcolm Rd UB10 .... 201 F4
Malden Cl HP6 .... 154 C1
Malders La Cookham SL6 .. 195 E2
  Maidenhead SL6 .... 195 E2
Malet Cl HP14 .... 158 C3
Malins Gate MK14 .... 34 C4
Malkin Dr HP9 .... 175 E2
Mallard Cl HP20 .... 101 F2
Mallard Croft HP17 .... 127 D4
Mallard Dr
  Buckingham MK18 .... 52 C4
  Slough SL1 .... 204 C3

Mallard Ho **5** HP11 .... 173 E3
Mallets End HP22 .... 85 D2
Malletts Cl MK11 .... 32 C3
Mallow Gate MK13 .... 34 C2
Mallow Park SL6 .... 195 E1
Malmers Well Rd HP11 ..... 173 D4
Malpas Rd SL2 .... 206 A3
Malt La NN13 .... 27 E4
Malthouse Sq HP9 .... 186 C4
Malting Cl MK16 .... 12 A3
Malting La Aldbury HP23 .. 120 B3
  Dagnall HP4 .... 107 E3
Maltings Cl Cranfield MK43 . 25 D1
  Stewkley LU7 .... 78 C4
Maltings The
  Chackmore MK18 .... 41 D2
  Olney MK46 .... 7 D2
  Tingewick MK18 .... 51 D3
Maltmans Green Sch for Girls
  SL9 .... 188 B4
Maltmans La SL9 .... 188 B4
Malton Ave SL1 .... 205 D3
Malvern Cl HP13 .... 172 C4
Malvern Ct SL3 .... 212 A4
Malvern Dr
  Leighton Buzzard LU7 .... 80 B4
  Milton Keynes MK11 .... 32 C2
Malvern Rd
  Aylesbury HP20 .... 116 B4
  Maidenhead SL6 .... 195 E1
Malyns Cl OX9 .... 147 E4
Manchester Terr HP14 ..... 171 D2
Mandela Ct UB8 .... 208 B4
Mandelyns HP4 .... 134 C4
Mandeville Dr MK10 .... 36 B1
Mandeville Mews HP21 .... 115 F2
Mandeville Rd
  Aylesbury HP21 .... 115 F3
  Prestwood HP16 .... 151 D4
Mandeville Sch The HP21 . 115 E2
Manfield Cl SL2 .... 198 A1
Manifold La MK5 .... 46 A2
Manor Cl
  Berkhamsted HP4 .... 135 E2
  Cosgrove MK19 .... 19 F1
  Hanslope MK19 .... 11 D1
  Milton Keynes MK10 .... 35 F2
  Salford MK17 .... 37 E2
  Stoke Hammond MK17 ...... 69 F4
  Tylers Green HP10 .... 163 D1
Manor Cotts
  Chorleywood WD3 .... 167 D2
  Milton Keynes MK12 .... 33 D4
Manor Court Yd HP13 .... 162 A1
Manor Cres
  Seer Green HP9 .... 176 B3
  Wendover HP22 .... 131 E3
Manor Ct
  Grendon Underwood HP18 . 83 D3
  Leighton Buzzard LU7 .... 70 C1
  Marlow SL7 .... 183 E2
  20 Slough SL1 .... 205 F2
Manor Ctyd MK16 .... 13 F1
Manor Dr Amersham HP6 . 154 A2
  Aylesbury HP20 .... 101 F1
  Haversham MK19 .... 20 C1
  Stewkley LU7 .... 78 C4
Manor Farm Cl Stone HP17 114 B3
  Weston Turville HP22 ..... 116 C1
  Windsor SL4 .... 209 F2
Manor Farm Cotts SL4 ..... 211 D1
Manor Farm Ct HP22 .... 87 D1
Manor Farm Cty Fst Sch
  HP15 .... 163 D1
Manor Farm Cty Mid Sch
  HP15 .... 163 D1
Manor Farm Ho SL4 .... 209 F2
Manor Farm La LU7 .... 90 B4
Manor Farm Way **4** HP9 176 B2
Manor Gdns
  High Wycombe HP13 .... 162 A1
  Maids Moreton MK18 .... 41 F1
  Wooburn Green HP10 ...... 185 F3
Manor House (Arts Ctr) The
  MK14 .... 21 F1
Manor House Cl HP20 ...... 101 F1
Manor House Hospl HP20 . 101 F1
Manor House La SL3 .... 211 D3
Manor La
  Gerrards Cross SL9 .... 188 B2
  Maidenhead SL6 .... 202 C2
Manor Park MK18 .... 41 F2
Manor Park Ave HP27 ...... 139 D2
Manor Pound Rd HP20 ..... 105 D4
Manor Rd Rkeley MK18 ..... 41 F4
  Aylesbury HP20 .... 101 F1
  Cheddington LU7 .... 104 C4
  Chesham HP5 .... 144 A1
  Chinnor OX9 .... 137 D3
  Haversham MK19 .... 20 C1
  Maidenhead SL6 .... 202 C2

Manor Rd
  Milton Keynes, Bletchley
    MK2 .... 58 C4
  Milton Keynes, Wolverton
    MK12 .... 33 D4
  Newport Pagnell MK16 ...... 22 A2
  Newton Longville MK17 ..... 57 E2
  Oakley HP18 .... 109 E3
  Oving HP22 .... 86 B4
  Princes Risborough HP27 139 D1
  Seer Green HP9 .... 176 B3
  Tring HP23 .... 119 D3
  Tylers Green HP10 .... 163 D1
  Wendover HP22 .... 131 E3
  Windsor SL4 .... 209 F3
  Wing HP22 .... 102 B4
Manor Way HP15 .... 163 D1
Manor View Ho HP13 .... 161 F1
Manor Way Chesham HP5 . 144 B1
  Coleshill HP7 .... 164 C2
  Yardley Gobion NN12 .... 18 C3
Manor Waye UB8 .... 201 E2
Manorfields Rd MK19 .... 32 A3
Mansard Ct **11** HP23 ... 119 D2
Manse Cl MK11 .... 32 B3
Mansfield Cl HP5 .... 144 A2
Mansel Cl Cosgrove MK19 . 19 F1
  Slough SL2 .... 206 A4
Mansell Cl
  Shenley Church End MK5 .. 46 A3
  Windsor SL4 .... 209 F3
Manshead Ct MK11 .... 32 C3
Mansion Dr HP23 .... 119 D2
Mansion Hill HP22 .... 131 F4
Mansion La Harrold MK43 ... 3 F3
  Iver SL0 .... 207 E3
Manton Rd LU6 .... 93 E3
Maple Ave UB7 .... 208 C3
Maple Cl
  High Wycombe HP12 .... 172 B3
  Maidenhead SL6 .... 202 B3
  Tylers Green HP15 .... 163 D2
Maple Cres SL2 .... 206 A3
Maple Cross Jun Mix Inf Sch
  WD3 .... 178 C3
Maple Ct
  Gerrards Cross SL9 .... 188 C3
  Marlow SL7 .... 183 F2
  Windsor SL4 .... 210 B2
Maple Gr
  Milton Keynes MK2 .... 58 C4
  Wooburn Sands MK17 .... 49 D2
Maple Leys MK18 .... 63 F2
Maple Lodge Cl WD3 .... 178 C3
Maple Pl UB7 .... 208 C3
Maple Rise SL7 .... 183 F2
Maplebeam MK12 .... 32 C4
Mapledurham MK7 .... 48 A2
Mapledurham Wlk SL6 ..... 195 F2
Maplefield La HP7 .... 166 A3
Maples The **15** SL6 ...... 185 D2
Maplewood Gdns HP9 ...... 175 D1
Maplin Park SL3 .... 207 D2
Marand Ct HP21 .... 115 F4
Marbeck Cl SL4 .... 209 E3
March Edge MK18 .... 41 F1
March Meadow MK7 .... 48 B4
March Pl HP19 .... 115 D4
Marchant Ct SL7 .... 184 A2
Mardle Rd LU7 .... 80 C3
Mare Leys MK18 .... 52 C4
Marcei Cl
  Leighton Buzzard LU7 .... 80 B4
  Milton Keynes MK2 .... 58 B3
Marefield Rd SL7 .... 183 E1
Marescroft Rd SL2 .... 197 F1
Margaret Smyth Ho SL9 .. 188 C3
Marie Cl OX6 .... 71 F2
Marigold Pl MK14 .... 34 C2
Marigold Wlk HP15 .... 162 C1
Marina Dr Dunstable LU6 .. 93 F4
  Milton Keynes MK12 .... 33 E4
Marina Rdbt MK6 .... 47 E4
Marina Way Burnham SL1 . 204 B3
  Iver SL0 .... 208 A3
Marish Ct SL3 .... 207 D2
Marish Inf Sch SL3 .... 207 D2
Marish La UB9 .... 189 E4
Marish Mid Sch SL3 .... 207 D2
Marish Wharf (Ind Est)
  SL3 .... 206 C2
Marjoram Pl MK14 .... 34 C2
Mark Dr SL9 .... 177 E3
Market Hill
  Milton Keynes MK6 .... 47 D4
  Whitchurch HP22 .... 86 C3
Market Ho **5** SL9 .... 177 E1
Market La SL3 .... 212 C3

Manor Par HP15 .... 163 D2
Market Pl Colnbrook SL3 .. 212 B4
  Gerrards Cross SL9 .... 177 E1
  Henley-on-T RG9 .... 191 E1
  Olney MK46 .... 6 C2
  Woburn MK17 .... 60 C4
Market Sq Amersham HP7 165 D4
  Aylesbury HP20 .... 115 E4
  Chesham HP5 .... 154 A4
  Hanslope MK19 .... 11 D1
  Marlow SL7 .... 183 E1
  Milton Keynes MK11 .... 32 B3
  Princes Risborough HP27 139 D2
  Uxbridge UB8 .... 201 E3
  Winslow MK18 .... 65 F2
Market St
  12 Aylesbury HP20 .... 115 E4
  Maidenhead SL6 .... 202 C4
  18 Windsor SL4 .... 210 B3
Markhams Ct MK18 .... 52 B4
Marlborough Cl SL6 .... 202 A3
Marlborough Ct SL1 .... 204 C4
Marlborough Gate MK4 ...... 34 C2
Marlborough Ho **5** SL6 . 202 C3
Marlborough
  Aylesbury HP21 .... 115 F2
  Maidenhead SL6 .... 202 A3
  Slough SL3 .... 206 C1
Marlborough St MK14 .... 34 C3
Marlborough Trad Est
  HP11 .... 172 C4
Marley Gr MK8 .... 45 F4
Marlin Cl HP4 .... 134 C3
Marlin Copse HP4 .... 135 D2
Marlin Ct SL7 .... 183 E1
Marlins Cl HP13 .... 133 D4
Marlins Cl WD3 .... 167 F4
Marlow Bottom SL7 .... 183 E3
Marlow Bridge La SL7 ...... 194 C4
Marlow CE Fst Sch SL7 ... 183 E2
Marlow Comm Hospl SL7 . 183 F1
Marlow Comm SL7 .... 182 C2
Marlow Dr MK16 .... 22 A2
Marlow Hill HP11 .... 173 D3
Marlow Lodge **13** SL6 . 202 C3
Marlow Mill SL7 .... 183 F1
Marlow Rd
  Beacon's Bottom HP14 ... 170 A4
  Bisham SL6 .... 194 C2
  Bourne End SL8 .... 184 B3
  Henley-on-T RG9 .... 191 F2
  High Wycombe HP11 .... 172 C2
  Lane End HP14 .... 171 F1
  Little Marlow SL7 .... 184 B3
  Maidenhead SL6 .... 202 C4
  Marlow Bottom HP14, SL7 183 E3
  Marlow Sta SL7 .... 183 F1
  Marmion Rd RG9 .... 191 F1
  Marquis Cl MK17 .... 60 C4
  Marram Cl MK6 .... 47 F3
  Marriott Terr WD3 .... 167 F3
  Marriotts Ave HP16 .... 142 C1
  Marriotts Cl HP17 .... 126 C3
  Marriotts La HP17 .... 126 C3
  Marriotts Way HP17 .... 126 C3
  Marrod's Bottom HP9 ...... 175 E4
  Marron La MK12 .... 33 E3
Marroway
  Stoke Mandeville HP22 ... 116 B1
  Weston Turville HP22 ..... 116 B1
Marsh Ct HP13 .... 173 F2
Marsh Cty Fst Sch HP11 .. 173 F2
Marsh Dr MK14 .... 21 F1
Marsh End Rd MK16 .... 22 B2
Marsh Gibbon CE Fst Sch
  OX6 .... 71 F2
Marsh La SL6 .... 203 F3
Marsh Lane HP22 .... 129 F4
Marsh Rd
  Great Kimble HP17 .... 129 E2
  Shabbington HP18 .... 124 B2
Marshall Court Ind Est
  MK1 .... 47 D1
Marshalls La MK15 .... 35 E1
Marshalls Lea HP22 .... 102 B2
Marsham Cl HP21 .... 116 A2
Marsham La SL9 .... 188 C3
Marsham Lodge SL9 .... 188 C3
Marsham Way SL9 .... 188 C3
Marshcroft La HP23 .... 119 E3
Marshfield SL3 .... 211 E3
Marshworth MK6 .... 47 E3
Marston Cl HP5 .... 144 A2
Marston Ct HP23 .... 104 A2
Marston Hill
  Cranfield MK43 .... 25 F1
  Oving HP22 .... 86 B4
Marston Rd
  Granborough MK18 .... 75 F3
  Thame OX9 .... 126 A1
Marstonfields Rd MK18 ..... 76 A1

Marsworth CE Fst Sch
  HP23 .... 105 D1
Marsworth Rd LU7 .... 105 E2
Martin Cl Buckingham MK18 52 C4
  Milton Keynes MK14 .... 34 C3
  Uxbridge UB10 .... 201 F2
  Windsor SL4 .... 209 E3
Martin Dell Cotts HP16 .... 142 C2
Martin Rd Maidenhead SL6 202 C4
  Slough SL1 .... 205 F2
Martin's Plain SL2 .... 198 C2
Martindale SL6 .... 200 B1
Martingale Pl MK14 .... 34 C3
Martins Dr The LU7 .... 80 C4
Martinsend La HP16 .... 151 F4
Martyrs Ct HP7 .... 165 E4
Marunden Green SL2 .... 197 F1
Marwood Cl MK4 .... 46 B2
Mary Bassett Lower Sch
  LU7 .... 80 C4
Mary Cross Cl HP23 .... 119 E1
Mary Macmanus Dr MK18 . 41 E1
Mary Morgan Ct SL1 .... 205 E4
Mary Towerton Cty Fst
  Sch The HP14 .... 159 E2
Marygold Wlk HP6 .... 166 B4
Maryland Coll MK17 .... 60 C3
Maryland Rd MK15 .... 35 D4
Maryot Cl MK16 .... 13 F1
Marys Mead HP15 .... 163 D3
Maryside SL3 .... 206 C2
Mascoll Path SL2 .... 197 F1
Masefield Cl MK16 .... 22 A2
Masefield Gr MK3 .... 58 A4
Maslin Dr MK6 .... 47 D3
Mason MK14 .... 34 B4
Mason's Ct Aylesbury HP21 115 D4
  Slough SL1 .... 204 C3
Masons Cl HP16 .... 151 E3
Masons Ct HP5 .... 144 B1
Masons Rd SL1 .... 204 C3
Masons Yd HP4 .... 135 E2
Massie Cl MK15 .... 35 D3
Mathieson Rd MK13 .... 34 A3
Mathisen Way SL3 .... 212 C3
Matilda Gdns MK5 .... 46 A3
Matlock Rd HP20 .... 101 F1
Matson Dr RG9 .... 191 F1
Matthew Ct MK5 .... 46 A3
Matthews Ct **13** HP20 . 101 F1
Maud Jane's Cl LU7 .... 105 F3
Maude Cl HP9 .... 176 A1
Maude Rd HP9 .... 176 A1
Maudsley Cl MK5 .... 46 B3
Maudsley Ho SL6 .... 203 D4
Mauduit Cl MK19 .... 11 D2
Maulden Gdns MK14 .... 35 D4
Maurice Mount HP15 .... 162 C3
Maxham MK5 .... 46 A2
Maxwell Dr HP15 .... 163 D3
Maxwell Rd
  Beaconsfield HP9 .... 175 F2
  West Drayton UB7 .... 208 C1
May Cl LU6 .... 92 C3
May Rd MK43 .... 8 C3
May Tree Cl SL7 .... 183 E3
Maybrook Gdns HP13 ...... 173 E4
Maybury Cl SL1 .... 204 B4
Maybush Wlk MK46 .... 6 C3
Maydale Ho HP15 .... 162 C3
Maydich Pl MK13 .... 34 B2
Mayer Gdns MK5 .... 46 B3
Mayfield Ave SL9 .... 188 B4
Mayfield Rd HP10 .... 185 F3
Mayflower Cl HP17 .... 114 C3
Mayflower Way
  Beaconsfield HP9 .... 186 A4
  Farnham Common SL2 .... 198 B4
Maygoods Cl UB8 .... 208 B4
Maygoods Green UB8 ...... 208 B4
Maygoods La UB8 .... 208 B4
Maygoods View UB8 .... 208 B4
Mayhall La HP5 .... 154 A2
Mayhew Cres HP13 .... 173 E4
Maylands Dr UB8 .... 201 E3
Maynard Cl MK13 .... 34 A2
Maynard Ct SL4 .... 210 A3
Maypole Rd SL6 .... 204 A4
Mays Way NN12 .... 18 B2
McConnell Dr MK12 .... 33 F3
McEwen Ride HP22 .... 117 E1
McKay Trad Est SL3 .... 212 C3
McKenzie Cl MK18 .... 52 B4
Mead Acre HP27 .... 139 D3
Mead Ave SL3 .... 207 D2
Mead Cl Denham UB9 ...... 190 A1
  7 Marlow SL7 .... 183 F2
  Princes Risborough HP27 139 D3
  Slough SL3 .... 207 D2
Mead Ho HP16 .... 196 B1
Mead Pk HP15 .... 163 E4
Mead Platt HP14 .... 158 B3

Mead Rd UB8 .... 201 E3
Mead St HP10 .... 174 A2
Mead The
  Beaconsfield HP9 .... 175 F1
  Soulbury LU7 .... 69 F2
Mead Way
  High Wycombe HP11 .... 173 F2
  Slough SL1 .... 204 B4
Mead Wlk SL3 .... 207 D2
Meades La HP5 .... 154 A4
Meadfield Ave SL3 .... 207 D2
Meadfield Rd SL3 .... 207 D2
Meadfurlong Cty Comb Sch
  MK6 .... 34 C1
Meadow Bank 18 SL8 .... 185 D2
Meadow Cl Aylesbury HP20 .. 102 A1
  Berkhamsted HP4 .... 135 D1
  Chesham HP5 .... 144 A2
  Cublington LU7 .... 78 B1
  High Wycombe HP11 .... 173 F2
  Marlow SL7 .... 183 F1
  Oakley HP18 .... 109 E2
  Old Windsor SL4 .... 211 D1
Meadow Cotd La HP7 .... 164 C2
Meadow Cotts
  Beaconsfield HP9 .... 175 F1
  Little Kingshill HP16 .... 152 A2
Meadow Dr
  Amersham HP6 .... 154 C1
  Longwick HP27 .... 138 B3
Meadow Gate
  Padbury MK18 .... 53 D1
  Prestwood HP16 .... 151 E2
Meadow Gdns MK18 .... 52 C3
Meadow La
  Beaconsfield HP9 .... 175 F1
  Eton SL4 .... 210 B4
  Milton Keynes Village
  MK10 .... 36 A2
  Pitstone LU7 .... 105 F2
Meadow Pk HP22 .... 116 B1
Meadow Rd
  Berkhamsted HP4 .... 135 D3
  Chinnor OX9 .... 147 E3
  Henley-on-T RG9 .... 191 F1
  Marlow Bottom SL7 .... 183 F3
  Slough SL3 .... 206 C2
Meadow Rise HP27 .... 149 F3
Meadow Sch The UB8 .... 208 C4
Meadow View
  Aspley Guise MK17 .... 49 E3
  Chalfont St Giles HP8 .... 177 D4
  Long Crendon HP18 .... 125 F2
  Pottersbury NN12 .... 18 B2
  Stanwell TW19 .... 213 D1
  Uxbridge UB8 .... 208 B4
Meadow Way
  Aylesbury HP20 .... 102 A1
  Dorney SL4 .... 203 F2
  Hyde Heath HP6 .... 153 E2
  Old Windsor SL4 .... 211 D1
  Thame OX9 .... 125 F1
  Wing LU7 .... 79 F2
Meadow Wlk
  Buckingham MK18 .... 41 E1
  Tylers Green HP10 .... 163 E1
Meadoway
  Steeple Claydon MK18 .... 63 F2
  Stone HP17 .... 114 C3
Meadowbank Cl HP18 .... 125 E4
Meadowbrook Cl SL3 .... 212 C3
Meadowcroft
  Aylesbury HP19 .... 101 D2
  Berkhamsted HP4 .... 134 B4
  Gerrards Cross SL9 .... 177 E1
Meadowcroft Cty Fst Sch
  HP19 .... 101 D1
Meadowcroft Cty Mid Sch
  HP19 .... 101 D2
Meadowlea Cl UB7 .... 213 E4
Meadows Cty Comb Sch The
  HP10 .... 185 F4
Meadows The
  Amersham HP7 .... 154 C1
  Flackwell Heath HP10 .... 185 D4
  Seer Green HP9 .... 176 B3
Meadowside HP9 .... 176 C2
Meadowsweet MK7 .... 48 A3
Meads Cl MK13, MK17 .... 34 A4
Meads The
  Berkhamsted HP4 .... 134 C3
  Eaton Bray LU6 .... 92 C3
  Tring HP23 .... 119 D2
  Uxbridge UB8 .... 201 F1
  4 Windsor SL4 .... 210 A3
Meadway
  Berkhamsted HP4 .... 135 F3
  Buckingham MK18 .... 52 C3
  Dunstable LU6 .... 93 F4
  Oving HP22 .... 76 C1

Meadway Ct LU6 .... 93 F4
Meadway The MK5 .... 46 A4
Meare Estate HP10 .... 185 F4
Meavy Cl HP10 .... 174 A2
Medhall Rd MK6 .... 47 D3
Medallion Pl SL6 .... 203 D4
Medbourne Rdbt MK8 .... 45 F3
Medeswell MK4 .... 46 C2
Medhurst MK8 .... 33 F1
Medland MK6 .... 47 E4
Medley Cl LU6 .... 92 C3
Medman Cl UB8 .... 201 E2
Medway Cl MK16 .... 22 C2
Meeting Oak La MK18 .... 66 A3
Megdale Pl HP20 .... 101 E1
Melbourne Ave SL1 .... 205 E4
Melbourne Cl HP21 .... 115 F3
Melbourne Rd HP13 .... 173 F3
Melbourne Terr MK13 .... 34 A4
Melford Gn HP19 .... 101 E2
Melfort Dr
  Leighton Buzzard LU7 .... 80 A3
  Milton Keynes MK2 .... 58 B2
Melick Rd MK6 .... 47 D2
Mellish Cl MK3 .... 47 D1
Mellstock Rd HP21 .... 115 F3
Melrose Ave MK3 .... 47 D2
Melrose Ct HP13 .... 162 A1
Melrose Wlk HP21 .... 115 F3
Melton MK14 .... 34 B4
Melton Dr Dunstable LU6 .... 93 F4
  Maidenhead SL6 .... 202 C3
Mendelssohn Gr MK7 .... 48 B2
Mendip Cl SL3 .... 207 D1
Mendip Way HP13 .... 172 C4
Mendy St HP11 .... 173 D4
Menmarsh Rd HP18 .... 123 F3
Menteith Cl MK2 .... 58 B3
Mentmore Cl HP22 .... 172 A3
Mentmore Crossroads
  HP22 .... 89 F3
Mentmore Ct MK8 .... 45 F4
Mentmore Gdns HP21 .... 115 F2
Mentmore Rd
  Cheddington LU7 .... 104 C4
  High Wycombe HP12 .... 172 A3
  Leighton Buzzard LU7 .... 80 C3
Mentmore View HP23 .... 118 C3
Mentone Ave MK7 .... 49 E2
Menzies Ct MK5 .... 46 A2
Mercer Wlk UB8 .... 201 E3
Mercers Dr MK13 .... 34 A3
Merchant La
  Cranfield MK43 .... 24 C1
  Cranfield MK43 .... 25 D1
Mercia Rd SL6 .... 202 B2
Mercian Way SL1 .... 204 B3
Mere Cl SL7 .... 183 F1
Mere Rd Finmere MK18 .... 50 B3
  Slough SL1 .... 205 F2
Meredith Dr HP19 .... 100 C1
Meriland Ct MK2 .... 58 C2
Merlebank HP5 .... 154 B4
Merlewood Cl HP11 .... 173 D2
Merlewood Dr MK5 .... 45 F2
Merlin Cl SL3 .... 212 A4
Merlin Ctr HP19 .... 101 E1
Merlin Wlk MK6 .... 47 D4
Merlins Croft HP4 .... 134 C4
Marrivale Mews UB7 .... 208 B3
Merry Down HP13 .... 161 E1
Merryfields UB8 .... 201 E2
Mersey Cl MK3 .... 46 C1
Mersey Way MK3 .... 46 C1
Merthen Gr MK4 .... 57 D4
Merton Cl SL6 .... 202 B2
Merton Dr MK6 .... 47 D2
Merton Rd
  Princes Risborough HP27 .... 139 D1
  Slough SL1 .... 206 A2
Merwin Way SL4 .... 209 E2
Mescar Ct HP21 .... 116 A3
Metcalfe Gr MK14 .... 22 A1
Michael Rd SL6 .... 202 B3
Michigan Dr
  Milton Keynes MK15 .... 35 D4
  Newport Pagnell MK15 .... 22 B1
Micklefield Cty Comb Sch
  HP13 .... 174 A4
Micklefield Rd HP13 .... 174 A4
Mid Cross La SL9 .... 177 F3
Midas Ind Est UB8 .... 201 D2
Midcot Way HP4 .... 134 C3
Midcroft SL2 .... 198 A1
Middle Cl HP6 .... 154 C1
Middle Cres UB9 .... 189 E2
Middle Dr HP9 .... 175 D3
Middle Field HP22 .... 116 C2

Middle Green SL3 .... 206 C3
Middle La HP3 .... 146 A1
Middle Mdw HP8 .... 177 F4
Middle Rd Aylesbury HP21 .. 116 A4
  Berkhamsted HP4 .... 135 E4
  Denham Green UB9 .... 189 E2
Middle Slade MK18 .... 52 B3
Middle Walk SL1 .... 197 E1
Middle Way OX9 .... 147 D3
Middlebrook Rd HP13 .... 161 F1
Middlefield Cl MK18 .... 41 F1
Middlegreen Rd SL3 .... 206 B3
Middlegreen Trad Est SL3 .. 206 B2
Middlesex Dr MK3 .... 46 C1
Middleton MK14 .... 34 C4
Middleway The HP12 .... 172 B3
Midhurst Cl HP21 .... 116 A3
Midland Rd MK 7 D3
Midsummer Arc MK9 .... 34 C1
Midsummer Bvd MK9 .... 34 C1
Midsummer Rdbt MK9 .... 34 B1
Miersfield HP12 .... 172 B2
Mikern Cl MK2 .... 58 B4
Milburn Ave MK6 .... 46 C4
Milburn Dr UB7 .... 208 C3
Mildenhall Rd SL1 .... 205 F4
Mildun Way HP12 .... 172 B3
Mile Elm SL7 .... 184 A2
Milebush LU7 .... 80 B4
Milecastle MK13 .... 34 A3
Miles Cl Aylesbury HP21 .. 116 A4
  Milton Keynes MK14 .... 22 A2
Miles End HP21 .... 115 D3
Milesmere MK8 .... 33 E1
Milfoil Ave MK14 .... 34 C2
Milford Ave MK11 .... 32 C2
Milford Cl SL1 .... 206 A2
Milk Hall Barns HP5 .... 154 C3
Mill Ave UB8 .... 201 E2
Mill Cl Chesham HP5 .... 154 C3
  West Drayton UB7 .... 208 B2
  Wingrave HP22 .... 89 D2
Mill Ct Horton SL3 .... 212 B2
  Milton Keynes MK12 .... 33 D3
  Waddesdon HP18 .... 99 D4
  West Drayton UB7 .... 208 B2
Mill End Rd HP12 .... 192 B4
Mill End Cl LU6 .... 92 C2
Mill End Rd HP12 .... 172 B4
Mill Gdns HP23 .... 119 D2
Mill Ho MK43 .... 8 B3
Mill La Amersham HP7 .... 165 D4
  Aspley Guise MK17 .... 49 E3
  Beaconsfield HP9 .... 175 F1
  Brackley NN13 .... 38 A3
  Buckingham MK18 .... 52 B4
  Chalfont St Giles HP8 .... 177 D4
  Chinnor OX9 .... 147 D4
  Cookham SL6 .... 196 B4
  Gerrards Cross SL9 .... 188 C3
  Great Brickhill MK17 .... 58 C1
  Haddenham HP17 .... 126 A2
  Horton SL3 .... 212 A2
  Horton-cum-S OX33 .... 108 A3
  Hurley SL6 .... 193 F2
  Milton Keynes, Bradville
  MK13 .... 34 A4
  Milton Keynes, Stony Stratford
  MK11 .... 32 B3
  Milton Keynes, Woolstone
  MK15 .... 35 E2
  Princes Risborough HP27 .. 139 D3
  Salford MK17 .... 37 E2
  South Heath HP16 .... 152 B4
  Stokenchurch HP14 .... 158 B3
  Taplow SL6 .... 203 E4
  Twyford MK18 .... 62 B1
  Upper Arncott OX6 .... 94 C4
  Westbury NN13 .... 39 D2
  Weston Turville HP22 .... 117 D1
  Windsor SL4 .... 210 A4
  Wingrave HP22 .... 89 E1
Mill Lane Cty Prim Sch
  OX9 .... 147 D4
Mill Mead HP22 .... 131 D3
Mill Pl SL3 .... 211 E3
Mill Rd Cranfield MK43 .... 25 E1
  2 Leighton Buzzard LU7 .. 80 C4
  Marlow SL7 .... 183 F1
  Milton Keynes MK2 .... 58 C4
  Oakley HP18 .... 109 E2
  Slapton LU7 .... 91 E4
  Stokenchurch HP14 .... 158 B3
  West Drayton UB7 .... 208 B2
  Whitfield NN13 .... 26 C2
Mill Sq MK12 .... 33 D3
Mill St Aylesbury HP20 .... 101 F1
  Berkhamsted HP4 .... 135 E2
  Colnbrook SL3 .... 212 B4
  High Wycombe HP11 .... 172 C4

Mill St
  Newport Pagnell MK16 .... 22 B3
  Slough SL2, SL3 .... 205 F3
Mill Terr MK12 .... 33 D3
Mill Tower LU6 .... 92 C3
Mill View Rd HP23 .... 118 C2
Mill Way
  Aspley Guise MK17 .... 49 E3
  Berkhamsted HP4 .... 135 E4
  Rickmansworth WD3 .... 167 F1
Millards Cl MK43 .... 25 E1
Millbank
  Leighton Buzzard LU7 .... 80 C4
  Marlow SL7 .... 183 F1
Millbank Pl MK7 .... 48 A3
Millboard Rd SL8 .... 185 D2
Millbridge Way SL3 .... 212 C3
Millbrook Pl HP18 .... 123 F3
Miller Pl SL4 .... 188 C4
Miller's La SL4 .... 211 D1
Millers Turn OX9 .... 147 D3
Millers Way
  MK1, MK12, MK13 .... 33 E3
Millfield HP4 .... 135 E2
Millfield Ave OX6 .... 71 F2
Millfield Cl Cranfield MK43 .. 25 D1
  Marsh Gibbon OX6 .... 71 F2
Millfields HP5 .... 154 B3
Millhayes MK14 .... 34 C4
Milliners The 18 HP20 .... 101 F1
Millington Gate MK15 .... 35 E4
Millshot Dr HP7 .... 165 E4
Millside SL8 .... 185 E2
Millstream HP22 .... 116 C1
Millstream La SL1 .... 204 C3
Millstream Way
  Leighton Buzzard LU7 .... 80 C4
  Wooburn Green HP10 .... 185 F4
Milner Rd SL1 .... 204 A4
Milton Ave SL9 .... 188 B3
Milton Cl Henley-on-T RG9 .. 191 E1
  Horton SL3 .... 212 A2
Milton Dr MK16 .... 22 C2
Milton Fields HP8 .... 177 D4
Milton Gdns HP27 .... 139 D1
Milton Gr MK3 .... 57 F4
Milton Hill HP5 .... 177 D4
Milton Keynes Central Sta
  MK9 .... 34 B1
Milton Keynes Coll MK6 .... 46 C4
  (Bletchley Ctr) MK3 .... 58 A4
Milton Keynes Coll,
  Wolverton Ctr MK12 .... 33 D3
Milton Keynes Gen Hospl
  MK3 .... 57 F2
Milton Keynes Prep Sch
  MK3 .... 57 E2
Milton Lawns HP6 .... 154 B2
Milton Rd
  Aston Clinton HP22 .... 117 F3
  Aylesbury HP21 .... 115 F3
  Chesham HP5 .... 144 A1
  Milton Keynes MK15 .... 35 E4
  Slough SL2 .... 198 B1
  Walton MK7 .... 47 F3
Milton Way UB7 .... 208 C1
Milton's Cott (Mus) HP8 .... 177 D4
Milverton Cl SL6 .... 202 A2
Mimas Cl HP21 .... 115 D3
Mina Ave SL3 .... 206 B2
Mineral La HP5 .... 154 B4
Minerva Cl TW19 .... 213 D1
Minerva Gdns MK7 .... 48 B4
Minerva Way HP9 .... 176 A1
Minniecroft Rd SL1 .... 197 D1
Minshull Cl MK18 .... 41 E1
Minster Way SL3 .... 206 C2
Minstrel Ct MK13 .... 34 A4
Minton Cl MK14 .... 22 A1
Minton Rise SL6 .... 204 A4
Mirador Cres SL2 .... 206 B3
Mirrie La UB9 .... 189 E3
Misbourne Ave
  Chalfont St Peter SL9 .... 177 F3
  High Wycombe HP13 .... 173 F3
Misbourne Cl
  Chalfont St Peter SL9 .... 177 F3
  Stoke Mandeville HP21 .... 115 E2
Misbourne Ct SL3 .... 207 D1
Misbourne Dr HP16 .... 152 A3
Misbourne Ho HP6 .... 166 B1
Misbourne Meadows UB9 .. 189 E2
Misbourne Prim Sch The
  HP6 .... 152 A3
Misbourne Vale SL9 .... 177 E3
Missenden Gdns SL1 .... 204 B3
Missenden Rd
  Chesham HP5 .... 154 A4
  Ellesborough HP17 .... 130 B1
  Great Kingshill
  HP15, HP16 .... 151 E1
  Winslow MK18 .... 65 F2

Miswell La HP23 .... 118 C2
Mitcham PH MK13 .... 34 B2
Mitcham Wlk HP19 .... 101 D1
Mitchell Cl Bovingdon HP1 . 145 F2
  Slough SL1 .... 205 D2
  Thame OX9 .... 125 F1
Mitchell Rd MK43 .... 25 E1
Mitchell Wlk HP6 .... 154 C1
Mithras Gdns MK7 .... 48 B3
Mitre Cl MK18 .... 52 B4
Mitre St MK18 .... 52 B4
Moat Cl Prestwood HP16 .. 151 E3
  Wendover HP22 .... 131 D3
Moat Dr Prestwood HP16 .. 151 E3
  Slough SL2 .... 206 B4
Moat End HP22 .... 102 A2
Moat La Aston Abbots HP22 . 88 B2
  Marsh Gibbon OX6 .... 71 F1
  Prestwood HP16 .... 151 E4
  Wingrave HP22 .... 89 D1
Moat Pl UB9 .... 201 D4
Mobwell Terr HP16 .... 152 A4
Model Row HP22 .... 117 F3
Moeran Cl MK7 .... 48 B3
Moffy Hill SL6 .... 195 F1
Mole Run HP13 .... 161 E1
Monellan Gr MK7 .... 48 A2
Monet Pl HP19 .... 100 C1
Money La UB7 .... 208 B2
Monkey Island La SL6 .... 203 F1
Monks Hollow SL7 .... 183 F3
Monks Rd SL4 .... 209 E3
Monks Risborough CE
  Comb Sch HP27 .... 139 E3
Monks Risborough Sta
  HP27 .... 139 D1
Monks Way
  Harmondsworth UB7 .... 213 F4
  Milton Keynes
  MK12, MK14, MK15, MK6 .. 34 B3
Monksfield Way SL2 .... 198 A1
Monkston Rdbt MK10 .... 36 A1
Monkswood Ct 6 SL7 .... 183 F1
Monkton-Waye HP27 .... 150 B3
Monmouth Cl HP19 .... 101 D1
Monro Ave MK4 .... 45 F4
Montabaur Rd NN13 .... 38 A4
Montagu Dr MK6 .... 47 D4
Montagu Rd SL3 .... 211 D3
Montague Rd
  Aylesbury HP21 .... 115 E4
  Berkhamsted HP4 .... 135 D2
  Slough SL1 .... 205 F3
  Uxbridge UB8 .... 201 F3
Montague St MK18 .... 52 B4
Montem Mid Sch (Annexe)
  SL1 .... 205 D2
Montem (The) Infs Sch
  SL1 .... 205 D2
Montgomerie Cl HP4 .... 135 D3
Montgomery Cres MK15 .... 35 D4
Montgomery Pl SL2 .... 206 B4
Montpellier Ct SL4 .... 210 B3
Montrose Ave Datchet SL3 . 211 E4
  Slough SL1, SL3 .... 205 D4
Montrose Dr SL6 .... 202 A3
Montrose Way SL2 .... 211 E4
Monument La SL9 .... 177 F3
Moor Cl SL1 .... 33 E3
Moor End Eaton Bray LU6 .. 92 C3
  Maidenhead SL6 .... 203 E1
Moor End Cl LU6 .... 92 C2
Moor End La LU6 .... 92 C3
Moor La
  Harmondsworth UB7 .... 213 E4
  High Wycombe HP13 .... 161 E2
  Maidenhead SL6 .... 195 F1
  Sarratt WD3 .... 156 C3
Moor Park Halton HP22 .... 131 D4
  Milton Keynes MK3 .... 57 E4
Moor Rd MK9 .... 154 B3
Moor Rdbt UB7 .... 213 E4
Moor's Farm Cotts HP5 .... 145 D2
Moorbridge Rd SL6 .... 203 D4
Moore Cl SL1 .... 205 D2
Moore Rd HP4 .... 134 C3
Moorend La Thame OX9 .... 125 F1
  Thame OX9 .... 126 A1
Moorend Rd NN12 .... 18 C3
Moores Hill MK46 .... 6 C3
Moores La SL4 .... 204 C1
Moores Cl MK17 .... 57 E2
Moorfield Rd
  Denham Green UB9 .... 190 A3
  Uxbridge UB8 .... 208 B4
Moorfield Terr SL6 .... 203 D4
Moorfoot MK11 .... 33 D2

Moorgate MK6 .... 46 C4
Moorhall Rd UB9 .... 190 A3
Moor Ct 7 HP20 .... 101 F2
Moorhen Way MK18 .... 52 C4
Moorhills Cres LU7 .... 79 F2
Moorhills Rd LU7 .... 79 F2
Moorings The MK6 .... 52 B4
Moorland Cty Fst Sch MK6 . 47 D3
Moorland Rd UB7 .... 213 E4
Moorlands LU7 .... 79 F2
Moorlands Rd LU7 .... 79 F2
Moorside HP10 .... 185 F4
Moorside Cl SL6 .... 195 F1
Moorstown Ct 7 SL1 ...... 205 F2
Mop End La HP7 .... 164 A4
Morar Cl LU7 .... 80 B4
Moray Dr SL2 .... 206 A4
Moray Pl MK3 .... 46 C1
Mordaunt Cl MK43 .... 8 C3
Mordaunts Ct MK15 .... 35 E1
More Ave HP21 .... 115 E4
Moreau Wlk SL3 .... 206 C4
Morebath Gr MK4 .... 46 B2
Morefields HP23 .... 119 D3
Moreland Ave SL3 .... 212 B4
Moreland Cl SL3 .... 212 B4
Morelands Dr SL9 .... 188 C2
Morello Dr SL3 .... 206 C3
Moreton Dr MK18 .... 41 F1
Moreton La HP17 .... 115 D1
Moreton Rd MK18 .... 41 E1
Moreton Way SL1 .... 204 B3
Morley Cl SL3 .... 206 C2
Morley Cres MK7 .... 48 B2
Morrell Cl MK5 .... 46 A3
Morrice Cl SL3 .... 207 D1
Morris Cl SL9 .... 177 F1
Morris Ct Aylesbury HP21 .. 115 E2
Windsor SL4 .... 209 F3
Morris Wlk MK16 .... 22 A2
Morrison Ct MK4 .... 45 F3
Mortain Cl MK7 .... 48 A2
Mortain Dr HP4 .... 134 C3
Morten Gdns UB9 .... 190 A2
Mortens Wood HP7 .... 165 F4
Mortimer Hill HP23 .... 119 D2
Mortimer Rd SL3 .... 206 B2
Mortimer Rise HP23 .... 119 D2
Morton Cl
North Marston MK18 .... 76 A1
Pitstone LU7 .... 106 C4
Morton King Cl HP18 .... 124 B2
Mortons Fork MK13 .... 33 F3
Moseley Rd HP14 .... 161 E4
Moses Plat La HP27 .... 150 A3
Moss Cl 2 HP9 .... 176 B2
Mossdale MK13 .... 34 A3
Mossway HP9 .... 175 E3
Mossy Vale SL6 .... 195 E1
Mount Ave MK1 .... 47 F2
Mount Cl
Aston Clinton HP22 .... 117 F2
Farnham Common SL2 .... 198 B4
High Wycombe HP12 ...... 172 C3
Mount Farm Ind Est MK1 ... 47 E2
Mount Farm Rdbt MK1 .... 47 E2
Mount Hill La SL9 .... 188 A1
Mount La UB9 .... 189 E1
Mount Nugent HP5 .... 144 A2
Mount Pleasant
Aspley Guise MK17 .... 49 F2
Aylesbury HP19 .... 101 E1
Lane End HP14 .... 171 D3
Milton Keynes MK17 .... 47 D2
Soulbury LU7 .... 69 F2
Steeple Claydon MK18 ..... 63 F1
Stoke Goldington MK16 .... 12 A4
Stoke Hammond MK17 ...... 69 F4
Whitchurch HP22 .... 86 C4
Yardley Gobion NN12 .... 18 C3
Mount Pleasant Ct MK18 .... 52 B4
Mount Pleasant Cotts 12
SL8 .... 185 D2
Mount St HP20 .... 115 E4
Mount The
Aspley Guise MK17 .... 49 E2
Milton Keynes MK6 .... 47 F2
Mount View RG9 .... 191 E1
Mount View Ct RG9 .... 191 E1
Mount Way HP27 .... 139 D2
Mountain Ash SL7 .... 183 E3
Mountbatten Cl SL1 .... 206 A2
Mountbatten Sq 8 SL4 ... 210 B3
Mounthill Ave MK46 .... 32 A4
Mountsfield Cl
Newport Pagnell MK16 ..... 22 B2
Stanwell TW19 .... 213 D1
Mow Mead MK46 .... 6 C3

Mowbray Dr LU7 .... 80 B4
Mowbray Rd HP20 .... 101 E1
Mowhills MK43 .... 3 F3
Moyleen Rise SL7 .... 183 E1
Mozart Cl MK7 .... 48 B2
Muddiford La MK4 .... 46 B2
Muirfield Dr MK3 .... 46 B1
Mulberry Cl Amersham HP7 165 F4
Tring HP23 .... 119 D3
Mulberry Ct HP15 .... 163 E4
Mulberry Dr SL3 .... 206 C1
Mulberry Wlk SL6 .... 202 B4
Mullen Ave MK14 .... 34 C2
Mullins Way HP19 .... 100 C1
Mullion Pl MK6 .... 35 D1
Mumfords La SL9 .... 188 A4
Munces Rd SL7 .... 183 E3
Munday's Farm HP21 .... 116 B4
Mundaydean La SL7 .... 183 D2
Mundesley Spur SL1 .... 205 F4
Murcott Rd OX6 .... 94 B3
Murray Rd HP4 .... 135 E3
Murrey Cl MK5 .... 46 B3
Murrin Rd SL6 .... 202 B3
Mursley CE Fst Sch MK17 ... 67 E3
Mursley Ct MK11 .... 32 C2
Mursley Rd
Little Horwood MK17 .... 55 F1
Mursley MK17 .... 67 D2
Museum St 15 HP23 ...... 119 D2
Musgrave Rd OX9 .... 147 E4
Musgrave Wlk HP14 .... 158 C3
Musgrove Pl MK5 .... 175 E1
Myddleton Rd UB8 .... 201 E2
Mylne Cl HP13 .... 172 C4
Mynchen Cl HP9 .... 175 E3
Mynchen End HP9 .... 175 E3
Mynchen Rd HP9 .... 175 E3
Myrke The SL3 .... 205 F1
Myrtle Bank MK12 .... 33 F3
Myrtle Cl Stanwell SL3 ...... 212 C3
Uxbridge UB8 .... 208 C4
West Drayton UB7 .... 208 C2
Myrtle Cres SL2 .... 205 F3

Nag's Head La
Great Kingshill HP16 .... 152 A2
Little Kingshill HP16 .... 152 A2
Nailzee Cl SL9 .... 188 C2
Nairdwood Cl HP16 .... 151 F2
Nairdwood La HP16 .... 151 E3
Nairdwood Way HP16 .... 151 F2
Nairn Ct MK3 .... 46 C1
Naisby Dr MK17 .... 59 E1
Nalders Rd HP5 .... 144 B1
Nan Aires HP22 .... 89 D2
Nancy Hall Ct HP12 .... 172 B2
Naphill Pl MK13 .... 34 B2
Napier Cl UB7 .... 208 C2
Napier Rd
Harmondsworth TW6 ...... 213 E4
Maidenhead SL6 .... 202 A3
Napier St MK2 .... 58 B4
Nappin Cl HP19 .... 101 D2
Nappins Cl HP18 .... 125 E3
Narberth Dr HP20 .... 116 A4
Narcot La
Chalfont St Giles HP8 ..... 177 D3
Gerrards Cross HP8 .... 177 D4
Narcot Rd HP8 .... 177 D4
Narcot Way HP8 .... 177 D3
Narrow La HP13 .... 161 F2
Narrow Path MK17 .... 49 D2
Naseby Cl
Newport Pagnell MK16 ..... 22 A2
Thame OX9 .... 126 A1
Naseby Ct
Buckingham MK18 .... 41 F1
Milton Keynes MK13 .... 34 A3
Nash Cl HP21 .... 116 A2
Nash Croft MK4 .... 57 D4
Nash Lee Rd HP22 .... 130 B3
Nash Rd
Great Horwood MK17 .... 55 D2
Slough SL3 .... 207 D1
Thornborough MK18 .... 54 A4
Whaddon MK17 .... 45 D1
Nashdom La SL1 .... 197 D3
Nashleigh Hill HP5 .... 144 B2
Nathanial Cl MK5 .... 46 A3
Nathaniel Wlk HP23 .... 119 D3
National Badminton Ctr
MK8 .... 34 A1
National Bowl The MK46 .... 46 C3
National Film Sch The
HP9 .... 175 F1
National Hockey Stadium
MK9 .... 34 C4
Natwoke Cl HP9 .... 175 E3
Neal Cl SL9 .... 189 D2
Neale Cl HP12 .... 172 B2

Neapland MK6 .... 47 D3
Near Town MK46 .... 7 D2
Near Town Gdns MK46 .... 7 D2
Neath Cres MK3 .... 47 D1
Neath Hill Rdbt MK15 .... 35 D3
Needham Cl SL4 .... 209 F3
Needlemakers HP18 .... 125 E4
Nedermead 6 MK6 .... 47 D3
Neilson Cl MK7 .... 48 B3
Nelson Cl Coleshill HP7 .... 164 B2
High Wycombe HP13 .... 173 F1
Shenley Church End MK8 ... 45 F3
Slough SL3 .... 206 B1
Nelson Ct MK18 .... 52 B4
Nelson Rd Dagnall HP4 .... 107 E1
Harmondsworth TW6 ...... 213 F3
Windsor SL4 .... 209 F2
Nelson St MK18 .... 52 B4
Nelson Terr HP20 .... 115 E4
Nene Cl Aylesbury HP21 ... 115 E2
Newport Pagnell MK16 ..... 22 B2
Nene Dr MK3 .... 57 F4
Ness Way MK2 .... 58 B3
Nether Cl NN13 .... 38 A4
Nether Gr MK5 .... 46 A2
Netherby Cl HP23 .... 119 E3
Nethercote La OX9 .... 157 D4
Netherfield Rdbt MK6 .... 47 E4
Netherwood Rd HP9 .... 175 E3
Nettlecombe MK4 .... 46 B2
Nettleden Rd HP4 .... 121 F2
Nettleton Rd UB10 .... 201 F4
Nevo Ho SL6 .... 202 C4
Nevill Cl MK19 .... 11 D1
Neville Cl SL2 .... 198 C3
Neville Ct SL1 .... 197 E1
Nevis Cl LU7 .... 80 B4
Nevis Gr MK2 .... 58 C2
New Chilterns HP7 .... 165 F4
New Cl RG9 .... 192 A4
New College Ct MK18 .... 41 D2
New Cotts HP18 .... 125 E3
New Ct
High Wycombe HP13 .... 173 E3
Marlow SL7 .... 183 E1
New Dr HP13 .... 173 F4
New Footpath HP5 .... 154 A4
New Garden Dr UB7 .... 208 C2
New Inn La MK18 .... 51 F2
New Meadow HP21 .... 116 B4
New Mill Terr HP23 .... 119 E3
New Par Chorleywood WD3 167 E3
West Drayton UB7 .... 208 C3
New Peachey La UB8 .... 208 B4
New Pond Rd HP15 .... 163 E4
New Rd
Amersham HP6, HP7 ...... 154 C1
Aston Clinton HP22 .... 117 F3
Aylesbury HP22 .... 116 C3
Berkhamsted HP4 .... 135 E3
Berkhamsted, Northchurch
HP4 .... 134 C4
Bourne End SL8 .... 185 D2
Castlethorpe MK19 .... 19 F3
Chipperfield WD4 .... 146 C1
Coleshill HP7 .... 164 C2
Cookham SL6 .... 195 F4
Datchet SL3 .... 211 D1
Dinton HP17 .... 113 F1
Drayton Parslow MK17 ...... 68 B3
Great Kingshill HP15 .... 162 B4
Harrold MK43 .... 3 E4
High Wycombe HP12 .... 172 B3
Hurley SL6 .... 193 F2
Lacey Green HP27 .... 149 F2
Lane End HP14 .... 170 C3
Leighton Buzzard LU7 ...... 80 C4
Little Chalfont HP8 .... 166 C3
Little Kingshill HP16 .... 152 A2
Marlow Bottom SL7 .... 183 E3
Prestwood HP16 .... 151 E3
Princes Risborough HP27 . 139 F2
Sarratt WD3 .... 156 C1
Slough SL3 .... 207 D2
Stokenchurch HP14 .... 158 C2
Tring HP23 .... 119 D3
Tylers Green HP10 .... 163 E1
Walter's Ash HP14, HP27 . 150 A1
Weedon HP22 .... 101 D4
Wilstone HP23 .... 118 B4
New Road Cl HP12 .... 172 B3
New Road Gdns HP12 ...... 172 B3
New Row MK46 .... 7 F4
New Sq SL1 .... 205 F2
New St Aylesbury HP20 ... 101 E1
Berkhamsted HP4 .... 135 E2
Cheddington LU7 .... 104 C4
Henley-on-T RG9 .... 191 F1
Milton Keynes MK11 .... 32 B3
Tingewick MK18 .... 51 D3
Waddesdon HP18 .... 99 D4
New Windsor St UB8 .... 201 E2

Newark Ct MK7 .... 48 A2
Newbarn La HP9 .... 176 C3
Newberry Cres SL4 .... 209 E3
Newbery Way SL1 .... 205 E2
Newbolt Cl NN12 .... 17 D4
Newbridge Oval MK4 .... 46 A2
Newbury Ct MK3 .... 57 E3
Newbury Cl MK3 .... 57 F3
Newby Pl MK4 .... 46 A1
Newchurch Rd SL2 .... 204 C4
Newcombe Rise UB7 .... 208 C4
Newcourt UB8 .... 208 B4
Newcroft Cl UB8 .... 208 C4
Newell Cl HP21 .... 116 A3
Newells Hedge LU7 .... 105 E3
Newfield Gdns SL7 .... 183 F2
Newfield Rd SL7 .... 183 F2
Newfield Way SL7 .... 183 F1
Newground Rd HP23 .... 120 A2
Newhall Cl HP3 .... 146 A2
Newhaven Spur SL2 .... 198 A1
Newhouse Rd HP3 .... 146 A3
Newland Ho UB8 .... 201 E2
Newlands Dr
Maidenhead SL6 .... 202 A4
Stanwell SL3 .... 212 C2
Newlands Gdns LU7 .... 79 F1
Newlands Sch SL6 .... 202 A4
Newlyn Pl MK6 .... 35 D1
Newlyn Place Cty Fst Sch
MK6 .... 35 D1
Newmans Ctyd MK17 .... 66 B3
Newmarket Ct MK10 .... 36 B1
Newmer Rd HP12 .... 172 B3
Newport Pagnell Rd MK43 .. 16 B2
Newport Rd Astwood MK16 . 15 E1
Emberton MK46 .... 13 F4
Hanslope MK19 .... 11 D1
Milton Keynes, Oakgrove
MK15, MK17, MK6 .... 35 E1
Milton Keynes Village MK10 36 B1
Milton Keynes, Woolstone
MK15 .... 35 E2
Moulsoe MK16 .... 36 B4
Slough SL2 .... 197 F1
Wavendon SL3 .... 206 C2
Newton Ct SL4 .... 211 D1
Newton La SL4 .... 211 D1
Newton Longville CE Comb Sch
MK17 .... 57 E2
Newton Rd
Drayton Parslow MK17 ...... 68 B4
Milton Keynes MK17, MK3 . 57 F3
Stoke Hammond MK17 ...... 69 E4
Turvey MK43 .... 3 E2
Newton Side Orch SL4 ..... 211 D1
Newton St MK46 .... 7 D2
Newtonside SL4 .... 211 D1
Newtown Cty Fst Sch HP5 . 144 B1
Newtown Rd Marlow SL7 .. 183 F2
New Denham SL0 .... 201 D2
Newville HP22 .... 87 E1
Newyears Green La UB9 ... 190 C3
Neyland Dr HP19 .... 101 E2
Nicholas Gdns HP13 .... 173 E4
Nicholas Mead MK14 .... 34 C4
Nicholls SL4 .... 209 E3
Nicholls Wlk SL4 .... 209 E2
Nicholsons Ctr 5 SL6 .... 202 C4
Nicholsons La SL6 .... 202 C4
Nickson Ct HP15 .... 163 D2
Nicol Cl SL9 .... 177 E1
Nicol End SL9 .... 177 E1
Nicol Rd SL9 .... 177 E1
Nigel Ct NN13 .... 38 A3
Nightingale Cl
Holmer Green HP15 .... 163 D3
Steeple Claydon MK18 ..... 63 F1
Nightingale Cres MK13 ...... 34 A4
Nightingale Ho 7 HP10 ... 174 A2
Nightingale Lodge HP4 .... 135 D2
Nightingale Park SL2 .... 197 F1
Nightingale Pl
Buckingham MK18 .... 41 F1
Cookham SL6 .... 195 F4
Nightingale Rd
Aylesbury HP21 .... 115 F3
Chesham HP5 .... 144 A1
Wendover HP22 .... 131 D3
Nightingale Way UB9 .... 189 F3
Nightingales Cnr HP7 ...... 166 B4
Nightingales Ct HP6 .... 166 B4
Nightingales La
Chalfont St Giles HP8 ..... 166 B2
Little Chalfont HP8 .... 166 B2
Nijinsky Ho UB8 .... 201 E2
Nine Elms Ave UB8 .... 208 B4
Nine Elms Cl UB8 .... 208 B4

Nine Stiles Cl SL0 .... 201 D3
Ninnings Rd SL9 .... 177 F2
Ninnings Way SL9 .... 177 F2
Nixey Cl SL1 .... 206 A2
Nixons Cl MK6 .... 46 C3
Noble Cl MK15 .... 35 D4
Nooke The MK15 .... 35 E4
Norbrek MK8 .... 33 F1
Norden Cl SL6 .... 202 B2
Norden Meadows SL6 ...... 202 B3
Norden Rd SL6 .... 202 B3
Norfolk Ave SL1 .... 204 C3
Norfolk Park Cotts SL6 .... 202 C4
Norfolk Rd
Maidenhead SL6 .... 202 C4
Turvey MK43 .... 8 C3
Uxbridge UB8 .... 201 E3
Norfolk Terr HP20 .... 101 F1
Norgrove Park SL9 .... 188 C4
Norjo-An Villas HP5 .... 154 B3
Norman Ave RG9 .... 191 F1
Norman Way LU6 .... 93 F4
Normandy Dr HP4 .... 135 D3
Normandy Way MK3 .... 46 C4
Normans Cl UB8 .... 208 C4
Normans Ct 4 HP13 ...... 173 F3
Normans The SL2 .... 206 A4
Normill Terr HP22 .... 117 D3
Norreys Dr SL6 .... 202 B2
Norrington MK8 .... 33 F1
Norris Ho SL6 .... 202 C4
Norris Rd OX6 .... 94 C4
North Bridge Rd HP4 .... 135 D3
North Burnham Cl SL1 ..... 197 D2
North Cl
Drayton Parslow MK17 ...... 68 B3
Medmenham SL7 .... 193 E4
Windsor SL4 .... 209 F3
North Common Rd UB8 .... 201 F4
North Cotts SL2 .... 198 B1
North Crawley CE Fst Sch
MK16 .... 24 A3
North Crawley Rd
Moulsoe MK16 .... 23 E2
Newport Pagnell MK16 ..... 23 E2
North Crawley MK16 .... 23 E2
North Croft Winslow MK18 .. 66 A2
Woodham Green HP10 .... 185 F3
North Dr Aylesbury HP21 .. 115 F3
Beaconsfield HP9 .... 186 A4
High Wycombe HP13 .... 173 F4
North Eastern Rd HP19 ... 101 E1
North Eighth St MK9 .... 34 C2
North Elder Rdbt MK9 .... 34 B1
North Eleventh St MK9 ...... 34 C2
North End Rd
Quainton HP22 .... 85 D3
Steeple Claydon MK18 ..... 63 E2
North Fifth St MK9 .... 34 B1
North Fourteenth St MK9 ... 34 C2
North Fourth St MK9 .... 34 B1
North Gate MK2 .... 47 E1
North Gn 8 SL6 .... 195 F1
North Green SL1 .... 205 F3
North Hill HP18 .... 96 A1
North La Chorleywood WD3 167 F4
Walton MK7 .... 47 F4
North Lee La HP22 .... 129 F4
North Lines Rd HP10 .... 174 A1
North Marston CE Fst Sch
MK18 .... 76 A1
North Marston La HP22 ..... 86 C4
North Mill Rd HP27 .... 138 A3
North Ninth St MK9 .... 34 C2
North Orbital Rd
Denham Green UB9 .... 189 F4
Maple Cross WD3 .... 178 C2
North Park
Gerrards Cross SL9 .... 188 C4
Iver SL0 .... 207 E2
North Rd Amersham HP6 .. 154 B2
Berkhamsted HP4 .... 135 D2
Chorleywood WD3 .... 167 E2
Holmer Green HP15 .... 162 B3
Maidenhead SL6 .... 202 C4
West Drayton UB7 .... 208 C2
North Ridge MK6 .... 35 D1
North Row Fulmer SL3 ..... 199 F4
Milton Keynes MK9 .... 34 C2
North Second St MK9 .... 34 B1
North Seventh St MK9 ...... 34 B1
North Sixth St MK9 .... 34 B1
North Skeldon Rdbt MK9 ... 35 D2
North Sq MK16 .... 22 B3
North St Castlethorpe MK19 19 F3
Milton Keynes, Bradville
MK13, MK19, MK2 .... 34 A4
Milton Keynes, Fenny Stratford
MK2 .... 47 E1
Thame OX9 .... 125 F1

North Tenth St MK9 .... 34 C2
North Third St MK9 .... 34 B1
North Thirteenth St MK9 ...... 34 C2
North Town Cl ■ SL6 .... 195 F1
North Town Mead ■ SL6 .... 195 F1
North Town Moor SL6 .... 195 F1
North Town Rd SL6 .... 195 F1
North Twelfth St MK9 .... 34 C2
North View HP22 .... 87 D2
North Way
  Deanshanger MK19 .... 31 F3
  Pottersbury NN12 .... 18 C1
  Uxbridge UB10 .... 201 F3
Northall Cl UL6 .... 92 B3
Northall Rd UL6 .... 92 B3
Northampton Ave SL1 .... 205 E4
Northampton Rd
  Brackley NN13 .... 26 A1
  Cosgrove MK19 .... 19 E1
  Grafton Regis NN12 .... 9 E2
  Lathbury MK16 .... 22 B3
  Lavendon MK46 .... 7 F4
  Yardley Hastings NN7 .... 1 A3
Northborough Rd SL22 ...... 198 A1
Northchurch La HP5 .... 134 B1
Northcliffe UL6 .... 92 C3
Northcroft
  Shenley Brook End MK5 .... 46 B3
  Slough SL2 .... 198 A1
  Weedon HP22 .... 87 E1
Northean ■ SL6 .... 195 F1
Northdown Rd SL9 .... 177 F2
Northend MK46 .... 5 F2
Northend Cl HP10 .... 185 E4
Northend Sq MK18 .... 41 E1
Northern Hts SL8 .... 185 D3
Northern Perimeter Rd (W)
  TW6 .... 213 F3
Northern Rd
  Aylesbury HP19 .... 101 E1
  Slough SL2 .... 198 B1
Northern Woods HP10 ...... 185 E4
Northfield Ct RG9 .... 191 E2
Northfield Dr MK15 .... 35 F3
Northfield End RG9 .... 191 E2
Northfield Rd
  Aylesbury HP20 .... 116 A4
  Eton SL4 .... 204 C1
  Maidenhead SL6 .... 195 F1
  Princes Risborough HP27 . 139 E2
Northfield Rdbt MK10 .... 36 A3
Northlands Dr SL1 .... 197 E2
Northlands Rd MK18 .... 53 F1
Northleigh MK4 .... 46 B1
Northmead Rd SL2 .... 204 C4
Northmill HP27 .... 138 C2
Northolt Rd TW6 .... 213 F3
Northumberland Ave
  HP21 .... 116 A3
Northumberland Cl TW19 . 213 F1
Northumbria Rd SL4 .... 202 A2
Northwich MK6 .... 47 E4
Northwood Rd TW6 .... 213 E3
Nortoft Rd SL9 .... 177 F3
Norton Leys MK7 .... 48 B4
Nortor Rd UB8 .... 201 E1
Norton's PI MK18 .... 52 B4
Nortons The MK7 .... 48 A2
Norvic Rd MK23 .... 105 D1
Norway Dr SL2 .... 206 A4
Norwich Ho
  High Wycombe HP13 .... 173 F4
  Maidenhead SL6 .... 202 C4
Norwood Cl HP20 .... 101 F1
Norwood La
  Newport Pagnell MK16 ...... 22 B2
  Uxbridge SL0 .... 200 B1
Norwood Rd HP10 .... 174 A1
Norwoods Cl HP7 .... 165 D4
Nottingham Ho ■ HP13 .... 173 F4
Nottingham Rd WD3 .... 167 E1
Nova Lodge MK4 .... 46 A1
Novello Croft MK7 .... 48 B2
Nugent Cl SL7 .... 183 F2
Nugent Ct HP5 .... 144 A2
Nup End Cl HP22 .... 89 D2
Nup End La HP22 .... 89 D2
Nurseries The UL6 .... 92 C3
Nursery Cl Amersham HP7 . 165 F4
  Aylesbury HP21 .... 115 E3
  Tylers Green HP10 .... 174 B4
Nursery Ct HP12 .... 172 B3
Nursery Dr HP14 .... 171 D3
Nursery Gdns
  Milton Keynes MK13 .... 34 A2
  Tring HP23 .... 119 D2
Nursery La Slough SL3 ..... 206 B3
  Tylers Green HP10 .... 174 B4
Nursery Rd SL6 .... 204 A4
Nursery Way TW19 .... 211 E1
Nursery Waye UB8 .... 201 E2

Nursery Wlk SL7 .... 183 D1
Nutfield La HP11 .... 172 C4
Nuthatch ■ HP20 .... 101 F2
Nutkin Wlk UB10 .... 201 F3
Nutkins Way HP5 .... 144 B1
Nutmeg Cl MK7 .... 48 A3
Nye Way HP3 .... 146 A2

O'Grady Way HP19 .... 101 D2
Oak Bank MK43 .... 25 D1
Oak Cres HP12 .... 172 B2
Oak Dr HP4 .... 135 E2
Oak End Dr SL0 .... 200 B2
Oak End Way Chinnor OX9 . 147 F3
  Gerrards Cross SL9 .... 188 C3
Oak Field HP5 .... 144 A1
Oak Green HP21 .... 115 E4
Oak Green Cty Mid Sch
  HP21 .... 115 E4
Oak La
  Buckland Common HP5 .. 133 D1
  Windsor SL4 .... 210 A3
Oak Rd HP27 .... 139 E2
Oak St HP11 .... 173 E2
Oak Stubbs La SL4 .... 203 F2
Oak Tree Ave SL7 .... 183 E2
Oak Tree Cl SL7 .... 183 E2
Oak Tree Dr HP14 .... 171 E3
Oak Tree Rd SL7 .... 183 E2
Oak View HP15 .... 162 B4
Oak Way MK18 .... 66 A2
Oak Wood HP4 .... 134 C2
Oakdene HP9 .... 175 F2
Oakdown Cres MK46 .... 6 C2
Oaken Gr SL6 .... 195 E1
Oakengrove HP16 .... 151 E3
Oakengrove Cl HP15 .... 163 E3
Oakengrove La HP15 .... 163 D2
Oakengrove Rd HP15 .... 163 D2
Oakeshott Ave HP14 .... 161 E3
Oakfield WD3 .... 167 F1
Oakfield Ave SL1 .... 205 D3
Oakfield Cl HP6 .... 154 B1
Oakfield Cnr HP6 .... 154 B1
Oakfield Est SL4 .... 210 A3
Oakfield Rd
  Aylesbury HP20 .... 116 A4
  Bourne End SL8 .... 185 D2
Oakhill Cl WD3 .... 178 C3
Oakhill Rd
  Maple Cross WD3 .... 178 B3
  Shenley Church End MK5 . 45 F3
Oakhurst SL6 .... 196 A2
Oakington Ave HP6 .... 166 C4
Oakland Way HP10 .... 174 A1
Oaklands HP4 .... 135 D2
Oaklawn ■ HP23 .... 119 D2
Oakley Ho HP10 .... 185 F4
Oakley Cres SL1 .... 205 F3
Oakley Gdns MK15 .... 35 D3
Oakley Green Rd SL4 .... 209 D3
Oakley La OX9 .... 147 D3
Oakley Parochial Comb Sch
  HP18 .... 109 E2
Oakley Rd OX9 .... 147 E3
Oakridge MK4 .... 46 C2
Oakridge Cl HP12 .... 172 B3
Oakridge Cty Fst Sch
  HP12 .... 172 C4
Oakridge Rd HP11 .... 172 C4
Oaks Rd TW19 .... 213 E1
Oaks The HP4 .... 135 D2
Oakside HP20 .... 201 D3
Oaktree Cl HP10 .... 163 D1
Oaktree Cl MK15 .... 35 E4
Oakview HP16 .... 153 E2
Oakway HP6 .... 154 A2
Oakwell Cl UL6 .... 93 F4
Oakwood HP10 .... 174 A1
Oakwood Dr MK2 .... 58 C4
Oatlands Dr SL1 .... 205 E4
Oban Ct SL1 .... 205 E2
Ockwells Rd SL6 .... 202 B1
Octagon Par ■ HP11 .... 173 D4
Octavian Dr MK13 .... 33 F3
Octavian Way NN13 .... 38 A4
Oddley La HP27 .... 148 B4
Oddy Hill HP23 .... 119 E1
Odell Cl MK6 .... 47 E4
Odencroft Rd SL2 .... 198 A1
Odney La SL6 .... 196 A4
Offas La MK18 .... 66 A3
Ogilvie Rd HP11 .... 172 C4
Okeford Cl HP23 .... 118 C2
Okeford Dr HP23 .... 118 C2
Okeley La HP23 .... 118 B2
Old Bakery The HP14 ...... 171 D2
Old Barn Cl MK18 .... 52 A2
Old Brewery Cl HP21 .... 115 F4
Old Burrs HP21 .... 115 E2
Old Coach Dr ■ HP10 ...... 174 A2

Old Court Cl SL6 .... 202 A2
Old Crown ■ SL1 .... 205 F2
Old Dashwood Hill HP14 . 159 F1
Old Dean HP3 .... 146 A2
Old End MK18 .... 53 D1
Old Farm Cl HP12 .... 105 E2
Old Farm Cl
  Beaconsfield HP9 .... 175 E3
  Worminghall HP18 .... 123 E3
Old Farm Ct HP18 .... 82 C3
Old Farm Rd
  High Wycombe HP13 ...... 161 F1
  West Drayton UB7 .... 208 B2
Old Ferry Dr TW19 .... 211 E1
Old Field Cl HP6 .... 166 C4
Old Fives Ct SL1 .... 197 D1
Old Forge Cl
  Maidenhead SL6 .... 203 D2
  Tingewick MK18 .... 51 D3
Old Forge Gdns HP22 ..... 102 A2
Old Forge Rd HP10 .... 174 B1
Old Forge The HP23 .... 104 A2
Old Garden Ctr The HP27 . 139 D2
Old Groveway MK6 .... 47 E3
Old Hardenwaye HP13 ..... 162 C1
Old Horns La SL7 .... 172 A2
Old House Ct SL3 .... 206 B4
Old Kiln Rd
  Flackwell Heath HP10 ... 185 D4
  Tylers Green HP10 .... 163 E1
Old Linslade Rd LU7 .... 70 C2
Old Lodge Dr HP9 .... 175 F1
Old Maltings The OX9 ...... 125 F1
Old Manor Cl
  Princes Risborough HP27 . 139 E4
  Whaddon MK17 .... 45 D1
Old Marsh La Dorney SL6 . 203 F2
  Taplow SL6 .... 203 F2
Old Mead SL9 .... 177 F2
Old Mill Cl HP17 .... 127 D3
Old Mill Furlong MK18 ...... 66 A3
Old Mill Gdns HP4 .... 135 E2
Old Mill La
  Maidenhead SL6 .... 203 E2
  Uxbridge UB8 .... 208 A4
Old Mill Rd UB9 .... 190 A1
Old Moor La HP10 .... 185 F4
Old Nursery Ct SL2 .... 187 E1
Old Oak Gdns HP4 .... 134 C4
Old Orchard OX7 .... 137 F1
Old Orchard Mews HP4 ... 135 E2
Old Orchards HP22 .... 102 A2
Old Oxford Rd HP14 .... 160 B1
Old Palace Ct SL3 .... 212 B3
Old Plough Cl HP18 .... 112 A1
Old Post Office La ■ SL6 . 202 C4
Old Rd LU7 .... 80 C4
Old Rectory La UB9 .... 189 F2
Old Risborough Rd HP22 . 130 A4
Old Sax La HP16 .... 143 E2
Old School Cl Halton HP27 . 117 E1
  Stokenchurch HP14 .... 158 C2
Old School Cotts HP5 ..... 145 E3
Old School Ct
  Buckingham MK18 .... 52 B4
  Eaton Bray LU6 .... 92 C3
Old School The HP10 ...... 185 E2
Old School Yd MK18 .... 63 E2
Old Shire La WD3, SL9 .... 167 D2
Old Slade La SL0 .... 207 F1
Old Station Way HP10 ..... 185 F3
Old Stoke Rd HP21 .... 115 E3
Old Stratford Prim Sch
  MK19 .... 32 A3
Old Tan Yard Cl MK18 ...... 65 F2
Old Town NN13 .... 38 A4
Old Town Cl HP9 .... 175 F1
Old Town Farm HP16 .... 152 A4
Old Uxbridge Rd WD3 ..... 178 C2
Old Vicarage Way HP10 ... 185 E2
Old Watery La HP10 .... 185 F4
Old Windmill Way HP18 ... 125 E4
Old Wolverton Rd MK12 .... 33 E4
Oldacres SL6 .... 203 D4
Oldbrook Bvd MK6 .... 46 C4
Oldbrook Fst Sch MK6 ...... 46 C4
Oldbury Gr HP9 .... 175 E3
Olde Bell Cl MK17 .... 69 F4
Olde Bell La MK5 .... 46 A4
Oldershaw Mews SL4 ...... 202 A4
Oldfield Prim Sch SL6 ..... 203 D3
Oldfield Rd SL6 .... 203 D3
Oldfield Rd Ind Est SL6 ... 203 D4
Oldhams Meadow ■ HP20 101 F1
Oldhouse Cl HP12 .... 172 C2
Oldway La SL1 .... 204 B3
Oliffe Cl HP20 .... 101 E2
Oliffe Way HP20 .... 101 E2
Oliver Rd MK2 .... 58 B4
Oliver's Paddock SL7 ...... 183 E3
Olivier Way HP20 .... 116 A4

Olleberrie La WD4 .... 156 B4
Olney Cty Fst Sch MK46 .... 6 C2
Olney Cty Mid Sch MK46 .... 6 C3
Olney Rd Emberton MK46 . 13 F4
  Lavendon MK46 .... 7 F4
One Pin La SL2 .... 187 E1
One Tree La HP9 .... 175 F2
Onslow Cl MK7 .... 48 A2
Onslow Dr OX9 .... 126 A1
Onslow Gdns HP13 .... 173 F4
Open University
  (Walton Hall) The MK7 ... 47 F4
Opendale Rd SL1 .... 204 A4
Orbell Cl HP27 .... 139 D2
Orbison Ct MK8 .... 45 E4
Orchard Ave
  Berkhamsted HP4 .... 135 D2
  Slough SL3 .... 204 B4
  Windsor SL4 .... 210 A3
Orchard Cl
  24 Aylesbury HP20 .... 101 F2
  Beaconsfield HP9 .... 175 E2
  Chorleywood WD3 .... 167 E3
  Chesham HP5 .... 144 B1
  Henley-on-T RG9 .... 191 F1
  Hughenden Valley HP14 . 162 A4
  Longwick HP27 .... 138 B4
  Maidenhead SL6 .... 203 D2
  Milton Keynes MK17, MK3 . 57 F4
  New Denham SL0 .... 201 D3
  Newton Longville MK17 ... 57 E2
  Oakley HP18 .... 109 E2
  Stoke Mandeville HP22 . 116 A1
  Waddesdon HP18 .... 99 D4
  Wendover HP22 .... 131 D3
  Wingrave HP22 .... 89 D2
  Yardley Gobion NN12 .... 18 C2
Orchard Ct Bovingdon HP3 146 A2
  Harmondsworth TW6 ..... 213 E4
Orchard Dr
  Aston Clinton HP22 .... 117 F2
  Chorleywood WD3 .... 167 E3
  Leighton Buzzard LU7 .... 80 B3
  Tylers Green HP15 .... 163 D2
  Uxbridge UB8 .... 201 E1
  Wooburn Green HP10 .... 185 E2
Orchard End
  Edlesborough LU6 .... 92 C2
  Holmer Green HP15 .... 163 D3
Orchard End Ave HP7 ...... 165 F4
Orchard Gate SL2 .... 198 B4
Orchard Gr
  Flackwell Heath HP10 ... 185 D4
  Gerrards Cross SL9 .... 177 E1
  Maidenhead SL6 .... 202 B4
Orchard Ho ■ SL8 .... 185 D2
Orchard La Amersham HP6 154 B1
  Harrold MK43 .... 3 F4
  Prestwood HP16 .... 151 E3
  Stewkley LU7 .... 78 C4
Orchard Mews ■ HP9 ..... 176 B2
Orchard Park HP15 .... 163 E3
Orchard Pl Uxbridge UB8 . 201 E3
  Westbury NN13 .... 39 D2
Orchard Rd
  Beaconsfield HP9 .... 175 F1
  Chalfont St Giles HP8 .... 177 E4
  High Wycombe HP14 ..... 174 A2
  Old Windsor SL4 .... 211 D1
  Seer Green HP9 .... 176 B3
Orchard Rise MK46 .... 6 C2
Orchard The
  Aston Clinton HP22 .... 117 F3
  Flackwell Heath HP10 ... 185 D4
  Halton HP22 .... 131 E4
  Holmer Green HP15 .... 163 D3
  Marlow SL7 .... 183 F2
  Pottersbury NN12 .... 18 B2
  Walter's Ash HP14 .... 161 F3
  Orchard View UB8 .... 201 E1
Orchard Way
  Aylesbury HP20 .... 101 F1
  Bovingdon HP3 .... 146 A2
  Chinnor OX9 .... 147 E3
  East Claydon MK18 .... 74 C3
  Eaton Bray LU6 .... 92 C3
  Tylers Green HP15 .... 163 E3
  Ivinghoe LU7 .... 105 F2
  North Crawley MK16 ...... 24 A3
  Slough SL3 .... 206 C3
  Wing LU7 .... 79 F1
Orchard Waye UB8 .... 201 E2
Orchard Wlk MK46 .... 7 F4
Orchards The
  Eaton Bray LU6 .... 92 C4
  Little Kingshill HP16 ...... 152 A1
  Tring HP23 .... 118 C2
Orchardville SL1 .... 197 D1
Orchehill Ave SL9 .... 188 B4
Orchehill Ct SL9 .... 188 C3

Orchehill Rise SL9 .... 188 C3
Oregano Cl MK7 .... 208 C3
Orford Ct MK5 .... 46 A3
Orkney Cl
  Milton Keynes MK3 .... 46 C1
  Stewkley LU7 .... 78 C4
Orkney Ct SL6 .... 196 C3
Ormesby Cl HP21 .... 116 A3
Ormond Rd OX9 .... 126 A1
Ormonde MK14 .... 34 B4
Orpington St MK13 .... 34 A3
Orne Gdns MK15 .... 35 D4
Orpington Gr MK5 .... 46 A2
Ortensia Dr MK7 .... 48 B4
Orwell Cl Aylesbury HP21 . 115 E2
  Newport Pagnell MK16 .... 21 F3
  Windsor SL4 .... 210 B2
Orwell Dr Aylesbury HP21 . 115 E2
  Stoke Mandeville HP21 . 115 E2
Osborn Rd UB8 .... 201 E3
Osborn's Ct MK46 .... 6 C2
Osborne Mews SL4 .... 210 B3
Osborne Rd SL4 .... 210 B2
Osborne St
  Milton Keynes MK2 .... 58 B4
  Slough SL1 .... 205 F2
Osborne Way HP23 .... 119 E1
Osbourne Ct SL4 .... 210 B3
Osbourne St MK12 .... 33 E3
Osier La MK5 .... 46 A2
Osier Way HP20 .... 115 F4
Osmington Pl HP23 .... 118 C2
Osney Rd HP21 .... 195 F1
Osprey Cl
  Milton Keynes MK6 .... 47 D4
  West Drayton UB7 .... 208 C2
Osprey The HP20 .... 101 F2
Osprey Wlk
  Aylesbury HP20 .... 101 F2
  Buckingham MK18 .... 52 C4
Ostler Gate SL6 .... 195 E1
Ostlers Ct ■ HP10 .... 174 A2
Ostlers La MK11 .... 32 B3
Otter Cl MK3 .... 46 B1
Otterfield Rd UB7 .... 208 C3
Otters Brook MK18 .... 52 C4
Otway Cl HP21 .... 115 F2
Oulton Cl HP21 .... 116 A3
Our Lady of Peace
  RC Inf Sch SL1 .... 204 B4
Our Lady of Peace
  RC Mid Sch SL1 .... 204 B4
Our Lady's RC Comb Sch
  HP6 .... 154 A2
Ousebank St MK16 .... 22 B3
Ousebank Way MK11 .... 32 B3
Ousedale Sch MK16 .... 22 A2
Ouseley Rd SL4 .... 211 E1
Outfield Rd SL9 .... 177 E2
Outlook Dr HP8 .... 177 E4
Ouzel Cl MK3 .... 46 A1
Oval The MK4 .... 46 C4
Oval Way SL9 .... 188 C4
Over Hampden HP16 .... 151 E4
Over The Misbourne SL9 . 189 D3
Overdale Rd HP5 .... 144 A2
Overdales HP15 .... 162 C2
Overend Cl MK13 .... 34 A2
Overgate MK9 .... 35 D2
Overn Ave MK18 .... 41 E1
Overn Cl MK18 .... 41 E1
Overn Cres MK18 .... 41 E1
Overshot Ho HP11 .... 174 B1
Oversley Ct MK14 .... 22 A1
Overstone Comb Sch LU7 . 79 F1
Overstrand HP22 .... 117 F3
Overstreet MK14 .... 35 D3
Overton Dr OX9 .... 126 A1
Oville Ct MK8 .... 46 A3
Oving Rd Oving HP22 .... 86 C4
  Whitchurch HP22 .... 86 C3
Ovitts Cl UB18 .... 66 A3
Owl Cl 10 HP20 .... 101 F2
Owlsears Cl HP9 .... 175 E2
Oxendon Ct LU7 .... 70 C1
Oxfield Cl HP4 .... 135 D2
Oxford Ave Burnham SL1 . 197 D2
  Slough SL3 .... 204 C4
Oxford Gdns UB9 .... 190 A1
Oxford Rd
  Denham UB9 .... 189 C1
  Gerrards Cross SL9 .... 188 B3
  High Wycombe HP11 ..... 173 D4
  Lane End HP14 .... 160 B1
  Marlow SL7 .... 183 E1
  New Denham UB8 .... 201 D3
  Oakley HP18 .... 109 E3
  Stokenchurch HP14 .... 158 B3

Oxford Rd
Stone HP17, HP18 .... 114 B3
Thame OX9 .... 125 F1
Windsor SL4 .... 210 B3
Oxford Rd E SL4 .... 210 B3
Oxford St
4 High Wycombe HP11 .. 173 D4
Lee Common HP16 .... 142 B3
Milton Keynes,
Fenny Stratford MK2 ...... 58 B4
Milton Keynes,
Stony Stratford MK11 ...... 32 B3
Milton Keynes, Wolverton
MK12 .... 33 E3
Oxley Park Rdbt MK5 ...... 45 F2
Oxleys MK46 .... 6 C2
Oxman La MK12 .... 33 D3
Oxwich Gr MK4 .... 57 D4

Pack & Prime La RG9 .... 191 E1
Packet Boat La UB7 .... 208 B4
Packhorse Rd SL9 .... 188 C3
Padbury CE Fst Sch MK18 .. 53 E1
Padbury Oaks TW6 .... 213 D3
Padcroft Rd UB7 .... 208 B3
Paddock Cl SL6 .... 202 A1
Paddock The
Aylesbury HP21 .... 116 B4
Chalfont St Peter SL9 .... 177 F3
Datchet SL3 .... 211 D3
Emberton MK46 .... 13 F4
Maidenhead SL6 .... 195 E1
Paddock Way MK2 .... 47 E1
Paddocks End 1 HP9 .. 176 B2
Paddocks Hospl The
HP27 .... 139 E2
Paddocks The
Chorleywood WD3 .... 167 F3
Flackwell Heath HP10 .... 185 D4
Haddenham HP17 .... 127 D3
High Wycombe HP12 ...... 172 A2
Leighton Buzzard LU7 .... 80 C4
Steeple Claydon MK18 ...... 63 F2
Wendover HP22 .... 131 D3
Padstow Ave MK6 .... 34 C1
Padstow Cl
Aylesbury HP20 .... 101 F1
Slough SL3 .... 206 C2
Page Hill Ave MK18 .... 41 F1
Page Hill Fy Fst Sch
MK18 .... 41 F1
Pages Croft HP4 .... 135 D3
Pages La UB8 .... 201 E3
Paget Cl SL7 .... 183 F2
Paget Dr SL6 .... 202 A2
Paget Rd SL3 .... 206 C1
Pagg's Ct MK16 .... 22 B2
Pagoda The SL6 .... 196 A1
Paines Orch LU7 .... 105 D4
Palace Cl SL1 .... 204 C3
Palace Sq MK6 .... 46 C4
Palliser Rd HP8 .... 177 D4
Palmer Ave
Aylesbury HP19 .... 115 E4
Upper Arncott OX6 .... 94 F4
Palmer's Moor La SL0 .... 201 D1
Palmers Cl SL6 .... 202 A2
Palmers Moor MK18 .... 54 A4
Palmers Rd MK46 .... 7 D2
Palmerston Ave SL3 .... 206 A2
Pankridge Dr HP16 .... 151 E4
Panleigh Cotts HP14 ...... 171 D2
Pannier Pl MK14 .... 35 D3
Pantile Row SL3 .... 207 D1
Pantile Wlk UB8 .... 201 E3
Paprika Ct MK7 .... 48 A3
Par The SL2 .... 198 B3
Parade The
Bourne End SL8 .... 185 D2
Uxbridge UB8 .... 208 B4
Windsor SL4 .... 209 E3
Paradise MK17 .... 57 E2
Paradise Mews RG9 .... 191 E1
Paradise Rd RG9 .... 191 E1
Parchment Cl HP6 .... 154 C1
Parish La SL2 .... 187 E1
Parish Piece HP15 .... 163 E4
Park Ave
Newport Pagnell MK16 .... 22 A2
Totternhoe LU6 .... 93 D4
Wraysbury TW19 .... 211 E2
Park Cl Cosgrove MK19 .... 19 F1
Hoggeston MK18 .... 77 E4
Lane End HP14 .... 171 E3
Windsor SL4 .... 210 B3
Park Cnr SL4 .... 209 F2
Park Crescent Sch HP12 .. 172 B2
Park Ct UB8 .... 201 E2

Park Cty Mid Sch The
HP15 .... 162 C3
Park Farm Rd HP12 .... 161 D1
Park Farm Way HP14 ...... 171 E3
Park Gate LU7 .... 79 F1
Park Gdns MK3 .... 47 D1
Park Gr HP8 .... 166 B3
Park Hill OX33 .... 122 A1
Park Ho
Berkhamsted HP4 .... 135 D3
Maidenhead SL6 .... 202 C3
Park La Beaconsfield HP9 .. 175 F1
Burnham SL1 .... 197 F4
Eaton Bray LU6 .... 92 B3
Horton SL3 .... 212 A2
Lane End HP14 .... 171 E3
Paulerspury NN12 .... 17 D4
Slough SL3 .... 206 A2
Stokenchurch HP14 .... 158 C3
Stoner RG9 .... 179 E3
Tylers Green HP15 .... 163 D2
Park Lawn SL2 .... 198 B1
Park Meadow MK27 .... 139 D2
Park Parade Ctr The
HP15 .... 163 D3
Park Pl HP6 .... 154 C1
Park Rd Amersham HP6 .. 154 C1
Farnham Common SL2 .... 198 D2
Granborough MK18 .... 75 F3
Grendon Underwood HP18 .. 82 C4
Hanslope MK19 .... 11 D1
Hartwell NN7 .... 10 B4
Henley-on-T RG9 .... 191 F1
Milton Keynes MK11 .... 32 B3
Sherington MK16 .... 14 A1
Stanwell TW19 .... 213 E1
Stoke Poges SL2 .... 198 C2
Tring HP23 .... 118 C1
Uxbridge UB8 .... 201 F3
Winslow MK18 .... 65 F3
Park Rd E UB8 .... 201 E2
Park Rd S MK18 .... 65 F2
Park Rise HP4 .... 134 C3
Park St HP20 .... 101 F1
Park St Aylesbury HP20 .. 115 F4
Berkhamsted HP4 .... 135 D3
High Wycombe HP11 ...... 173 E3
Maidenhead SL6 .... 202 C4
Princes Risborough
HP27 .... 139 D2
Slough SL1, SL3 .... 205 F2
Stanwell SL3 .... 212 B3
Tring HP23 .... 119 D2
Windsor SL4 .... 210 B3
Woburn MK17 .... 60 C4
Park Street Ind Est HP20 .. 115 F4
Park View
Newport Pagnell MK16 .... 22 B2
West Drayton UB7 .... 208 C3
Park View Ct
Berkhamsted HP4 .... 135 D2
High Wycombe HP12 ...... 172 B4
11 Leighton Buzzard LU7 .. 80 C4
Park View Rd
Berkhamsted HP4 .... 135 D2
Uxbridge UB8 .... 208 C4
Parker Cl MK13 .... 34 A3
Parker Wlk HP19 .... 101 E2
Parkfield WD3 .... 167 F3
Parkfield Ave HP6 .... 154 B1
Parkgate SL1 .... 197 E1
Parkland Ave SL3 .... 206 B1
Parklands MK14 .... 21 E1
Parkside
Gerrards Cross SL9 .... 188 C4
Henley-on-T RG9 .... 191 E1
Maidenhead SL6 .... 195 E1
Milton Keynes MK4 .... 46 C2
Walter's Ash HP14 .... 150 A1
Parkside Wlk SL1 .... 206 A2
Parkview
Flackwell Heath HP10 .... 185 D4
Maidenhead SL6 .... 202 C4
Parkview Chase SL1 .... 204 C4
Parkway
Bow Brickhill MK17 .... 48 B1
Marlow SL7 .... 184 A2
Woburn Sands MK17 .... 49 D3
Parkway The SL0 .... 200 B2
Parkwood HP4 .... 150 A1
Parlaunt Park Comb Sch
SL3 .... 207 D2
Parlaunt Rd SL3 .... 207 D1
Parliament Cl HP16 .... 151 D4
Parliament La SL6 .... 196 C3
Parliament Rd OX9 .... 125 F1
Parmoor La RG9 .... 170 C1
Parneleys MK10 .... 35 F2
Parrock La MK10 .... 36 A1
Parrott Cl HP21 .... 115 D3
Parrott's La HP23 .... 133 D2

Parrs Rd HP14 .... 158 C2
Parry Cotts SL9 .... 177 F3
Parry Green N SL3 .... 206 C1
Parry Green S SL3 .... 207 D1
Parsley Cl
Aston Clinton HP22 .... 117 E3
Walton MK7 .... 48 A3
Parslow Cl HP21 .... 115 E2
Parslow Ct HP21 .... 115 E2
Parson's Fee HP20 .... 115 E4
Parson's Wood La SL2 .... 198 B3
Parsonage Cl
High Wycombe HP13 ...... 173 E3
1 Tring HP23 .... 119 D2
Parsonage Ct 2 HP23 .... 119 D2
Parsonage Farm HP22 .... 89 D2
Parsonage Gdns SL7 ...... 183 F1
Parsonage La
Farnham Common SL2 .... 198 B2
Windsor SL4 .... 210 A3
Parsonage Pl
Amersham HP7 .... 165 E4
Tring HP23 .... 119 D2
Parsonage Rd HP7 .... 165 E4
Parsons Cl Stewkley LU7 .. 78 C4
Winslow MK18 .... 65 F2
Parsons Cres MK5 .... 46 B3
Parsons La HP22 .... 102 A2
Parsons Wlk HP15 .... 163 E3
Parton Cl HP22 .... 131 D3
Parton Rd HP20 .... 116 A4
Partridge Cl
Buckingham MK18 .... 52 C4
Chesham HP5 .... 144 C2
Partridge Mead SL6 .... 195 F1
Partridge Piece MK43 ...... 25 E2
Partridge Way
12 Aylesbury HP20 .... 101 F2
High Wycombe HP15 ...... 161 E1
Pascomb Rd LU6 .... 93 F4
Passalewe La MK7 .... 48 B4
Passmore MK6 .... 47 E3
Pastern Pl MK14 .... 35 D3
Pastures The
Aylesbury HP20 .... 102 A1
Edlesborough LU6 .... 92 C2
High Wycombe HP15 ...... 161 E1
Patch Cl UB10 .... 201 F2
Patches Field SL7 .... 183 F3
Paterson Rd HP21 .... 115 E3
Patricia Cl SL1 .... 204 C3
Patrick Haugh Rd OX6 .... 94 C4
Patrick Way HP21 .... 116 A2
Patrick's La MK19 .... 31 F2
Patrington Cl UB8 .... 201 F2
Patriot Dr MK13 .... 34 A1
Patrons Dr UB9 .... 189 F3
Patterson Rd HP5 .... 144 A2
Pattison La MK15 .... 35 E2
Paul's Row HP11 .... 173 D3
Paulerspury CE Sch NN12 .. 17 D4
Pauls Hill HP10 .... 174 C3
Pavers Ct HP21 .... 115 E2
Pavilion Cl HP20 .... 116 A4
Pavilion Way HP6 .... 166 B4
Paxton Ave SL1 .... 205 E2
Paxton Cl MK46 .... 6 C2
Paxton Cres MK5 .... 46 A3
Paxton Rd HP4 .... 135 E2
Paynes Dr MK5 .... 46 A4
Pea La HP4 .... 134 B4
Peace La SL6 .... 195 F3
Peach Meadows HP22 .... 131 D4
Peachey Cl UB8 .... 208 B4
Peachey La UB8 .... 208 B4
Peacock Hay MK4 .... 46 B1
Peacock Rd SL7 .... 184 A2
Peacocks Cl HP4 .... 134 C3
Pear Tree Ave UB8 .... 208 C4
Pear Tree Cl
Amersham HP7 .... 165 F4
Seer Green HP9 .... 176 B2
Pearce Cl Aylesbury HP21 .. 115 F2
Maidenhead SL6 .... 195 F1
Pearce Rd Chesham HP5 .. 144 A1
Maidenhead SL6 .... 195 F1
Pearces Orch RG9 .... 191 E2
Pearl Gdns SL1 .... 205 D3
Pearse Gr MK7 .... 48 A2
Pearson Cl HP21 .... 115 D3
Peartrees UB7 .... 208 B3
Peascod Pl 3 SL4 .... 210 B3
Peascod St SL4 .... 210 B3
Peascroft HP18 .... 125 E4
Pebble Brook Sch HP21 .. 115 E4
Pebble La Aylesbury HP20 .. 115 E4
Brackley NN13 .... 38 A4
Pebblemoor LU6 .... 92 C2
Peckover Ct MK8 .... 33 F1
Pednor Bottom HP16 ...... 143 D2
Pednor Rd HP5,HP16 ...... 143 F1

Pednormead End HP5 .. 154 A4
Peebles Pl MK3 .... 46 C2
Peel Cl SL4 .... 210 A2
Peel Ct SL1 .... 205 D4
Peel Rd MK12 .... 33 E3
Peel Way UB8 .... 208 C4
Peerless Dr UB9 .... 190 B4
Peers Dr MK17 .... 49 F2
Peers La MK5 .... 46 A3
Peggs La HP22 .... 117 F3
Pelham Cl SL6 .... 202 C4
Pelham Pl MK14 .... 34 C3
Pelham Rd OX9 .... 126 A1
Pelton Ct MK5 .... 46 B3
Pemberton Cl HP21 .... 115 F3
Pemberton Rd SL2 .... 197 F1
Pembridge Chase HP3 .... 146 A2
Pembridge Cl HP3 .... 146 A2
Pembridge Rd HP3 .... 146 A2
Pembroke Rd HP20 .... 101 F1
Pencarrow Pl MK6 .... 35 D1
Pendeen Ct SL1 .... 205 D3
Pendrill Ho 5 HP12 .... 172 C4
Penfold HP22 .... 116 C1
Penfold Cotts HP15 .... 163 E4
Penfold La
Holmer Green HP16 .... 152 C1
Hyde Heath HP16 .... 152 C1
Penina Cl MK3 .... 46 B1
Penington Rd HP9 .... 186 A4
Penlee Rise MK4 .... 57 D4
Penley Cl OX9 .... 117 F2
Penling Cl SL6 .... 195 F3
Penmoor Cl HP12 .... 172 B4
Penn Ave HP5 .... 144 A1
Penn Bottom HP10 .... 163 F1
Penn Cl Chorleywood WD3 .. 167 E2
Uxbridge UB8 .... 201 E1
Penn Ct 8 SL7 .... 183 F1
Penn Dr UB9 .... 189 F3
Penn Gaskell La SL9 ...... 177 F3
Penn Haven SL9 .... 188 C3
Penn Meadow SL2 .... 198 C2
Penn Rd Aylesbury HP21 .. 115 E4
Beaconsfield HP9 .... 175 E3
Chorleywood WD3 .... 167 E1
Gerrards Cross SL9 .... 177 E1
Milton Keynes MK2 .... 58 C4
Slough SL3 .... 198 B1
Tylers Green HP15 .... 163 D2
Penn St HP9 .... 175 D3
Penn Sch Raymers HP10 .. 174 B4
Penn Way WD3 .... 167 E2
Penn Wood View HP7 .... 144 A2
Pennefather Ct 9 HP21 .. 115 F4
Pennine Rd SL2 .... 205 D4
Pennington Pl OX9 .... 126 A1
Pennington Rd
Gerrards Cross SL9 .... 177 E2
High Wycombe HP13 ...... 173 F3
Penningtons The HP6 ...... 154 C1
Pennycress Way MK14 .... 21 F2
Pennylets Gn SL2 .... 199 D3
Pennyroyal MK7 .... 48 A4
Penrith Cl UB8 .... 201 E3
Penrith Way HP21 .... 116 A4
Penryn Ave MK6 .... 35 D1
Penshurst Cl SL9 .... 177 E1
Penshurst Rd SL6 .... 202 B3
Pentewan Gate MK13 ...... 34 C1
Pentland Rd
Aylesbury HP21 .... 115 F3
Slough SL2 .... 205 D4
Pentlands MK11 .... 32 C2
Pentlands Cl 9 HP10 ...... 174 A2
Pentlands The HP10 ...... 174 A2
Penwith Cty Fst Sch MK6 .. 34 C1
Penwood Ct SL6 .... 202 A4
Penwood La SL7 .... 183 E1
Penyston Rd SL6 .... 202 B4
Penzance Spur SL2 .... 198 A1
Peplow Cl UB7 .... 208 B3
Peppard Meadow HP16 .. 151 E3
Pepper Hill Cty Fst Sch
MK13 .... 34 A4
Peppet's Green HP5 .... 143 E4
Peppiatts The LU6 .... 92 A3
Pepys Cl SL3 .... 212 A4
Pepys Dr HP16 .... 151 E3
Perch Cl SL7 .... 194 B4
Percheron Pl MK14 .... 34 C3
Percy Bush Rd UB7 .... 208 C2
Percy Pl SL3 .... 211 D3
Percy Terr HP8 .... 177 D4
Peregrine HP20 .... 101 F2
Peregrine Bsns Pk HP10 .. 174 A2
Peregrine Cl MK6 .... 47 D4
Perks La HP16 .... 151 E2
Permayne MK13 .... 34 A4
Perracombe MK4 .... 46 C1
Perran Ave MK6 .... 35 D1

Perrin Springs La RG9 .. 170 C1
Perry Hill HP18 .... 73 D1
Perry Ho SL1 .... 197 D1
Perry La HP27 .... 138 B1
Perry Oaks Dr TW6 .... 213 E3
Perry St HP22 .... 131 D3
Perrycroft SL4 .... 209 F2
Perryfields Way SL1 .... 197 D1
Perryman Way SL2 .... 197 F1
Perrys The HP22 .... 131 D3
Perth Ave SL1 .... 205 D4
Perth Cl MK3 .... 46 C1
Perth Cl MK11 .... 46 C1
Perth Rd HP13 .... 173 E4
Perth Trad Est SL1 .... 205 D4
Peter's Cl HP16 .... 151 E3
Peter's Pl HP4 .... 134 B4
Peterborough Ave HP13 .. 173 E4
Peterborough Gate MK15 .. 35 E3
Peterhill Cl SL9 .... 177 E2
Peterley Rd HP16 .... 151 F2
Peterley Ave HP16 .... 151 F2
Peters La Prestwood HP27 .. 139 F2
Princes Risborough HP27 .. 139 F2
Petersfield HP22 .... 116 B2
Petersfield Ave SL2 .... 206 A3
Petersham Cl MK16 .... 22 B1
Pettifer Way HP12 .... 172 B3
Pettingrew Cl MK7 .... 48 A3
Petty Pl SL6 .... 202 B2
Petworth MK8 .... 33 F1
Petworth Cl SL4 .... 210 A3
Petworth Ho MK8 .... 33 F1
Pevensey Cl
Aylesbury HP21 .... 116 A3
Milton Keynes MK3 .... 57 F4
Pevensey Rd SL2 .... 205 D4
Peverel Dr MK1 .... 47 D2
Peveril Cl HP21 .... 116 A3
Pevers La MK46 .... 6 A1
Pheasant Cl
Berkhamsted HP4 .... 135 E2
Tring HP23 .... 119 D3
Pheasant Dr HP13 .... 161 E1
Pheasant Hill HP8 .... 177 E4
Pheasant Rise HP5 .... 154 B3
Pheasant Wlk SL9 .... 177 F3
Pheasants Croft SL6 ...... 202 A2
Pheasants Dr HP15 .... 163 D3
Pheasants Ridge SL7 ...... 183 E4
Philip Dr HP10 .... 185 E4
Philip Rd HP13 .... 173 E4
Phillimore Cl MK15 .... 35 D3
Phillip Ct MK5 .... 46 A3
Philpots Cl UB7 .... 208 B3
Philps Cl HP14 .... 171 E2
Phipps Cl SL6 .... 202 A1
Phipps Rd SL1 .... 204 C4
Phoebe La MK17 .... 48 C3
Phoebe's Orch MK17 .... 69 F4
Phoenix Dr MK6 .... 46 C4
Phygtle The SL9 .... 177 F2
Phyllis Ct Dr RG9 .... 191 F2
Picasso Pl HP19 .... 100 C1
Pickering Dr MK4 .... 46 A1
Pickford Dr SL3 .... 206 C3
Picts La HP27 .... 139 D1
Piddington La HP14 .... 171 D4
Piddington Rd HP18 .... 96 A4
Pield Heath Rd UB8 .... 201 F1
Pierson Rd SL4 .... 209 E3
Pigeon Farm Rd HP14 .... 158 C3
Piggott's Hill HP14 .... 150 C1
Piggotts End HP7 .... 165 D4
Piggotts Orch HP7 .... 165 D4
Pightle Cres MK18 .... 41 E1
Pightle The
Buckingham MK18 .... 41 E1
Maids Moreton MK18 ...... 41 F2
Oving HP22 .... 86 B4
Pigott Dr MK5 .... 46 A3
Pigott Orch HP22 .... 85 D3
Pike Cl Marlow SL7 .... 194 B4
Uxbridge UB10 .... 201 F2
Pike Cnr HP21 .... 116 B3
Pilch La MK17 .... 54 B2
Pilgrim St MK9 .... 35 D2
Pilgrims Cl HP27 .... 139 D3
Pimms Cl HP13 .... 174 A3
Pimms Gr HP13 .... 174 A3
Pimpernel Gr MK7 .... 48 A3
Pinchfield WD3 .... 178 B3
Pinders Croft MK12 .... 33 D3
Pine Chase HP12 .... 172 A2
Pine Cl Berkhamsted HP4 .. 135 D2
Maidenhead SL6 .... 202 A4
Tylers Green HP15 .... 163 D2
Pine Crest Mews LU7 ...... 80 C3
Pine Gr MK17 .... 49 D2
Pine Hill HP15 .... 162 C2
Pine Road LU6 .... 106 C4
Pine Trees Dr UB10 .... 201 F4

Pine Wlk
Berkhamsted HP4 ...... 134 B4
Tylers Green HP15 ...... 163 D2
Pineapple Rd HP7 ...... 165 F4
Pinecroft SL7 ...... 183 E2
Pinels Way HP12 ...... 172 C2
Piner Cotts SL4 ...... 209 F2
Pines Cl Amersham HP6 ...... 154 A1
Little Kingshill HP15 ...... 152 A2
Pines The Feldon HP1 ...... 146 C4
Tylers Green HP10 ...... 163 D1
Pinetree Cl SL9 ...... 177 E2
Pinewood Ave UB8 ...... 208 C4
Pinewood Cl
Gerrards Cross SL9 ...... 188 C2
Iver Heath SL0 ...... 200 B3
Pinewood Dr MK2 ...... 58 C4
Pinewood Film Studios
SL0 ...... 200 A3
Pinewood Green SL0 ...... 200 B3
Pinewood Mews TW19 ...... 213 E1
Pinewood Rd
High Wycombe HP12 ...... 172 B4
Iver Heath SL0 ...... 200 A2
Pinfold MK7 ...... 48 A3
Pinglestone Cl UB7 ...... 213 F4
Pinions Rd HP13 ...... 173 F3
Pink Hill HP27 ...... 149 F4
Pink La SL1 ...... 197 D2
Pink Rd HP27 ...... 149 F4
Pinkard Ct MK6 ...... 47 E4
Pinkneys Dr SL6 ...... 195 D1
Pinkneys Rd SL6 ...... 202 A4
Pinkworthy MK4 ...... 46 B2
Pin Cl UB8 ...... 208 B4
Pipard MK14 ...... 34 C4
Pipers Cl SL1 ...... 197 E1
Pipers Corner Sch HP14 ...... 162 A4
Pipers Croft LU6 ...... 93 F4
Pipers Ct SL1 ...... 197 E1
Pipers La HP15 ...... 162 B4
Pipit Gdns 4 HP20 ...... 101 F2
Pipit Wlk 3 HP20 ...... 101 F2
Pippins Cl UB7 ...... 208 B2
Pippins The SL3 ...... 206 C3
Pipston Gn MK7 ...... 48 A4
Pitch Pond Cl HP9 ...... 175 E3
Pitch The HP14 ...... 159 E2
Pitchcott Rd HP22 ...... 86 A3
Pitcher La MK5 ...... 46 A4
Pitchford Ave MK18 ...... 41 F1
Pitfield MK11 ...... 33 D2
Pitt Green MK18 ...... 41 F1
Pitters Piece HP18 ...... 125 D4
Pitts Rd SL1 ...... 205 E3
Place Farm Ho HP27 ...... 139 D3
Place Farm Way HP27 ...... 139 D3
Plackett Way SL1 ...... 204 B3
Plaiters Cl HP23 ...... 119 D2
Plantain Ct MK7 ...... 48 A3
Plantation Rd
Amersham HP6 ...... 154 C1
High Wycombe HP13 ...... 174 A4
Leighton Buzzard LU7 ...... 70 C2
Platt The HP7 ...... 165 D4
Playing Field Rd NN13 ...... 39 D2
Pleasant Cotts SL0 ...... 200 A1
Pleasant Pl HP13 ...... 178 C2
Pleasaunce The HP22 ...... 117 F3
Pleshey Cl MK5 ...... 46 A3
Plested Ct HP22 ...... 116 B1
Plomer Green Ave HP13 ...... 161 E1
Plomer Green La HP13 ...... 161 E2
Plomer Hill HP13 ...... 161 E1
Plough Cl HP21 ...... 115 F2
Plough La Sarratt WD4 ...... 156 C3
Stoke Poges SL2 ...... 199 D2
Ploughlees La SL1 ...... 205 F3
Ploughley Rd OX6 ...... 94 C4
Plover Cl
Buckingham MK18 ...... 52 C4
Newport Pagnell MK16 ...... 22 C2
Plover The HP20 ...... 101 F2
Plover Wlk 2 HP20 ...... 101 F2
Plowman Cl MK12 ...... 33 D3
Plum Park La NN12 ...... 17 E4
Plumer Rd HP11 ...... 172 C4
Plumstead Ave MK13 ...... 34 B2
Plym Cl HP21 ...... 115 E3
Plymouth Rd SL1 ...... 204 C4
Pocock Ave UB7 ...... 208 C2
Pococks La SL4 ...... 205 F1
Poets Chase HP21 ...... 115 F3
Points The SL4 ...... 202 A2
Pole Hill Chesham HP5 ...... 144 A1
Sarratt WD3 ...... 156 C3
Police Ho's SL9 ...... 189 D2
Polidoris La HP15 ...... 163 E4
Polish Ave HP22 ...... 131 F4
Pollard Ave UB9 ...... 189 F3
Pollard Cl SL4 ...... 211 D1

Pollards WD3 ...... 178 B3
Pollywick Rd HP23 ...... 119 E1
Polruan Pl MK6 ...... 35 D1
Pomander Cres MK7 ...... 48 A4
Pomeroy Cl HP7 ...... 165 E4
Pond App HP15 ...... 163 E4
Pond Cl Coleshill HP7 ...... 164 B2
Newton Longville MK17 ...... 57 E1
Tring HP23 ...... 119 D2
Pond Cotts HP14 ...... 171 D2
Pond La SL9 ...... 177 D1
Pond Park Rd HP5 ...... 144 A1
Pondgate MK7 ...... 48 A4
Pondwicks HP7 ...... 165 D4
Pool La SL1 ...... 205 F3
Poolmans Rd SL4 ...... 209 E2
Pope Way HP21 ...... 115 F2
Popes Acre HP17 ...... 126 C3
Popes Cl Amersham HP6 ...... 154 C1
Colnbrook SL3 ...... 212 A4
Popes La SL6 ...... 195 E4
Poplar Ave
Amersham HP7 ...... 165 F4
West Drayton UB7 ...... 208 C3
Poplar Cl Aylesbury HP20 ...... 102 A1
Stanwell SL3 ...... 212 C3
Poplar Ho SL3 ...... 206 C1
Poplar Rd
Aylesbury HP20 ...... 102 A1
New Denham UB9 ...... 201 E3
Poplars Cl HP18 ...... 114 B3
Poplars Gr SL6 ...... 196 A1
Poplars Rd MK18 ...... 52 B4
Poplars The HP22 ...... 131 E3
Poppy Rd HP27 ...... 139 D1
Porlock La MK4 ...... 46 B2
Port Field Farm MK16 ...... 21 F3
Portal Cl UB10 ...... 201 F3
Portal Rd HP22 ...... 131 E3
Portchester Ct MK8 ...... 33 F1
Porter's Cl MK19 ...... 31 F2
Porters Way UB7 ...... 208 C2
Portfield Cl MK18 ...... 52 C4
Portfield Way MK18 ...... 52 C4
Portfields Cty Fst Sch
MK16 ...... 22 A3
Portfields Cty Mid Sch
MK16 ...... 22 A3
Portholme Rd MK16 ...... 22 A2
Porthcawl Gn MK4 ...... 57 E4
Porthleven Pl MK6 ...... 35 D1
Porthmellion Cl MK4 ...... 57 D4
Portland Bsns Ctr SL3 ...... 211 D3
Portland Cl SL2 ...... 197 E1
Portland Dr MK5 ...... 35 E4
Portland Ho HP13 ...... 173 E4
Portland SL7 ...... 183 E1
Portlock Rd SL6 ...... 202 B4
Portmarnock Cl MK3 ...... 57 E4
Portnall Pl MK43 ...... 25 D1
Portobello Cl HP5 ...... 144 A1
Portrush Cl MK3 ...... 57 E4
Portsmouth Ct SL1 ...... 205 F3
Portway
Milton Keynes MK15, MK9 ...... 35 E3
North Marston MK18 ...... 76 A1
Stone HP17 ...... 114 C2
Portway Dr HP12 ...... 161 D1
Portway Rd MK18 ...... 62 A3
Post Meadow SL0 ...... 200 B1
Post Office Cotts SL2 ...... 199 D3
Post Office La
Beaconsfield HP9 ...... 175 E2
Slough SL3 ...... 206 B4
Whitchurch HP22 ...... 87 D3
Potash La HP18 ...... 104 A3
Potkiln La HP9 ...... 176 B1
Potter Row HP16 ...... 142 B1
Potters Cl HP16 ...... 151 D4
Potters Cross SL0 ...... 200 C1
Pottersupy Lodge Sch
NN12 ...... 18 A3
Poulcott TW19 ...... 211 F1
Pound Cl
Steeple Claydon MK18 ...... 63 E2
Wicker MK16 ...... 31 D2
Pound Cres SL7 ...... 183 E1
Pound Hill MK16 ...... 59 E1
Pound La
Little Marlow SL7 ...... 184 B2
Marlow SL7 ...... 183 E1
North Crawley MK16 ...... 24 A4
Preston Bissett MK18 ...... 62 A4
Pound St HP22 ...... 131 D2
Pound The Cookham SL6 ...... 195 F4
Slough SL3 ...... 197 E1
Syresham NN13 ...... 27 D4
Poundfield La SL6 ...... 195 F4
Poundfield Rd NN12 ...... 18 C1
Poundlands HP27 ...... 149 F3

Pounds Cl MK43 ...... 25 D1
Powis Cl SL6 ...... 202 A2
Powney Rd SL6 ...... 202 B4
Poyle 14 Trad Est SL3 ...... 212 C2
Poyle Cl Inf Sch SL3 ...... 212 C3
Poyle La SL1 ...... 197 D2
Poyle New Cotts SL3 ...... 212 C3
Poyle Rd SL3 ...... 212 C3
Poyle Tech Ctr The SL3 ...... 212 C3
Poynings SL0 ...... 207 F1
Pratt Ho HP20 ......*...... 154 C1
Prebendal Ave HP21 ...... 115 E4
Prebendal Cl HP20 ...... 115 E4
Prebendal Ct 10 HP20 ...... 115 E4
Prebendal Ct 1 HP20 ...... 115 E4
Precedent Dr MK13 ...... 34 A2
Precincts The SL1 ...... 197 E1
Prentice Gr MK5 ...... 46 A2
Prescott Rd SL3 ...... 212 C3
Prescotts The UB9 ...... 189 F2
Presley Way MK8 ...... 45 F4
Press Rd UB8 ...... 201 E3
Preston Ct MK15 ...... 35 D4
Preston Hill HP5 ...... 144 B1
Preston Rd SL2 ...... 206 B3
Prestwick Cl MK3 ...... 57 E4
Prestwood Cl SL2 ...... 206 A4
Prestwood Cl 4 HP12 ...... 172 B4
Prestwood Cty Fst Sch
HP16 ...... 151 E4
Prestwood Lodge Sch
HP16 ...... 151 E3
Prestwood Pl HP16 ...... 151 E3
Pretoria Rd HP13 ...... 173 E4
Primatt Cres MK5 ...... 46 A3
Primrose Cotts HP14 ...... 150 C1
Primrose Ct HP21 ...... 115 D3
Primrose Dr HP21 ...... 115 D3
Primrose Gn HP15 ...... 162 C3
Primrose Hill HP15 ...... 162 C4
Primrose Terr HP18 ...... 110 A4
Prince Andrew Cl SL6 ...... 196 A1
Prince Andrew Rd SL6 ...... 196 A1
Prince Consort Cotts SL4 ...... 210 B3
Prince Edward St HP4 ...... 135 E2
Prince Philip Ave MK43 ...... 24 B1
Prince's Rd HP21 ...... 115 F4
Princes Cl
Berkhamsted HP4 ...... 135 D3
Chilton HP18 ...... 111 D2
Eton SL4 ...... 204 C1
Princes Ct LU7 ...... 80 C4
Princes Est HP27 ...... 138 C2
Princes Gdns HP27 ...... 139 D2
Princes La HP16 ...... 142 B3
Princes Rd SL8 ...... 185 E2
Princes Risborough Sta
HP27 ...... 138 C1
Princes Risborough
Upper Sch HP27 ...... 139 E1
Princes St Lane End HP14 ...... 160 A1
Slough SL1 ...... 206 A2
Princes Way HP22 ...... 58 B4
Princes Way Rdbt MK2 ...... 58 A4
Princess Ave SL4 ...... 210 A2
Princess Margaret Hospl The
SL4 ...... 210 B3
Princess Margaret Royal
Free Sch The SL4 ...... 210 B3
Princess Mary's Hospl
HP22 ...... 131 E3
Princess St SL6 ...... 202 C3
Printers End HP19 ...... 101 D1
Prior Gr HP5 ...... 144 B1
Priors Cl Maidenhead SL6 ...... 203 D1
Slough SL1 ...... 206 A2
Priors Pk MK4 ...... 46 B1
Priors Rd SL4 ...... 209 E2
Priors Way SL6 ...... 203 D1
Priory Ave
High Wycombe HP13 ...... 173 D4
South Harefield UB9 ...... 190 B4
Priory Cl Aylesbury HP19 ...... 101 E1
Denham UB9 ...... 190 A1
Horton-cum-S OX33 ...... 108 A3
Newport Pagnell MK16 ...... 22 C2
South Harefield UB9 ...... 190 B4
Priory Common Cty Fst Sch
MK13 ...... 34 A2
Priory Cotts UB9 ...... 190 B4
Priory Cres HP19 ...... 101 E1
Priory Ct HP4 ...... 135 E2
Priory Cty Jun & Inf Sch
SL1 ...... 204 B4
Priory Gdns
Berkhamsted HP4 ...... 135 E2
South Harefield UB9 ...... 190 B4
Priory Rd Burnham SL1 ...... 204 B4
Gerrards Cross SL9 ...... 188 B4
High Wycombe HP13 ...... 173 D4

Priory St MK16 ...... 22 C2
Priory Way Datchet SL3 ...... 211 D4
Gerrards Cross SL9 ...... 188 B4
Harmondsworth UB7 ...... 213 F4
Pritchard Ct MK14 ...... 34 C4
Progress Bsns Ctr SL1 ...... 204 B4
Progress Rd HP12 ...... 172 A4
Promenade SL4 ...... 210 B4
Prospect Cl MK17 ...... 68 B3
Prospect Cotts HP14 ...... 161 E4
Prospect Ct HP14 ...... 171 D3
Prospect Pl
Castlethorpe MK19 ...... 19 F3
Hurley SL6 ...... 193 F2
3 Windsor SL4 ...... 210 B2
Wing LU7 ...... 79 F1
Prospect Rd Marlow SL7 ...... 183 E1
Milton Keynes MK11 ...... 32 B3
Prothero Field MK7 ...... 48 B2
Providence Pl
Maidenhead SL6 ...... 202 C4
Milton Keynes MK13 ...... 34 A2
Providence Rd UB7 ...... 208 C3
Prudential Bldgs 8 SL1 ...... 205 F2
Pryors Field HP9 ...... 176 C2
Pudding La HP9 ...... 176 C2
Puffin Way HP20 ...... 101 F2
Pulborough Cl MK3 ...... 46 B1
Pulford Rd LU7 ...... 80 C3
Pullfields HP5 ...... 144 A1
Pulpit Cl HP5 ...... 144 A1
Pulpit La HP22 ...... 76 B1
Pump La N SL7 ...... 183 F3
Pump La S SL7 ...... 184 A2
Pump Meadow HP16 ...... 152 A4
Pumpkin Hill SL1 ...... 197 F3
Pumpus Green MK18 ...... 66 A2
Punch Bowl La HP5 ...... 154 B4
Purbeck MK14 ...... 34 B3
Purbeck Cl HP21 ...... 116 A3
Purcel Dr MK15 ...... 22 A2
Purssell Cl SL6 ...... 202 A2
Purssell Pl HP27 ...... 139 D3
Purssells Meadow HP14 ...... 161 E4
Purton Ct SL2 ...... 198 B3
Purton La SL2 ...... 198 B3
Pury Rd NN12 ...... 9 D1
Pusey Way HP14 ...... 171 E3
Putlowes Dr HP18 ...... 100 B2
Putman Ho MK5 ...... 46 B3
Putman Pl RG9 ...... 191 F1
Putnams Dr HP22 ...... 117 E3
Puxley Rd MK19 ...... 31 E3
Pyebush La HP9 ...... 187 D4
Pyghtle The Olney MK46 ...... 6 C2
Turvey MK43 ...... 8 B3
Pyghtles The HP22 ...... 85 D3
Pym Wlk OX9 ...... 125 F1
Pymcombe Cl HP27 ...... 139 D3
Pynefield Ho WD3 ...... 167 F1
Pyxe Ct MK7 ...... 48 A2

Quadrangle The HP13 ...... 173 D4
Quadrans Cl MK14 ...... 35 D4
Quadrant The
High Wycombe HP13 ...... 162 C1
Maidenhead SL6 ...... 203 D3
Quainton Cc Comb Sch
HP22 ...... 85 D3
Quainton Railway Ctr
HP22 ...... 84 C1
Quainton Rd
North Marston MK18 ...... 76 A1
Waddesdon HP18 ...... 99 D4
Quaker's Mead HP22 ...... 116 C2
Quaker's Mede HP17 ...... 127 D3
Quantock Cl SL3 ...... 207 D1
Quantock Cres MK4 ...... 46 B1
Quarrendon Ave HP19 ...... 101 D1
Quarrendon Rd HP7 ...... 165 F4
Quarrendon Upper Sch
HP19 ...... 101 E1
Quarry Cl HP18 ...... 125 E4
Quarry Wood Rd SL6 ...... 195 D4
Quarrydale Dr SL7 ...... 183 F1
Quaves Rd SL3 ...... 206 B2
Quebec Rd HP13 ...... 173 F3
Queen Alexandra Rd
HP11 ...... 173 D3
Queen Anne Fst Sch The
SL4 ...... 210 B2
Queen Anne St MK13 ...... 33 F4
Queen Anne's Cl 10 SL4 ...... 210 B3
Queen Anne's Ct SL4 ...... 210 B3
Queen Catherine Rd MK18 ...... 63 F1
Queen Charlotte St 19
SL4 ...... 210 B3
Queen Cl RG9 ...... 191 F1
Queen Eleanor St MK11 ...... 32 B3
Queen Mother's Dr UB9 ...... 189 F3
Queen Sq 7 HP11 ...... 173 D4

Queen St Aylesbury HP20 ...... 116 A4
Henley-on-T RG9 ...... 191 F1
High Wycombe
HP13, HP14 ...... 173 E4
Lane End HP14 ...... 160 A1
Leighton Buzzard LU7 ...... 80 C4
Maidenhead SL6 ...... 202 C4
Milton Keynes MK11 ...... 32 C3
Pitstone LU7 ...... 105 E2
Tring HP23 ...... 119 D2
Waddesdon HP18 ...... 98 C3
Queen Victoria Rd HP11 ...... 173 D3
Queen's Acre SL4 ...... 210 B2
Queen's Cl SL4 ...... 211 D1
Queen's Ct SL1 ...... 205 F3
Queen's Dr The WD3 ...... 167 F1
Queen's Gate SL4 ...... 210 B2
Queen's La 8 SL6 ...... 202 C4
Queen's Pk HP21 ...... 115 F4
Queen's Rd Datchet SL3 ...... 211 D4
Marlow SL7 ...... 183 E1
Slough SL1 ...... 205 F3
Uxbridge UB8 ...... 201 E1
Windsor SL4 ...... 210 B3
Queen's Terr 5 SL4 ...... 210 B3
Queens Acre HP13 ...... 173 E3
Queens Acre Ho 6 SL4 ...... 210 B2
Queens Ave MK16 ...... 22 B2
Queens Cl OX9 ...... 125 F1
Queens Ct 3 HP21 ...... 173 E3
Queens Mead HP16 ...... 116 B4
Queens Rd
Berkhamsted HP4 ...... 135 D3
Chesham HP5 ...... 144 B1
Eton SL4 ...... 204 C1
High Wycombe HP13 ...... 173 E3
Princes Risborough HP27 ...... 139 E2
West Drayton UB7 ...... 208 C2
Queens Wlk Mall 3 SL6 ...... 202 C4
Queensmead Ho HP13 ...... 211 D3
Queensmead Rd HP10 ...... 174 B1
Queensmere Rd SL1 ...... 206 A2
Queensway
Maidenhead SL6 ...... 195 F1
Milton Keynes MK2 ...... 58 B4
Tylers Green HP15 ...... 163 D2
Queensway The SL9 ...... 188 B4
Quickberry Pl HP7 ...... 165 E4
Quickley Brow WD3 ...... 167 D2
Quickley La WD3 ...... 167 E2
Quickley Rise WD3 ...... 167 D2
Quill Hall La HP6 ...... 154 C1
Quilter Meadow MK7 ...... 48 B3
Quilters Way HP22 ...... 130 B4
Quinbrookes SL2 ...... 206 B4
Quince Cl MK7 ...... 48 A3
Quinton Cl MK13 ...... 34 A2
Quoiting Sq SL7 ...... 183 E1
Quoitings Dr SL7 ...... 183 E1

Raans Rd Amersham HP6 ...... 154 C1
Little Chalfont HP6 ...... 154 C1
Rabans Cl HP19 ...... 100 C1
Rabans Ct HP19 ...... 100 C1
Rabbs Farm Prim Sch
UB7 ...... 208 C3
Rabels Way HP5 ...... 154 B3
Rackstraw Gr MK7 ...... 48 B3
Radcliffe Sch The MK12 ...... 33 D3
Radcliffe St
Milton Keynes MK12 ...... 33 E3
Milton Keynes MK12 ...... 33 E4
Radclive Rd MK18 ...... 51 F3
Radcot Ave SL3 ...... 207 D2
Radford Cl SL6 ...... 195 F2
Radman Gr MK12 ...... 33 D3
Radnage CE Fst Sch
HP14 ...... 159 E3
Radnage Common Rd
HP14 ...... 159 E3
Radnage La HP14 ...... 148 B1
Radnor End HP20 ...... 101 F1
Radnor Way SL3 ...... 206 C1
Radworthy MK4 ...... 46 B2
Raeside Cl HP9 ...... 176 B3
Ragmans Cl SL7 ...... 183 E4
Ragmans La SL7 ...... 172 B1
Ragnall's La OX33 ...... 108 A3
Ragstone Rd SL1 ...... 205 F2
Ragstones HP10 ...... 174 A1
Railway Cotts
Steeple Claydon MK18 ...... 64 A1
Wigginton HP23 ...... 119 F3
Railway St 3 HP21 ...... 115 F4
Railway Terr SL2 ...... 205 F3
Rainborough Gdns HP20 ...... 101 F1

Rainbow Dr MK6 .... 46 C4
Rainsborough MK14 .... 35 D4
Rainsborough Chase SL6 . 202 A2
Rake Way HP21 .... 115 E2
Raleigh Cl SL1 .... 205 D3
Ralphs Retreat HP15 ...... 162 C2
Rambler Cl MK14 .... 204 A4
Rambler La SL3 .... 206 B2
Ramsay View HP15 .... 163 D2
Ramsey Ct SL2 .... 197 E1
Ramsgill Ct MK13 .... 34 B3
Ramsons Ave MK14 .... 34 C2
Ramsthorn Gr MK7 .... 48 A3
Ramworth Way HP21 ...... 116 A3
Randall Cl SL3 .... 206 C1
Randall Cl SL4 .... 211 D1
Randolph Rd SL3 .... 206 C2
Ranelagh Gdns MK16 ...... 22 B1
Rangers Ct MK3 .... 33 F1
Rannal Dr OX9 .... 147 E3
Rannoch Cl MK2 .... 58 A3
Rannock Gdns LU7 .... 80 B4
Ranston Cl UB9 .... 189 F3
Rashleigh Pl MK6 .... 46 C4
Ratcliffe Cl UB8 .... 201 E1
Rathbone Cl MK8 .... 45 F4
Raven 🔢 HP20 .... 101 F2
Raven Cres HP18 .... 98 B3
Raven Rd HP14 .... 158 C2
Ravens Field SL3 .... 206 B2
Ravens La HP4 .... 135 E2
Ravens Wharf HP4 .... 135 E2
Ravensbourne Pl MK6 ..... 35 D1
Ravensbourne Rd HP21 ... 115 E2
Ravenscar Ct MK4 .... 46 A1
Ravenscourt SL7 .... 184 A2
Ravenscroft Rd RG9 .... 191 E1
Ravenshoe Cl SL8 .... 185 D2
Ravensmead
  Chalfont St Peter SL9 ... 177 F3
  Chinnor OX9 .... 147 E3
Ravenstone Mill Rd MK46 .. 12 C4
Ravensworth Rd SL2 ..... 198 A1
Ravigill Pl MK12 .... 33 E2
Rawcliffe Ho SL6 .... 203 D3
Rawling Rd MK13 .... 34 A2
Rawlings La HP9 .... 176 B4
Ray Dr SL6 .... 203 D4
Ray Ho 🔢 SL8 .... 185 D2
Ray Lea Cl SL6 .... 203 D4
Ray Lea Rd SL6 .... 203 D4
Ray Lodge Mews SL6 ...... 203 D4
Ray Mead Ct SL6 .... 196 B1
Ray Mead Rd SL6 .... 203 E4
Ray Meadow SL6 .... 196 A1
Ray Mill Rd E SL6 .... 196 A1
Ray Mill Rd W SL6 .... 203 D4
Ray Park Ave SL6 .... 203 D4
Ray Park La SL6 .... 203 D4
Ray Park Rd SL6 .... 203 D4
Ray St SL6 .... 203 D4
Ray's Hill
  Buckland Common HP5 .. 133 E1
  Cholesbury HP5 .... 133 E1
Rayfield SL6 .... 203 D4
Raylands Mead SL9 .... 188 B3
Rayleigh Cl MK5 .... 46 A3
Raylens HP12 .... 172 A3
Raymond Cl SL3 .... 212 C3
Raymond Rd
  Maidenhead SL6 .... 202 B4
  Slough SL3 .... 207 D2
Rayners Ave HP10 .... 174 A2
Rayners Cl
  Colnbrook SL3 .... 212 B4
  Loudwater HP10 .... 174 B2
Rays Ave SL4 .... 209 F4
Rays La HP10 .... 163 E1
Read Dr HP22 .... 102 B2
Reade Cl SL2 .... 198 B3
Reading Cl HP19 .... 101 D2
Reading Rd RG9 .... 191 F1
Readings The WD3 .... 167 F3
Reads La LU7 .... 78 B2
Recreation Rd SL8 .... 185 D2
Rectory Ave HP13 .... 173 E4
Rectory Cl
  Farnham Common SL2 ... 198 B1
  Marsh Gibbon OX6 .... 71 F2
  Slapton LU7 .... 91 E3
  Windsor SL4 .... 210 A3
Rectory Ct
  🔢 High Wycombe HP13 .. 173 F3
  Lewknor OX9 .... 157 D4
Rectory Dr HP18 .... 99 D3
Rectory Fields MK15 .... 35 D3
Rectory Gdns HP8 .... 177 D4
Rectory Hill HP6, HP7 ..... 165 E4
Rectory La Amersham HP7 165 D4
Berkhamsted HP4 .... 135 E2
Yardley Hastings NN7 ...... 1 A4
Rectory Meadow OX9 ...... 147 E4
Rectory Orch MK46 .... 7 F4
Rectory Rd SL6 .... 196 C1
Rectory Terr SL2 .... 198 B2
Red Cottage Mews SL3 ... 206 B2
Red Ct SL1 .... 205 F3
Red House Cl
  Beaconsfield HP9 .... 175 D2
  Newton Longville MK17 ... 57 E2
Red Leaf Cl SL3 .... 206 C3
Red Leys UB10 .... 201 F3
Red Lion Cl MK43 .... 25 D1
Red Lion Cotts SL2 .... 199 D1
Red Lion Dr HP14 .... 158 B3
Red Lion St HP5 .... 154 B4
Red Lion Way HP10 .... 185 F3
Red Lodge Gdns HP4 ..... 135 D2
Redborne Cl SL3 .... 322 C3
Redbourne MK14 .... 34 B4
Redcliffe Wlk HP10 .... 101 D1
Redcote Manor MK7 .... 48 A2
Redding Dr HP6 .... 154 A1
Redding Gr MK8 .... 45 F3
Reddings Cl HP22 .... 131 D3
Reddington Dr SL3 .... 206 C1
Redfern Cl UB8 .... 201 E2
Redfield Cl LU6 .... 93 F4
Redford Rd SL4 .... 209 E3
Redford Way UB8 .... 201 E3
Redhill UB9 .... 189 E2
Redhouse Cl HP12 .... 172 C2
Redhuish Cl MK4 .... 46 B2
Redland Dr MK5 .... 46 B4
Redland Way HP21 .... 116 A2
Redman Rd HP12 .... 172 A2
Redriff Cl SL6 .... 202 B3
Redshaw Cl MK18 .... 41 F1
Redshots Cl SL7 .... 183 F2
Redvers Gate MK15 .... 35 D4
Redway Sch The MK6 ...... 47 E3
Redwing HP20 .... 101 F2
Redwood SL1 .... 197 D2
Redwood Cl
  Tylers Green HP15 .... 163 D2
  Wing LU7 .... 79 F1
Redwood Dr
  Aylesbury HP21 .... 115 F4
  Wing LU7 .... 79 F1
Redwood Gate MK5 .... 46 B2
Redwood Gdns SL1 .... 205 E3
Redwood Glade LU7 .... 70 C2
Redwoods The SL4 .... 210 B2
Reed Cl SL0 .... 207 F4
Reeves Croft MK12 .... 33 E3
Reform Rd SL6 .... 203 D4
Regal Ct 🔢 HP23 .... 119 D2
Regency Ct HP21 .... 116 A4
Regent Cl
  🔢 Maidenhead SL6 ...... 202 C4
  Slough SL1 .... 205 F4
  Windsor SL4 .... 210 B3
Regent Ho HP27 .... 139 D2
Regent Rd HP21 .... 116 A4
Regent St MK2 .... 58 B4
Reid Ave SL3 .... 202 C3
Reliance La MK2 .... 58 A3
Rembrandt End HP19 .... 100 C1
Remenham Church La
  RG9 .... 192 A2
Remenham La RG9 .... 191 F2
Remenham Terr RG9 ..... 192 B1
Remus Gate NN13 .... 38 A3
Rendlesham MK15 .... 35 E3
Rendlesham Way WD3 ... 167 E2
Renfrew Way MK3 .... 46 A2
Rennie Cl HP13 .... 161 F1
Repton Cl SL6 .... 202 B2
Retreat La HP14 .... 148 B1
Retreat The
  Little Chalfont HP6 ...... 166 C4
  Milton Keynes MK11 ...... 32 B4
  Princes Risborough HP27 139 D2
Revel Rd HP10 .... 185 E4
Revesby Cl SL6 .... 202 B2
Reyners Gn HP16 .... 152 A2
Reynold Dr HP21 .... 102 A1
Reynolds Cl
  Cranfield MK43 .... 24 C2
  High Wycombe HP13 .... 173 F4
Reynolds Rd HP9 .... 175 E2
Reynolds Wlk HP5 .... 144 A2
Rhodes Pl MK6 .... 46 C4
Rhondda Cl MK1 .... 47 F4
Rhoscolyn Dr MK4 .... 57 E4
Rhuddlan Cl MK5 .... 45 F4
Rhymer Cl MK19 .... 10 C2
Ribble Cl MK16 .... 22 C2
Ribble Cres MK3 .... 57 E4
Ribstone Rd SL6 .... 202 A2
Ricardo Rd SL4 .... 211 D1
Richard Gdns HP13 .... 173 F4
Richards Way SL1 .... 205 D3
Richardson Pl MK6 .... 34 C1
Richardson St HP11 ...... 172 C4
Richborough MK13 .... 34 A3
Richings Way SL0 .... 207 F2
Richmond Cl
  Amersham HP6 .... 154 C1
  Milton Keynes MK3 .... 46 B1
Richmond Cres SL1 .... 204 B3
Richmond Ct 🔢 HP13 ... 173 E4
Richmond Rd HP20 .... 116 B4
Richmond Way MK16 ...... 22 C1
Rick Yd The MK16 .... 13 F1
Rickard Cl
  Stoke Mandeville HP21 .. 114 C4
  West Drayton UB7 .... 208 B2
Rickford's Hill HP20 ...... 115 E4
Rickley Cty Mid Sch MK3 .. 57 F4
Rickley La MK3 .... 58 A4
Rickman's La SL2 .... 198 C3
Rickmansworth La SL9 ... 177 F2
Rickmansworth Rd
  Chorleywood WD3 .... 167 F3
Rickyard Cl
  Milton Keynes MK13 ...... 34 A2
  Whitchurch HP22 .... 87 D4
Ride The LU6 .... 93 D3
Riders Way OX9 .... 147 E3
Ridge Cl Lane End HP14 .. 171 E2
  Stoke Mandeville HP21 .. 115 E2
Ridge Side HP14 .... 160 A4
Ridge View HP23 .... 119 E3
Ridge Way
  High Wycombe HP13 .... 162 B1
  Iver SL0 .... 207 F3
Ridgebank SL1 .... 204 C3
Ridgemont End SL9 .... 177 F3
Ridgeway
  Berkhamsted HP4 .... 134 C2
  High Wycombe HP13 .... 173 D4
Ridgeway Cl
  Chesham HP5 .... 144 A2
  Marlow SL7 .... 183 F2
Ridgeway Cotts MK17 ...... 62 D2
Ridgeway Ct 🔢 HP20 ... 101 F1
Ridgeway Meads HP27 ... 138 A1
Ridgeway Rd HP5 .... 144 A2
Ridgeway The
  Gerrards Cross SL9 ...... 188 C4
  Marlow SL7 .... 183 F2
Ridgeway Trad Est The
  SL0 .... 207 F3
Ridgmont Cl MK19 .... 31 F3
Ridgmont Ct MK19 .... 31 F3
Ridgway MK17 .... 49 D3
Riding Court Rd SL3 ...... 211 F4
Riding Ct SL3 .... 211 E4
Riding La HP9 .... 174 C2
Riding The MK19 .... 31 F3
Ridings Cotts HP15 .... 163 E3
Ridings The
  Amersham HP6 .... 154 B2
  Iver SL0 .... 207 F1
  Latimer HP5 .... 155 E2
  Maidenhead SL6 .... 202 A4
Ridings Way LU7 .... 78 A1
Rignall Rd HP16 .... 151 F4
Riley Rd SL7 .... 183 E1
Rillington Gdns MK4 .... 46 A2
Rimsdale Ct MK2 .... 58 B2
Ring Rd HP10 .... 173 F1
Ring Rd E MK7 .... 47 F4
Ring Rd N MK7 .... 47 F4
Ring Rd W MK7 .... 47 F4
Ringsall Dr HP4 .... 121 D4
Ringshall Rd HP4 .... 107 D2
Ringstead Way HP7 .... 165 E3
Ripley Cl
  High Wycombe HP13 .... 173 D4
  Slough SL3 .... 206 C1
Ripon Ho HP21 .... 115 F3
Ripon St 🔢 HP20 .... 101 E1
Risborough Rd
  Maidenhead SL6 .... 202 C4
  Stoke Mandeville HP22 .. 130 A4
Rise The Amersham HP7 . 165 E4
  Gawcott MK18 .... 51 F2
  Holmer Green HP15 ...... 163 D3
  Loudwater HP10 .... 174 A2
  Uxbridge UB10 .... 201 F2
Riseley Rd SL6 .... 202 B4
Risings The HP13 .... 162 A1
River Cl MK16 .... 22 B2
River Ct SL6 .... 203 E4
River Gdns SL6 .... 203 E2
River Park Ind Est HP4 .. 135 D3
River Rd SL6 .... 203 E4
River Side MK16 .... 22 B2
River Side Cotts HP10 ... 185 F4
River St SL4 .... 210 B4
River View HP10 .... 185 D4
River Wlk UB9 .... 201 E4
Rivercrest Rd MK19 .... 32 A3
Rivermead Ct SL7 .... 194 B4
Riverpark Dr SL7 .... 183 F1
Rivers Cty Fst Sch MK43 .. 46 C1
Rivers Edge HP11 .... 174 A2
Riverside Bsns Ctr 🔢
  HP11 .... 172 C4
Riverside Cotts UB7 ..... 208 B1
Riverside Cty Fst Sch
  MK16 .... 22 C2
Riverside Pk MK43 .... 135 D3
Riverside Park SL3 .... 212 C3
Riverside Pl MK19 .... 173 F1
Riverside Rd TW19 .... 211 E3
Riverside Way SL0 .... 207 D2
Riverside Wlk Olney MK46 .. 7 D3
  Windsor SL4 .... 210 B4
Riverswood Gdns HP10 . 174 A2
Riverwalk Mews MK18 .... 52 B3
Riverwood Cl SL7 .... 184 A1
Riverwoods Ave SL7 ...... 184 A1
Riverwoods Dr SL7 .... 184 A1
Rivetts Cl MK46 .... 6 C2
Rixband Cl MK7 .... 48 A2
Rixman Cl SL6 .... 202 B3
Rixon Cl SL3 .... 206 C4
Roade Hill NN7 .... 9 F4
Robert Rd SL2 .... 187 E1
Robert's Dr HP19 .... 101 E1
Roberts Cl Stanwell TW19 . 213 D1
  West Drayton UB7 .... 208 C3
Roberts La SL9 .... 178 A3
Roberts Rd
  Haddenham HP17 .... 127 D3
  High Wycombe HP13 .... 173 D4
Roberts Ride HP15 .... 163 D3
Roberts Way HP21 .... 115 F3
Roberts Wood Dr SL9 ... 177 F3
Robertson Cl MK5 .... 45 F4
Robertson Cnr LU6 .... 93 F2
Robertswood Comb Sch
  SL9 .... 177 F2
Robeson Cl MK4 .... 46 A2
Robin Cl Aylesbury HP20 .. 101 F2
  Buckingham MK18 .... 52 C4
  Great Kingshill HP15 .... 151 E1
Robin Hill HP4 .... 135 E2
Robin Ho 🔢 HP20 .... 174 A2
Robin Hood Cl SL1 .... 204 C3
Robin Par 🔢 SL2 .... 198 B4
Robin Willis Way SL4 ..... 211 D1
Robins Cl
  Little Marlow HP12 .... 172 B2
  Uxbridge UB8 .... 208 B4
Robins Hill MK6 .... 47 D3
Robins Orch SL9 .... 177 F2
Robins Platt OX9 .... 147 D3
Robinson Rd HP10 .... 174 A2
Robinswood
  Beaconsfield HP9 .... 175 E3
  Leighton Buzzard LU7 ... 70 C1
Roblin Cl HP21 .... 115 F2
Robson Cl HP13 .... 177 F3
Robson Ct HP16 .... 152 A4
Roche Gdns MK3 .... 58 A4
Rochester Ct MK5 .... 46 A3
Rochester Pl HP21 .... 115 D4
Rochford Way SL6 .... 204 A4
Rochfords MK6 .... 46 C3
Rochfords Gdns SL2 ...... 206 B3
Rock Cl LU7 .... 80 B3
Rock La LU7 .... 80 B3
Rockall Ct SL3 .... 207 D2
Rockingham Cl UB8 ...... 201 E2
Rockingham Dr MK14 .... 34 C2
Rockingham Par UB8 .... 201 E3
Rockingham Rd UB8 ..... 201 E2
Rockingham Wharf UB8 . 201 D2
Rockleigh Ct 🔢 LU7 ..... 80 A4
Rockspray Gr MK7 .... 48 A3
Rodney Way SL3 .... 212 C3
Rodwell Gdns MK7 .... 48 B2
Roebuck Ave HP13 .... 173 F3
Roebuck Gn SL1 .... 204 C3
Roebuck Way MK5 .... 46 B3
Roeburn Cres MK4 .... 46 B1
Rogers Croft MK6 .... 47 E4
Rogers La SL2 .... 198 C2
Roker Park Ave UB10 .... 201 F4
Rokesby Rd SL2 .... 197 F1
Rolfe Cl HP9 .... 175 F1
Rolvenden Gr MK7 .... 48 A4
Roman Lea SL6 .... 195 F4
Roman Way
  Bourne End SL8 .... 185 D2
  Brackley NN13 .... 38 A4
Romans Field Sch MK3 ... 46 C1
Roman Ct MK1 .... 47 E3
Romney Ct 🔢 SL7 .... 183 F2
Romney Lock Rd SL4 ..... 210 B4
Romney Rd HP21 .... 115 F2
Romsey Cl SL3 .... 206 C2
Romsey Dr SL2 .... 187 E1
Romsey Way HP11 .... 173 D2
Romulus Way NN13 .... 38 A3
Ronald Rd HP9 .... 175 F1
Ronaldsay Spur SL1 ..... 205 F4
Rook Rd HP10 .... 185 F3
Rook Wood Way HP16 ... 152 A3
Rookery Cl SL7 .... 183 E1
Rookery La HP18 .... 72 C1
Rookery Meadow HP15 .. 163 E4
Rookery Way MK18 .... 63 F2
Rooks Terr UB7 .... 208 C2
Rooksley Rdbt MK13 ...... 34 A2
Ropa Ct LU7 .... 80 C4
Rosary The HP15 .... 163 D1
Rose Ave Aylesbury HP19 . 101 E2
  Tylers Green HP15 .... 163 D1
Rose Cnr HP14 .... 158 C3
Rose Cotts SL6 .... 202 B2
Rose Ct Chesham HP5 ... 154 B3
  Eaton Bray LU6 .... 92 B3
Rose Dr HP5 .... 154 B4
Rose Hill SL1 .... 197 D3
Rose Ind Est SL7 .... 183 E3
Rose La RG10 .... 193 D3
Rose Wlk SL2 .... 205 D4
Roseary Cl UB7 .... 208 B1
Rosebank Cl SL6 .... 195 F4
Rosebank Cotts HP10 .... 174 A2
Rosebay Cl MK7 .... 48 A3
Rosebery Ave
  High Wycombe HP13 .... 173 F3
  Leighton Buzzard LU7 ... 80 C4
Rosebery Ct 🔢 LU7 ...... 80 C4
Rosebery Mews LU7 .... 90 B2
Rosebery Rd HP22 .... 117 D3
Rosebery Way HP23 ..... 119 D3
Rosecomb Pl MK5 .... 46 A2
Rosehill HP4 .... 135 D2
Rosehill Cl MK18 .... 62 B1
Rosehill Ct SL1 .... 206 A2
Roseleigh Cl SL6 .... 202 A4
Rosemary Cl HP12 .... 161 D3
Rosemary Ct
  High Wycombe HP13 .... 161 D1
  Walton MK7 .... 48 A3
Rosemary La HP17 .... 127 D4
Rosemead HP22 .... 117 D3
Rosemullion Ave MK4 ..... 57 D4
Rosery The SL8 .... 185 D2
Roses Cl SL17 .... 78 A3
Roses La SL4 .... 209 E3
Rosetree Cl HP16 .... 151 E3
Rosewood Gdns HP12 ... 172 B2
Rosewood Way SL2 .... 198 B4
Rosken Gr SL2 .... 198 A2
Roslyn Ct MK5 .... 35 E4
Ross Rd Aston Abbots HP22 . 88 B3
  Maidenhead SL6 .... 202 C2
Ross Way MK3 .... 46 C1
Rossal Pl MK12 .... 33 E2
Rossendale MK14 .... 34 B4
Rossetti Pl HP15 .... 163 E4
Rossey Pl SL4 .... 205 E1
Rossiter Cl SL3 .... 206 C1
Rossway La HP23 .... 134 A4
Rostrevor Gdns SL0 ...... 200 B2
Rothersthorpe MK14 ..... 35 D4
Rothesay Cl HP20 .... 101 F1
Rothesay Ho HP4 .... 135 D2
Rothschild Ave HP22 .... 117 F3
Rothschild Rd
  Leighton Buzzard LU7 ... 80 C4
  Wing LU7 .... 79 F1
Rotten Row MK17 .... 59 E3
Roughwood La HP8 .... 166 C2
Round Hill HP17 .... 114 B3
Round Wood Rd HP6 ..... 154 C1
Roundabout Dr OX9 ...... 125 F1
Roundhead End HP9 ..... 175 D2
Roundwood Rd HP22 .... 172 B4
Roveley Ct MK11 .... 32 C3
Row The Cholesbury HP5 . 133 E1
  Coleshill HP7 .... 164 B2
  Lane End HP14 .... 171 D2
Rowan Ave HP13 .... 173 F4
Rowan Cl Aylesbury HP21 . 115 F2
  Beaconsfield HP9 .... 175 D1
  Tylers Green HP15 .... 163 D2
Rowan Dr MK19 .... 20 B3
Rowan Gdns SL0 .... 200 B2

Rowan Ho **1** SL8 .... 185 D2
Rowan Pl HP6 .... 154 C1
Rowan Rd UB7 .... 208 B1
Rowan Way SL2 .... 205 D4
Rowanhurst Dr SL2 .... 198 B4
Rowans The SL9 .... 188 B4
Rowborough Rd HP22 ..... 131 E4
Rowland Cl SL4 .... 209 E2
Rowland Way HP21 .... 115 D4
Rowlands Cl MK2 .... 58 C4
Rowle Cl MK14 .... 34 C4
Rowley Furrows LU7 .... 80 B4
Rowley La Iver Heath SL3 .. 199 E2
Stoke Poges SL3 .... 199 E2
Rowleys Pl UB7 .... 208 C2
Rowliff Rd HP12 .... 172 B3
Rowsham Dell MK14 .... 21 F1
Rowsham Rd HP22 .... 102 B3
Roxburgh Way MK3 .... 46 C2
Roxhill Rd MK43 .... 25 F2
Roxwell Cl SL1 .... 204 C3
Roxwell Path **5** HP20 .... 101 F1
Royal Buckinghamshire
Hospl The HP19 .... 101 E1
Royal Cl UB8 .... 208 C4
Royal Cotts SL6 .... 195 E4
Royal Ct HP23 .... 120 A3
Royal Free Ct **22** SL4 ..... 210 B3
Royal Gram Sch HP13 ...... 162 B1
Royal La Uxbridge UB7 .... 208 C4
West Drayton UB8 .... 209 D4
Royal Latin Sch The MK18 .. 52 B4
Royal Mansions RG9 .... 191 F1
Royal Mead HP17 .... 130 B3
Royal Windsor Race Course
SL4 .... 209 F4
Royce Cl LU6 .... 93 F4
Royce Rd MK43 .... 24 B2
Royle Cl SL9 .... 177 F2
Royston Way SL1 .... 204 B4
Rubbra Cl MK4 .... 48 B3
Rubens Cl HP19 .... 100 C1
Ruby Cl SL1 .... 205 D2
Ruckles Way HP7 .... 165 E4
Rudchesters MK13 .... 33 F3
Rudd's La HP17 .... 127 D4
Ruddlesway SL4 .... 209 E3
Rudds Cl MK18 .... 66 A3
Rudsworth Cl SL3 .... 212 B4
Rugwood Rd HP10 .... 173 F1
Rumptons Paddock HP18 .. 82 C3
Run Furrow HP17 .... 127 D4
Runford Ct MK5 .... 46 B3
Runnymede MK14 .... 21 F1
Runrig Hill HP6 .... 154 C2
Rupert Ave HP12 .... 172 C2
Rupert Cl RG9 .... 191 F2
Rupert House Sch RG9 ..... 191 F1
Rupert Way OX9 .... 126 A1
Rupert's La RG9 .... 191 F2
Ruscombe Gdns SL3 .... 211 D4
Rushall Rd OX9 .... 126 A1
Rushbrooke Cl HP13 .... 162 C1
Rushburn HP10 .... 185 F3
Rushdon Furlong LU7 ...... 105 E3
Rushes Mead UB8 .... 201 E2
Rushes The SL6 .... 203 D3
Rushington Ave SL6 .... 202 C3
Rushmere CI MK17 .... 48 B1
Rushmere La HP5 .... 145 D2
Rushmere Ret Pk MK1 .... 47 E1
Rushmoor Ave HP15 .... 163 D2
Rushton Ct MK8 .... 45 F4
Ruskin Ct MK16 .... 22 B1
Ruskin Way HP20 .... 101 E1
Rusland Cir MK4 .... 46 B2
Russell Ave HP21 .... 115 E3
Russell Cl
Little Chalfont HP6 .... 166 B4
Tylers Green HP10 .... 163 D1
Russell Ct Aylesbury HP21 . 115 E3
Chesham HP5 .... 144 B1
Maidenhead SL6 .... 202 C4
Walter's Ash HP14 .... 161 E4
Wendover HP22 .... 131 D3
Russell City Fst Sch MK11 ... 32 B3
Russell City Prim Sch
WD3 .... 167 D3
Russell Ho **9** SL8 .... 185 D2
Russell Sch The WD3 .... 167 D3
Russell St
Milton Keynes MK11 .... 32 B3
Windsor SL4 .... 210 B3
Woburn Sands MK17 ...... 49 D2
Russet Cl TW19 .... 212 C1
Russet Rd SL6 .... 202 B2
Russets The SL9 .... 177 E1
Russett Hill SL9 .... 188 C4
Rustlings Gate HP14 .... 171 E3
Rutherford Cl SL4 .... 209 F3

Rutherford Gate MK5 .... 46 B3
Rutherford Rd HP21 .... 115 F2
Ruthven Cl MK2 .... 58 B2
Rutland Ave
High Wycombe HP12 ...... 172 B3
Slough SL1 .... 205 E4
Rutland Ct HP11 .... 173 D3
Rutland Gate SL6 .... 202 B3
Rutland Pl SL6 .... 202 B3
Rutland Rd SL6 .... 202 B3
Rutland St HP11 .... 173 D3
Ryans Mount SL7 .... 183 E1
Rycote La OX9 .... 136 B3
Rycotewood Coll OX9 ...... 125 F1
Rycroft Milton Keynes MK4 .. 46 C2
Windsor SL4 .... 209 F2
Rydal Way
High Wycombe HP12 ...... 172 A3
Milton Keynes MK2 .... 58 B3
Ryder Cl HP3 .... 146 A2
Rydings SL4 .... 209 F2
Rye Cl Aylesbury HP21 .... 115 E2
Maidenhead SL6 .... 202 A2
Rye Ct SL1 .... 206 A2
Rye The LU6 .... 92 A4
Rye View HP13 .... 173 E4
Ryecroft Rd HP5 .... 154 A4
Ryeland MK11 .... 32 C3
Ryeland Cl UB7 .... 208 C4
Rylstone Cl
Maidenhead SL6 .... 202 B2
Milton Keynes MK13 ...... 34 A2
Ryman Ct WD3 .... 167 E2
Rymill Cl HP3 .... 146 A2
Ryton Pl MK4 .... 46 B2
Ryvers Comb Sch SL3 ..... 206 B2
Ryvers Rd SL3 .... 206 C2

Sabina Cl HP12 .... 172 C3
Sacred Heart RC
Prim Sch The RG9 .... 191 E1
Saddington MK6 .... 47 E3
Saddlers Gn MK17 .... 49 D3
Saddlers Pl MK14 .... 35 D3
Sadlers Mews SL6 .... 203 D4
Saffron Cl SL3 .... 211 D3
Saffron Ct **1** HP13 .... 173 E3
Saffron Rd HP13 .... 173 E3
Saffron Rise LU6 .... 92 C3
Saffron St MK2 .... 58 B4
Saham Croft Cl MK18 ...... 65 F2
St Adrian's Cl SL6 .... 202 A2
St Agnes HP6 .... 166 A4
St Aidan's Cl MK3 .... 57 F3
St Alban's Rd MK18 .... 65 F2
St Alban's St SL4 .... 210 B3
St Albans CE **16** SL4 ..... 210 B3
St Andrew's Ave SL4 .... 209 F3
St Andrew's CE Inf Sch
OX9 .... 147 E4
St Andrew's CE Jun Sch
OX9 .... 147 E4
St Andrew's CE Prim Sch
UB8 .... 201 E2
St Andrew's Cl
High Wycombe HP13 ...... 162 C1
Old Windsor SL4 .... 211 D1
Wraysbury TW19 .... 211 F1
St Andrew's Cres SL4 ..... 209 F3
St Andrew's Ho **1** OX9 .. 147 E3
St Andrew's Rd RG9 .... 191 F1
St Andrews Way Ind Est
HP19 .... 101 E1
St Ann's HP10 .... 174 B1
St Ann's Ct HP10 .... 174 B1
St Anne's Cl
Henley-on-T RG9 .... 191 E1
Wendover HP22 .... 131 D3
St Anne's Rd
Aylesbury HP21 .... 115 D4
South Harefield UB9 ...... 190 B4
St Anthony's Cl HP21 ..... 115 D4
St Anthony's Cl HP9 .... 186 B4
St Anthony's Pl MK4 .... 57 D4
St Anthony's RC Comb Sch
SL2 .... 198 B1
St Augustine's RC Comb Sch
HP11 .... 173 D2
St Bartholomew's CE Sch
HP23 .... 119 E1
St Bees MK10 .... 36 A1

St Bernard's Convent Sch
SL3 .... 206 B2
St Bernard's Prep Sch SL1 .206 A2
St Bernard's RC Sec Sch
HP11 .... 173 D2
St Bernards CE **4** HP13 .. 173 E3
St Bernards Rd SL3 .... 206 B2
St Birinus HP10 .... 174 C1
St Botolphs MK10 .... 36 A1
St Brides Cl MK6 .... 35 E1
St Catherine's Ave MK3 ... 57 E3
St Catherine's Ct HP21 ... 115 D4
St Catherine's RC Sch
UB7 .... 208 B2
St Catherines Ct **3** SL4 .. 210 A3
St Chad's Rd SL6 .... 202 A2
St Christopher Rd UB8 .... 208 B4
St Christopher's Cl HP16 . 152 A2
St Christophers Ct WD3 ... 167 E3
St Clement Cl UB8 .... 208 B4
St Clement Danes Sch
WD3 .... 167 E4
St Clement's Dr MK3 .... 57 E3
St-Cloud Way SL6 .... 203 D4
St Columba's Cl SL6 .... 202 A2
St David Cl UB8 .... 208 B4
St David's Cl
Iver Heath SL0 .... 200 B2
Maidenhead SL6 .... 202 A2
St David's Ct NN13 .... 38 A4
St David's Par SL0 .... 200 B2
St David's Rd MK3 .... 57 F3
St Dunstans MK6 .... 47 D3
St Edmund Campion RC
Prim Sch SL6 .... 202 A3
St Edmund's Cl HP21 ...... 115 D4
St Edmund's Rd HP4 ...... 135 E2
St Edward's RC Mid Sch
HP21 .... 116 A4
St Edward's RC Sch SL4 .. 210 A3
St Edwards Ct MK14 .... 34 C4
St Elmo Cl SL2 .... 198 B1
St Elmo Cres SL2 .... 198 B1
St Ethelbert's RC Comb Sch
SL2 .... 206 A4
St Faith's Cl MK17 .... 57 E2
St Francis de Sales Ind RC
Day Sch HP23 .... 118 C2
St Francis Rd
Beacon's Bottom HP14 ... 159 E2
Denham Green UB9 .... 189 F3
St George HP6 .... 166 A4
St George's CE Fst Sch
HP7 .... 165 F4
St George's Cl
High Wycombe HP13 ...... 173 E4
Windsor SL4 .... 209 F3
St George's Cres SL1 ..... 204 B3
St George's Dr UB10 .... 190 C1
St George's Rd MK3 .... 57 F3
St George's Sch SL4 .... 210 B4
St Georges Ct **2** HP12 ... 172 B4
St Georges Ind Est HP7 ... 165 F4
St Georges Way MK12 ..... 33 E4
St Giles Mews MK11 .... 32 B3
St Giles St MK13 .... 33 F4
St Govans Cl MK4 .... 57 D4
St Helen Cl UB8 .... 208 B4
St Hilda's Cl HP21 .... 115 D4
St Hilda's Way HP10 .... 174 A1
St Huberts Cl SL9 .... 188 C1
St Huberts Cotts SL9 ...... 188 C2
St Huberts La SL9 .... 188 C1
St Hugh HP6 .... 166 A4
St Hugh's Ave HP13 .... 173 F3
St Hugh's Cl HP14 .... 158 C2
St Hugh's Pl HP14 .... 158 C2
St Ives Rd SL6 .... 203 D4
St James CtMK19 .... 11 D1
St James Ctyd **4** SL7 .... 183 F1
St James Pl SL1 .... 204 B4
St James St MK13 .... 33 F4
St James Way HP22 .... 102 A2
St James Wlk SL0 .... 207 F2
St John St MK16 .... 22 B2
St John's Ave HP10 .... 174 A4
St John's CE Comb Sch
HP27 .... 149 F2
St John's Cl UB8 .... 201 D2
St John's Ind Est HP10 ... 163 D1
St John's La MK19 .... 31 D2
St John's Rd
Milton Keynes MK15 ...... 57 F3
Tylers Green HP15 .... 162 C1
Uxbridge UB8 .... 201 D2
St John's St HP20 .... 101 F1
St John's Terr MK16 .... 22 B2
St John's Well Ct HP4 ..... 135 D3

St John's Well La HP4 ..... 135 D3
St Johns Cl HP10 .... 163 D1
St Johns Cres MK12 .... 33 E3
St Johns Dr SL4 .... 210 A3
St Johns Rd Slough SL2 .. 206 A3
Stone HP17 .... 114 B3
Tylers Green HP10 .... 163 D1
Windsor SL4 .... 210 A3
St Joseph's Cath High Sch
SL2 .... 206 A4
St Joseph's RC Comb Sch
SL9 .... 188 B4
St Joseph's RC Fst Sch
HP21 .... 116 A4
St Josephs Cl MK46 .... 6 C2
St Jude HP6 .... 166 A4
St Katherine HP6 .... 166 A4
St Katherine's Way HP4 .. 134 C4
St Laurence CE Jun Sch
UB8 .... 208 B4
St Laurence Cl UB8 .... 208 B4
St Laurence Rd MK18 ...... 65 F2
St Laurence Way SL1 ..... 206 A2
St Lawrence Cl HP21 ...... 146 A2
St Lawrence View MK13 ... 34 A2
St Leger Ct MK14 .... 34 C4
St Leger Rd MK14 .... 34 C4
St Leonard's Ave **20** SL4 . 210 B3
St Leonard's Rd
Oakley Green SL4 .... 209 E1
Windsor SL4 .... 210 B2
St Leonard's Way LU6 ...... 92 C1
St Leonards Hill SL4 .... 209 F2
St Leonards Rd HP6 .... 154 C2
St Leonards Wlk SL0 ...... 207 F2
St Louis RC Comb Sch
HP20 .... 101 F1
St Luke HP6 .... 166 A4
St Luke Cl UB8 .... 208 B4
St Luke's CE Prim Sch
SL6 .... 202 C4
St Luke's Rd
Maidenhead SL6 .... 202 C4
Old Windsor SL4 .... 211 D1
Uxbridge UB10 .... 201 F3
St Margaret Cl MK2 .... 58 C4
St Margaret's Cl
Berkhamsted HP4 .... 135 E2
Iver Heath SL0 .... 200 B2
St Margaret's Gate SL0 ... 200 B2
St Margaret's Rd SL6 ...... 202 A4
St Margarets Cl MK16 ...... 22 C2
St Margarets Ct SL0 .... 200 B2
St Margarets Gr HP15 ..... 151 F1
St Mark's Cres SL6 .... 202 A4
St Mark's Hospl SL6 .... 202 B4
St Mark's Pl SL4 .... 210 B3
St Mark's Rd
Aylesbury HP21 .... 115 E4
Henley-on-T RG9 .... 191 F1
Maidenhead SL6 .... 202 B4
Windsor SL4 .... 210 B3
St Martin Cl UB8 .... 208 B4
St Martin's Cl UB7 .... 208 B2
St Martin's Rd UB7 .... 208 B2
St Martin's St MK2 .... 58 B4
St Mary & All Saints CE
Comb Sch HP9 .... 175 F2
St Mary Magdalene RC
Comb Sch MK12 .... 33 D3
St Mary St
High Wycombe HP11 ..... 173 D3
Milton Keynes MK13 ...... 33 F4
St Mary & St Giles CE
Mid Sch MK11 .... 32 C3
St Mary's Ave
Berkhamsted HP4 .... 134 B3
Milton Keynes MK6 .... 57 F4
Milton Keynes, Stony Stratford
MK11 .... 32 C3
St Mary's CE Comb Sch
Amersham HP7 .... 165 D4
Datchet SL3 .... 211 D3
Slough SL1 .... 206 A2
St Mary's CE Fst Sch
HP20 .... 115 E4
St Mary's Cl
Maidenhead SL6 .... 203 D4
South Harefield UB9 ...... 190 A4
Wavendon MK17 .... 48 C4
St Mary's Glebe LU6 .... 92 C2
St Mary's Ind Day Sch
for Girls SL9 .... 188 C4
St Mary's La HP16 .... 142 B3
St Mary's RC JMI Prim Sch
SL6 .... 195 F1
St Mary's RC Prim Sch
Maidenhead SL6 .... 195 F1
Uxbridge UB8 .... 201 E2

St Mary's Rd
Denham Green UB9 .... 189 F3
Slough SL3 .... 206 C2
South Harefield UB9 ...... 190 A4
St Mary's Row **5** HP20 .. 115 E4
St Mary's Sch HP4 .... 134 C3
St Mary's Sq **2** HP20 .... 115 E4
St Mary's Way
Chesham HP5 .... 154 A4
Gerrards Cross SL9 ...... 177 E1
Leighton Buzzard LU7 .... 80 C4
St Mary's Wlk SL6 .... 202 C4
St Marys Ct
East Claydon MK18 .... 74 C4
Mursley MK17 .... 67 E3
St Marys Rd MK18 .... 51 D4
St Matthew Cl UB8 .... 208 B4
St Matthew's CE Prim Sch
UB7 .... 208 C3
St Matthews Ct MK3 .... 57 F3
St Michael's CE Comb Sch
LU7 .... 68 C1
St Michael's Cl HP22 ...... 117 E1
St Michael's Ct SL2 .... 197 E1
St Michael's Green HP9 ... 175 F2
St Michael's Way MK18 ... 63 F2
St Michaels Cl
Halton HP22 .... 131 E4
Stewkley LU7 .... 68 C1
St Michaels Ct MK7 .... 9 F4
St Michaels Dr MK7 .... 47 F4
St Monica's RC Comb Sch
MK14 .... 34 C3
St Nicholas CE Comb Sch
SL6 .... 196 C1
St Nicholas Cl
Cublington LU7 .... 78 A1
Little Chalfont HP6 .... 166 A4
Uxbridge UB8 .... 208 B4
St Patrick's Cl SL6 .... 202 A2
St Patrick's Way MK3 .... 57 F3
St Paul Cl UB8 .... 208 B4
St Paul's CE Comb Sch
HP10 .... 185 E2
St Paul's Rd MK3 .... 57 F3
St Pauls Ave SL2 .... 206 A3
St Pauls Cl MK11 .... 32 B3
St Pauls Sch MK16 .... 46 C4
St Pauls Yd MK16 .... 22 B2
St Peter St SL7 .... 183 F1
St Peter's Ave HP19 .... 101 E2
St Peter's CE Comb Sch
SL1 .... 197 D1
St Peter's (CE) Mid Sch
SL4 .... 210 C1
St Peter's Cl Burnham SL1 . 197 D1
Old Windsor SL4 .... 211 D1
St Peter's Ct **2** SL2 ...... 177 F1
St Peter's Hill HP23 .... 119 D2
St Peter's RC Comb Sch
SL7 .... 183 E2
St Peter's Rd
Brackley NN13 .... 38 A4
Maidenhead SL6 .... 195 E1
Uxbridge UB8 .... 208 B4
St Peters Cl
Lacey Green HP27 .... 150 B2
Loudwater HP10 .... 174 A1
St Peters Gate NN13 .... 38 A4
St Peters Way
Chorleywood WD3 .... 167 D3
Milton Keynes MK13 ...... 34 A4
St Pirans Ind Day Sch
SL6 .... 195 F1
St Rumbold's La MK18 ..... 52 B4
St Stephen's CE Prim Sch
UB7 .... 208 B3
St Stephens Dr MK15 ...... 35 D4
St Teresa's Sch HP27 ..... 139 D2
St Teresas Cl HP27 .... 139 D2
St Thomas Aquinas RC
Comb Sch MK3 .... 57 E4
St Thomas More RC Sch
HP4 .... 135 D2
St Thomas Walk SL3 ...... 212 B4
St Vincents MK2 .... 49 E2
Salden Cl
Drayton Parslow MK17 ... 68 B3
Shenley Church End MK5 .. 46 A3
Salford Rd MK18 .... 49 E4
Salisbury Ave SL2 .... 205 E4
Salisbury Cl
Amersham HP7 .... 165 F4
Princes Risborough HP27 . 139 E2
Salisbury Ct SL6 .... 202 C3
Salisbury Gr MK14 .... 21 F1

Salisbury Mews SL2 .... 198 B1
Salisbury Rd
  High Wycombe HP13 ...... 162 B1
  Uxbridge UB8 .... 201 D2
Salmons La HP16 .... 151 E3
Salt Hill Ave SL1 .... 205 E3
Salt Hill Cl UB8 .... 201 F4
Salt Hill Dr SL1 .... 205 E3
Salt Hill Mansions SL1 ...... 205 E3
Saltash Cl HP10 .... 174 A2
Salter's Cl HP4 .... 134 C3
Salters Cl SL6 .... 203 D4
Salters La HP18 .... 96 B4
Salters Mews MK14 .... 34 C3
Salters Rd SL6 .... 203 D4
Salters Row HP10 .... 186 A2
Salton Link MK4 .... 46 A1
Samphire Ct MK7 .... 48 A3
Sampsons Green SL2 .... 197 F1
Sampsons Hill HP7 .... 164 C1
San Remo Rd MK17 .... 49 F2
Sanctuary Rd HP15 .... 163 D3
Sandage Rd HP14 .... 171 D3
Sandal Ct MK5 .... 46 A3
Sandbrier Cl MK7 .... 48 A3
Sandbrook La HP23 .... 104 B1
Sandels Way HP9 .... 175 E2
Sandelswood End HP9 ...... 175 E3
Sanders La NN12 .... 18 B2
Sanderson Rd UB8 .... 201 E3
Sandford Gdns HP11 .... 173 D2
Sandhill Rd MK18 .... 74 C4
Sandholme MK18 .... 63 F2
Sandhurst Dr MK18 .... 52 B4
Sandisplatt Rd SL6 .... 202 A3
Sandiers End SL2 .... 198 A1
Sandon Cl HP23 .... 118 C2
Sandown Ct MK3 .... 57 E3
Sandown Rd SL2 .... 204 C4
Sandpiper HP20 .... 101 F2
Sandpit Hill MK18 .... 50 C3
Sandpit Hill Cotts HP23 .... 133 D2
Sandpit La HP27 .... 138 A2
Sandpits La HP10 .... 174 B4
Sandringham Ct
  Newport Pagnell MK16 .... 22 A2
  Slough SL1 .... 204 B4
Sandringham Pl MK2 .... 58 B4
Sandringham Rd
  Maidenhead SL6 .... 195 F1
  Stanwell TW19 .... 213 F1
Sands Cty Fst Sch HP12 .... 172 B4
Sands Cty Mid Sch HP12 ... 172 B4
Sands Farm Dr SL1 .... 197 E1
Sands End Fst HP12 .... 172 A4
Sandwell Ct MK8 .... 33 E1
Sandy Cl Buckingham MK18 . 52 C4
  Milton Keynes MK14 .... 34 B4
Sandy La
  Aspley Heath MK17 .... 49 D1
  Leighton Buzzard LU7 ...... 70 C2
  Long Crendon HP18 .... 125 D3
Sandy Mead SL6 .... 203 E1
Sandy Rise SL9 .... 177 F1
Sandycroft Rd HP6 .... 155 E1
Sandygate Cl SL7 .... 183 E2
Sandygate Rd SL7 .... 183 E2
Sandywell Dr MK15 .... 35 D3
Santen Gr MK7 .... 58 B2
Sargeants Cl UB8 .... 201 E1
Sarum Complex UB8 .... 201 D2
Satis Ho SL3 .... 211 E4
Saunders Cl MK7 .... 48 B3
Saunders Cl 🔲 HP13 .... 173 F3
Saunders End HP6 .... 153 E3
Saunders Rd UB10 .... 201 F3
Saunders Wood Copse
  HP14 .... 158 C2
Saunderton Sta HP14 .... 149 E1
Savay Cl UB9 .... 190 A2
Savay La UB9 .... 190 A3
Savernake Rd HP19 .... 101 E2
Savill Way SL7 .... 183 F1
Sawmill Rd HP27 .... 138 B4
Sawpit Hill HP15 .... 163 D3
Sawyer's Cl SL4 .... 209 F4
Sawyers Cl SL6 .... 202 A1
Sawyers Cres SL6 .... 202 A1
Saxeways Bsns Ctr HP16 .. 143 F2
Saxhorn Rd HP14 .... 171 E2
Saxon Cl Amersham HP6 ... 154 B1
  Dunstable LU6 .... 93 F4
  Slough SL3 .... 206 C2
  Uxbridge UB8 .... 208 C4
Saxon Ct
  High Wycombe HP12 .... 172 B4
  Stanwell TW19 .... 213 D1

Saxon Gdns SL6 .... 196 B1
Saxon St
  Milton Keynes, Ashland
  MK1, MK6, MK2, MK14 ..... 47 E2
  Milton Keynes, Leadenhall
  MK1, MK14, MK2 .... 34 B3
Saxon Way
  Harmondsworth UB7 .... 213 E4
  Old Windsor SL4 .... 211 D1
Saye & Sele Cl HP18 .... 82 C3
Sayers Gdns HP4 .... 135 D3
Sayward Cl HP5 .... 144 B1
Scafell Rd SL2 .... 204 C4
Scampton Rd TW19 .... 213 F1
Scarborough Way SL1 ...... 205 D2
Scardale MK13 .... 34 B3
Scarlett Ave HP22 .... 131 F3
Scatterdells La WD4 .... 146 C1
Scatterill Cl MK13 .... 34 A2
Scholars Way HP6 .... 154 C1
Scholars Wlk SL9 .... 177 F2
School Cl
  Great Kingshill HP15 ...... 162 B3
  High Wycombe HP11 .... 173 D2
  High Wycombe, Downley
  HP13 .... 161 E1
  Holmer Green HP15 .... 163 E4
  Ickford HP18 .... 124 A2
School Dr MK17 .... 57 E2
School End MK17 .... 54 C2
School Hill
  Charndon MK18 .... 73 D3
  North Marston MK18 .... 76 A1
School Ho TW19 .... 213 E1
School La Amersham HP7 . 165 D4
  Buckingham MK18 .... 52 B4
  Castlethorpe MK19 .... 19 F3
  Chalfont St Giles HP8 ..... 177 D4
  Chearsley HP18 .... 112 A1
  Cookham SL6 .... 196 A4
  Cookham, Cookham Dean
  SL6 .... 195 D4
  Eaton Bray LU6 .... 92 C3
  Gerrards Cross SL9 .... 177 E1
  Ibstone RG9 .... 169 F2
  Little Marlow SL7 .... 184 B3
  Maidenhead SL6 .... 195 F1
  Medmenham SL7 .... 193 D3
  Milton Keynes MK5 .... 46 A4
  Oakley HP18 .... 109 E3
  Preston Bissett MK18 ...... 62 A4
  Seer Green HP9 .... 176 B2
  Shabbington HP18 .... 124 B2
  Sherington MK16 .... 14 A1
  Stoke Hammond MK17 .... 69 F4
  Stoke Poges SL2 .... 199 D2
  Twyford MK18 .... 62 B1
  Tylers Green HP7 .... 164 A3
  Waddesdon HP18 .... 99 D3
  Waddesdon, Upper Winchendon
  HP18 .... 99 D1
  Weston Turville HP22 ..... 116 C1
  Yardley Gobion NN12 ..... 18 C3
School Rd
  Harmondsworth UB7 .... 213 E4
  Tylers Green HP10 .... 174 B4
  Wooburn Green HP10 ...... 185 F3
School St MK13 .... 33 F4
School The HP23 .... 118 B4
School Way HP11 .... 174 A1
Schorne La MK18 .... 76 A1
Schumann Cl MK7 .... 48 B2
Scotlands Dr SL2 .... 198 A3
Scotney Gdns MK3 .... 57 F4
Scotsgrove Cotts HP17 .... 126 A2
Scotswood Cl HP9 .... 175 E3
Scott Cl
  Farnham Common SL2 .... 198 B4
  West Drayton UB7 .... 208 C1
Scott Dr MK16 .... 22 A3
Scott End HP19 .... 100 C1
Scott Evans Ct MK18 .... 66 A3
Scotts Cl
  Marsh Gibbon OX6 .... 72 A2
  Stoke Hammond MK17 .... 69 F4
Scotts Farm Cl MK18 .... 41 F2
Scotts La Adstock MK18 ... 53 F1
  Marsh Gibbon OX6 .... 71 F1
Scriven Ct MK15 .... 35 F4
Scriveners La MK12 .... 17 D4
Scrubb's La HP14 .... 160 A4
Seacourt Rd SL3 .... 207 D1
Seaford Rd TW19 .... 213 E1
Seagrave Ct MK7 .... 48 A2
Seagrave Rd HP4 .... 175 E2
Sears The LU6 .... 92 A3
Seaton Dr HP21 .... 115 E2
Secklow Gate MK9 .... 34 C2
Second Ave MK1 .... 47 E1
Second Cres SL1 .... 205 E4

Second St HP11 .... 173 E2
Sedgemere MK8 .... 33 E1
Sedgemoor Dr OX9 .... 126 A1
Sedgmoor Gdns HP10 ...... 185 D4
Sedgmoor La HP10 .... 185 D4
Sedgmoor Rd HP10 .... 185 D4
Sedley Gr UB9 .... 190 B4
Sedrup La HP17 .... 114 C2
Seeleys Cl HP9 .... 175 E2
Seeleys Farm HP9 .... 175 E2
Seeleys Rd HP9 .... 175 E2
Seer Green CE Comb Sch
  HP9 .... 176 B2
Seer Green & Jordans Sta
  HP9 .... 176 B2
Seer Green La HP9 .... 176 C2
Seer Mead HP9 .... 176 B2
Sefton Cl SL2 .... 198 C2
Sefton Paddock SL2 .... 199 D3
Sefton Park Cotts SL2 ..... 199 D2
Sefton Way UB8 .... 208 B4
Selbourne Ave MK3 .... 57 F4
Selby Gr MK5 .... 46 A3
Selkirk Ave HP19 .... 101 E1
Selkirk Gr MK3 .... 46 C1
Selwood Cl TW19 .... 213 E1
Selwood Gdns TW19 .... 213 E1
Selwood Way HP13 .... 161 F1
Selworthy MK4 .... 46 B2
Selwyn Cl HP21 .... 116 A3
Selwyn Pl SL1 .... 204 C3
September Ct U88 .... 201 E2
Serjeants Green MK14 ..... 34 C3
Series Cl MK6 .... 47 D3
Serpentine Ct MK2 .... 58 B3
Servite Ho SL6 .... 203 D4
Seven Acre Ho HP10 .... 174 B1
Seven Acres HP18 .... 125 D4
Sevenhills Rd SL0 .... 200 B3
Severalls Ave HP5 .... 144 B1
Severn Cres SL3 .... 212 A4
Severn Dr MK16 .... 22 C2
Severn Ho HP13 .... 173 F4
Severn Way MK3 .... 46 C1
Sewell Cl HP19 .... 100 C1
Seymour Cl
  Flackwell Heath HP10 .... 173 F1
  Maidenhead SL6 .... 202 A2
Seymour Court La SL7 ..... 183 D3
Seymour Court Rd SL7 .... 183 E2
Seymour Ct HP4 .... 134 C3
Seymour Ho
  High Wycombe HP12 .... 172 C3
  Slough SL3 .... 206 C2
Seymour Park Rd SL7 ...... 183 E2
Seymour Plain SL7 .... 183 E3
Seymour Rd
  Berkhamsted HP4 .... 134 C3
  Chalfont St Giles HP8 ..... 177 E3
  Slough SL1 .... 205 D3
Shackleton Ct 🔲 TW19 ... 213 F1
Shackleton Pl MK6 .... 34 C1
Shackleton Rd
  High Wycombe HP12 .... 172 C3
  Slough SL1 .... 205 F3
Shaftesbury Cres MK3 ..... 47 D1
Shaftesbury Ct
  Maidenhead SL6 .... 202 C3
  🔲 Slough SL1 .... 205 F2
Shaftesbury Ho HP21 ...... 116 B4
Shaftesbury St HP11 .... 172 C4
Shaftsbury Cl MK18 .... 65 F3
Shaggy Calf La SL2 .... 206 A3
Shakespear Cl MK16 .... 22 B3
Shakespeare Orch HP18 .. 82 C3
Shakespeare Way HP20 ... 116 A4
Shamrock Cl MK7 .... 48 A3
Shannon Ct Chesham HP5 . 144 B1
  Milton Keynes MK14 .... 35 D1
Shantock Hall La HP3 ...... 145 F1
Shantung Pl HP5 .... 154 B3
Sharman Wlk MK13 .... 34 A2
Sharney Ave SL3 .... 207 D2
Sharp Cl HP21 .... 115 F3
Sharp's Cl HP18 .... 99 D3
Sharrow Vale HP12 .... 172 C4
Shaw Cl Aylesbury HP20 . 116 A4
  Newport Pagnell MK16 .... 22 A3
Shaw Ct Old Windsor SL4 . 211 D1
  Stoke Mandeville HP21 ... 115 F2
Shaw The SL6 .... 195 F3
Shawfield Ct UB7 .... 208 C2
Shaws Cl HP16 .... 151 E3
Shearmans MK11 .... 33 D2
Sheehy Way SL3 .... 206 A3
Sheep St MK18 .... 66 A2
Sheepcoat Cl MK5 .... 46 A3
Sheepcote Cl HP9 .... 175 E2
Sheepcote Cotts HP15 .... 163 E4
Sheepcote Dell Rd HP15 . 163 F4

Sheepcote Gdns UB9 ...... 190 A3
Sheepcote La SL1 .... 186 A1
Sheepcote Rd Eton SL4 ... 205 D1
  Windsor SL4 .... 209 F3
Sheepfold La HP7 .... 165 E4
Sheephouse Rd SL6 .... 196 A1
Sheepridge La
  Bourne End SL7 .... 184 C4
  Flackwell Heath SL7 ...... 184 C4
Sheerstock HP17 .... 126 C3
Sheerwater HP20 .... 101 F2
Sheet St SL4 .... 210 B3
Sheet Street Rd SL4 .... 210 B1
Sheffield Dr HP21 .... 115 F3
Sheffield Rd SL1 .... 205 E4
Shelburne Ct HP12 .... 172 C2
Shelburne Cty Fst Sch
  HP12 .... 172 B2
Shelburne Rd HP12 .... 172 C2
Sheldon Cl MK8 .... 33 F1
Sheldon Rd HP18 .... 124 A2
Shelduck Cl 🔞 HP20 ...... 101 F2
Shelley Cl
  Medmenham SL7 .... 193 E4
  Newport Pagnell MK16 .... 22 A2
  Slough SL3 .... 206 C1
  Wooburn Green HP10 ...... 185 F4
Shelley Dr MK3 .... 57 F4
Shelley Rd Chesham HP5 . 144 A1
  High Wycombe HP11 .... 172 C3
  🔢 Marlow SL7 .... 183 F2
Shellin Gr MK2 .... 58 B2
Shelsmore MK14 .... 35 D4
Shelton Ct Slough SL3 ..... 206 B2
  Wooburn Sands MK17 ..... 49 D2
Sheney Rd MK3 .... 57 F4
Shenley Brook End Sch
  MK3 .... 47 D1
Shenley Rd Milton Keynes
  MK17, MK3, MK5 .... 46 C1
  Shenley Church End MK5 . 46 A3
  Whaddon MK17 .... 56 A4
Shenley Rdbt MK5 .... 46 A3
Shenley Rise MK18 .... 66 A2
Shenley Way HP5 .... 154 B3
Shepherdswell Cty Fst Sch
  MK6 .... 35 D1
Sheppards Cl MK16 .... 22 B2
Sheppards La MK18 .... 66 A1
Shepperds Gn MK5 .... 45 F3
Shepperton Cl MK19 .... 19 F3
Sheraton Dr HP13 .... 162 B1
Sheraton Ho WD3 .... 167 E3
Sherborne Cl SL3 .... 212 C3
Sherborne Ct SL6 .... 202 C3
Sherborne Dr
  Bow Brickhill MK7 .... 48 A2
  Maidenhead SL6 .... 202 B2
  Windsor SL4 .... 209 F2
Sherborne Wlk SL2 .... 198 B4
Shergold Way SL6 .... 195 F3
Sheridan Cl HP21 .... 115 E2
Sheridan Ct
  Maidenhead SL6 .... 203 D4
  Slough SL1 .... 204 C3
Sheriff Cl HP21 .... 115 D4
Sherington CE Fst Sch
  MK16 .... 14 A1
Sherington Rd
  Lathbury MK16 .... 22 C4
  Sherington MK16 .... 22 C4
Sherman Rd SL1 .... 205 F4
Shernfold MK7 .... 48 A4
Sherriff Cotts HP18 .... 99 D4
Sherwood Cl SL3 .... 206 C2
Sherwood Ct
  Colnbrook SL3 .... 212 B4
  Slough SL3 .... 206 C1
Sherwood Dr
  Maidenhead SL6 .... 202 A3
  Milton Keynes MK3 .... 47 D1
Shields Ct HP10 .... 163 D1
Shifford Cres SL6 .... 195 F2
Shilling Cl MK15 .... 35 D4
Shillingridge Pk SL7 .... 182 C3
Shinfield Cl MK18 .... 63 E1

Ship Hill SL1 .... 186 C2
Ship Rd LU7 .... 80 C3
Ship St HP11 .... 173 D4
Shiplake Ho SL8 .... 185 D2
Shipley Rd MK16 .... 22 A2
Shipman Ct MK15 .... 35 D4
Shipton Hill MK13 .... 34 A3
Shipton Rd U88 .... 201 F4
Shire Ct MK14 .... 35 D3
Shire La
  Chalfont St Peter SL9 ..... 178 A3
  Cholesbury HP23 .... 133 D2
  Chorleywood WD3 .... 167 E2
  Hastoe HP23 .... 133 D2
  North Crawley MK16 .... 24 B2
Shires Bsns Pk The NN13 . 38 A3
Shires Rd MK18 .... 38 A3
Shirley Ave SL4 .... 209 F3
Shirley Moor MK7 .... 48 A4
Shirley Rd SL6 .... 202 B3
Shirwell Cres MK5 .... 46 B3
Shogmoor La RG9 .... 170 B1
Sholto Rd TW19 .... 213 F1
Shootacre Cnr HP27 .... 149 D4
Shootacre La
  Lacey Green HP27 .... 149 D4
  Princes Risborough HP27 . 149 D4
Shootersway HP4 .... 134 C2
Shootersway La HP4 .... 134 C2
Shootersway Park HP4 .... 134 C2
Shop La NN7 .... 1 A3
Shoppenhanger's Rd SL6 . 202 C2
Shoredicke Cl UB10 .... 190 C1
Shoreham Rd (E) TW19 ... 213 F1
Shoreham Rd (W) TW19 .. 213 F1
Shoreham Rise SL2 .... 197 E1
Shorham Rise MK8 .... 33 F1
Short Massey MK46 .... 6 C3
Short Rd TW19 .... 213 F1
Short St HP11 .... 172 C4
Shortborough Ave HP27 . 139 D3
Shortfern SL2 .... 206 B4
Shortway Amersham HP6 . 154 B1
  Chesham HP5 .... 144 A1
Shotfield Rd HP14 .... 171 E2
Shothanger Way HP3 ...... 146 B3
Shouler Cl MK5 .... 46 A3
Shrimpton Cl HP9 .... 175 E3
Shrimpton Rd
  Beaconsfield HP9 .... 175 E3
  High Wycombe HP12 ...... 172 A2
Shrubbery Rd HP13 .... 173 D4
Shrublands Ave HP4 .... 135 D2
Shrublands Rd HP4 .... 135 D3
Shugars Gn HP23 .... 119 D3
Shupp's La HP18 .... 112 A1
Shutlanger Rd NN12 .... 9 D4
Shuttleworth Gr MK7 ...... 48 B3
Sibleys Rise HP16 .... 152 B4
Side Rd UB9 .... 189 E2
Sidings Ind Est The NN13 . 38 A4
Sidlow Ct MK11 .... 32 C2
Sidney Rd SL4 .... 209 E2
Sidney Terr HP22 .... 131 D3
Silbury Arc MK9 .... 34 C2
Silbury Bvd MK9 .... 34 B1
Silbury Rdbt MK9 .... 34 B1
Silchester Ho SL6 .... 203 D4
Silchester House Sch SL3 . 203 E4
Silco Dr SL2 .... 202 C3
Silicon Ct MK5 .... 46 B3
Silk Mill Way HP23 .... 119 D3
Silk St HP18 .... 99 D3
Sillswood MK46 .... 6 C2
Silsden Cres HP8 .... 177 E4
Silver Birch Cl UB10 .... 201 F4
Silver Cl SL6 .... 202 A3
Silver End MK46 .... 7 D2
Silver Hill HP8 .... 177 D4
Silver St
  🔲 Aylesbury HP20 .... 115 E4
  Cublington LU7 .... 78 A1
  Milton Keynes MK11 .... 32 B3
  Newport Pagnell MK16 .... 22 B2
Silverbirches La MK17 .... 49 D1
Silverdale Cl
  🔲 Aylesbury HP20 .... 101 E1
  Tylers Green HP10 .... 163 D1
Silvermead HP18 .... 123 E3
Silverstone Motor Racing
  Circuit MK18 .... 28 C4
Silvertrees Dr SL6 .... 202 A3
Silverweed Ct MK7 .... 48 A3
Simatt Ho HP10 .... 174 B1
Simdims MK43 .... 25 D1
Simmons Cl SL3 .... 207 D1
Simmons Ct HP21 .... 115 F2
Simmons Rd RG9 .... 191 E2
Simmons Way
  Lane End HP14 .... 171 E2
  Thame OX9 .... 125 F1

Simnel MK6 .... 47 D3
Simon Dean HP3 .... 146 A2
Simons Lea MK13 .... 34 A2
Simonsbath MK4 .... 46 B1
Simpson Cl SL6 .... 203 D4
Simpson Cty Comb Sch
  MK6 .... 47 E3
Simpson Dr MK6 .... 47 F3
Simpson PI HP21 .... 115 F3
Simpson Rd Milton Keynes
  MK1, MK2, MK6 .... 47 F2
  Walton MK1, MK2, MK6 ... 47 F2
Sinclair Ct MK1 .... 47 D2
Singer La RG9 .... 191 F1
Singleborough La MK17 ... 54 C2
Singret PI UB8 .... 201 E1
Sion Terr MK18 .... 51 D3
Sipson Rd UB7 .... 208 C2
Sipthorp Cl MK7 .... 48 B3
Sir Frank Markham Sch
  .... 47 D4
Sir Henry Floyd Gram Sch
  .... 115 E4
Sir William Borlase's
  Gram Sch SL7 .... 183 E1
Sir William Ramsay Sch
  HP15 .... 163 D2
Sitwell Cl MK16 .... 21 F3
Sixth St HP11 .... 173 E2
Sixty Acres Rd HP16 ..... 151 E3
Skeats Wharf MK15 .... 35 D4
Skeldon Gate MK9 .... 35 D2
Skeldon Rdbt MK9 .... 35 D2
Skelton Cl HP9 .... 186 A4
Skene Cl MK2 .... 58 B2
Skerries Ct SL3 .... 207 D1
Skimmers Cl HP15 .... 163 E3
Skimmers End HP15 .... 163 E3
Skimmers Field HP15 ..... 163 E3
Skippon Way OX9 .... 125 F1
Skipton Cl MK15 .... 35 E3
Skittle Green HP27 .... 138 A1
Skydmore Path SL2 .... 197 F1
Skylark Rd UB9 .... 189 E2
Skyport Dr UB7 .... 213 E4
Skytech Ctr SL3 .... 212 C2
Skyway 14 Trad Est SL3 ... 212 C2
Slad La HP27 .... 149 F2
Slade Hill HP21 .... 115 D4
Slade La MK11 .... 33 D2
Slade Oak La UB9 .... 189 E3
Slade Rd HP14 .... 158 C2
Slade The MK17 .... 57 E2
Slapton La LU6 .... 91 F3
Slated Row MK12 .... 33 D4
Slated Row Sch MK12 ...... 33 D4
Slater St HP13 .... 173 E3
Slattenham Cl HP21 ...... 115 D4
Slave Hill HP17 .... 126 C3
Slayter Rd HP14 .... 171 E2
Slickett's La LU6 .... 92 C2
Slipe The LU7 .... 105 D4
Slough & Eton Comp Sch
  SL1 .... 205 E2
Slough Gram Sch SL3 .... 206 A2
Slough Rd Datchet SL3 ... 211 D4
  Eton SL4 .... 205 F1
  Iver Heath SL0 .... 200 C2
  Slough SL3 .... 205 F1
Slough Trad Est SL1 ...... 205 D4
Sly Cnr HP16 .... 142 C2
Smabridge Wlk MK15 .... 35 E4
Small Cres MK18 .... 52 C4
Smalldean La HP14, HP27 ... 149 F1
Smarden Bell MK7 .... 48 A4
Smeaton Cl
  Aylesbury HP19 .... 100 C3
  Milton Keynes MK14 ..... 22 A1
Smith Cl HP20 .... 116 A4
Smith Hospl RG9 .... 191 D3
Smith's La SL4 .... 209 F3
Smithergill Ct MK13 .... 34 B3
Smithfield End MK17 .... 66 C2
Smithfield Rd SL6 .... 202 A2
Smithsons PI MK9 .... 35 D2
Smithstore Cres MK5 .... 46 A4
Snakeley Cl HP10 .... 174 B1
Snape Spur SL1 .... 205 F4
Snells Wood Ct HP7 ...... 166 B4
Snelshall St MK4 .... 56 C4
Snowball Hill SL6 .... 202 A1
Snowberry Cl MK12 .... 33 E3
Snowden Cl SL4 .... 209 E2
Snowdon Dr MK4 .... 46 B4
Snowdrop Way HP15 ...... 162 C4
Snowhill Cotts HP5 .... 144 C4
Snowshill Ct MK14 .... 21 F1
Soane Wlk HP13 .... 173 D4
Soho Cres HP10 .... 185 E2
Soho Mills Ind Est HP10 ... 185 E2

Sokeman Cl MK12 .... 33 D3
Solar Ct MK14 .... 21 F1
Solent Rd HP19 .... 213 F1
Solesbridge Cl WD3 ...... 167 F3
Solesbridge La WD3 ...... 167 F3
Solters Cl HP18 .... 96 B4
Somerford Cl MK6 .... 203 D4
Somerford PI HP9 .... 175 E2
Somersby Cres SL6 .... 202 C2
Somerset Cl MK3 .... 46 C1
Somerset Lodge 3 SL6 ... 202 C3
Somerset Way SL0 .... 207 F2
Somerville Rd SL4 .... 205 E1
Somerville Way HP21 ..... 115 D4
Sorrell Dr MK16 .... 21 F2
Soskin Dr MK14 .... 34 B3
Sospel Ct SL2 .... 198 B2
Soulbury Rd
  Leighton Buzzard LU7 ... 80 B4
  Stewkley LU7 .... 68 C1
  Wing LU7 .... 79 E2
South Bank Rd HP4 .... 134 C3
South Cl Burnham SL1 ... 204 B3
  Medmenham SL7 .... 193 E4
  West Drayton UB7 .... 208 C2
South Common Rd UB8 ... 201 F3
South Cott Dr WD3 .... 167 F2
South Cotts Gdns WD3 ... 167 F2
South Cres MK17 .... 79 E4
South Dr Beaconsfield HP9 ... 186 A4
  High Wycombe HP13 ... 173 E4
South Eighth St MK9 .... 34 C1
South End HP17 .... 126 C3
South End La LU6 .... 92 A2
South Enmore Rdbt MK6 ... 35 D2
South Field Cl SL4 .... 204 B2
South Fifth St MK9 .... 34 C1
South Fourth St MK9 .... 34 B1
South Green SL1 .... 205 F3
South Hills HP18 .... 96 A1
South Hollow MK1 .... 47 E2
South Lawne MK3 .... 57 F4
South Maundin HP14 ...... 162 A4
South Meadow La SL4 .... 210 B4
South Ninth St MK9 .... 34 C1
South Overgate Rdbt MK6 ... 35 D2
South Park SL9 .... 188 C3
South Park Ave WD3 ...... 167 F2
South Park Cres SL6 ...... 188 C4
South Park Dr SL9 .... 188 C4
South Park Gdns HP4 ..... 135 D3
South Park View SL9 ...... 188 C4
South Path SL4 .... 210 B3
South PI SL7 .... 183 F1
Southall Cty Comb Sch
  SL7 .... 183 D3
Spinfield La SL7 .... 183 D3
Spinfield Mount SL7 ...... 183 D1
Spinfield Park SL7 .... 183 D1
Spinners Wlk Marlow SL7 ... 183 E1
  Windsor SL4 .... 210 B3
Spinney SL1 .... 205 D3
Spinney Bglws LU7 .... 91 E3
Spinney Cl
  Steeple Claydon MK18 ... 63 F1
  West Drayton UB7 .... 208 C3
Spinney Cres LU6 .... 93 F4
Spinney Hill Rd MK46 ...... 6 C2
Spinney La MK17 .... 49 F2
Spinney The
  Berkhamsted HP4 .... 134 C2
  Chesham HP5 .... 144 B1
  High Wycombe HP11 ... 173 E2
  Holmer Green HP15 .... 163 E4
  Milton Keynes MK13 .... 34 A3
  Winslow MK18 .... 66 A3
Spinneys The HP13 .... 174 A4
Spittal St SL7 .... 183 E1
Spoonbill La HP22 .... 99 E3
Spooney Wood MK13 .... 33 F3
Sportsfield App HP9 ...... 176 B3
Sportsman Cl MK18 .... 63 E2
Spout La TW19 .... 213 D2
Spout La N TW19 .... 213 D2
Sprigs Holly La HP14 ..... 159 D4
Spring Cl
  Great Horwood MK17 .... 55 D1
  High Wycombe HP13 ... 173 F4
  Latimer HP5 .... 155 E2
  Maidenhead SL6 .... 195 F3
Spring Coppice HP14 ..... 171 F3
Spring Coppice La
  Prestwood HP27 .... 150 B3
  Walter's Ash HP27 ...... 150 B3
Spring Field Rd HP4 ...... 135 D3
Spring Gardens Arts Ctr
  HP11 .... 173 E3
Spring Gardens Rd 6
  HP13 .... 173 F3
Spring Gdns
  Bourne End SL8 .... 185 D2
  Marlow SL7 .... 183 F2

Southfield Gdns SL1 ..... 204 A4
Southfield Rd
  Aylesbury HP20 .... 116 A4
  Flackwell Heath HP10 ... 174 A1
  High Wycombe HP13 ... 161 E1
  Princes Risborough HP27 ... 139 E2
Southgate Ho SL6 .... 202 C4
Southlea Rd SL3 .... 211 D3
Southview Rd SL7 .... 183 F2
Southwick Ct MK8 .... 45 F4
Southwold Cl HP21 .... 116 A3
Southwood Spur SL3 ..... 207 E2
Southwood Cty Mid Sch
  MK13 .... 34 C3
Southwood Gdns SL6 .... 195 F3
Southwood Rd SL6 .... 195 F3
Sovereign Cl MK18 .... 75 F4
Sovereign Ct
  Aylesbury HP20 .... 101 E1
  High Wycombe HP13 ... 173 E3
Sovereign Dr MK15 .... 35 D4
Sovereign Lodge MK15 ... 35 D4
Spa Cl HP18 .... 110 A4
Spackmans Way SL1 ..... 205 E2
Spade Oak Meadow SL8 ... 184 C2
Spark Way MK16 .... 21 F3
Sparrow Cl HP20 .... 101 F2
Sparsholt Cl MK4 .... 46 B1
Spearing Rd HP12 .... 172 B3
Spearmint Cl MK7 .... 48 A3
Specklands MK5 .... 46 A4
Speedwell PI MK14 .... 34 C2
Speen CE First Sch HP27 ... 150 A2
Speen Rd
  HP14, HP16, HP27 ..... 150 B1
Speldhurst Ct MK7 .... 48 A4
Spen MK4 .... 34 B4
Spencer Cl UB8 .... 201 E1
Spencer Rd SL3 .... 206 C2
Spencer St MK13 .... 33 F4
Spencers Cl SL6 .... 202 B4
Spencers La SL6 .... 195 F3
Spencers Rd SL6 .... 202 B4
Spenlows Rd MK3 .... 47 D2
Spenser Ho HP21 .... 115 F3
Spenser Rd HP21 .... 115 F3
Sperling Rd SL6 .... 195 F1
Spickett's La HP18 .... 113 D2
Spier's La OX6 .... 71 F1
Spiert The HP18 .... 114 B3
Spindle Cl HP15 .... 163 D2
Spindle Ct 9 HP22 ...... 172 C4
Spinfield Cty Comb Sch
  SL7 .... 183 D3

Spring Gdns
  Newport Pagnell MK16 .... 22 B2
  Wooburn Green HP10 ... 185 F4
Spring La Alderton NN12 ... 9 D1
  Clifton Reynes MK43 ...... 7 E2
  Cookham SL6 .... 195 E3
  Farnham Common SL2 ... 198 B3
  Flackwell Heath HP10 ... 173 F2
  Great Horwood MK17 .... 55 D1
  Olney MK46 .... 6 C2
  Slough SL1 .... 204 C3
Spring Meadow HP18 ...... 97 D1
Spring Valley Dr HP14 .... 162 A4
Springate Field SL3 ...... 206 C2
Springett PI HP6 .... 154 C1
Springfield Olney MK46 ... 6 C2
  Slough SL1 .... 206 A2
Springfield Bvd MK6 .... 35 D1
Springfield Cl
  Chesham HP5 .... 154 B4
  Windsor SL4 .... 210 A3
Springfield Ct
  13 Leighton Buzzard LU7 ... 80 C4
  Maidenhead SL6 .... 203 D4
  Milton Keynes MK6 .... 35 D1
Springfield Cty Mid Sch
  MK6 .... 35 D1
Springfield Gdns
  Chinnor OX9 .... 147 E4
  Deanshanger MK19 ..... 31 F2
Springfield La SL7 .... 183 D1
Springfield Park SL6 ...... 203 D4
Springfield Rd
  Eaton Bray LU6 .... 93 E3
  Leighton Buzzard LU7 ... 80 B4
  Stokenchurch HP14 .... 158 C2
  Windsor SL4 .... 210 A3
Springfield Rdbt MK6 ...... 35 D1
Springfield Way MK43 ..... 25 E1
Springfields
  Amersham HP6 .... 154 B1
  Padbury MK18 .... 53 E1
  Tylers Green HP10 ...... 163 E1
Springfields Cl MK18 ...... 53 E1
Springfields Ct MK18 ..... 53 E1
Springhill (HM Prison)
  HP18 .... 73 D1
Springhill Rd HP18 .... 83 D4
Springs Cl HP17 .... 130 A1
Springs La HP17 .... 130 A2
Springside 14 LU7 .... 80 C4
Springwater Mill HP11 ... 173 F2
Springwood HP27 .... 150 B2
Spruce Ct 20 SL1 .... 205 F2
Spruce Dene HP15 .... 162 C1
Spur The SL1 .... 204 B4
Spurgrove La RG9 .... 170 C1
Spurlands End Rd HP15 ... 162 C4
Spurt La HP18 .... 112 C2
Square Close Cotts RG9 ... 169 F2
Square The Akeley MK18 ... 41 F4
  Aspley Guise MK17 .... 49 F3
  Harmondsworth TW6 ... 213 D3
  Long Crendon HP18 .... 125 E3
  Milton Keynes MK12 .... 33 E3
  Preston Bissett MK18 .... 62 A4
  South Heath HP16 ...... 152 A4
  Waddesdon HP18 .... 99 D3
  Yardley Hastings NN7 ... 1 A3
Squires Cl MK6 .... 47 D3
Squirrel La HP12 .... 172 B3
Squirrel Rise SL7 .... 183 E3
Squirrels Way MK18 .... 52 C4
Stable Cl MK18 .... 50 B4
Stable Cotts SL7 .... 194 B2
Stable La HP9 .... 176 B2
Stable Rd HP22 .... 131 F4
Stablebridge Rd HP22 ... 117 F2
Stables Ct SL7 .... 183 D1
Stacey Ave MK12 .... 33 F2
Stacey Bushes Trad Ctr
  MK12 .... 33 F2
Stacey Ho HP12 .... 172 C2
Stacey's Ct HP8 .... 177 E4
Stafferton Way SL6 .... 203 D3
Stafford Ave SL2 .... 198 B1
Stafford Cl SL6 .... 204 A4
Stafford Gr MK5 .... 46 A3
Stag Ct WD3 .... 157 F1
Stag La Berkhamsted HP4 ... 135 D3
  Chorleywood WD3 ...... 167 F2
  Great Kingshill HP15 ... 151 E1
Stainby Cl UB7 .... 208 C2
Stainton Dr MK13 .... 34 B2
Stamford Ave MK6 .... 35 D1
Stamford Rd SL6 .... 203 D3
Stanbridge Cl HP27 ...... 127 D4
Stanbridge Ct MK11 .... 32 C3
Stanbridge Rd HP17 ...... 127 D3

Standing Way
  MK10, MK4, MK6 .... 47 E4
Standring PI MK20 .... 101 F1
Stanhope Cl HP22 .... 131 D4
Stanhope Heath TW19 ... 213 E1
Stanhope Rd
  Aylesbury HP20 .... 116 A4
  Slough SL1 .... 204 B4
Stanhope Way TW19 ..... 213 E1
Stanier Rise HP4 .... 134 C4
Stanier Sq 8 MK2 .... 58 B4
Stanley Ave HP5 .... 154 A4
Stanley Cl Marlow SL7 ... 183 F2
  Uxbridge UB8 .... 201 E2
Stanley Cotts SL2 .... 205 F3
Stanley Cl MK46 .... 6 C2
Stanley Gdns HP23 ...... 118 C2
Stanley Green E SL3 ..... 206 C1
Stanley Green W SL3 .... 206 C1
Stanley Hill HP7 .... 165 F4
Stanley Hill Ave HP7 .... 165 F4
Stanley Ho SL4 .... 211 D1
Stanley Rd HP12 .... 172 B4
Stanmore Gdns MK14 .... 22 A1
Stanstead PI HP7 .... 165 E4
Stanton Ave MK13 .... 34 A3
Stanton Cty Mid Sch
  .... 34 A4
Stanton Gate MK13 .... 34 B4
Stanton Way SL3 .... 206 C1
Stantonbury Campus
  MK13 .... 34 B4
Stanway Cl MK15 .... 35 D3
Stanwell Cl TW19 .... 213 E1
Stanwell Gdns TW19 ..... 213 E1
Stanwell Moor Rd
  Harmondsworth
  TW6, TW19 .... 213 D2
  Stanwell TW6, TW19 ... 213 D2
Stanwell Rd Horton SL3 ... 212 B2
  Stanwell SL3 .... 212 B2
Staple Hall Rd MK1 .... 47 F1
Stapleton Cl SL7 .... 183 F2
Stars La HP17 .... 113 F1
Startins La SL6 .... 195 E4
Starveall Cl UB7 .... 208 C3
Starwood Ct SL3 .... 206 B2
Staters Pound MK15 .... 35 D4
Statham PI MK6 .... 46 C4
Station App
  Amersham HP6, HP7 ... 154 B1
  Chorleywood WD3 ...... 167 E3
  Denham Green UB9 ..... 189 E2
  Gerrards Cross SL9 .... 188 C3
  Little Chalfont HP6 ..... 166 B4
  Maidenhead SL6 .... 202 C3
  Marlow SL7 .... 183 F1
  South Heath HP16 ...... 152 A4
  Wendover HP22 .... 131 D2
  West Drayton UB7 ...... 208 C3
Station Cotts UB9 .... 189 F2
Station Hill SL6 .... 195 F4
Station Par
  Beaconsfield HP9 .... 175 E2
  Cookham SL6 .... 195 F3
  Denham Green UB9 .... 190 A2
Station Rd Aldbury HP23 ... 120 A3
  Amersham HP6, HP7 ... 165 E4
  Berkhamsted HP4 .... 135 E2
  Blackthorn OX6 .... 81 D2
  Bourne End SL8 .... 185 D2
  Bow Brickhill MK17 ..... 48 B3
  Buckingham MK18 .... 52 B4
  Castlethorpe MK19 ...... 19 F3
  Chesham HP5 .... 154 B4
  Chinnor OX9 .... 147 E3
  Cookham SL6 .... 195 F4
  Gerrards Cross SL9 .... 188 C3
  Haddenham HP17 .... 126 C3
  Henley-on-T RG9 .... 191 F1
  High Wycombe HP13 ... 173 E3
  Ivinghoe LU7 .... 105 F3
  Leighton Buzzard LU7 ... 80 C4
  Long Marston HP23 ..... 104 A2
  Loudwater HP10 .... 174 B1
  Marlow SL7 .... 183 F1
  Marsh Gibbon OX6 .... 71 F2
  Mentmore LU7 .... 91 D1
  Mursley MK17 .... 67 D4
  Newport Pagnell MK16 ... 22 B2
  Padbury MK18 .... 53 D1
  Princes Risborough HP27 ... 139 D1
  Quainton HP22 .... 85 D2
  Slough SL1 .... 204 C4
  Slough, Langley SL3 .... 207 D2
  Stoke Mandeville HP22 ... 116 A1
  Taplow SL6 .... 203 F4

Station Rd
Tring HP23 .... 119 E2
Uxbridge UB8 .... 201 E1
West Drayton UB7 .... 208 C2
Winslow MK18 .... 66 A3
Woburn Sands MK17 .... 49 D3
Wraysbury TW19 .... 212 A1
Station Rise SL7 .... 183 F1
Station St HP20 .... 115 F4
Station Terr
Buckingham MK18 .... 52 B4
Milton Keynes MK14 .... 21 F1
Station Way HP20 .... 115 E4
Staunton Rd SL2 .... 205 E4
Staveley Cl HP21 .... 116 B3
Stavordale MK10 .... 36 A1
Staying La MK14 .... 34 C3
Stephenson Cl
Aylesbury HP21 .... 115 D4
High Wycombe HP13 ...... 161 F1
Leighton Buzzard LU7 ...... 80 C3
Stephenson Ct **21** SL1 ... 205 F2
Stephenson Dr SL4 .... 210 A4
Stepnells HP23 .... 105 D1
Steppingstones LU6 .... 93 F4
Stevens Cl
Holmer Green HP15 .... 162 B4
Prestwood HP16 .... 151 E3
Stevens Field MK7 .... 48 B3
Stevens Ho HP7 .... 165 D4
Stevenson Rd SL2 .... 187 E1
Stewart Ave SL1 .... 205 F4
Stewarts Dr SL2 .... 198 A4
Stewarts Way SL7 .... 183 E4
Stewkley La MK17 .... 67 F2
Stewkley Rd
Cublington LU7 .... 78 B1
Soulbury LU7 .... 69 E1
Wing LU7 .... 79 D4
Stile Meadow HP9 .... 175 F2
Stile Rd SL3 .... 206 B2
Stilebrook Rd MK46 .... 6 C2
Stirling Ave HP20 .... 101 F1
Stirling Cl
Milton Keynes MK15 .... 35 D3
Uxbridge UB8 .... 201 E1
Windsor SL4 .... 209 E3
Stirling Ho
2 High Wycombe HP13 ... 173 F4
Milton Keynes MK3 .... 57 E4
Stirling Rd Slough SL1 .... 205 D4
Stanwell TW19 .... 213 F1
Stock Field Cl HP15 .... 163 D2
Stock La MK17 .... 45 D1
Stockdale MK13 .... 34 B3
Stockdales Rd SL4 .... 204 C1
Stocken Cl MK46 .... 6 C2
Stockgrove Country Pk
LU7 .... 70 C4
Stockhall Cres LU7 .... 64 B8
Stocking Green Cl MK19 .. 11 D2
Stocking La HP14 .... 161 F4
Stocklake Aylesbury HP20 .. 101 F1
Bierton HP20 .... 101 F1
Stocklands Way HP16 .... 151 E3
Stockleys La MK18 .... 51 D3
Stockport Rd WD3 .... 167 E1
Stocks Rd HP23 .... 120 B4
Stocks The MK19 .... 19 F1
Stockway HP22 .... 87 E1
Stockwell HP17 .... 127 D3
Stockwell Furlong HP17 .. 127 D3
Stockwell La
Longwick HP27 .... 139 D4
Wendover MK17 .... 48 A4
Stockwells SL6 .... 196 B1
Stoke Bruerne CE Sch
NN12 .... 9 D4
Stoke Common Rd
Fulmer SL3 .... 199 D4
Stoke Poges SL3 .... 199 D4
Stoke Court Dr SL2 .... 198 C2
Stoke Farm La HP21 ..... 115 F2
Stoke Gdns SL1 .... 205 F3
Stoke Gn SL2 .... 199 D1
Stoke Goldington CE Fest Sch
MK16 .... 12 A3
Stoke La MK17 .... 59 F2
Stoke Leys Sch HP21 .... 115 F2
Stoke Mandeville Cty
Comb Sch HP22 .... 116 A1
Stoke Mandeville Hospl
HP21 .... 115 F2
Stoke Mandeville Sta
HP22 .... 116 A1
Stoke Park Ave SL2 ...... 198 B1
Stoke Poges Cty Fst Sch
SL2 .... 199 D3

Stoke Poges La SL1, SL2 ... 205 F4
Stoke Poges Sch The SL2 198 C3
Stoke Rd Ashton NN7 .... 9 F4
Aylesbury HP21 .... 115 F3
Leighton Buzzard LU7 ..... 70 C1
Milton Keynes MK2 .... 58 C3
Newton Longville MK17 .... 57 F2
Slough SL2 .... 205 F4
Stoke View SL1 .... 205 F3
Stoke Wood SL2 .... 198 C4
Stokenchurch Cty Fst Sch
HP14 .... 158 C2
Stokenchurch Cty Mid Sch
HP14 .... 158 C2
Stokenchurch Pl MK13 ... 34 B2
Stokes Croft HP17 .... 127 D4
Stokes End HP17 .... 127 D4
Stokes La HP17 .... 127 D4
Stokesay SL2 .... 205 F3
Stokesley Rise HP10 ..... 185 F4
Stomp Rd SL1 .... 204 A4
Stompits Rd SL6 .... 203 E1
Stone CE Comb Sch
HP17 .... 114 B3
Stone Cl UB7 .... 208 C3
Stone Croft HP17 .... 114 B3
Stone Ct MK46 .... 13 F4
Stone Hill MK8 .... 33 E1
Stone House La SL6 ...... 184 B1
Stone View HP22 .... 86 B3
Stonebridge Field SL4 ... 205 D1
Stonebridge Rd HP19 ... 101 D2
Stonebridge Rdbt MK13 .. 33 F4
Stonechat HP20 .... 101 F2
Stonecroft HP16 .... 153 E2
Stonecroft Ave SL0 ...... 200 F4
Stonecrop Pl MK14 .... 34 C2
Stonefield Pk SL6 .... 202 B4
Stonefield Rd HP14 ...... 161 E4
Stonegate MK13 .... 34 B3
Stonehaven Rd HP19 ... 101 D1
Stones Row HP11 .... 173 F2
Stones Way MK17 .... 68 B3
Stoney Cl HP4 .... 134 C3
Stoney Croft HP23 .... 120 B3
Stoney Dean Sch HP7 ... 165 F4
Stoney Grove HP5 .... 144 C2
Stoney La Bovingdon HP3 . 146 B3
Burnham SL2 .... 198 A2
Chipperfield WD4 .... 146 C1
Stoney Meade SL1 .... 205 D3
Stoney Ware SL7 .... 194 C4
Stoney Ware Cl SL7 ...... 194 C4
Stonor Ct MK8 .... 45 F4
Stonor Ho RG9 .... 180 A4
Stony Hill NN12 .... 34 B2
Stony La Cheenies HP6 .. 155 F1
Little Chalfont HP6 .... 166 C4
Little Kingshill HP16 ..... 152 B2
Stooksdale HP22 .... 89 E4
Stork Cl **8** HP20 .... 101 F2
Stotfold Ct MK11 .... 32 C2
Stour Cl Aylesbury HP21 ... 115 E2
Milton Keynes MK3 .... 57 F4
Newport Pagnell MK16 .... 22 C2
Slough SL1 .... 205 D2
Stovell Rd SL4 .... 210 A4
Stowe Ave SL6 .... 41 D2
Stowe Cl MK18 .... 44 C4
Stowe Cl MK14 .... 34 B4
Stowe Gardens MK18 .... 40 C4
Stowe Rd SL1 .... 204 C3
Stowe Rise MK18 .... 41 E1
Stowe Sch MK18 .... 40 C4
Stowe View MK18 .... 51 D4
Straight Bit HP10 .... 185 D4
Straight Rd SL4 .... 211 D1
Strand La SL6 .... 195 F3
Strand The HP22 .... 85 D3
Strand View Wlk SL6 ..... 195 F3
Strangers La MK18 .... 51 D3
Strangford Dr MK2 .... 58 B3
Stranraer Gdns SL1 ...... 205 F3
Stranraer Rd **3** TW19 ... 213 F1
Stranraer Way **2** TW19 . 213 F1
Stratfield Ct
Maidenhead SL6 .... 203 D4
Milton Keynes MK8 .... 33 F1
Stratfield Rd SL1 .... 205 D2
Stratford Arc MK11 .... 32 B3
Stratford Ave UB10 .... 201 F2
Stratford Cl SL2 .... 197 E1
Stratford Dr
Aylesbury HP21 .... 115 D3
Wooburn Green HP10 ... 185 E2
Stratford Gdns SL6 .... 202 B2
Stratford Rd
Buckingham MK18 .... 41 F1
Cosgrove MK19 .... 19 E1
Maids Moreton MK18 ...... 42 B1
Milton Keynes MK12,MK13 . 33 E4

Stratford Rd Nash MK17 ... 44 B1
Whaddon MK17 .... 45 D1
Stratfords Way HP17 ..... 127 D3
Strathcona Cl HP10 ...... 185 E4
Strathcona Way HP10 ... 185 E4
Strathnaver Pl MK12 ...... 33 E2
Stratton Chase Dr HP8 . 177 D4
Stratton Gn HP21 .... 116 A3
Stratton Rd
Beaconsfield HP9 .... 175 D1
Princes Risborough
HP27 .... 139 D2
Strauss Gr MK7 .... 48 B2
Strawberry Cl HP16 ...... 151 E3
Streamside Wlk HP21 ... 115 E3
Streatham Pl MK13 .... 34 B1
Stretton Cl HP10 .... 174 B4
Stretton Pl HP6 .... 154 C3
Stringers Cotts **1** SL9 ... 177 E1
Stringfellow Cl MK43 ...... 24 C1
Stroma Ct SL1 .... 204 B3
Stroud Cl SL4 .... 209 E2
Strudwick Dr MK6 .... 46 C4
Stuart Cl
Milton Keynes MK2 .... 47 E1
Windsor SL4 .... 209 F3
Stuart Ct HP6 .... 154 B1
Stuart Rd HP13 .... 173 E3
Stuart Way Thame OX9 . 126 A1
Windsor SL4 .... 209 F3
Stubbles La SL6 .... 195 D3
Studdridge Ct HP14 ...... 158 B2
Studham La HP4 .... 107 E2
Studland Cl HP21 .... 116 A3
Studley Knapp MK7 .... 48 A3
Sturdridge La HP27 ...... 150 A2
Sturges Cl MK7 .... 48 A3
Stylecroft Rd HP8 .... 177 E4
Styles Cl OX6 .... 71 F1
Styles Ct HP18 .... 99 D4
Sudgrove Ho MK15 .... 35 D3
Suffield Rd HP11 .... 172 C4
Suffolk Cl
Milton Keynes MK3 .... 46 C1
Slough SL1 .... 204 C4
Suffolk Cl OX6 .... 71 F2
Suffolk Rd SL6 .... 202 B2
Sulby Cl HP21 .... 115 E3
Sulgrave Cres HP23 ..... 119 E3
Sulgrave Ct MK8 .... 45 F4
Sullivan Cres MK7 .... 48 B3
Sumburgh Way SL1 ...... 205 F4
Summerfield Cty Comb Sch
MK13 .... 34 B2
Summergill Ct MK13 .... 34 B3
Summerhayes La MK17 ... 34 C4
Summerhouse La UB7 ... 213 E4
Summerlea SL1 .... 205 D3
Summerleaze Rd SL6 .... 196 A1
Summerleys Lo 92 C2
Summerleys Rd
Longwick HP27 .... 138 C2
Princes Risborough
HP27 .... 138 C2
Summers Rd SL1 .... 197 E1
Summerson Rd MK6 .... 46 C3
Summit Ctr UB7 .... 213 E4
Sumner Ct MK5 .... 46 A4
Sun Cl SL4 .... 210 B4
Sun Cres HP18 .... 109 E3
Sun La SL6 .... 202 C4
Sun Pas SL4 .... 210 B3
Sunbury Cl MK13 .... 34 A3
Sunbury Ct SL4 .... 210 B4
Sunbury Rd SL4 .... 210 B4
Sunderland Ct **4** TW19 . 213 F1
Sunderland Rd SL6 ...... 202 A4
Sunningdale Cl HP12 .... 172 A3
Sunningdale Way MK3 ... 57 E4
Sunny Bank
Cheddington LU7 .... 104 C4
Holmer Green HP15 ..... 162 C3
Sunny Croft HP13 .... 161 E1
Sunny View NN7 .... 1 A3
Sunnybank SL7 .... 183 E2
Sunnybrook Cl HP22 .... 117 E3
Sunnyhill Rd WD3 .... 178 B2
Sunnymeads Sta TW19 . 211 F2
Sunnymede Ave HP5 .... 144 C2
Sunnymede Cotts SL6 ... 196 A1
Sunnyside Rd HP15 ...... 144 B1
Sunray Ave UB7 .... 208 B2
Sunridge Cl MK16 .... 22 B2
Sunrise Parkway MK14 ... 34 C3
Sunset Cl MK2 .... 58 B4
Sunset Wlk MK9 .... 34 C1
Sunters End HP12 .... 172 A4
Sunters Wood Cl HP12 . 172 A3
Surly Hall Wlk SL4 .... 209 F3

Surrey Ave SL2 .... 198 B1
Surrey Pl
Milton Keynes MK3 .... 46 C1
Tring HP23 .... 119 D2
Surrey Rd MK3 .... 46 C1
Sussex Cl
Aylesbury HP19 .... 101 D2
Chalfont St Giles HP8 ... 177 D4
High Wycombe HP13 .... 162 B1
Slough SL1 .... 206 A2
Sussex Ho SL2 .... 198 B3
Sussex Keep SL1 .... 206 A2
Sussex Lodge **7** SL6 .... 202 C3
Sussex Pl SL3 .... 206 A2
Sussex Rd MK3 .... 46 C1
Sussex Way UB9 .... 189 F3
Sutcliffe Ave MK6 .... 34 C1
Sutherland Gr MK3 .... 46 C2
Sutherland Grange SL4 . 209 E4
Sutherland Wlk HP21 ... 115 F3
Sutleye Ct MK5 .... 46 A3
Sutton Ave SL3 .... 206 B2
Sutton Cl Cookham SL6 . 196 A4
Maidenhead SL6 .... 202 B3
Tring HP23 .... 119 D3
Sutton La SL3 .... 207 E1
Sutton Pl SL3 .... 212 A4
Sutton Rd SL6 .... 196 A3
Swabey Rd SL3 .... 207 D1
Swains Cl UB7 .... 208 C2
Swains La HP10 .... 174 A1
Swains Mkt HP10 .... 174 A1
Swakeleys Rd UB10 ..... 201 F4
Swale Rd HP21 .... 115 E3
Swallow Cl MK18 .... 52 C4
Swallow Dr HP15 .... 163 D3
Swallow Ho SL2 .... 184 A1
Swallow La MK17 .... 67 D1
Swallow St Iver SL0 ..... 200 B1
Swallow St Iver SL0 ..... 207 E4
Iver Heath SL0 .... 200 B1
Swallowdale SL0 .... 200 B1
Swallowfield MK8 .... 33 F1
Swallowfield Lower Sch
MK17 .... 49 D3
Swallowsprings LU6 .... 93 F1
Swan Cl Aylesbury HP20 .. 101 F2
Buckingham MK18 .... 52 C4
Chesham HP5 .... 144 A2
Ivinghoe LU6 .... 92 A1
Whitchurch HP22 .... 87 D3
Swan Cotts HP17 .... 129 E1
Swan Ct
Chorleywood WD3 .... 167 E3
Leighton Buzzard LU7 .... 80 C3
Olney MK46 .... 7 D2
Swan Dr MK18 .... 52 C4
Swan Hill HP18 .... 112 C2
Swan La OX6 .... 72 A2
Swan Mews HP22 .... 131 D3
Swan Rd Iver SL0 .... 207 F4
West Drayton UB7 .... 208 B2
Swan Terr MK11 .... 32 B3
Swan Wharf UB8 .... 201 E2
Swan's Way MK18 .... 75 E1
Swanbourne CE Fst Sch
MK17 .... 67 D2
Swanbourne House Sch
MK18 .... 66 C2
Swanbourne Rd MK17 .... 67 E2
Swann Rd HP22 .... 131 E4
Swansons Lo 92 C2
Swayne Rise MK10 .... 36 A2
Sweetcroft La UB10 ...... 201 F3
Sweetlands Cnr MK7 ...... 48 A4
Swift Cl Aylesbury HP20 . 101 F2
Newport Pagnell MK16 ... 22 A3
Swift Ho SL7 .... 184 A1
Swinbridge La MK4 .... 46 B2
Swinden Ct MK3 .... 34 A2
Swinfens Yd MK11 .... 32 B3
Swing Gate La HP4 .... 135 E1
Swing Gate Sch HP4 ..... 135 E2
Switchback Cl SL6 .... 195 E1
Switchback Rd SL6 .... 195 F2
Switchback Rd N
Cookham SL6 .... 195 F2
Maidenhead SL6 .... 195 F2
Switchback Rd S SL6 .... 195 F1
Switchback The SL6 ...... 195 E1
Sycamore Ave MK2 .... 58 B3
Sycamore Cl
Amersham HP6 .... 154 B1
13 Bourne End SL8 .... 185 D2
Buckingham MK18 .... 52 C4
Chalfont St Giles HP8 ... 177 D4
Long Crendon HP18 ..... 125 E3
Maidenhead SL6 .... 202 A4
Stewkley LU7 .... 68 B1
West Drayton UB7 .... 208 C3
Sycamore Cnr HP6 .... 154 B1

Sycamore Ct
Aylesbury HP19 .... 101 E1
High Wycombe HP12 .... 172 B2
Windsor SL4 .... 210 B2
Sycamore Dene HP5 ..... 144 B2
Sycamore Dr
Marlow Bottom SL7 ...... 183 E1
Tring HP23 .... 119 D2
Sycamore Ho
Amersham HP6 .... 154 B1
Princes Risborough HP27 . 139 D2
Sycamore Leys MK18 ..... 63 F1
Sycamore Pl HP6 .... 154 B1
Sycamore Rd
Amersham HP6 .... 154 B1
Chalfont St Giles HP8 ... 177 D4
High Wycombe HP12 .... 172 B2
Sycamore Rise
Berkhamsted HP4 .... 135 E2
Chalfont St Giles HP8 ... 177 D4
Sycamore Way HP15 .... 163 D2
Sycamore Wlk SL3 .... 206 C4
Sycamores The HP3 ..... 146 C4
Sydney Gr SL1 .... 205 E4
Syke Cluan SL0 .... 207 F2
Syke Ings SL0 .... 207 F2
Sykes Rd SL1 .... 205 D4
Sylvana Cl UB10 .... 201 F1
Sylvester Rd SL6 .... 195 F4
Sylvia Cl HP16 .... 152 A2
Symington Ct MK5 .... 46 A3
Syon Gdns MK16 .... 22 B3
Syresham CE Prim Sch
NN13 .... 27 E4

Tabard Gdns MK16 .... 22 B3
Tachbrook Rd UB8 .... 201 E2
Tackneill Dr
Shenley Brook End MK5 . 46 A2
Shenley Church End MK5 . 35 D3
Tadmarton MK15 .... 35 D3
Tadmere MK8 .... 33 E1
Talbot Ave
High Wycombe HP13 ..... 161 E1
Slough SL3 .... 206 C2
Talbot Ct
Milton Keynes MK15 ...... 35 E3
Windsor SL4 .... 210 A2
Talbot Pl SL3 .... 211 E3
Talbot Rd HP22 .... 117 F3
Talbots Dr SL6 .... 202 A3
Talbots Hyde MK46 .... 6 C2
Tall Oaks HP6 .... 154 B1
Tall Trees SL3 .... 212 C3
Talland Ave MK6 .... 34 C1
Tallis La MK7 .... 48 B3
Tamar Cl Aylesbury HP21 . 115 E2
Loudwater HP10 .... 174 A2
Tamar Ho
13 High Wycombe HP13 ... 173 F4
Milton Keynes MK3 .... 46 C1
Tamar Way SL3 .... 207 D1
Tamarisk Ct MK7 .... 48 A3
Tamarisk Way SL1 .... 205 D2
Tamworth Stubb MK7 .... 48 A3
Tancred Rd HP13 .... 162 A1
Tandra MK6 .... 47 D3
Tandys Cl MK43 .... 8 C3
Tangier Cl SL4 .... 210 B4
Tangier La SL4 .... 210 B4
Tank House Rd MK18 ..... 66 A3
Tanners Dr MK14 .... 22 A1
Tannery Rd HP10 .... 174 A2
Tansman La MK7 .... 48 B3
Tapestries The SL4 ...... 211 D3
Taplin Way HP10 .... 163 E4
Taplow Common Rd
Burnham SL1 .... 197 D2
Taplow SL1 .... 197 D2
Taplow Rd SL6 .... 204 A4
Taplow Sta SL6 .... 203 F4
Tapping Rd HP14 .... 171 E3
Taranis Cl MK7 .... 48 B4
Tarbay La SL4 .... 209 D3
Tarbert Cl MK2 .... 58 B3
Tarmac Way UB7 .... 213 D4
Task The MK46 .... 7 D2
Taskers Ho LU6 .... 92 C2
Taskers Row LU6 .... 92 C2
Tatchbrook Cl SL6 .... 203 D4
Tate Rd SL9 .... 177 F3
Tathams La MK17 .... 67 D2
Tatling Gr MK7 .... 48 A3
Tattam Cl MK15 .... 35 E3
Tattenhoe La MK3 .... 57 F4
Tattenhoe St MK5 .... 45 F3
Tattershall Ct MK5 .... 46 A3
Tattlers Hill HP22 .... 89 D2
Taunton Deane MK4 .... 46 B3
Taurus Cl MK18 .... 63 E1
Tavelhurst MK8 .... 33 E1

averner CI MK7 .... 48 B3
avistock CI
  Maidenhead SL6 .... 202 A4
  Woburn Sands MK17 ... 49 D3
avistock Rd UB7 .... 208 B3
avistock St MK2 .... 47 E1
avistock Wlk HP20 ..... 101 F1
ry Rd MK3 .... 46 C3
aylor Rd HP21 .... 115 E3
aylor's CI SL7 .... 183 F1
aylor's Ride LU7 ...... 70 C1
aylors Ct SL6 .... 202 A4
aylors Mews MK14 .... 34 C3
aylors Rd HP5 .... 144 B3
aylors Turn HP13 ..... 161 E2
aymouth PI MK9 ...... 35 D2
eale CI MK14 .... 34 C3
easel Ave MK14 ...... 34 C3
edder CI UB10 .... 201 F3
edder Rd HP22 ...... 131 E3
ees Way MK3 .... 46 A3
eesdale Rd SL2 ...... 204 C4
eign CI MK16 .... 22 B2
eikyo Sch SL3 .... 199 E3
elford CI HP19 ...... 100 C1
elford Dr SL1 .... 205 D2
elford Way
  High Wycombe HP13 ... 162 A1
  Milton Keynes MK14 .. 22 B1
elston CI SL8 .... 185 D3
emperance Terr MK11 . 32 B3
emplars PI SL7 ...... 183 F1
emple MK14 .... 34 B4
emple CI
  Buckingham MK18 .... 41 F1
  Milton Keynes MK3 .. 57 E4
emple End HP13 .... 173 D4
emple La SL7 ...... 194 B3
emple Mill Cotts SL7 . 194 B3
emple Mill Island SL7 . 194 B3
emple Mill La HP13 .. 173 D4
emple Park SL6 ..... 193 F2
emple Rd SL4 ...... 210 B3
emple Sq [14] HP20 .. 115 E4
emple St
  Aylesbury HP20 ..... 115 E4
  Brill HP18 .... 96 A1
  High Wycombe HP11 . 173 D4
emple Way SL2 ..... 198 B4
emplecroft Terr HP17 . 114 A2
emplewood HP14 ... 150 A1
emplewood La SL2 .. 198 B4
ene Acres MK5 ..... 45 F3
ennis La MK18 ..... 66 A2
ennyson Dr MK16 .. 22 A2
ennyson Gr MK3 ... 57 F4
ennyson Rd HP11 .. 173 D3
ennyson Way SL2 .. 197 F1
enterden Cres MK7 . 48 A4
enzing Dr HP13 .... 173 F3
errace The
  Aspley Guise MK17 .. 49 F3
  Maidenhead SL6 .... 203 E2
  [10] Tring HP23 .... 119 D2
errent Ct SL4 ...... 210 A3
erriers Cty Mid Sch
  HP13 .... 162 C1
errington Hill SL7 .. 183 D1
erry Dr HP19 ...... 101 E2
erry Orch HP13 .... 173 E4
erry Rd HP13 ...... 173 E4
erry's La SL6 ...... 195 F4
erryfield Rd HP13 .. 173 F3
ess Rd HP21 ...... 115 E3
estwood Rd SL4 ... 209 E3
etherdown HP16 ... 151 E3
ews End La NN12 .. 17 D4
hackeray End HP19 . 100 C1
hame Ho [11] HP21 . 173 D4
hame Rd
  Aylesbury HP21 .... 115 E4
hames Ave SL4 .... 210 B4
hames CI
  Bourne End SL8 ... 185 D2
  Milton Keynes MK3 . 57 F4
hames Cres SL6 ... 196 A1
hames Dr MK16 ... 22 C2
hames Ind Est SL7 . 183 F1
hames Mead SL4 .. 209 F3
hames Rd SL3 .... 207 D2
hames Reach SL7 .. 193 E3

Thames Side
  Henley-on-T RG9 .... 191 F1
  Windsor SL4 .... 210 B4
Thames St SL4 ...... 210 B4
Thames Valley Univ SL1 . 205 F3
Thamesbourne Mews SL8 . 185 D2
Thamesfield Gdns SL7 ... 183 F1
Thane Ct MK14 ..... 34 B4
Thatcher CI UB7 .... 208 C2
Thatchers Dr SL6 ... 202 A3
Thellusson Way WD3 .. 167 F1
Theydon Ave MK17 .. 49 D2
Thicket The
  Tylers Green HP10 .. 163 D1
  West Drayton UB7 .. 208 C4
Third Ave Marlow SL7 . 183 F1
  Milton Keynes MK1 . 47 D1
Third Cres SL1 ..... 205 E4
Third St SL11 ...... 173 D2
Thirkleby CI SL1 .... 205 E3
Thirlby La MK5 ..... 46 A3
Thirlmere Ave
  Burnham SL1 ...... 204 B4
  Milton Keynes MK2 . 58 B3
Thirsk Gdns MK3 ... 57 F3
Thistle Ct HP21 .... 115 E3
Thomas Coram Sch The
  HP4 .... 135 E1
Thomas Ct HP4 .... 134 C3
Thomas Dr MK16 ... 22 A2
Thomas Harding Cty Mid Sch
  HP5 .... 154 A4
Thomas Rd HP10 ... 185 E2
Thompkins La SL2 .. 198 A3
Thompson CI SL3 .. 207 D1
Thompson Rd UB10 . 201 F3
Thompson St MK13 . 34 A4
Thomson Wlk HP21 . 115 D3
Thorn Dr SL3 ..... 206 C4
Thornbury PI HP10 . 185 F4
Thornbank CI TW19 . 213 D1
Thornborough Cty Fst Sch
  MK18 .... 54 A4
Thornborough Rd MK17 . 55 D4
Thornbridge Rd SL0 . 200 B2
Thorncliffe MK8 ... 33 E1
Thorndike SL2 .... 205 D4
Thorne Rd HP14 ... 171 E2
Thorne Way
  Aylesbury HP20 ... 101 F1
  Drayton Beauchamp HP23 118 A2
Thorney La N SL0 .. 207 F3
Thorney La S SL0 .. 207 F1
Thorney Mill La SL0 . 208 A2
Thorney Mill Rd SL0 . 208 A2
Thorney Park Golf Course
  SL0 .... 208 A2
Thorneycroft La MK15 . 35 D3
Thornhill MK18 .... 54 A4
Thornhill Ct MK17 .. 165 D4
Thornhill Rd UB10 .. 201 F4
Thorniea Croft MK46 . 6 C2
Thornley Croft MK4 . 46 B1
Thorns CI HP27 .... 139 E3
Thornton Ave UB7 .. 208 C2
Thornton CI UB7 ... 208 C2
Thornton Coll (RC
  Convent Sch) MK17 ... 43 A1
Thornton Cres HP22 . 131 D3
Thornton Rd MK17 .. 44 A1
Thorntree Dr HP23 . 118 C2
Thorpe House Prep Sch
  SL9 .... 188 C4
Thorwold PI MK5 ... 46 A3
Thrasher Rd HP21 .. 115 E3
Three Close La HP4 . 135 E2
Three Gables HP9 .. 175 F1
Three Households HP5 . 176 C3
Three Oaks CI UB10 . 190 C1
Three Points La MK18 . 74 A3
Thresher Gr MK12 .. 33 D3
Thrift La MK18 .... 202 B1
Thrift View MK43 .. 25 E1
Thrupp CI MK19 ... 20 A3
Thrush CI
  [1] Aylesbury HP20 . 101 F2
  High Wycombe HP12 . 172 B2
Thurlby Way SL6 ... 202 B2
Thurleys Cotts SL2 . 199 D2
Thurne CI MK16 ... 22 C2
Thursby CI MK15 ... 35 E4
Thurston Rd SL1 ... 205 D4
Tibbys La HP18 .... 112 C2
Ticehurst CI MK7 .. 48 A4
Tichborne WD3 .... 178 B3
Tickford Arc MK16 . 22 B2
Tickford St MK16 .. 22 C2
Tidbury CI MK17 ... 49 D2
Tierney Ct [10] SL7 . 183 F1

Tiffany CI MK2 ..... 58 B3
Tilbrook Ind Est MK7 . 48 A2
Tilbrook Rdbt MK7 .. 48 A1
Tilburywood CI HP13 . 161 E1
Tilbury CI RG9 .... 191 E1
Tilecotes CI SL7 ... 183 E1
Tilehouse Cty Comb Sch
  UB9 .... 189 F3
Tilehouse La UB9 .. 189 F3
Tilehouse Way UB9 . 189 F2
Tilers Rd MK11 .... 33 D1
Tilling Cres HP11 .. 174 A4
Tilman CI MK8 .... 33 E3
Tilstone Ave SL4 ... 204 C1
Tilstone CI SL4 .... 204 C1
Tilsworth Rd HP9 .. 175 E1
Timber La MK17 ... 60 C4
Timber Way SX9 ... 147 E3
Timbers Wlk MK9 .. 202 A3
Timberscombe MK4 . 46 B2
Timbold Dr MK7 ... 48 A4
Timor Ct MK11 .... 32 B3
Timpsons Row MK46 . 7 D2
Tindal Rd HP20 ... 101 F1
Tingewick Cty Fst Sch
  MK18 .... 51 D3
Tingewick Rd
  Buckingham MK18 .. 52 A4
  Chackmore MK18 .. 51 F4
Tingewick Road Ind Pk
  MK18 .... 52 A4
Tinkers La
  Berkhamsted HP23 . 134 A3
  Windsor SL4 ...... 209 E3
Tinkers Wood Cty Comb Sch
  HP13 .... 161 F1
Tinkers Wood Rd HP13 . 161 F1
Tintagel CI MK6 ... 47 D4
Tintagel Ho SL1 ... 205 E3
Tintern CI SL1 .... 205 E2
Tinterne CI HP21 .. 116 B3
Tippet CI MK7 .... 48 B2
Tippings HP14 .... 158 C3
Tiree Ho SL1 ..... 205 D4
Titchmarsh Ct MK6 . 46 C4
Tithe Barn Dr SL6 . 203 F1
Tithe CI SL6 ..... 203 E1
Tithe CI SL3 ..... 207 D1
Tithe La TW19 .... 212 A1
Titmus Rd HP22 ... 131 F4
Tiverton Cres HP19 . 101 E2
Tockley Way SL1 ... 197 D1
Todd CI Aylesbury HP21 115 D3
  Holmer Green HP15 . 163 D3
Tolcarne Ave MK6 .. 35 D1
Tollgate SL6 ..... 202 A3
Tollgate CI WD3 ... 167 F3
Tolman Ct HP21 ... 115 D3
Tomkins CI HP22 .. 117 F2
Tomlin Rd SL2 .... 197 F1
Tompion Rd HP19 .. 100 C1
Tompkins CI MK45 . 44 C2
Tompkins La OX6 .. 71 F1
Toms Hill Rd HP23 . 120 B3
Toms Turn HP15 ... 162 C3
Tongwell La MK16 .. 22 C1
Tongwell St
  Milton Keynes MK15 . 35 F4
  Milton Keynes Village MK7 . 48 A4
  Walton MK7 ...... 48 B3
Top Angel MK18 ... 52 B3
Top Farm CI HP9 .. 175 D1
Top Meadow MK7 .. 48 B3
Top Park SL9 ..... 188 B3
Top Station Rd NN13 . 38 A4
Topaz CI SL1 ..... 205 D3
Topland Rd SL9 ... 177 E2
Topping La UB8 ... 201 E1
Torbay HP22 ..... 85 E2
Tornay Ct LU7 .... 91 E3
Torquay Spur SL2 .. 198 A1
Torridge MK3 ..... 47 D1
Torridge Rd
  Aylesbury HP21 ... 115 E2
  Slough SL3 .... 212 A4
Torridon Ct MK2 .. 58 B2
Torrington Rd HP4 . 135 D2
Tortoiseshell Way HP4 134 C3
Torwood CI HP4 ... 134 C2
Totteridge Ave HP13 173 E3
Totteridge Dr HP13 . 162 C1
Totteridge La HP13 . 162 C1
Totteridge Par HP13 173 E4
Totteridge Rd HP13 . 173 E4
Totternhoe Lower Sch LU6 . 93 D4
Totternhoe Rd
  Dunstable LU6 .... 93 F4
  Eaton Bray LU6 ... 92 B4
Towan Ave MK6 ... 35 D1
Towcester Dr NN12 . 18 A2
Towcester Rd MK19 . 32 A4

Tower CI
  Berkhamsted HP4 ... 135 D2
  Emberton MK16 ... 13 E3
  Flackwell Heath HP10 . 185 E4
Tower Cres MK14 ... 34 C3
Tower Ct HP27 .... 34 C4
Tower Dr MK14 .... 34 C4
Tower Hill WD4 ... 146 C1
Tower Ho Iver SL0 . 207 F4
  [4] Slough SL1 ... 205 F2
Tower Rd HP7 .... 165 D2
Tower St HP13 .... 162 B1
Toweridge La
  High Wycombe HP12 . 172 B4
  High Wycombe, Towerage
  HP14 .... 160 C1
Towers Lea HP13 .. 173 E4
Towersey Way HP21 . 115 D4
Town Bridge Ct MK5 . 154 A4
Town CI MK18 .... 50 B3
Town End Cres MK16 . 12 A3
Town End Rd HP14 .. 159 E4
Town Farm LU7 ... 105 D4
Town Field La HP8 . 177 E4
Town La Stanwell TW19 213 E1
  High Wycombe HP10 . 185 E2
Town Sq [17] SL1 .. 205 F2
Townfield HP5 .... 154 B4
Townfield Rd [5] HP13 173 E4
Townlands Hospl RG9 . 191 E1
Townsend OX6 .... 71 F1
Townsend Cotts MK17 55 D2
Townsend Gr MK13 . 34 A4
Townsend La OX6 .. 71 F1
Townsend Piece HP19 101 E1
Townsend Rd HP5 .. 144 B1
Townside
  Edlesborough LU6 .. 92 C2
  Haddenham HP17 .. 126 C3
Tozer Wlk SL4 .... 209 E2
Trafalgar Ave MK3 . 46 C1
Trafford CI HP16 .. 152 A3
Trafford Rd HP16 .. 152 A4
Tramhill HP18 .... 96 A1
Tranlands Brigg MK13 34 A2
Trapp's Ct HP5 ... 154 B3
Trapp's La HP5 ... 154 B3
Travell Ct MK13 .. 34 A2
Travic Rd SL2 .... 197 F1
Travis Ct SL2 .... 198 A1
Treacher's CI HP5 . 154 A4
Treadaway Hill
  Flackwell Heath HP10 174 A1
  Loudwater HP10 .. 174 A1
Treadaway Rd HP10 . 174 A1
Treborough MK4 ... 46 B1
Tredington Gr HP4 . 148 A2
Tree Cathedral (NT) LU6 93 F1
Treehanger CI HP23 . 119 D2
Trees Ave HP14 ... 158 C3
Trees Rd Bourne End SL8 . 185 D2
  Hughenden Valley HP14 . 162 A3
Treeside CI UB7 ... 208 B1
Treesmill Dr SL6 .. 202 B2
Trelawney Ave SL3 . 206 C2
Tremayne Ct MK6 .. 47 D4
Trenchard Ave HP22 . 131 E3
Trenches La SL3 .. 207 D3
Trengothal Ct NN13 . 26 B2
Trent Dr MK16 .... 22 B2
Trent Rd
  Milton Keynes MK3 . 46 C1
  Slough SL3 ...... 212 A4
Trent Villas Est SL3 . 211 D3
Trentishoe Cres MK4 . 46 B2
Tresco Rd HP4 .... 134 C3
Tresham Ct MK5 .. 46 A4
Trevelyan Mid Sch SL4 210 A3
Trevelyan Way HP4 . 135 D3
Treves Gn HP21 .. 115 F3
Trevithick La MK5 . 46 A3
Trevone CI MK6 ... 47 D4
Trevor Ct TW19 ... 213 D1
Trevose Ho SL2 ... 198 A1
Trewarden Ave SL0 . 200 B2
Triangle Bsns Pk HP22 130 B4
Trident Ind Est SL3 . 212 C2
Tring Bsns Ctr HP23 . 118 C2
Tring Ford Rd HP23 . 119 D4
Tring Hill HP23 ... 118 B2
Tring Rd
  Aylesbury HP20, HP22 116 A4
  Berkhamsted HP4 .. 134 B4
  Dunstable LU6 .... 93 F4
  Edlesborough LU6 . 106 C4
  Long Marston HP23 . 104 A2
  Wendover HP22 ... 131 E3
  Wingrave HP22 ... 89 E1
Tring Sch HP23 ... 119 D2
Tring Sta HP23 ... 120 A3
Trinity Ave SL3 ... 183 E2

Trinity CI TW19 ... 213 E1
Trinity Ct HP5 .... 154 B4
Trinity Ho SL6 .... 195 F3
Trinity PI SL4 .... 210 B3
Trinity Rd Marlow SL7 . 183 E1
  Milton Keynes MK12 . 33 D4
Tylers Green HP15 .. 162 C2
Trinity St Stephens CE
  Fst Sch SL4 ..... 210 A3
Tripps Hill CI HP8 . 177 D4
Trispen Ct MK4 ... 47 D4
Trooper Rd HP23 .. 120 B3
Trout CI SL7 ..... 194 B4
Trout La UB7 .... 208 B3
Trout Rd UB7 .... 208 B3
Troutbeck MK6 ... 47 E4
Trubys Gdn MK6 .. 47 D4
Trueman PI MK6 .. 46 C4
Truesdale Dr UB9 . 190 B4
Trumper Way Slough SL1 . 204 C3
  Uxbridge UB8 .... 201 E2
Trumpton La MK7 . 48 B4
Trunk Furlong Est MK17 49 E3
Truro CI SL6 ..... 202 A4
Trustees Way UB9 . 189 F3
Tubwell Rd SL2 ... 199 D2
Tucker CI HP13 ... 173 E4
Tuckers Dr HP15 .. 163 E4
Tudeley Hale MK7 . 48 A4
Tudor Ct Amersham HP6 . 154 B1
  Lane End HP14 ... 160 B1
  [9] Leighton Buzzard LU7 . 80 C4
  Maidenhead SL6 .. 196 B1
  [5] Stanwell TW19 . 213 F1
Tudor Dr MK11 ... 185 E4
Tudor Gdns Burnham SL1 204 B4
  Milton Keynes MK11 . 32 C2
Tudor Mill HP10 .. 185 F3
Tudor Orch HP4 .. 134 C3
Tudor Park HP6 .. 154 B1
Tudor Rd HP15 ... 163 E2
Tudor Way SL4 ... 209 F3
Tuffnell CI MK15 .. 35 F4
Tulkers CI HP16 .. 151 E3
Tulla Ct MK2 .... 58 B2
Tummell Way MK2 . 58 B3
Tunbridge Gr MK7 . 48 A4
Tunmers Ct SL9 .. 177 E1
Tunmers End SL9 . 177 E1
Tunmers Ho SL9 .. 177 E1
Tuns La Henley-on-T RG9 . 191 F1
  Slough SL1 ...... 205 E2
Turks Head Ct SL4 . 210 B4
Turnberry CI MK3 . 57 E4
Turner CI HP20 ... 101 F2
Turner Rd SL3 ... 206 B2
Turner Wlk [2] HP20 . 101 F2
Turners Dr HP13 .. 173 F4
Turners Field HP13 . 161 F2
Turners Mews MK14 . 34 C3
Turners PI HP15 .. 163 E3
Turners Wood Dr HP8 . 177 E4
Turneys Dr MK12 .. 33 D3
Turnfields HP13 ... 124 A2
Turnfurlong HP21 .. 115 F4

Turnfurlong HP21 .. 116 A3
Turnfurlong Cty Fst Sch
  HP21 .... 116 A3
Turnfurlong Cty Mid Sch
  HP21 .... 116 A3
Turnfurlong La HP21 . 116 A3
Turnip CI HP18 ... 112 A1
Turnmill Ave MK6 . 35 D1
Turnmill Ct MK6 .. 35 D1
Turnoak Park SL4 . 209 F2
Turnpike End HP21 . 115 F3
Turnpike La UB10 . 201 F1
Turnpike Rd HP22 . 172 B2
Turnpike The HP18 . 109 E3
Turnpike Way HP12 . 172 B2
Turnstone Way HP20 . 101 F2
Turpins Dr SL6 ... 202 A3
Turpyn Ct MK6 ... 47 E4
Turton Way SL1 .. 205 E2
Turvy CI HP22 ... 117 F3
Turvey Lower Sch MK43 . 8 C3
Turvey Mill MK43 . 8 B3
Turvey Rd Astwood MK16 . 15 F3
  Carlton MK43 .... 3 F1
Turville Rd HP22 .. 116 B3
Turweston Rd NN13 . 26 A1
Tweed CI HP4 .... 135 D3
Tweed Dr MK3 ... 46 B1
Tweed Rd SL3 ... 212 A4
Tweedale CI MK17 . 67 E4
Tweenways HP5 .. 144 C1
Twelve Leys HP22 . 89 D2
Twinches La SL1 .. 205 D3
Twinflower MK7 .. 48 A3

Twist The HP23 .... 119 E1
Twitchell La HP22 .... 117 F3
Twitchell Rd HP16 .... 152 A4
Twitchell's La HP4 .... 176 C3
Twitchen La MK4 .... 46 B2
Two Dells La HP5 .... 145 D2
Two Gates La HP5 .... 143 E4
Two Mile Ash Cty Mid Sch
  MK8 .... 33 F1
Twyford CE Fst Sch MK18 ... 62 B1
Twyford La MK7 .... 48 B3
Twynham Rd SL6 .... 202 A4
Tyburn Ave MK6 .... 35 D1
Tyle Pl SL4 .... 211 D1
Tylers Cres HP15 .... 163 D1
Tylers Green MK13 .... 34 B2
Tylers Green Cty Fst Sch
  HP10 .... 174 B4
Tylers Green Cty Mid Sch
  HP10 .... 174 A4
Tylers Hill Rd HP5 .... 154 C4
Tylers Rd HP15 .... 163 D1
Tylsworth Cl HP6 .... 154 B1
Tyne Rd HP21 .... 115 E2
Tyne Sq MK3 .... 46 C4
Tyneham Cl HP21 .... 116 A2
Tyrell Cl MK18 .... 52 B4
Tyrell Gdns SL4 .... 209 F2
Tyrells Gdns MK17 .... 69 F4
Tyrells Rd MK17 .... 69 F4
Tyrill MK14 .... 34 B4
Tyson Pl MK6 .... 46 C4
Tythe Cl LU7 .... 78 C4
Tythe Gdns LU7 .... 78 C4
Tythe Mews LU6 .... 92 C2
Tyzack Rd HP13 .... 162 C1

Ufton Court Yd SL8 .... 185 D2
Ufton Ct SL8 .... 185 D2
Ullswater Cl SL1 .... 204 B4
Ullswater Dr LU7 .... 80 B4
Ulverscroft MK10 .... 36 A1
Ulyett Pl MK6 .... 46 C4
Umberville Way SL2 .... 197 F1
Underhill Cl SL6 .... 202 C3
Underwood Cotts HP7 .... 164 B1
Underwood Pl MK6 .... 46 C4
Underwood Rd HP13 .... 173 E4
Union St
  High Wycombe HP11 .... 173 D4
  Newport Pagnell MK16 ...... 22 B3
Univ of Buckingham
  Buckingham MK18 .... 52 B4
  Buckingham MK18 .... 52 C4
Up Corner Cl HP8 .... 177 D4
Upcroft SL4 .... 210 A2
Upland Ave HP5 .... 144 A2
Uplands SL7 .... 183 E3
Uplands Cl
  Gerrards Cross SL9 .... 188 C2
  High Wycombe HP13 .... 173 F4
Uplands Cl HP5 .... 144 B1
Uplands The SL7 .... 188 C1
Upper Abbotts Hill HP21 ... 115 D4
Upper Ashlyns Rd HP4 ...... 135 D2
Upper Belmont Rd HP5 ...... 144 A2
Upper Bray Rd SL6 .... 203 E2
Upper Church St HP18 .... 112 C2
Upper Coombe LU7 .... 80 C4
Upper Dr HP9 .... 175 E3
Upper Fifth St MK9 .... 34 B1
Upper Fourth St MK9 .... 34 B1
Upper George St HP5 .... 144 B1
Upper Gladstone Rd HP5 ... 144 B1
Upper Hall Park HP4 .... 135 F1
Upper Hollis HP16 .... 151 F4
Upper Hundreds Way
  HP20 .... 115 F4
Upper Icknield Way
  Aston Clinton HP22 .... 117 F1
  Bledlow HP27 .... 149 D4
  Drayton Beauchamp HP22 117 F1
  Halton HP22 .... 117 F1
  Pitstone LU7 .... 105 F1
  Princes Risborough HP27 149 D4
  Princes Risborough,
    Whiteleaf HP27 .... 139 F1
Upper Lees Rd SL2 .... 198 A1
Upper Lodge La HP15 .... 162 C3
Upper Meadow HP5 .... 144 A1
Upper Rd UB9 .... 189 E2
Upper Riding HP9 .... 175 D1
Upper Second St MK9 .... 34 B1
Upper St Quainton HP22 .... 85 D3
  Tingewick MK18 .... 51 D3
Upper Stonehayes MK14 ..... 34 C4
Upper Third St MK9 .... 34 B1
Upper Ventnor Cotts SL6 .. 195 E4

Upper Way MK17 .... 59 E1
Upton Cl Henley-on-T RG9 .. 191 F1
  Slough SL1 .... 205 F2
Upton Court Rd SL3 .... 206 A1
Upton Gr MK5 .... 46 B2
Upton Hospl SL1 .... 205 F2
Upton House Sch SL4 .... 210 B3
Upton Lea Par SL2 .... 206 A3
Upton Park SL1 .... 205 F2
Upton Rd Dinton HP17 ...... 114 A2
  Slough SL1 .... 206 A2
Upton Terr HP17 .... 114 A2
Upway SL9 .... 177 F1
Uxbridge Coll UB8 .... 201 F3
Uxbridge High Sch UB8 .... 201 E2
Uxbridge Ind Est UB8 .... 201 D2
Uxbridge Rd
  Slough SL1, SL2, SL3 ...... 206 B4
  Uxbridge UB10 .... 201 F1
  Uxbridge UB8 .... 201 E3

Vache La
  Chalfont St Giles HP8 ..... 177 E4
  Shenley Church End MK5 ... 45 F3
Vale Cl SL9 .... 177 E1
Vale Ct MK43 .... 25 F1
Vale Gr SL1 .... 205 F2
Vale House HP21 .... 115 E4
Vale Ind Cntr The HP19 ..... 101 E1
Vale Park Dr HP20 .... 115 F4
Vale Rd Aylesbury HP20 .... 101 F1
  Chesham HP5 .... 144 B2
  Windsor SL4 .... 209 F3
Vale Rise HP5 .... 144 B2
Vale Sch The, Peveral Court
  HP17 .... 114 C2
Vale The SL9 .... 177 E1
Valens Cl MK8 .... 45 F4
Valentine Ct MK8 .... 45 F4
Valentine Way HP8 .... 177 E4
Valley Cl MK18 .... 38 A4
Valley Cres NN13 .... 38 A4
Valley Ctr The HP13 .... 173 E3
Valley End SL3 .... 199 E1
Valley Rd
  Berkhamsted HP4 .... 134 C3
  Brackley NN13 .... 38 A4
  Buckingham MK18 .... 52 C4
  Finmere MK18 .... 50 B3
  Henley-on-T RG9 .... 191 F1
  Hughenden Valley HP14 .. 162 A3
  Uxbridge UB10 .... 201 F2
Valley Rise NN13 .... 38 A4
Valley View HP5 .... 144 A1
Valley Way SL9 .... 188 B3
Valpy Cl HP23 .... 119 E1
Van Der Bilt Ct MK13 .... 33 F3
Van Diemens Cl OX9 .... 147 F4
Vandyke Cl MK17 .... 49 D3
Vane Rd OX9 .... 126 A1
Vanguard Ho **8** TW19 .... 213 F2
Vansittart Est SL4 .... 210 B3
Vansittart Rd Bisham SL7 .. 194 C4
  Windsor SL4 .... 210 A3
Vantage Ct MK16 .... 22 C2
Vantage Rd SL1 .... 205 D3
Vanwall Bsns Pk SL6 .... 202 B3
Vanwall Rd SL6 .... 202 B2
Varnell Terr RG9 .... 181 E1
Vaughan Copse SL4 .... 205 E1
Vaughan Gdns SL4 .... 204 C1
Vaughan Way SL2 .... 197 F1
Vauxhall MK13 .... 34 A3
Vellan Ave MK6 .... 35 D1
Venables La MK15 .... 35 D4
Venetian Cl MK7 .... 48 B4
Ventfield Cl OX33 .... 108 A3
Venus Hill HP3 .... 156 A4
Verbena Cl UB7 .... 208 B1
Verdi Cl MK7 .... 48 B3
Verdon Ct SL2 .... 198 A1
Verdon Dr MK15 .... 35 D4
Verity Pl MK6 .... 34 C1
Verley Cl MK6 .... 47 E4
Vermont Rd SL2 .... 197 F1
Verney Ave HP12 .... 172 B2
Verney Avenue Sch HP12 . 172 C2
Verney Cl
  Berkhamsted HP4 .... 134 C3
  Buckingham MK18 .... 41 E1
  Marlow SL7 .... 183 E1
  Tring HP23 .... 119 E3
Verney Farm Cl MK18 ...... 174 C4
Verney Rd Slough SL3 ..... 207 D1
  Winslow MK18 .... 65 F2
Verney Wlk HP21 .... 115 E4
Verona Cl UB8 .... 208 B4
Verwood Rd HP20 .... 101 F1
Veryan Pl MK6 .... 35 D1
Vicarage Cl Cookham SL6 . 196 A4
  Seer Green HP9 .... 176 B2

Vicarage Cl
  Steeple Claydon MK18 ...... 63 E1
  Wendover HP22 .... 131 D3
  Yardley Gobion NN12 .... 18 C3
Vicarage Dr SL6 .... 203 E2
Vicarage Flats SL4 .... 210 B4
Vicarage Gdns
  Leighton Buzzard LU7 .... 80 C3
  Marsworth HP23 .... 105 D1
  Milton Keynes MK13 .... 34 A2
Vicarage La
  Bovingdon HP3 .... 146 A2
  Ivinghoe LU7 .... 105 F3
  Piddington OX6 .... 95 F3
  Steeple Claydon MK18 ...... 63 E1
  Wing LU7 .... 79 F1
Vicarage Rd
  Aylesbury HP21 .... 115 E3
  Henley-on-T RG9 .... 191 F1
  Leighton Buzzard LU7 .... 80 C3
  Maidenhead SL6 .... 202 C4
  Marsworth HP23 .... 105 D1
Milton Keynes, Bradwell
  MK11, MK13, MK17, MK2 .. 34 A2
Milton Keynes, Fenny Stratford
  MK2 .... 58 C4
Milton Keynes, Stony Stratford
  MK11 .... 32 B3
  Pitstone LU7 .... 105 E2
  Whaddon MK17 .... 56 A4
  Wigginton HP23 .... 119 E1
  Winslow MK18 .... 65 F2
Vicarage St MK17 .... 49 E2
Vicarage Wlk
  Maidenhead SL6 .... 203 E2
  Milton Keynes MK11 .... 32 B3
Vickers Ct **11** TW19 ...... 213 F1
Vickery Way HP21 .... 115 F3
Victor Cl SL6 .... 202 A4
Victor Rd SL4 .... 210 B2
Victoria CE Sch HP4 .... 135 E2
Victoria Cres SL0 .... 208 A3
Victoria Ct
  Henley-on-T RG9 .... 191 F1
  2 High Wycombe HP11 . 172 C4
  2 Marlow SL7 .... 183 F1
  Slough SL1 .... 205 D3
Victoria Fst Sch HP4 .... 135 E2
Victoria Gdns HP11 .... 172 C2
Victoria Ho SL4 .... 211 D1
Victoria Rd
  Berkhamsted HP4 .... 135 E2
  Chesham HP5 .... 144 B1
  Eton SL4 .... 204 C1
  Farnham Common SL2 .... 198 B3
  Leighton Buzzard LU7 .... 80 C3
  Marlow SL7 .... 183 F1
  Milton Keynes MK2 .... 47 F1
  Slough SL2 .... 206 A3
  Uxbridge UB8 .... 201 E3
Victoria Row MK18 .... 52 B4
Victoria St
  Aylesbury HP20 .... 115 F4
  High Wycombe HP11 .... 172 C4
  Milton Keynes MK12 .... 33 E3
  18 Slough SL1 .... 205 F2
  Windsor SL4 .... 210 B3
Victory Ct MK1 .... 47 D1
Victory Rd
  Berkhamsted HP4 .... 135 D3
  Steeple Claydon MK18 ...... 63 E1
  Wendover HP22 .... 131 D3
Vienna Gr MK13 .... 33 F3
Villa Pk MK17 .... 37 F4
Village Cl MK16 .... 13 F1
Village La SL4 .... 187 E2
Village Rd Coleshill HP7 .. 164 C2
  Denham UB9 .... 190 A2
  Dorney SL4 .... 204 A2
Village Sh Ctr The **13**
  SL1 .... 205 F2
Village Way HP6 .... 166 B4
Villier St UB8 .... 201 E2
Villiers Cl MK18 .... 41 F1
Villiers Ct SL4 .... 210 A4
Villiers Rd SL2 .... 197 F1
Vimy Rd LU7 .... 80 C4
Vincent Ave MK8 .... 45 F4
Vincent Cl HP19 .... 101 D2
Vincent Dr UB10 .... 201 F2
Vincents Way HP14 .... 161 E3
Vine Cl Stanwell TW19 ..... 213 D1
  Tylers Green HP15 .... 163 D2
Vine Ct SL2 .... 199 D3
Vine Gr UB10 .... 201 F3
Vine Rd SL2 .... 198 C3
Vine St UB8 .... 201 E2

Vine The HP18 .... 124 B2
Vinetrees HP22 .... 131 D2
Vineyard Dr SL8 .... 185 D3
Vineyards The HP27 .... 138 A1
Vinio House Sch HP12 ...... 172 B2
Vinlake Ave UB10 .... 190 C1
Vintners Mews MK14 .... 34 C3
Violet Ave Uxbridge UB8 ... 208 C4
  West Drayton UB8 .... 208 C4
Violet Cl HP27 .... 149 E3
Violets Cl MK16 .... 24 A3
Virginia MK6 .... 47 D4
Virginia Gdns HP14 .... 159 F4
Viscount Cl **14** HP20 ... 101 F1
Viscount Cl **17** SL4 ...... 210 B3
Viscount Trad Est SL3 ..... 212 C2
Viscount Way MK2 .... 47 E1
Vivien Cl SL6 .... 195 F3
Vyne Cres MK8 .... 33 F1
Vyners Sch UB10 .... 201 F4

Waborne Rd SL8 .... 185 D2
Waddesden Cty Comb Sch
  HP18 .... 99 D3
Waddesdon Hill HP18 .... 99 E2
Waddesdon Manor (NT)
  HP18 .... 99 D4
Wade Dr SL1 .... 205 D3
Wadesmill La
  Bow Brickhill MK7 .... 48 A2
  Walton MK7 .... 48 A2
Wadhurst La MK7 .... 48 A4
Wagner Cl MK7 .... 48 B3
Wainers Croft MK12 .... 33 D2
Wainwrights HP18 .... 125 E3
Waits Green MK18 .... 112 A1
Waivers Way HP21 .... 116 A3
Wakefield Cl MK14 .... 34 C4
Wakefield Cres SL2 .... 198 C3
Wakelins End SL6 .... 195 F4
Wakeman Rd SL8 .... 185 D2
Walbrook Ave MK6 .... 35 D2
Walbrook Dr MK5 .... 46 A2
Waldeck Rd SL6 .... 203 D4
Waldens Cl SL8 .... 185 D2
Walducks Cl LU7 .... 78 C4
Walford Rd UB8 .... 201 E2
Walgrave Dr MK13 .... 34 A4
Walk House Cl MK43 .... 25 D1
Walk The Eton SL4 .... 205 D1
  Winslow MK18 .... 65 F2
Walk Wood Rise HP9 .... 186 B4
Walker Rd SL6 .... 203 D2
Walkers Rd HP27 .... 138 B4
Walkham Cl HP10 .... 174 A2
Walkhampton Ave MK13 .... 34 B2
Walkwood End HP9 .... 175 E1
Wallace Cl Marlow SL7 ..... 183 F2
  Uxbridge UB10 .... 201 F2
Wallace Dr LU6 .... 92 C3
Wallace End HP21 .... 116 A3
Wallace Mews LU6 .... 92 C3
Wallace St MK13 .... 33 F4
Wallace Wlk SL4 .... 205 F1
Wallbridge Cl HP21 .... 115 D4
Wallbridge Dr HP9 .... 175 F1
Wallinger Dr MK5 .... 46 A2
Wallingford MK13 .... 34 A3
Wallingford Gdns HP11 .... 173 D2
Wallingford Rd UB8 .... 201 D1
Wallington Rd HP5 .... 144 A1
Wallis Ct SL1 .... 206 A2
Wallmead Gdns MK5 .... 46 A4
Walnut Cl
  Long Crendon HP18 .... 125 E4
  Newport Pagnell MK16 ..... 22 A2
  South Heath HP16 .... 152 A4
  Stoke Mandeville HP22 ... 116 B1
Walnut Cres HP27 .... 138 B3
Walnut Dr
  Maids Moreton MK18 .... 41 F2
  Milton Keynes MK2 .... 58 C4
Walnut Tree Cl
  Bourne End SL8 .... 185 D1
  High Wycombe HP12 .... 172 B4
Walnut Tree Ct HP22 .... 116 B2
Walnut Tree Ho HP10 .... 174 A2
Walnut Tree La LU7 .... 79 F2
Walnut Tree Rd MK7 .... 48 B3
Walnut Way
  Bourne End SL8 .... 185 D1
  Hyde Heath HP6 .... 153 E2
Walnuts Sch The MK6 .... 47 E2
Walpole Rd SL1 .... 204 B4
Walsh's Manor MK13 .... 34 B4
Walsingham Gate HP11 .... 173 D2
Walters Ash Mid Sch
  HP14 .... 150 A1
Walton Cl HP13 .... 162 C1
Walton Court Ctr HP21 ..... 115 E3
Walton Dene HP21 .... 115 F4

Walton Dr
  High Wycombe HP13 .... 162 C3
  Walton MK7 .... 47 F3
Walton End MK7 .... 48 B3
Walton Gdns MK18 .... 41 F3
Walton Gr HP21 .... 115 F4
Walton Green MK7 .... 115 F4
Walton Heath MK3 .... 57 F4
Walton La SL2 .... 197 F3
Walton Park Rdbt MK7 .... 48 A3
Walton Pl HP22 .... 116 C2
Walton Rd
  Aylesbury HP21 .... 115 F4
  Bow Brickhill MK7 .... 48 A2
  Walton MK7 .... 48 A3
  Wavendon MK17 .... 48 B2
Walton St HP20, HP21 ...... 115 F4
Walton Way HP21 .... 116 A4
Wandlebury MK14 .... 35 D4
Wandsworth Pl MK13 .... 34 B2
Wannions Cl HP5 .... 145 D3
Wantage Cl LU7 .... 79 F2
Wantage Cres LU7 .... 79 F2
Wappenham Rd NN13 .... 27 D4
Wapping HP18 .... 125 E2
Wapseys La SL2 .... 187 F2
Ward Cl SL0 .... 207 F4
Ward Gdns SL1 .... 204 C3
Ward Pl HP7 .... 165 D4
Ward Rd Brackley NN13 ..... 38 A3
  Milton Keynes MK1 .... 47 F2
Ward Royal **6** SL4 .... 210 B3
Ward Royal Par **3** SL4 . 210 B3
Wardes Cl HP16 .... 151 E3
Wardle Pl MK6 .... 46 C4
Wardrobes La HP27 .... 149 E4
Wardstone End MK4 .... 46 A3
Ware Leys Cl OX6 .... 71 F2
Wargrave Rd RG9 .... 191 F3
Warmstone Cl HP18 .... 99 D3
Warmstone La HP18 .... 99 D3
Warneford Ave MK7 .... 131 E1
Warner Cl SL1 .... 204 C1
Warners Cl MK17 .... 59 E3
Warners Hill SL6 .... 195 E4
Warren Bank MK6 .... 57 E2
Warren Bank MK6 .... 47 F3
Warren Cl
  Buckingham MK18 .... 52 C4
  Slough SL3 .... 206 C2
Warren Ct
  7 Farnham Common SL2 198 B4
  Little Horwood MK17 .... 55 F1
Warren Field SL0 .... 200 B2
Warren Ho HP19 .... 101 D3
Warren Rd
  Ickenham UB10 .... 201 F4
  Yardley Gobion NN12 .... 18 C3
Warren The
  Chalfont St Peter SL9 ..... 177 F2
  Chartridge HP16 .... 143 F2
  Holmer Green HP15 .... 163 D1
  Warren Wood Dr HP11 .... 173 E1
  Warren Yd MK12 .... 33 D2
Warrendene Rd HP14 .... 162 A4
Warrender Rd HP5 .... 144 C1
Warren's La SL1 .... 205 E4
Warrington Rd Olney MK46 ... 7 D4
  Warrington MK46 .... 7 D4
Warwick Ave
  High Wycombe HP12 .... 172 A3
  Slough SL2 .... 198 B3
Warwick Cl
  Aston Clinton HP22 .... 117 F1
  Maidenhead SL6 .... 202 A1
Warwick Ct
  Beaconsfield HP9 .... 175 E2
  Chorleywood WD3 .... 167 F3
  34 Windsor SL4 .... 210 B3
Warwick Dr LU7 .... 79 F1
Warwick Ho **7** HP13 .... 173 F4
Warwick Pl
  Milton Keynes MK3 .... 57 F4
  Uxbridge UB10 .... 201 E3
Warwick Rd
  Beaconsfield HP9 .... 175 E2
  Hanslope MK19 .... 11 D2
  Milton Keynes MK3 .... 57 F4
  West Drayton UB7 .... 208 C2
Wash Hill HP10 .... 185 F2
Wash Hill Lea HP10 .... 185 F2
Washfield MK4 .... 46 B1
Washingleys MK43 .... 25 E1
Washington Ct SL7 .... 184 A2
Washington Dr
  Slough SL1 .... 204 B3
  Windsor SL4 .... 209 F2
Washington Row HP7 .... 165 D4
Wastel MK6 .... 47 D3
Watchcroft Dr MK18 .... 41 F3
Watchet Ct MK4 .... 46 B1

Watchet La
Holmer Green HP16 .... 152 B1
Little Kingshill HP16 .... 152 B1
Water Eaton Rd MK2, MK3 .. 58 B4
Water End Rd HP14 .... 159 E2
Water La
Berkhamsted HP4 .... 135 E2
Bovingdon HP3 .... 146 A1
Brackley NN13 .... 38 A4
Chesham HP5 .... 154 A4
Dinton HP17 .... 128 A4
Lacey Green HP27 .... 150 B2
Leighton Buzzard LU7 .... 80 C4
Sherington MK16 .... 13 F1
Water Meadow
Aylesbury HP20 .... 101 F2
Chesham HP5 .... 154 A4
Water Stratford Rd
Tingewick MK18 .... 51 D4
Water Stratford MK18 .... 40 A1
Water Tower Cl UB8 .... 201 F4
Waterbeach Rd SL1 .... 205 E4
Watercroft Rdbt MK4 .... 46 A1
Waterfield W03 .... 167 E1
Waterford Ho UB7 .... 208 B2
Waterglades The HP9 .... 175 E3
Waterhall Comb Sch MK2 .. 58 B2
Waterhouse Cl MK16 .... 22 B2
Waterlily ◼ HP20 .... 101 F2
Waterloo Ct MK3 .... 46 C1
Waterloo Rd
Leighton Buzzard LU7 .... 80 C3
Uxbridge UB8 .... 201 E2
Waterlow Cl MK16 .... 22 B1
Watermead HP20 .... 101 F2
Watermill Way HP22 .... 116 C1
Waterperry Gdns OX33 .... 123 D1
Waterperry Rd HP18 .... 123 E3
Waterside
Berkhamsted HP4 .... 135 E2
Chesham HP5 .... 154 B3
Edlesborough LU6 .... 92 C2
Milton Keynes MK6 .... 47 E4
Uxbridge UB8 .... 208 B4
Wooburn Green HP10 .... 185 F4
Waterside Ct HP5 .... 154 B4
Waterside Cty Comb Sch
HP5 .... 154 B3
Waterside Dr SL3 .... 207 D2
Waterslade Pens HP17 .... 126 C3
Watersmeet Ct MK4 .... 46 B2
Watery La
Beachampton MK19 .... 44 A3
Brackley NN13 .... 38 A4
Frieth RG9 .... 170 A1
Marsworth HP23 .... 104 C1
Wooburn Green HP10 ...... 185 F4
Watling St
Bow Brickhill MK17 .... 58 C4
Milton Keynes MK19 .... 33 D1
Pottersbury NN12 .... 18 B2
Watling Terr MK2 .... 47 F1
Watling Way Cty Fst Sch
MK11 .... 32 C2
Watling Way Cty Mid Sch
MK11 .... 32 C2
Wattington Ct HP16 .... 152 A4
Wattington Rd OX9 .... 157 D4
Watten Ct MK2 .... 58 C2
Wattleton Rd HP9 .... 175 F1
Watts Cl MK19 .... 11 D2
Wavell Ct MK15 .... 35 D4
Wavell Gdns SL2 .... 197 F1
Wavell Rd
Beaconsfield HP9 .... 176 A1
Maidenhead SL6 .... 202 A3
Wavendon Cty Fst Sch
MK17 .... 48 C4
Wavendon Fields MK17 .... 48 C3
Wavendon House Dr MK17 . 49 D4
Wavendon Rd MK17 .... 37 E1
Waveney Cl MK16 .... 22 C2
Waverley Rd SL1 .... 205 E4
Waverley Wlk HP20 .... 101 E1
Waxwing Cl HP20 .... 101 F2
Wayfarers Pk HP4 .... 134 C2
Wayside
High Wycombe HP13 ...... 173 E4
Lacey Green HP27 .... 150 B2
Wayside Ct HP6 .... 154 B1
Wayside Gdns SL9 .... 188 B2
Wayside Mews SL6 .... 202 C4
Wealdstone Pl MK6 .... 35 D1
Weasel La MK3 .... 57 E3
Weatherby LU6 .... 93 F4
Weathercock Cl MK17 .... 49 D3
Weathercock Gdns HP15 . 163 E4
Weathercock La
Aspley Guise MK17 .... 49 E2
Woburn Sands MK17 .... 49 E2
Weavers End MK19 .... 11 D1

Weavers Hill MK11 .... 33 D2
Weavers Rd HP23 .... 118 C2
Webb Cl Chesham HP5 .... 144 A1
Slough SL3 .... 206 B1
Webber Heath MK7 .... 48 B2
Webster Cl
Maidenhead SL6 .... 202 A3
Thame OX9 .... 125 F1
Webster Rd HP21 .... 116 A3
Wedgewood Ave MK4 ...... 22 A1
Wedgewood Dr HP14 ...... 162 A3
Weedon Cl SL9 .... 177 D1
Weedon Hill HP6 .... 153 E2
Weedon La HP6 .... 154 A2
Weedon Rd HP19 .... 101 E1
Weekes Dr SL1 .... 205 D2
Weir Rd HP21 .... 116 A2
Weir La Blackthorn OX6 .... 81 D2
East Claydon MK18 .... 74 C3
Whitchurch HP22 .... 86 C3
Welbeck Ave HP21 .... 116 B3
Welbeck Rd SL6 .... 202 B3
Welby Cl SL6 .... 202 A2
Welden SL2 .... 206 B4
Welders La
Chalfont St Giles SL9 ...... 177 D2
Gerrards Cross SL9 .... 177 D2
Seer Green SL9 .... 177 D2
Welford Way HP18 .... 112 C2
Well Croft LU7 .... 105 F3
Well Head Rd LU6 .... 93 E3
Well La LU7 .... 79 F1
Well St MK18 .... 52 B4
Welland Cl SL3 .... 212 A4
Welland Dr MK16 .... 22 C2
Welland Ho MK3 .... 57 F4
Welland Rd HP21 .... 115 E3
Wellbank SL6 .... 196 C1
Wellbrook Mews ◼ HP23 119 D2
Wellcroft LU7 .... 105 F3
Wellcroft Rd SL1 .... 205 D3
Weller Cl HP6 .... 154 C1
Wellesbourne Gdns HP13 162 B1
Wellesley Ave SL0 .... 207 F2
Wellesley Cl SL0 .... 207 F2
Wellesley Path SL1 .... 206 A2
Wellesley Rd SL1 .... 206 A2
Welley Ave TW19 .... 211 F2
Welley Rd Horton TW19 .. 211 F1
Wraysbury TW19 .... 211 F1
Wellfield HP15 .... 163 D2
Wellfield Ct MK15 .... 35 E4
Wellfield Rd HP14 .... 171 D4
Wellhayes MK14 .... 34 C4
Wellhouse Rd SL6 .... 195 F1
Wellhouse Way HP14 ...... 161 F3
Wellingborough Rd MK46 .... 6 C3
Wellington Ave HP27 ...... 139 D2
Wellington Pl
Aylesbury HP21 .... 115 F2
Milton Keynes MK3 .... 58 A4
Wellington Rd
Aylesbury HP21 .... 115 F2
High Wycombe HP12 .... 172 C3
Maidenhead SL6 .... 202 B4
Uxbridge UB8 .... 201 E2
Wellington St SL1 .... 206 A2
Wells Cl SL4 .... 210 A4
Wellsmead Cty Fst Sch
MK3 .... 46 C1
Wellsmead Cty Mid Sch
MK3 .... 46 C1
Welsh La MK18 .... 40 B3
Welton Rd HP21 .... 116 A4
Wendover CE Mid Sch
HP22 .... 131 D3
Wendover House Sch
HP22 .... 131 E2
Wendover Hts HP22 .... 131 E3
Wendover Rd Aylesbury
HP17, HP21, HP22 .... 116 B2
Bourne End SL8 .... 185 D3
Burnham SL1 .... 204 A4
Ellesborough HP17 .... 130 B2
Stoke Mandeville HP22 .. 116 B2
Wendover St HP11 .... 172 C4
Wendover Sta HP22 .... 131 D2
Wendover Way
Aylesbury HP21 .... 115 F3
High Wycombe HP11 .... 173 D3
Wenlack Cl UB9 .... 190 A1
Wenning La MK4 .... 46 A1
Wentworth Ave SL2 .... 198 A1
Wentworth Cl HP13 .... 173 E4
Wentworth Cres SL6 ...... 202 B3
Wentworth Way MK3 ...... 57 E4
Wenwell Cl HP22 .... 118 A2
Werner Ct HP21 .... 115 F2
Werner Terr MK18 .... 73 D3
Werth Dr MK17 .... 49 D1

Wescott Way UB8 .... 201 E2
Wesley Dene ◼ HP13 .... 173 D4
Wesley Hill HP5 .... 144 A1
Wessex Ct ◼ TW19 .... 213 F1
Wessex Inf Sch SL6 .... 202 A2
Wessex Jun Sch SL6 ...... 202 A2
Wessex Rd
Bourne End SL8 .... 185 D1
Harmondsworth TW6 .... 213 F2
Wessex Road Ind Est SL8 185 D1
Wessex Way SL6 .... 202 A2
Wessons Hill SL6 .... 195 E4
West Acres HP7 .... 165 E4
West Ave HP10 .... 163 E1
West Cl SL7 .... 193 E4
West Comm SL0 .... 188 B3
West Common Cl SL9 .... 188 C3
West Common Rd UB8 .... 201 E3
West Cres SL4 .... 209 F3
West Dales MK13 .... 34 B3
West Dean SL6 .... 202 C4
Wot Dr HP13 .... 173 E4
West Drayton Park Ave
UB7 .... 208 C2
West Drayton Prim Sch
UB7 .... 208 C2
West Drayton Sta UB7 .... 208 C3
West Edge OX6 .... 71 F1
West End HP22 .... 116 C1
West End Ct SL2 .... 198 C2
West End La SL2 .... 198 C2
West End Pl HP22 .... 116 C1
West End Rd
Cheddington LU7 .... 104 C4
High Wycombe HP11 .... 172 C4
West End St HP11 .... 172 C4
West Farm Way MK46 ...... 13 F4
West Furlong MK18 .... 53 D1
West Hill MK17 .... 49 E2
West Hyde La SL9 .... 178 A2
West La Bledlow HP27 .... 138 A1
Emberton MK46 .... 13 F4
West Leith HP23 .... 118 C1
West Mead SL6 .... 195 F1
West Pas ◼ HP23 .... 119 D2
West Point SL1 .... 204 B3
West Rd
Berkhamsted HP4 .... 135 D3
Cranfield MK43 .... 24 B1
Maidenhead SL6 .... 202 C4
West Drayton UB7 .... 208 C2
Woburn Sands MK17 ...... 49 D3
West Ridge SL8 .... 185 D2
West Side Rise MK46 .... 6 C2
West Sq SL0 .... 207 F4
West St Adstock MK18 .... 53 F1
Aylesbury HP19 .... 101 E1
Buckingham MK18 .... 41 E1
Dunstable LU6 .... 93 F4
Henley-on-T RG9 .... 191 E1
Leighton Buzzard LU7 ...... 80 C4
Maidenhead SL6 .... 202 C4
Marlow SL7 .... 183 E1
Olney MK46 .... 6 C2
Steeple Claydon MK18 .... 63 E1
West View Chesham HP5 144 B1
Hardwick HP22 .... 87 D2
West Way HP9 .... 174 C1
West Waye HP13 .... 162 B1
West Well Cl MK18 .... 51 D3
West Well La MK18 .... 51 D3
West Wycombe City
Comb Sch HP14 .... 160 C1
West Wycombe Hill Rd
HP14 .... 160 C1
West Wycombe Ho HP14 . 160 C1
West Wycombe Rd HP13 . 161 E1
West Yard Ind Est HP14 .. 160 B4
Westanley Ave HP7 .... 165 E4
Westborne Ct MK13 .... 34 A3
Westborough Ct SL6 ...... 202 B3
Westborough Rd SL6 ...... 202 B3
Westbourne St HP11 ...... 172 C4
Westbrook Cl MK15 .... 203 F1
Westbrook End MK17 ...... 57 E2
Westbury Cl MK16 .... 22 A2
Westbury Ho ◼ HP20 .... 101 E1
Westbury La MK16 .... 22 A3
Westcliffe MK8 .... 33 E1
Westcott CE Fst Sch HP18 .. 98 A4
Westcott Slough SL2 ...... 198 A1
Tring HP23 .... 119 D2
Westdean La HP16 .... 143 E2
Western Ave
Buckingham MK18 .... 41 E1
New Denham UB9 .... 201 E4
Uxbridge UB8 .... 201 E4
Western Dene HP15 ...... 163 D3
Western Dr
Hanslope MK19 .... 11 D2
Wooburn Green HP10 .... 185 F3

Western House Inf Sch
SL1 .... 204 C3
Western La MK18 .... 65 F2
Western Perimeter Rd
Harmondsworth
TW6,TW19 .... 213 D2
Stanwell TW6,TW19 ...... 213 D2
Western Perimeter Road Rdbt
TW19 .... 213 E1
Western Rd
Great Horwood MK17 ...... 55 D2
Milton Keynes, Fenny Stratford
MK2 .... 47 E1
Milton Keynes, Wolverton
MK12 .... 33 E3
Tring HP23 .... 118 C2
Westfield
Hyde Heath HP6 .... 153 E2
Stoke Mandeville HP21 .. 115 F2
Westfield Ave MK19 .... 31 E3
Westfield Bglws SL7 ...... 192 C3
Westfield Cotts SL7 ...... 192 C3
Westfield Fst Sch HP4 .... 134 C3
Westfield Rd
Beaconsfield HP9 .... 175 E1
Berkhamsted HP4 .... 134 C3
Dunstable LU6 .... 93 F4
Maidenhead SL6 .... 202 A4
Milton Keynes MK2 .... 58 B4
Slough SL2 .... 198 A1
Westfield Sch SL8 .... 185 D2
Westfield Wlk HP12 ...... 172 B3
Westfields
Buckingham MK18 .... 52 A4
Princes Risborough HP27 . 139 E2
Westgate Cres SL1 .... 204 C3
Westgate Ct HP10 .... 174 A2
Westgate Sch The SL1 .... 205 D3
Westhill MK14 .... 34 B4
Westhope Rd SL7 .... 183 F2
Westland Ct ◼ TW19 .... 213 F1
Westlands Ave SL1 .... 204 B4
Westlands Cl SL1 .... 204 B4
Westlands Rd HP27 ...... 149 F3
Westlington La HP17 ...... 113 F1
Westlington Lea HP17 .... 113 F1
Westmead
Princes Risborough HP27 139 D3
Windsor SL4 .... 210 A2
Westminster Cl
Brackley NN13 .... 38 A4
High Wycombe HP11 .... 173 D2
Westminster Dr
Aylesbury HP21 .... 115 F3
Milton Keynes MK3 ...... 47 D1
Westmorland Ave HP21 .. 116 A3
Westmorland Rd SL6 ...... 202 B3
Westmount Ave HP7 ...... 165 E4
Weston Ct HP22 .... 117 E3
Weston La OX9 .... 136 C4
Weston Rd
Aston Clinton HP22 .... 117 E3
Lewknor OX9 .... 157 D4
Olney MK46 .... 6 C2
Ravenstone MK46 .... 5 F1
Slough SL1 .... 204 C4
Weston Underwood MK46 .... 6 C2
Weston Turville CE Comb Sch
HP22 .... 116 C2
Weston Way HP22 .... 116 A1
Westover Ct HP13 .... 161 E1
Westover Rd HP13 .... 161 E1
Westpitts MK46 .... 13 F4
Westrick Walk HP16 ...... 151 E3
Westside Rd MK16 .... 12 A3
Westwood HP12 .... 172 A2
Westwood Cl
Little Chalfont HP6 .... 166 B4
Milton Keynes MK8 .... 45 F4
Westwood Dr HP6 .... 166 B4
Westwood Rd SL7 .... 183 E1
Westwood Wlk ◼ HP20 .. 101 F1
Wetherburn Ct ◼ MK2 .... 58 B4
Wetherby Gdns MK3 ...... 57 E3
Wetherel Dr SL1 .... 204 A4
Wethered Rd SL7 .... 183 E1
Wexford Ct SL6 .... 203 D4
Wexham Cl SL2 .... 206 B4
Wexham Court Comb Sch
SL2 .... 206 B4
Wexham Park La HP4 ....
Iver Heath SL3 .... 199 E1
Stoke Poges SL3 .... 199 E1
Wexham Pl SL2 .... 199 D3
Wexham Park Hospl SL2 . 199 E1
Wexham Rd SL1, SL2 ...... 206 A3
Wexham St SL3 .... 199 D2
Wexham Woods SL3 ...... 206 B4
Wey La HP5 .... 154 A4

Whadden Rd MK4, MK5 .... 45 F1
Whaddon CE Fst Sch
MK17 .... 56 A4
Whaddon Chase HP19 .... 101 E1
Whaddon Rd
Mursley MK17 .... 67 E4
Nash MK17 .... 44 B1
Newport Pagnell MK16 .... 22 A2
Newton Longville MK17 .... 57 E2
Shenley Brook End MK5 .. 46 A2
Slough SL2 .... 206 B4
Whales La OX6 .... 71 F1
Wharf Cl MK13 .... 47 D1
Wharf Cl HP22 .... 131 D3
Wharf Ct UB8 .... 201 E1
Wharf La
Berkhamsted HP4 .... 134 B4
Bourne End SL8 .... 185 D2
Henley-on-T RG9 .... 191 F1
Old Stratford MK19 .... 32 B4
Wharf Rd HP22 .... 131 D3
Wharf The
Maidenhead SL6 .... 203 E4
Milton Keynes MK2 .... 58 C3
Milton Keynes, Giffard Park
MK14 .... 21 F1
Wharf View MK18 .... 41 F1
Wharf Way HP23 .... 118 A2
Wharfside MK2 .... 47 F1
Wharfside Mkt HP4 .... 41 F1
Wharton Ho ◼ HP20 ...... 101 E1
Whatmore Cl TW19 .... 213 D1
Wheat Cl HP21 .... 115 F2
Wheatbutts The SL4 ...... 204 C1
Wheatcroft Cl MK6 .... 47 D3
Wheatfield Cl SL6 .... 202 A2
Wheatlands Rd SL3 .... 206 B2
Wheatley Campus
(Brookes Univ) OX33 .. 122 B1
Wheatley Cl MK4 .... 46 B1
Wheatley Park Sch
OX33 .... 122 A1
Wheatley Way SL9 .... 177 F2
Wheatsheaf Par SL4 ...... 211 D1
Wheeler Ave HP10 .... 174 B4
Wheeler Cl HP20 .... 116 A4
Wheeler Rd OX9 .... 147 E3
Wheelers Flats HP10 ...... 174 B4
Wheelers La MK43 .... 34 A3
Wheelers Orch SL9 .... 177 F2
Wheelers Yd HP16 .... 152 A4
Wheelwright Mews
MK14 .... 34 C3
Wheelwright Rd HP27 .... 138 B4
Wheelwrights HP22 ...... 116 C1
Wheelwrights Pl SL3 ...... 212 B4
Whetstone Cl MK13 ...... 34 A2
Whichcote Gdns HP5 .... 154 B3
Whichert Cl HP9 .... 175 E3
Whichford MK14 .... 22 A1
Whielden Cl HP7 .... 165 D4
Whielden Green HP7 .... 165 D4
Whielden La
Amersham HP7 .... 165 D3
Coleshill HP7 .... 164 C3
Whielden St HP7 .... 165 D4
Whichat HP20 .... 101 F2
Whincup Cl HP11 .... 172 C2
Whinneys Rd HP10 .... 174 B2
Whipass Hill HP9 .... 176 A3
Whipsnade Park Golf Course
HP4 .... 107 F3
Whipsnade Rd LU6 .... 93 F3
Whipsnade Wildlife
Animal Pk HP4 .... 107 F4
Whitby Cl MK3 .... 47 D1
Whitby Rd SL1 .... 205 E3
Whitchurch Cl
Maidenhead SL6 .... 195 F2
Westcott HP18 .... 98 A4
Whitchurch Cty Comb Sch
HP22 .... 86 C4
Whitchurch La HP22 ...... 86 B4
Whitchurch Rd LU7 .... 78 A1
White Alder MK12 .... 33 F3
White Cl
High Wycombe HP13 .... 161 E1
Slough SL1 .... 205 E3
White Cross HP22 .... 131 E4
White Hart HP18 .... 96 A4
White Hart Close HP8 .... 177 D4
White Hart Field HP22 .... 85 D2
White Hart La HP17 ...... 127 D3
White Hart Meadow HP7 . 175 F1
White Hart Rd
◼ Maidenhead SL6 ...... 202 C4
Slough SL1 .... 205 E2
White Hart St ◼ HP11 .. 173 D4

White Hill
Ashley Green HP5 .... 145 E4
Beaconsfield HP9 .... 185 F4
Chesham HP5 .... 144 B1
High Wycombe HP13 .... 162 A1
Remenham Hill RG9 .... 192 A1
Wooburn Green HP9 .... 185 F4
White Hill Cl HP5 .... 144 B1
White Horse Dr MK4 .... 46 B1
White Horse La HP22 .... 87 D3
White Horse Rd SL4 .... 209 E3
White House Cl SL9 .... 177 F2
White Lilies Island SL4 ..... 210 A4
White Lion Cl HP7 .... 166 A4
White Lion Rd
Amersham HP7 .... 166 A4
Little Chalfont HP7 .... 166 A4
White Lodge Cl SL7 .... 183 E3
White Paddock SL6 .... 202 A1
White Rock SL6 .... 196 A1
White Spire Sch MK3 .... 46 C1
White View 22 HP20 .... 101 F2
Whiteacres Dr SL6 .... 203 D1
Whitebaker Ct MK14 .... 34 C3
Whitecross Rd HP17 .... 126 C3
Whitefield La HP16 .... 152 A3
Whiteford Rd SL2 .... 205 F4
Whitegate Cross MK6 .... 47 D3
Whitehall SL6 .... 196 A1
Whitehall
Berkhamsted HP4 .... 135 E3
Olney MK46 .... 6 C3
Whitehall Ave MK10 .... 36 B1
Whitehall Cl UB8 .... 201 E2
Whitehall Inf Sch UB8 ...... 201 E2
Whitehall Jun Sch UB8 ..... 201 E2
Whitehall La TW19 .... 212 A1
Whitehall Rd UB8 .... 201 E2
Whitehall St 6 HP21 .... 101 E1
Whitehaven SL1 .... 205 F3
Whitehill
Berkhamsted HP4 .... 135 E3
Olney MK46 .... 6 C3
Whitehill Ct HP4 .... 135 E3
Whitehills Cl SL7 .... 183 E3
Whitehorns MK16 .... 22 A2
Whitehorse Yd MK11 .... 32 B3
Whitehorse Way SL4 .... 210 C1
Whitehouse La HP, H10 .... 174 C1
Whitehouse Way SL0 .... 200 B1
Whitelands Ave WD3 .... 167 D3
Whitelands Rd HP12 .... 172 A4
Whitelands Way HP21 ...... 172 B4
Whiteleaf Way HP27 .... 139 E3
Whiteley SL4 .... 209 F4
Whiteley Cres MK3 .... 57 F3
Whitepit La HP10 .... 185 E4
Whites La SL3 .... 211 D4
Whitethorn Ave UB7 .... 208 C3
Whitethorn Pl UB7 .... 208 C3
Whitewood Rd HP4 .... 135 D2
Whitfield Rd HP14 .... 162 A3
Whitfield Way WD3 .... 167 F1
Whitley Cl TW19 .... 213 F1
Whitley Ct HP21 .... 115 F2
Whitmees Cl MK46 .... 6 C2
Whitsun Pasture MK15 ..... 35 D4
Whittaker Rd SL2 .... 197 F1
Whittenham Cl SL2 .... 206 A3
Whittle Parkway SL1 .... 204 B4
Whitton Way MK16 .... 22 B2
Whitworth La MK5 .... 46 A4
Whurley Way SL4 .... 195 F1
Whyteladyes La SL6 .... 195 F3
Whytingham Rd HP23 ...... 119 E2
Wick Rd HP23 .... 133 E4
Wicken Rd MK18 .... 30 C1
Wickets The SL6 .... 202 B4
Widbrook Rd SL6 .... 196 A2
Widdenton View HP14 ..... 171 E3
Widecroft Rd SL0 .... 207 F4
Widewater Bsns Ctr UB9 .. 190 B3
Widmer End Cty Comb Sch
HP15 .... 162 C3
Widmere Field HP16 .... 151 E3
Widmere La SL7 .... 183 D1
Widmore Cl HP5 .... 143 F3
Wigan's La HP27 .... 148 B3
Wiggington Bottom HP23 . 133 E4
Wigmore Ct HP19 .... 101 D1
Wigmore Rd HP19 .... 101 D1
Wigwell Gdns MK17 .... 55 D1
Wildacre Rd MK5 .... 46 A2
Wilderness The HP4 .... 135 E2
Wildgreen N SL3 .... 207 D1
Wildgreen S SL3 .... 207 D1
Wildwood Ct WD3 .... 167 F3
Wilford Cl HP15 .... 35 E1
Wilford Rd SL3 .... 206 C1
Wilfrids Wood Cl SL8 .... 185 D3

Willen Cty Comb Sch
MK15 .... 35 E4
Willen La MK14 .... 34 C4
Willen Park Ave MK15 ...... 35 D4
Willen Rd
Milton Keynes MK10 .... 35 F2
Newport Pagnell MK16 .... 22 B2
Willets Rise MK5 .... 46 A3
Willetts La UB9 .... 200 C4
Willey Ct MK11 .... 32 C2
William Bandy Cl LU7 ...... 79 F2
William Burt Cl HP22 .... 116 C1
William Durrant Cty
Mid Sch The HP5 .... 144 A2
William Ellis Cl SL4 .... 211 D1
William Harding Cl HP21 .. 115 F4
William Harding Cty Fst Sch
HP21 .... 116 A3
William Harding Cty Mid Sch
HP21 .... 115 F3
William Hill Dr HP22 .... 102 B2
William Ho 7 HP13 .... 173 F3
William Moulder Ct HP5 ... 144 A2
William Penn Comb Sch
SL2 .... 198 B1
William St
Berkhamsted HP4 .... 135 E2
Slough SL1 .... 205 F3
Windsor SL4 .... 210 B3
William Sutton Ho MK6 .... 46 A3
Williams Circ MK7 .... 48 A2
Williams Cl
Aylesbury HP19 .... 101 E1
Hanslope MK19 .... 10 C2
Williams Way HP27 .... 138 B3
William Smith Cl MK5 ...... 35 E2
Willis Rd HP17 .... 127 D3
Willoners SL2 .... 205 D4
Willoughby Rd SL3 .... 207 D2
Willoughby's Wlk HP21 .... 161 E1
Willow Ave
High Wycombe HP12 .... 172 A2
New Denham UB9 .... 201 E3
West Drayton UB8 .... 208 C3
Willow Bank SL7 .... 183 E3
Willow Chase HP15 .... 162 C2
Willow Cl Colnbrook SL3 .. 212 B4
Flackwell Heath HP10 .... 185 D3
Moulsoe MK16 .... 36 B4
Willow Cres E UB9 .... 201 E4
Willow Cres W UB9 .... 201 E4
Willow Ct Aylesbury HP19 . 101 D1
High Wycombe HP11 ...... 173 F2
Walter's Ash HP14 .... 161 E4
Willow Dr
Buckingham MK18 .... 52 C4
Maidenhead SL6 .... 203 D1
Willow End HP22 .... 116 C1
Willow Gr MK19 .... 32 A3
Willow Herb HP20 .... 101 F2
Willow La HP7 .... 165 F3
Willow Par SL3 .... 207 D2
Willow Park SL2 .... 199 D3
Willow Pl SL4 .... 210 B4
Willow Rd
Aylesbury HP19 .... 101 E1
Brackley NN13 .... 38 A3
Chinnor OX9 .... 147 E3
Great Horwood MK17 ..... 55 D2
Stanwell SL3 .... 212 C3
Thame OX9 .... 125 F1
Willow Rise HP17 .... 127 D4
Willow Way
Loudwater HP10 .... 174 A1
Milton Keynes MK2 .... 58 B4
Princes Risborough HP27 139 D2
Wing LU7 .... 79 F2
Willow Wlk HP15 .... 163 D2
Willowbank HP22 .... 131 D4
Willowbank Terr 8 HP21 .. 115 F4
Willowbrook Slough SL4 ... 205 E1
Wendover HP22 .... 131 D4
Willowford MK13 .... 33 F3
Willowmead HP17 .... 114 C3
Willowmead Cl 10 SL7 ..... 183 F2
Willowmead Cty Fst Sch
HP21 .... 115 E3
Willowmead Gdns SL7 ..... 183 F2
Willowmead Rd 6 SL7 ..... 183 F2
Willowmead Sq 9 SL7 ..... 183 F2
Willows Rd SL8 .... 185 D2
Willows The
Amersham HP6 .... 154 A2
14 Bourne End SL8 .... 185 D2
High Wycombe HP12 ...... 172 C4
Longwick HP27 .... 138 C3
Windsor SL4 .... 209 E4
Wilmar Cl UB8 .... 201 E3
Wilmin Gr MK5 .... 46 A4
Wilmot Rd SL1 .... 197 D1
Wilsley Pound MK7 .... 48 A4

Wilson Ct MK8 .... 45 F4
Wilton Ave MK3 .... 58 A4
Wilton Cl UB7 .... 213 E4
Wilton Cres
Beaconsfield HP9 .... 175 F2
Windsor SL4 .... 209 E2
Wilton Hollow HP9 .... 175 F2
Wilton La HP9 .... 174 C2
Wilton Rd HP9 .... 175 F2
Wiltshire Ave SL2 .... 198 B1
Wiltshire Lodge 2 SL6 ..... 202 C3
Wiltshire Rd SL7 .... 183 F2
Wimbledon Pl MK13 .... 34 B2
Wimblington Dr MK6 .... 47 D2
Wimborne Cres MK4 .... 45 F1
Wimpole Rd UB7 .... 208 B3
Winbury Ct SL6 .... 202 C4
Winbury Sch SL6 .... 203 D2
Wincanton Hill MK3 .... 57 E3
Winchbottom La
SL7 ,HP10 .... 184 A4
Winchendon Rd HP18 ...... 112 A1
Winchester Circ MK10 ..... 36 A1
Winchester Cl
Amersham HP7 .... 165 F4
Stanwell SL3 .... 212 C3
Winchester Ct HP10 .... 174 A2
Winchester Dr SL6 .... 202 A2
Winchester Ho HP21 .... 115 F3
Windermere Dr MK2 .... 58 B3
Windermere Cl
Aylesbury HP21 .... 116 A3
Chorleywood WD3 .... 167 E2
Windermere Gdns LU7 ..... 80 B4
Windermere Way
Slough SL1 .... 204 B4
West Drayton UB7 .... 208 C3
Windmill Cl
Buckingham MK18 .... 41 F1
Ivinghoe LU7 .... 105 F3
Windsor SL4 .... 210 A3
Windmill Dr HP15 .... 162 C3
Windmill Hill
Chipperfield WD4 .... 156 C4
Coleshill HP7 .... 164 C1
Princes Risborough HP27 139 D1
Windmill Hill Dr MK3 ..... 57 E4
Windmill Hill Rdbt MK4 .. 46 B1
Windmill La HP15 .... 162 C4
Windmill Par HP15 .... 162 C3
Windmill Rd
Cookham SL6 .... 195 D3
Fulmer SL3 .... 199 E4
Gerrards Cross SL9 .... 177 E2
Haddenham HP17 .... 126 C3
Slough SL1, SL3 .... 205 E3
Thame OX9 .... 126 C1
Windmill St HP18 .... 96 A1
Windmill Way
Cranfield MK43 .... 25 E2
Tring HP23 .... 118 C2
Windmill Wood Ho MK4 ... 154 A1
Windrush Ave SL3 .... 207 D2
Windrush Cl UB10 .... 201 F4
Windrush Ct
Aylesbury HP21 .... 115 E2
High Wycombe HP13 ...... 173 F4
Windsor SL4 .... 210 D3
Windsor SL6 .... 202 C4
Windsor Ave
Leighton Buzzard LU7 .... 80 C4
Newport Pagnell MK16 ... 22 B2
Windsor Boys Sch SL4 ..... 210 A3
Windsor Bsns Ctr The
SL4 .... 210 B4
Windsor Castle SL4 .... 210 C4
Windsor Cl Bovingdon HP3 146 A2
Burnham SL1 .... 197 E1
Windsor Cres HP10 .... 174 B1
Windsor Ct HP6 .... 154 B1
Windsor Dr HP13 .... 162 B1
Windsor End HP9 .... 186 C4
Windsor Rd
Aylesbury HP21 .... 116 A4
Chesham HP5 .... 144 A2
Datchet SL3 .... 211 D4
Gerrards Cross SL9 .... 188 B2
Maidenhead SL6 .... 203 E1
Oakley Green SL6 .... 203 E1
Slough SL1, SL2, SL3 ..... 205 F2
Wraysbury TW19 .... 211 F1

Windsor St
Milton Keynes MK2 .... 58 B4
Milton Keynes, Wolverton
MK12 .... 33 E3
Uxbridge UB8 .... 201 E3
Winemar Cl MK19 .... 11 D2
Winer Cl SL7 .... 183 E1
Wing Rd Cublington LU7 .. 78 B2
Leighton Buzzard LU7 .... 80 B3
Stewkley LU7 .... 78 C3
Wingate Ave HP13 .... 173 F4
Wingate Circ MK7 .... 48 A2
Wingate Cl HP13 .... 173 F4
Wingate Walk HP20 .... 116 A4
Wingrave CE Comb Sch
HP22 .... 89 D2
Wingrave Crossroads
HP22 .... 88 C2
Wingrave Rd
Aston Abbotts HP22 ...... 88 C2
Long Marston HP23 .... 104 B1
Tring HP23 .... 119 D3
Winkers Cl SL9 .... 177 F1
Winkers La SL9 .... 177 F2
Winkfield La SL4 .... 209 D1
Winkfield Rd SL4 .... 209 F1
Winnock Rd UB7 .... 208 B3
Winsford Hill MK4 .... 46 C2
Winslow CE Comb Sch
MK18 .... 66 A3
Winslow Cty Fst Sch
MK18 .... 66 A2
Winslow Field HP16 .... 151 F4
Winslow Gdns SL3 .... 174 A4
Winslow Rd
Granborough MK18 .... 75 F4
Great Horwood MK17 .... 54 C1
Little Horwood MK17 ..... 55 E1
Mursley MK17 .... 67 D2
Nash MK17 .... 55 E4
Swanbourne MK17 .... 66 C2
Wingrave MK17 .... 89 D2
Winstane Cl HP6 .... 154 A3
Winstanley La MK5 .... 46 B2
Winston Gdns HP4 .... 134 C2
Winston Ho HP11 .... 174 A2
Winter Hill SL6 .... 184 B1
Winter Hill Rd
Cookham SL6 .... 195 D2
Maidenhead SL6 .... 195 D2
Winterburn MK13 .... 34 A3
Winters Way HP15 .... 163 E4
Winterton Dr HP21 .... 115 F2
Wintoun Path SL2 .... 197 F1
Winvale SL1 .... 205 F2
Winwood Slough SL2 ...... 206 B4
Windsor SL4 .... 209 F3
Windsor Dr HP22 .... 85 D3
Wise La UB7 .... 208 B1
Wishart Gn MK7 .... 48 C3
Wisley Ave MK13 .... 34 B2
Wistmans MK4 .... 46 B2
Witan Gate MK9 .... 34 B1
Witchell HP22 .... 131 D2
Witham Ct MK3 .... 46 B1
Witham Way HP21 .... 115 E2
Witheridge La HP9 .... 175 D4
Withey Cl SL4 .... 209 F3
Withington MK13 .... 34 A3
Withycombe MK4 .... 46 C2
Withycroft SL3 .... 206 C4
Witney Cl UB10 .... 201 F4
Wittington Cotts SL7 ..... 193 E3
Wittmills Oak MK18 ...... 41 F1
Wivelsfield LU6 .... 92 C3
Woad La MK14 .... 34 C4
Woburn Ave MK12 .... 33 E4
Woburn Golf & Ctry Club The
MK17 .... 59 F4
Woburn La MK17 .... 49 F2
Woburn Lower Sch MK17 . 60 C4
Woburn Rd
Aspley Heath MK17 ...... 60 B3
Heath MK17 .... 60 B1
Little Brickhill MK17 ..... 59 F2
Woburn Sands MK17 .... 48 B2
Woburn Sands Sta MK17 . 49 D3
Wodehouse Wlk MK16 .... 22 A2
Wolf La SL4 .... 209 F2
Wolfcote La MK4 .... 46 A2
Wolsey Gdns MK3 .... 34 A2
Wolstan Cl UB9 .... 190 A1
Wolverton Rd
Castlethorpe MK19 .... 20 A3
Milton Keynes, Giffard Park
MK14 .... 21 F1
Milton Keynes, Wolverton
MK12,MK19 .... 33 F4
Newport Pagnell MK16 ... 22 A2
Wolverton Sta MK12,MK19 . 33 F4

Woburn Common Rd
SL1 .... 186 A1
Wooburn Grange HP10 ... 185 E2
Wooburn Green La HP9 ... 186 A4
Wooburn Manor Park
HP10 .... 185 F3
Wooburn Mews HP10 ..... 185 F3
Wood Cl SL4 .... 210 B2
Wood End
Little Horwood MK17 .... 55 F1
Nash MK17 .... 55 E4
Wood End Cl SL2 .... 187 E1
Wood End Cty Fst Sch
MK13 .... 34 B4
Wood End La MK16 .... 23 F1
Wood La
Aspley Guise MK17 .... 49 E2
Iver SL0 .... 207 E4
Milton Keynes MK14,MK17 34 C4
Pottersbury NN12 .... 18 C2
Slough SL1, SL2 .... 205 D2
South Heath HP16 .... 152 C4
Weston Underwood MK46 . 6 A1
Wood Lane Cl SL0 .... 200 A1
Wood Pond Cl HP9 .... 176 B2
Wood Rd MK43 .... 3 F4
Wood St
Milton Keynes MK13 ..... 33 F4
Waddesdon HP18 .... 99 D4
Woburn Sands MK17 .... 49 D2
Wood Way HP9 .... 174 C1
Woodbank HP27 .... 149 E3
Woodbank Ave SL9 .... 188 B3
Woodbank Dr HP8 .... 177 E4
Woodbine Cotts SL9 ...... 188 B4
Woodbridge Ho UB8 ...... 201 E3
Woodbury Cl SL8 .... 185 E2
Woodchester Park HP9 ... 175 E3
Woodcock HP14 .... 161 D4
Woodcote SL6 .... 202 B3
Woodcote Green HP13 ... 161 E1
Woodcote Lawns HP5 .... 144 A2
Woodcroft Rd HP5 .... 144 B2
Woodfield HP27 .... 149 E3
Woodfield Dr SL6 .... 202 A3
Woodfield Park HP6 ...... 154 A2
Woodford Way SL2 .... 198 A1
Woodhall Cl UB8 .... 201 E4
Woodhill Ave SL9 .... 189 D3
Woodhill Ct
Amersham HP6 .... 154 B1
Gerrards Cross SL9 ...... 188 C2
Woodhouse Ct MK14 ..... 34 B3
Woodhurst Dr UB9 .... 189 F3
Woodhurst Rd SL6 .... 196 A1
Woodhurst South SL6 ... 196 B1
Woodland Ave
Leighton Buzzard LU7 ... 70 C1
Slough SL1 .... 205 E3
Windsor SL4 .... 209 F2
Woodland Cl
High Wycombe HP12 ..... 172 B3
Marlow SL7 .... 183 F2
Tring HP23 .... 118 C1
Woodland La WD3 .... 167 E3
Woodland Rd WD3 .... 178 B3
Woodland View
Chesham HP5 .... 154 B3
Milton Keynes MK12 ..... 33 E3
Woodland Way
Marlow SL7 .... 183 F2
Woburn Sands MK17 .... 49 D2
Woodlands SL9 .... 188 C3
Woodlands Ave HP4 ..... 135 E2
Woodlands Bsns Pk SL6 . 202 A1
Woodlands Cl
Buckingham MK18 .... 41 F1
Gerrards Cross SL9 ...... 189 D3
Holmer Green HP15 ..... 163 E3
Woodlands Cotts 4 SL2 . 198 B4
Woodlands Cres HP16 ... 41 E1
Woodlands Dr
Beaconsfield HP9 .... 175 E2
Walter's Ash HP14 ...... 161 E4
Woodlands Glade
Beaconsfield HP9 .... 175 E2
Farnham Common SL2 .. 187 E1
Woodlands Hill HP9 ..... 186 C3
Woodlands Park Ave SL6 . 202 A1
Woodlands Park Prim Sch
SL6 .... 202 A1
Woodlands Park Rd SL6 . 202 A2
Woodlands The
Amersham HP6 .... 154 B2
Tylers Green HP15 ...... 162 C2
Woodlands View HP13 ... 174 A4
Woodlane Cl HP10 .... 173 F1
Woodley Headland MK6 . 47 E4
Woodley Hill HP5 .... 154 B3
Woodman Cl LU7 .... 79 F2

Woodmoor End SL6 .... 196 A4
Woodpiece Rd OX6 .... 94 C4
Woodruff Ave MK14 .... 34 C2
Woodrush CI MK6 .... 47 D2
Woods PI **18** Tring HP23 ... 119 D2
Wendover HP22 .... 131 D2
Woodside
  Aspley Guise MK17 .... 49 E2
  Eaton Bray LU6 .... 92 C3
  Flackwell Heath HP10 ...... 185 E3
  Milton Keynes MK11 .... 32 C3
Woodside Ave
  Amersham HP6 .... 154 B2
  Beaconsfield HP9 .... 175 E2
  Flackwell Heath HP10 ...... 185 E4
Woodside CI
  Beaconsfield HP9 .... 175 E2
  Gerrards Cross SL9 .... 177 F1
  Loudwater HP10 .... 174 A1
Woodside Cty Mid Sch
  HP6 .... 154 C1
Woodside Hill SL9 .... 177 F1
Woodside Rd
  Amersham HP6 .... 154 B1
  Beaconsfield HP9 .... 175 E2
  High Wycombe HP13 .... 174 A4
Woodside Way
  Leighton Buzzard LU7 ...... 80 B3
  Tylers Green HP10 .... 174 B4
Woodstock Ave SL3 .... 206 B1
Woodstock CI
  Aylesbury HP21 .... 116 A3
  Maidenhead SL6 .... 195 F1
Woodstock Ct MK13 .... 34 A4
Woodstock Dr UB10 .... 201 F4
Woodview Dr HP27 .... 150 B3
Woodville OX9 .... 147 E3
Woodville Cres NN12 .... 18 C3
Woodway HP27 .... 149 E3
Woodways HP17 .... 127 D3
Woollerton Cres HP22 ...... 131 E3
Woollerton Ct HP27 .... 139 D2

Woolmans MK11 .... 33 D2
Wootton Dr HP10 .... 185 F4
Wootton Gn OX6 .... 72 C3
Wootton La HP17 .... 113 F1
Wootton Way SL6 .... 202 B3
Worcester CI
  Maidenhead SL6 .... 202 B2
  Newport Pagnell MK16 ...... 22 A2
Worcester Gdns SL1 .... 205 E2
Worcester Rd UB8 .... 208 B4
Wordsworth Ave MK16 ...... 22 A2
Wordsworth Dr MK3 .... 58 A4
Wordsworth Rd
  High Wycombe HP11 .... 173 D3
  Slough SL2 .... 197 E1
Wordsworth Way UB7 ...... 208 C1
Worlds End La HP22 .... 130 C4
Worminghall Rd
  Ickford HP18 .... 123 F2
  Oakley HP18 .... 109 E2
Wormsley Cres HP14 .... 158 B2
Worple The TW19 .... 211 F1
Worrelle Ave MK10 .... 36 A2
Worster Rd SL6 .... 195 F3
Worthies The HP7 .... 165 D4
Worthington Rd LU6 .... 93 F4
Wotton End HP18 .... 96 B4
Wotton Path HP21 .... 115 F2
Wotton Rd HP18 .... 97 F1
Woughton Campus MK6 .... 46 C4
Wraysbury Cty Comb Sch
  TW19 .... 211 F1
Wraysbury Sta TW19 .... 212 A1
Wren CI MK18 .... 52 C4
Wren Ct SL3 .... 207 D2
Wren Dr UB7 .... 208 B2
Wren Rd HP16 .... 151 E3
Wren Vale HP13 .... 173 D4
Wren Wlk LU6 .... 92 C2
Wrens Pk MK10 .... 36 A1
Wrensfield SL7 .... 183 E1
Wright SL4 .... 209 E3

Wright Sq SL4 .... 209 E2
Wright Way SL4 .... 209 E2
Wright's La HP16 .... 151 E3
Wrights CI HP14 .... 171 D3
Wyatt CI HP13 .... 172 C4
Wyatt Rd SL4 .... 209 E2
Wyatt's Rd W03 .... 167 F3
Wychwood HP16 .... 152 A2
Wychwood Gdns HP12 .... 172 B3
Wychwood Rise HP16 ...... 152 A2
Wyclands Ho HP12 .... 161 D1
Wycombe Abbey (Sch)
  HP11 .... 173 D3
Wycombe Air Park SL7 .... 172 A1
Wycombe End HP9 .... 175 F1
Wycombe General Hospl
  HP11 .... 173 D3
Wycombe High Sch HP11 . 172 C2
Wycombe Ind Mall HP11 .. 172 C4
Wycombe La HP10 .... 185 F4
Wycombe Rd
  Beacon's Bottom HP14 .... 159 E2
  Bledlow Ridge HP27 .... 149 D2
  Holmer Green HP15 .... 163 D3
  Lacey Green HP27 .... 149 D2
  Lane End HP14 .... 159 F1
  Marlow SL7 .... 183 F2
  Prestwood HP16 .... 151 E3
  Princes Risborough HP27 . 149 D2
  Stokenchurch HP14 .... 159 E2
Wycombe View HP10 ...... 174 A1
Wycombe West Sch &
  Collegiate Ctr HP13 ...... 161 E2
Wye CI Aylesbury HP21 .... 115 E3
  Milton Keynes MK3 .... 46 C1
Wye Est HP11 .... 173 F3
Wye Rd HP10 .... 185 F4
Wye Valley Sch The SL8 .. 185 D2
Wykeham Gate HP17 ...... 126 C3
Wykeham Rise OX9 .... 147 E3
Wykeham Way HP17 ...... 126 C3
Wykeridge CI HP5 .... 144 A2

Wylands Rd SL3 .... 207 D1
Wymering Rd HP21 .... 116 B3
Wymers CI SL1 .... 197 D2
Wymers Wood Rd SL1 ...... 197 D2
Wymondham MK10 .... 36 B1
Wynbury Dr HP13 .... 162 C1
Wyndale CI RG9 .... 191 F1
Wyndham Ave HP13 .... 161 F1
Wyndham Cres SL1 .... 197 D2
Wyness Ave MK17 .... 59 F3
Wynford Gn HP21 .... 115 F3
Wyngates LU7 .... 80 C3
Wyngrave PI HP9 .... 175 E3
Wynn Gr HP15 .... 163 D3
Wynne Jones Ctr HP21 .... 115 F4
Wynnstay Gdns SL7 .... 183 F3
Wynnswick Rd HP9 .... 176 B3
Wynyard CI MK46 .... 6 C4
Wyre CI HP17 .... 127 D3
Wyvern Cty Fst Sch MK12 .. 33 E3
Wyvern Way UB8 .... 201 D3

Yalts Brow MK4 .... 46 A1
Yardley Ave LU7 .... 105 E2
Yardley Gn HP20 .... 101 F1
Yardley Gobion CE Prim Sch
  NN12 .... 18 C3
Yardley Hastings Prim Sch
  NN7 .... 1 A4
Yardley Rd Cosgrove MK19 .. 19 E1
  Olney MK46 .... 6 C3
  Potterspury NN12 .... 18 C2
Yarmouth Rd SL1 .... 205 E3
Yarrow PI MK14 .... 34 C2
Yarrowside HP7 .... 166 A4
Ye Meads SL6 .... 203 F3
Yeates CI Thame OX9 ...... 125 F1
  Winslow MK18 .... 65 F2
Yeats CI MK16 .... 21 F3
Yeomans CI NN13 .... 38 A4
Yeomans Dr MK14 .... 22 A1
Yeovil Rd SL1 .... 204 C4

Yew Ave UB7 .... 208 C3
Yew Tree CI
  Beaconsfield HP9 .... 175 F1
  Botley HP5 .... 145 D3
  Eaton Bray LU6 .... 92 C3
  Ivinghoe LU7 .... 105 F2
  Maidenhead SL6 .... 202 C4
  Newton Longville MK17 .... 57 E2
  Stoke Mandeville HP22 .... 116 A1
Yew Tree Dr
  Bovingdon HP3 .... 146 A2
  Holmer Green HP15 .... 162 C3
Yew Tree Rd Slough SL1 .. 206 A2
  Uxbridge UB10 .... 201 F2
Yew Wlk HP15 .... 163 D2
Yiewsley Ct UB7 .... 208 C3
Yolsum CI HP17 .... 126 C3
Yonder Slade MK18 .... 52 C3
York Ave Slough SL1 .... 205 E4
  Windsor SL4 .... 210 A3
York CI HP7 .... 165 F4
York Ct **E** LU7 .... 80 C4
York Ho
  High Wycombe HP13 ...... 173 F4
  Milton Keynes MK3 .... 57 F4
York PI HP21 .... 115 F4
York Rd Henley-on-T RG9 .. 191 E1
  Maidenhead SL6 .... 203 D4
  Marlow SL7 .... 183 E1
  Milton Keynes MK11 ...... 32 B3
  Uxbridge UB8 .... 201 E3
  Windsor SL4 .... 210 A3
York Way HP12 .... 172 C2
Yorke CI HP22 .... 117 F3
Youens Rd HP12 .... 172 B3
Young CI HP21 .... 116 A3

Zealand Ave UB7 .... 213 E4
Zetland Ct SL6 .... 203 D4

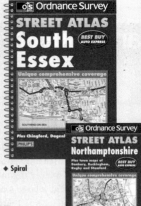